FAMILY STRESS

To a new generation of family stress scholars. May you celebrate the inevitable differences in families as you discover new ways to understand resilience and family stress management.

FAMILY STRESS

Classic and Contemporary Readings

Editor

PAULINE BOSS

University of Minnesota

with Carol Mulligan

SAGE Publications
International Educational and Professional Publisher
Thousand Oaks ▪ London ▪ New Delhi

For information:

Sage Publications, Inc.
2455 Teller Road
Thousand Oaks, California 91320
E-mail: order@sagepub.com

Sage Publications Ltd.
6 Bonhill Street
London EC2A 4PU
United Kingdom

Sage Publications India Pvt. Ltd.
M-32 Market
Greater Kailash I
New Delhi 110 048 India

Printed in the United States of America

Library of Congress Cataloging-in-Publication Data

Family stress: classic and contemporary readings / edited by Pauline Boss, with Carol Mulligan.
    p. cm.
Includes bibliographical references and index.
ISBN 0-7619-2612-7 (P)
  1. Family—Psychological aspects. 2. Family—Mental health. 3.
Stress (Psychology) I. Boss, Pauline. II. Mulligan, Carol.
HQ734 .F24188 2002
306.85--dc21

              2002008927

This book is printed on acid-free paper.

03 04 05 06 10 9 8 7 6 5 4 3 2 1

Acquisitions Editor:	Jim Brace-Thompson
Editorial Assistant:	Karen Ehrmann
Production Editor:	Sanford Robinson
Copy Editor:	Gillian Dickens
Typesetter:	C&M Digitals (P) Ltd., Chennai, India
Indexer:	Julie Grayson
Cover Designer:	Michelle Lee

CONTENTS

PREFACE

Nowhere has the need for contextual family stress theory been more evident than in New York City after the terrorist attacks of September 11, 2001. My colleagues, students, and I worked there with many families experiencing the same crisis but within vastly different contexts. In the aftermath of the disaster, we saw what worked and what did not. Theories were tested as we designed interventions on the spot. New questions emerged as we worked with families from more than 20 different cultures and religions. Many spoke no English. We learned quickly that what we did had to fit diverse beliefs and values. We learned that new directions are needed in an area of study that has at times been excessively focused on the norm.

With conceptual and pragmatic goals, this book of classic and contemporary readings is designed to accompany *Family Stress Management* (Boss, 2002) (hereafter *FSM*). *Conceptually*, its purpose is to add depth to the contextual model presented in *FSM*. It is also designed to stimulate continued development of more general family stress theories to guide prevention, treatment, and policy in an era of multiculturalism. *Pragmatically*, the book provides a new generation of family stress professors and their students with convenient access to a sampling of articles by past and present researchers, theorists, and clinicians. All exemplify new directions or critical thought in family psychology, family social science, family therapy, social work, nursing, family sociology, and cultural psychiatry.

Medical researchers have documented well the idea that stress can make people sick. Psychologists have shown that stress affects emotional well-being and work productivity. The challenge now to family scholars is to document how diverse families in diverse contexts manage to remain resilient despite stress or crisis. Culture, history, economic status, development, heredity, and chronic discrimination are examples of a family's *external context* (Boss, 2002). The family's *internal context,* more amenable to change, consists of *structural*, *psychological,* and *philosophical* dimensions. These are discussed fully in *FSM* (Boss, 2002), but relevant examples are provided in this book.

This collection of readings is meant for graduate students and upper-level undergraduates in family studies, family psychology, social work, child psychology, sociology, nursing, and family life education. It is also a resource for professors, scholars, and military personnel interested in discovering new ways to help contemporary families manage stress, avert crisis, recover from trauma, and maximize resilience.

After reading this book, you should

- be more familiar with classic and contemporary writings in family stress research, theory development, and intervention;
- understand better how culture, history, economics, development, heredity, and discrimination influence a family's meaning of stress or crisis and thus better shape interventions to manage and maintain their resilience;
- understand more varied examples of coping (e.g., spirituality) by paying more attention to the family's construction of their reality, listening to each person's unique interpretations, and also eliciting community or tribal perceptions;

- know how to apply one or two family stress models with the couples and families you see in your practice or research;
- know how to use family stress theory and research more effectively to assess and aid families experiencing catastrophic as well as normative situations.

Although the articles in this reader were intentionally selected to stimulate critical thinking and to augment the contents of *FSM*, you may read them in whatever order meets your needs. There was not space, however, to include an article to illustrate every section or subsection. We identify the following deviations from the original outline in *FSM*. First, a section specific to coping, adapting, resilience, and managing is not included because many articles throughout this book are intrinsically about coping and especially resilience. See especially Part 1 on spirituality and meanings, Part 4 on developing tolerance for ambiguity, Part 5 on minimizing ambivalence, Part 6 on values and beliefs, and Part 7 on the family's external context. Second, due to an increasing focus on health, function, and strength, we prefer the constructs of "managing" or "staying resilient" rather than "coping," which may connote "putting up with" or enduring. To sustain an emphasis on resilience throughout the book, we therefore do not include a section specifically on coping. For a full discussion of coping, adapting, resilience, and managing, see *FSM* (Boss, 2002, chap. 4).

Third, a section specifically on denial is omitted due to space limitations, so we especially recommend a 1992 article written by Stephen R. Connor, titled "Denial in Terminal Illness: To Intervene or Not to Intervene." See also *FSM* (Boss, 2002, chap. 7) for more discussion about denial as a barrier or buffer.

Finally, a specific section on family crisis and overcoming traumatization and victimization is not included because several other sections in this book contain information about these phenomena. Kirmayer et al. (2000) address this topic in Part 6, as do Campbell and Demi (2000) in Part 5. See also *FSM* (chap. 10) for a discussion on this topic. We also recommend Laurence Kirmayer, Allan Young, and Barbara Hayton's (1995) article, "The Cultural Context of Anxiety Disorders," in which they discuss the anxiety and suffering caused by cultural bereavement after ethnic annihilation. They describe destruction and cultural loss of North American Indians and also people worldwide, including those in Cambodia, Nigeria, Middle East, Asia, the Caribbean, Puerto Rico, and Hawaii. Kirmayer and colleagues (1995) write, "The levels of economic deprivation, uncertainty, violence, and trauma in many war-torn parts of the world, as well as in inner city neighborhoods, may make anxiety endemic" (p. 517). Because we believe that the culture of anxiety detailed by Kirmayer et al.—now magnified by the terrorist attacks of September 11, 2001, and global terrorism—will test family resilience, articles about trauma and troubles are more numerous in this book than articles on the normative stressors of everyday family life. Although Kirmayer et al.'s (1995) work is not about family crisis per se, I highly recommend their article to expand our thinking about the processes and outcomes people face when their culture and way of life are taken from them. With the current influx of immigrants and refugees escaping from war-torn countries bent on ethnic cleansing, family stress scholars cannot avoid this topic and must incorporate cultural loss and ethnic discrimination into every aspect of family stress assessment and intervention.

Aside from these changes, the sequencing of articles in this book adheres to the following order established in *FSM*:

Chapter 1: What Is New?

The mind-body-family connection

The introduction of resilience to the family stress field

Recognition of spirituality and faith as important in family stress management

Growth in the knowledge and treatment of post-traumatic stress disorder

The widespread use of critical incident or disaster teams

Growth in research-based interventions for families with chronic illness (mental and physical) and disabilities

To be sure, theoretical pragmatism shaped this book; articles were selected for conceptual and clinical usefulness in a contemporary context. The process was collaborative. A jury of unnamed professors reviewed and voted on the proposed list of articles. Most of the articles or topics that received their votes are included. Although the panel members heavily influenced the book's content, they are in no way responsible for omissions. Indeed, worthy articles had to be eliminated due to space limitations and high copyright costs. References for those articles are given within the text of each chapter.

I invite you to participate in the collaborative process that will shape revisions of this book. Please suggest articles to include (or delete) in future editions.

REFERENCES

Boss, P. (2002). *Family stress management* (2nd ed.). Thousand Oaks, CA: Sage.

Connor, S. R. (1992). Denial in terminal illness: To intervene or not to intervene. *Hospice Journal, 8*(4), 1-15.

Kirmayer, L., Young, A., & Hayton, B. (1995). The cultural context of anxiety disorders. *Cultural Psychiatry, 18* (3), 503-521.

Pauline Boss, Professor
Department of Family Social Science
College of Human Ecology
University of Minnesota

ACKNOWLEDGMENTS

I wish to thank Carol Mulligan for her first-rate skill and collaboration in compiling this book of readings. I also thank the reviewers who influenced the selection of articles for this book: Priscilla Blanton, Deborah B. Gentry, Raeann R. Hamon, Melanie Lutenbacher, and Rhea Williams. Thanks also to Clara Schreiber and Jessie Paulson for their technical help. Finally, I thank the editorial staff at Sage Publications—including Sanford Robinson, my production editor, and my editor Jim Brace-Thompson and his assistant Karen Ehrmann—for seeing that the book was really needed by instructors and students increasingly frustrated by obtaining copyrights and copying packets of articles to supplement lectures and texts. Finally, I thank the authors whose articles make up this collection. Whether classic or contemporary, may they stimulate even newer directions in family stress theory.

PART 1

WHAT IS NEW IN FAMILY STRESS THEORY AND RESEARCH?

T he new ideas in family stress theory can be summarized by the following:

1. emphasis on health rather than dysfunction, using a biopsychosocial approach. We call this the mind-body-family connection for managing stress;

2. focus on family resilience by expanding individual to more systemic perspectives that include family attachments and interactions.

3. recognition of spirituality and religiosity as major influences on how people perceive and manage stress, crisis, or traumatic events;

4. growth in the knowledge and treatment of posttraumatic stress disorder with children and families;

5. increased use of on-site disaster teams for victims and workers;

6. growth in research-based interventions for caregiving families stressed with chronic illness (mental and physical) or disabilities;

7. concern about stress from balancing work and family in both single- and duo-parent families; and

8. postmodern emphasis on meanings and perceptions, individually and collectively, about the family's stress or crisis situation. This includes community perceptions.

This section starts with Antonovsky and Sourani's (1988) article that introduces the idea of a "family sense of coherence," an indicator of health (salutogenesis). Antonovsky originated the terms *salutogenesis* and *sense of coherence* (SOC), the latter meaning that one can nevertheless make sense of and view as manageable his or her particular situation of stress, crisis, or trauma. In this article, Antonovsky and Sourani expand the original SOC measure to the family level. Although they found validity for the construct of "family SOC," pay special attention to their discussion following their research report.

Wood, Klebba, and Miller's (2000) article is included next to show how contemporary research modes link mind, body, and family—the psychological, physiological, and social—as a way to understand the impact of family stress on health. In this case, the focus is on children with asthma and the effect that parental conflicts have on their ability to breathe. Such interdisciplinary links in recent research are helping us understand how stress in the family environment can lower a child's resilience—in this case, actually lower the oxygen level for those with asthma.

Next is Garmezy's (1987) classic work on "competence" in children stressed by having a parent with mental illness. At this point, you will recognize that articles placed in one section overlap with others. Both Antonovsky and Garmezy laid the groundwork for what we now call "resilience." Hawley and DeHaan (1996) provide much-needed direction for integrating the separate streams of study in psychology and family science regarding individual versus family resilience. It is essential now to integrate knowledge on resilience across disciplines, and thus Hawley and DeHaan's article, among others, is pivotal, stimulating new directions that merge ideas from psychology and family social science, as well as sociology, social work, family therapy, and nursing.

Also in this section on "what's new," McAdoo (1995), Strang and Strang (2001), and Wright (1997) add the construct of spirituality (and religiosity) for our consideration. Clinicians who work directly with families have long been aware that spirituality provides belief systems and rituals that are frequently used to lower stress and to manage feelings of helplessness or hopelessness. It was said that Rose Kennedy's going to Mass every morning helped her stay strong despite her many losses. Only recently have researchers recognized, defined, and studied spirituality systematically. Only recently has suffering been added to scholarly study. The series of articles here is meant to provide conceptual groundwork and nuances for increased analysis of the links between spirituality, meaning, resilience, and stress management.

To illustrate the postmodern shift to meaning, we present a thought-provoking article defining three levels of meaning as conceptualized by Patterson and Garwick (1994). As scientist-practitioners, they provide us with new insights for working with families of children with disabilities.

In addition to the articles here, we recommend Jon C. Stuckey's (2001) article, titled "Blessed Assurance: The Role of Religion and Spirituality in Alzheimer's Disease Caregiving and Other Significant Life Events."

A dearth of family-focused research addresses the stress of work and family, so we recommend as a start the review of literature by Maureen Perry-Jenkins, Rena L. Repetti, and Ann C. Crouter (2000), titled "Work and Family in the 1990s." Although this review does not focus on family stress, we recommend it to stimulate more research on the stress of balancing work and family.

We could not find research documenting the systemic effectiveness of critical incident teams with *families,* so this category is omitted for the time being. Discussion of post-traumatic stress within a cultural context is critical and overlaps with Parts 1, 6, and 7.

REFERENCES

Perry-Jenkins, M., Repetti, R. L., & Crouter, A. C. (2000). Work and family in the 1990s. *Journal of Marriage and the Family, 62*(4), 981-998.

Stuckey, J. C. (2001). Blessed assurance: The role of religion and spirituality in Alzheimer's disease caregiving and other significant life events. *Journal of Aging Studies, 15,* 69-84.

1

Family Sense of Coherence and Family Adaptation

Aaron Antonovsky
Talma Sourani

The sense of coherence (SOC) is a construct that refers to the extent to which one sees one's world as comprehensible, manageable, and meaningful. This article applies the SOC construct to the study of family adaptation. A family SOC scale was developed to measure the perceived coherence of family life. The study tested the hypothesis that the strength of the SOC, central to successful coping with family stressors, is associated with adaptation, here defined in terms of perceived satisfaction with intrafamily and family-community fit. A sample of 60 married Israeli males who were disabled by injury or illness completed SOC and adaptation scales, along with their wives. The data provide strong support for the hypothesis and show a considerable degree of consensus among spouses. The discussion considers the dual meaning of the term "the family SOC," the nature of the links between coherence and adaptation, and the variable conceptions of adaptation.

The Family Sense of Coherence

The purpose of this paper is dual: *(a)* to consider the possibility of translating the sense of coherence (SOC) construct from the individual to the family level; and *(b)* to test the hypothesis that the family SOC is related to family adaptation. In doing so, we hope to advance the growing link between the different theoretical and research traditions of the fields of family stress and life events and illness, as exemplified in Walker's (1985) paper. It is not our intention to enter into all the theoretical complexity

Reprinted from the *Journal of Marriage and the Family* 50 (1988): 79-92. Copyright © 1988 by the National Council on Family Relations, 3989 Central Ave. NE, Suite 550, Minneapolis, MN 55421. Reprinted by permission. This article is based on an MSW thesis submitted by Talma Sourani to the School of Social Work, University of Haifa, 1983.

of the work done in this area, but rather, using empirical data from a modest study, to make a contribution toward clarifying this complexity.

The life events literature, from Selye through Holmes and Rahe to the present day, presents an overwhelming emphasis on risk factors as causally related to pathological outcomes. In the mid-seventies, with the appearance of the first Dohrenwend volume (Dohrenwend and Dohrenwend, 1974) and the Rabkin and Struening paper in *Science* (1976), attention was increasingly paid to mediating and buffer variables. The underlying philosophical hypothesis continued to be that life events, stressors, or psychological risk factors eventuate in physical and/or emotional pathology. What was now added was that it was important to see what factors might attenuate this relationship. Occasionally in the more recent papers, especially on social support, a new note is detected: the possibility that such factors might have a direct and positive effect on not getting sick.

The family stress literature, by contrast, tends to show a somewhat different orientation, or at least to be hospitable to one. True, in Hill's classic work (1949, 1965), the dependent variable was crisis. But as this model was developed by Burr (1973) and McCubbin and Patterson (1983), not only was central attention given to the family's resources and its definition of the stressor; regenerative power, reorganization after a period of crisis, and adaptation as fit became central concepts as well.

Starting from a different philosophical orientation than that of the life events literature, Antonovsky, having earlier worked on "resistance resources" (1972), developed a "salutogenic model" (1979). Stressors, he argued, are ubiquitous in human existence; heterostasis is normative; the deviance of illness is far from rare. It is at least of equal importance to seek to explain the origins of health—of successful coping with stressors—as it is to explain the origins of pathology. Moreover, the two questions are seen as radically different. (For a detailed development of this argument, see Antonovsky, 1987, chapter 1.)

The proposed answer to the salutogenic question came to be called the *sense of coherence*. It is derived from a theoretical analysis of what a large variety of "generalized resistance resources" seem to have in common that might explain *how* they work. Briefly put, such resources as social support, money, religious faith, work role autonomy, and cultural stability provide continuing life experiences with three characteristics: consistency (see Cassel's 1974 discussion of feedback); an underload-overload balance; and participation in socially valued decision making. Over the course of time, a person with many such experiences comes to see the world as one that makes sense; or in terms of information theory, one that provides information rather than noise. Formally, this world view, the sense of coherence, is defined as (Antonovsky, 1987: 19)

a global orientation that expresses the extent to which one has a pervasive, enduring though dynamic feeling of confidence that (1) the stimuli deriving from one's internal and external environments in the course of living are structured, predictable and explicable; (2) the resources are available to one to meet the demands posed by these stimuli; and (3) these demands are challenges, worthy of investment and engagement.

The three inextricably intertwined components of the SOC are called, respectively, comprehensibility, manageability, and meaningfulness. A tendency to expect the world to be ordered, or orderable, facilitates cognitive clarification of the nature of the problems stressors pose. A tendency to expect the demands posed by these problems to be manageable leads one to search out the appropriate resources potentially available to one. And a tendency to see life as meaningful provides the motivational drive to engage in confrontation with the problems. It should be noted that the SOC is not at all a specific coping style, active or otherwise. Its hallmark, rather, is flexibility in selecting coping behaviors that are judged to be appropriate. These may vary radically according to the situation and the culture. This approach proposes that if one has a strong SOC, the motivational and cognitive bases exist for transforming one's potential resources, appropriate to a given stressor, into actuality, thereby promoting health.

The formal definition of the SOC includes the phrase "a global orientation," that is, a general view of the world not limited to this or that area of life.

The theory assumes that one's view of the world tends to be of whole cloth. When this is not the case, the implication is that one has a weak SOC. Obviously, this assumption will sooner or later have to be tested. In recent work (Antonovsky, 1987, chapter 2) the concept of "boundaries" is introduced, suggesting that what matters is not that *all* stimuli be perceived as coherent, but only those that one defines as important in one's life. For one person, the boundaries might be wide; for another, narrow. But this caveat is qualified by the insistence that no one can so narrow the boundaries as to put beyond the pale of significance four spheres—one's inner feelings, one's immediate interpersonal relations, one's major activity, and existential issues— and yet maintain a strong SOC.

For purposes of the present study, however, we decided to focus on one sphere of life: one's family. The instrument we used to measure the family sense of coherence (FSOC) refers only to this sphere, which brings us to another issue.

In the original formulation of the SOC construct (Antonovsky, 1979), occasional reference was made to the SOC as applicable to the group as well as the individual. But this thought was never seriously developed. It was only with the planning of the present study that the complexity of the problem began to become clear. What does it mean, we asked ourselves, to say that *a family* has a strong, or a weak, SOC? A family has size, structure, division of labor and power, social functions, myths, and so on. But how can a family have a dispositional orientation, a way of seeing the world? We speak of family ambience, morale, atmosphere, and the like, but how do we know such things about a given family?

The clinician, working with the individual person, tends to rest content with obtaining data about the individual's perception of how the family presumably sees things. One can make a case for arguing that this is what matters. Or can one? If the "reality" of how other family members see things is at variance with the individual's perception, this has consequences for what happens to him or her; which brings us back to whether "the family" sees things.

Family researchers, by and large, have ignored the issue. As Walker puts it (1985: 832), "those who study family stress continue to postulate the existence and importance of the family's definition of the event, even though it has yet to be operationalized or measured." (For a detailed discussion of this issue, see Fisher, Kokes, Ransom, Phillips, and Rudd, 1985.) The tendency has been to collect data on the perceptions of reality by different family members. If these perceptions coincide, the problem is "solved." If not, one averages the ratings. When the consistency of family members' perceptions is on the high side, one can reasonably feel that little violence has been done to the data. One can ignore the fact that one has avoided the theoretical problem.

The problem is particularly salient when the issue of concern is a construct like the SOC. Its very essence as a group property requires that there be consensus among family members if one is to speak of a strong family SOC. To use one person's report, or to average data, is to risk the danger that there is dissensus, in itself evidence of a weak family SOC. On the other hand, consensus about seeing the world as incoherent, paradoxically, might hint that there is some order.

Two problems have been raised here with regard to the "family sense of coherence": *(a)* the focus on family life versus the world as a whole as the *object* of the perception of coherence; and *(b) who* does the perceiving. The wisdom and problematics of our resolution of these issues in the present study will be considered in the discussion.

FAMILY ADAPTATION

In the development of the salutogenic model (Antonovsky, 1979), great care was taken to avoid tautology. The SOC was carefully defined, and later operationalized, to avoid any reference to health. Health was specified as referring to one type of "well-being," essentially physical health; thus the slippery concept of mental health was avoided. If a link was indeed found between the SOC and health, one could have some confidence that how a person sees the world of stimuli and how his or her organism functions physiologically are distinct though related variables. But the SOC construct, posited to explain successful coping with stressors or crises, can reasonably be hypothesized to be related to morale, satisfaction, general well-being—or adaptation (see

Antonovsky, 1987, chapter 7). Yet how are the two to be measured independently?

Family stress researchers have long wrestled with the problem. However, as Lavee and McCubbin (1985: 1-2) put it in a recent and most significant paper,

> family adaptation is but a descriptive criterion of family post-crisis outcome rather than a purely defined construct with an operationalized set of measures. . . . Specifically, in adopting family adaptation as a dependent variable in family stress research we are faced with the challenge of ensuring the independence of the predictors, such as family resources (e.g., family integration and communication) or family appraisal (e.g., coherence), from the criterion measure of family adaptation.

In the present study, "adaptation" was conceptualized in a way consistent with the literature (McCubbin and Patterson, 1983; Lazarus and Folkman, 1984) and pushed one step further. Specifically, we followed Lavee and McCubbin's (1985: 1) definition of adaptation as "a *fit* at two levels—between the family members and the family unit and between the family unit and the community." We departed, however, from their definition when it came to operationalizing the concept, choosing to measure adaptation by asking about the *satisfaction* with fit (while they chose to operationalize it by asking about general well-being, satisfaction, and family distress). Once again, the wisdom of our decision will be considered in the discussion.

In sum, the present study deals *(a)* with the degree of spouse consensus about the family's perception of the coherence of family life (FSOC); and *(b)* with the presumed consequences for the perception by spouses of the family's satisfaction with its adaptation to its internal and external environments (FAS).

SAMPLE AND DATA COLLECTION

Sample

The sample for this study was drawn from the Rehabilitation Branch files of a central Israeli city office of the National Security Institute (Israel's Social Security Administration). All potential respondents who met the following criteria were selected: male, formally recognized disability of at least 40%, disabled from 2 to 10 years, aged 25 to 50 at the time of onset of disability, and married (to the same spouse) with at least one child at home at time of onset and at time of study. These criteria were set in keeping with the purpose of the study, which focused on coping with a family crisis. Of the 65 families identified in the files, 7 refused to be interviewed and 3 could not be traced. The files of an adjacent small community office contained records for another 5 men who met these criteria, and they were included in the sample. The final sample comprised 60 men and their wives.

It should be noted that the sample only includes persons disabled in civilian life. Those disabled while on army duty are registered in the Ministry of Defense Rehabilitation Branch. Among the respondents, then, were persons injured in traffic, at work or in other accidents, or as a result of illness.

The modal male respondent had been disabled for 3 to 5 years (48.3%), had a 51-80% disability (i.e., of sufficient seriousness to warrant institutional assistance in rehabilitation and with reasonable grounds, as the NSI saw it, to anticipate reemployment; 50%), had experienced a decline in occupational status and income after onset (75%), was unemployed and not looking for work (48.3%), had been 41-50 years old at onset (70%), was born in Asia or Africa (53.3%), had had 5 to 8 years of schooling (38.4%), and had three or more children (76.7%). Thus the sample may generally be characterized as a working-class population.

Data Collection

Talma Sourani, an experienced rehabilitation social worker, visited each family at home after an appointment had been made. After the purposes of the study were explained, each spouse was requested to complete the questionnaire, separately and simultaneously. After the forms were collected, any further necessary explanations were given. In nine cases, male respondents were unable to complete the questionnaire by themselves. While the wife was doing so elsewhere, the questions were read aloud and responses recorded. In two of these cases, an adolescent child read the questions to the wife, who was also unable to read and write Hebrew.

Measures

The self-completion questionnaire (see Appendix) opened with a general statement that the items refer to the family's behavior as a whole. The 26-item FSOC measure opened the questionnaire, followed by 9 demographic items. The third part contained the 10-item Family FAS and a single item on overall satisfaction with family life. The questionnaire took, on the average, 20 minutes to complete. Case workers were also asked to evaluate the adaptation of each of "their" families, using a single global 7-point item.

The *Family Sense of Coherence Scale* (FSOC) consisted of 26 semantic differential items, scored from 1 to 7, with extreme anchor phrases. High scores indicate a strong FSOC. Fourteen of the items were phrased so that the higher the number checked, the weaker the coherence; these were reversed in scoring.

The initial basis for constructing the scale was Antonovsky's (1987, chapter 4) questionnaire designed to measure the SOC of the individual as a global orientation. As indicated above, the present study focuses on family life only. Those items that could not easily be adapted to a family context were dropped. Other items referring to issues that come up in everyday life were constructed. In each case, the underlying frame of an item was the extent to which the respondent perceives family life as comprehensible, manageable, or meaningful. Two brief pretests, with 5 and 14 couples, respectively (each with a disabled spouse not included in the sample), led to the construction of the final questionnaire.

The internal reliability of the FSOC was quite high. Cronbach's alpha for the entire sample ($N = 120$) was .921; for husbands separately, .923, and for wives separately, .920. Systematic removal of each item had no impact on the alpha.

The *Family Adaptation Scale* (FAS) consisted of 10 semantic differential items scored from 1 to 7. In each case, the extreme anchor phrases were "completely satisfied" and "dissatisfied." Given the propensity shown in many surveys to give positive answers to such questions, the imbalance was intentional

(i.e., the fact that "completely dissatisfied" was not used). Six of the items were phrased so that the higher the number checked, the poorer the adaptation; these were reversed in scoring, so that a high score indicates good adaptation. Five of the items referred to satisfaction with internal family fit (Items 1, 4, 5, 7, and 10); 2 items referred to family-community fit (Items 8, 9); and the 3 others were less specific, covering both facets of fit. Cronbach's alpha for the 10-item scale was .874 for the whole sample (.851 for husbands, .895 for wives).[1]

RESULTS

Preliminary Analyses

Our concern in this study is to test the hypothesis that the *family* construction of family reality is related to the perception of family adaptation. Before doing so, we present data on the individual scores. The mean score on the 26-item FSOC scale was 128.63 ($SD = 33.35$) for husbands and 130.85 ($SD = 33.99$) for wives, or 4.95 and 5.03, respectively, per item. In keeping with many other survey results, these means seem to be on the high, optimistic side, if we consider that 7 is the most positive reply. Since the scale has never been used with any other population, no comparisons can be made. The 29-item individual SOC scale, however, has been used (Antonovsky, 1987, chapter 4). Adjusted mean scores of most of the populations are considerably lower, suggesting that it seems easier for persons to be less optimistic about themselves, at least in survey questionnaires, than about their families. Since many of the items differ on the two scales, however, such a generalization can only be tentative. The important point, for present purposes, is that "high" scores have no inherent meaning, and can only be used for comparative purposes within the same study or across studies when the same instrument is used.

In order to examine the relationship between the FSOC and the FAS, we set cutting points to divide both husbands and wives into three groups as equal as possible on each scale. In each case, the two variables are strongly related. Among men, 46 (77%) of the 60 are in the same third on the two variables, with one extreme deviant (low on FSOC, high on FAS). Among women, 35 (58%) of 60 are in the same third, while 3 are extreme deviants. The correlation coefficient between the two variables for men is 0.89; for women, 0.85 ($p < .001$).

We have, then, initial evidence that does not allow us to reject the FSOC-FAS hypothesis. But this hypothesis relates to the *family's* SOC and the *family's* adaptation, not to the perception by each spouse of the coherence of family life and adaptation. What can the data tell us about this question?

Spouse Consensus on Coherence and Adaptation

To what extent, we now ask, do spouses share a construction of reality, in this case the perception of the FSOC and of the FAS? Many studies ignore the problem by assigning a family score based on the mean spouse score. When few couples in a sample differ substantially—an empirical issue—using mean scores to test hypotheses perhaps does little harm. But when the construct under study bears a very direct relationship to the issue of agreement, as in the present case, it becomes impossible to ignore the matter. The very idea of a family sense of coherence is based on spouse agreement. When spouses disagree, there is by definition a weak SOC.

The correlation between husband's and wife's FSOC is .77 ($p < .001$). As noted, the scores of each gender were trichotomized into groups as nearly equal as possible. Of the 60 couples, 35 (58%) were in the diagonal cells, indicating agreement, whereas only 4 were extreme deviants (husband high—wife low, or the reverse) (chi-square = 20.9, 4 *df*, $p < .001$).

One further way of examining consonance between spouses was taken: examination of the 26 FSOC item-by-item differences. The range of possible mean item differences is from 0 to 6.0. In reality, 19 of the couples (32%) had a mean item difference of less than 1; another 28 (47%), from 1.01 to 2; and the remaining 13 between 2.01 and 4.

Thus it can be concluded that by and large there is a substantial degree of spouse agreement. This proves to be the case on the FAS as well. The correlation between husband's and wife's FAS is .68 ($p < .001$). Again, the scores of each gender were trichotomized into groups as nearly equal as possible. Of the 60 couples, 33 (55%) were in the diagonal

cells, indicating agreement, and only 4 were extreme deviants (chi-square = 18.0, 4 *df*, $p < .001$).

Having shown that there is indeed a considerable degree of consensus between spouses, which suggests that, at least in this case, it makes sense to speak of a *family* SOC (as well as of a family perception of adaptation), we may turn to the hypothesis of the study and examine the relationship between the two. But it is of value to analyze the "deviant" cases—in this instance, the spouses whose perceptions of the FSOC are discordant. The correlation between spouses is not perfect; 42% of the couples are not in the same third on the trichotomized scores; 22% of the couples had a mean item difference of 2.01 or more. Most, then, though not all, spouses have a similar construction of family reality. How does this relate to family adaptation? Or, to put the problem in another way: do the separate levels of husband and wife FSOC matter more or less than the fact that they agree or disagree on FSOC?

Family Coherence and Adaptation

Our first way of jointly analyzing the level of FSOC and the extent of spouse agreement as related to FAS was to use the tripartite divisions of spouses on FSOC and on FAS. The small number of cases obviates a very detailed breakdown. Nonetheless, the data, presented in Table 1.1, are suggestive. There are 13 cases in which both husband and wife had a high FSOC score, that is, they were both high and in agreement with each other. Using the husband's FAS score as criterion, we can see that none of the 13 had a low score. In the wife's perception, only one had a low score. Almost all these husbands (12 of 13) and a majority of the wives (8 of 13) report high adaptation. By contrast, the 13 couples in which both spouses agree that the family has a weak SOC are concentrated in the "poor adaptation" group (11 of the 13 by husband's perception, 12 of the 13 by wife's). The four intermediate groups on FSOC are clearly also intermediate on FAS.

But is the FSOC score more or less important than consensus in relation to the FAS? This issue was examined in two ways. We first compared two sets of two groups from the six in Table 1.1: the medium-high versus the medium-medium FSOC

Table 1.1   Distribution of Joint Spouse Family Sense of Coherence by Husband's and by Wife's Perception of Family Adaptation

| | Joint Spouse FSOC | | | | | |
Adaptation	*High-High*	*High-Medium*	*Medium-Medium*	*Medium-Low*	*High-Low*	*Low-Low*
			Husband FAS			
High	92.3%	45.5%	0.0%	20.0%	25.0%	0.0%
Medium	7.7	54.5	77.8	20.0	50.0	15.4
Low	0.0	0.0	22.2	60.0	25.0	84.6
n	(13)	(11)	(9)	(10)	(4)	(13)

chi-square = 54.3, 10 *df, p* < .001

			Wife FAS			
High	61.5%	36.4%	33.3%	40.0%	0.0%	0.0%
Medium	30.8	54.5	44.4	40.0	50.0	7.7
Low	7.7	9.1	22.2	20.0	50.0	92.3
n	(13)	(11)	(9)	(10)	(4)	(13)

chi-square = 33.2, 10 *df, p* < .001

groups; and the medium-low versus the low-low. If the average FSOC level is more important than consensus, then the former in each pair should have a higher adaptation score; if consensus is more important, the opposite should be the case. Using first the husband's FAS and then the wife's FAS as criterion measures, we tested the null hypothesis four times. In all four cases, even though the numbers are small, the mean FAS scores of the discordant FSOC pair are higher than the concordant but lower FSOC average couples. (In three of the four cases, the difference is statistically significant.) Thus, for example, comparing the mean husband's FAS scores of the medium-high and medium-medium couples, $t = 3.15, p < .006$.

We next examined the question using the above-noted mean FSOC single-item differences. The 60 couples were trichotomized into low, medium, and high mean differences. Again using the husband and wife FAS scores as criteria, we compared the three mean item difference groups pairwise. None of the comparisons show statistically significant *t* test differences, though the low-difference group has a bit higher FAS score than

the medium, and the medium a higher score than the high-difference group. But even the low-high comparison falls short of significance.

We may conclude, then, that it seems to matter more for adaptation that at least one spouse has a relatively strong FSOC than that the spouses agree. This observation should make those who use average family scores a bit more comfortable. This is not to say that consensus makes no difference. The correlations between the mean item differences and the FSOC of husbands is −.25 ($p < .027$); of wives, −.29 ($p < .012$). The correlations between the differences and the FAS of the husbands and wives, respectively, are −.14 and −.24 ($p < .069$ and .032). Consensus, then, is related to both coherence and adaptation, but it seems less powerful than the average level of coherence.

The Problem of Contamination

Evidence has been provided that the FSOC, whether measured by individual spouse score or joint couple score, is very strongly related to the FAS. In order to confront empirically the question of tautology raised earlier, that is, whether the FSOC and FAS measure the same thing, two steps were taken. First, the individual FSOC items were compared to the individual FAS items in terms of substantive overlap. This subjective comparison led to the identification of 9 FSOC items that seemed to us too close for comfort to FAS items. Thus, for example, FAS Item 7 refers to satisfaction with communication among family members. FSOC Item 1 refers to a feeling of mutual understanding; Item 8 refers to clarifying problems together; Item 14, to others sensing one's feelings. These 9 items (the above 3 and Items 5, 11, 19, 23, 25, and 26) were eliminated and a new scale was constructed on the basis of the remaining 17 items.

Once again, the correlation between husband's and wife's FSOC scores is highly significant (.71, $p < .001$, a bit lower than the .77 of the original scores). Of greater importance, the correlations between the new scores and the FAS scores remain highly significant: .84 ($p < .001$) for husbands and .81 ($p < .001$) for wives. This time, further, we calculated the correlations between husband FSOC and wife FAS scores and vice versa in the attempt to decrease contamination. The correlations were indeed somewhat lower but remained very highly significant (husband FSOC–wife FAS, .57; wife FSOC–husband FAS, .68; $p < .001$ in both cases).

Our final attempt at removing contamination between the two variables seems to be a strict test. We had asked the social workers in the rehabilitation office to provide a global estimate, on a scale of 1 to 7, of each family's level of adaptation. By and large, the worker was most familiar with the disabled husband. We obtained social worker ratings of the overall adaptation of 47 families. The correlations between these and the four major measures of the study are as follows: husband FSOC, .64; wife FSOC, .62; husband FAS, .51; wife FAS, .55 (in all cases, $p < .001$). Thus, even with a totally independent measure of adaptation, which is highly correlated with the respondents' perception of adaptation, there is a strong relationship between the sense of coherence and adaptation. This provides an independent confirmation of our consistent finding.

DISCUSSION

This study was designed to apply the concept of sense of coherence to the level of the family and to test the hypothesis that the family SOC is related to family adaptation. A sample was selected consisting of 60 families who had confronted a severe life stressor or crisis—the disablement of the head of the family—at least two years earlier, an acute event followed by the pileup of stressors involved in the inevitable need to reorganize family life. The data strongly support the hypothesis that those families with a strong family SOC—measured by the perception by spouses that family life is comprehensible, manageable, and meaningful—are more likely to be well adapted, more likely to have reached a high level of reorganization after a period of crisis, as measured by the satisfaction with family fit, internally and vis-à-vis the social environment.

Examination of this brief summary of the study points up a number of conceptual problems that are central to family stress theory. It may well be that the major contribution of this study goes beyond the modest empirical finding and is found in conceptual clarification. These are the issues to which we now turn. We will first consider the meaning of the two central variables of the study, "the family SOC" and "family adaptation." We then will turn to the relationship between the two.

The SOC construct was originally formulated to apply to the individual's perception of the world of stimuli that bombard one. In the present study, we have undertaken to examine whether the construct can be applied to the family. But the word "family" as used in the phrase "the family sense of coherence" has a dual meaning. First, it refers to the *stimuli* generated by interaction among family members and between family members and nonfamily units—to *what* is perceived as more or less coherent. In this sense, the term is narrower than the focus of the original concept. The latter is similar to the focus in Reiss's (1981) concept of "reality." Reiss too encompasses a very broad range and asks how this reality is "constructed" in the minds of the people he studies. The broader scope is also similar to what Lavee and McCubbin (1985: 9) call "family schema," defined as "the family's world view or appraisal of the total situation . . . the most enduring and stable of the family's levels of appraisal." The narrower use of the construct in the present study is analogous to Lavee and McCubbin's Level 3, called "family coherence" and defined as "the family's appraisal of the overall circumstances, particularly, the family's *fit* within the community in which it lives, its sense of manageability about life events, the predictability about circumstances, and the sense of control and trust the family has over present and future events." It also would seem closely related to the Mooses' concept of the family environment (Moos & Moos, 1976).

We have raised these parallels in order to call attention to the distinction between broader and narrower foci, a distinction that has received little attention and is often blurred, particularly when it comes to operationalization. We chose to study the construction of *family* reality, rather than the global orientation of the original SOC concept, following the Moos and Lavee-McCubbin approach. In retrospect, this choice may be regrettable. First, it increased the danger of contamination with the dependent variable (an issue dealt with below). Second, it may have involved the loss of power of the broader concept, which, precisely because it encompasses a global view of the world, promises to be relevant in coping with a wide variety of stressors. On the other hand, limiting the focus of attention to family reality increased the chances that spouses would agree (whereas they are more likely to have divergent views of their major activities, social relations, etc.). Moreover, since coping with family reorganization in the face of the acute and ongoing stressors of disablement is a family issue par excellence, we thought it more appropriate to make the choice we did. Further study would be required to test the hypothesis that global coherence would be a better predictor to adaptation than coherence about family life. A further crucial question for study is the relationship between the global perception of the world as coherent and the perception of family life as coherent. Our important point is that the two should be studied separately. It might be noted that, while Reiss explicitly claims to be studying the construction of all reality, his methodology of observing family interaction in essence compels him to *assume*

that how family members interact in coping with problems reflects how they see the world.

The second meaning of "family" refers to the *family* sense of coherence, thus posing the question of what it means to say that "the family" perceives a reality (whether that reality is broader or narrower), or the question of *who* is the perceiver. This question too has been slighted in the literature, the tendency being to assume that the technical device of averaging individual perceptions gives the "family" perception. At the operational level, Moos and Moos (1981) have given attention to this issue in developing and applying the Family Incongruence Score. In a rather different context, Kohn (1983: 6) has also raised the issue, when he writes: "The second issue is so obvious as to be embarrassing to raise, yet it has received surprisingly little attention in the research literature: Mothers and fathers often do not have the same values."

One possibility is to follow Moos and Moos, asking the individual respondent about his or her perceptions. Alternatively, one can, as Reiss (1981) does, obtain data by observing family interaction; the family as a unit, in this case, provides the data directly. In the present study, we sought a solution to the problem by combining the technically easier way of obtaining data from individuals with, in the stage of data analysis, considering spouse consensus as relevant to the SOC. The fact that our data show that consensus is a less powerful predictor of adaptation than is the average perception does not mean that the problem of group perception can be disregarded. We know, however, of no way other than Reiss's method of systematic observation of behavior to get at the orientation of the family as a unit.

We may summarize this issue by proposing a fourfold table of study designs. One may ask, focusing on *who* does the perceiving, about the perceptions of *(A)* individual family members or *(B)* the family as a unit. Second, one may ask, focusing on *what* is perceived, about the extent of coherence in *(a)* family life or *(b)* all of life. In design the present study is of the *Aa* type, asking: To what extent does each spouse perceive family life as coherent? In the analysis, by dealing with the consensus between spouses, we sought to introduce *B*. The fact that we found a high degree of spouse consensus, making it difficult to compare consensual and dissensual families, does not do away with the theoretical problem. This may have been a result of something unique about our sample. These families have all experienced a similar, major, nonnormative stressor and have remained intact. This may have effected a process of greater shared construing as a way to adapt.

The distinctions between *A* and *B,* and between *a* and *b,* may contribute to understanding the rather surprising finding that Moos and Moos's Family Environment Scale and Reiss's Card Sort Procedure showed no empirical association, despite seeming conceptual overlap (Oliveri and Reiss, 1984). The FES represents an *Aa* approach, its scores expressing the average of how individual family members perceive different aspects of family life. The CSP represents a *Bb* approach. Family interactional behavior is observed and scored directly; the focus of attention is on how the "family views the world" (p. 36). In addition to the contribution of methodological differences in obtaining data, Oliveri and Reiss attribute the lack of association to the possibility that "the FES and the CSP are tapping essentially unrelated domains of family functioning . . . one domain consists of the family processes or properties that govern how individual family members perceive the family and describe it to an investigator and the other domain consists of the family processes or properties that govern how family groups behave in a situation with unclear external demands" (p. 47).

The next issue to which we turn is the conceptualization and operationalization of the "dependent" variable, adaptation. Antonovsky's original work on the coherence-adaptation hypothesis focused on physical health. When this limitation is observed, the problem arises whether it should be measured in terms of "objective" or "subjective" criteria. The former, in practice, comes down to axiomatic acceptance of a medical mode of thinking, which also has its problems of reliability and which poses no less difficulty than the use of self-report. Once one moves to self-report, whether of physical health, psychological well-being, or social functioning, one enters dangerous waters.

On the one hand, one faces the Scylla of determination by the investigator of what is good adaptation, an inevitably value-shaped determination. At the conceptual level, the solution seems to be easy. One can use terms like integration, homeostasis, level of entropy or disorganization, fit among members and between the family and the nonfamily environment, or the balance between demands and capabilities. These are the terms with which the literature is replete. But when it comes down to operationalization, this approach leads to problems. Thus one might ask which of three families is best adapted: when both husband and wife agree that she continue to be a maid-chauffeur? when the wife rebels, against the husband's wishes? or when both agree that the time has come for a radical revision of her role? Residents of Fresno and Berkeley are likely to give quite different answers. Or one might ask about the number of friends spouses have jointly, or how many organizations they both belong to, or how often there are family fights, or whether problems are solved by letting time do its work or by actively discussing them. In each case, the investigator, wishing to rank respondents on adaptation, introduces his or her own values.

On the other hand, one faces the Charybdis of conceptualizing adaptation as satisfaction. Operationally, one can seek to avoid asking directly about satisfaction by asking about physical or psychological symptoms, financial or legal problems, sense of well-being (cheerful, happy, etc.), and so on. But in each case, the underlying question is always one of satisfaction, for it is reasonable to presume that no one is particularly pleased by having symptoms or problems, or by being tense, morose, or miserable. Or one can ask about satisfaction directly, avoiding the investigator's values by the reasonable assumption that a family that is highly satisfied in a variety of life areas is a family that is in dynamic homeostasis.

This latter is the choice we made, in essence asking how well the respondent thought his or her family fitted together and fitted into the community. We have called this choice a preference for Charybdis because it presented the danger of making a valid test of the SOC-adaptation hypothesis impossible. Had we been interested, say, in social class or ethnic differences in adaptation, there would have been no problem. These are zeroing-in variables, not contaminated with the dependent variable, but they are not helpful, except as points of departure, in the task of explaining bon- or maladaptation. Use of the FSOC—or any other presumably explanatory variable, such as perceived resources, definition of the stressful situation, or marital quality—carries the danger of implicitly or explicitly asking about satisfaction with family life.

We tried to avoid this danger by constructing FSOC items that avoid direct reference to satisfaction. In all but a few cases, however, there are clearly desirable answers. But what differentiates the FSOC questionnaire from other measures is that it is constructed on the basis of a theoretical guide. Each item is explicitly constructed to ask about the perception of comprehensibility, manageability, or meaningfulness of a given family issue. On the other hand, the FAS was constructed with the use of the concept of fit.

How, then, are the two variables related? The population selected for study was clearly one whose members had all faced a serious crisis from 2 to 10 years earlier, when the head of the family (in Israeli culture at present, for better or for worse, the husband-father is defined as such) had become seriously disabled because of illness or injury. Though we did not investigate the matter, it is reasonable to assume that, since the onset of disability, there had been a "pileup" of stressors; for example, 75% of the husbands reported a decline in occupational status and income after onset. Was the FSOC, we asked, associated with adaptation?

The data provided strong support for the hypothesis. Whether one looks at husband, wife, or joint perception, the relationship is extremely strong. Correlations of .89 and .85 are not often found in the social sciences. When the FSOC measure was refined by omitting items that seemed overlapping to reduce contamination between the two variables, the correlations were only slightly reduced (to .84 and .81). And when a truly independent measure of adaptation was used, the evaluation by case workers, the correlations remained highly significant (.64 and .62).

These findings are consistent with those of the only other study we know of in which the SOC construct was used to study family adaptation (Lavee, McCubbin, and Olson, 1987, based on

Lavee's doctoral dissertation). In a large U.S. national sample of families, the sense of coherence was hypothesized to enhance family well-being. Since the SOC scale developed by Antonovsky was not yet available (Antonovsky, 1983), the researchers used two brief scales that represented the concept: a 4-item scale measuring confidence that problems can be handled by the family, and a 3-item scale measuring acceptance and positive appraisal of stressful situations as part of life. "Well-being" was measured by a scale that "measures family members' satisfaction with various aspects of their lives in areas such as health, work, the family, and the community" (Lavee et al., 1987: 863). "The results show," the authors write, "that sense of coherence has a positive impact upon family well-being [and] acts as a *stress-buffer*" (p. 868).

The study by Lavee et al. (1987) is far more sophisticated, in plan and analysis, than is suggested by this brief reference. Its importance, in the present context, is that there is a commitment to providing an explanation of the link between SOC and well-being. Their emphasis, in keeping with the original discussion of the SOC construct (Antonovsky, 1979, especially chapter 5), is on the cognitive processes, the factors of appraisal and perception, that facilitate coping with stressors. Our study takes us two steps further, going beyond a strictly cognitive emphasis and incorporating components that are emotional (confidence in the availability of resources) and motivational (viewing the stressor as a challenge).

Neither Lavee and associates nor we have solved the problem of contamination. But we have, we believe, taken a step in the right direction. Some may prefer to see both studies as using two scales that represent a single construct, or as studies of concurrent validity. But the hope is that both contribute to the clarification required for advancing research.

The solution to the problem we would propose at this stage is that a variety of conceptualizations and operationalizations of family adaptation be used. But we would insist, in each case, that it is incumbent on the researcher to specify the *mechanisms* through which the independent variables and one's variant of adaptation are linked. (On this issue, see the exchange between Trost and Spanier in the November 1985 issue of this journal, pp. 1072-1074.) In the present case, such specification provides, we believe, at least some theoretical basis for claiming that the FSOC and the FAS are conceptually distinct and that the hypothesis of the study has been tested.

One final comment is in order. Correlation is not causation. The results of a cross-sectional study cannot demonstrate that a strong SOC is causally predictive of family adaptation. Whatever the plausibility of a theoretical account of a chain of events, the data cannot demonstrate that the SOC indeed precedes adaptation. This can only be tested in a longitudinal study. Moreover, in real life, we would anticipate interactional influence: a strong SOC does foster, by its contribution to successful coping with stressors, a high level of family adaptation; but such adaptation, in turn, leads the family to experiences that reinforce the SOC. To study this process over time is indeed a challenge for research.

CONCLUSION

Our underlying concern in this study has been to bridge two research traditions that have generally disregarded each other. The SOC construct was developed in the context of life events and coping theory, which primarily seeks to explain physical (and sometimes psychological) illness. Family stress theory, on the other hand, has been concerned with family adaptation (though one of the indices sometimes used is physical distress). Both traditions deal with crises, stressors, coping, and the consequences of the process. There is little doubt that a married couple, experiencing a relatively severe disablement of the husband, confronts both a serious acute stressor and an ongoing stress situation. The study has demonstrated that the levels of the "family sense of coherence" of husband and wife, taken singly and taken jointly, are very closely associated with the extent to which the spouses are satisfied with different aspects of family life. Whether such strong results would have been obtained had an alternative conception of adaptation been adopted remains a matter for future research. Moreover, since the study was cross-sectional, we have no evidence for a causal relationship. The theory proposed points to such causality in that it argues that a strong SOC, particularly one shared by spouses, provides

the motivational, perceptual, and behavioral basis for successful resolution of both the instrumental and emotional problems posed by stressors. Such resolution—note, not the absence of stressors, but their successful resolution—should provide one with a sense of satisfaction about family life. Were one to carry on study of the process, one might see that such satisfaction reinforces coherence. But if, at any given time, one wishes to predict which families will resolve crises successfully, the SOC seems to be a promising bet.

NOTE

1. The inevitable limitations of a one-person endeavor prevented fulfilling the desirable requirement of obtaining data that would test the validity of the FSOC and FAS, for example, by administering the Moos and Moos (1981) Family Environment Scale. Our empirical findings, then, must be treated with due precaution. But since our major concern in this study was to advance theoretical clarification, we felt justified in using the data at least to illustrate our concepts. Clearly, the scales proposed here will have to be examined further for their psychometric properties before they can be adopted.

REFERENCES

Antonovsky, Aaron. 1972. "Breakdown: A needed fourth step in the conceptual armamentarium of modern medicine." Social Science and Medicine 6: 537-544.

Antonovsky, Aaron. 1979. Health, Stress, and Coping. San Francisco: Jossey-Bass.

Antonovsky, Aaron. 1983. "The sense of coherence: Development of a research instrument." Newsletter and Research Report 1: 11-22, W. S. Schwartz Research Center for Behavioral Medicine, Tel Aviv University.

Antonovsky, Aaron. 1987. Unraveling the Mystery of Health. San Francisco: Jossey-Bass.

Burr, Wesley, R. 1973. Theory Construction and the Sociology of the Family. New York: Wiley.

Cassel, John. 1974. "Psychosocial processes and 'stress': Theoretical formulation." International Journal of Health Services 4: 471-482.

Dohrenwend, Barbara S., and Bruce P. Dohrenwend (eds.). 1974. Stressful Life Events: Their Nature and Effects. New York: Wiley.

Fisher, Lawrence, Ronald F. Kokes, Donald C. Ransom, Susan L. Phillips, and Pamela Rudd. 1985.

"Alternative strategies for 'relational' family data." Family Process 24: 213-224.

Hill, Reuben. 1949. Families Under Stress. New York: Harper and Row.

Hill, Reuben. 1965. "Generic features of families under stress." Pp. 35-52 in H. J. Parad (ed.), Crisis Intervention: Selected Readings. New York: Family Service Association of America.

Kohn, Melvin L. 1983. "On the transmission of values in the family: A preliminary formulation." Pp. 1-12 in A. C. Kerckhoff (ed.), Research in Sociology of Education and Socialization (Vol. 4). Greenwich, CT: JAI Press.

Lavee, Yoav, and Hamilton I. McCubbin. 1985. "Adaptation in family stress theory: Theoretical and methodological considerations." Paper presented at the annual meeting of the National Council on Family Relations, Dallas (November).

Lavee, Yoav, Hamilton I. McCubbin, and David H. Olson. 1987. "The effect of stressful life events and transitions on family functioning and well-being." Journal of Marriage and the Family 49: 857-873.

Lazarus, Richard S., and Susan Folkman. 1984. Stress, Appraisal, and Coping. New York: Springer.

McCubbin, Hamilton I., and Joan M. Patterson. 1983. "The family stress process: The double ABCX model of adjustment and adaptation." Pp. 7-37 in H. McCubbin, M. B. Sussman, and J. M. Patterson (eds.), Social Stress and the Family: Advances and Development in Family Stress Theory and Research. New York: Haworth.

Moos, Rudolf H., and Beatrice S. Moos. 1976. "A typology of family social environments." Family Process 15: 357-372.

Moos, Rudolf H., and Beatrice S. Moos. 1981. Family Environment Scale Manual. Palo Alto, CA: Consulting Psychologists Press.

Oliveri, Mary E., and David Reiss. 1984. "Family concepts and their measurement: Things are seldom what they seem." Family Process 23: 33-48.

Rabkin, Judith G., and Elmer L. Struening. 1976. "Life events, stress, and illness." Science 194: 1013-1020.

Reiss, David. 1981. The Family's Construction of Reality. Cambridge, MA: Harvard University Press.

Spanier, Graham B. 1985. "Improve, refine, recast, expand, clarify—Don't abandon." Journal of Marriage and the Family 47: 1073-1074.

Trost, Jan E. 1985. "Abandon adjustment!" Journal of Marriage and the Family 47: 1072-1073.

Walker, Alexis J. 1985. "Reconceptualizing family stress." Journal of Marriage and the Family 47: 827-837.

APPENDIX

THE FAMILY SENSE OF COHERENCE SCALE AND THE FAMILY ADAPTATION SCALE

In the data-gathering phase of this study, the written questionnaire was introduced to respondents as follows:

> This questionnaire contains questions about the way your family handles various daily problems. The questions relate to your immediate family: spouse and children. In answering, try to think of the behavior of the entire family, and not only of specific individuals. But don't include little children to whom the questions don't apply. There are no right or wrong answers. Each family has its own way of behaving in different situations.

The semantic differential technique was explained next, and the 26 FSOC items were introduced. These were followed by 9 sociodemographic items and the 10 FAS items, again in semantic differential format. The first FSOC item is given here in the format in which it appeared in the questionnaire (translated from the Hebrew). All other items are given with the anchor responses in parentheses, the response appearing under 1 presented first.

In the marginal notations on the FSOC items, "R" shows that the response is reversed for scoring purposes, so that 7 is always a high FSOC. "C," "MA," and "ME" indicate that the item is a comprehensibility, manageability, or meaningfulness item.

Family Sense of Coherence

C   1.   Is there a feeling in your family that *everyone* understands everyone else well?

R

1	2	3	4	5	6	7
There's full understanding among all family members.						There's no understanding among family members.

MA   2.   When you have to get things done that depend on cooperation among all members of the family, your feeling is: (there's almost no chance that the things will get done . . . the things will always get done)

R MA   3.   Do you have the feeling that it's always possible, in your family, to get help one from another when a problem arises? (you can always get help from all family members . . . you can't get help from family members)

C   4.   Let's assume that unexpected guests are about to arrive and the house isn't set up to receive them. Does it seem to you that: (the job will fall on one person . . . all the members of the family will pitch in to get the house ready)

R MA   5.   In case an important decision has to be taken which concerns the whole family, do you have the feeling that (a decision will always be taken that's for the good of all family members . . . the decision that will be taken won't be for the good of all family members)

R ME   6.   Family life seems to you (full of interest . . . totally routine)

C   7.   Does it happen that someone in the family feels as if it isn't clear to him/her what his/her jobs are in the house? (this feeling exists all the time . . . this feeling exists very rarely)

ME   8.   When a problem comes up in the family (like: unusual behavior of a family member, an unexpected overdraft in the bank account, being fired from work, unusual tension), do you think that you can together clarify how it happened? (very little chance . . . to a great extent)

R MA   9.   Many people, even those with a strong character, sometimes feel like sad sacks (losers). In the past, has there been a feeling like this in your family? (there's never been a feeling like this in the family . . . this feeling always exists)

R MA   10.   Think of a situation in which your family moved to a new house. Does it seem to you that (all family members would be able to adjust easily to the new situation . . . it would be very hard for family members to adjust to the new situation)

MA   11.   Let's assume that your family has been annoyed by something in your neighborhood. Does it seem to you that (nothing can be done to prevent the annoyance . . . it's possible to do a great deal to prevent the annoyance)

ME   12.   Until now your family life has had (no clear goals or purpose at all . . . very clear goals and purpose)

R ME   13.   When you think about your family life, you very often (feel how good it is to be alive . . . ask yourself why the family exists)

C   14.   Let's say you're tired, disappointed, angry, or the like. Does it seem to you that *all* the members of the family will sense your feelings? (no one will sense my feelings . . . all the family members will sense my feelings)

R C   15.   Do you sometimes feel that there's no clear and sure knowledge of what's going to happen in the family? (there's no such feeling at all . . . there's always a feeling like this)

MA   16.   When the family faces a tough problem, the feeling is (there's no hope of overcoming the difficulties . . . we'll overcome it all)

ME   17.   To succeed in things that are important to the family or to one of you (isn't important in the family . . . is a very important thing for all family members)

R C	18.	To what extent does it seem to you that family rules are clear? (the rules in the family are completely clear . . . the rules aren't clear at all)
ME	19.	When something very difficult happened in your family (like a critical illness of a family member), the feeling was (there's no point in going on living in the family . . . this is a challenge to go on living in the family despite everything)
MA	20.	When you think of possible difficulties in important areas of family life, is the feeling that (there are many problems which have no solution . . . it's possible in every case to find a solution)
R C	21.	Think of your feeling about the extent of planning money matters in your family (there's full planning of money matters . . . there's no planning about money matters at all in the family)
R MA	22.	When you're in the midst of a rough period, does the family (always feel cheered up by the thought of better things that can happen . . . feel disappointed and despairing about life)
ME	23.	Does it happen that you feel that there's really not much meaning in maintaining the family framework? (we always have this feeling . . . we've never had a feeling like this in our family)
R C	24.	Think of your feeling about the extent of order in your home. Is the case that (the house is well-ordered . . . the house isn't at all ordered)
R ME	25.	Let's assume that your family is the target of criticism in the neighborhood. Does it seem to you that your reactions will be (the whole family will join together against the criticism . . . family members will move apart from each other)
R ME	26.	To what extent do family members share sad experiences with each other? (there's complete sharing with all family members . . . we don't share our sad experiences with family members)

Family Adaptation Scale

Two anchor replies, printed under scores 1 and 7, were standard for all 10 items: I'm not satisfied . . . I'm completely satisfied. However, to avoid a set, the negative reply was placed under 7 on Items 1, 2, 4, 6, 9, and 10. These items, then, need to be reversed so that a high score represents high satisfaction. Item 11 represents an overall measure of adaptation, scored after reversing.

1. Are you satisfied in belonging to your family?

2. Are you satisfied about the way the children are being raised? (like with their education, their behavior, their activities?)

3. Are you satisfied with the family's way of life?

4. Are you satisfied with the possibility of expressing what you feel in your family?

5. Are you satisfied with the extent to which family members are close to each other?

6. Are you satisfied with how the family spends its leisure time?

7. Are you satisfied with the way family members communicate with each other?

8. Are you satisfied with how your family fits into the neighborhood?

9. Are you satisfied with the social relations your family has?

10. Are you satisfied with the way the family relates to the wishes of all the family members?

11. And now, think of what for you would be an ideal family, one which is perfectly adjusted. Where on the scale would you rank your family compared to the ideal family? (1 = ideally adjusted family; 7 = a family which is not at all adjusted)

2

EVOLVING THE BIOBEHAVIORAL FAMILY MODEL

The Fit of Attachment

BEATRICE L. WOOD
KENDRA B. KLEBBA
BRUCE D. MILLER

The 1993 Biobehavioral Family Model (BBFM) posits that family relational patterns and biobehavioral reactivity interact so as to influence the physical and psychological health of the children. The revised 1999 BBFM incorporates parent-child attachment as a pivotal construct. The current study tests the 1999 BBFM by predicting, in asthmatic children, that child perception of parental relationship quality, triangulation of child in marital conflict, and parent-child security of relatedness will be associated with hopelessness and vagal activation (one mechanism of airway compromise in asthma). In this study, 22 children with asthma (11 males/11 females, aged 8 to 16), watched, alone, an emotionally challenging movie, then engaged in family discussion tasks (problem solving, loss, conflict, cohesion) and completed the Children's Perception of Interparental Scale, the Relatedness Questionnaire, The Multidimensional Scale of Anxiety in Children, and the Hopelessness Scale for Children. Heart rate variability, measured at baseline and throughout the movie and family tasks, was used to compute respiratory sinus arrhythmia (RSA)—an inferential measure of vagal activation. The child's perception of parental conflict showed trends of association with triangulation and insecure father-child relatedness. Triangulation and hopelessness also were associated with insecure father-child relatedness, all of which were associated with vagal activation. Insecure mother-child relatedness was correlated only with hopelessness. Anxiety was not related to any variables. These findings lend support to the 1999 BBFM, and suggest a key role for parent-child attachment.

Reprinted by permission from *Family Process* 39 (2000): 319-44. This research was supported by a National Institute of Mental Health K01-MH01291-04 Career Development Award to the first author.

The original Biobehavioral Family Model (BBFM), a biopsychosocial model, posits that particular patterns of family relationship influence and are influenced by the psychological and physiological processes of individual family members (Wood, 1993; Wood, in press). Specifically, the BBFM proposes that family proximity, generational hierarchy, parental relationship, triangulation, and interpersonal responsivity are processes that influence one another and interact with individual (family member) psychological and emotional processes in ways that either buffer or exacerbate biological processes related to disease activity in children. It is also posited that individual psychological and emotional processes, in turn, influence and shape the specific family patterns. Figure 2.1 represents the 1993/1999 BBFM (shaded portions represent the 1993 version).

Proximity is defined as the extent to which family members share personal space, private information, and emotions. *Generational hierarchy* refers to the extent to which caregivers are in charge of the children by providing nurturance and limits through strong parental alliance and absence of cross-generational coalitions (Wood, 1995). *Parental relationship quality* refers to interaction patterns, which include mutual support, understanding, and adaptive disagreement (respectful and resolving) versus hostility, rejection, and conflict. Parental relationship quality is conceived as a family-level construct because it refers to the external expression of relationship, which influences family process. Other, more private, aspects of the parental relationship, such as marital satisfaction, disappointment, distance, commitment, and attachment, are likely to impact indirectly through influence on parent-child relationship, but the BBFM focuses on the direct impact of these relational processes on the children. Hence, child-experienced parental conflict vs. respect and support is the key aspect of this variable. *Triangulation* refers to involving a child in the parental conflictual process in ways that render the child responsible, blamed, scapegoated, or in loyalty conflict. *Responsivity* refers to the extent to which family members are behaviorally, emotionally, and physiologically responsive to one another. Responsivity depends, in part, on the *biobehavioral* (that is, *emotional) reactivity* of each family member. Moderate levels of emotional/physiological responsivity allow for empathic response among family members. Extremely high levels of responsivity can exacerbate maladaptive emotional/physiological resonance in the family, possibly worsening psychologically influenced emotional or physical disorders. Extremely low levels of responsivity may be part of a general pattern of neglect or avoidance, leaving family members unbuffered from internal, familial, or environmental stressors. Levels of responsivity reflect family-level patterns of emotion regulation, stemming, in part, from the confluence of individual family members' ways of regulating emotion. Emotion regulation or dysregulation is reflected in the quality and intensity of biobehavioral reactivity.

Biobehavioral reactivity, the pivotal construct that links psychological to biological processes in the BBFM, is conceptualized as the degree or intensity with which an individual family member responds physiologically, emotionally, and behaviorally to emotional stimuli (Boyce, 1992; Jemerin & Boyce, 1990, 1992; Wood, 1993). Biobehavioral reactivity reflects the ability of the individual to regulate emotion, and is mediated, in part, by autonomic nervous system (sympathetic and parasympathetic) arousal processes.[1] Biobehavioral reactivity/ emotion regulation is presumed to be influenced both by temperament (Kagan, Reznick, & Snidman, 1988; Suomi, 1987) and by external influences, particularly by patterns of caregiving (Calkins, 1994;

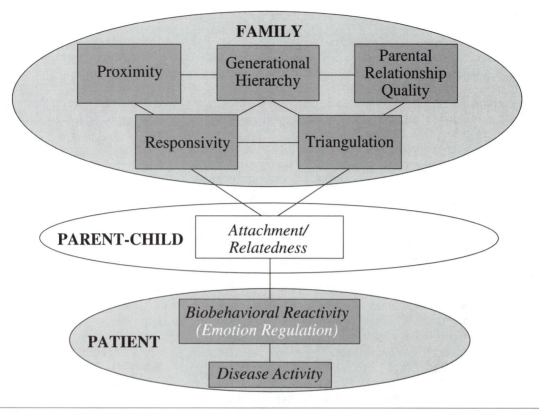

Figure 2.1   1993/1999 Biobehavioral Family Model

NOTE: Shaded portions represent the 1993 BBFM.

Cassidy, 1994; Field, 1994). Ongoing emotional conditions such as anxiety or hopeless depression are reflected in biobehavioral reactivity, with the former being characterized by relatively greater sympathetic nervous system activity, and the latter by relatively greater parasympathetic activity. Depending on which physiological processes are activated or deactivated by particular patterns of emotion dysregulation, such processes may influence specific psychological or physical diseases, depending upon the presence of a pathogenic pathway. For example, in cardiovascular disease, or in illnesses for which immune function is critical (cancer, infectious disease, certain types of diabetes), sympathetic arousal or activation may be pathogenic, such that chronic anxiety, anger, fear, and interpersonal relationship stress may negatively impact on the disease process. Mental illnesses,

such as schizophrenia or bipolar disorder, may also be susceptible to high sympathetic arousal (Tarrier, Vaughn, Lader, & Leff, 1979). For other illnesses, such as asthma or gastrointestinal disorders, different psychophysiological processes, such as emotionally induced parasympathetic (vagal) activation, may be more problematic (Lehrer, 1998; Lehrer, Isenberg, & Hochron, 1993; Miller, 1987; Miller & Wood, 1994, 1997). Biobehavioral reactivity thus encompasses a variety of emotional and physiological processes. Different configurations of proximity and hierarchy structure maintain, contain, or magnify the mutual influence that patterns of parental relationship, triangulation, responsivity, and individual biobehavioral reactivity have on one another. (See Wood, 1993, and Wood, in press, for further explication of the BBFM with clinical application.)

The Scope of the BBFM. To date, the BBFM has concentrated on physiological processes and physical illness in children. However, the model, in principle, could be focused to address the processes affecting *any* family member (adult or child) suffering from physically *and/or* psychologically manifested disease. This broad developmental application is justified by the ill person's likely dependence upon, and high levels of involvement with, the family, regardless of age or developmental status. The broad interpretation of "disease" is justified by research developments that increasingly demonstrate the mutual contribution of psychological and biological factors to both physically and psychologically manifested disease. Indeed it could be argued that the dichotomy of psychological versus physical disease is an outmoded dichotomy (Wood, 1995). (See Figure 2.2 for the Biobehavioral Continuum of Disease.)

Figure 2.2 suggests that all disease has both biological and psychological influences, and that these influences interact to affect the disease, but that they may have differential levels of contribution, depending on the disease or life circumstance. Therefore, stressful (or supportive) family process may either exacerbate (or buffer) the impact of psychosocial factors on psychological and/or physical disease, For example, a given child with asthma may have disease that is equally influenced by psychosocial and biological factors. However, if parental conflict becomes intense and prolonged and involves the child, particularly in ways that challenge attachment to one or both parents, then psychosocial factors might assume greater proportional influence on the disease process, thus shifting the disease toward the psychosocial end of the continuum. This recognition of relative influences on the disease is crucial for effective intervention. In this case, giving more medication might not have the desired ameliorative effect. Intervention to support security of attachment, and detriangulate the child might "treat" the asthma more successfully.

THE REVISED 1999 BBFM

Incorporating Parent-Child Attachment

Attachment refers to the biologically based, life-long tendency of human beings under conditions of stress to seek some form of proximity (physical or emotional) with specific other persons who are perceived as protective or comforting, such that one's emotional and physiological equilibrium are restored (Bowlby, 1969, 1973). Bowlby, who is considered the father of attachment theory, also published what was perhaps the first family therapy article (Bowlby, 1949). Although Bowlby ultimately decided to focus on the mother-dyad attachment relationship because it was a more manageable unit of investigation, he always believed that once the dyadic relationship had been understood, that the full range of family attachment relationships would then need to be explored (Byng-Hall, 1991). Wynne (1984) identified attachment/caregiving as the first stage upon which rests the development of adaptive patterns of communication, joint problem solving, and intimacy in families. Byng-Hall extended and articulated a framework of family scripts in which he applied attachment theory to the treatment of families (Byng-Hall, 1991). Patricia Minuchin (1988) and Marvin and Stewart (1990) also have elaborated family systems frameworks in which attachment may be studied. Cobb (1996) has developed a method of assessing—through laboratory-based direct observation—adolescent-parent attachment style and shown that these styles relate to Reiss' family problem-solving styles (Reiss, 1989). Mikulincer and Florian (1999) have demonstrated independent and differential contributions of family dimensions (cohesion and adaptability) and adult attachment to offspring attachment style. These theoretical and empirical developments indicate the increasing appreciation of the importance of integrating attachment and family systems theory and research.

The importance of integrating attachment and family systems theory is reinforced by developmental research indicating the central role played by security of attachment in psychological and behavioral outcomes (Bretherton, 1985; Cole, Michel, & Teti, 1994; Cummings & Davies, 1996; Masten, Best, & Garmezy, 1990). There is evidence that secure attachment can buffer a child from difficult life events (Beeghly & Cicchetti, 1996; Cummings, 1990; Masten et al., 1990; Sroufe & Waters, 1977), including divorce (Leckman, Peterson, Anderson, et al., 1997; Petersen & Zill, 1986). Furthermore,

Psychologically Manifested Disease

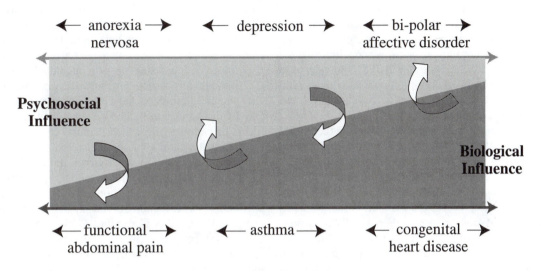

Figure 2.2   Biobehavioral Continuum of Disease

Cowan, Cowan, Cohn, and Pearson (1996) show that parental attachment style and marital quality predict behavior and emotional problems in young children. Wood (1999) has proposed that relationship and attachment processes also play an important role for children with chronic physical illnesses and their families.

Attachment findings specific to the biobehavioral link in the 1999 BBFM show that insecure attachment is related to depressive symptoms (Salzman, 1996; Toth & Cicchetti, 1996; West, Rose, Verhoef, et al., 1998), and that attachment history shapes the child's capacity for, and patterns of, emotion regulation (Cicchetti, Ganiban, & Barnett, 1991; Cooper, Shaver, & Collins, 1998; Siegel, 1999; Sroufe, 1996). Since emotional process is tied to physiological process, emotion dysregulation and physiological dysregulation are also likely to be tightly linked (Cassidy, 1994; Field, 1994) with potential influence on physical or psychological diseases through psychophysiological processes and pathways (Cole et al., 1994; Liang & Boyce, 1993; Porges, 1996; Schore, 1996).

It may appear to the reader that the construct of attachment overlaps with the constructs of proximity and generational hierarchy included in the BBFM. However, we believe that the constructs are actually quite distinct, suggesting potentially independent influence on child functioning. Proximity, as conceptualized in the BBFM, refers merely to the amount and intensity of physical and emotional exchange among all family members. In contrast, the construct of attachment refers to dyadic relations, and includes not only the child's seeking of proximity, when under threat or stress, but also the attunement (that is, sensitive attentiveness, perception, and response) of the caregiver, which helps the child modulate the emotional/physiological response. Thus attachment involves the notion of safety and emotion regulation, but proximity, by itself, does not. The constructs are related, however. The degree of family or child-parent proximity (or lack thereof) constrains the expression of attachment interactions. The nurturance aspect of generational hierarchy is also not equivalent to attachment, because nurturance is a broader construct addressing a more general fostering of the child's well-being. Nurturance and attachment are likely to be closely related, however, because secure parent-child attachment interactions are unlikely to occur in the absence of a nurturant relationship. For these reasons, we conclude that the addition of attachment to the BBFM may address a separate domain of family function, which could have unique influence on child psychological and physiological outcomes.

Given the above research findings and theoretical rationale, it seems likely that secure parent-child attachment may buffer, and insecure attachment exacerbate, the impact of stressful family process (or life events) on disease-related psychological and physiological processes in children (Bleil, Ramesh, Miller, & Wood, in press; Wood, 1999). Furthermore, patterns of proximity, generational hierarchy, and responsivity are likely to shape and constrain (and be constrained by) attachment configurations in the family. Taking all these factors into consideration, we propose to integrate attachment into the revised 1999 BBFM (see Figure 2.1).

Literature Review

To date, there have been no studies reported that test the full BBFM. However, there is research relevant to components of the model. We will not review the literature on proximity, hierarchy, and responsivity since these aspects of the model are not the focus of the current study. We will review parental conflict, triangulation of the child in that conflict, and the biobehavioral reactivity link.

Parental conflict, a key aspect defining the quality of parental relationship, has negative consequences for children, including depression, poor academic performance, and conduct-related problems (Davies & Cummings, 1994; Emery & O'Leary, 1982; Grych & Fincham, 1990; Reid & Crisafulli, 1990). Katz and Gottman (1994) concluded that marital conflict was the strongest familial predictor of childhood behavior problems. Cowan and colleagues (1996) found parental conflict to mediate the relationship between parents' individual distress and child externalizing problems. Although most of the research in this area has focused on the behavioral indicators of child distress, and identified relations between marital conflict and externalizing problems, marital conflict has also been identified as a prime risk factor in childhood depression (Seligman, Reivich, Jaycox, & Gillham, 1995). It is also likely that underlying the externalizing behavioral expressions of distress there may be intense emotional experience of depression, despair, and hopelessness.

Although the association between marital conflict and child problems has been shown repeatedly, few studies have investigated systematically mechanisms or pathways by which parental conflict may impact on the child's emotional and physical well-being. One exception to this is Grych and Fincham's (1990) cognitive-contextual model, proposing that the impact of parental conflict is mediated by children's understandings and appraisal of the conflict. Davies and Cummings (1994) emphasize the central role that emotions play in children's response to parental conflict. Some studies extend the investigation to physiological responses in the child. El-Sheikh (1994) found that girls from high-conflict homes exhibited greater, and boys lower, heart rate reactivity in response to an argument between two adults in a laboratory setting. Katz and Gottman (1995) hypothesize that marital conflict evokes physiological and emotional dysregulation in the child, causing increased levels of stress hormones and longer time to recover from arousal in response to emotional events. They also found an association between parental conflict in the laboratory and higher vagal tone in the child (Gottman & Katz, 1989). Gottman and Katz interpret the child's increased vagal tone as an indication of a buffering system that is activated by the conflict (vagal activation modulates level of sympathetic arousal). However, we have found that vagal activation was associated with feelings of depressed hopelessness evoked in a laboratory paradigm (Miller & Wood, 1997), which is consistent with other findings in the literature. We propose, therefore, that vagal activation may also accompany the emotional state of depressed hopelessness that is evoked in the child by chronic parental conflict. Furthermore, we propose that, for some diseases (for example, asthma or irritable bowel syndrome), high levels of emotionally engendered vagal activation may potentiate vagally mediated disease process (for example, airway constriction in asthma).

Triangulation. Children may become involved in parental conflict when they attempt to regulate emotions (Davies & Cummings, 1994). Such involvement increases with increasing intensity of the conflict (Cummings, Zahn-Waxler, & Radke-Yarrow, 1981; Emery, 1989), and has negative outcomes for children (Davies & Cummings, 1994; Vuchinich, Emery, & Cassidy, 1988). In a more direct laboratory-based assessment, Wood (Wood, Watkins, Boyle, et al., 1989) observed and rated marital discord and triangulation of children with inflammatory bowel disease. Findings indicated that marital discord and triangulation were related to increased disease activity, whereas poor family conflict resolution, enmeshment, and overprotection were not.

Each of the components of the BBFM appear to have important relations to both psychological and physical well-being in children. However none of the studies to date have directly investigated the mechanisms by which family patterns might impact on child physical well-being or disease. The following section addresses that psychophysiological link.

The Biobehavioral Reactivity-Disease Activity Link. One type of biobehavioral reactivity may be conceptualized as high stress-reactivity, rendering children vulnerable to a number of physical and psychological illness outcomes (Boyce, Chesney, Alkon, et al., 1995; Liang & Boyce, 1993). In the "stress" research view of biobehavioral reactivity, it is posited that vagal (parasympathetic) influence modulates the stress response (sympathetic arousal), and is, therefore, positive or protective (Katz & Gottman, 1995; Porges, 1995). However, for individuals with asthma, higher vagal activation may be problematic because vagal activation is one mechanism of airways constriction. Thus, for asthma, and other illnesses mediated by parasympathetic (vagal) activation, vagal activation becomes the specific "biobehavioral reactivity" that is of concern. For these reasons, we identify vagal activation as the specific *type* of "biobehavioral reactivity" examined in this study of children with asthma.

Asthma is defined as a chronic inflammatory disorder of the airways in which inflammation causes recurrent episodes of wheezing, breathlessness, chest tightness, and coughing associated with airflow obstruction that is reversible (National Heart, Lung and Blood Institute, 1997). It is widely recognized that airway constriction is mediated by cholinergic/vagal (parasympathetic nervous system) pathways and by immune/inflammatory processes (Middleton, Ellis, Yunginger, et al., 1998). Thus, these mechanisms of airway constriction in asthma point to two possible biobehavioral pathways by which emotions may influence airway function: 1) psychoneuroimmunological, and 2) psychophysiological (vagal). Previous research on children with asthma has linked hopelessness or despair to airway constriction and poor course of illness through the psychophysiological mechanism of vagal activation (Miller, 1987; Miller & Strunk, 1989; Miller & Wood, 1995, 1997). Thus the proposed BBFM pathway under investigation will be particular patterns of family process (parental conflict, triangulation of the child, and insecure parent-child attachment) which evoke states of hopelessness with concomitant vagal activation in children with asthma.

Current Study

The study presented here is part of a larger project testing Wood's BBFM and Miller's Autonomic Nervous System (ANS) Dysregulation Model of the Impact of Emotions on Asthma (Miller & Wood, 1995). The goal of the present study was two-fold: 1) to assess the value of incorporating attachment into the BBFM; 2) to test key family psychophysiological pathways proposed by the revised 1999 BBFM. Attachment was estimated according to the child's perception of the security of parent-child relatedness. The linkages tested were among the child's perception of *parental conflict* and *triangulation,* the child's perception of *security of relatedness with each parent,* and the child's biobehavioral reactivity. For this study, the biobehavioral reactivity construct encompasses the psychological state of *depressed hopelessness* and physiological function of *vagal activation.*

METHODS

Design and Rationale

This study uses a multimethod, multimeasure design in which emotions and family interactions

Table 2.1   Description of Movie Scenes and Family Tasks

Movie Scenes	Family Tasks (Five Minutes Each)
• Baseline Before movie begins—television is blank	• Card House Family builds a house out of playing cards
• Parental Conflict Elliott reveals to his mother at the family dinner that her ex-husband is away with a girl friend	• Patient Problem Family discusses the patient's biggest problem
• Death Elliott delivers a soliloquy over the "dead" body of E.T.	• Loss Family discusses the greatest loss or saddest experience of the patient
• Alive E.T.'s "heart" lights up—Elliott discovers E.T. is alive	• Patient Disagreement Family discusses a source of disagreement between patient and parents
• Separation End of movie—E.T. and Elliott say goodbye	• Parent Disagreement Parents discuss a source of disagreement between themselves with the children present
• Total Movie From the opening credits to the end of the movie	• Cohesion Each family member says what they like best about everyone else in the family
	• Total Family Protocol Compilation of all family tasks

are evoked in a controlled laboratory setting, and self-reports are obtained to provide data regarding the child's emotional status and his or her perception of family relationships. An emotionally challenging movie ("E.T., the Extra-Terrestrial") and family discussion tasks were used to evoke a variety of emotional/physiological responses, some of which are based in content relevant to family conflict, triangulation, and parent-child attachment. (See Table 2.1 for description of scenes and family tasks.) The evoked physiological responses were then correlated with the child's report of parental conflict, triangulation, security of parent-child relatedness (at home), and of ongoing hopelessness, in order to assess linkages between the child's experience of family relationships and emotional condition, on the one hand, and the child's physiological responses to emotional challenge on the other. Physiological data (heart rate and vagal activation) was also collected during a 5-minute rest period (baseline) before the movie began.

The following **Hypotheses** were tested:

1. Child perception of parental conflict is associated with hopelessness and increased vagal activation. Something changed here?

2. Triangulation in parental conflict is associated with hopelessness and increased vagal activation.

3. Insecure patterns of mother-child or father-child relatedness are associated with hopelessness and with increased vagal activation.

4. Hopelessness is associated with increased vagal activation.

We used two levels of approach in testing connections between the family and child psychological variables in relation to the child's physiological process (vagal activation). The first level of approach examined whether children showed characteristic vagal activation levels that were related to (and hypothetically influenced by) the family and/or child psychological variables, but which were carried across laboratory-evoked content, and even during resting baseline. To test hypotheses 1-4, we tested the predicted correlations among child perception of parental conflict, triangulation, security of parent-child relatedness, hopelessness, and anxiety with vagal activation at baseline, throughout the movie, and averaged across all family tasks. The patterns of correlation among parental conflict, triangulation, and insecure relatedness also were explored. Anxiety was assessed in relation to these variables to test the specificity of hopelessness as an emotional psychophysiological link to vagal activation in children with asthma.

The second level of approach explored whether vagal activation evoked in the laboratory during content-specific movie scenes (e.g., parent conflict or separation/loss/attachment), or during specific types of family interaction (e.g., parent conflict or parent-child conflict) was differentially related to child report of parental conflict, insecure parent-child attachment, and/or hopelessness, as it occurs at home. This approach tested the effects of specific family-sensitized "emotional triggers" of vagal activation. We reasoned that parental conflict, triangulation, and insecure attachment may sensitize children to respond to conflict and attachment-relevant laboratory exposures with hopelessness accompanied with vagal activation. If this were the case, then we would expect that the variance in vagal activation during parental conflict or separation/loss/attachment exposures would be associated with the child's self-report of parent conflict, triangulation, and parent-child relatedness occurring at home. In contrast, we would not expect such associations during laboratory exposures that have other emotional content.

Although the sample size was too small to justify formal analysis, we tested the following **Hypotheses** on an exploratory basis:

5. The degree of vagal activation during laboratory-based movie scenes or family interactions involving parental conflict will be specifically related to the child's report of parental conflict, triangulation, and hopelessness.

6. The degree of vagal activation during laboratory-based movie scenes or family interactions involving

separation/loss or attachment will be specifically related to the child's report of security of parent-child relatedness, and hopelessness.

It should be noted that we are *not* predicting that the actual *level* of vagal activation will be the greatest during the parent-conflict and separation/loss content exposures. Other content might evoke equally high or even higher levels of vagal activation. However, the level of vagal response to this other content would *not* be expected to be related to the child's report of parental conflict, triangulation, or parent-child relatedness. Rather, the level of vagal activation in these scenes would be primarily due to other factors. Thus, the testing of hypotheses 5 and 6 require focus on the *links* among variables, and not on the absolute levels of the variables measured.

Subjects

Twenty-two mildly to moderately asthmatic children, 11 male, 11 female (mean age = 12, $SD = 2.34$) and their mothers, fathers, and closest-aged siblings were recruited from a suburban allergist's office. Families were told that we were interested in understanding how children and their families solve problems and adapt to asthma. Diagnosis of asthma was confirmed, and disease severity was determined, by the child's allergist using National Heart, Lung and Blood Institute Guidelines (National Heart, Lung and Blood Institute, 1997). Included were children between the ages of 8 to 16 who had diagnosis of asthma and no other major medical illness; who were living with two parents (could be step-parents) for at least the last 2 years; and who had at least one other sibling. Parents signed a consent and children an assent form. The study was approved by the Children's Hospital of Buffalo Human Subjects Review Board. Recruitment success was about 33%, with shortage of time being the primary reason given for refusal. The children who participated in the current study did not differ from those who declined with respect to socioeconomic status or disease severity.

Variables and Measures

Parental conflict (i.e., negative parental relationship quality) was indexed by the score on the *conflict properties scale* (compilation of frequency, intensity, and resolution subscales) of the Children's Perception of Interparental Conflict Scale (CPIC; Grych, Seid, & Fincham, 1992). The CPIC is a 52-item self-report scale in which items are answered not true, sort of true, and true. This subscale of the CPIC was derived from factor analysis, and has been shown to have good reliability, with alpha coefficients of .90 and .89 (Grych et al., 1992). The alpha coefficient for the current sample was .94. The test-retest correlation for this subscale was .70. This subscale was related to child adjustment difficulties as measured on the Child Behavioral Checklist, thus supporting predictive validity (Grych et al., 1992).

Convergent data on parental relationship/conflict was obtained by husband and wife independent self-report of marital satisfaction on the Dyadic Satisfaction scale of the Dyadic Adjustment Scale (DAS; Spanier, 1976) and the Kansas Marital Satisfaction scale (KMS; Miller & Wood, 1995). The Dyadic Satisfaction subscale of the DAS has shown good reliability, with alpha coefficients of .94 (Spanier, 1976). The alpha coefficient of the current sample was .88. The KMS has also shown good reliability, with alpha coefficients of .93 (Miller & Wood, 1995). Current sample alpha coefficient was .97.

Triangulation (Self-Blame/Content Scale of CPIC). Although the self-blame/content scale is not labeled as "triangulation" by the authors of the CPIC, the items and concepts of self-blame, and child belief that they cause parental conflict are seen by family systems theorists and researchers as key aspects of triangulation (Bowen, 1971; Haley, 1967; Minuchin, 1974). The reliability of these two subscales of the CPIC has also been shown to be adequate with coefficient alphas of .78 and .84 for the CPIC self-blame and content subscales (Grych et al., 1992). The coefficient alpha for the current sample was .71 for the self-blame/content scale. The test-retest correlation for the CPIC self-blame/content scale has been shown to be .76. Validity of the self-blame/content scale of the CPIC is supported by the relationship of scores on this scale to children's perceptions that a child in marital conflict vignettes was at fault for the conflict (Grych et al., 1992).

Attachment is estimated by the Relatedness questionnaire, a 17-item questionnaire completed by the child, once for each parent (Lynch & Cicchetti, 1991, 1997). "Relatedness" describes the quality of the child's self-reported relationship patterns with his or her parents (Connell, 1990). The relatedness construct and instrument include two dimensions: "Psychological Proximity Seeking" and "Emotional Quality." "Psychological Proximity Seeking" refers to the child's desire to be "closer" to the person about whom the child is answering the questionnaire. For example, the child may endorse items stating that he or she wishes to be "better understood" by, or "spend more time" with, the parent. It is proposed that endorsing proximity-seeking items reflects insufficiency of attachment connection. "Emotional Quality" refers to the positive and negative emotions that the child feels when in the presence of the parent.

The configurational combination of scores on each dimension yields five qualitatively distinct patterns of relatedness, 2 secure and 3 insecure (Lynch & Cicchetti, 1991, 1997), which parallel attachment patterns (Lynch & Cicchetti, 1997). Children with *optimal* patterns of relatedness report higher than average levels of positive emotions and lower than average amounts of psychological proximity-seeking. *Average* children report levels of emotional quality and psychological proximity-seeking within one standard deviation from the mean for each dimension. These children feel positive and secure in their relationships, and they are satisfied with existing degrees of closeness. Children with *deprived* (ambivalent) patterns of relatedness report lower than average levels of emotional quality, but higher than average amounts of psychological proximity-seeking. These children desire to feel closer to others, but their relationships are characterized by feelings of negativity and insecurity. Children with *disengaged* (avoidant) patterns of relatedness report lower than average levels of emotional quality and lower than average amounts of psychological proximity-seeking. These children have predominantly negative feelings about others and do not want to be any closer to them. *Confused* children report high levels of emotional quality as well as extremely high amounts of psychological proximity-seeking. To achieve the power necessary for a small *n,* and in a manner consistent with the way in which relatedness has been treated in past research (Cicchetti, Toth, & Lynch, 1995), these categories were combined into a secure relatedness group and an insecure relatedness group. Children identified as reporting optimal and adequate patterns of relatedness were identified as having "secure" patterns of relationship, and children identified as reporting deprived, avoidant, or confused patterns of relatedness were identified as "insecure."

This questionnaire has been used with children aged 8 to 13. Cronbach's alpha coefficient for psychological proximity seeking ranges from .83 to .93, and for emotional quality from .67 to .83. In the current sample of children, Cronbach's alpha for psychological proximity-seeking was .86 to .90, and for emotional quality was .86 to .92, for mothers or fathers, respectively. The validity of the Relatedness Questionnaire is supported by its ability to differentiate maltreated from nonmaltreated children, and to predict psychosocial outcomes in these children (Toth & Cicchetti, 1996).

The *Hopelessness Scale for Children* (*HSC*; Kazdin, Rodgers, & Colbus, 1986) is a 17-item true-false self-report questionnaire with an internal consistency coefficient alpha ranging from .75-.97 (Kazdin, French, Unis, et al., 1983; Kazdin et al., 1986). Cronbach's alpha for the current sample was .73. The scale correlates moderately in the positive direction with measures of depression and with suicidality (Marciano & Kazdin, 1994) and in the negative direction with self-esteem, thus supporting construct validity.

The *Multidimensional Anxiety Scale for Children* (MASC; March, Parker, Sullivan et al., 1997) was used to assess the level of anxiety. The MASC is a 39-item self-report questionnaire that provides an overall anxiety score and scores on four factors (physical symptoms, harm avoidance, social anxiety, and separation anxiety). The alpha reliability coefficients have been reported to range from .6-.9. The alpha coefficient for the current sample was .87. Test-retest reliability is in the satisfactory to excellent range (March et al., 1997).

Vagal Activation. Heart period (rate) fluctuations were used to compute respiratory sinus arrhythmia (RSA), an inferential measure of vagal activation.

Fluctuations in heart period were detrended using a moving polynomial and band pass filter, and were analyzed to compute the natural logarithm of the variance of the resulting inter-beat interval signal (Porges, 1992). RSA's during baseline, movie, and family tasks were highly intercorrelated (*r*'s range from .7 to .9, $p < .001$), indicating the reliability of this measure and within subject stability of this variable. Heart rate was also computed to clarify further the physiological response.

Procedure

Movie Protocol. All children arrived between 7:30 and 8:00 AM in order to minimize effects of circadian rhythm on physiological measures. According to previously accepted procedure, medications were withheld for 12 hours prior to the study (Miller & Wood, 1994). The children answered questionnaires, had the physiological sensors placed, and rested for 5 minutes to obtain baseline heart rate and respiration rate. Then they viewed the movie ("E.T., the Extra-Terrestrial") alone, while having their heart period continuously recorded. After the movie, the children resumed their normal daily activities until the family protocol in the late afternoon. Previous research has demonstrated the reliability and validity of this movie in evoking asthma-relevant emotional and physiological responses, regardless of the number of times the movie was previously viewed (Miller & Wood, 1994). See Table 2.1 for a description of the scenes.

Family Protocol. In the late afternoon, the children and their mothers, fathers, and closest-aged siblings answered questionnaires and participated in six emotionally challenging family discussion tasks. Before coming together family members independently identified problems, losses, and conflicts for later discussion during the tasks. A research assistant read the family the instructions for each task, and then left after saying that s/he would return in a few minutes (see Table 2.1 for the content of the discussion tasks). After the family protocol, the children and their families were given an opportunity to ask questions and make comments and suggestions to the investigators.

Table 2.2   Descriptive Statistics

	N	M	SD
Parental Conflict Properties	22	10.82	8.23
Triangulation—Self-Blame	22	3.32	3.18
Hopelessness Scale for Children (HSC)	22	3.00	2.49
MASC Total Score (anxiety)	22	52.00	10.44
Baseline Vagal Activation	22	7.92	0.94
Total Movie Vagal Activation	22	7.86	0.84
Total Family Protocol Vagal Activation	20†	6.58	1.08
	N Secure	*N* Insecure	% Secure
Mother Relatedness	17	5	77.3
Father Relatedness	12	10	54.5

† Artifact compromised the physiological measures in two families, hence the *N* of 20 for total Family Vagal Activation.

Data Reduction and Analysis

Heart rate (HR) and vagal activation (RSA) were computed for baseline, the whole movie, and for specific preselected movie scenes (parent conflict; E.T. death; E.T. revives; E.T. and Elliott say goodbye). For the family tasks, HR and RSA were computed for each 5-minute task, and then averaged across tasks to obtain whole family task scores.[2] The hypothesized associations among variables were tested using Pearson product-moment correlations. Heart rate was not systematically related to any of the variables and will not be discussed further in this report.

RESULTS

Father and mother self-reported marital satisfaction scores were inversely related to the child's perception of conflict intensity, frequency, and resolution (DASF: $r = -.63$, $p < .005$; KMSF: $r = -.77$, $p < .0001$; DASM: $r = -.45$, $p < .05$; KMSM: $r = -.43$, $p < .05$), thus indicating convergence on the phenomenon of negative parental relationship quality. However, the hypothesized (Hypothesis 1) relationship between child-perceived parental conflict and hopelessness and vagal activation was not supported. See Table 2.2 for descriptive statistics and Table 2.3 for correlations. Note that shaded cells in Table 2.3 contain the correlations hypothesized *a priori*.

Hypothesis two, positing that triangulation would be associated with hopelessness and vagal activation, was partially supported. Triangulation was associated with increased vagal activation during the baseline ($r = .52$, $p < .05$), the movie ($r = .47$, $p < .05$), and the family tasks ($r = .57$, $p < .01$), but was not significantly associated with hopelessness ($r = .25$, ns).

Most of the children reported secure relatedness with mother (77%), whereas only 54% reported secure relatedness with father. (The preponderance of secure relatedness reports for mother may have diminished the statistical power necessary to achieve significant associations between mother-child relatedness and the other variables. Nonetheless, it should be noted that in many cases the correlations, themselves, are very small for mothers as compared to fathers.) The test of Hypothesis three regarding security of parent-child relatedness and hopelessness and vagal activation yielded different results for fathers and mothers. Insecure father relatedness was associated with hopelessness ($r = .53$, $p < .05$) and increased vagal activation (RSA) during the baseline ($r = .59$, $p < .005$), the movie ($r = .63$, $p < .005$), and the family tasks ($r = .47$, $p < .05$). Insecure mother relatedness was associated with hopelessness ($r = .45$, $p < .05$) but not with vagal activation. (See Table 2.3.)

Hypothesis four, positing that hopelessness (HSC) would be associated with increased vagal activation (RSA) received partial support. HSC and RSA approached significant correlation for the movie ($r = .40$, $p < .06$), and was significantly correlated across family tasks ($r = .44$, $p < .05$). (See Table 2.3.)

Table 2.3   Correlations Between Parental Conflict, Triangulation, Parent Child Relatedness, and Vagal Activation

		PC	T-SB	HSC	MASC	RL-M	RL-F
Perception of Parental Conflict (PC)	r p						
Triangulation—Involvement (T-I)	r p	.55 †					
Triangulation—Self-Blame (T-SB)	r p	.38 †					
Hopelessness (HSC)	r p	.12 —	.25 —				
MASC Total Score (MASC)	r p	.10 —	−.26 —	.13 —			
Relatedness With Mother (RL-M)	r p	.22 —	.15 —	.45 *	.10 —		
Relatedness With Father (RL-F)	r p	.40 †	.64 ****	.53 *	.10 —	.38 †	
Baseline Vagal Activation	r p	.25 —	.52 *	.32 —	.11 —	.17 —	.59 ***
Total Movie Vagal Activation	r p	.26 —	.47 *	.40 †	.18 —	.29 —	.63 ***
Total Family Protocol Vagal Activation	r p	.15 —	.57 **	.44 *	−.22 —	.20 —	.47 *

NOTE: Shaded cells indicate relations tested in hypotheses.

$†p < .10$, $*p < .05$, $**p < .01$, $***p < .005$, $****p < .001$.

Hypothesis five (exploratory) predicted that the degree of vagal activation during laboratory-induced movie scenes or family interactions involving parental conflict would be specifically related to the child's report of parental conflict, triangulation, and hopelessness. The parental conflict movie scene, in contrast to the E.T. death and E.T. alive scenes, showed vagal activation correlated with triangulation self-blame ($r = .52$, $p < .05$), but not the parental conflict nor hopelessness. Vagal activation also was associated (but not predicted to be) with insecure patterns of relatedness with father ($r = .57$, $p < .005$) during the parent conflict scene.

Among the family tasks, we predicted that the hypothesized pattern would be most prominent in the parent disagreement task. For this task, vagal activation was correlated with triangulation ($r = .51$, $p < .05$) and with hopelessness ($r = .49$, $p < .05$), but not parental conflict. Vagal activation also was associated (but not predicted to be) with insecure patterns of relatedness with father ($r = .48$, $p < .05$) during the parent conflict task. However, the hypothesized pattern was also obtained in the neutral card task. (See Table 2.4.)

Hypothesis six (exploratory) predicted that the degree of vagal activation during laboratory-

Table 2.4   Exploratory Analysis of Family-Related Vagal Activation Specific to Family Tasks

		PC	T-SB	HSC	MASC	RL-M	RL-F
Movie Vagal Activation							
Parental Conflict Scene	r	.32	.52	.28	.08	.35	.57
	p	—	*	—	—	—	***
Death Scene	r	.12	.26	.15	−.11	.06	.25
	p	—	—	—	—	—	—
Alive Scene	r	.11	.14	.34	−.03	.20	.37
	p	—	—	—	—	—	†
Separation Scene	r	.31	.32	.41	.15	.12	.55
	p	—	—	†	—	—	**
Family Protocol Vagal Activation							
Card House	r	.12	.62	.53	−.11	.15	.64
	p	—	***	*	—	—	***
Patient Problem	r	.07	.60	.36	−.27	.20	.43
	p	—	**	—	—	—	†
Loss Discussion	r	.10	.56	.36	−.28	.04	.35
	p	—	*	—	—	—	—
Patient Disagreement	r	.08	.59	.41	−.27	.39	.48
	p	—	*	†	—	—	*
Parent Disagreement	r	.23	.51	.49	−.06	.19	.48
	p	—	*	*	—	—	*
Cohesion Discussion	r	.14	.46	.41	−.15	.21	.34
	p	—	*	†	—	—	—

NOTE: Shaded cells indicate relations tested in hypotheses. PC = Perception of Parental Conflict; T-SB = Triangulation—Self-Blame; HSC = Hopelessness; MASC = Multidimensional Anxiety Scale for Children; RL-M = Relatedness—Mother; RL-F = Relatedness—Father.

$†p < .10, *p < .05, **p < .01, ***p < .005, ****p < .001.$

induced movie scenes or family interactions involving separation/loss or attachment would be related to the child's report of insecurity of parent-child relatedness and hopelessness. We predicted that the E.T.-Elliott separation scene at the end of the movie should reveal this pattern. In this scene vagal activation was correlated with insecure father-child relatedness ($r = .55, p < .01$) and approached significant correlation with hopelessness ($r = .41, p < .06$). This pattern was not found in the parental conflict, E.T. death, or alive scenes. With regard to actual family interaction, we predicted that the parent-child disagreement would most strongly reveal the predicted pattern, reasoning that disagreement involves an emotional "separation." For this task, vagal activation was correlated with insecure father-child relatedness ($r = .48, p < .05$) and approached significant correlation with hopelessness ($r = .41, p < .1$). (The loss task was not selected because often the children presented very benign or nonrelational losses). However the hypothesized pattern also held for the neutral task and the parent disagreement task. In

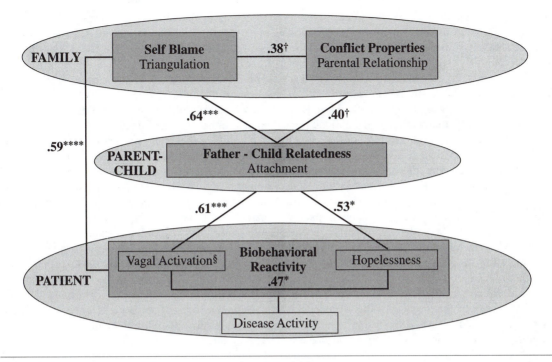

Figure 2.3   Summary of Relationships Among Study Variables

NOTE: † *p* < .10, * *p* < .05, *** *p* < .005, **** *p* < .001 *p*, § average of movie and family data

general, the patterns were not very specific for family task type. Triangulation self-blame was fairly robustly correlated with vagal activation throughout the family discussions, whereas it was not in the movie scenes. Insecure father relatedness was correlated with vagal activation in three of the six family tasks (the disagreement tasks and the card house task) and in two of the four movie scenes (the parental conflict scene and the separation scene). In conclusion, the exploratory testing of hypotheses 5 and 6 received only partial support. (See Table 2.4.)

Assessment of other linkages revealed a trend in association between perceived parental conflict and triangulation (*r* = .38, *p* < .09), but triangulation in parental conflict was not associated with hopelessness (*r* = .25, *ns*). Although we had no specific *a priori* hypothesis regarding how perception of parental conflict would relate to quality of relatedness, we found a trend toward association between perceived parental conflict and insecure father relatedness (*r* = .40, *p* < .07), but not for mother relatedness. Furthermore, insecure relatedness with father was associated with triangulation (*r* = .64, *p* < .005) as well as hopelessness (*r* = .53, *p* < .05). Anxiety

(MASC) symptoms were not systematically related to any of the variables. (See Figure 2.3 for a summary of the relations among variables.)

DISCUSSION

The results reported must be interpreted with considerable caution, given the preliminary nature of this study and the small sample size. Nonetheless certain patterns are robust, others intriguing, and taken together, the findings raise important questions and considerations for future research.

Relations Among Parental Conflict, Triangulation, and Parent-Child Attachment. The most unexpected finding is that the child's perception of level of parental conflict (intensity, frequency, and resolution) was not reliably related to hopelessness, anxiety, or vagal activation. There was a trend toward parental conflict being related to triangulation, but this correlation did not achieve significance, perhaps because of the small sample size. This lack of association between perceived level of parental conflict and the psychological and physiological variables is particularly surprising since the correlations between parent self-report of marital satisfaction and the child's perceptions of conflict converge, lending support to the validity of the assessment of parental discord. Perhaps it is not simply the perceived characteristics of the intensity and frequency of parental conflict that matters to the child, but the meaning of the discord for the child, or the way the child is involved in the conflict. This interpretation is supported by the finding that while parent conflict is *not* associated with vagal activation, triangulation is. These findings are consistent with Grych and Fincham's theory that the impact of parent conflict on a child importantly depends upon the interaction of this process with the child's interpretation of the conflict and with his or her personality and/or cognitive style (Grych, 1998; Grych & Fincham, 1990).

It is noteworthy that vagal activation is associated with both the self-blame focus of this index of triangulation (that is, the child's perception that s/he is to blame for the conflict) and with insecure relatedness with father. Previous research indicates that insecure attachment is associated with shame (Lopez, 1997; Lutwak, 1997; Schore, 1994, 1996), and with shame proneness and self-blame (Tangney, 1999); and shame has been shown to be characterized by parasympathetic (vagal) activation (Schore, 1994, 1996). It is possible that the child's perception of responsibility and self-blame for parental conflict also may be accompanied by feelings of shame. Thus one might speculate that a child's shame could be an important psychophysiologically compromising link between parental conflict, insecure attachment, and compromised disease function in asthma.

The quality of the child's attachment to each parent clearly plays an integral role. The association between parental conflict and children's psychological functioning has been shown to be at least partially mediated by parent-child relationships (Black & Pedro-Carroll, 1993; Harold, Fincham, Osborne, & Conger, 1997; Osborne & Fincham, 1996). The current finding that the child's security of relatedness with father was associated (a trend) with perception of parental conflict, and robustly with triangulation is consistent with the literature. Owen and Cox (1997) found that marital conflict before the birth of the couple's first child predicted

insecurity in the child's later attachment relationships with its parents, especially with fathers. Similarly, Howes and Markman (1989) found that father's reports of marital conflict before the child was born predicted dependency in the child. These and the current findings suggest either that parental conflict, for which the child blames herself or himself, undermines father-child security, or that insecurity of father-child attachment renders marital conflict and self-blame more salient for the child. One might speculate that this association could be the result of father's marital conflict spilling over to the child, impairing the security of the relationship, perhaps in part through overt blaming of the child. The lack of relationship between mother-child relatedness and self-blame might be due to mothers being better able to compartmentalize their marital conflict. Alternatively, it is also conceivable that a personality inclination toward self-blame might make the child overly sensitive to negative-relating experiences both with father and within the marital relationship, and a tendency to self-blame may also lead children to blame themselves for whatever marital discord they perceived.

The lack of findings for mother relatedness is inconsistent with the literature. Howes and Markman (1989) found that lower marital satisfaction reported by mothers before the birth of the couple's child predicted insecure attachment in the child. It is possible that the predominant reports of secure mother-child patterns of relatedness in our sample (77% secure with mothers vs. 54% secure with fathers) may account for the lack of findings. Alternatively, mothers may be better able than fathers to compartmentalize their marital dissatisfaction if the dissatisfaction is less intense or long-lived. Our sample may have included couples with milder marital dissatisfaction than was typified in the Howes and Markman (1989) sample.

Attachment Assumes a Central Position Among the BBFM Variables. The overall pattern of results places relatedness/attachment in a central position among the interrelating variables: insecure relatedness with father is associated with hopelessness and triangulation, all of which are related to vagal activation (see Figure 2.3). One possible interpretation is that compromised attachment may engender both hopelessness and shame, each of which are physiologically accompanied by vagal activation (Lopez, 1997; Lutwak, 1997; Schore, 1994, 1996). Self-blame and responsibility for parental conflict are also likely to be accompanied by feelings of shame. It thus appears that there may be two distinct psychophysiological pathways to vagal activation in attachment insecurity: one via insecure father-child attachment and self-blame/shame regarding parental conflict, and one via insecure father-child attachment and hopelessness. If this suggestion is valid, the implication is that the quality of attachment would be exquisitely important with regard to psychophysiological vulnerability in asthma or other psychological or physical illnesses mediated by vagal activation.

The small sample size in this study precludes tests of parent-child relatedness as a moderating or mediating factor in the relationship between family process and individual child psychological and physiological function. However the pattern of results suggests that relatedness (a proposed index of attachment) plays a central role, and thus justifies more specific investigation regarding the pathways by which relatedness influences psychological and physiological factors. The findings of this study are consistent with the 1999 BBFM, which includes an attachment component, and supports the heuristic value of such a revision of the 1993 model.

General Versus Scene-Specific and Task-Specific Relations Among Variables. The association between triangulation, self-blame, insecure father relatedness, and hopelessness, each to vagal activation throughout the baseline, movie, and family discussions, indicates that children who experience these processes carry around a generally elevated level of vagal activation. Such a state would render asthmatic children, or any patient whose disease is worsened by vagal activation, vulnerable to exacerbations and a worse course of disease. This interpretation is consistent with both the 1999 BBFM, which proposes interpersonal pathways influencing psychophysiological processes, and with Miller's Autonomic Nervous System (ANS) Dysregulation Model of Emotional Influence on Asthma (Miller, 1987; Miller & Wood, 1995), which posits a pathogenic synergy between hopelessness and cholinergically mediated airway constriction. The current findings also provide a possible explication of the pathways by which family dysfunction may operate

as a risk factor for morbidity and mortality in asthma (Miller & Strunk, 1989). The finding in the current study indicating a self-blame link with vagal activation, which is independent of the hopelessness-vagal activation link (that is, no correlation between hopelessness and self-blame), suggests that self-blame (and/or shame) may also exacerbate cholinergically mediated airway constriction in asthma.

In addition to the influences that family, parent-child attachment, and psychological factors may have on chronic vagal activation, there may also be acute and specific effects. That is to say, these family relational influences may potentiate vagal activation that is triggered in response to parental conflict or attachment related themes, or emotional experiences engendered inside or outside the family. The findings offered weak support for such specificity within the movie. The limitations in specificity of the movie scenes themselves with respect to emotional content may have attenuated the findings for specificity in emotional triggering. For example, the so-called parental conflict scene included reference to mother's and father's unhappy separation, but also made reference to father's absence, which may account for the observed, but not predicted, *a priori* correlation between vagal activation and insecure father-child relatedness.

The observation that there is only weak, if any, specificity of patterns of associations based on family task type suggests that the tasks are also less effective than originally expected in their ability to evoke the specific emotional interactions. Perhaps the task demands were not strong enough to evoke sufficiently differentiated family process. More likely, family patterns of relational interaction may be stronger than, or transcend, the particular content of discussions. Furthermore, it is also likely that the child's physiological and emotional experience of the family process has been conditioned by years of patterned process, so that his or her experience of the family relating is more continuous than differentiated, even when the family engages in a variety of emotional and relational processes.

Summary

There appears to be evidence of disease-relevant psychophysiological influence associated with triangulation in parental conflict, insecure parent-child attachment, and hopelessness. This association appears to be in the form of a continuous vagal activation bias, regardless of the emotional content of the immediate context. These findings are consistent with the 1999 BBFM and justify further investigation of the model. There is also weak, but intriguing evidence for another level of influence, that being the family-related potentiation of vagal response to particular emotional themes or family processes. The intriguing nature of these findings, and the fact that methodological limitations may have diminished the strength of the specificity effects, suggest the value of further investigation in this area.

Limitations of This Study

The small sample size in this preliminary study requires the exercise of caution in interpreting the results. Furthermore, limitations in power precluded investigating with more specificity the nature of the relationships among the variables. In addition, this study included only the child's perceptions of parent conflict, triangulation, and parent relatedness, so there is likely to be some shared method variance in the reported associations. This would not, of course, be the case for the associations of the family and psychological variables in relation to the physiological variables.

The family tasks did not always evoke in families the emotional conditions we were seeking. Sometimes people would joke and say nice things to each other in the conflict tasks and sometimes conflict and tension would arise even when families were asked to say nice things about each other (cohesion task). Thus there was not a one-to-one relationship between the task type (neutral, conflict, loss, cohesion) and type of family process. Basing inferences regarding the emotional climate according to the content of the task assigned may have falsely attenuated our assessment of specificity of emotional themes and particular family processes (that is, parental conflict and loss) to evoke vagal activation in children (potentiation hypothesis).

The attachment construct was measured by self-report of parent-child relatedness, which appears to be closely linked to traditional concepts of attachment. However, the instrument has not yet been validated against the currently accepted measures of attachment. Furthermore, limitations in sample size precluded assessment of specific types of insecure relatedness in association with the other variables, thus limiting interpretation and application of the findings.

Finally, the children in this study were restricted in range in terms of severity and stability of asthma (mild to moderate), and reported only mild to moderate hopelessness. Furthermore more than half (77%) of the children reported secure relatedness with mother, possibly precluding the discovery of associations between mother relatedness and the other variables. Finally, the marital discord in most of these families was rather modest. These restrictions may have limited the power and precluded finding associations that would be obtained with a sample containing broader ranges of parent conflict, parent-child relatedness, hopelessness, and asthma disease severity.

Future Research

As part of the larger project from which these findings emerge, we will assess, through observation ratings, particular patterns of family process during the tasks as they relate to the physiological responses, including vagal activation, of the children. This will address the problem of the lack of one-to-one relationship between the task type (neutral, conflict, loss, cohesion) and type of family process. Associating specific ratings for parental conflict, triangulation, invalidation, and support with concomitant physiological processes in the child will allow more specific understandings of how patterns of parental conflict, triangulation, and expressions of quality of attachment impact on emotional and physiological processes in the child. This will permit a better test of the specificity of potentiation of emotional and physiological responses to emotional provocation.

Future research will assess relatedness or attachment through observation measures as well as by child self-report. Focus will be on assessing how secure attachment may buffer, or insecure attachment exacerbate, the impact of family process on children's psychological and physiological processes. The types of insecure attachment and their effects will be specifically studied. Care will be taken to consider fathers and mothers separately with regard to their child's attachment. The current sample was too small and skewed toward secure mother-child relatedness to allow assessment of the relative impact on the child of having two secure, versus one secure, versus no secure parent-child attachments. This configurational aspect of attachment in families warrants investigation.

Future research will also track how patterns of parental conflict interact with the child's perceptions of their conflict, along with the child's individual temperament and cognitive styles. Consideration will be given to the possibility that the child's conscious perceptions and interpretations of parental conflict and the unconscious effects of parental conflict may each have important, but non-overlapping, impact on child psychological and physiological outcomes.

Clinical Implications

The findings of this study are too preliminary to suggest firm clinical implications, but it seems safe to infer that supporting secure attachment processes between the child and each parent is always important, but perhaps critical in the context of marital strife. Secondly, fathers are at least as important as mothers in terms of potential positive and negative influences on the child's well-being. If the findings hold up, they would suggest prioritizing helping fathers to relate supportively to their children during times of marital difficulties. These implications are made with regard to the emotional well-being of children, in general. However, attending to parental conflict, compromised parent-child attachment, hopelessness, and perhaps, self-blame or shame, in children with asthma may be of critical importance for their physical, as well as emotional, well-being.

Notes

1. The autonomic nervous system is that part of the nervous system concerned with regulating the activity of cardiac muscle, smooth muscle, and glands. It is composed of the sympathetic nervous system, which organizes the organism to respond to demands of the environment, and the parasympathetic (that is, vagal) nervous system, which organizes the resting and recuperative aspects of physiological function. The sympathetic and parasympathetic branches regulate one another. High sympathetic arousal, which evokes high heart rate and respiration, is a preparation for action. Parasympathetic (vagal) activation, which is accompanied by low and variable heart rate, can counteract sympathetic arousal to modulate adaptive levels of arousal.

2. Artifact compromised the physiological measures in two families, hence the N of 20 for total Family Vagal Activation.

References

Beeghly, M., & Cicchetti, D. (1996). Child maltreatment, attachment, and the self system: Emergence of an internal state lexicon in toddlers at high social risk (pp. 127-166). In M. E. Hertzig & E. A. Farber (eds.), *Annual progress in child psychiatry and child development*. New York: Brunner/Mazel.

Black, A. E., & Pedro-Carroll, J. (1993). Role of parent-child relationships in mediating the effects of marital disruption. *Journal of the American Academy of Child & Adolescent Psychiatry 32:* 1019-1027.

Bleil, M. E., Ramesh, S., Miller, B. D., & Wood, B. L. (in press). The influence of parent-child relatedness on depressive symptoms in children with asthma: Tests of moderator and mediator models. *Journal of Pediatric Psychiatry*.

Bowen, M. A. (1971). The use of family theory in clinical practice (pp. 159-192). In J. Haley (ed.), *Changing families: A family therapy reader*. New York: Grune & Stratton.

Bowlby, J. (1949). The study and reduction of group tension in the family. *Human Relations 2:* 123-128.

Bowlby, J. (1969). *Attachment and Loss: Vol. 1, Attachment*. New York: Basic Books.

Bowlby, J. (1973). *Attachment and Loss: Vol. 2, Separation*. New York: Basic Books.

Boyce, W. T. (1992). The vulnerable child: New evidence, new approaches. *Advances in Pediatrics 39:* 1-33.

Boyce, W. T., Chesney, M., Alkon, A., Tschann, J. M., Adams, S., Cohen, F., Kaiser, P., Folkman, S., & Wara, D. (1995). Psychobiologic reactivity to stress and childhood respiratory illnesses: Results of two prospective studies. *Psychosomatic Medicine 57:* 411-422.

Bretherton, I. (1985). Attachment theory: Retrospect and prospect. *Monographs of the Society for Research in Child Development 50*(1-2): 167-193.

Byng-Hall, J. (1991). The application of attachment theory to understanding and treatment in family therapy (pp. 199-215). In C. M. Parkes, J. Stevenson-Hinde, & P. Marris (eds.), *Attachment across the life cycle*. New York: Routledge.

Calkins, S. D. (1994). Origins and outcomes of individual differences in emotion regulation. *Monographs of the Society for Research in Child Development 59:* 53-72.

Cassidy, J. (1994). Emotion regulation: Influences of attachment relationships. *Monographs of the*

Society for Research in Child Development 59: 228-249.

Cicchetti, D., Ganiban, J., & Barnett, D. (1991). Contributions from the study of high-risk populations to understanding the development of emotion regulation (pp. 15-48). In J. Garber & K.A. Dodge (eds.), *The development of emotion regulation and dysregulation.* New York: Cambridge University Press.

Cicchetti, D., Toth, S. L., & Lynch, M. (1995). Bowlby's dream comes full circle: The application of attachment theory to risk and psychopathology. *Advances in Clinical Child Psychology 17:* 1-75.

Cobb, C. L. H. (1996). Adolescent-parent attachments and family problem-solving styles. *Family Process 35:* 57-82.

Cole, P. M., Michel, M. K., & Donnell Teti, L. O. (1994). The development of emotion regulation and dysregulation: A clinical perspective. *Monographs of the Society for Research in Child Development 59:* 73-100.

Connell, J. P. (1990). Context, self, and action: A motivational analysis of self-esteem processes across the life-span (pp. 61-97). In D. Cicchetti & M. Beeghly (eds.), *The self in transition: Infancy to childhood.* Chicago: University of Chicago Press.

Cooper, M. L., Shaver, P. R., & Collins, N. L. (1998). Attachment styles, emotion regulation, and adjustment in adolescence. *Journal of Personality & Social Psychology 74:* 1380-1397.

Cowan, P. A., Cowan, C. P., Cohn, D. A., & Pearson, J. L. (1996). Parents' attachment histories and children's externalizing and internalizing behaviors: Exploring family systems models of linkage. *Journal of Consulting & Clinical Psychology 64:* 53-63.

Cummings, E. M. (1990). Classification of attachment on a continuum of felt security: Illustrations from the study of children of depressed parents (pp. 311-338). In M. T. Greenberg, D. Cicchetti, & E. M. Cummings (eds.), *Attachment in the preschool years: Theory, research, and interview.* Chicago: University of Chicago Press.

Cummings, E. M., & Davies, P. (1996). Emotional security as a regulatory process in normal development and the development of psychopathology. *Development and Psychopathology 8:* 123-139.

Cummings, E. M., Zahn-Waxler, C., & Radke-Yarrow, M. (1981). Young children's responses to expressions of anger and affection by others in the family. *Child Development 52:* 1274-1282.

Davies, P. T., & Cummings, E. M. (1994). Marital conflict and child adjustment: An emotional security hypothesis. *Psychological Bulletin 116:* 387-411.

El-Sheikh, M. (1994). Children's emotional and physiological responses to interadult angry behavior: The role of history of interparental hostility. *Journal of Abnormal Child Psychology 22:* 661-678.

Emery, R. E. (1989). Family violence. *American Psychologist 44:* 321-328.

Emery, R. E., & O'Leary, K. D. (1982). Children's perceptions of marital discord and behavior problems of boys and girls. *Journal of Abnormal Child Psychology 10:* 11-24.

Field, T. (1994). The effects of mother's physical and emotional unavailability on emotion regulation. *Monographs of the Society for Research in Child Development 59:* 208-227.

Gottman, J. M., & Katz, L. F. (1989). Effects of marital discord on young children's peer interaction and health. *Developmental Psychology 25:* 373-381.

Grych, J. H. (1998). Children's appraisals of interparental conflict: Situational and contextual influences. *Journal of Family Psychology 12:* 437-453.

Grych, J. H., & Fincham, F. D. (1990). Marital conflict and children's adjustment: A cognitive-contextual framework. *Psychological Bulletin 108:* 267-290.

Grych, J. H., Seid, M., & Fincham, F. D. (1992). Assessing marital conflict from the child's perspective: The children's perception of interparental conflict scale. *Child Development 63*(3): 558-572.

Haley, J. (1967). Toward a theory of pathological systems (pp. 11-27). In G. H. Zuk & I. Boszormenyi-Nagy (eds.), *Family therapy and disturbed families.* Palo Alto CA: Science and Behavior Books.

Harold, G.T., Fincham, F. D., Osborne, L. N., & Conger, R. D. (1997). Mom and dad are at it again: Adolescent perceptions of marital conflict and adolescent psychological distress. *Developmental Psychology 33:* 333-350.

Howes, P., & Markman, H. J. (1989). Marital quality and child functioning: A longitudinal investigation. *Child Development 60:* 1044-1051.

Jemerin, J. M., & Boyce, W. T. (1990). Psychobiological differences in childhood stress response: II. Cardiovascular markers of vulnerability. *Journal of Developmental & Behavioral Pediatrics 11:* 140-150.

Jemerin, J. M., & Boyce, W. T. (1992). Cardiovascular markers of biobehavioral reactivity. *Developmental and Behavioral Pediatrics 13:* 46-49.

Kagan, J., Reznick, J. S., & Snidman, N. (1988). Biological basis of childhood shyness. *Science 240:* 167-171.

Katz, L. F., & Gottman, J. M. (1994). Patterns of marital interaction and children's emotional development (pp. 49-74). In R. D. Parke & S. G. Kellman (eds.), *Exploring family relationships with other social contexts.* Hillsdale NJ: Lawrence Erlbaum Associates.

Katz, L. F., & Gottman, J. M. (1995). Marital interaction and child outcomes: A longitudinal study of mediating and moderating processes (pp. 301-342). In D. Cicchetti & S .L. Toth (eds.), *Emotion, cognition, and representation.* Rochester NY: University of Rochester Press.

Kazdin, A. E., French, N. H., Unis, A. S., Esveldt-Dawson, K., & Sherick, R. B. (1983). Hopelessness, depression, and suicidal intent among psychiatrically disturbed inpatient children. *Journal of Consulting and Clinical Psychology 51:* 504-510.

Kazdin, A. E., Rodgers, A., & Colbus, D. (1986). The Hopelessness Scale for Children: Psychometric characteristics and concurrent validity. *Journal of Consulting and Clinical Psychology 54:* 241-245.

Leckman, J. F., Peterson, B. S., Anderson, G. M., Arnsten, A. F. T., Pauls, D. L., & Cohen, D. J. (1997). Pathogenesis of Tourette's Syndrome. *Journal of Child Psychology and Psychiatry and Allied Disciplines 38:* 119-142.

Lehrer, P. M. (1998). Emotionally triggered asthma: A review of research literature and some hypotheses for self-regulation therapies. *Applied Psychophysiology and Biofeedback 23:* 13-41.

Lehrer, P. M., Isenberg, S., & Hochron, S. M. (1993). Asthma and emotion: A review. *Journal of Asthma 30:* 5-21.

Liang, S. W., & Boyce, W. T. (1993). The psychobiology of childhood stress. *Current Opinion in Pediatrics 5:* 545-551.

Lopez, F. G. (1997). Attachment styles, shame, guilt, and collaborative problem-solving orientations. *Personal Relationships 4:* 187-199.

Lutwak, N. (1997). Understanding shame in adults: Retrospective perceptions of parental–bonding during childhood. *Journal of Nervous & Mental Disease 185*(10): 595-598.

Lynch, M., & Cicchetti, D. (1991). Patterns of relatedness in maltreated and nonmaltreated children: Connections among multiple representational models. *Development & Psychopathology 3:* 207-226.

Lynch, M., & Cicchetti, D. (1997). Children's relationships with adults and peers: An examination of elementary and junior high school students. *Journal of School Psychology 35:* 81-99.

March, J. S., Parker, J. D. A., Sullivan, K., Stallings, P., & Conners, K. (1997). The Multidimensional Anxiety Scale for Children (MASC): Factor structure, reliability, and validity. *Journal of the American Academy of Child and Adolescent Psychiatry 36*(4): 554-555.

Marciano, P. L., & Kazdin, A. E. (1994). Self-esteem, depression, hopelessness, and suicidal intent among psychiatrically disturbed inpatient children. *Journal of Clinical Child Psychology 23:* 151-160.

Marvin, R. S., & Stewart, R. B. (1990). A family systems framework for the study of attachment (pp. 51-86).

In M. Greenberg, D. Cicchetti, & E. M. Cummings (eds.), *Attachment in the preschool years: Research and intervention.* Chicago: University of Chicago Press.

Masten, A.S., Best, K. M., & Garmezy, N. (1990). Resilience and development: Contributions from the study of children who overcome adversity. *Development & Psychopathology 2:* 425-444.

Middleton, E., Jr., Ellis, E. F., Yunginger, J. W., Reed, C. E., Adkinson, N. F., Jr., & Busse, W. W. (eds.). (1998). *Allergy principles and practice.* St. Louis MO: C. V. Mosby.

Mikulincer, M., & Florian, V. (1999). The association between parental reports of attachment style and family dynamics, and offspring's reports of adult attachment style. *Family Process 38:* 243-257.

Miller, B. D. (1987). Depression and asthma: A potentially lethal mixture. *Journal of Allergy and Clinical Immunology 80:* 481-486.

Miller, B. D., & Strunk, R. C. (1989). Circumstances surrounding the deaths of children due to asthma. *American Journal of Diseases of Children 143:* 1294-1299.

Miller, B. D., & Wood, B. L. (1994). Psychophysiologic reactivity in asthmatic children: A cholinergically mediated confluence of pathways. *Journal of the American Academy of Child and Adolescent Psychiatry 33:* 1236-1245.

Miller, B. D., & Wood, B. L. (1995). "Psychophysiologic reactivity" in asthmatic children: A new perspective on emotionally triggered asthma. *Pediatric Asthma, Allergy and Immunology 9:* 133-142.

Miller, B. D., & Wood, B. L. (1997). Influence of specific emotional states on autonomic reactivity and pulmonary function in asthmatic children. *Journal of the American Academy of Child and Adolescent Psychiatry 36*(5): 669-677.

Minuchin, P. (1988). Relationships within the family: A systems perspective on development (pp. 7-26). In R.A. Hinde & J. Stevenson-Hinde (eds.), *Relationships within families.* New York: Oxford University Press.

Minuchin, S. (1974). *Families & family therapy.* Cambridge: Harvard University Press.

National Heart, Lung and Blood Institute (1997). National Heart, Lung and Blood Institute, National Asthma Education Program Expert Panel Report. Guidelines for the diagnosis and management of asthma.

Osborne, L. N., & Fincham, F. D. (1996). Marital conflict, parent-child relationships, and child adjustment: Does gender matter? *Merrill-Palmer Quarterly 42:* 48-75.

Owen, M. T., & Cox, M. J. (1997). Marital conflict and the development of infant-parent attachment relationships. *Journal of Family Psychology 11:* 152-164.

Petersen, J. L., & Zill, N. (1986). Marital disruption, parent-child relationships, and behavior problems in children. *Journal of Marriage & the Family 48:* 295-307.

Porges, S. W. (1992). Vagal tone: A physiologic marker of stress vulnerability. *Pediatrics 90:* 498-564.

Porges, S. W. (1995). Cardiac vagal tone: A physiological index of stress. *Neuroscience and Biobehavioral Reviews 19:* 225-233.

Porges, S. W. (1996). Psychological regulation in high-risk infants: A model for assessment and potential intervention. *Development and Psychopathology 8:* 43-58.

Reid, W. J., & Crisafulli, A. (1990). Marital discord and child behavior problems: A meta-analysis. *Journal of Abnormal Child Psychology 18:* 105-117.

Reiss, D. (1989). *The family's construction of reality.* Cambridge: Harvard University Press.

Salzman, J. P. (1996). Primary attachment in female adolescents: Association with depression, self-esteem, and maternal identification. *Psychiatry 59:* 20-33.

Schore, A. N. (1994). *Affect regulation and the origin of the self: The neurobiology of emotional development.* Hillsdale NJ: Lawrence Erlbaum Associates.

Schore, A. N. (1996). The experience-dependent maturation of a regulatory system in the orbital prefrontal cortex and the origin of developmental psychopathology. *Development and Psychopathology 8:* 59-87.

Seligman, M. E. P., Reivich, K., Jaycox, L., & Gillham, J. (1995). *The optimistic child.* Boston: Houghton Mifflin.

Siegel, D. J. (1999). *The developing mind.* New York: Guilford Publications.

Spanier, G. B. (1976). Measuring dyadic adjustment: New scales for assessing the quality of marriage and similar dyads. *Journal of Marriage and the Family 38:* 15-28.

Sroufe, L. A. (1996). *Emotional development: The organization of emotional life in the early years.* New York: Cambridge University Press.

Sroufe, L. A., & Waters, E. (1977). Attachment as an organizational construct. *Child Development 48:* 1184-1199.

Suomi, S. J. (1987). Genetic and maternal contributions to individual differences in rhesus monkey behavioral development (pp. 397-419). In N. A. Krasnegor, E. M. Blass, & M. A. Hofer (eds.), *Perinatal development: A psychobiological perspective.* Orlando FL: Academic Press.

Tangney, J. P. (1999). The self-conscious emotions: Shame, guilt, embarrassment and pride (pp. 541-568). In T. Dalgleish & M. J. Power (eds.), *Handbook of cognition and emotion.* New York: John Wiley & Sons.

Tarrier, N., Vaughn, C., Lader, M. H., & Leff, J. P. (1979). Bodily reactions to people and events in schizophrenia. *Archives of General Psychiatry 36:* 311-315.

Toth, S. L., & Cicchetti, D. (1996). Patterns of relatedness, depressive symptomatology, and perceived competence in maltreated children. *Journal of Consulting & Clinical Psychology 64:* 32-41.

Vuchinich, S., Emery, R. E., & Cassidy, J. (1988). Family members and third parties in dyadic family conflict: Strategies, alliances and outcomes. *Child Development 59:* 1293-1302.

West, M., Rose, M. S., Verhoef, M. J., Spreng, S., & Bobey, M. (1998). Anxious attachment and self-reported depressive symptomatology in women. *Canadian Journal of Psychiatry—Revue Canadienne de Psychiatrie 43:* 294-297.

Wood, B., Watkins, J. B., Boyle, J. T., Nogueira, J., Zimand, E., & Carroll, L. (1989). The "psychosomatic family" model: An empirical and theoretical and empirical analysis. *Family Process 28:* 399-417.

Wood, B. L. (1993). Beyond the "psychosomatic family": A biobehavioral family model of pediatric illness. *Family Process 32:* 261-278.

Wood, B.L. (1995). A developmental biopsychosocial approach to the treatment of chronic illness in children and adolescents (pp. 437-455). In R. H. Mikesell, D. Lusterman, & S. H. McDaniel (eds.), *Integrating family therapy: Handbook of family psychology and systems theory.* Washington DC: American Psychological Association.

Wood, B. L. (1999). Editorial: Relationship matters. *Families, Systems & Health 17:* 145-147.

Wood, B. L. (in press). Physically manifested illness in children and adolescents: A biobehavioral family approach. *Child and Adolescent Psychiatric Clinics of North America.*

Wynne, L. C. (1984). The epigenesis of relational systems: A model for understanding family development. *Family Process 23:* 297-381.

3

STRESS, COMPETENCE, AND DEVELOPMENT

Continuities in the Study of Schizophrenic Adults, Children Vulnerable to Psychopathology, and the Search for Stress-Resistant Children

NORMAN GARMEZY

The evolution of an ongoing research study into stress-resistant factors in children is traced from the early work on adult schizophrenia through the identification of risk factors in children vulnerable to stress. Future directions for the research are explored, including the necessity for defenses against possible politicization of the findings.

This paper will present a somewhat broadened history of a research program that initially studied adaptive and maladaptive performance of schizophrenic adults. In collaboration with Eliot Rodnick at Duke University and subsequently undertaken at the University of Minnesota, the later research turned to children vulnerable to psychopathology and, finally, in our most recent efforts, to an attempt to uncover the sources of stress resistance in children. The focus of this research was summarized more than a decade earlier in an article published in this Journal:[23]

From *The American Journal of Orthopsychiatry*, (1987), *57*(2): 159-174. Copyright © 1987 by the American Orthopsychiatric Association, Inc. Reproduced by permission.

In the study of high risk and vulnerable children, we have come across another group of children whose prognosis could be viewed as unfavorable on the basis of familial or ecological factors, but who upset our prediction tables and in childhood bear the visible indices that are hallmarks of competence: good peer relations, academic achievement, commitment to education and to purposive life goals, early and successful work histories. . . . School principals not only believe they can identify such children but . . . they can produce instances from their own school settings of children whose intellectual and social skills are not destroyed by the misfortunes they encounter in home and street. . . . Were we to study the forces that move such children to survival and to adaptation, the long range benefits to our society might be far more significant than our many efforts to construct models of primary prevention designed to curtail the incidence of vulnerability. (p. 114)

At that time, the study of children vulnerable to schizophrenia and other forms of psychopathology was prominent in the research commitment of our Project Competence team at the University of Minnesota. We termed our research program Project Competence, not only for the positive (and prophetic, as reflected in the normal behavior of many of our "at risk" children) image it evoked, but also because the competence theme dominated our formulations and our measures.

We had evolved a research program that occupied our attention for a 12-year period and we were part of a productive international consortium of research groups that were attempting to provide empirically grounded data on the development of children born to schizophrenic mothers. The output of those consortium groups has recently been summarized in an extensive volume edited by Watt et al.[73]

That long-term research commitment came to serve as the foundation stone of our current decade-long preoccupation with stress-resistant children. At first glance, the transition from a concern with developmental precursors to psychopathology would seem discontinuous with a search for children resilient under stress. But, as with most researchers' lives, the threads of continuity are visible on close scrutiny of directional shifts in the research output. A look at an earlier period of research reveals the natural progression that followed.

REVIEW OF EARLY RESEARCH

The study of children at risk for schizophrenia had numerous forebears in the area of adult schizophrenia. Historically, schizophrenia was associated with childhood. In 1850 Morel,[2] in observing deteriorated mental patients, traced their case histories and concluded that the illness had begun in adolescence. Thus, he assigned the term, *demence prècoce,* to such cases to summarize an end point of dementia that began with its initial and premature expression in puberty. Kraepelin[38] also recognized cases such as these and assumed a psychosis originating in adolescence. He thought it organically based, the result of some autotoxin in the brain which produced a mental condition marked by hallucinations, delusions, bizarre behavior, and a deteriorative, irreversible course. It was the combination of age of onset and symptom expression that led to its identification as *dementia praecox.*

A window was opened into the fixed notions of the early emergence of the disorder and the pattern of irreversibility by Eugen Bleuler,[8] who retitled the disorder *schizophrenia* to reflect the psychic splitting of affect and cognition that he observed. His clinical experience suggested that in many cases adolescence was not the starting point of the disease and that deterioration did not invariably follow.

This broadening of the concept, although it came a half-century prior to the first systematic effort to study the development and attributes of children of schizophrenic mothers, suggested that the clinical course was variable and that development in those predisposed to the disorder might also be variable and thus worthy of systematic study.

Three other factors, in addition to these historical psychiatric transitions, served to advance the cause of risk research. The first was the impact of a genetic model for the etiology of schizophrenia—a model widely accepted in Europe, though delayed in its acceptance here until the stability of data drawn from familial, twin, and adoption studies made recognition of a genetic substrate inevitable. The fact that the incidence rate for schizophrenia in a random sample of the population approximated 1%, but that the same outcome for offspring born to a schizophrenic parent produced a ten-fold increase in that rate, not only seemed supportive of the genetic proposition, but also suggested to the pioneering team of Mednick and Schulsinger[46] that here was a method for selecting children at risk for schizophrenia that heightened the probability of a schizophrenic endpoint in a carefully selected cohort.

The second factor came from retrospective studies of the life span development of the schizophrenic patient.[70,77] Bleuler had initially observed a varied pattern of outcomes. Later systematic studies of the patient's premorbid patterns of adaptation[78] were shown to coincide with varied outcomes. Evidence of social engagement, work performance, and cognitive competencies in childhood and adolescence, as opposed to incompetencies in early childhood histories, seemed to be coordinate with relatively rapid recovery in the former, chronicity in the latter.[22,58,59,79]

A third factor arose from family studies. Clinical therapists of great acumen, exemplified by Frieda Fromm-Reichmann[21] and other leading spirits in the Washington School of Psychiatry, noted a consistent pattern of mother-patient interactions in hospital that was marked by a compound of criticism, hostility, rebuff, and emotional overinvolvement. Inappropriately, Fromm-Reichmann interpreted such behavior as a causative agent and thus did inadvertent injury to the already overburdened mothers of schizophrenic adults. A fascinating sidelight on these observations of the tragically termed "schizophrenogenic mother" was the discovery, 30 years later, by psychiatric researchers in Great Britain[11,12,72] that some families of schizophrenic patients did indeed evidence a prevailing climate of interactions that came to be labeled, *expressed emotions* (EE).[39] EE was derived from three elements evident in interviews with a number of identifiable families who had a schizophrenic offspring or spouse. These elements, supported by tonal and gestural patterns, were hostility, marked emotional involvement, and the number of critical comments made by the relatives; these were directed at the patient without reflection on the contribution that an extreme pathological state was making to the sick member's provocative behavior.

Patients subjected to EE were more likely to relapse and return to the hospital, whereas patients not so emotionally targeted were more likely to remain in the community. Further, two forms of intervention were shown to stabilize the patients' recovery: a maintenance schedule of neuroleptic drugs, and educational and social intervention aimed at modifying family resistances or behavior. The combination of these two interventions reduced the patients' relapse rate in one study from 50% to 9%.[72] Such data suggested that while the family *per se* may not have been a primary etiologic agent, in terms of the longitudinal skein of schizophrenia family climate could play an important role in maintaining or attenuating the deviant behavioral patterns of the schizophrenic patient; these, in turn, could affect remission or relapse.

Thus, over time, genetic data, competence data, and family data joined by the investigative challenge from developmentally-oriented, research-minded psychologists and psychiatrists sparked the emergence of two decades of study of children deemed to be at risk for schizophrenia. The Minnesota project was part of that movement, now superbly chronicled in a recently published volume.[73]

STRESS-RESISTANT CHILDREN

At Minnesota the approach to studying the biological children of schizophrenic parentage provided the threads of continuity from pathological precursors into the area of stress-resistance.

Two major questions immediately confront a risk researcher who is launching a developmentally-oriented program of investigations: who to study and what to study? So far as the first question is concerned, the Minnesota project was marked by an extended cohort comparison strategy. Instead of simply comparing children of schizophrenic parents with a normal control group, it was decided that multiple comparison groups were necessary within both the psychopathology and the normal control cohorts. (Extended descriptions of the Minnesota at-risk program can be found elsewhere.[24,28])

Accordingly, we selected children of schizophrenic mothers for our central focus and added a group of children of nonpsychotic depressive and personality disordered mothers. To evaluate whether these index children were moving in a developmental direction consistent with maladaptive as opposed to normal children, we added subsets of similarly-aged children who had been referred by school personnel to community child guidance clinics. These separate groups included those diagnosed as conduct disordered (externalizers), over-inhibited (internalizers), and hyperactive. These various groups of children were, of course, distributed over many schools in the community. Therefore, for controls we paired each child with two same-sex classmates, one matched demographically (age, SES, IQ) with the target child, the other randomly selected from the class list; both controls were drawn from a pool of children identified by the teacher as getting along reasonably well in the classroom.

All over the city school system these triads (target, matched, and random control) were formed and studied in terms of two major variables. The first variable was social and motivational competence as indexed by sociometric measures by peers, and by teacher ratings to complement the peer judgements. There is linkage here to the adult schizophrenia studies in which levels of premorbid competence were found to be associated with positive and negative outcomes in schizophrenia and other forms of psychopathology.[58,59,77,78]

The second variable was the emphasis placed on the child's attentional functioning—a decision that was rooted in two premises. First, poorer attentional functioning has recurrently characterized the performance of adult schizophrenic patients in comparison with others—an observation reiterated by clinicians and researchers alike.[45,68] We reasoned that, in a subset of children of schizophrenic mothers who were truly at risk, early precursor signs of such an attentional deficit would occur. A second basis for our choice was that acquisition and the development of cognitive, social, and occupational skills presupposes the ability to pay attention.

Both variables proved to have merit. At-risk-for-schizophrenia children in various studies were found to be rated lower on social attributes by peers. However, it was not this group but the antisocial children who occupied the bottom rung of peer and teacher acceptance. Combined with their restricted competence skills, antisocial children seem tagged as the truly endangered group among the multiple risk groups studied in the Minnesota project.

As for attentional functioning, several studies pointed to a subset within the at-risk-for-schizophrenia group who showed such deficits.[25] Parenthetically, I might add that in a reaction time study,[40] run under various motivating conditions, including one invoking a genteel gambling game, the at-risk-for-schizophrenia group revealed deficits that were not overcome in the gambling condition; the antisocial children, in contrast, raised their scores to a normal level when this gambling quality was introduced into the experiment.

Another attention task that was employed[50] involved a vigilance task—the Continuous Performance Test (CPT) in which (blurred) numerical stimuli were presented at rapid time exposures to the subject who was required to respond by pressing a button whenever a predesignated number appeared on the screen but not pressing it when any other number was presented.

This research by Keith Nuechterlein[50] provides an example of a creative effort to track the relationship of attentional dysfunction to at-risk-for-schizophrenia. Again Nuechterlein used multiple subject groups including 1) children of schizophrenic mothers, 2) children of non-psychotic but psychiatrically disturbed mothers, 3) hyperactive children, and 4) conduct-disordered children. Again there was matching on sex, SES, age, sociometric status, and reading achievement in securing classroom controls.

Nuechterlein was able to use signal detection analysis[33,71] with his data to calculate two indices: one, d', reflects the child's ability to discriminate relevant from the irrelevant stimuli; the second, β (beta), measures a test-taking response pattern of incaution. Nuechterlein hypothesized that the offspring of the schizophrenic mother would show the basic d' deficit, whereas the hyperactive child, incautious in his approach to stimuli, would be deficient with regard to the β response. The data supported the hypothesis, with d' characteristic for a subset of the at-risk-for-schizophrenia children.

This finding of two different dimensions of attentional deficit, reflecting two different internal processes, introduced a new and highly sophisticated element into the study of attentional parameters in children at risk.[5,19] For one thing it pointed to an interrelationship between this perceptual deficit and possible subtle impairments in brain function as suggested by a subsequent finding, reported by O'Dougherty, Nuechterlein and Drew,[54] that children who in their early years had been exposed to chronic brain anoxia as a result of a congenital heart defect and had then had successful open heart surgery that ameliorated the condition, also showed the d' deficit but not the β deficit when tested years later in middle childhood.

For schizophrenia, complementary evidence has now been secured by Nuechterlein and his colleagues[51-53] at UCLA that has provided further construct validation of the d' variable. They have demonstrated that college students whose MMPI profiles showed peak elevations on depression, psychasthenia, and schizophrenia—a 2-7-8 profile characteristic of latent schizophrenia, schizotypal personality, and perhaps affective disorder as well—also showed the d' deficit on the CPT when compared with other subjects who had clearly normal MMPI profiles or with those whose configural multiphasic peaks were suggestive of other types of psychiatric disorder.

Using a different selection strategy, another study[4] approached unemployed persons to participate in a CPT experiment. These volunteers were subsequently split into two groups based on their overall CPT perceptual sensitivity (d') index and then evaluated on their MMPI profiles. Low d' subjects showed significantly higher scores on the schizophrenia scale and also on recently developed scales of schizotypy and psychosis-proneness.[14]

Many more findings that now characterize children-at-risk-for-schizophrenia have been widely reported.[73] Of particular interest is the new literature now emerging on children at risk for affective disorders.[7,47,57,60,74] In addition, there continue to be numerous studies of that most widely researched and consistent disorder of all in terms of risk variables—and these relate to the development of conduct disorder, adolescent delinquency, and adult antisocial disorder.[20,35,56,62,66,75,76]

A survey of the Minnesota data showed that, except for the conduct-disordered group of children, only a minority of our at-risk children seemed deficit ridden. Thus, presuming that these children were at risk, the absence of disorder in the majority suggested as yet unknown protective factors. (Antonovsky[3] referred to these as "resistance resources.") Recently, Masten and I have examined findings on actualized and nonactualized risk in children who have been designated as vulnerable.[42]

In these and other recent writings, we have described our latest research program, "Studies of Stress-Resistant Children," as one involving "the search for protective factors" in an effort to account for the adaptational adequacy of particular children exposed to stress and adversity. In many ways this research, too, has continuities with the past, in terms of its developmental orientation; the centrality of manifest competence as a presumed predictor of adaptation under stress; and the inclusion of multiple stressed cohorts, two disadvantaged by medical and physical handicaps, and a community cohort of stressed families that might conceivably contribute disproportionately to the proneness of their offspring to psychopathology.[30,32]

Problems in Research

Despite this presumed continuity in research, the study of stress-resistant children in many ways poses more difficult problems than the investigation of children at risk for schizophrenia and other forms of psychopathology, for here there are neither guidelines nor previous research programs to which one can turn. This truly fascinating phenomenon, children who reveal competence and strength despite the presence of adversities, has been inexplicably neglected. A number of studies of stress in various forms provide reports of children's behavior that is marked by adaptability and competence. Examples of such studies can be found in an earlier report by the author[27] on the search for protective factors and in the epidemiological investigations by Rutter and his colleagues.[63-65]

Changing treatment paradigms in medicine show awareness of coping mechanisms and new pairings can now be found side by side with older ones: stress and coping; illness and health maintenance; treatment and prevention; medical care and patient self-management. Areas of professional activity have been relabeled—health psychology, behavioral medicine, environmental medicine—the last name having its counterpart in Cassel's[13] view that except in rare instances the prevention of disease has not resulted from the identification and treatment of the sick, but rather from modification of those environmental factors that affect the incidence of disease.

As Medawar[36] wisely wrote, "... it is not informative to study variations of behavior unless we know beforehand the norm from which the variants depart." Health, not illness, is the norm of society; resistance, not capitulation, to mental disorder is the norm; adaptation and recovery from stress, and not breakdown, is the way of the majority.

In Minnesota we have witnessed the adaptive range of many so-called "at risk" children over more than a decade of experimental study. Responding to our own admonitions, we turned over the coin of risk to look at what we first termed "invulnerable" children—a term we later dropped for the less dramatic one of "stress-resistant" or "resilient" to describe such children.

Nevertheless, the neglect by the scientific community of a phenomenon so ubiquitous in the real world remains a matter for wonder. I once suggested[26] that the exclusive focus of the mental health disciplines on pathogenic processes can best be explained by philosopher Abraham Kaplan's[37] "law of the hammer." Simply put, the law's basic postulate is: "Give a child a hammer and everything the kid sees will need pounding." Armed with our hammer of psychopathology, everywhere we turn in our clinics and waiting rooms we perceive primarily disorders, symptoms, and their dynamics. So we pound away, even though our overarching goal is mental health, not mental disorder. The roots of the disciplines of psychology, social work, and pediatrics require basic attention to the normative; even psychiatry, with its accent on abnormality, must bend to the words of Medawar and to those of Lois Murphy,[48] distinguished advocate of children's coping behavior:

It is something of a paradox that a nation which has exulted in its rapid expansion and its scientific technological achievements, should have developed so vast a "problem" literature: a literature often expressing difficulties, social failures, blocked potentialities, and defeat . . . in applying clinical ways of thinking formulated out of experience with broken adults, we were slow to see how the language of adequacy to meet life's challenges could become the subject matter of psychological science. (p. 2)

Looking for data to support the hypothesis that there are children who are demonstrably resilient under stress, several types of strategies and findings can be identified. Numerous clinical case studies are housed in a broad literature[27,31] that reflects children's adaptation to a variety of stressors: poverty, migration, war, the Holocaust, loss and bereavement, divorce, chronic illness, physical handicap, parental psychopathology, natural disasters and many more; these accounts offer dramatic proof of the phenomenon we seek to study.

Next is the epidemiological evidence drawn from surveys of children's adaptation in different locales. Among the best known are the studies of Rutter and his colleagues[63,65] on the incidence of psychiatric disorder in ten-year-old children residing in two strikingly different geographic areas, the Isle of Wight and an inner borough of London.

Risk Factors

In these investigations the researchers identified six familial "risk" factors seemingly correlated with childhood psychiatric disorders: *1*) severe marital distress, *2*) low social status, *3*) overcrowding or large family size, *4*) paternal criminality, *5*) maternal psychiatric disorders, *6*) admissions of children into foster home placement.

In examining rates of disorder in terms of the cumulative frequency of these risk factors, an increasing progression of negative outcomes was noted: if one risk factor was present, the likelihood of children having a psychiatric disorder was not appreciably greater than that for children whose families were free of any risk factors (this itself provides one indication of adaptive functioning). Two risk factors, by contrast, provided a four-fold increase in the likelihood of a psychiatric disorder; four factors increased the risk ten-fold.

Here is clear evidence of the critical importance of risk status in the context of multiple stressors and chronic stress exposure. Its generalization, noted Rutter, could be extended to acute stressors as well. Thus, a single hospital admission of a child appeared to exercise minimum deleterious effects, but multiple admissions greatly increased the child's risk for subsequent psychiatric disorders.

Protective Factors

Given these findings, how does an investigator use epidemiological data to search for stress-resistance factors? Rutter, who has pioneered the study of protective factors, took his clues from studies of children in institutions. In these settings, the establishment of a stable child-adult relationship was correlated with a better social adjustment of the child.

Since marital discord and parental psychopathology were strong risk factors in earlier studies, Rutter[63] chose a sample of children living with their biological parents who met these twin criteria. In all cases discordant marital relationships marked the households. But in comparing the adaptation of children who benefitted from some degree of parental affection with others who lacked good relationships with either parent, the incidence of psychiatric disorder was found to be 25% in the first group and approximately 75% in the latter group. Similar findings in another study of the prevalence of conduct disorder in children who were removed from their parental homes and placed in harmonious foster homes showed approximately 2½ times fewer cases of conduct disorder than did the children placed with families marked by hostility and discord. One can suggest then that there is a protective component provided by a supportive, stable, and cohesive family climate.[44]

A third potential protective factor emerges in a comparison by Rutter et al.[67] of manifestations of competence in children exposed to two school settings housed in similar disadvantaged areas. The two schools had marked differences in pupils' rates of delinquency, behavioral disturbances, attendance patterns, and academic attainments—differences that remained even when statistical controls were initiated to insure similarities in the children's backgrounds and characteristics, and in the types of schools they had attended in their primary years. Despite the controls for background factors implicated in delinquent behavior, the rates of delinquency in one school were three times those of the other. The school with the lower delinquency rate showed greater effectiveness in classroom management techniques such as high structure in the classroom, preparation and planning, an emphasis on homework and exams, allowing pupils to assume responsibility for their actions and activities, and the maintenance of a prosocial atmosphere. Age and size of school and availability of space were not the predictors of enhanced competence. Rather, the ethos of the school and of its teachers and administrators seemed to nurture a major protective factor in the developing child and adolescent: the acquisition of cognitive and social competencies that forms the basis for survivorship in a stressful world.

In a recent publication,[27] I reviewed a heterogeneous array of relevant articles in a search for additional protective factors that seemed to be recurrent across studies. The result was the preliminary identification of three broad categories of variables: 1) the personality dispositions of the child; 2) a supportive family milieu; 3) an external support system that encourages and reinforces a child's coping efforts and strengthens these by inculcating positive values.

The personality dispositions of the child are virtually unexplored so far as systematic efforts to measure adaptive temperament and personality traits across time, stressors, and studies are concerned. A supportive family milieu asserts the importance of a wholesome family ecology but not the underlying processes that are reflected in supportive and nonsupportive family milieus. The third factor taps into a rapidly expanding literature on support systems but one that largely ignores the diversity of correlates that attach to active support, the initiating acts that awaken it, and the processes whereby supporter and supported become linked. Although these three categories of variables appear, on the surface, to be essentially psychosocial in nature, I believe that fundamental biological parameters are reflected as well within each category.

Whatever the components of these variables, qualitative rather than quantitative elements predominate at this point; but there remains a strong suggestion that we stand on the threshold of a research area of considerable importance. What is needed now are interdisciplinary investigative groups ready, willing, and able to cross over that threshold, bringing with them an orientation to potential variables and sophisticated methods for the study of children's development under stressful conditions.

THE MINNESOTA STUDY

At Minnesota we have attempted to do so in a research context of discovery, hoping to learn what lies on the other side of that threshold. Our study of stress-resistant children began with a focus on three questions:

1. Could we identify several different cohorts of stress-resistant children whose lives were marked by exposure to different types of stressors?

2. Within such cohorts was there a subset of children identifiable by characteristic patterns of competence-related behaviors that differed from those of their less adaptive counterparts?

3. Did developmental factors also differentiate the two groups of children?

These questions required that we define a variety of stressors, and set out specific criteria for rating adaptability in adversity. Methods and measures for defining stressors were readily available; defining adaptability in adversity proved to be a more difficult task.

In meeting the second requirement we had two options. One was to provide behavioral indicators of different categories of coping responses, but such coping scales are ineffective when the stressor is a chronic one, and they provide little evidence of trans-situational generality. Furthermore, some instruments that presume to measure coping pose hypothetical stress situations and equally hypothetical modes of responding; they thus provide a picture of coping that is both arbitrary and unreliable, often disposing a respondent to employ a "social desirability" response set—a pattern of "faking good" (or sometimes "faking poor")—a shortcoming not uncommon to many inadequate self-report inventories.[9,18] The second option involved measures of social, cognitive and motivational competence, as well as of work performance, which possess stability and can be used as generalized indicators of sustained effectiveness and adaptability. In keeping with our previous research programs, we chose to focus on competence rather than on today's more popular coping styles.

Subjects

We began the research program with three cohorts of children, each of which had been exposed to different types of stress events. Cohort I was a community-based sample of approximately 200 families drawn from two physically contiguous elementary schools located in the central city. Cohort II constituted a small group of 32 children who had suffered a life-threatening congenital heart defect—Transposition of the Great Arteries (TGA)—since birth. Cohort III was comprised of 29 severely physically handicapped children who had spent a large part of their young lives in a special school and then were confronted with the additional stressful challenge of being mainstreamed into a regular classroom of a larger public school.

Cohort II and some of the results that were obtained with these heart defect children have been described and reported in detail elsewhere[55] and will not be detailed here. In sum, the study laid more emphasis on the risk side of such children than on the presence of protective factors. In creating a risk model based on cardiac, medical, surgical, and family stress factors in the 31 heart defect children, the investigators sought to test the power of the prediction model by examining the children's school, psychological, and neurological adaptation years after successful open heart surgery when the mean age of the children was approximately nine years.

On the basis of the medical record, the risk model consisted of factors hypothesized to heighten the probability of adverse developmental outcomes. Those included failure of palliative surgery to alleviate hypoxia, prolonged hypoxia, growth failure, congestive heart failure, absence of ameliorating shunting heart defects, stroke, CNS infection, and two psychosocial moderator variables: socioeconomic status and current life stress. Early hospital medical records of the children were read to tabulate the presence or absence of each risk factor, thus providing a "cumulative risk" index score for each child. These scores proved to be highly correlated with a composite neurologic outcome ($r = .62$), IQ ($r = -.66$), school achievement test data ($r = -.60$), and tests of perceptual-motor function ($r = -.48$). Intelligence test performance of children grouped for low, moderate, and high risk scores revealed IQs of 112, 102, and 79 respectively. Socioeconomic status of the family related primarily to children's verbal ability. Stress assessed by a Life Events Questionnaire related significantly to the psychological measures ($r = -.31$ to $-.44$). (A subsequent partial replication of the predictive power of the Minnesota model has since been reported by a group of Harvard investigators.[49])

Unfortunately, limitations of time, personnel, funding, and distance of families from the University Hospital precluded more intensive follow-up studies that might have suggested the operation of familial protective factors to explain the distinct variability in adaptation that was evidenced by some of the children in the cumulated moderate and high risk groups.

Cohort III, the mainstreamed, handicapped group, involved two major doctoral studies. One[69] emphasized an intensive set of interviews, two-thirds of which replicated the Cohort I mothers' interviews, thus providing a large normative comparison group. This study produced a structured, clinical-like account of mothers' reactions to, and modes of coping with, situations and problems evoked by having a severely handicapped offspring in the family, as well as mothers' devices for teaching their children alternative modes of adaptation to the disability, often in response to the thoughtless behavior of other people to the child's handicap. The second coordinated study[10,61] was a carefully wrought ethological/observational account of the modes of response used by the physically handicapped offspring of these mothers to everyday problems (social, cognitive, motor, etc.) encountered in their mainstream and special school setting. In comparing the handicapped children with their non-disabled classroom peers in terms of their efficacy in coping with normal, everyday problems, measures of academic, behavioral, and social competence were employed.

Although the handicapped students received more help and encountered more frequent problem situations, their patterns of responding proved to be similar to those of their non-handicapped classmates. There was a surprising lack of group differences evident in how handicapped students handled problems compared with non-handicapped students in mainstream classes.

Analysis of Cohort I

Cohort I, the central city community-based cohort, consisted of some 200 volunteer families who received the heaviest concentration of activity from our research group. Among the data we gathered were six hours of interviews with mothers and two hours of additional interviewing of the index children. The children were also given an individual achievement test, an abbreviated intelligence test, and a variety of laboratory procedures designed to measure social cognition, problem-solving, divergent thinking, humor comprehension, humor appreciation, humor generation, delay of gratification, and impulsivity-reflectiveness. In addition, cumulative school records were analyzed, sociometric data were secured from classmates with their cooperation, and teachers rated all the children in the class on aspects of the child's motivation, irrespective of the ability level of children in this group.[32]

The amount of data collected in the course of three years of research activity was extremely large. Thus a great portion of our recent activities has been devoted to exploring relations among a number of major environmental and individual variables, using multiple indicators of stress exposure, competence and the like, to insure the stability of our constructs. The first stage of our analyses required extensive correlational and factor-analytic explorations of the internal structure of specific domains. In this manner we replaced many single indicators with a smaller number of composite measures representing such major behavioral domains as competence, social cognition, reflectiveness-impulsiveness, stress (measured by life events schedules and the interviewers' ratings after six hours of interviews with mothers), socioeconomic status, and so on.

In the next stage of the analysis we explored the relations between domains through multiple regression procedures. Examples of such analyses included social class and cognitive variables in relation to measures of competence, and the combining of social class ratings, stress, and measures of effective social-problem solving in relation to competence.

Each of the measures we developed and used became a technical report that included literature reviews and provided the psychometric properties of the project instruments, including evidence of their reliabilities, validities, and intercorrelations with other variables. The net result of this careful mapping of our variables resulted in a 300-page manual of technical reports. This discussion touches on some of the research problems and some of the results of our first wave (Time 1) of data-gathering.

The Problems. The issues of recruitment and attrition were of particular importance. We began with a letter of solicitation inviting parents of children in one of two possible schools to complete a Life Events Questionnaire and asked permission for the research group to review the children's academic records. We paid our families for their participation, inducing many to join in the initial survey. On our second contact with the families, we asked them to join the larger-scale project that involved multiple interviews and laboratory demands. Our invitation was carefully constructed and it urged parents to contact us or the school principal if they had any questions. Initial failures to respond were overcome by repeated solicitations, including phone calls. Those who dropped out and failed to respond were primarily from families that had reported significantly more stressful life events in the first mailing and their children could be identified by significantly lower ratings of academic, social, and behavioral competence as indexed by cumulative school records and other ratings. Thus, we were left with a cohort bias, a final study sample that was not fully representative of the first wave of respondents.

Fortunately, the second school had been held in reserve to correct the anticipated errors. In our approach to School B parents, we observed a similar proportion of responders and non-responders to our second wave of letters as we had witnessed from School A. To avoid the same sample bias, we sent interviewers into the field to contact this potential attrition group. Repeated visits were often necessary to establish contact. Some non-responding families had moved several times—probably an unobtrusive measure of their exposure to stressful circumstances.

The interview staff of social workers and psychology graduate students were able to recapture 33 of the first 39 non-responding families. Our mode of entry at the doorstep was to inquire about the reasons for the parents' non-participation, with no indication of our desire to change their decision. Invariably invited in, the interviewers proceeded to describe the project and its goals and before leaving asked the mother whether, if she had to do it all over again, she would want to join the project. Some 71% indicated that they would and they were signed up immediately. Recognizing the probable fragility of their commitment to the study, we gave first priority to interviewing and testing this group of families.

Findings

The following are some of the results of our first wave study. In it we sought to measure competence by sociometric methods with peers (social competence); motivational and citizenship qualities via teacher judgements divorced from the child's ability; and cognitive competence by an evaluation of the abbreviated IQ test, longitudinal school record, and an individually administered achievement test.

- Factor analyses of peer and teacher ratings of the competence qualities of the participating children resulted in two factors reflecting a portion of the competence domain which we have identified as Engaged-Disengaged and Classroom Disruptiveness.
- Four potential modifying factors of the stress-competence relationship were analyzed: *a)* the child's sex (girls > boys); *b)* IQ (high *vs* low); *c)* SES (high *vs* low); and *d)* parental competence qualities (stability and cohesion *vs* a lack of these attributes).
- Children with greater assets (higher IQ, higher SES, and positive family attributes of stability and cohesion) appeared to be more competent and, under stress, more socially engaged with their peers and in their classroom.[41]
- Children with fewer assets appeared to be more disruptive, particularly under stress.
- Higher SES, IQ, and, for girls, more positive family attributes appeared to be protective factors against disruptive-aggressive response to stress. These family attributes were derived from a Family Rating Scale completed by interviewers after six hours of interviewing mothers. Positive Family Attributes (PFA) embraces such elements as quality of the parent-child relationship, adequacy of family communication, degree of parents' perceptiveness

about the child, and overall competence of the parent.

- The behavioral style of stress response varied according to personal and environmental characteristics with stress effects differing for different aspects of competence.
- The quality of a child's social engagement in school was related not only to IQ and SES but also to social comprehension—a factor that reflects interpersonal understanding, problem-solving ability, and humor comprehension, appreciation, and production. This composite element was related to the two global indices of Engagement-Disengagement and Disruptiveness.
- Factor analysis of portions of an extensive parent interview provided two potential family-related modifiers of competence and stress: family stability and organization (as indexed by such things as numbers of family moves, marriages, jobs, and the upkeep of the home) and family cohesion, (indexed by frequency of family activities, level of manifest affection, presence of rules regarding offspring's behavior, adequacy of communication in the family, etc.). Children with these more advantageous family characteristics were more intelligent, more competent, and less likely to become disruptive under high levels of stress.[43]
- Children in families with lower SES and fewer positive qualities of stability, organization, and cohesion were more likely to be exposed to stressful life events and were, as well, less competent and less intellectually able.
- The effects of stressful events and these multiple risk factors on children appear to be cumulative in terms of reducing qualities of engagement and enhancing disruptiveness.

FUTURE RESEARCH

These analyses will continue as we plumb the extensive data set derived from our first wave investigations. In coordination with this work we have begun a follow-up study of our community cohort 6-7 years after the families were originally seen. Our recontact efforts have been strikingly successful: of our original group of 205 target children, now in their early and late adolescent years, we have located 188 (92%) and have elicited a positive response to participation from 184 respondents (90% of the original cohort).

Via mail questionnaires, we have secured new data on stressful life events, current family status, competence ratings of the child provided by the mother, and a form of clinical status as derived from her ratings of the target offspring using the Achenbach Child Behavior Checklist.[1]

Comparable data have been secured from the adolescents themselves, including their self-perception of their competence qualities.[34] These data have been coded and tabulated. Our intention now is to bring mother and index child back for interviews while the offspring will again be engaged in comparable but more complex laboratory tasks that tap similar dimensions to those that characterized the first wave of testing. We hope to be able to identify and trace the power of those risk and protective factors related to personal dispositions and familial factors in childhood as these may relate to competence and resilience under stress in adolescence and early adulthood. In addition, our interviews with the adolescents will cover broad domains of competence in multiple areas (*e.g.* school, work, social relationships, future perspective-taking, long-term plans, and their response to a highly significant specific stressful event identified by them as having been particularly critical in their lives).

This research program has been seven years in its preparation and execution. In considering the implications of research on risk and protective factors for the practicing clinician, we recently concluded a review[42] of various areas of risk studies with this commentary:

> Given limited resources, it is important to identify target groups for intervention, to know who is at greatest risk, and who can benefit from specific interventions. It is also crucial to know what can be changed and how to change it. Some risk factors are preventable, others may not be. In some cases it may be most effective to change the environment, in other cases to change the individual, and in still others to modify the transactional change between them. Knowing how best to promote change will require knowledge of the developmental processes linking risk and protective factors with psychopathology and with competence.
>
> The task will not be simple given the complex role of modifiers and interaction effects implicated

in the development of psychopathology. Similar complexity exists in the measurement of competence and the necessity of attending to its manifestation in multiple domains using psychometrically sophisticated measuring instruments.

For such goals to be realized, collaboration among basic and applied researchers and clinical practitioners will be essential. The sharing of knowledge across these groups will require that investigators in those camps become both teachers and students in the collaborative research enterprise.[29] The results of such an alliance will benefit legions of people who are now perceived to be at risk, but for whom negative outcomes need not be the inevitable consequence of their current status. (pp. 42-43)

THE POLITICIZATION OF PROTECTIVE FACTORS

The concept of protective factors is potentially a political weapon. Resilient children and the countless numbers of successful adults who demonstrate their escape from poverty and disadvantage can be used by political advocates of an ideological viewpoint that holds the resiliency of some to be proof of its possession by all: that anyone can emulate such achievements if they only try harder. These advocates use the evidence of individual differences to generalize to a collective, clearly a false assumption. The very fact of individual variations in competence suggests the need for greater assistance to some while lesser assistance may be directed to others. A wise society and a compassionate government see this position not as inconsistency, but rather as an exercise of mature, non-ideological judgment and equity.

Government, by providing protective factors, enables some who would otherwise be lost to a fruitful life to move above the threshold of competence needed to survive in an increasingly complex, technological society. Such governmental assistance seems congruent with what citizens have a right to expect from a responsible government confronted with a period of heightened risk for many of its children.

We are not discussing abstractions. The Children's Defense Fund[15-17] has gathered some disquieting, even grim, statistics that attest to the crisis of risk for subsets of America's children. Compared to five years ago, the Fund reports, America's black children are now *twice* as likely as white children to die in the first year, be born prematurely, suffer low birth weight, have mothers who received late or no prenatal care, and have no employed parent. They are *three* times as likely to have their mothers die in childbirth, be in foster care, or die of known child abuse. They are *four* times as likely to live with neither parent and be supervised by a child welfare agency and to be murdered before one year of age or as a teenager. They are *five* times as likely to be dependent on welfare or become pregnant as teenagers. They are *twelve* times as likely to live with a parent who never married. Nor is this an issue limited to black children; it touches white children, Chicano children, and other American racial and ethnic groups as well. After all, two of every three poor children in this country are white; almost one-half of all black children in America live in poverty; almost two of every five Hispanic children in America occupy a similar status; and more than half the children in female-headed households are poor. It is evident that poverty in America's families traverses a broad range of our varied population.

That our wealthy nation should lead the world in military expenditures while it stands fourteenth in the world in terms of the life expectancy of its infants over the first year of their lives is an anomaly. Reflecting on ways to protect America's children, one could conclude that changing children's program entitlements and folding them into the Department of Defense might prove the most productive. Our school lunch program might then be retitled *Nutritional Care of Future Infantrymen (Infantrypersons?)* while prenatal care programs could be listed as *Early Maintenance of Air Force and Naval Personnel.*

What better way to throw a protective umbrella over our most significant resources? Otherwise we face budgetary expenditures and decisions that may well ensure more stressors on children in poor families with long-term deleterious consequences that will likely accrue not only to the children, but to the nation as a whole.

Who is the supporter and who are the supported in the social support relationship that involves government and its citizens? The stereotypical view is that government plays the role of supporter, while recipients of government's largesse are the supported. That is not the way it works. I commend to you the proposition that there is a sequence of shifting roles in that relationship and that children who are assisted by their government in a democratic society to become competent, healthy adults, in time reverse the roles and become the supporters and protectors of their government, thus making government the supported.

Simply stated, the long-term well-being of a nation is a function of the long-term well-being of its people. Unfair, unequal burdens placed on the many who are disadvantaged, in time affect the more favored few. A democratic society is truly measured by how it treats the least advantaged of its citizens through efforts to reduce the vulnerability gap among its people. A permanent underclass imperils a nation. Only wise leadership can prevent such permanency.

These are discouraging times for members of the mental health disciplines. At high levels of our society, compassion and concern for the poor appear to be in short supply. Nevertheless, countless allies support the philosophy of those in the helping professions. Justice Benjamin Cardozo,[6] one of the great liberal jurists in the history of the Supreme Court once wrote:

> There is in each of us a stream . . . whether you choose to call it philosophy or not which gives coherence or direction to thought and action. Judges cannot escape that current any more than other mortals. (p. 126)

If at this moment the current we favor runs sluggish, the "coherence or direction" to our thought and action must not. The pendulum of history continues to swing. Time is on the side of the expression of compassion and concern and extension of the helping hand, for that view is supported by millions of as yet uncounted Americans.

REFERENCES

1. ACHENBACH, T. M. AND EDELBROCK, C. S. 1983. Manual for The Child Behavior Checklist and Revised Child Behavior Profile. Queen City Printers, Burlington, Vt.

2. ALEXANDER, F. G. AND SELESNICK, S. T. 1966. The History of Psychiatry. Harper & Row, New York.

3. ANTONOVSKY, A. 1979. Health, Stress, and Coping. Jossey-Bass, San Francisco.

4. ASARNOW, R. F., NEUCHTERLEIN, K. H. AND MARDER, S. R. 1983. Span of apprehension, neuropsychological functioning, and indices of psychosis-proneness. J. Nerv. Ment. Dis. 171: 662-669.

5. ASARNOW, R. F. ET AL. 1977. An attentional assessment of foster children at risk for schizophrenia. J. Abnorm. Psychol. 86:267-275.

6. BAUM, L. 1981. The Supreme Court. Congressional Quarterly Press, Washington, D.C.

7. BEARDSLEE, W. R. ET AL. 1983. Children of parents with major affective disorder: a review. Amer. J. Psychiat. 140:825-832.

8. BLEULER, E. 1950. Dementia Praecox or The Group of Schizophrenias (1911). International Universities Press, New York.

9. BLOCK, J. 1965. The Challenge of Response Sets. Appleton-Century-Crofts, New York.

10. BLOM, S. D., LININGER, R. S. AND CHARLESWORTH, W. R. 1987. Ecological observation of emotionally and behaviorally disordered students: an alternative method. Amer. J. Orthopsychiat. 57(1): 49-59.

11. BROWN, G. W., BIRLEY, J. L. T. AND WING, J. K. 1972. Influence of family life on the course of schizophrenic disorders: a replication. Brit. J. Psychiat. 121:241-258.

12. BROWN, G. W. AND RUTTER, M. 1966. The measurement of family activities and relationships: a methodological study. Hum. Relat. 19:241-263.

13. CASSEL, J. 1976. The contribution of the social environment to host resistance. Amer. J. Epidem. 104:107-123.

14. CHAPMAN, L. J., CHAPMAN, J. P. AND RAULIN, M. L. 1976. Scales for physical and social anhedonia. J. Abnorm. Psychol. 85:374-382.

15. CHILDREN'S DEFENSE FUND. 1985. Black and White Children in America: Key Facts, Washington, D.C.

16. CHILDREN'S DEFENSE FUND. 1986. A Children's Defense Budget. Government Printing Office, Washington, D.C.

17. CHILDREN'S DEFENSE FUND. 1986. Maternal and Child Health Data Book: The Health of

America's Children. Government Printing Office, Washington, D.C.

18. EDWARDS, A. L. 1957. The Social Desirability Variable in Personality Assessment and Research. Dryden Press, New York.

19. ERLENMEYER-KIMLING, L. AND CORNBLATT, B. 1978. Attentional measures in a study of children at risk for schizophrenia. J. Psychiat. Res. 14:93-98.

20. FARRINGTON, D. P. 1978. The family background of aggressive youths. *In* Aggression and Antisocial Behaviors in Childhood and Adolescence, L. A. Hersov, M. Berger and D. Shaffer, eds. Pergamon Press, Oxford.

21. FROMM-REICHMANN, F. 1948. Notes on the development of treatment of schizophrenics by psychoanalytic psychotherapy. Psychiatry 11: 263-273.

22. GARMEZY, N. 1970. Process and reactive schizophrenia: some conceptions and issues. Schiz. Bull. No. 2:30-74.

23. GARMEZY, N. 1971. Vulnerability research and the issue of primary prevention. Amer. J. Orthopsychiat. 41:101-116.

24. GARMEZY, N. 1975. The experimental study of children vulnerable to psychopathology. *In* Child Personality and Psychopathology: Current Topics, Vol. II, A. Davids, ed. John Wiley, New York.

25. GARMEZY, N. 1978. Attentional processes in adult schizophrenia and in children at risk. J. Psychiat. Res. 14:3-34.

26. GARMEZY, N. 1981. Children under stress: perspective on antecedents and correlates of vulnerability and resistance to psychopathology. *In* Further Explorations in Personality, A. I. Rabin et al., eds. John Wiley, New York.

27. GARMEZY, N. 1985. Stress-resistant children: the search for protective factors. *In* Recent Research in Developmental Psychopathology, J. E. Stevenson, ed. Pergamon Press, Oxford.

28. GARMEZY, N. AND DEVINE, V. 1994. Project Competence: the Minnesota studies of children vulnerable to psychopathology. *In* Children at Risk for Schizophrenia: A Longitudinal Perspective, N. F. Watt et al., eds. Cambridge University Press, Cambridge.

29. GARMEZY, N. AND MASTEN, A. S. 1986. Stress, competence, and resilience: common frontiers for therapist and psychopathologist. Behav. Ther. 17:500-521.

30. GARMEZY, N., MASTEN, A. S. AND TELLEGEN, A. 1984. The study of stress and competence in children: a building block for developmental psychopathology. Child Devlpm. 55:97-111.

31. GARMEZY, N. AND RUTTER, M. 1985. Acute reactions to stress. *In* Child Psychiatry: Modern Approaches (2nd Ed.), M. Rutter and L. Hersov, eds. Blackwell Scientific Press, Oxford.

32. GARMEZY, N. AND TELLEGEN, A. 1984. Studies of stress-resistant children: methods, variables, and preliminary findings. *In* Advances in Applied Developmental Psychology, Vol. I, F. Morrison, C. Lord and D. Keating, eds. Academic Press, New York.

33. GREEN, D. M. AND. SWETS, J. A. 1966. Signal Detection Theory and Psychophysics. John Wiley, New York.

34. HARTER, S. 1982. The perceived competence scale for children. Child Devlpm. 53:87-97.

35. HERSOV, L. A., BERGER, M. AND SHAFFER, D., eds. 1978. Aggression and Anti-Social Behaviour in Childhood and Adolescence. Pergamon Press, Oxford.

36. JONES, N. B., ed. 1972. Ethological Studies of Behavior. Cambridge University Press, Cambridge.

37. KAPLAN, A. 1964. The Conduct of Inquiry. Chandler Publishing, San Francisco.

38. KRAEPELIN, E. 1971. Dementia Praecox and Paraphrenia (1919). Robert E. Krieger, Huntington, N.Y.

39. LEFF, J. AND VAUGHN, C. 1985. Expressed Emotion in Families. Guilford Press, New York.

40. MARCUS, L. M. 1972. Studies of attention in children vulnerable to psychopathology. Unpublished doctoral dissertation, University of Minnesota, Minneapolis.

41. MASTEN, A. S. 1986. Patterns of adaptation to stress in middle childhood. Presented to the American Psychological Association, Washington, D.C.

42. MASTEN, A. S. AND GARMEZY, N. 1985. Risk, vulnerability, and protective factors in developmental psychopathology. *In* Advances in Clinical Child Psychology, Vol. VIII, B. B. Lahey and A. E. Kazdin, eds. Plenum Press, New York.

43. MASTEN, A. S. ET AL. 1986. Family factors related to stress and competence in children. Presented to the American Psychological Association, Los Angeles.

44. MASTEN, A. S. ET AL. Competence and stress in school children: the moderating effects of individual and family qualities. (in preparation)

45. MC GHIE, A. 1970. Attention and perception in schizophrenia. *In* Progress in Experimental Personality Research, Vol. V, B. A. Maher, ed. Academic Press, New York.

46. MEDNICK, S. A. AND SCHULSINGER, F. 1968. Some premorbid characteristics related to breakdown in children with schizophrenic mothers. *In* The Transmission of Schizophrenia, D. Rosenthal, and S. S. Kety, eds. Pergamon Press, Oxford.

47. MORRISON, H. L., ed. 1983. Children of Depressed Parents: Risk, Identification, and Intervention. Grune and Stratton, New York.

48. MURPHY, L. B. 1962. The Widening World of Childhood. Basic Books, New York.

49. NEWBURGER, J. W. ET AL. 1984. Cognitive function and age at repair of Transposition of the Great Arteries in children. New Eng. J. Med. 310(23): 1495-1499.

50. NUECHTERLEIN, K. H. 1983. Signal detection in vigilance tasks and behavioral attributes among offspring of schizophrenic mothers and among hyperactive children. J. Abnorm. Psychol. 92:4-28.

51. NUECHTERLEIN, K. H. 1985. Converging evidence for vigilance deficit as a vulnerability indicator for schizophrenic disorders. *In* Controversies in Schizophrenia, M. Alpert, ed. Guilford Press, New York.

52. NUECHTERLEIN, K. H. AND DAWSON, M. E. 1984. Information processing and attentional functioning in the developmental course of schizophrenic disorders. Schiz. Bull. 10:160-203.

53. NUECHTERLEIN, K. H. AND DAWSON, M. E. 1984. A heuristic vulnerability/stress model of schizophrenic episodes. Schiz. Bull. 10:300-312.

54. O'DOUGHERTY, M., NUECHTERLEIN, K. H. AND DREW, B. 1984. Hyperactive and hypoxic children: signal detection, sustained attention and behavior. J. Abnorm. Psychol. 93:178-191.

55. O'DOUGHERTY, M. ET AL. 1983. Later competence and adaptation in infants who survive heart defects. Child Devlpm. 54:1129-1142.

56. OLWEUS, D. 1979. Stability of aggressive reaction patterns in males: a review. Psychol. Bull. 86: 852-875.

57. ORVASCHEL, H. 1983. Maternal depression and child dysfunction: children at risk. *In* Advances in Clinical Child Psychology, Vol. VI, B. B. Lahey and A. E. Kazdin, eds. Plenum Press, New York.

58. PHILLIPS, L. 1953. Case history data and prognosis in schizophrenia. J. Nerv. Ment. Dis. 6:515-525.

59. PHILLIPS, L. 1968. Human Adaptation and Its Failures. Academic Press, New York.

60. PUIG-ANTICH, P. 1980. Affective disorders in childhood. Psychiat. Clin. N. Amer. 3:403-424.

61. RAISON, S. B. 1983. Coping behavior of main-streamed physically handicapped students. Doctoral dissertation, University of Minnesota. (Dissert. Abstr. Inter. 43(8):2635A; ERIC No. DA8301992)

62. ROBINS, L. N. 1966. Deviant Children Grown Up. Williams and Wilkins, Baltimore.

63. RUTTER, M. 1979. Protective factors in children's responses to stress and disadvantage. *In* Primary Prevention of Psychopathology, Vol. III, Social Competence in Children, M. W. Kent and J. Rolf, eds. University Press of New England, Hanover, N.H.

64. RUTTER, M. 1985. Resilience in the face of adversity: protective factors and resistance to psychiatric disorder. Brit. J. Psychiat. 147:598-611.

65. RUTTER, M. ET AL. 1975. Attainment and adjustment in two geographical areas—I: The prevalence of psychiatric disorder. Brit. J. Psychiat. 126: 493-509.

66. RUTTER, M. AND GILLER, H. 1983. Juvenile Delinquency: Trends and Perspectives. Penguin Books, Middlesex, England.

67. RUTTER, M. ET AL. 1979. Fifteen Thousand Hours: Secondary Schools and Their Effects on Children. Harvard University Press, Cambridge.

68. Schizophrenia Bulletin. 1977. The Psychology and Psychopathology of Attention (Special Issue, N. Garmezy and S. Matthysse, eds.). 3(3):358-482.

69. SILVERSTEIN, P. R. 1982. Coping and adaptation in families of physically handicapped school children. Unpublished doctoral dissertation, University of Minnesota, Minneapolis.

70. STEPHENS, J. H. 1978. Long term prognosis and followup in schizophrenia. Schiz. Bull. 4:25-47.

71. SWETS, J. A. 1973. The relative operating characteristic in psychology. Science 182:990-1000.

72. VAUGHN, C. E. AND LEFF, L. P. 1976. The influence of family and social factors on the course of psychiatric illness. Brit. J. Psychiat. 129:125-137.

73. WATT, N. F. ET AL. 1984. Children at Risk for Schizophrenia: A Longitudinal Perspective. Cambridge University Press, Cambridge.

74. WEISSMAN, M. M. ET AL. Children of depressed parents: increased psychopathology and early onset of major depression. Arch. Gen. Psychiat. (in press)

75. WEST, D. J. 1982. Delinquency, Its Roots, Careers, and Prospects. Harvard University Press, Cambridge.

76. WEST, D. J. AND FARRINGTON, D. P. 1973. Who Becomes Delinquent? Heinemann Educational Books, London.

77. ZIGLER, E. AND PHILLIPS, L. 1961. Social competence and outcome in psychiatric disorder. J. Abnorm. Soc. Psychol. 63:264-271.

78. ZIGLER, E. AND PHILLIPS, L. 1962. Social competence and the process-reactive distinction in psychopathology. J. Abnorm. Soc. Psychol. 65:215-222.

79. ZIGLER, E. AND GLICK, M. 1986. A Developmental Approach to Adult Psychopathology. John Wiley, New York.

4

TOWARD A DEFINITION OF FAMILY RESILIENCE

Integrating Life-Span and Family Perspectives

DALE R. HAWLEY

LAURA DeHAAN

Family resilience is a relatively new construct that describes how families adapt to stress and bounce back from adversity. Literature pertaining to resilience as a family-level variable is reviewed. An overview of the developmental psychopathology literature dealing with individual resilience is also presented. Implications for extending the study of family resilience drawn from research on individual resilience are discussed and a definition of family resilience is proposed.

In recent years there has been a movement in the family field toward strengths-based and away from deficit-based models. For example, in family therapy the solution-focused and narrative models assume that clients possess resources that will allow them to resolve their difficulties (Berg & Miller, 1992; White & Epston, 1990). An emphasis on resilience in clients has often accompanied this focus on strengths. For instance, Wolin and Wolin (1993) decry the damage model that underlies many traditional approaches to therapy. They offer an alternative—the Challenge Model—that is based on seven resiliencies they have observed in clients who have resisted victimization in poorly functioning

Reprinted from *Family Process* 35 (1996): 283-98. Copyright © 1996 by Family Process Inc. Reproduced with permission of Family Process Inc. in the format Other Book via Copyright Clearance Center.

families of origin. Arguing for a less pathological approach to therapy, Barnard (1994) cites a number of individual and family correlates of resiliency.

This clinical interest in resilience and families has been paralleled by growing attention to the construct of resilience in the family field in general. In the recent past, family resilience has been the focus of a number of articles in the family literature, several national conferences (sponsored by the University of Wisconsin–Madison), and a USDA Extension Service network on the Internet (the National Network for Family Resiliency). While this area of study offers considerable potential, a clear definition of what family resiliency entails or how it can be operationalized has not emerged. Nor does it appear to draw on the well-established literature on individual resiliency found in the area of developmental psychopathology.

Doherty, Boss, LaRossa, et al. (1993) indicate that clarity of concepts is a necessary component for communication among scholars in the evaluation of theories. Family resilience is a relatively new concept around which theoretical notions are beginning to emerge (see McCubbin & McCubbin, 1988; 1993). It is also in the early stages of definitional development. The goal of this article is to make a contribution toward clarifying family resilience by drawing on both the family and developmental psychopathology literatures. We will review each of these literatures for components that are instrumental in constructing a viable definition of resilience. We will then seek to integrate findings from both perspectives.

We propose a definition of family resiliency informed by both the family and developmental psychopathology literatures. This would examine family resiliency as a whole (rather than focusing on individuals within families) and would draw on unique contributions from developmental psychopathology. This article is concerned with addressing three questions believed to prove useful in clarifying family resilience as a construct: 1) Does the concept of family resilience make a new and distinct contribution to the literature?; 2) Can resiliency legitimately be considered a family-level variable?; and 3) How can the study of resilience on the individual level influence the study of resilience on the family level?

RESILIENCE AND THE FAMILY

Resilience has been variously defined in the family literature. McCubbin and McCubbin (1988) define family resilience as "characteristics, dimensions, and properties of families which help families to be resistant to disruption in the face of change and adaptive in the face of crisis situations" (1988, p. 247). Their emphasis in this area focuses on the adaptive qualities of families as they encounter stress, particularly those processes promoting coping, endurance, and survival (McCubbin, McCubbin, & Thompson, 1993). The Family Resiliency Network of the USDA Extension Service defines family resilience as "the family's capacity to cultivate strengths to positively meet the challenges of life" (Silliman, 1994, p. 1). Valentine and Feinauer (1993) refer to resiliency as "the power or ability to return to original form or position after being bent, compressed, or stretched, as well as the ability to overcome adversity, survive stress, and rise above disadvantage" (1993, p. 222), while Wolin and Wolin (1993) see resilience as the capacity to bounce back, to withstand hardship, and to repair one's self.

Several common threads seem evident in these definitions. First, resilience is seen as surfacing in the face of hardship. It refers to qualities that enable a family to maintain its equilibrium as it experiences crisis. Terms like endurance, withstand, survival, and coping imply that families encounter adversity and that those with greater resilience show a capacity to adapt in ways that are productive for their well-being. In this sense, it is similar to the systems concept of morphogenesis (Speer, 1970; Whitchurch & Constantine, 1993), which posits that families must sometimes make fundamental changes in their rules and processes in order to survive.

Second, resilience carries a property of buoyancy. The ability to bounce back or to return to a previous way of functioning suggests that families may temporarily be thrown off course under stressful conditions but that they will resist altering their basic structure and will return to a semblance of their previous functioning following the storm. This is reminiscent of Hill's (1958) Roller Coaster Model, which hypothesized that, following a crisis, families return to a level of functioning below, at, or above their precrisis level. Resilient families are presumed to return to a level of functioning at or above their precrisis level.

Third, resilience tends to be viewed in terms of wellness rather than pathology. As Goddard and Allen (1991) suggest, there is something "innately appealing about the study of resilience" (p. 2) because it addresses ways in which families are successful rather than ways in which they fail. Antonovsky (1987) terms this a "salutogenic orientation" (p. 2). Rather than looking at factors associated with deficits, salutogenesis is concerned with discovering characteristics that contribute to healthy functioning in families. This is similar in approach to research conducted on family strengths (for example, Curran, 1983; Lewis, 1979; Stinnett & DeFrain, 1985) and is especially reflected in the definition proposed by the Family Resiliency Network and in the work of McCubbin and McCubbin (1988).

A review of the literature reveals at least two units of analysis at the intersection of resiliency and the family. In some cases, resiliency is seen as an individual factor with family serving as a protective or a risk factor while in other cases it is viewed as a systemic quality shared by the family unit as a whole. The following sections review literature from each of these streams of study.

Family as a Protective Factor

Family often serves as an important protective factor for resilient individuals. In a review of family correlates of resilience, Barnard (1994) cites several familial factors that appear to be related to resilience, including a good fit between parent and child, maintenance of family rituals, proactive confrontation of problems, minimal conflict in the home during infancy, the absence of divorce during adolescence, and a productive relationship between a child and his or her mother. Families exhibiting warmth, cohesion, and stability appear to be correlated with resilient children (Garmezy, 1993; Wyman, Cowen, Work, et al., 1992) while strong parentchild relationships marked by positive interactions, nurturance, affection, and consistent discipline are also related to resilience in children (Rutter, 1979; Werner, 1989; Werner & Smith, 1982; Wyman et al., 1992).

Family as a Risk Factor

Families may also serve as a risk factor for children. Severe marital discord, maternal mental illness, overcrowded housing, and limited parenting abilities have all been identified as factors associated with the development of psychiatric disorders and criminality in children (Kolvin, Miller, Fleeting, & Kolvin, 1988; Rutter, 1979). Some research in the family field has focused on how children have overcome adverse circumstances found in their families of origin to become productive adults. Valentine and Feinauer (1993) interviewed 22 adult female survivors of sexual abuse and found that their ability to find emotional support outside their family, a strong sense of self-regard, a dependence on religion or spirituality, external attributions of blame surrounding the abuse, and an inner-directed locus of control emanating from internal values were important factors in helping them overcome the abuse. Based on his work with children of alcoholics, Wolin has developed the Challenge Model, which suggests that some children buffer themselves from family-inflicted, potential damage by developing at least one of seven resiliencies: insight, independence, relationships, initiative, humor, creativity, and morality (Wolin & Wolin, 1993).

Family Resilience

A growing body of literature considers resilience as a family-level construct. McCubbin and McCubbin (1988; 1993) have recently proposed the Resiliency Model of Family Stress, Adjustment, and Adaptation. Coming out of a family stress conceptual framework, they expand the adaptation phase of the Double ABCX Model developed by McCubbin and Patterson (1983) to include family type and family schema as salient factors in determining a family's level of adaptation to stressors. Family type is based on a threefold typology consisting of regenerative, rhythmic, and resilient families (McCubbin & McCubbin, 1988), each of which emphasize different aspects of family functioning. Regenerative families tend to exhibit patterns of functioning that stress coherence and hardiness; rhythmic families focus on family time and routines as a way of coping with change; and resilient families are seen as those with high degrees of flexibility and bonding. Family type interacts with a family's resources and social support, their appraisal of the situation and schema, and their problem-solving and coping skills to mediate their level of adaptation to a crisis.

Family schema describes a family's shared values, goals, priorities, expectations, and world view (McCubbin, McCubbin, & Thompson, 1993). This is an extension of the appraisal or C factor in the Double ABCX Model, which focuses on how families define the stressor and the surrounding situation. Family schema takes appraisal to another level of abstraction, emphasizing the overall meaning a family gives to a situation, given its collective view of the world. Families with a strong schema stress their investment in the family unit, exhibiting a shared orientation that emphasizes a collective "we" more than "I"; they also tend to adopt a relativistic view of life and show a willingness to accept less than perfect solutions to life's demands (McCubbin, McCubbin, & Thompson, 1993). Family schema appears to have taken a central role in this model in that it is seen as a stable component that allows families to assign meaning to stressful events in their lives and to develop congruency between those meanings and their patterns of functioning (McCubbin & McCubbin, 1993). Patterson and Garwick (1994) have developed a similar concept they call family world view, which focuses on the family's interpretation of reality, its assumptions about its environment, and its existential beliefs about its place in the world.

A related concept to schema and world view is sense of coherence, developed by Antonovsky (1979, 1987). Primarily an individual construct consistent with Antonovsky's salutogenic orientation, sense of coherence is a global concept that assesses the extent to which individuals feel confident that the outcome of a situation will turn out favorably (Antonovsky, 1987). There are three components to sense of coherence: comprehensibility, or the degree to which events surrounding a situation make sense cognitively; manageability, or the degree to which one perceives she or he has adequate resources to meet their demands; and meaningfulness, or the degree to which one feels that life makes sense emotionally. A high sense of coherence is viewed as a salient factor influencing one's ability to adapt to life's demands.

Recently, several researchers have explored whether sense of coherence might be considered a family-level construct. McCubbin, Thompson, Thompson, et al. (1994) have defined family coherence as a shared world view expressing the family's feelings of confidence, and have taken steps to incorporate it into their resiliency model. Using data from 1,140 husbands and wives in a LISREL model, Lavee, McCubbin, and Olson (1987) examined causal relationships among stressors and strains, marital adjustment, family well-being, and family coherence. They found coherence to be positively related to family well-being, indicating that families who are able to reframe problems as resolvable are better off than families without this capacity. They also unexpectedly discovered a positive relationship between sense of coherence and family strain when marital adjustment was controlled for. This may suggest that the experience of overcoming demanding situations can enhance a family's sense of coherence. Antonovsky and Sourani (1988) found a substantial level of agreement between spouses on a family version of the Sense of Coherence scale, supporting the notion that this construct may have validity on the family level of analysis. They also discovered that families with a strong family sense of coherence were more likely to be well-adapted than those with lesser levels. In a study of families with serious illnesses, Anderson (1994) discovered a strong link between family sense of coherence and quality of family life.

Silliman (1994) suggests that resiliency can be described at individual, family, and community levels, each of which is unique yet interdependent. Resiliency may be viewed in terms of values, attitudes, and behavioral dimensions. It is a dynamic quality through which families focus on their strengths and coping assets to build competence, to avoid negative stressors, and to address adversity. Resilience is also seen as contextual, suggesting that a family's capacity to be resilient depends on the fit between their strengths and the circumstances of a specific situation. Drawing primarily on family strengths literature, Silliman identifies several resiliency factors including commitment, communication, cohesion, adaptability, spirituality, connectedness, time together, and efficacy.

Finally, family resilience can vary according to cultural contexts. For example, McCubbin, McCubbin, Thompson, and Thompson (1995) suggest that family schema in many Native American Indian and Hawaiian families is strongly influenced by several factors less prominent in Anglo families, including an emphasis on the group over the individual, a present-time orientation, and a heightened focus on spiritual beliefs and on the land. Zimmerman, Ramirez, Washienko, et al. (1995) found enculturation, or a close connection to one's cultural roots, to be an important protective factor for Native American youth. Genero (1995) and Dalla and Gamble (1995) found informal support networks to be a vital resource for African American and Navajo mothers, respectively. Thus, outcome criteria for evaluating the resilience of families may depend to some degree on their cultural background.

INDIVIDUAL RESILIENCE

Developmental psychologists have become increasingly cognizant that children are often able to withstand extreme stress during childhood and yet mature into well-adjusted, successful adults. These children, often described as "resilient," are currently the subject of much research and debate. Many developmentalists have begun to focus on individual adaptive patterns associated with later adjustment, more specifically on how prior adaptations leave children either protected or defenseless against stressful events, as well as how "particular patterns of adaptation, at different developmental periods, interact with a changing external environment" (Sroufe & Rutter, 1984, p. 27). This area of study, termed developmental psychopathology, has been described as the "origins and course of individual patterns of behavioral maladaptation" (Sroufe & Rutter, 1984, p. 18), and focuses on the development of pathological behaviors over time.

Resilience has been defined in various ways within the field of developmental psychopathology. Rutter (1987) describes it as "individual variation in

response to risk" (p. 317), with the assumption that the same stressors will be experienced differently by different people. He also maintains that individuals will also differ in their ability to respond to stressful circumstances throughout the life course, as "continuities and discontinuities are to be expected" (Rutter, 1989, p. 26).

Several have placed emphasis on an individual's ability not only to cope with stress, but to prosper because of it, such as Werner's (1989) definition of "successful adaptation following exposure to stressful life events" (p. 72), and Garmezy's (1993) focus on the "power of recovery" and "functioning following adversity" (p. 129). Burger (1994) describes resilient children as those who can "endure and thrive in the harshest of circumstances" with an emphasis on "long-term patterns of mastery and competence" (p. 7).

The field of developmental psychopathology has several unique features that could inform an understanding of family resiliency. First, there is considerable focus on developmental transitions, and their impact on adaptation to stress (Luthar & Zigler, 1991). For example, the entrance of a family into poverty has been found to affect adolescents more adversely than young children (Elder, Liker, & Cross, 1984), while young children, who have a limited understanding of what death means (Smith, 1991), are often more vulnerable to experiencing the death of a parent than are older children. Differences in short and long-term reaction are also possible, in that individuals may successfully cope with divorce throughout childhood and adolescence, but later experience difficulties in developing romantic relationships (Hetherington, Cox, & Cox, 1985). True resilience encompasses both short and long-term coping styles, with a focus on continued adaptability and flexibility in the long term.

This focus on the long term also necessitates the importance of identifying behaviors that are not pathological at present, but are precursors of later maladjustment. For example, the death of a father may result in increased intimacy between mother and daughter, which is not in itself pathological; but this intimacy may make it more difficult for the daughter to negotiate leaving home upon completion of adolescence.

Another key construct is the idea of adaptability of coping styles (Compas, 1987). Compas distinguishes between problem-focused and emotionally based coping styles, arguing that both children and adolescents use these strategies. Resilient children are considered more able to adapt their coping styles flexibly to a specific situation, as well as evaluate the effectiveness of their coping efforts.

Another important feature of developmental psychopathology centers on the identification of risk and protective factors. Risk factors are those that, if present, increase the likelihood of a person developing an emotional or behavioral problem at some point. Protective factors are defined as attributes of individuals and environments, which serve as buffers between a person and stressful situations (Garmezy, 1985). Broad categories of risk factors have been developed such as poverty and parental death, divorce, or mental illness, with poverty being the most commonly researched risk factor (Luthar, 1991). Rutter (1979) argues that most children can effectively cope with at least two risk factors simultaneously, but the presence of three or more risk factors almost always results in emotional or behavioral problems.

Garmezy (1985) has identified three broad classes of protective factors as well. These include possessing what is considered an "easy" temperament, or having a flexible and adaptable personality. Another important protective factor is the presence of at least one adult who takes a strong interest in the child. Bronfenbrenner (1990) describes this person as someone who loves with an irrational emotional involvement, as well as a rational commitment to provide more complex challenges in life. Sometimes this person is described as a polestar, or someone who can guide the path of a child. The third protective factor is a well-defined, social support network. Other identified protective factors include intelligence, adequate financial resources within the family, sense of humor, empathy, and internal locus of control (Luthar, 1991).

What is important to consider about risk and protective factors is that they are not static entities, but are elastic and changing in nature. Rutter (1989) argues that risk and protective factors are largely inert on their own, but often serve as catalysts and buffers for stressful events. Therefore, it is impossible to make assumptions or predictions based on the knowledge of certain events, without understanding how that event interacts with other life circumstances. The goal, therefore, is not to uncover static traits or experiences that produce risk or provide comfort, but to develop possible trajectories or "developmental pathways" of how life circumstances may interact with development in positive or negative ways (Rutter, 1990). These pathways are sometimes described as "chain effects" and describe typical patterns of behavior that often lead to problematic outcomes. For example, Patterson, DeBaryshe, and Ramsey (1989) document a commonly followed path for juvenile delinquents, beginning with conflict-ridden and inconsistent parenting in early childhood, followed by rejection by peers and academic failure in middle childhood. This leads to commitment to a deviant peer group and actual delinquent behavior during adolescence. It is argued that identifying precursors to actual problem behaviors can set up earlier and more effective points for intervention.

Another element of the elastic nature of risk and protective factors is that they are often renegotiated. Rutter (1989) argues that today's protective factor often becomes tomorrow's risk factor. For example, the "compulsive compliance," or conforming to maternal demands, that many abused infants exhibit in response to their parental treatment is an effective strategy for coping or possibly even reducing abusive acts, and therefore would be considered a protective factor in the short term (Crittenden & DiLalla, 1988). However these infants, who seemed to be effective in maintaining at least some control over their environment, were found to have difficulty relating to peers and other adults at 36 months, indicating that this coping strategy may be impeding their social development. This behavior therefore becomes a risk factor in the long term.

Rutter (1989) also argues that risk and protective factors must be examined within the context of a person's life because risk and protective factors are embedded in an individual's context. Events such as parental death or divorce do not influence everyone equally. Timing of experience, the person's temperament, specific environmental context, and past coping behaviors influence how stressful events are experienced. Having a close and supportive relationship with parents may serve as a protective factor for most situations, but may make the event of divorce or leaving home more difficult. Intelligence, often considered a protective factor, has been found to place some inner-city children at risk for loneliness or depression (Luthar, 1991). Rutter calls for examining the interplay between development and a given environment, as well as identifying connections between past experiences and current adaptation. He writes, "Particular attention needs to be paid to the mechanisms operating at key turning points in people's lives, when a risk trajectory may be redirected onto a more adaptive path" (Rutter, 1990, p. 210).

DISCUSSION

While the relationship between families and individual resilience appears to be well established, the notion of family units being resilient has only recently surfaced in the literature. Family resilience would seem to be a reasonable and fruitful area of exploration, but there are several questions worthy of discussion at this juncture. Several of these are highlighted in this section.

Does the Concept of Family Resilience Make a New and Distinct Contribution to the Literature?

Lavee (1995) has suggested that while the term "resilience" is relatively new in family studies, the concept itself is not. Literature focusing on the characteristics and strengths of families successfully facing crisis date back to the 1930s (Angell, 1936; Cavan & Ranck, 1938; Hill, 1949; Koos, 1946). Both the family stress (Hansen & Johnson, 1979; McCubbin & Patterson, 1983) and the family strengths (Otto, 1962, 1963; Stinnett, 1979) literatures have provided a rich history focusing on resources a family brings to bear when it faces significant difficulties.

The current family resiliency literature appears to expand upon these themes. The model proposed by McCubbin and McCubbin (1988; 1993) represents an extension of the ABCX model, which is based on a family stress conceptual framework. At the same time, many of the characteristics attributed to resilient families are derived from the family strengths literature (McCubbin & McCubbin, 1988; Silliman, 1994). One may wonder whether the study of family resilience is found at the intersection of the two frameworks. Does resilience simply describe how families use their strengths in times of crisis?

At this point, it appears that the literature on family resilience primarily represents a refinement of the family stress and family strengths literatures. Perhaps the most distinct conceptual contribution in the budding family resilience literature has been the development of the notion of a family ethos (that is, schema, world view, sense of coherence), which attempts to describe a shared set of values and attitudes held by a family unit that serves as the linchpin of its resilience.

Can Resiliency Legitimately Be Considered a Family-Level Construct?

Is resilience mutually constructed and shared by the family as a whole, or is it a collective of individual resiliencies exhibited by family members? While the idea of individual resilience is supported in the developmental psychopathology literature, is there a basis for believing that families as units can exhibit resiliency?

Several interactive variables including flexibility and cohesion (McCubbin & McCubbin, 1988) and a variety of family strengths (Silliman, 1994) have been associated with resilience in families. Such variables are often observed and assessed in family research. However, socially constructed variables such as schema and coherence may be problematic. Can such concepts, which rely on the cognitive constructions of individual family members, be shared?

Wamboldt and Wolin (1989) have grappled with this issue by distinguishing between family realities and family myths. Family realities are viewed as shared group perceptions that serve as a template for group behavior and interaction. They are influenced by what Reiss (1981) calls family paradigms (or the family's perceptions about the nature of the outside world and its place in it), and by what Bennett, Wolin, and McAvity (1988) term family identity (or a family's subjective sense of its own character). Family myths, on the other hand, are the maps of family reality, which reside within individual members. These are the stories each member has about his or her family and they may differ from the family reality. Wamboldt and Wolin maintain that a family may have a shared view of reality, such as a schema or a sense of coherence, which relies on cognitive construction and which is distinct from the myths carried by individual family members.

The difficulty, however, lies in measuring this shared family reality. On the one hand, Wamboldt and Wolin (1989) indicate that it can be inferred through observation of family interactions, but cannot be assessed through verbal discussion, which would entail tapping into individual interpretations or family myths. Antonovsky and Sourani (1988) concur. They cite Reiss's (1981) observational methods in studying family paradigms as successful, but go on to say: "We know, however, of no way other than Reiss's method . . . to get at the orientation of the family as a unit" (p. 87). Patterson and Garwick (1994), on the other hand, cite preliminary evidence that suggests that a family's world view can be assessed through conjoint family interviews. In any case, it seems clear that, from a theoretical standpoint, resilience can logically be construed as a family-level construct. However, researchers may encounter difficulties in operationalizing those portions of the concept that rely on shared perceptions of reality.

How Can the Study of Resilience on the Individual Level Influence the Study of Resilience on the Family Level?

Clearly a number of similarities can be found in the two literatures. Definitions from both levels of analysis argue that resilience is developed in response to stress, distinguishing between people who are well-adjusted because they have never faced a potentially damaging stressor, and those who have managed to prosper in spite of difficult circumstances. Resiliency, therefore, cannot be tracked until some degree of stress is faced. Both

levels also stress the ability to "bounce back" or return to previous levels of functioning from stressful circumstances, from Garmezy's (1993) "power of recovery" to Valentine and Feinauer's (1993) "ability to return to original form." In addition, families are cited as an important risk and protective factor for resilient individuals, and the importance of context in predicting resilient outcomes is emphasized for both individual and family resilience.

Nevertheless, there are a number of differences between the two literatures. While it can be expected that resilience will take on a different nature at varying levels of analysis, the more recently established exploration of family resilience may benefit from work already done on resilience at the individual level.

First, literature related to resilience in individuals appears to place a significant emphasis on developmental issues. The role of developmental transitions and the emphasis on long-term reactions to stress highlight the importance of considering the life cycle of resilience. In an early article on family resilience, McCubbin and McCubbin (1988) identify a number of strengths and stressors found at various stages in the family life cycle. Their resiliency model, however, appears to focus on a family's response to a stressor and its context at a given point in time. Similarly, Silliman's (1994) comments on the dynamic nature of resilience underscore the importance of looking at process but do not address the idea that resilience in a family may follow a consistent trajectory over a long period of time.

Resilience is partially defined at both the individual and family levels in terms of the passage of time. The ability to "bounce back" implies a former and a latter state of being. Although both perspectives acknowledge the importance of time, the developmental psychopathologists' focus is on long-term adaptation. This stems from the assumption that certain behaviors, although not problematic at present, may make future development or adjustment more difficult. The ultimate goal of this perspective is to predict which early behaviors will lead to later problems, in order to intervene at an early and arguably more effective point. Models conceptualizing family resilience may need to consider the salience of the development of families over time as a means of identifying potential threats to family well-being.

Second, while the literature on individual resilience emphasizes both risk and protective factors, family resilience primarily emphasizes protective factors. Risk factors are not ignored in the family resilience literature (note the pileup of demands in McCubbin and McCubbin's [1993] model), but the central focus is on strengths such as resources, sense of coherence, and schema. This is undoubtedly a reflection of the philosophical orientation found in the roots of family resilience, such as salutogenesis (Antonovsky, 1987) and family strengths research. These approaches place greater emphasis on family health than on pathology because they assume it produces a qualitatively different set of discoveries. Developmental psychopathologists focus on strengths and wellness, but they also place greater emphasis on pathology than the current family resilience literature. The literature on individual resilience stresses the dual nature of risk and protective factors. The notion that today's protective factors may become tomorrow's risk factors (and vice versa) suggests that these are not separate entities. Rather, context and development can determine whether a given factor represents risk or protection for a family. For example, intense bonding may be a protective factor for a family dealing with a serious illness but a risk factor for a family in the process of launching one of its members. The goal is not, therefore, to develop a list of static risk and protective factors, but to examine how experiences are mediated by context and developmental level. Consequently, while resilience is connected with positive processes such as adaptiveness and buoyancy, models of family resilience may need to give greater consideration to the role played by risk factors, specifically in identifying common family trajectories that lead into pathology.

While some may argue that this focus on pathology is counterproductive, and may even represent a step backwards (Lavee, 1995), the connection between pathology and opportunities for resiliency must be made. This consideration differs from past research on family stress because of its focus on how pathways of pathology are developed by families over time. When we gain a clearer understanding of how earlier behaviors (whether pathological or not) link to current maladaptive behaviors, we can compare the trajectories of those families that show resilient behaviors with those that do not. This focus also allows us to examine which behaviors contribute to long-term growth, as well as aid our understanding of whether early resiliencies in fact may lead to long-term risks.

Third, how do resilient individuals influence the resilience of the family unit as a whole? The effects of family dynamics on individual resiliency have been well established, but is the process bidirectional? McCubbin and McCubbin (1993) indicate that personal strengths are one type of resource used by a family in mediating the effects of a stressor. The systems concept of mutual causality suggests that the actions of one family member impact the entire family. Thus, we might assume that individual resilience has an effect on family resilience. Silliman (1994) suggests that the individual, family, and community levels of resilience are interrelated. Extensions of a family resiliency framework may consider what form this interaction takes.

DEFINITION OF FAMILY RESILIENCE

Based on the above discussion, we offer the following definition as an initial attempt to integrate contributions from the literatures addressing individual and family resilience:

> Family resilience describes the path a family follows as it adapts and prospers in the face of stress, both in the present and over time. Resilient families respond positively to these conditions in unique ways, depending on the context, developmental level, the interactive combination of risk and protective factors, and the family's shared outlook.

This definition suggests that resilience at the family level describes the trajectory a family follows as it positively adapts to and bounces back from stressful circumstances. Resilience-enabling family processes allow a family to create a path that is adaptive and may even permit them to grow and thrive in response to the stressors. As such, resilience should not be conceptualized as a static set of strengths or qualities as much as a developmental process unique to each family, which leads to similar, adaptive outcomes, much like the systems concept of equifinality (Whitchurch & Constantine, 1993).

Furthermore, family resilience should be viewed through both short and long-term lenses, recognizing that time and development are contributing factors. Resilience in families is affected by their unique context, including developmental factors, risk and protective factors, and worldview considerations. The goal, therefore, is not to develop a resiliency scale, but to bring a more longitudinal focus to our consideration of family stresses and strengths in order to maximize our intervention effectiveness.

This definition draws on and seeks to integrate those previously set forth in the literature on family resilience. McCubbin and McCubbin (1988) describe resilient families as "resistant to disruption in the face of change and adaptive in the face of crisis situations" (p. 247). In our view, adaptation encompasses both of these processes, drawing on the interplay of morphostasis and morphogenesis (Whitchurch & Constantine, 1993). It seeks to capture the concept of buoyancy (Valentine & Feinauer, 1993; Wolin & Wolin, 1993) by suggesting that resilient families have the capacity to rise above setbacks and prosper. It also recognizes the foundational base of the resilience model proposed by McCubbin and McCubbin by including risk factors (pileup of demands), protective factors (resources/strengths), and shared outlook (schema).

However, we have also sought to include dimensions that have received greater emphasis in the literature on individual resilience than on family resilience. These include: 1) an increased focus on the role of time, including current and longterm views of resilience and the place of developmental level; 2) a clear acknowledgment of the role of risk factors as well as protective factors; and 3) an emphasis on resilience as a developmental process rather than as a static entity.

CLINICAL IMPLICATIONS

Implications for clinical practice can be drawn from this definition of family resilience. First, the notion of family schema or world view suggests that family members may bring to therapy a common perception of themselves, which, if identified, could be therapeutically useful. Helping individuals discover positive meanings to distress is a common procedure in strengths-based therapies. Wolin and Wolin (1993), for example, highlight the "survivor's pride" (p. 8) they see in resilient clients, while White and Epston (1990) seek to help clients discover their "lived experiences" (p. 15) that provide preferred alternatives to their dominant stories. However, most of these approaches focus on meanings held by *individuals*. Resilience as a family-level construct suggests that it may be fruitful to identify how a commonly perceived family ethos is useful in helping families frame their distress more positively. Clinicians need to bear in mind, however, that the shared perceptions a family brings to therapy may be destructive and that a part of the therapeutic process involves developing a schema that is empowering to the family.

Second, this definition suggests that resilience is best detected by observing families over time and in their unique contexts. Developmental stage has long been seen as a key treatment consideration with families (Carter & McGoldrick, 1988; Haley, 1973; Solomon, 1973). Resilience, however, is less concerned with a cross-sectional approach, which looks for commonalities between families at a particular developmental stage, than it is with the trajectory describing how a given family functions at points across the life cycle. Clinically, this may highlight the importance of discovering interaction patterns that helped families exhibit resilience at points in their past. However, therapists should also be aware that today's protective factor may be tomorrow's risk factor.

Interventions that worked in the past may be ineffective in a present or future context and may even contribute to problem development. Family resilience may also suggest that therapeutic outcomes are not easily measured in the short term. Some families who appear to make remarkable progress in brief therapy may show low levels of resilience over time. Conversely, other families, who appear to be making little progress in therapy, could be developing qualities that will enable them to be highly resilient in future struggles.

IMPLICATIONS FOR RESEARCH

Perhaps the key issue for furthering the study of family resilience is operationalization. Burr, Hill, Nye, and Reiss (1979) distinguish between concepts that vary along an identifiable dimension (variables) and those that do not (nonvariables). An important conceptual question concerns into which of these categories family resilience best fits. Furthermore, if family resilience is a variable, is it categorical (suggesting that some families are resilient while others are not) or continuous (suggesting that all families are resilient, but to varying degrees)?

In our definition, family resilience would be regarded as a nonvariable construct. As mentioned above, family resilience is primarily concerned with the trajectory a family displays through a variety of stress points within the life cycle. Operationalization of family resilience has less to do with the specific content of the family processes themselves (for example, variables such as communication and cohesion) than it does with the pathways a family follows in its response to stressors. Family resilience can be evaluated by assessing whether a family has returned to or exceeded pre-stressor levels of functioning at some point subsequent to the stressor. While there may be some resilience-enabling processes that are common to all families facing stress, they have not been clearly identified in past research. Therefore, the specific variables used as outcome measures for these paths depend on what the literature suggests as important factors to consider in how a particular population responds to stress. For example, the same set of resilience-enabling variables may not apply to families responding to a health crisis as would apply to families coping with the stress of cross-cultural reentry. However, both sets of families may exhibit similar trajectories over a length of time. Thus, longitudinal designs, which capture family processes at multiple points of time, are better suited for evaluating resilience than cross-sectional research designs, which assess family resilience at one point in time.

CONCLUSION

Family resilience is a relatively new construct that describes how families adapt to stress and bounce back from adversity. The study of how families maintain resilience holds excellent potential for improving efforts in primary prevention and clinical intervention. Initial work in this area has moved beyond viewing resilience as a characteristic of individuals influenced by their families, to providing a useful framework for conceptualizing resilience as a systemic quality of families. While areas of resilience, which depend on cognitive constructions of multiple family members (for example, schema and coherence) may present methodological challenges for assessment, resilience appears to be a viable family-level construct.

We have suggested that the developmental psychopathology literature, which focuses on resilience in individuals, is a profitable source for extending family resilience. Resilience is similarly defined in both literatures, as might be expected since it is the same concept addressed at different levels of analysis. However, the roots of each stream of study differ. Family resilience comes out of family stress and family strengths—conceptual orientations that tend to emphasize wellness and adaptability; individual resilience is grounded in a pathologically oriented framework, which is concerned with the long-term development of resilience and the discovery of risk and protective factors.

The interactive focus of family studies suggests that similar concepts often take on a different nature at the family level of analysis. Nevertheless, researchers and theorists of resilience in families would do well to consider implications from developmental psychopathology. Of particular importance are the influence of developmental transitions on resilience and the identification of potential risk factors at the family level of analysis. Family science has a rich heritage of exploring the influences of development and identifying precursors of pathology; conceptualizations of family resilience can draw on these sources as they continue to seek clarification. Finally, it should be noted that the learning curve is bidirectional. Although it is less well established as an area of investigation, theoretical advances and research findings in family resilience can also contribute to growth in the study of individual resilience.

REFERENCES

Anderson, K. H. (1994). Family sense of coherence: As collective and consensus in relation to family quality of life after illness diagnosis (pp. 169-187). In H. I. McCubbin, E. A. Thompson, A. I. Thompson, & J. E. Fromer (eds.), *Sense of coherence and resiliency: Stress, coping and health*. Madison WI: University of Wisconsin Press.

Angell, R. C. (1936). *The family encounters the Depression*. New York: Charles Scribner.

Antonovsky, A. (1979). *Health, stress, and coping: New perspectives on mental and physical well-being*. San Francisco: Jossey-Bass.

——— (1987). *Unraveling the mystery of health: How people manage stress and stay well*. San Francisco: Jossey-Bass.

Antonovsky, A. and Sourani, T. (1988). Family sense of coherence and family adaptation. *Journal of Marriage and the Family 50:* 79-92.

Barnard, C. P. (1994). Resiliency: A shift in our perception? *American Journal of Family Therapy 22:* 135-144.

Bennett, L. A., Wolin, S. J. and McAvity, K. J. (1988). Family identity, ritual, and myth: A cultural perspective on life cycle transitions (pp. 211-234). In C. J. Falicov (ed.), *Family transitions: Continuity and change over the life cycle*. New York: Guilford Press.

Berg, I. K. and Miller, S. (1992). *Working with the problem drinker*. New York: W. W. Norton.

Bronfenbrenner, U. (1990). Discovering what families do (pp. 27-38). In D. Blankenhorne, S. Bayme, & J. B. Elshtain (eds.), *Rebuilding the nest*. Milwaukee WI: Family Service of America.

Burger, J. V. (1994). Keys to survival: Highlights in resilience research. *Journal of Emotional and Behavioral Problems 3:* 6-10.

Burr, W. R., Hill, R., Nye, F. I. and Reiss, I. L. (1979). Meta-theory and diagramming conventions (pp. 17-24). In W. R. Burr, R. Hill, F. I. Nye, & I. L. Reiss (eds.), *Contemporary theories about the family (Vol. 1): Research-based theories*. New York: Free Press.

Carter, E. and McGoldrick, M. (1988). *The changing family life cycle: A framework for family therapy* (2nd ed.). New York: Gardner Press.

Cavan, R. S. and Ranck, K. H. (1938). *The family and the Depression*. Chicago: University of Chicago Press.

Compas, B. E. (1987). Coping with stress in childhood and adolescence. *Psychological Bulletin 101:* 393-403.

Crittenden, P. M. and DiLalla, D. L. (1988). Compulsive compliance: The development of an inhibitory coping strategy in infancy. *Journal of Abnormal Child Psychology 16:* 585-599.

Curran, D. (1983). *Traits of a healthy family*. Minneapolis: Winston.

Dalla, R. L. and Gamble, W. C. (1995). Social networks and systems of support among American Indian Navajo adolescent mothers (pp. 183-198). In H. I. McCubbin, M. A. McCubbin, A. I. Thompson, & J. E. Fromer (eds.), *Resiliency in ethnic minority families: Native and immigrant American families, Volume 1*. Madison WI: University of Wisconsin Press.

Doherty, W. J., Boss, P. G., LaRossa, R., Schumm, W. R. and Steinmetz, S. K. (1993). Family theories and methods: A contextual approach (pp. 3-30). In P. G. Boss, W. J. Doherty, R. LaRossa, W. R. Schumm, & S. K. Steinmetz (eds.), *Sourcebook of family theories and methods: A contextual approach*. New York: Plenum Press.

Elder, G. H., Liker, J. K. and Cross, C. E. (1984). Parent-child behavior in the Great Depression: Life course and intergenerational influences. *Life Span Development and Behavior 6:* 109-158.

Garmezy, N. (1985). Stress resistant children: The search for protective factors (pp. 213-233). In J. E. Stevenson (ed.), Recent research in developmental psychopathology. *Journal of Child Psychology and Psychiatry Book Suppl. No. 4*. Oxford: Pergamon Press.

——— (1993). Children in poverty: Resilience despite risk. *Psychiatry 56:* 127-136.

Genero, N. P. (1995). Culture, resiliency, and mutual psychological development (pp. 31-48). In H. I. McCubbin, M. A. McCubbin, A. I. Thompson, & J. A. Futrell (eds.), *Resiliency in ethnic minority families: African-American families, Volume 2*. Madison WI: University of Wisconsin Press.

Goddard, H. W. and Allen, J. D. (1991). Using the ABCX model to understand resilience. Paper presented at the Theory Construction and Research Methodology Workshop, Denver CO, November 1991.

Haley, J. (1973). *Uncommon therapy: The psychiatric techniques of Milton H. Erickson, M.D.* New York: W. W. Norton.

Hansen, D. A. and Johnson, V. A. (1979). Rethinking family stress theory: Definitional aspects (pp. 582-603).

In W. R. Burr, R. Hill, F. I. Nye, & I. L. Reiss (eds.), *Contemporary theories about the family (Vol. 1): Research-based theories*. New York: Free Press.

Hetherington, E. M., Cox, M. and Cox, R. (1985). Long-term effects of divorce and remarriage on the adjustment of children. *Journal of American Academy of Psychiatry 24:* 518-530.

Hill, R. (1949). *Families under stress: Adjustment to the crises of war, separation, and reunion*. New York: Harper & Brothers [reprinted 1971, Westport CT: Greenwood Press].

——— (1958). Generic features of families under stress. *Social Casework 49:* 139-150.

Kolvin, I., Miller, F. J. W., Fleeting, M. and Kolvin, P. A. (1988). Social and parenting factors affecting criminal offense rates: Findings from the Newcastle Thousand Family Study, 1947-1980. *British Journal of Psychiatry 152:* 80-90.

Koos, E. L. (1946). *Families in trouble*. New York: King's Crown Press.

Lavee, Y. (1995). Discussant's comments on Dale R. Hawley and Laura DeHaan's "Toward a definition of family resilience: Integrating life-span and family perspectives." Paper presented at NCFR Theory Construction and Research Methodology Workshop, Portland OR, November 1995.

Lavee, Y., McCubbin, H. I. and Olson, D. H. (1987). The effect of stressful life events and transitions on family functioning and well-being. *Journal of Marriage and the Family 49:* 857-873.

Lewis, J. (1979). *How's your family?* New York: Brunner/Mazel.

Luthar, S. S. (1991). Vulnerability and resilience: A study of high risk adolescents. *Child Development 62:* 600-612.

Luthar, S. S. and Zigler, E. (1991). Vulnerability and competence: A review of research on resilience in childhood. *American Journal of Orthopsychiatry 61:* 6-22.

McCubbin, H. I. and McCubbin, M. A. (1988). Typologies of resilient families: Emerging roles of social class and ethnicity. *Family Relations 37:* 247-254.

McCubbin, H. I., McCubbin, M. A. and Thompson, A. I. (1993). Resiliency in families: The role of family schema and appraisal in family adaptation to crises (pp. 153-177). In T. H. Brubaker (ed.), *Family relations: Challenges for the future*. Newbury Park CA: Sage Publications.

McCubbin, H. I., McCubbin, M. A., Thompson, A. I. and Thompson, E. A. (1995). Resiliency in ethnic families: A conceptual model for predicting family adjustment and adaptation (pp. 3-48). In H. I. McCubbin,
M. A. McCubbin, A. I. Thompson, & J. E. Fromer (eds.), *Resiliency in ethnic minority families: Native and immigrant American families, Volume 1*. Madison WI: University of Wisconsin Press.

McCubbin, H. I. and Patterson, J. M. (1983). The family stress process: The Double ABCX model of adjustment and adaptation. *Marriage and Family Review 6:* 7-37.

McCubbin, H. I., Thompson, A. I., Thompson, E. A., Elver, K. M. and McCubbin, M. A. (1994). Ethnicity, schema, and coherence: Appraisal processes for families in crisis (pp. 41-67). In H. I. McCubbin, E. A. Thompson, A. I. Thompson, & J. E. Fromer (eds.), *Sense of coherence and resiliency: Stress, coping and health*. Madison WI: University of Wisconsin Press.

McCubbin, M. A. and McCubbin, H. I. (1993). Family coping with health crises: The resiliency model of family stress, adjustment, and adaptation (pp. 21-64). In C. Danielson, B. Hamel-Bissell, & P. Winstead-Fry (eds.), *Families, health, and illness*. St. Louis MO: C. V. Mosby.

Otto, H. A. (1962). "What is a strong family?" *Marriage and Family Living 24:* 77-81.

——— (1963). Criteria for assessing family strength. *Family Process 2:* 329-338.

Patterson, G. R., DeBaryshe, B. D. and Ramsey, E. (1989). A developmental perspective on antisocial behavior. *American Psychologist 44:* 329-335.

Patterson, J. M. and Garwick, A. W. (1994). Theoretical linkages: Family meanings and sense of coherence (pp. 71-89). In H. I. McCubbin, E. A. Thompson, A. I. Thompson, & J. E. Fromer (eds.), *Sense of coherence and resiliency: Stress, coping and health*. Madison WI: University of Wisconsin Press.

Reiss, D. (1981). *The family's construction of reality*. Cambridge: Harvard University Press.

Rutter, M. (1979). Protective factors in children's responses to stress and disadvantage (pp. 49-74). In M. W. Kent & J. E. Rolf (eds.), *Primary prevention of psychopathology, Vol. 3: Social competence in children*. Hanover NH: University Press of New England.

——— (1987). Psychosocial resilience and protective mechanisms. *American Journal of Orthopsychiatry 57:* 316-331.

——— (1989). Pathways from childhood to adult life. *Journal of Child Psychology and Psychiatry 30:* 23-51.

——— (1990). Psychosocial resilience and protective mechanisms (pp. 181-214). In J. E. Rolf, A. S. Masten, D. Cicchetti, K. H. Nuechterlein, & S. Weintraub (eds.), *Risk and protective factors in the development of psychopathology*. Cambridge, England: Cambridge University Press.

Silliman, B. (1994). Rationale for resilient families concept paper. National Network for Family Resiliency.

Smith, I. (1991). Preschool children "play" out their grief. *Death Studies 15:* 169-176.

Solomon, M. A. (1973). A developmental, conceptual premise for family therapy. *Family Process 12:* 179-188.

Speer, D. C. (1970). Family systems: Morphostasis and morphogenesis, or "Is homeostasis enough?" *Family Process 9:* 259-278.

Sroufe, L. A. and Rutter, M. (1984). The domain of developmental psychopathology. *Child Development 55:* 17-29.

Stinnett, N. (1979). In search of strong families (pp. 257-274). In N. Stinnett, B. Chesser, & J. DeFrain (eds.), *Building family strengths*. Lincoln NE: University of Nebraska Press.

Stinnett, N. and DeFrain, J. (1985). *Secrets of strong families*. Boston: Little, Brown.

Valentine, L. and Feinauer, L. L. (1993). Resilience factors associated with female survivors of childhood sexual abuse. *American Journal of Family Therapy 21:* 216-224.

Wamboldt, F. S. and Wolin, S. J. (1989). Reality and myth in family life: Changes across generations. *Journal of Psychotherapy and the Family 4:* 141-165.

Werner, E. E. (1989). High-risk children in young adulthood: A longitudinal study from birth to 32 years. *American Journal of Orthopsychiatry 59:* 72-81.

Werner, E. E. and Smith, R. S. (1982). *Vulnerable but invincible: A longitudinal study of resilient children and youth*. New York: McGraw-Hill.

Whitchurch, G. G. and Constantine, L. L. (1993). Systems theory (pp. 325-352). In P. G. Boss, W. J. Doherty, R. LaRossa, W. R. Schumm, & S. K. Steinmetz (eds.), *Sourcebook of family theories and methods: A contextual approach*. New York: Plenum Press.

White, M. and Epston, D. (1990). *Narrative means to therapeutic ends*. New York: W. W. Norton.

Wolin, S. J. and Wolin, S. (1993). *The resilient self*. New York: Villard Books.

Wyman, P. A., Cowen, E. L., Work, W. C., Raoff, A., Cribble, P. A., Parker, G. R. and Wannon, M. (1992). Interviews with children who experienced major life stress: Family and child attributes that predict resilient outcomes. *Journal of the American Academy of Child and Adolescent Psychiatry 31:* 904-910.

Zimmerman, M. A., Ramirez, J., Washienko, K. M., Walter, B. and Dyer, S. (1995). Enculturation hypothesis: Exploring direct and protective effects among Native American youth (pp. 199-220). In H. I. McCubbin, M. A. McCubbin, A. I. Thompson, & J. E. Fromer (eds.), *Resiliency in ethnic minority families: Native and immigrant American families, Volume 1*. Madison WI: University of Wisconsin Press.

5

STRESS LEVELS, FAMILY HELP PATTERNS, AND RELIGIOSITY IN MIDDLE- AND WORKING-CLASS AFRICAN AMERICAN SINGLE MOTHERS

HARRIETTE PIPES MCADOO

In this survey of 318 middle- and working-class African American mothers, stress and female-related stress were found to be intense and frequent. Women experienced serious life changes. Younger mothers, with younger children, had more stress than older mothers, and college-educated women had more stress than those without a college education. Religion was important; women prayed frequently but tended not to attend church services. Faith provided strong emotional support, especially for the working class and those in stress, but women who were not religious had the lowest stress.

Unmarried mothers are a growing phenomenon in the United States as divorce and pregnancy without marriage increase in all segments of our society. Now that single parenting has been recognized as a problem that faces all U.S. women, including Black and White alike, empirical studies are needed to address the issues of an increasingly typical family type: a mother alone with her children. Poverty, and its attending stresses, is a major consequence of single parenting (D'Ercole, 1988; Edelman, 1991; Farley & Allen, 1987; Kamerman & Kahn, 1988). Poverty causes

Reprinted from the *Journal of Black Psychology* 21 (1995): 424-49. Funds for this research were provided by the National Institutes of Mental Health, Department of Health and Human Services, Grant 5 R1O MN32159.

many of the strains of single parenting, not just the fact of rearing children alone without a husband. Black children in single-parent households are among the poorest in the nation (Edelman, 1987). This article examines how women of different economic and marital status cope with the acute stresses they face as household head. It is proposed that the support of extended family and friends and religiosity are important factors for single mothers.

National attention has been focused on the problems of Black single mothers, and various myths have been mixed with reality (such as matriarchy, the welfare mother) to explain the demographic changes that have occurred in the past 20 years (Kaplan, 1988). These stereotypes often became "truth" in policy discussions, and the result is curtailed federal assistance funds.

Family trends for all groups are similar, but for African Americans it appears that patterns emerge a generation earlier than for Whites (Farley & Allen, 1987; McAdoo, 1988). Whereas the unmarried adolescent pregnancy rate for Blacks is higher than for Whites, the rate dropped for several years and then rose for Black girls in comparison to White girls (Alan Guttmacher Institute, 1981; Edelman, 1987; Hayes, 1987; Kaplan, 1988). Other family patterns that have converged are childbearing expectations and childlessness rates (Glick, 1988). There are indications that late first marriages and the long period between divorce and remarriage are the result of young men having difficulty gaining permanent employment (Edelman, 1987; Farley & Allen, 1987; Wilson & Neckerman, 1986).

More than half of all African American children under age 18 live with their mother alone (Danziger & Danziger, 1993). Divorce is the greatest contributor to Black mothers being single (Kamerman & Kahn, 1988; McAdoo, 1988). The second source is birth of a child to young unmarried women, and a small but growing source is birth by choice to stable, older unmarried women (Mechaneck, 1987). As the number of single mothers of all races has increased, the literature has moved from condemnation to the realization that single parenting is here to stay, that one can socialize and rear children effectively without being married (D'Ercole, 1988; Yankelovich, 1981).

Mothers who parent alone are confronted with multiple role demands, financial issues, and child-rearing concerns that require social support and resources. An inadequate standard of living and role overload have been found to be significant predictors of stress in single mothers (D'Ercole, 1988). McLanahan and Booth (1989) offer a comprehensive explanation of the issues and stressors that single mothers face. They point out that stress in a single-parent home is greater than in other forms of family structure. The major stressor is financial, particularly when the father of the child does not provide sufficient support.

An extensive support network among family members and fictive kin, who become as family, is true for people of all socioeconomic statuses (Farley & Allen, 1987; McAdoo, 1988) and different family structures (Taylor, Chatters, Tucker, & Lewis, 1990). The extended family network can be especially helpful to single mothers, as it can mean options in schooling or career (Martin & Martin, 1978).

Social support apparently buffers stress, and friendships or secondary relationships with other women, family members, and coworkers have been found to be helpful to single mothers (Garfinkel & McLanahan, 1986; Brown & Gary, 1985). If stress becomes too great upon mothers, either mental or physical illness soon follows (Holmes & Masuda, 1974). Women survive by adopting certain patterns of support from the family situations in which they find themselves. Women receive help more frequently from female relatives. When family is available and the relationship with kin is harmonious, the family can be the source of support. Single mothers tend to be more involved with their parents, and this pattern is extended to increased interaction with kin (Marks & McLanahan, 1993).

Although not present in all families, kin help absorb the life stresses of family members and provide emotional support for kin and fictive kin (Aschenbrenner, 1973; McAdoo, 1991a, 1991b; Stack, 1974). The cohesion of families often has a direct linear relationship with positive outcomes. Because the needs of single mothers may exceed the resources of kin, nonrelatives often become closely aligned to the family and also provide support. These fictive kin (McAdoo, 1988; Stack, 1974) become as close to the mother as her own kin and in some cases closer. Because the helping arrangements are similar for kin and fictive kin, both relatives and friends must be examined in looking at the help given to single mothers. There is no agreement on the support patterns that are present in single-mother families, although the work of Horowitz (1992) indicates that a hierarchy of obligations determines which kin provide care to family members. To look only at actual kin ignores an important source of support, however, and female fictive kin should not be overlooked.

Social support from extended family and fictive kin is associated with the involvement of fathers in child rearing. The more support the father gives and the more invested he becomes, the more involved he becomes with the child. The support system among family and fictive kin has been titled *generalized mutual obligations* (Scanzoni & Marsiglio, 1993). If a mother requests assistance from one person in her network and that person is unable to help, then she can turn to another individual. But there are reciprocal obligations (McAdoo, 1988). Mothers who receive help find that their resources must be kept available for others in the network. Family support systems are sometimes overextended and overwhelmed with increasing economic and social pressures and chronic illness (McAdoo, 1993; Reiss, 1989). Interactions with relatives may be problematic for single mothers (Belle, 1982).

Grandparents play an important role in many African American families. They are a source of support and also an important link in the intergenerational history and knowledge within the family (Cherlin & Fustenberg, 1986; Kivett, 1993). Yet many grandmothers are themselves trapped in low-paying jobs with no hope of upward mobility. They may not be able to provide financial aid, but there are many ways that help can be exchanged; sometimes it is important to have a shoulder to cry on.

In a study of very poor urban families, Burton (1992) found that if a parent was addicted to drugs and the grandmother had to step in and rear the children, other kin did not provide the necessary help. These families are extremely stressed and overwhelmed by the grandmother's assumption of the main parenting role. The situation is not typical of African American families, and it also is not typical that the grandmother not receive the help she needs. Indeed, her assumption of the parenting role illustrates the concept of extended kin help common in African American families.

Stressors of Single Parenting

The stressors related to being African American and to being female have been well noted. The stress faced by single mothers, whether divorced or never married, has become more evident as more women move into this status. The severity of that stress is affected by the economic and emotional resources available. Poor mothers must deal with poverty, high-crime areas, and poor educational facilities, whereas mothers who do not have the same basic economic needs may be more concerned with child care and household tasks. Quinn (1989) found that single mothers were concerned about lack of time and child care. Their sample represented all three socioeconomic groups, similar to the study sample here. The chronic shortage of time was experienced by employed single mothers.

There is an emotional adjustment to single mothering and bearing the sole responsibility for children. Women with young children and women who are no longer married have more stress than other women (McAdoo, 1991b; McLanahan & Booth, 1989). Blacks have a high divorce rate, and divorced women undergo many changes in roles and social position that cause stress to them and their children (Garfinkel & McLanahan, 1986; Hannam & Eggebeen, 1993; McAdoo, 1991a). Future marriage or remarriage often is unlikely for single mothers because of the imbalance in the sex ratios (Darity & Myers, 1991; Tucker & Mitchell-Kernan, 1992). The patterns and interactions of the extended family often work against the entry of another spouse into very poor families (Stack, 1974). The family needs the younger member's help, which would be lost if a marriage were to occur. And some families may interfere with the mother's child-rearing style (Fine, McKinry, Donnelly, & Voydanoff, 1992).

The stressors are affected by any change or significant life event. The lifestyle changes that are found when women move in and out of marriage or go in or out of poverty are significant and cause changes in both women and their children. These changes have been found to be disruptive to women and their children (McAdoo, 1991b).

Taylor, Henderson, and Jackson (1991) found that the stressors leading to depression and poor health emanated from the many life changes that the women in their sample faced. Any change in the environment may cause depressive symptoms and stress. When these changes occur, the perceived availability and involvement of friends are very important. Females in general are more vulnerable than men, and African American women are more vulnerable to depression than are Caucasian females. Single mothers have fewer psychological problems than those who are married (Taylor et al., 1991).

Religiosity

A religious orientation is a belief in a supreme being, and religiosity may not mean church attendance or membership. As used in this study, religiosity refers to the importance of religion in the woman's life. The traditional Black churches offer solace, warmth, and nurturance, and the "church family" may assume many functions of a kinship network: informal adoptions, job referrals, emotional support, and social contacts. This assistance is in addition to the religious function.

The importance of religion and the church in coping in the lives of African Americans has been well documented (Billingsley, 1968, 1992; Frazier, 1963; Hill, 1971; Pipes, 1992). Brown and Gary (1985) found that religious participation is a source of support with anxiety-related problems. Other studies have shown that the church provides emotional well-being (Neighbors & Jackson, 1984) and that women are more religiously involved than men (Taylor, Thornton, & Chatters, 1987). Therefore, it is important to understand religion as one of the coping strategies available to single mothers.

Although one would expect religiosity to have a direct and positive effect on stress and coping, the women who are very stressed have the greatest religiosity (McAdoo, 1988). A high religious orientation has a direct relationship with depressive symptoms in

mothers; that is, the more religious a mother is, the greater is her depression. Women high in religiosity tend to be less involved in their social support network (Taylor, 1991), and a religious orientation seems to have a culturally oppressive rather than liberating effect on women. This finding was corroborated in two other large-scale studies (Jackson, 1991; Taylor & Jackson, 1990).

In summary, as noted in McAdoo (1994), extended family support is available in many families, but help from kin becomes more activated when the mothers are single, when families are facing greater stress, or when economic resources are more limited. Socioeconomic status (SES) and family structure are directly related because the resources that are available to parents as they rear their children are diminished when mothers are parenting alone.

THE HYPOTHESES

This study examines how women of different status cope with the acute stresses they face as household head. What are their sources of support and how do these sources differ for women of different social class and marital status? Four issues were addressed: (a) the factors in personal and family backgrounds that contribute to the ability to face stress; (b) the levels of stress; (c) whether female-related stressors are an addition to regular stress; and (d) the roles of religion.

Hypothesis 1: Stress levels will be similar for both the previously married and never-married women.

Hypothesis 2: Working-class mothers will have significantly higher stress levels than will middle-class mothers.

Hypothesis 3: The roles of religion will be similar for women in both marital status and SES groups.

METHODOLOGY

Procedures

National probability studies with large samples (Jackson, 1991) can provide representative samples, but this research involved a regional sample. Interviewers were able to take time to develop a relationship with the mothers, to follow up on the answers, and to probe in detail for more information. All the interviewers were African American, and half were single mothers. The interviews ranged from 2.5 to 3 hours.

A systematic sampling procedure could not be used because residences of single Black mothers were not randomly distributed across the city. Three methods were used to obtain subjects. First, a sample was drawn from an income-stratified list of all the day care centers approved by the Baltimore Department of Social Service that had an approximate Black enrollment of at least 25. That procedure resulted in a predominance of mothers with younger children. Second, to obtain the names of mothers with older children, ads asking for participants were placed in the local White and Black newspapers. Third, volunteers were obtained from the Women's Center, an employment service center.

Telephone contact was made to explain the project and establish eligibility criteria. Subjects were interviewed at home, but in a few instances, because of privacy, mothers preferred to be interviewed on their job or in our Baltimore office. Each mother was given $20 as a small gift of appreciation for her time and effort. The interviewers were trained, and most had previous interview experience.

Instruments

Stress Intensity. The Significant Life Events (SLE) scale was used to obtain an intensity score. The Holmes and Rahe (1967; Holmes & Masuda, 1974) Scale of Recent Events was used to secure universal events, that is, 49 events weighted on actual populations across the country. This scale gives a higher score for major changes (divorce, 73; death of a child, 63) and a lower score for less traumatic events (vacation, 13). Based on clinical follow-ups, Holmes grouped the scores into three stress categories: mild (150-199), moderate (200-299), and major (300 +). Those in the higher stress groups had a greater probability of becoming physically or mentally ill within a shorter period.

Stress Frequency. Frequency was a simple count of whether a stressful event had occurred in a specified period. The Holmes and Rahe SLE scale used 2 years as the time during which change is measured. For this study, that period was used, and an additional two-step temporal scale was developed. Mothers were asked to indicate whether the event had occurred within the past 6 months or the past 7 to 24 months. For example, a family may be subjected to one major event (such as personal injury, 53 points) in 2 years or may have five smaller events (with lower stress scores each) within 6 months. The latter may yield a lower Holmes and Rahe score but may be equally or more traumatic for the family because they all occur within a shorter period.

Female Stress. Because many of the stress events on the SLE were oriented toward men and families but not women, 16 events from Belle's (1980) study were added. These items were going on or off welfare; starting an intimate relationship; having an unfaithful lover; widowhood; marriage of a former husband or lover; undesired miscarriage or abortion; unwanted pregnancy and birth; adoption or taking in of a child; changed child care arrangements; giving up custody of a child; death of a child; menopause; rape or molestation; becoming a crime victim; nervous breakdown; and joining a self-help group. These items could not be weighed as were the others on the SLE, but the frequency of occurrences was noted, as in the stress frequency scoring.

Religion. Five areas were examined: religious denomination membership; religiosity; church attendance; frequency of prayer; and what religion does for one. Religiosity was a subjective assessment of how religious the women felt they were and the importance of spirituality in their lives.

Sample Characteristics

The sample of 318 single Black women lived in the Baltimore area, where they maintained independent households. All were employed and had full custody of their children, all of whom were under age 19. The women had an average of 1.53 children (.89 boys and 1.02 girls); the younger the mother at her first pregnancy, the more children she tended to have. The average age in the sample was

30.24 years, ranging from 20 to 50 years. More than half (54%) had been age 19 or older when their first child was born.

Forty-four percent had never been married, and 56% had been married at one time; of these latter, 29% were divorced, 26% were separated and considered their marriage to be over, and 2% were widowed (see Table 5.1). Most of the women (70%) had grown up in two-parent homes, and their present single-parent status was not due to direct modeling of their families of procreation. Their parents had been in their mid-20s (mothers) or late 20s (fathers) when these women were born. They tended to be either the first and only or the second child born to their parents.

Two thirds of the subjects (73%) were not married at the birth of their first child. Half of that group later married, not always to the father of their first child. Very few of the women (5%) had men living within the home. Their present family structures were diverse. The forms were as follows: attenuated nuclear (mother and children, 66%), attenuated extended (mother, children, and relatives, 25%), augmented attenuated nuclear (mother, children, and nonrelative, 7%), and augmented extended (mother, children, relative, and nonrelative, 2%) (see Table 5.2).

Socioeconomic Status (SES). SES was assessed in two different ways. All subjects were coded using the Hollingshead-Redlick Social Position Scale (1958), which places greater emphasis on the occupation than on the education of an individual. This method allowed comparisons with other data sets. The approach does not seem satisfactory, however, for those who face gender and racial discrimination in the occupational market (McAdoo, 1988; Scanzoni, 1977). Therefore, a method suggested by Baldwin (1973) was used, which gives more weight to education than to occupation.

With the modified scoring, the distribution of the sample by SES status was as follows: 11% Class I; 20% Class II; 53% Class III; 15% Class IV; and 1% Class V. For this study, the classes were combined into two groups: middle-class mothers, Classes I and II (31%), and working-class mothers, Classes III, IV, and V (69%).

The education levels were high school (37%), 1 or 2 years of college (29%), 3 or 4 years of college (19%), and graduate or professional degree (12%). Eighty-nine percent worked full time, 11% part time. Most of the women were clerical workers (47%), followed by executives or professionals (25%) and administrative/personnel (12%). Many had been unemployed at some time in their life; being in college (32%) and pregnancy and child rearing (22%) were the most frequent reasons for unemployment.

Those who had never married tended to be working class, $\chi^2 = 5.69$, $p < .02$, had fewer children, $\chi^2 (1) = 68.27$, $p < .000$, and lived within a three-generation family. Middle-class women who had never married had more people in the home, $F(3, 314) = 4.58$, $p < .03$. This large household size was due to the fact that these women had taken in more elderly persons, $F(3, 310) = 7.15$, $p < .008$, than had those who were working class. They were in a better financial position to do so and were older than the working-class women. These elderly adults were often the persons who had helped the middle-class women when they were young single mothers.

Income. The median income was $12,000; the range was from $3,000 to more than $40,000. The net income for previously married mothers was higher than for those never married, $\chi^2 (7) = 20.64$, $p < .004$. As expected, the middle-class mothers had higher net incomes, $\chi^2 (7) = 67.44$, $p < .000$; the working-class mean was $9,500, and the middle-class mean was $16,500. The mother's income was the major source of support (94% of the sample) for her family. Child support was received by half the mothers, but it was more irregular (51%) than regular (49%).

Because of the low wages they were paid, 84 (26%) of the women received welfare despite their working. Of those receiving welfare, 57% received it regularly, 43% irregularly.

Religion. The largest group was Baptist (59%), followed by Methodist (18%), Catholic (14%), and all other Protestants combined (15%). The change in denomination over three generations on both the paternal and maternal side was examined. The pattern

Table 5.1   Demographic Characteristics of African American Mothers in Sample (*N* = 318)

| | *Marital Status* | | *Socioeconomic Status* | | |
	Ever (%)	Never (%)	Middle Class (%)	Working Class (%)	Total (%)
Variable					
Total	56	44	31	69	100
Marital status					
Separated	26	46	0	24	27
Divorced	29	51	0	40	24
Widowed	2	3	0	3	1
Never married	44	0	100	34	48
Total	101	100	100	101	100
Education					
Junior high	3	4	2	3	3
High/trade school	37	31	44	0	53
1-2 years college	29	26	32	5	39
3-4 years college	19	21	17	53	4
Graduate/professional	12	17	6	39	0
Total	100	99	101	100	99
Occupation					
Executive/major professional	25	29	19	77	1
Administrative personnel	12	10	14	10	12
Clerical/business owner	47	47	48	13	63
Skilled/semiskilled	14	12	16	0	20
Unskilled	3	2	4	0	4
Total	101	100	101	100	100
Income ($)					
3,000-8,999	17	17	36	4	35
9,000-11,999	12	22	27	18	27
12,000-14,999	18	18	20	20	19
15,000-23,999	33	33	15	47	16
24,000-40,000	7	10	3	13	4
Total	100	100	100	101	101
Religion					
Baptist	45	49	53	41	52
Methodist	18	20	15	29	13
Catholic	14	13	16	15	14
Other Protestant (combined)	11	13	9	4	14
Fundamentalist	4	6	2	8	2
No religion	4	3	5	2	5
Total	100	100	100	99	100

NOTE: Rounding errors resulted in subtotals of 99 and 101.

Table 5.2 Frequency Distribution of Structure of Family of Orientation and Family of Procreation by Socioeconomic Status and Marital Status

Family Structure	Total f	Total %	Socioeconomic Status Middle %	Socioeconomic Status Working %	χ^2	df	p	Marital Status Ever %	Marital Status Never %	χ^2	df	p
Family of origin					2.71	2	ns			5.54	2	ns
Nuclear	169	53	51	55				48	60			
Extended	130	41	47	39				47	34			
Augmented	17	5	3	7				5	6			
Total	316	99	101	101				100	100			
N	316		99	217				177	139			
Simple nuclear	126	40	43	38	20.55	7	.005	38	42	11.46	7	ns
Attenuated nuclear	41	13	6	16				9	19			
Simple extended	83	26	37	21				32	19			
Attenuated extended	46	15	8	18				15	14			
Augmented nuclear	6	2	3	1				2	1			
Augmented extended	6	2	1	2				2	2			
Augmented attenuated nuclear	5	2		2				1	1			
Augmented attenuated extended	3	1	1	1				1	1			
Total	316	101	100	99				100	99			
N	316		99	217				177	139			
Present family of procreation					2.65	4	ns			14.54	5	.01
Attenuated nuclear	211	66	64	68				72	59			
Simple extended	23	7	10	6				5	11			
Attenuated nuclear	55	17	16	18				15	21			
Augmented attenuated nuclear	23	7	8	6				8	5			
Augmented attenuated extended	6	2	2	2				1	4			
Total	318	99	100	100				101	100			
N	318		98	216				179	139			

NOTE: Structural definitions: augmented = parents, child, nonrelative; augmented attenuated extended = 1 parent, child, relative, nonrelative; nuclear = parents, child; attenuated nuclear = 1 parent, child; augmented attenuated nuclear = 1 parent, child, nonrelative; extended = parents, child, relative; attenuated extended = 1 parent, child, relative.

of distribution among denominations had remained constant, but membership had steadily decreased. For example, among Baptists, 70% of grandparents, 62% of parents, and 49% of the present generation were members of this denomination (see Table 5.1).

Regular church attendance, weekly or at least three times a month, was reported by 25% of the sample; 12% attended once a month. The largest number of women (35%) went only a few times a year, and 15% reported that they never attended church; 52% reported little contact with an organized denomination. Yet frequent prayers were reported by 72% of the women, 25% prayed sometimes, and only 3% said they never prayed.

Social class was associated with different religious memberships, $\chi^2 (5) = 25.50$, $p < .0001$. Most of the Baptists (74%) and Catholics (67%) were working class. Methodists (51%) and other Protestants (Episcopalian, Presbyterian, Lutheran, 62%) tended to be middle class. Chi-square analyses were used to compare occupations. The majority were clerical for all religious groups except other Protestants, who were predominately middle class (62%). Methodists were evenly divided between middle class (51%) and working class (49%) (see Table 5.3).

Marital status at the first pregnancy was associated with religious denomination, $\chi^2 (5) = 13.93$, $p < .02$. The majority of mothers in each religious group were not married, except for the combined Protestants group (other than Baptist), Methodists, and Catholics.

RESULTS

Stress

Hypothesis 1 was not supported, for even though all of the women had very high stress intensity scores, stress levels did differ based on marital status.

The mothers had a mean stress score of 367.33, considered to be a very high level (see Table 5.4). Holmes would consider this entire group to be under major stress (300 +) and vulnerable to physical or mental illness, which have been found significantly related to the level of stressful changes in life. Stress intensity levels were high for all subgroups and were not related to age, SES, or age and marital status at

first pregnancy. For the 2-year period, previously married mothers ($M = 186.27$) had higher stress intensity scores than those never married ($M = 154.00$), $F(313) = 3.88$, $p < .05$. The stress score that was assigned to divorce (73) is a factor. Those who did not experience a marriage that had gone bad and a subsequent divorce would, indeed, have lower stress.

The second measure of stress was the frequency of stressful life events that had occurred, regardless of intensity. The average was 16.31 events over 2 years, 9.13 within the 6 months prior to the interview. The mothers had, in addition, experienced an average of 2.05 female stress events during the 2-year period. The average for the combined measures over the 2 years was 18.26 events (see Table 5.4).

All the stress measures for the three periods intercorrelated significantly ($p < .001$) with all the other stress scores. Mothers who experienced stress in one area were high in all other stress.

The demographic variables were regressed against stress intensity, and all were significant. Mothers who were under less stress had residential stability, sufficient income and occupation, were never married, were older, had few people and children in the home, and were moderately educated (see Table 5.5). A positive direct relationship was found for the number of years the mother had lived in the same house, $r(308) = .174$, $p < .01$, and for sufficient income, $r(308) = .144$, $p < .01$.

Women who were older and more experienced with the demands of their lives, who had time to work out their living arrangements, who had children who were older and less physically demanding, who were educated enough to have stable jobs, and who were responsible for fewer people in their homes perceived their lives as less stressful.

Mothers who had been married and given birth during their teen years had experienced more female stress life events, $F(3, 294) = 3.74$, $p < .05$, than those who had never married or who were older than 19 years when first giving birth. College-educated women had experienced more stress intensity, $F(1, 311) = 5.52$, $p < .004$, than those with less education.

When incomes were considered, those who made less were under greater strain. Women who earned less than $9,000, $F(1, 310) = 5.47$, $p < .02$, and those who earned less than $12,000 were higher in all

Table 5.3 Cross-Tabulations of Type of Religion and Occupation, Socioeconomic Status, and Marital Status at 1st Pregnancy

	Total	Baptist	Methodist	Catholic	Fundamentalist Protestant[a]	Other Protestant[b]	No Religion	χ^2	df	p
Occupation								45.39	10	.000
Executive	25	19	46	24	11	54	8			
Clerical	60	63	49	67	51	39	92			
Unskilled	15	18	5	9	37	8	0			
Total	100	100	100	100	100	100	100			
N	318	155	57	45	35	13	13			
Socioeconomic status								25.50	5	.0001
Middle class	31	27	51	33	11	62	15			
Working class	69	74	49	67	89	39	85			
Total	100	101	100	100	100	101	100			
N	318	155	57	45	35	13	13			
Marital status at 1st pregnancy								13.93	5	.02
Married	27	22	35	20	23	62	39			
Not married	73	78	65	80	77	39	62			
Total	100	100	100	100	100	101	101			
N	316	153	57	45	35	13	13			

NOTE: Rounding errors resulted in subtotals of 99 and 101.
a. Fundamental Protestants = Pentecostal, Jehovah's Witness, Moorish, Seventh-Day Adventist.
b. Other Protestants = Episcopal, Presbyterian, Lutheran.

Table 5.4 Means and Standard Deviations of Stressful Life Events (SLE): Intensity and Frequencies of Experiences (*N* = 317)

Stress Variables	M	SD
Stress intensity		
Past 6 months	194.81	125.73
Past 6 months–2 years	172.22	149.63
Entire 2 years (original SLE scoring)	367.33	205.92
Stress frequency		
Past 6 months	9.31	5.39
Past 6 months–2 years	7.03	5.88
Entire 2 years	16.31	8.54
Female-related stress frequency		
Past 6 months	1.01	1.14
Past 6 months–2 years	1.05	1.18
Entire 2 years	2.05	1.77
Total stress frequency		
Past 6 months	10.32	6.03
Past 6 months–2 years	8.08	6.48
Entire 2 years	18.26	9.61

NOTE: SLE was score of stress intensity over the entire three year period. A temporal dimension was added: stress over the past six months; stress experienced between 7 months and 2 years.

Table 5.5 Regression Analyses of Stress Intensity

	Cumulative			
	r	R^2	*β*	*F*
Number of years in same house	.174*	.03	−.11	8.80*
Family income	.144*	.05	−.16	6.87*
Marital status	.109	.06	.22	6.40**
Age	−.079	.07	−.13	5.78**
Number of people in house	−.125	.09	−.11	5.59**
Education	.086	.09	.08	5.05**
Number of children	−.039	.09	−.04	4.36**
Occupation	−.035	.10	−.01	3.81**

NOTE: *df* = 8,274.
*$p < .01$. **$p < .09$.

three stress scores. Women who needed income from a number of sources were higher in stress intensity, frequency, and female stress over each of the three periods (significant at the .01 level or higher). Mothers who were highly stressed had fewer people contributing to the family income and living in the house with them. Mothers experienced fewer stress events in either the 6-month or 2-year period when more people lived in and helped out financially ($r = −.094$, $p < .05$).

Younger mothers were higher on the stress intensity scores; age was negatively correlated with stress in the past 6 months ($r = −.127$, $p < .01$) and over the 2-year period ($r = −.150$, $p < .03$). Younger mothers had experienced more frequent stress events in the past 6 months ($r = -.174$, $p < .001$) and over the whole 2 years ($r = -.132$, $p < .000$). The younger mothers had even more female stress ($r = -.235$, $p < .000$). Older mothers experienced less stress in all areas.

In addition to the regression, analyses of variance were used to determine the relation between age at first pregnancy and stress. Age at first pregnancy (below or above 19 years) did not relate to stress levels. As noted earlier, however, mothers who had been married and had given birth during their teens had experienced more female stress life events, $F(3, 294) = 3.74$, $p < .05$, than those who had married but gave birth later, those who never married but gave birth as teens, or those who never married but gave birth later.

The age of the woman's parents at her birth was related to female stress. Women had higher female stress scale scores when their own fathers ($r = .158$) and mothers ($r = .136$) were younger. Women who reported more frequent female stress also had younger mothers ($r = .146$, $p < .007$). The younger the mother at her first pregnancy, the more children she tended to have. These women had more girls than boys. The ages of the children appeared to make a difference in female-related stress but not in stress intensity in general. Mothers with higher scores on the female stress events scale, in the past six months ($r = .101$, $p < .04$) and in the entire two years, had more young children between the ages of 2-5 years old. The older the children, the lower the stress, which was borne out by the fact that mothers with older children had less stress of all kinds. Mothers of older children, 15 to 18 years old, tended to have lower frequency scores in the 6-month period ($r = -.132$, $p < .009$) and in the 2-year period ($r = -.113$, $p < .02$). Mothers had experienced fewer female-related stress events in the period of 6 months to 2 years when their children tended to be 10-14 years old.

The more children living at home the less stress intensity was reported in the past 6 months to 2 years ($r = -.112$, $p < .02$). Women with more children living at home had also experienced fewer female-related stress events in the immediate previous 6 months ($r = -.122$, $p < .02$); 6 months to 2 years ($r = -.105$, $p < .04$); and over the whole period ($r = -.107$, $p < .03$). Mothers with more children in the 15-to-18 age group had lower stress intensity scores for the previous 6 months ($r = -.121$, $p < .03$) and over the 2-year period ($r = -.105$, $p < .03$). These same mothers had lower female stress scores for the 6-month ($r = -.143$, $p < .007$) and 2-year ($r = -.130$, $p < .01$) periods as well as fewer female stress occurrences in the 6-month to 2-year period ($r = -.102$, $p < .04$) and for the whole 2 years ($r = -.121$, $p < .02$).

The Role of Religion

Most of the women reported that they were fairly religious (75%), some said very religious (19%), and some not religious at all (6%). The importance of religion was shown in that it provided emotional support for 86% of the women. Moral support was mentioned by 11%. Two percent said that religion answered prayers, and the same percentage said that it did nothing. When the women were asked what religion did for their family, the most frequent responses were that it provides emotional support (39%) and moral support (36%). Religion was considered to help by fostering family unity (6%), by just being there (5%), and by answering prayers (3%). Eleven percent of the sample felt that religion did nothing for their family.

Most of the mothers felt that the church had helped Blacks function in this society (76%). The positive comments were that churches gave strong support to families (42%) and provided a system of beliefs (21%). Mention was also made of persons who had stopped drugs and alcohol, and emphasis was placed on the churches' role in fostering civil rights. The negative comments referred to hypocritical practices, insensitivity, and the promotion of beliefs that cloud reality and pacify Blacks into accepting less (see Table 5.6).

Stress intensity differed significantly by the three major denominations that represented 83% of the sample, $F(2, 253) = 3.61$, $p < .03$. Baptists, the largest group, had the highest stress scores ($M = 390.29$), much higher than the overall mean for the sample ($M = 367.33$). Catholics ($M = 338.96$) and Methodists ($M = 310.22$) had much lower scores.

Table 5.6   Description of the Role of Religion

Variable	%
How religious	
Very	19
Fairly	75
Not at all	6
Total	100
N	316
How often pray	
Often	72
Sometimes	25
Never	3
Total	100
N	315
Attends services	
Once a week	18
3 times a month	17
Once a month	12
Few times a year	37
Never	15
Total	99
N	314
What religion does for subject	
Emotional support	86
Moral support	11
Answers prayers	2
Nothing	2
Total	101
N	303
What religion does for subject's family	
Emotional support	39
Moral support	36
Nothing	11
Helps family unity	6
Just helps	5
Answers prayers	3
Total	100
N	305
How church affects Blacks	
Positive	
Strong support	42
Something to believe in	21
Only alternative	6
People stopped using drugs/alcohol	4
Supported civil rights	4
Negative	
Hypocritical practices	7
Insensitive to needs of people	4
Pacifies, clouds reality	4
No difference	8
Total	100
N	275

The working-class predominance among the Baptists and the middle-class status of many of the Methodists could account for the difference.

Religiosity was also related to stress intensity, $F(2, 312) = 3.10$, $p < .05$. Those who were fairly religious had higher stress scores ($M = 18.71$) than those who were very religious ($M = 18.14$). The lowest stress was found among women who were not at all religious ($M = 12.87$).

DISCUSSION

This sample of middle-class and working-class Black single mothers was highly stressed. Within the past 6 months they had experienced enough stressful events ($M = 194.81$) to be considered under moderate stress on the Holmes and Rahe (1967) scale, even if it was spread over 2 years. They were experiencing stress that can be considered destructive. It was so intense and occurring so frequently that one wonders how they managed to function from day to day.

Intensity scores were higher for more recent (last 6 months) than more distant (7 months to 2 years) stress. This would indicate that their stress was accelerating or that they had forgotten more distant stress after a certain amount of time. Regardless of the measurement issues, this sample had experienced life changes sufficiently serious to become debilitating without intervention or some form of external support (Holmes & Masuda, 1974).

Stress intensity and frequency were important measures of changes within their lives that required adjustment. Only 2.05 of the 16 female stress items had occurred, on the average, but female stress appeared to be an important issue, as it differentiated the women in many respects.

One interesting pattern was that a woman with younger parents, regardless of her present age or her age when she became pregnant, experienced more female stress but not stress intensity. These women born to young parents were experiencing the most difficulty with their own stress related to childbearing, their lovers, and other female stress. They may not have had the benefit of parents who had learned a few of life's lessons before they had children, and therefore these women were relatively unprepared.

This could be related to our finding that previously married women who had given birth in their teen years had higher female stress. Young marriage, especially when hastened by an impending pregnancy, may not be wise. The young girl may lose some family support and the wisdom that comes from having parents around a little longer.

Younger mothers had more stress than older women. Women who had younger children (aged 2 to 5 years) at home had more female stress but not more stress intensity. Younger women may still be finding themselves while facing the multiple pressures of parenting alone. They may be experiencing the changes that come with their age, they may face exploitation in the work place, and they may be more dependent. Older women with older children may have learned how to fend for themselves, may not be as attractive, and may be more experienced at not putting themselves in situations where they can be exploited. They have learned their lessons and may be retreating to their family and children. Children make fewer demands on a mother when they become older; the demands may be emotionally taxing, but at least the physical care is easier.

College-educated women experienced more stress. Although this appears contrary to the data on income, one must also look at the household arrangements under which they lived. There are fewer marriage partners with comparable education available to them (McAdoo, 1988), a situation complicated by the presence of children. In comparison to the older women, more of them had taken elderly people into their homes. Those middle-class women who had never married had a home significantly longer, allowing them to amass the resources that enabled them to be more supportive of more relatives. These women, who had been pregnant and not married, had earlier been dependent on their family members and now were obligated to assist them in their old age, a reversal of roles.

Never-married women tended to be working class, have fewer children, and live in three-generational families. Low income did contribute to higher stress, as was found by Edelman (1987). But stress was lower when the mother could depend on many people for support.

Women who were Baptist or Catholic were working class; Methodists and other Protestants tended to be middle class. Baptists had the highest stress intensity levels, much higher than the overall average score of the women. Whereas most women were single at the birth of their first child, those in the combined Protestants group tended to be married, probably because of the higher social class of the participants in those denominations.

Our subjects were basically unchurched, as attested by their lack of attendance regardless of denomination. This indicates a need that the churches, especially in the Black community, should address. More attention needs to be paid to this population because of the high levels of single parenting within these communities. The women reported praying frequently, so religion still plays an important role in their life (Frazier, 1963). They may be overwhelmed by responsibilities and unable to attend church.

These single mothers, of both middle and working class, felt that they were fairly religious and that their religion provided emotional support. Yet, the fairly religious women had higher stress scores. In fact, the lowest mean score belonged to the women who were not religious at all. But for those with stress, though they may not go to a church service, praying and having faith appears to be a readily available coping strategy.

This is consistent with the role that religion has played through the years (Pipes, 1992). Women under great stress have used religion as a resource, not unlike the way they have used the other members of their family. Consistent with the findings of Brown and Gary (1985), religion appears to be a recourse for the women studied here. They pray often to release anxiety. They may not be able to solve their problems, but they have the strength to go on and face up to their life.

Implications

The overall impression is that these women are facing tremendous stress. Its alleviation should be a priority, for more families in all communities are adopting the family structure of single mothers. The financial stress could be lessened by court-ordered and -enforced child support payments. Only half of African American women are granted such an order, and only half of those ever receive any money (Pearce & McAdoo, 1981). More recent data are similar, and this situation accounts for the increased poverty of millions of women and children.

There are implications from these findings for counselors and therapists, the churches, social service deliverers, and family life educators. For these who provide counseling and advisory services, it is important to be aware of the family support and helping systems. Providers should attempt to become familiar with the literature about these families (Boyd-Franklin, 1989). Services should not try to replace but should augment the existing cultural patterns. Reciprocal help is a tradition in many African American families, and the *familism* among Hispanics is very similar. One cannot generalize, however, for there are real differences in the overall patterns. Whereas most families are available to help, not all African Americans are involved in their family network, not all live in close proximity, and not all have lifestyles consistent with their other relatives.

Services should meet the diversity of family support patterns. One cannot make assumptions about a woman's social network. Women differ in their approaches to receiving help; some are in intensive family help patterns, some are in cooperative arrangements with women in similar situations, and a few women are going it all alone. It will be necessary to gather background data, more than is needed for most service providers.

One cannot make assumptions about why a single mother is in her situation. Myths should not cloud our thinking. It is often difficult for service providers to remain free of the stereotypes that prevail about Black women, welfare, and teen pregnancy. Most Black mothers were formerly married, and only 30% were mothers while unmarried in their teens (Edelman, 1991). The rate of divorce is twice that of Whites and has risen to an alarming extent. The important point is that Black single mothers are not a monolithic group (Campbell & Moen, 1993; McAdoo, 1991b).

Counselors should look at the importance of female stress, for this is more problematic than the type measured by the typical male-oriented scales. The female component should always be used when assessing stressful significant life changes. Support groups could be started to address relevant concerns. Effective use of time is an important topic, for time is what the mothers do not have. Indeed, support groups must be made highly relevant, or the women will not make time for them. Groups should meet in the neighborhoods or the homes of the women. Those running the programs should provide child care and perhaps transportation. I found in an intervention project for single mothers that once these women are interested in what is going on in a support group, they will not let anything stop them from getting there.

The religious institutions, whether Protestant, Catholic, or Muslim, need to work more with single mothers through targeted programs and outreach in which other women, preferably single mothers, visit the homes to disseminate pertinent information and supportive services. Churches should look at the attendance of single mothers, for they are religious but do not go to services. Religious groups sometimes are reluctant to 'work with a divorced woman or a young girl who becomes pregnant when unmarried, but there is work to be done in the churches, for the level of single mothers is increasing. Churches can be sources of support beyond the religious aspect, such as augmenting existing family patterns or forming supportive networks where none exist.

As mothers are provided help, there must be emphasis on related policy issues: child support enforcement; adequate quality child care available 24 hours; housing discrimination that prevents women with children and African Americans from moving to convenient locations with good schools; and the maintenance of income above the poverty level. There will be more single African American mothers in the future, and it is imperative that efforts are made to help them be self-sufficient and able to cope with their many roles.

REFERENCES

Alan Guttmacher Institute. (1981). *Fact book on teenage pregnancy.* New York: Author.

Anne E. Casey Foundation. (1992). *Kids count data book.* Washington, DC: Center for the Study of Social Policy.

Aschenbrenner, J. (1973). Extended families among Black Americans. *Journal of Comparative Family Studies, 4,* 257-268.

Baldwin, C. (1973, March). Comparison of mother-child interaction at different ages and in families of different education levels and ethnic backgrounds. Paper presented at the annual meeting of the Society for Research in Child Development, Philadelphia.

Belle, D. (1982). Social ties and social support. In D. Belle (Ed.), *Lives in stress: Women and depression* (pp.133-144). Newbury Park, CA: Sage.

Billingsley, A. (1968). *Black families in White America.* Englewood Cliffs, NJ: Prentice-Hall.

Billingsley, A. (1992). *Climbing Jacob's ladder: The enduring legacy of African-American families.* New York: Simon & Schuster.

Boyd-Franklin, N. (1989). *Black families in therapy: A multisystems approach.* New York: Guilford.

Brown, D., & Gary, L. (1985). Social support network differentials among married and nonmarried Black females. *Psychology of Women Quarterly, 9,* 229-241.

Burton, L. (1992). Black grandparents rearing children of drug-addicted parents: Stressors, outcomes, and social service needs. *The Gerontologist, 32,* 744-751.

Campbell, M., & Moen, P. (1993). Job-family role strain among employed mothers of preschoolers. *Family Relations, 41,* 205-211.

Cherlin, A., & Fustenberg, F. (1986). *The new American grandparents.* New York: Basic Books.

Danziger, S., & Danziger, S. (1993). Child poverty and public policy: Toward a comprehensive antipoverty agenda. America's childhood. *Daedalus: Journal of the American Academy of Arts and Sciences, 122*(l), 57-84.

Darity, W., & Myers, S. (1991, March). Sex ratios, marriageability, and the marginalization of Black males. Paper presented at the biennial meeting of the Society for Research in Child Development, Seattle, WA.

D'Ercole, A. (1988). Single mothers: Stress, coping, and social support. *Journal of Community Psychology, 16,* 41-54.

Edelman, M. (1987). *Families in peril: An agenda for social change.* Cambridge, MA: Harvard University Press.

Edelman, M. (1991). *The measure of our success: Letter to my children and yours.* Boston: Beacon Hill.

Farley, R., & Allen, W. (1987). *The color line and the quality of life in America.* New York: Russell Sage.

Fine, M., McKinry, P., Donnelly, B., & Voydanoff, P. (1992). Perceived adjustment of parents and children: Variations by family structure, race, and gender. *Journal of Marriage and the Family, 54,* 118-127.

Frazier, F. (1963). *The Negro church in America.* New York: Schocken.

Garfinkel, I., & McLanahan, S. (1986). *Single mothers and their children.* Washington, DC: Urban Institute.

Glick, P. (1988). A demographic picture of Black families. In H. McAdoo (Ed.), *Black families* (2nd ed., pp. 116-137). Newbury Park, CA: Sage.

Hayes, C. (Ed.). (1987). *Risking the future: Adolescent sexuality, pregnancy, and childbearing.* Washington, DC: National Academy Press.

Hill, R. (1971). *The strengths of Black families.* New York: Prentice Hall.

Hollingshead, A., & Redlich, F. (1958). *Social class and mental illness: A community study. The index of social position.* New York: Wiley.

Holmes, T., & Masuda, M. (1974). Life changes and illness susceptibility. In B. Dohrenwend & B. Dohrenwend (Eds.), *Stress life events, their nature and effects* (pp. 45-72). New York: John Wiley.

Holmes, T., & Rahe, R. (1967). The social readjustment rating scale. *Journal of Psychosomatic Research, 11,* 213-218.

Horowitz, F. D. (1992). John B. Watson's legacy: Learning and environment. *Developmental Psychology, 28,* 360-367.

Jackson, J. (1991). *Life in Black America.* Newbury Park, CA: Sage.

Kamerman, S., & Kahn, A. (1988). *Mothers alone, strategies for a time of change.* Dover, MA: Auburn House.

Kaplan, E. (1988). Where does the Black teenage mother turn? *Feminist Issues, 8*(l), 51-83.

Kivett, V. (1993). Racial comparisons of the grandmother role: Implications for strengthening the family support system of older Black women. *Family Relations, 42,* 165-172.

Marks, N., & McLanahan, S. (1993). Gender, family structure, and social support among parents. *Journal of Marriage and the Family, 55,* 481-493.

Martin, E., & Martin, J. (1978). *The Black extended family.* Chicago: University of Chicago Press.

McAdoo, H. (1988). *Changes in the formation and structure of Black families: The impact of Black women* (Working Paper No. 182). Wellesley, MA: Wellesley College Center for Research on Women.

McAdoo, H. (1991a). The ethics of research and intervention with ethnic minority parents and their children. In C. B. Fisher & W. W. Tryon (Eds.), *Ethics in applied developmental psychology* (pp. 273-283). Norwood, NJ: Ablex.

McAdoo, H. (1991b). Portrait of African American families in the United States. In S. Rix (Ed.), *The American women: A status report* (pp. 71-93). New York: Norton.

McAdoo, H. (1993). The social cultural contexts of ecological developmental family models. In P. Boss, W. Doherty, R. LaRossa, W. Schumm, & S. Steinmetz

(Eds.), *Sourcebook of family theories and methods: A contextual approach* (pp. 298-301). New York: Plenum.

McAdoo, H. (1994). Family equality and ethnic diversity. In K. Altergott (Ed.), *One world, many families* (pp. 52-55). Minneapolis, MN: National Council on Family Relations.

McLanahan, S., & Booth, K. (1989). Mother-only families: Problems, prospects, and politics. *Journal of Marriage and the Family, 55,* 557-580.

Mechaneck, R. (1987). Single mothers by choice: A family alternative. *Women and Therapy, 6*(1/2), 263-281.

Neighbors, H., & Jackson, J. (1984). The use of informal and formal help: Four patterns of illness behavior in the Black community. *American Journal of Community Psychology, 12,* 629-644.

Pearce, D., & McAdoo, H. (1981, September). Women and children: Alone and in poverty. Washington, DC: National Advisory Council on Economic Opportunity, September.

Pipes, W. (1992). *Say amen, brother!* Detroit: Wayne State University Press.

Quinn, W., & Allen. (1989). Family treatment of adolescent drug abuse: Transitions and maintenance of drug-free behavior. *American Journal of Family Therapy, 17*(3), 229-243.

Reiss, D. (1989). Families and their paradigms: An ecological approach to understanding the family in its social world. In C. Ramsey (Ed.), *Family systems in medicine* (pp. 298-301). New York: Guilford.

Scanzoni, J. (1977). *The Black family in modern society: Patterns of stability and security.* Chicago: University of Chicago Press.

Scanzoni, J., & Marsiglio, W. (1993). New action theory and contemporary families. *Journal of Family Issues, 14,* 1005-1032.

Stack, C. (1974). *All my kin: Strategies for survival in a Black community.* New York: Harper & Row.

Taylor, J. (1991). Extended family networks of older Black adults. *Journal of Gerontology, 46,* S210-S217.

Taylor, R., Chatters, L., Tucker, B., & Lewis, E. (1990). Developments in research on Black families: A decade review. *Journal of Marriage and the Family, 52,* 993-1014.

Taylor, J., Henderson, D., & Jackson, B. (1991). A holistic model for understanding and predicting depressive symptoms in African American women. *Journal of Community Psychology, 19,* 306-320.

Taylor, J., & Jackson, B. (1990). Factors affecting alcohol consumption in Black women. *International Journal of Addictions, 25,* 1407-1419.

Taylor, R., Thornton, M., & Chatters, L. (1987). Black Americans' perceptions of the sociohistorical role of the church. *Journal of Black Studies, 18,* 123-138.

Tucker, B., & Mitchell-Kernan, C. (1992). Sex ratio imbalance among Afro-Americans: Conceptual and methodological issues. In R. Jones (Ed.), *Advances in Black Psychology, 1.* Berkeley, CA: Cobb & Henry.

Wilson, W., & Neckerman, K. (1986). Poverty and family structure: The widening gap between evidence and public policy issues. In S. Danziger & D. Weinburg (Eds.), *Fighting poverty: What works and what doesn't* (pp. 237-262). Cambridge, MA: Harvard University Press.

Yankelovich, D. (1981). A world turned upside down. *Psychology Today, 15*(4), 35-91.

6

Spiritual Thoughts, Coping and 'Sense of Coherence' in Brain Tumour Patients and Their Spouses

Susan Strang
Peter Strang

When a person is diagnosed with a life-threatening disease, existential questions are easily triggered. The aims of this study were to explore to what extent brain tumour patients and their next of kin were able to cope, understand and create meaning in their situation, to explore whether spirituality could be supportive and to analyse whether these concepts are related to Antonovsky's concept of sense of coherence. Using a purposive sampling technique, 20 patients and 16 of their next of kin took part in tape-recorded interviews. A content and context analysis was performed using a hermeneutic approach.

We found that comprehensibility was to a large extent constructed by the patient's own thoughts and theories, despite an insecure situation. Manageability was achieved by active information-seeking strategies, by social support and by coping, including positive reinterpretation of the situation. Meaningfulness was central for quality of life and was created by close relations and faith, as well as by work. A crucial factor was whether the person had a 'fighting spirit' that motivated him or her to go on. As only three patients were believers, trust in God had generally been replaced by a belief and confidence in oneself, in science, in positive thinking and by closeness to nature.

Sense of coherence as a concept can explain how exposed persons handle their situation. In its construction, sense of coherence integrates essential parts of the stress/coping model (comprehensibility, manageability) and of spirituality (meaning).

From *Palliative Medicine* 15 (2001): 127-34. Reprinted with permission of Arnold Publishers. This paper is based on the winning entry in the Postbasic Section of the Doyle Prize, 2000.

INTRODUCTION

A malignant brain tumour means a double threat, not only to life itself but also to the individual's personality, as many patients are stricken with functional and cognitive deficits as the tumour progresses. Therefore, not only the physical, psychological and social, but also spiritual dimensions should be integral parts of palliative care[1,2] and all care systems that claim to be holistic.[3,4] However, most of the studies on patients' reactions deal with physical or psychosocial aspects, and patients' spiritual needs have not been adequately addressed.[5,6] Every person wrestles at times with existential and spiritual issues, but these questions are accentuated when a person is diagnosed with a serious disease.[7,8]

Among people stricken with an illness, certain individuals manage relatively well and have a good quality of life, while others give up under the pressure, despite the fact that the external circumstances are the same. Besides the coping and defence mechanisms used by patients and their spouses, meaning is central for one's quality of life. Antonovsky[9] developed the useful, salutory model of health, sense of coherence, where the crucial component is meaningfulness. Individuals who experience a high level of coherence despite a difficult situation can still experience a good quality of life. Sense of coherence includes three main categories:

1) comprehensibility—implying that the stimuli are predictable and explicable;

2) manageability—meaning that resources are available to meet the demands;

3) meaningfulness—meaning that the demands are challenges worthy of emotional investment.

Since, for example, good relationships can provide a sense of meaning, a severely ill person may still experience a good quality of life, knowing that he or she is important to his or her family, that there is a meaning in his or her life. The component of meaningfulness creates motivation and is therefore central. Frankl[10] supports this by stating 'there is nothing in the world that would so effectively help one to survive even the worst conditions as the knowledge that there is a meaning in one's life'. The sense of coherence is the extent to which a person is able to cope with a severe crisis and create meaning in his or her life. Other studies in various contexts have shown that people with a high sense of coherence experience a better quality of life, regardless of the level of symptoms or functional health.[11]

Sense of coherence has many similarities with the concept of coping, as effective coping increases manageability and information-seeking coping strategies increase comprehensibility. During the Second World War, Anna Freud[12] studied how children coped with the stress of the bombing of London. She introduced the term 'cope', but not until the 1960s did coping become an established psychological term. Lazarus[13] emphasizes coping as a process and defines coping as ongoing cognitive and behavioural efforts to manage specific demands that are appraised as taxing the resources of a person. Coping is today also more clearly related to meaningfulness by the introduction of meaning-based coping processes.[14] In these strategies even spiritual beliefs and practices are now included.

Meaning is a central component not only in sense of coherence, but also in the spiritual/existential dimension; spirituality can in that sense be related to sense of coherence. Spirituality is also related to the other two components of sense of coherence, namely comprehensibility and manageability, as religion and faith provide explanations of existential questions and result in increased manageability, as the individual accepts the situation.[15,16]

There is no homogenous description of the concept of 'spiritual dimension'.[17,18] As concluded by Peter Speck[19] the words 'spiritual' and 'religion' are often used interchangeably. He stresses that spirituality does not necessarily need to be synonymous with religiosity and that a wider understanding of the word spiritual, as relating to the search for existential meaning within any given life experience, allows us to consider spiritual needs and issues in the absence of any clear practice of a religion or faith.

Religion pertains to the outward practice of spiritual understanding and/or the framework for a system of beliefs, values, codes of conduct and rituals.[19] Religion can be helpful in coping with illness, and is a source of well-being and hope for many individuals.[16] The familiar religious rituals may comfort and provide meaning to everyday life and help the patients through chaotic, threatening situations.

Thus, the concept of meaning is emphasized in spirituality as well as in sense of coherence, although partly from different points of view. This is true even for existentialism, a philosophical movement that deals with the questions of the basic conditions of being a human. An individual struggling with questions of life has to find his or her own answers to the challenging life questions and thus find meaning by himself or herself.[20]

The Aims of the Study

The aims of this study were:

- to explore to what extent brain tumour patients and their next of kin were able to cope, understand and create a meaning or sense of coherence in their stressful situation;
- to explore the extent to which spirituality could give support or be a hindrance;
- to analyse how the above mentioned aspects are related to Antonovsky's concept of sense of coherence.

METHODS

Patients

Twenty patients with malignant brain tumours of grade II-IV were included. When possible, their next of kin were also enrolled in the study ($n = 16$). Exclusion criteria were functional and cognitive deficits that would impair participation in interviews. Purposive, information-rich, maximum-variation sampling was aimed for, with respect to age, sex, ethnicity or ethnic origin and education. The number of interviews was not decided in advance; the study continued until a satisfactory conclusion was reached (saturation).[21] The interviews were analysed successively and data were compared with previous interviews. Recruitment was stopped when no new descriptions were found.

Study

A pilot study was performed with four patients, who were not included in the main study. The purpose was to practise and evaluate data collection and observe the patients' reactions.

All consecutive participants were sent a letter outlining the study. The researcher asked them 1 week later by telephone whether they were willing to participate in the study. The interviews, which were explorative and semistructured, were tape-recorded and then transcribed slightly modified from verbatim. Initial field notes were made immediately after each interview.[22] The interviews focused on four comprehensive issues:

1) comprehensibility;

2) manageability/coping strategies;

3) meaningfulness, for example what creates meaning in life;

4) whether spirituality contributes to a sense of coherence.

Analysis

In accordance with the interpretative process described by Richoeur,[23,24] three main steps were followed. In the first step all interviews were read through in order to get an overall picture. The second step consisted of a structural analysis (interpretative reading) based on the hermeneutic circle (see below). The third step involved a final interpretation of the whole.

The interpretation of data was performed using a hermeneutic approach[22-25] and interpreted in light of Antonovsky's concept of sense of coherence.[9] The scientific assumptions were mainly derived from existential hermeneutics, as developed by Heidegger[26] and Gadamer.[27] A central idea of hermeneutics is to pay attention to context and original purpose in order to enrich the previous understanding. The basis for the analysis has the following seven components.

1) The hermeneutic circle is used (a continuous movement between the whole and the parts, a dialogue with the text, in which the meaning of separate parts is determined by the global meaning of the text).

2) The interpretation of the meaning is finished when a coherent concept without contradictions is attained.

3) Partial interpretations are compared with other sources of knowledge about the patient.

4) The autonomy of the text is emphasized (which means that the researcher should interpret how the text itself describes a theme).

5) The comprehension of the themes of the text is essential for the interpretation.

6) The researcher must be aware of his or her assumptions and presuppositions; there is no unprejudiced interpretation of the text and the researcher cannot neglect his or her own comprehension.

7) Creativity is to be used, so that the interpretation enriches the previous understanding of the themes.[25]

Reliability

A dialogical validation[28] was made with the patients, as similar questions were addressed several times during the interview, to ensure that the patients' genuine perception was caught. A dialogical intersubjectivity was aimed at:[28] the interviews were analysed separately by the study's two authors and then compared for similarities and differences. The material and the interpretations were discussed until agreement was reached (communicative validity).

Ethics

As the questions about the meaning of life and death are deeply personal, the ethical issues were discussed thoroughly before the actual study. Approval to conduct the study was obtained from the regional research ethics committee.

RESULTS

Comprehensibility—The Cognitive Component

Most of the patients gave biological explanations for the origin of their disease. These included heredity, hormonal disturbances, head injury, tinnitus, immune defence impairment, chemicals, smoking and environmental influence. There were different opinions about the impact of psychosocial factors, however. Some respondents stressed that when a person is out of balance, or under mental stress, diseases such as brain tumours can develop. Others, however, stated that psychological health had no influence on the matter and considered the idea ridiculous.

Besides physical/biological explanations such as radiation, heredity, injury and obstetric injuries, the spouses were more convinced about the impact of the psyche on development of brain tumours. Despite these explanatory models, both patients and their spouses expressed insecurity as to the origin of brain tumours, because, as they put it, 'not even the doctors knew for sure'.

> He hit his head 30 years ago. He is convinced that this incident gave him the tumour. I think that he has had it latent for a long time but I know that it is the stress and infections that have provoked it.

The value of detailed information about the illness, symptoms and future was emphasized, while uncertainty obstructed comprehensibility and increased the sense of chaos and anxiety. Many efforts to intellectualize, redefine and diminish the seriousness of the disease were made.

None of the respondents perceived their illness to be some kind of punishment from God or any other external power. Still, there were many questions about justice. 'Why is this happening to me, when I have lived an honest life, while less conscientious people are not afflicted?' Thus, besides the apparently evident biological and psychological explanations, both patients and spouses had unresolved existential questions that hampered the comprehensibility, such as 'Why?', 'Why me?', 'What is the meaning, where is the justice?'.

Manageability—The Behavioural Component

A characteristic feature of individuals who managed to cope with life was that they had strong inherent resources of their own. They expressed confidence in themselves and in their own strength. They were actively seeking information, engaged in being cured and made positive reinterpretations in which hope played a prominent part.

> A man with malignant tumour, grade IV said: 'At first I sought for information and then I decided to recover. One has to believe and I am going to defeat this tumour . . . '.

The respondents presented various types of coping and defence mechanisms, such as rationalization, bargaining, control, distancing, humour and repression, in order to increase manageability. As an example, a 30-year-old man, who, due to his illness, was about to lose both his job and his family, could manage his everyday life by using coping mechanisms such as distancing, rationalization and repression.

> Now this tumour has hit me and I have to solve the situation. Personally, I still think that this has turned out very well.

Family, close friends and hospital staff were very helpful in coping with the situation. Work and hobbies were of great importance for some, mainly as a distraction. Religious faith generally did not increase manageability, as only three respondents were believers. One of these three especially stressed prayer as a powerful tool in this exposed situation, whereas several of the non-believers mentioned that religious faith is probably helpful for religious people, but not for themselves.

Factors that impaired the sense of manageability were depression and isolation, lack of information and a feeling of being deserted or being a victim of circumstances. Not to be recognized as a complete person was humiliating and increased the feeling of loneliness. Relatives who failed them, bad treatment by the staff and an abrupt manner in giving the diagnosis were factors that often hampered coping.

> A woman in her 40s who has had a low-grade brain tumour for 10 years: 'The illness itself has not changed my life. What has changed me is that people have not believed me or my fears, my misgivings'.

The spouses referred not so much to their internal resources as to the external ones. They tried to get social support from various conversation partners such as therapists, doctors, colleagues and friends. Work, hobbies and everyday matters took much of their time and by doing so they could partly keep the illness at a distance, that is they used distraction as coping. As the partner's personality gradually changed, much of the responsibility was transferred to the healthy spouse. Many of them assumed a protective attitude and took on responsibility for the survival of their spouses; by doing so, they could better control the situation.

> My greatest sorrow is that I have lost a part of the man I was married to. But if I had not been there, he would have been dead by now, because he does not notice anything himself and the hospital does not check up on things.

While many patients showed a fighting spirit and believed in cure, more rapid acceptance was seen in the spouses due to the fact that they noticed the change in personality.

> Soon I won't have my husband any more; he is going to die. He, himself, is not aware of that. But I have already planned the whole funeral.

At the same time, the spouses experienced a severe sense of powerlessness from just standing by. Since everything centred on the patient, it was not easy for the spouse to get any attention. This situation was difficult to manage.

> I have shown a great deal of consideration for my husband, but he has difficulties listening to my problems. Because he says that there is nothing wrong with me.

Meaningfulness—The Motivational Component

Despite the exposed situation, there were areas in the patients' lives, mainly close relations to children and family, that were of great emotional importance and that gave meaning to life. It also appeared that good relations became better, while other frail relations broke down because the marriage could not stand the pressure from the onset of the disease. Other factors that gave meaning to life were music, work and hobbies. A complicating factor was that many of the patients lost their jobs and therefore had to redefine its importance. However, many adapted to the new situation and reached a sort of acceptance.

> A man who had always regarded his work as most important said: 'Yes, I have got a new outlook. My job was really important before, but now it is not. Even though it used to be . . .' .

The acceptance was characterized by a component of reappraisal of life. Many respondents said that they now took better care of their lives, that their personality had grown stronger and that they were more positive about life. Living close to death had given them new dimensions. In some patients it was difficult, though, to distinguish between what was the result of an active crisis process that led to acceptance and what was an illusory acceptance due to the brain damage.

Factors that increased meaninglessness were functional deficits, personality changes and unresolved death anxiety. Further, many of the respondents mentioned spontaneously that their reduced financial circumstances made everyday life limited and therefore less valuable. However, some stressed the opposite, that money and position had lost their importance.

In the husband-wife relationship, the roles were changed. The marriage became unequal as most of the patients went through some kind of personality change including regression. Although the spouses had new values in life in many ways and felt needed, they expressed conflicting feelings.

Spirituality was related to meaning, although the value of a religious faith was ambiguous. Two informants stressed that religion helped them to create meaning in their lives, while for the third religious person, her faith became almost a burden and increased her sense of meaninglessness.

> I only feel hopelessness; who could help me? Why has God sent me this illness, what have I done, what is the meaning of it?

While traditional religion had little importance for most of the respondents, they still had some kind of spiritual or existential experience that helped them to create meaning. That could consist of a belief in a power beyond oneself, a life after death, destiny, the goodness of life or the grandness of nature. The experience of church was equivocal: a few could experience peace when being in a church while others considered that the church might be good for some people, but not for them. Some of the respondents considered themselves agnostic, and had no faith at all or trusted mainly in their own strength, or in their doctor.

> I suppose I have a belief, but not of the kind that helps. It is my mental stability, my inner strength that has helped me.

DISCUSSION

The need for information is profound, especially as regards life-threatening diseases such as brain tumours, as comprehensibility is important for coping, which is in good agreement with other studies.[29] It is therefore not surprising that information seeking is a recognized and often used coping mechanism that increases both comprehensibility and manageability. Information also constituted a partly unmet need in this study. To listen to patients and to inform them is therefore of utmost importance.[30] Antonovsky stresses the value of clearing away unrealistic interpretations to create order out of chaos and increase the sense of comprehensibility. Illness, accidents and death are not desirable, but when they occur, they should at least be comprehensible in order to achieve acceptance.[9]

The main goal of coping strategies is to increase manageability, although some strategies also facilitate comprehensibility. Coping mechanisms identified in this study that had clear components of comprehensibility were information-seeking, intellectualization, redefinition and rationalization. To specifically increase manageability, various coping mechanisms as described by Lazarus[13] can be used.

These include confrontative behaviour coping, distancing, self-controlling, seeking social support, accepting responsibility, escape-avoidance, planful problem-solving and positive reappraisal.[13] In this study, positive reappraisal and redefinition and believing in one's own strength were the most prominent strategies. This is in good agreement with Shelly Taylor,[31] who states that coping that enhances and focuses on the positive parts is important for maintenance of health. Hope was prominent in many respondents, although its content changed during the course of the disease, which is in agreement with other studies.[32]

Motivational parts of the sense of coherence component of meaningfulness consisted of children, family, friends, work, hobbies and faith. Yet, these were not questions of decisive importance in every case. There were individuals who had both a family and work but still experienced life as meaningless, while others, despite great losses, had much to fight for. The existential philosopher Karl Jaspers denotes stressful events in life as 'border situations', where the crisis either leads to meaninglessness and emptiness or to an increased positive valuing of life.[33] Those who possessed a 'fighting spirit' managed relatively well. By fighting spirit, we mean persons that had:

- faith—in God or other powers or confidence in oneself, others (for example, doctors);
- hope—a positive attitude to life, although the reasons for hoping changed during the course of the disease;
- love—of family, friends or work.

These findings have similarities with a study conducted by Akechi et al.[34] comprising 455 cancer patients. In that study 'fighting spirit' was correlated with relations and social interaction, support from physicians and with the performance status of the patient.[34] Akechi et al. refer to Moorey and Greer's description of fighting spirit: 'the patient sees the diagnosis as a challenge, has an optimistic view of the future, believes it is possible to exert some control over the illness and manifests confrontative coping responses'. That life's vicissitudes might be seen as a challenge is pointed out by Greer in a 15-year prospective study of women with breast cancer.[35] They found that those women who showed 'fighting spirit', that is saw cancer as a challenge and had a purpose and meaning, had the best disease outcome.

The losses that the respondents experienced during the period of illness (for example loss of work, money, relationships) affected their lives deeply. In this context, too, it was obvious that individuals with 'fighting spirit', or, as Antonovsky expresses it, a profound sense of coherence, experienced life as meaningful despite the losses. Meaningfulness represents the most important part, because without it neither comprehensibility nor manageability will last long. Those people who take an active part in life and are willing to invest energy have better chances of finding resources for problem-solving.

In many modern countries, such as Sweden, people have lost their religious beliefs to a large extent and replaced them with secular values, founded in scientific rationality.[36] A specific religious faith, which gave comprehensibility and guidance for life to earlier generations, is rare today.[37] Nevertheless, the respondents struggled with existential issues such as the meaning of life, death and destiny. An example of this is the question of justice. In a secularized country it is unusual today to believe that illness is inflicted by God or by any other power. Yet the question is addressed beyond the individual: 'Why have I been afflicted with this disease? Where is the [divine] justice?'. Faith in God has not been replaced by any clear philosophical alternatives and therefore persons may feel abandoned. Today, faith is partly replaced by confidence in, for example, oneself, in the doctor, in positive thinking. In other, less secularized, countries, religious tradition plays an important part in people's lives.[38] As Burton states,[17] 'Spirituality/religion is a significant element in the life of most Americans'.

We have used sense of coherence as our main model to understand the patients' and the spouses' strategies for handling their stressful situation. As shown in the results, coping mechanisms can be understood using this model, as coping enhances manageability and comprehensibility and, to a certain extent, also meaning, if meaning-based coping is used.[14] In the same way, spiritual and existential issues were possible to allocate, especially to the central sense of coherence category of 'meaning/meaningfulness'. This does not mean that the three models (coping–sense of coherence–spirituality) are interchangeable, but a clear relationship does exist.

The models can be distinguished as follows: the central question in a stress-coping model would be: 'What/which are the stressors and what are my resources to handle them?'. Spirituality, including existentialism from a philosophical point of view would be more concerned with the question 'What is the higher, inherent meaning of this? How can I create meaning in this situation?'. Sense of coherence is the intermediate position joining the coping model and the spiritual/existential issues.

ACKNOWLEDGEMENTS

This study was supported by Timmermansorden and by The Cancer Foundation at Sahlgrenska University Hospital, Gothenburg.

REFERENCES

1 Doyle D, Hanks G, MacDonald N, eds. *Oxford textbook of palliative medicine*, 2nd edition. Oxford: Oxford University Press, 1998.

2 Strang P. Palliative medicine. A new research field with specific demands. *Läkartidningen* 1999;**96**: 26-29.

3 Watson J. *Nursing: human science and human care: a theory of nursing*. New York: National League for Nursing, 1988.

4 Ross L. Spiritual aspects of nursing. *J Adv Nurs* 1994;**19**:439-47.

5 Highfield M, Cason C. Spiritual needs of patients: are they recognised? *Cancer Nurs* 1983;**6**: 187-92.

6 Giorgiella M, Berkman B, Robinson M. Spirituality and quality of life in gynecologic oncology patients. *Cancer Practice* 1998;**6**:333-38.

7 Choen R, Barry D, Clarke J, *et al*. Well being at the end of life. Part 1. A research agenda for psychosocial and spiritual aspects of care from the patient's perspective. *Cancer Prevent Control* 1997;**1**:334-43.

8 Adelbratt S, Strang P. Death anxiety in brain tumour patients and their spouses. *Palliat Med* 2000;**14**: 499-507.

9 Antonovsky A. *Unraveling the mystery of health: how people manage stress and stay well*. San Francisco, CA: Jossey-Bass, 1987.

10 Frankl V. *Man's search for meaning*. London: Hodder & Stoughton, 1987.

11 Buchi S, Sensky T, Allard S, *et al*. Sense of coherence—a protective factor for depression in rheumatoid arthritis. *J Rheumatol* 1998;**25**:869-75.

12 Freud A, Burlingham D. *War and children*. New York: International University Press, 1943.

13 Lazarus R. Coping theory and research: past, present and future. *Psychosom Med* 1993;**53**:234-37.

14 Folkman S. Positive psychological states and coping with severe stress. *Soc Sci Med* 1997;**45**:1207-21.

15 Greisinger A, Lorimor R, Aday L, Baile W. Terminally ill cancer patients: their most important concerns. *Cancer Practice* 1997;**5**:147-54.

16 Fehring R, Miller J, Shaw C. Spiritual well-being, religiosity, hope, depression, and other mood states in elderly people coping with cancer. *Oncol Nurs Forum* 1997;**24**:663-71.

17 Burton LA. The spiritual dimension of palliative care. *Semin Oncol Nurs* 1998;**14**:121-28.

18 Elkins D, Hedstrom LJ, Hughes L, Saunders C. Towards a humanistic-phenomenological spirituality: definition, description and measurement. *J Human Psychol* 1998;**28**:5-18.

19 Speck PW. *Being there: pastoral care in time of illness*. London: SPCK, 1988.

20 Yalom I. *Existential psychotherapy*. New York: Basic Books, 1980.

21 Patton MQ. *Qualitative evaluation and research methods*. Newbury Park, CA: Sage Publications, 1990.

22 Kvale S. *InterViews*. Thousand Oaks, CA: Sage Publications, 1996.

23 Richoeur P. *Interpretation theory: discourse of the surplus of meaning*. Fort Worth, TX: Christian University Press, 1976.

24 Richoeur P. *Hermeneutics and the social sciences*. New York: Cambridge University Press, 1981.

25 Radnitzky G. *Contemporary schools of metascience*. Gothenburg: Akademiförlaget, 1970.

26 Heidegger M. *Being and time*. Oxford: Basil Blackwell, 1962.

27 Gadamer HG. *Philosophical hermeneutics*. Berkeley, CA: University of California Press, 1976.

28 Kvale S. To validate is the question. In: Kvale, S., ed. *Issues of validity in qualitative research*. Lund: Studentlitteratur, 1989, 73-92.

29 van der Molen B. Relating information needs to the cancer experience: 1. Information as a key coping strategy. *Eur J Cancer Care* 1999;**8**:238-44.

30 Rose K. A qualitative analysis of the information needs in informal carers of terminally ill cancer patients. *J Nurs* 1999;**8**:81-88.

31 Taylor S. *Positive illusions*. New York: Basic Books, 1989.

32 Salander P. Qualities in short life. PhD thesis. Umeå: Umeå University, 1996.

33 Wikstrom O. *Dödsångest. [Death anxiety.]* Stockolm: Socialstyrelsen (Swedish National Board of Health and Welfare), 1999, vol. 1999-00-08-6.

34 Akechi T, Okamura H, Yamawaki S, Uchitomi Y. Predictors of patients' mental adjustment to cancer: patient characteristics and social support. *Br J Cancer* 1998;**77**:2381-85.

35 Greer S. Mind-body research in psychooncology. *Adv Mind-Body Med* 1999;**15**:236-44.

36 Kallenberg K. Spiritual and existential issues in palliative care. *Illness, Crisis, Loss* 2000;**8**:120-30.

37 Bondeson L. Seder och bruk kring dodsfall i gamla tider. *Socialmed Tidskrift* 1994;**71**:77-81. [In Swedish.]

38 Mytko J, Knight S. Body, mind and spirit: towards the integration of religiosity and spirituality in cancer quality of life research. *Psycho-oncology* 1999;**8**:439-50.

7

SUFFERING AND SPIRITUALITY

The Soul of Clinical Work With Families

LORRAINE M. WRIGHT

I first experienced suffering from illness in my childhood. My grandmother, who lived with us, suffered chronic pain from arthritis. I observed the suffering that one can experience from chronic pain, whether it be firsthand, as my grandmother suffered, or secondhand, as I emotionally suffered with her. I also learned that this chronic pain controlled all of our lives, especially how well my brother and I would behave on any given day, how much my grandmother was able to "mother," and how we children were invited to be more compassionate because of having a pain sufferer in the family. My grandmother was the center of our family, but the chronic pain she suffered ruled her. The disease severely disfigured her hands, caused her knees to be swollen much of the time, resulted in her walking with a limp, and dictated how well she was able to live her life day to day. But those disfigured hands made us apple pie, weeded our garden, and lifted numerous cups of tea while we exchanged stories of our lives with her. *However, I do not recall as a child hearing her own stories of suffering with chronic pain.* Perhaps I did not listen. Perhaps they were not told. But now I have several questions that I would like to ask of her. What meaning did she give to this life of chronic pain? What did she believe helped alleviate some of her suffering? What made it worse? What made it better? What did she believe we as children did to help or hinder her suffering? Was the physical suffering worse than the emotional suffering or vice versa? I wonder if conversations that included the answers to these questions would have been a part of the healing for both my grandmother and me.

WHAT IS SUFFERING?

The alleviation of suffering has always been the cornerstone of caring. "Suffering gives caring its own character and identity, and all forms of caring aim, in one way or another, to alleviate suffering"

Reprinted from the *Journal of Family Nursing* 3 (1997): 3-14.

(Lindholm & Eriksson, 1993, p. 1354). But what is suffering? Morse and Johnson (1991) offer the idea that suffering is a comprehensive concept that includes the experience of both acute and chronic pain, the strain of trying to endure, the alienation of forced exclusion from everyday life, the shock of institutionalization, and the uncertainty of anticipating the ramifications of illness. Hinds (1992) suggests that suffering is a phenomenon with physical and emotional components. A very interesting study by Lindholm and Eriksson (1993) examined suffering as perceived by both patients and nurses. This study revealed that patients described suffering and nurses tended to explain it. The descriptions of suffering included struggle, despair, pain, lack of strength, inner obstacle, a longing for home, a longing for love, "something that hurts," and breakdown in relationships.

In another study, the suffering of family caregivers of noninstitutionalized cancer patients revealed such descriptions as fear of loneliness; uncertainty about the future; communication breakdown; and lack of support (Hinds, 1992). It can be seen that suffering from illness manifests itself in many ways. Although I concur with these efforts to define and describe suffering, I most readily resonate with a patient who once described his suffering as "just feeling awful and heavy most of the time."

Individual beliefs of patients and family members are involved both in the experience of suffering and in inferences to suffering. Certain beliefs may conserve or maintain an illness; others may exacerbate symptoms; others alleviate suffering (Wright, Watson, & Bell, 1996). If nurses can invite persons to reflect on their beliefs, those persons are free to consider other possibilities. Lindholm and Eriksson (1993) offer a finding from their study that "suffering itself has no meaning, but man can give meaning to his own experienced suffering" (p. 1360). Frankl (1963) believes that the highest level of suffering is to find meaning in our experiences. In an eloquent and illuminating explanation of illness experiences, Frank (1995) offers another idea of how persons make meaning of their suffering. He asserts that people tell stories of their illness to make sense of their suffering; and when they turn their diseases into stories, they find healing. From my own clinical practice and research with families, I have come to strongly believe that talking about experiences with illness can often alleviate emotional, physical, and spiritual suffering (Wright, Watson, & Bell, 1996). To me, this talking and listening about illness stories in therapeutic conversations becomes the context from which suffering can be alleviated and healing begins.

SUFFERING AND SPIRITUALITY

The most significant learning about suffering that I have gleaned in my clinical work with families over 20 years is that a discourse of suffering frequently opens up a discourse of spirituality. Suffering invites us into the spiritual domain. A shift to and emphasis on spirituality is frequently the most profound response to suffering from illness. If nurses are to be helpful, we must acknowledge that suffering and, often, the senselessness of it are ultimately spiritual issues (Patterson, 1994).

The influence of family members' religious and spiritual beliefs on their illness experience has been one of the most neglected areas in family work. Yet our clinical experience with families has taught us that the experience of suffering becomes transposed to one of spirituality as family members try to make meaning out of their suffering and distress. To understand how family members offer compassion and what efforts are made to alleviate suffering, it is useful to explore religious and spiritual beliefs in clinical work with families. It is through a discourse of beliefs about spirituality and religion that a manner of understanding, explaining, conversing, and creating changes and healing with families becomes possible. It is important and helpful to make a distinction between religion, which is extrinsic, and spirituality, which is intrinsic. Spirituality generally refers to a personal belief in and experience of a supreme being or an ultimate human condition, along with an internal set of values and active investment in those values, a sense of connection, a sense of meaning, and a sense of inner wholeness (Mackinnon, Helmeke, & Stander, 1994), within or outside of formal religious structures.

It has been my clinical experience that persons and families with illness cope more effectively if there is an absence of spiritual distress. Spiritual distress is the inability to invest life with meaning (Burnard, 1987). To find meaning in all events that arise in our lives seems to be a basic human need. By being clear about our view of life and possessing facilitative beliefs about life, we are less threatened by unexpected or unusual experiences of illness. In short, we suffer less.

The challenge for nurses in working with family members who are experiencing spiritual distress is to avoid falling into the trap of offering ready answers but rather to listen, accept, and be curious. In so doing one hopes that family members will discover their own meanings for illness and reason for believing what they do about their illness. It is further hoped that the beliefs they adopt will assist them to alleviate or diminish their suffering (Wright, Watson, & Bell, 1996).

One clinical family that I and my clinical nursing team were privileged to know, learn from, and assist at the Family Nursing Unit, University of Calgary, consisted of a common-law couple and their 9-year-old daughter. The mother's presenting concern was her daughter's behavior problems at school and aggressive behavior toward the mother at home. During the first meeting (mother only present), the mother's belief about the connection between the child's behavior, the mother's recurrent breast cancer, and the recent separation of the parents was revealed. Also, the mother expressed concern about the potential relationship between the daughter and father after her death. The following dialogue occurred in the third session, with the mother (M), father (F), and child (Natasha [N] present (with clinician [C]).

C: How much do you think Natasha understands about death or about dying?

F: I think Natasha has a peaceful understanding of that because of the church, reincarnation and perpetuation of the soul.

M: Natasha was born with these ideas.

C: And what are your religious beliefs about death?

M: I don't have religious beliefs, I just have a spiritual philosophy.

C: Yes, and what is that?

M: I believe that my soul is immortal and no one can touch it except me. I am the only one who can change it . . . it doesn't stop if my body dies.

C: (directed to the mother) And what do you think Natasha's beliefs are?

N: Christian Scientist Sunday School . . . and prayer can heal headaches.

C: Natasha, can you help me understand what your mom is saying. When your mom is sick and if she does die, what do you believe will happen? [Long pause]

C: Can you tell me what you think? It's a pretty tough question, a hard one isn't it?

F: (to daughter) Have you thought about it much?

N: No.

C: Natasha, do you believe that when people are sick they can make themselves better? [Natasha nods yes]

C: Do you think there are ever times when people get sick and no matter how hard they pray or what they do that they can't get better, that their body can't do what they want and they still might die? Can that happen?

N: Yes.

C: [Later in session] Do you think at this point in time that Natasha is doing quite well with her understanding of your illness and the possibility of your life's being shortened?

M: She has a good basic foundation . . . but there is some denial there because she does believe that if I wanted to get well I could . . . but I'm at peace. I don't mind moving on.

This uncovering of the family members' beliefs was quite significant. We learn that this young mother is at peace with the possibility that her life will be shortened. But her young daughter believes that if her mother wanted to be well, then she would be. We later discovered that the father's belief was similar and was concerned that the mother had given up and was not trying anymore. Discussing these ideas openly and frankly with the family members proved to be a very useful exercise to reduce the family's, and in particular this young girl's, suffering. The young mother did die some months later and we again had the privilege to work with Natasha and her father. Natasha was concerned about keeping her mother's memory alive, and we discussed ways that she was already doing that and other ideas that she might entertain.

WAYS TO ALLEVIATE SUFFERING

In my clinical work with families, I believe my goal and my obligation is to alleviate or heal emotional, physical, or spiritual suffering. My colleagues, Wendy Watson and Janice Bell, and I have evolved an advanced practice approach to assist with the alleviation of suffering in families (Wright, Watson, & Bell, 1996). Some of the ways we have found useful to alleviate suffering are acknowledging suffering; telling, listening to, and witnessing suffering; connecting suffering and spirituality, creating a healing environment, inviting reflections about suffering; and helping students help families to alleviate suffering.

Acknowledging Suffering

One beginning effort to alleviate suffering is to acknowledge that suffering exists. Our aim is consistent with that of Janice Morse and Joy Johnson (1991), who suggested that the "goal of those involved in the illness experience is to decrease the suffering of the ill person or the shared suffering, thereby increasing well-being" (p. 315). Suffering is the illness experience, whether it is short and intense or prolonged and pervasive. Suffering is part of our human existence from stories of Job to stories of Holocaust victims to stories of illness.

Telling, Listening to, and Witnessing Stories of Suffering

Telling, listening to, and witnessing illness stories provides a powerful validation of an important human experience. Nurses are in a privileged position to hear and affirm illness narratives. By acknowledging illness narratives, we engage in the essential, ethical practice of recognizing the ill person as the *suffering other* (Frank, 1994). In our

clinical practice, we also want to open possibilities, through our therapeutic conversations, for recognizing the ill person and other family members as the heroic other, the joyful other, the giving other, the receiving other, the compassionate other, the passionate other, and the strengthened other. We want to open space for a breath of human experiences with illness to be spoken by each family member. In our clinical experience, the deliberate and open acknowledgment of suffering frequently opens the door for the disclosure of other fears or worries not previously expressed.

Positive responses and reduction in emotional and physical suffering have convinced us of the necessity to invite family members to tell their illness stories. In our professional encounters with families, we move beyond social conversation about the illness to purposeful therapeutic conversations. We direct the conversation in a manner that we hope will give voice to the human experiences of suffering and symptoms as well as to the experiences of courage, hope, growth, and love. Through the telling of the story, "the patient can interpret her own suffering [and, we would add, strength]; the role of witness is to provide moral affirmation of the struggle to find that interpretation. Thus the patient's voice must be cultivated, not cut off" (Frank, 1994, p. 14).

By providing a context for the sharing among family members of their illness experiences, intense emotions are legitimized. Kleinman (1988) proffered the idea that an inquiry into the meanings (beliefs) of illness is a journey into relationships. By inviting family members to share their illness narratives, which include stories of sickness and suffering, one allows them, as Frank (1994) has suggested, to reclaim their right to tell what are their own experiences and to reclaim a voice over and against the medical voice and a life beyond illness. I have had many families tell me that having someone listen to their stories, ask questions about their stories, and commend them for their courage in the face of suffering has enabled them to gain a new and sometimes renewed appreciation of their ability to cope. In many instances, it has even alleviated physical symptoms and familial conflict and alleviated emotional or spiritual suffering.

One of our most difficult duties as human beings is to listen to the voices of those who suffer. The voices of the ill are easy to ignore, because these voices are often faltering in tone and mixed in message. . . . Listening is hard, but it is also a fundamental moral act; to realize the best potential in postmodern times requires an ethics of listening. The moment of witness in the story crystallizes a mutuality of need, when each is *for* the other. (Frank, 1995, p. 25)

Connecting Suffering and Spirituality

Nurses' beliefs can hinder or enhance the possibilities for alleviating suffering (Wright, Bell, Watson, & Tapp, 1995). One belief frequently offered to those suffering with illness is that "life could be worse." This belief is offered to provide comfort and encouragement. One woman, suffering from endometriosis, did not find this belief useful, however. She responded: "I know life could be worse. I could have only one eye or leg, and I am very fortunate to have all I do have. . . . But those philophies do not solve the disease, do not get rid of the pain, the tears, the frustration, or the heartaches that come with the problems" (Donoghue & Siegel, 1992, p. 55). This example highlights the need for nurses to recognize that each person's suffering with illness is unique and that attempting to have persons "count their blessings" can inadvertently trivialize suffering from illness.

Creating a Healing Environment

The ultimate desired outcome is to create a healing environment for family members for the relief of suffering from their illness experiences. Remen (1993) eloquently offered the following notion:

Healing is different from curing. . . . Healing is a process we're all involved in all the time. . . . Sometimes people heal physically, and they don't heal emotionally, or mentally, or spiritually. And sometimes people heal emotionally, and they don't heal physically. (p. 344)

In his book, Frank (1995) offers the powerful metaphor that ill people are more than victims of disease or patients of medicine; they are wounded storytellers. He argues that people tell stories to make sense of their suffering; when they turn their diseases into stories, they find healing. This coincides with a strong belief that exists in our North American health care culture that eliciting, discussing, and expressing one's illness story and accompanying emotions can be very healing. Families also share this cultural belief and have often remarked in our clinical practice how they appreciated the opportunity to talk about the effect of illness on their lives and relationships. A study by Robinson (1994) about families, illness, and intervention conducted within the Family Nursing Unit, University of Calgary, gives further validation that families find nurses' invitations to engage in meaningful conversation about the effect of illness on their lives to be one of the most useful interventions in assisting families to move beyond and overcome problems. The capacity of nurses to be witnesses to the stories of suffering of patients and families is central to providing care; it is frequently the genesis of healing, if not curing (Frank, 1994; Kleinman, 1988).

Inviting Reflections About Suffering

To alter existing beliefs, nurses need to invite family members to a reflection about their constraining beliefs (Wright, Watson, & Bell, 1996). Through these reflections, a person begins to entertain different or alternative beliefs to get out of a state of confusion, struggle, or suffering.

One example of inviting reflections about suffering occurred with a family with a 34-year-old man experiencing multiple sclerosis (MS). A heart-to-heart conversation between this young man and myself later proved to be a turning point in his healing from his intense emotional suffering. In the final session, his parents reported that they believed one of the most useful aspects of the sessions was having their son talk about his illness story, something they claimed he had never done before. Inviting reflections about suffering began with my drawing a distinction about his possible affective responses to illness, specifically anger versus sadness (clinician [C], son with MS [Mark], mother [M], father [F]).

C: I see you get sad about your MS. Do you ever get angry about having MS? (Mark nods yes) Which emotion is more common for you to feel about your MS? Do you feel more sad or more angry about it?

Mark: Sad.

C: At this moment?

Mark: Sad.

C: More sad about it. And which one is easier for you to deal with? Which emotion do you feel more comfortable with? Is it easier to be sad about it or to be angry about it?

Mark: Angry.

C: Easier to be angry. The sadness is harder? Can you tell me about that?

Mark: Well, it's just letting off steam, it's easier than feeling bad about it.

C: (looks at M and F) Do you agree with that? Do you think it's easier? Do you notice that it's easier for him to be angry than to be sad?

M/F: Yeah, oh yeah.

C: That's a harder emotion. What about for you? What's the harder one for you to see your son experiencing, sadness or . . .

F: Sadness.

C: Or anger? Sadness.

F: I'm glad when he's angry and shouts and screams and lets it out, then he's good for awhile. But when he's sad and sits there and we ask "What's the matter, Mark?" And he says "Nothing" . . .

M: Doesn't say anything, just sits.

F: No conversation, just watches TV.

C: Actually in some ways it probably takes more strength to be sad, doesn't it, than to be angry. Because, like you say, when you're angry, it's over.

M: Oh yeah, it's over.

C: But it takes a lot of strength to be sad. When you're sad, do you cry on the inside or do you cry on the outside Mark?

Mark: Both, I guess (very softly).

M: Sometimes he cries.

F: Oh yeah, he has incidents of crying.

C: Because I've had other patients with MS and other illnesses tell me that crying on the inside takes more energy. They find when they cry on the outside and let the tears come, that it doesn't take as much energy. Do you find that?

Mark: Yeah.

C: It's harder and it seems like it saps your energy more if you just cry on the inside? So sometimes you allow yourself to cry on the outside?

Mark: Yes.

C: Good. That's good. Do you understand what I mean?

M/F: Oh yeah. I wish he would do it that way all the time.

C: That he cries on the outside.

F: Have a darn good cry and then . . .

C: Just like anger then, it's out, doesn't take as much energy, but being sad all the time on the inside, you're always being angry on the inside.

F: It's eating away . . .

C: It saps your energy, doesn't it?

F: Oh yes, it's hard, yep.

C: Do you ever hold back or cry on the inside because you're afraid it might upset your mom and dad? (Pause) Would you ever hold it back because you're . . .

F: I hope he doesn't. I wish, if he wants to cry, let him cry.

Mark: I don't think I purposely do.

In this short but intense focus on affect, I drew a distinction between anger and sadness, exploring which affect is easier for the son to experience and which is easier for his parents to observe. From the family members responses, both facilitative and constraining family beliefs were drawn forth: (1) It is okay to be angry; (2) it is not okay to be sad; and (3) it is weak to cry and weak to be sad. I challenged the constraining beliefs by embedding the suggestion and offering a facilitative belief that sadness—a difficult emotion for this family—is normal and takes courage. As the parents watch me explore these issues with their son, they are hearing the unspeakable (his sadness) being spoken in front of them. The wonderfully facilitative distinction between crying on the inside and crying on the outside led to further reflection about the son's experience of illness. I combined an exploration of affect with an exploration of cognition and behavior. I also had an intense affective experience of sadness while listening to this young man and, for a few moments, suffered with him as well as being a witness to his suffering. To be touched in some way by another in a conversation can alleviate human suffering.

Helping Students Help Families Who Are Suffering

Our graduate students specializing in family systems nursing take practicums within the Family Nursing Unit at the University of Calgary (Wright, Watson, & Bell, 1990). During these practicums, students participate as a clinical team member or interviewer (or both) of families who present suffering from chronic illness, life-threatening illness, or psychosocial problems. During our clinical work with families, I routinely ask our students, "Who do you think is suffering the most in this family? Who the least?" At the end of our clinical day with families, I will also ask the students, "Have we helped this family today? Have we made a difference? Have we reduced any suffering? If so, how did we do that?" By asking such questions, students are invited into the domain of acknowledging suffering, witnessing suffering, and assessing the alleviation of suffering, and again, it becomes a recursive phenomenon because ill persons also teach us. As Frank (1995, p. 145) suggests, the primary truth that the ill have to teach us is the "pedagogy of suffering."

CONCLUSION

The depth of one person's suffering is distinguished from others by each person's unique experience. I have ached, cried, and lamented when I have suffered for others, but only my own experiences of suffering have I experienced firsthand. Suffering experiences cannot be compared, but comparisons are indeed made about which sufferings we believe are the most horrific. For example, some of us may believe that it is more horrific to suffer from cancer than from ALS, or that pain is more unbearable from shingles than from a renal stone. The most important role we have as nurses is to be listeners and witnesses to others' sufferings. Then we must acknowledge suffering and ask questions that will challenge any constraining beliefs that may be exacerbating their suffering. Through this exchange between family members and nurse, a domain of spirituality is encountered. This journey into spirituality manifests itself in the offering of true compassion and love between and among family members and nurse. Likewise, these efforts to alleviate suffering cross the border into healing; a healing that is not reserved only for family members but also for nurses. Through this process of exchange, suffering and spirituality become the soul of clinical work with families.

REFERENCES

Burnard, P. (1987). Spiritual distress and the nursing response: Theoretical considerations and counseling skills. *Journal of Advanced Nursing, 12,* 377-382.

Donoghue, P. J., & Siegel, M. E. (1992). *Sick and tired of being sick and tired: Living with invisible chronic illness.* New York: Norton.

Frank, A. W. (1994). Interrupted stories, interrupted lives. *Second Opinion, 20,* 11-18.

Frank, A. W. (1995). *The wounded storyteller: Body, illness and ethics.* Chicago: University of Chicago Press.

Frankl, V. E. (1963). *Man's search for meaning: An introduction to logotherapy.* New York: Washington Square Press.

Hinds, C. (1992). Suffering: A relatively unexplored phenomenon among family caregivers of non-institutionalized patients with cancer. *Journal of Advanced Nursing, 17,* 918-925.

Kleinman, A. (1988). *The illness narratives.* New York: Basic Books.

Lindholm, L., & Eriksson, K. (1993). To understand and alleviate suffering in a caring culture. *Journal of Advanced Nursing, 18,* 1354-1361.

Mackinnon, D., Helmeke, K., & Stander, V. (1994, November). *Integrating spirituality and religion into family therapy*. Paper presented at the American Association for Marriage and Family Therapy Annual Conference, Chicago.

Morse, J. M., & Johnson, J. L. (1991). Toward a theory of illness: The Illness-Constellation Model. In J. M. Morse & J. L. Johnson (Eds.), *The illness experience: Dimensions of suffering* (pp. 315-342). Newbury Park, CA: Sage.

Patterson, R. B. (1994, June). Learning from suffering. *Family Therapy News,* 11-12.

Remen, R. N. (1993). Wholeness. In B. Moyers (Ed.), *Healing and the mind* (pp. 343-363). New York: Doubleday.

Robinson, C. A. (1994). *Women, families, chronic illness and nursing interventions: From burden to balance.*

Unpublished doctoral dissertation, University of Calgary, Alberta, Canada.

Wright, L. M., Bell, J. M., Watson, W. L., & Tapp, D. (1995). The influence of the beliefs of nurses: A clinical example of a post-myocardial-infarction couple. *Journal of Family Nursing, 1,* 238-256.

Wright, L. M., Watson, W. L., & Bell, J. M. (1990). The Family Nursing Unit: A unique integration of research, education and clinical practice. In J. M. Bell, W. L. Watson, & L. M. Wright (Eds.), *The cutting edge of family nursing* (pp. 95-109). Calgary, Canada: Family Nursing Unit Publications.

Wright, L. M., Watson, W. L., & Bell, J. M. (1996). *Beliefs: The heart of healing in families and illness.* New York: Basic Books.

8

Levels of Meaning in Family Stress Theory

JOAN M. PATTERSON
ANN W. GARWICK

Major stressful life events, particularly those that have chronic hardships, create a crisis for families that often leads to reorganization in the family's style of functioning. A major factor in this reorganization is the meaning the family gives to the stressful event. Often the meaning extends beyond the event itself and leads to a changed view of the family system and even to a changed view of the world. Building on other family stress models, we elaborate the family's definition of the stressor into three levels of family meanings: (1) situational meanings, (2) family identity, and (3) family world view. Examples from clinical work and studies of families adapting to chronic illness are used to illustrate the relationship between these three levels of meaning, particularly as they change in response to crisis. Implications for clinical and empirical work are discussed.

Within family stress theory, one of the critical constructs that has been more difficult and elusive to conceptualize and to operationalize is family meanings. Beginning with Reuben Hill's (1949, 1958) focus on the family's definition of the stressor event, many family scholars have contributed to family stress theory through empirical studies designed to understand how families adapt to various types of stressful experience (see Boss, 1987, for a comprehensive review).

Included in these studies is our own research on families living with chronic illness and disability

Reprinted from *Family Process* 33 (1994): 287-304. Preparation of this article was supported by the National Institute on Disability and Rehabilitation Research Grant #H133890012. It was first presented at the Theory Construction and Research Methodology Workshop at the Annual Meeting of the National Council on Family Relations, Orlando FL, November 1992.

(Garwick, 1991; Garwick, Detzner, & Boss, 1994; Patterson, 1989b; Patterson, Budd, Goetz, & Warwick, 1993; Patterson & Leonard, 1994; Patterson, Leonard, & Titus, 1992; Patterson, McCubbin, & Warwick, 1990). In our effort to understand those factors associated with adaptation to the chronic stress of disabling conditions, cognitive factors have emerged as very important. These cognitive factors go beyond the definition the family gives to the stressor (the onset of disability) as families search for meaning in a life that, in many ways, has been shattered by added demands, multiple losses, and a change in routines, roles, and expectations. From our research, it appears that there are multiple levels of family meanings. Furthermore, the meanings a family holds are often reconstructed after the experience of chronic illness; and, conversely, the different levels of family meanings influence and shape the processes and outcomes of family adaptation to chronic stress.

The focus of this theoretical article is on these levels of family meaning. Specifically, based on our clinical and empirical work with families who care for a member with chronic illness or disability, we propose that families, as a whole, construct and share meanings about (1) specific stressful situations, (2) their identity as a family, and (3) their view of the world. These meanings represent three levels of abstraction and stability that are dynamically interrelated. The family's world view is the most abstract, usually implicit, and often something the family is not consciously aware of nor readily able to articulate. It evolves slowly and is the most stable. It provides the framework for the family's identity as well as for its style of defining stressful situations as they are encountered. Situational meanings are the most concrete and more immediately available in the family's consciousness. They are also the most responsive to change. From our observations of families having a member with chronic illness, a major part of the adaptation process is defining the situation, or attributing meaning to the illness event that has imposed itself on their lives. This is often followed by a change at the other two levels of meaning: family identity changes in a way that allows for the illness and its associated hardships to have a place in the family life, and this in turn often evokes a change in the family world view or how family

members see themselves in relationship to the rest of the world.

FAMILY MEANINGS

We begin by emphasizing that the family system is the unit of analysis for the discussion in this article.[1] Our focus is on *meanings* that exist only *as a property of the whole family unit.* Family meanings are distinct from the meanings held by an individual family member. Furthermore, family meanings are distinct from a consensus about meanings held by individuals. *Family meanings* are the interpretations, images, and views that have been collectively constructed by family members as they interact with each other; as they share time, space, and life experience; and as they talk with each other and dialogue about these experiences. They are the family's social constructions, the product of their interactions; they belong to no one member, but to the family as a unit. Berger and Luckmann's (1966) classic text, *The Social Construction of Reality,* provides the theoretical grounding for this premise that all meanings are created and maintained through social interaction. Images of reality are created by human actors in the process of social interaction. Meanings are collectively constructed for these images and these meanings are expressed through language. According to cybernetician Humberto Maturana, people survive by fitting in with one another in social space, what he calls "structural coupling"—that is, "the relationship between a structure-determined entity and the medium in which it exists" (Dell, 1985, p. 12). To maintain this coupling and to coordinate complex interaction patterns, implicit and shared assumptions and meanings emerge about themselves in relationship to each other, and about themselves as a unit in relationship to systems beyond their boundaries. This structural coupling is, in essence, an emergent family that, over time, evolves an increasingly complex set of images, assumptions, and meanings to guide day-to-day behavior. Reiss (1981), who has elaborated most eloquently on the theoretical basis for family constructions of reality, emphasizes that shared explanatory systems play a crucial role in organizing and maintaining group process. Shared meanings reduce ambiguity and uncertainty about a complex array of stimuli and make coordination of response among group members possible. This, in turn, contributes to group stability. It also creates an identity for the group, which sets it apart from its context, creating a boundary between who is in and who is out of the group that we are calling "family."

Reiss (1981) emphasizes that these family constructions of reality emerge from the family's shared process and that this process is different from simple agreement or consensus among family members. In other words, the presence of disagreement does not imply the absence of sharing. If one were to ask one family member to report about family's meanings, that person's version would be his or her story, what Wamboldt and Wolin (1988) call the "family myth," or what David Reiss (1989) calls the "represented family." It is what the individual has internalized and can recall from his or her immersion in family experiences. This subjective account by one family member is essentially an individual-level variable, and one in which the notion of consensus or disagreement between individual subjective accounts would be relevant. This subjective account should be differentiated from what actually happens when family members are engaged with each other, what Reiss (1989) calls the "practicing family" and what Wamboldt and Wolin (1988) call "family reality." The implication of this is that we know about family-level meanings primarily by assessing the language that emerges from family interaction.

Wamboldt and Wolin (1988) point out a critical difference between *interaction* and *transaction* that is relevant to family constructions. All interaction is not transaction. Interaction becomes transaction when the persons engaged in the interaction undergo internal change, allowing for individual beliefs, emotions, behaviors, and so on, to be modified during the interaction process. There is a kind of reciprocal transformation, and something new is created or emerges. It belongs to no one person, but rather is a product of their transaction.

Reiss (1981) has identified two levels of family constructions of reality—*shared family constructs* and *family paradigms*. Family constructs are more situation-specific than family paradigms, and there are two types: (1) ordinary constructs, which are the family's conceptions of everyday, routine family interactions, and (2) crisis constructs, which are the family's conceptions of a crisis event and its response to the event. From the perspective of family stress theory, Reiss expands on Hill's (1958) "definition of the event" by emphasizing the collective family's initiative and involvement in interpreting the stressful event. Essential aspects of the family's constructions of stressful events are incorporated into the family paradigm, which is the central organizer of the family's shared constructs, sets, expectations, and fantasies about its social world. These meanings, or family constructions, are not static, but rather change over time as the family responds to new experiences, particularly stressful life experience. It is the nature of a stressor, inherent in its definition, that it is an event of change, a deviation from the status quo, and that it calls for a new response from the person or unit experiencing it (Patterson, 1988, 1989b).

LEVELS OF MEANING

Meaning Construct in Early Stress Models

In the earliest family stress models (Hill, 1949, 1958), the family's definition was focused solely on the stressor event, what Lazarus (1966) has called "primary appraisal." This definition interacted with the resources the family had and used to manage the stressor. For example, a parent who believed that her critically ill infant was going to die might resist emotional bonding with the infant as a way to minimize the pending loss. Or conversely, if she blamed herself for having caused the illness, she might invest more attention in the infant as a way to ease her guilt.

In the Double ABCX Model (McCubbin & Patterson, 1982, 1983a,b), the family's perception of the original stressor event was expanded to include the family's perception of other stressors and strains, plus their perceptions of family resources. This latter perception is what Lazarus (1966) called secondary appraisal, that is, appraisal of capabilities or the ability to manage the stressors and strains. Another way that meanings were included in the Double ABCX Model was in terms of "coping," which was defined to include both cognitive and behavioral strategies. For example, a parent, believing that her infant could live if given the best medical care, might search the country for the best specialist. In this model, a coping strategy that functioned to alter meanings so as to make a situation manageable was also emphasized (for example, believing this is God's will for our family and we were chosen because we can handle it). In addition, a more generalized meaning construct was added, called a sense of coherence (Antonovsky, 1979, 1987), which was defined as the family's ability to balance control and trust—that is, knowing when to take charge and when to trust in or believe in the authority and/or power of others. In an effort to emphasize *adaptation* as the central outcome of the stress process, the Double ABCX Model is now called the "The Family Adjustment and Adaptation Response (FAAR) Model" (Patterson, 1988, 1989a), to emphasize potentially positive outcomes. This focus on adaptation is consistent with the many studies now focusing on family and individual resilience in the face of stressors and risk factors.

In the FAAR Model, the meaning factor was differentiated into two levels of meaning: situational meanings and global meanings (Patterson, 1988, 1989a). Situational meanings referred to the individual's and family's subjective definitions of their demands, their capabilities, and of these two factors relative to each other. Global meanings were defined as transcending any given situation and comprising a more stable cognitive set of beliefs about the relationships of family members to each other, and the relationship of the family unit to the larger community.

Concurrent to the development of the FAAR Model, Boss (1987, 1988) developed the Contextual Model of Family Stress in which she also emphasized family perceptions. One of the critical constructs related to perceptions in Boss's work is *boundary ambiguity*, which she defines as "a state when family members are uncertain in their perception of who is in or out of the family or who is performing what roles and tasks within the family system" (Boss, 1987, p. 709). Boss has argued that both the *physical* and *psychological* presence of family members should be considered in defining boundaries. Boundary ambiguity can occur when a family member (1) is physically present but psychologically absent, or (2) is physically absent but psychologically present.

Garwick's (1991; Garwick et al., 1994) work studying families with a member with Alzheimer's disease is a prime example of the first type of boundary ambiguity; families with a husband/father missing-in-action in Viet Nam has been studied by Boss (1977) as an example of the second. Greater boundary ambiguity is believed to thwart the family's successful adaptation to stressors, and has been associated with greater individual and family dysfunction (Boss, 1987).

Integrating the situational and global meanings constructs from the FAAR Model and the concept of boundary ambiguity from the Boss Contextual Model, we propose that there are three levels of meaning that are important when considering family adaptation to stressful life experiences: situational meanings, family identity, and family world view (see Figure 8.1). Case illustrations and examples from previously published research will be used to illustrate these levels of meaning.

Level One: Situational Meanings

The first level still involves situational meanings as defined in the FAAR Model. As family members talk with each other about the stressful situation, they begin constructing meanings about the stressor event or the pileup of demands, as well as their capabilities as a family to manage the demands. This is consistent with Reiss's (1981) emphasis on *shared constructs,* which emerge from the collective family's initiative and involvement in interpreting stressful experience.

When a stressor event first occurs, family members begin a process of constructing meanings as they interact with each other. It may take time for a shared definition to emerge. This, in fact, is part of the process of family adaptation (McCubbin & Patterson, 1983b). It is highly unlikely that agreement will always occur among all family members, and it probably is not necessary for families to agree in order to still function well. A shared definition does not necessarily imply agreement among family members. Family members may agree to disagree. There are many domains of family life where individuals act independently (although families have implicit rules for how much independence is tolerated, which is part of our second level of family

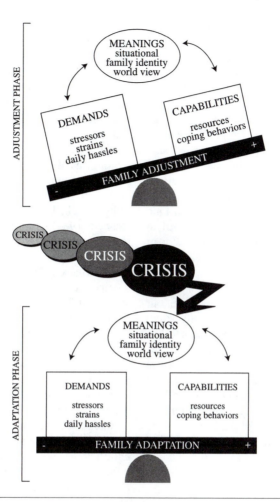

Figure 8.1   Levels of Meaning in the Family Adjustment and Adaptation Response Model

meanings). However, when a coordinated family behavioral response is necessary for effective functioning, the need for agreement on situational definitions will be more important. For example, when deciding whether a child who is experiencing severe respiratory distress should be taken to the emergency room, parents who can arrive at consensus quickly (both define the situation as a life-threatening medical emergency) will be more effective problem-solving units. Because family members share social space, time, and experience, they influence each other in their ways of appraising situations. In cohesive families, joined by bonds of unity, there

is likely to be mutual influence in arriving at these appraisals.

In families that have a member with chronic illness or disability, there are numerous examples of the role of situational meanings in the coping and adaptation process. In our study of families that have a medically fragile child (Patterson & Leonard, 1994), it was not unusual for parents to report positive aspects of having a child with intense medical needs: the child's warmth and responsiveness; the tenacity and perseverance of the child to endure that made the parents want to invest more of their effort; the closeness felt in the family unit by pulling together to manage; the assertiveness and skill that they as parents developed in response to caring for the child, as well as learning to deal with multiple providers and third-party payers; and the growth in empathy and kindness in their other children. In other words, parents selectively attended to the positive aspects of their child's personality and behaviors while minimizing the limitations or health problems. In addition, many parents emphasized the growth and development of the self or the family unit in response to the challenges. These efforts at positive attributions are examples of situational meanings about capabilities that have been referred to by others as a kind of secondary control, or accommodating oneself to existing realities by maximizing perceived benefits of things that cannot be changed (Weisz, Rothbaum, & Blackburn, 1984).

Another example of the role of situational meanings in adaptation to chronic illness is from our research on the relationship between family stress and coping variables and health outcomes in children with cystic fibrosis. Families rated the difficulty of intrafamily strains they had experienced in the last year (situational meaning for sources of stress). High subjective intrafamily strain scores were positively associated with a 3-month decline in weight-for-height ratios in the child with cystic fibrosis (Patterson, McCubbin, & Warwick, 1990).

Level Two: Family Identity

The second level of meaning refers to how families view themselves—the family identity. This global view about family relationships is more stable than situational meanings about demands and capabilities. How a family defines itself is reflected in its structure (who is in the family) as well as in its functioning (the patterns of relationship linking members to each other). Implicit rules of relationship guide family members in how they are to relate to each other. These rules include (1) definitions of external boundaries (who is in the family) and internal boundaries (such as subsystem alliances), (2) role assignments for accomplishing family tasks, and (3) rules and norms for interactional behavior.

The construct of family identity is more abstract than situational meanings, and, if asked, family members would probably be unable to articulate

their identity. However, it is through routines and rituals that family identity is developed and maintained, and it is through observing these patterned interactions that an outsider may be able to gain insight into a family's identity. This construct builds on the work of several family scholars who have examined the role of family rituals in maintaining a family's sense of itself as a collective whole, in establishing shared rules, attitudes, and ways of relating, as well as in maintaining continuity and stability in family functioning over time (Bennett, Wolin, & McAvity, 1988; Bossard & Boll, 1950; Imber-Black, Roberts, & Whiting, 1988; Wolin & Bennett, 1984). Families vary in their commitment to rituals, and there is some evidence that under-ritualized families may experience more dysfunction (Imber-Black et al., 1988). Rituals are often used therapeutically to help families establish boundaries, mark transitions, or develop a clear sense of their own identity. In empirical studies of factors associated with alcoholism, high levels of commitment to family rituals were a protective factor in reducing the intergenerational transmission of alcoholism (Bennett, Wolin, Reiss, & Teitelbaum, 1987; Steinglass, Bennett, Wolin, & Reiss, 1987; Wolin, Bennett, Noonan, & Teitelbaum, 1980).

Included in the many types of family rituals are rituals for family boundary changes, such as when a child is born, when someone gets married, or when a family member dies. When family boundaries are *not* clear, the family identity is challenged. This usually increases strain and adds to the pileup of demands in the family. Boss's (1987, 1988) work on boundary ambiguity is particularly relevant to this second level of family meanings. When there is incongruence between a family member's physical presence and psychological presence, the resultant ambiguity increases family stress because the boundary about who is "in" the family and who is "out" is unclear. Families experiencing chronic illness are particularly vulnerable to this kind of boundary ambiguity. For example, the birth of a premature infant who spends many months in a neonatal, intensive care unit is an example of psychological presence in the family system but with physical absence, which may be exacerbated even further by uncertainty about the infant's survival. Another example related to functional loss associated with some disabilities is the person who is cognitively impaired or demented. For example, is a person with Alzheimer's disease, who is physically present but psychologically absent, "in" or "out" of the family system? Our point here is that chronic illness or disability can and usually does have a significant impact on a family's identity, usually challenging an old identity and calling for something new.

Rituals and routines provide some sense of stability as well as an identity for a family, and they can serve to provide a kind of anchoring point and a sense of balance when stressful events happen that call for changes in the family system. Steinglass and his colleagues (Gonzalez, Steinglass, & Reiss, 1989; Reiss, Steinglass, & Howe, 1993; Steinglass & Horan, 1987) have emphasized how chronic illness can disrupt normal family regulatory processes, such as routines and rituals. In an effort to meet the demands associated with the chronic illness, for example, a different diet, home therapies, activity restrictions, and valued aspects of family life may be altered significantly or even given up. Families that have children with cystic fibrosis are asked to follow a daily routine of aerosol treatments, bronchial drainage treatments, exercise, special diet, and medications, which can take as long as 2 to 4 hours a day (Patterson, 1985). Such demands have a way of "taking over the family" and, in so doing, giving the family an identity as a "cystic fibrosis family." This kind of family reorganization around an illness often has negative implications for the course of development of all family members, including the child with the illness, as well as the course of development of the family unit (Reiss et al., 1993). For example, can a child whose family's organization and identity is based primarily on his or her illness ever leave home?

In her research on family caregiving, Garwick (1991; Garwick, Detzner, & Boss, 1994) found that each family had a unique construction of the reality of living with a member in the early stages of Alzheimer's disease. The disease clearly disrupted the fabric of everyday life in these families. In listening to the family talk together about this impact, it was possible to identify a family's meaning about the experience and a sense of its own changed identity in relation to it.

A family system also establishes a role structure for accomplishing basic tasks, for example, earning the family income, child care, meal preparation, and household maintenance. Families vary in how segregated (each gender performing separate roles) or egalitarian (both genders share most roles) they are. When the family boundaries expand to include a new member or contract when someone leaves home or dies, these roles often have to be renegotiated. Similarly, the diagnosis of a chronic illness often calls for role changes.

In our study of families with a medically fragile child (Patterson & Leonard, 1994), many mothers had to leave the work force totally or partially to care for their sick child. In many instances, this led to fathers working longer hours to earn more income and/or to assure job security. In other words, bringing the child home led to reorganization in the family's roles and rules, which then impacted how the family defined itself. This family definition of itself, which we call the family identity, is more stable than level-one situational meanings of stressors and capabilities, but it, too, can change over time.

Level Three: Family World View

At the third level of family meaning, the focus is on the family members' orientation toward the world outside of the family: how they interpret reality, what their core assumptions are about their environment, as well as their existential beliefs, such as the family's purpose in life. This is the most abstract of the three levels of meaning, and most families probably would not be able to describe their world view if asked. Our method for learning about the variability in family world views has been through qualitative analysis of the language used in conjoint family interviews where family members talk with each other about issues of consequence to them, such as a member's chronic illness and its impact on their lives. Because we are referring to a *family world view*, our emphasis is on an orientation and meanings that the family shares as a collective.

Our conceptualization of family world view has been influenced by the work of several theorists who have focused on this global orientation as a way to explain what helps persons adapt to or manage challenging circumstances in life. The construct of world view has been applied to persons, to families, and to cultures, recognizing that the views of each system are in part shaped by the larger context in which it is embedded.

At the individual level, Antonovsky (1979, 1987) has suggested that a *sense of coherence* is a personal trait associated with better individual health. He defined coherence as "the pervasive, enduring, though dynamic feeling of confidence that internal and external environments are predictable and there is a high probability that things will work out as well as can reasonably be expected" (Antonovsky, 1979, p. 123). Three dimensions underlie a sense of coherence: meaningfulness, manageability, and comprehensibility (Antonovsky, 1987). In a similar vein, Kobasa, Maddi, and Kahn (1982) have identified personal *hardiness* as a trait of individuals who adapt better to stress. The hardy personality shows commitment to life, willingness to take on challenges, and a belief in personal control of circumstances.

Ransom, Fisher, and Terry (1992) have applied the worldview construct to the family system, focusing on its relationship to individual health outcomes in parents. Eight dimensions of world view were included in their self-report assessment: optimism, religiousness, life engagement, child-adult separateness, child-centeredness, chance locus of control, powerful others locus of control, and internal locus of control. They found that family optimism and family religiousness were positively associated with good emotional health in parents, and a locus of control emphasizing chance or powerful others was negatively associated with emotional health.

It is Reiss's (1981) family paradigm construct that is most consistent with our conceptualization of family world view. His emphasis is on the *collective* family's world view as opposed to any one individual's report about the family's world view. His research group has reported that individuals engage in different problem-solving strategies (indicative of their paradigm) if they are solving problems with the whole family compared to solving problems alone (Reiss & Oliveri, 1980; Reiss, Oliveri, & Curd, 1983). According to Reiss, there are three dimensions to the family paradigm: configuration or a sense of mastery, coordination of effort with other family members, and closure or the degree of openness to new information.

In an earlier article, Patterson (1988) observed the similarity in the dimensions of world view identified by each of the four theoretical approaches discussed here, and suggested that there appeared to be five dimensions underlying their combined work: (1) shared purpose—having a shared ideology; (2) collectivity—seeing the family as part of something larger than itself; (3) frameability—optimism that is grounded in reality; (4) relativism—living in the context of present circumstances; and (5) shared control—balancing internal control with trust in others. Each dimension represents a continuum along which a family could vary from low to high. Support for these five dimensions of world view has been reported from our study of families who have a child that is medically fragile (Patterson, 1993). For example, these families reported a greater commitment to life and to working for the needs of those with disabilities (shared purpose). They felt stronger connections within the family unit and with the health team and people in their community as they managed their child's needs (collectivity). They developed a new outlook on life, valuing their strengths and what they had (frameability). They lived more in the present and were more flexible (relativism). They realized they had less control over life than they thought; they learned to let go and trust others, and became more aware of a higher power (shared control). At the same time, parents talked about taking responsibility for managing their child's care and for teaching him or her how to take age-appropriate responsibility for his or her own care.

A family's world view has its roots in the culture of which the family is part. For example, the dimension we have called "shared control" varies considerably among different cultural groups. In the US, the cultural experience of most Americans of European descent is one that values taking charge, being independent, and having a high sense of being personally able to control life circumstances. This orientation is associated with the opportunity to experience self-efficacy and mastery. Hence, a belief and value of taking charge is part of the world view for many middle and upper-class American families. In contrast, in less developed countries where social conditions preclude the same kind of opportunity, there may be a more fatalistic, passive orientation to control. In India, for example, there is a predominant spiritual orientation called "karma," which leads to an acceptance of one's circumstances as God's will. How well one accepts one's place is believed to influence whether one is reincarnated into a higher caste in the next life. Antonovsky's (1979, 1987) sense-of-coherence concept is somewhere between these two extremes. Evidence for a sense of coherence as a critical component of an individual's orientation to life originally emerged through interviews with Holocaust victims, who were able not only to survive torture and dehumanizing living conditions, but also were able to move on to loving, productive, and successful lives (Antonovsky, 1979). Culture, in and of itself, does not determine world view. Within any cultural group, there is still wide variation, which is influenced by the experiences of life. Thus, a family's world view evolves from shared experience. Major stressful events have the potential to change this world view, sometimes in dramatic ways.

CHANGING FAMILY MEANINGS

Clearly these three levels of meaning are interrelated. World view includes an orientation, values, and beliefs that influence how relationships are structured. Thus, world view influences the formation of the family identity. Both family identity and world view will influence how a given situation is viewed. And moving in the other direction, a newly experienced event, especially one that is more severe, disastrous, or victimizing, is likely to lead to changed relationship structures and changes in the family world view.

Several theorists have articulated a meaning-making process that evolves from disastrous events experienced by individuals. Janoff-Bulman and Frieze's (1983) assumptive worldview perspective holds that persons see the world as benevolent and meaningful and the self as worthwhile. Disastrous events shatter this world view, which must be rebuilt to incorporate the negative event. In contrast, Taylor (1983) argues that persons who experience disastrous events adapt by selectively distorting negative views of self, relationships, and the world as a way to reduce the threat; in doing so, they build illusions containing

meaning, mastery, and self-enhancing cognitions. Thompson and Janigian (1988) propose a life-scheme framework that provides a sense of order and purpose in life. When negative events challenge the life scheme, persons search for new meanings and purpose and challenge their life scheme.

What evidence is there that families engage in a similar search for meaning? In our research with families of infants with chronic conditions, parents often report that their expectations for themselves, their children, and their futures change when they discover that their child has a chronic illness or disability (Garwick, Patterson, Blum, & Bennett, 1993). For example, parents who expect a "perfectly healthy" baby are challenged to incorporate not only a new member into the family, but the chronic condition as well. Parents often report feeling shocked to learn that their newborn has a chronic illness, especially when there is no family history and the pregnancy has been uneventful. The family's world view influences how parents react to the news that their child has a health problem. For instance, parents with a mastery orientation who have deliberately taken measures to provide for the health of the child (through prenatal care and avoiding risk factors such as cigarettes, drugs, and alcohol) may struggle to find a "just" reason for their child's disability. As parents adjust to living with a chronic condition, they often report that their own personal experiences change their attitudes and orientations toward persons with disabilities.

As described, individuals come to hold a set of beliefs and assumptions about the meaning and purpose of life, about how relationships should be structured, and about ways to interpret experienced stimuli from their collective experience in social groups, particularly the family. When a couple begins dating, and particularly when they move toward marriage, the partners begin to forge a new shared belief system and pattern of interacting that represents what they each bring from their earlier life experience, primarily from their families of origin (Wamboldt & Reiss, 1989; Wamboldt & Wolin, 1988). Over time and through shared experience, they develop a family identity that influences their structure (who is in the family) and functioning. The family develops shared rules about relationships to coordinate their interaction patterns. Using language and a process of interpolation (one member fills in what is missing for another) and extrapolation (generalizing from one experience to a similar one), the family develops shared meanings and expectations (Reiss, 1981). The regulatory process that emerges reduces uncertainty and maintains stability of relationships within and outside the family.

At the beginning of a relationship, there is likely to be some consensus about core values and existential beliefs comprising an orientation to life, which, over time and through shared experience, emerges as a shared set of assumptions and a family orientation to the world. How much is shared or a true property of the group versus what is unique to individual family members is influenced by the implicit rules of relationship about how much members need to agree. In some families, individuality is highly valued, and they agree to disagree. In other families, the implicit rule is that all must agree. Reiss (1981) calls the latter "consensus-sensitive" families and the former "distance-sensitive" families. As already indicated, this rule about how much the family needs to see "eye to eye" changes normatively over the life cycle. For example, families with adolescents are often challenged to incorporate new views of life, relationships, and risks. Some families respond by insisting on greater consensus as a way to insure the safe passage of their adolescent children into adulthood. Other families may relax some of their rules and even change some of their views as a way to facilitate the adolescent's development of his or her own identity. In addition to normative life-cycle transitions, families construct new meanings when major, nonnormative life events occur. The diagnosis of chronic illness or disability in a family member is a prime example.

Chronic Illness and Level-One Meanings

In many instances, the diagnosis of chronic illness happens suddenly and unexpectedly. A first reaction may be one of disbelief or denial. This is an example of how someone else's situational definition of an event (such as the doctor's) doesn't fit the family's definition of itself (for example, children are supposed to be healthy, grow up to be independent, and live longer than parents) or perhaps the family's world view (for example, we should be able to control what happens to us if we live right and work hard). Family members search for a cause— "Why did this happen?" Their present world view and their family identity will likely influence the definition they give this stressor—"We are being punished for our misdeeds"; "The doctors made a mistake"; "You didn't take care of yourself during the pregnancy."

In addition to interpretations about what caused the disease, the family also will have or develop expectations about who is responsible for managing the illness. These two aspects of locus of control have been referred to as the locus of cause and the locus of consequence (Patterson, 1989b). This is an example of the family world view influencing the situational definition of a stressor event. A family's orientation may vary from internal control, to external control via chance, to external control via powerful others (Levenson, 1981; Ransom et al., 1992). This orientation about control has implications for behavioral compliance with treatment regimens and the relationship families develop with health providers. Belief in chance may result in marginal connections to the health care system. Belief in powerful others may lead to searches for cures or to passivity in managing disease processes. High internal control may lead to more active management.

Chronic Illness and Level-Two Meanings

The second level of meaning, the family's identity, also is affected by the presence of illness or disability. Normal family regulatory processes are disrupted (Gonzalez et al., 1989; Reiss et al., 1993; Steinglass & Horan, 1987). Routines for managing the illness tasks, role reallocations, and rule changes need to be developed. Disruption of the family's organizational structure may precipitate a crisis, which is defined as persistent disruptiveness when the family's old structural organization is no longer adequate to meet the new demands (Patterson, 1988, 1989a). The nature of the change called for is at the second meaning level where rules of relationship need to be changed. In the FAAR Model, this has been referred to as the adaptation phase, that is, where second-order structural change in the family system is called for (Patterson, 1988, 1989a). The way in which the family restructures itself to accommodate the illness demands may have an impact on the family's identity and sense of purpose in life. It has been emphasized that in some families faced with chronic illness, there may be a tendency to direct a disproportionate share of their resources toward the illness needs, reducing resources needed for normative family needs (Gonzalez et al., 1989; Reiss et al., 1993). This skew can lead to a family illness identity—"the diabetic family" versus the family who has a diabetic member. It is possible, of course, that one parent may orient this way, making the child with chronic illness the central focus, while the other parent resists, trying to maintain more balance in family functioning. In this latter example, when the parents' orientations diverge, they could change their relationship identity and agree to disagree and have less coordinated family behavior. Or this divergence in relationship rules could extend to other values and beliefs, perhaps an inability to agree on a family relationship identity, and ultimately result in the dissolution of the family system. In essence, family breakdown and dissolution occurs when family members can no longer agree sufficiently on the rules for their relationship. The structure becomes uncoupled and two separate family units result.

Or the opposite may occur and the family system restructures in a way that makes it stronger. It is a principle of physics that in order to "harden" steel, you place stress on it. Families, too, may be strengthened by learning to cope with adversity. In our sample of families with a medically fragile child, it was striking how frequently parents reported that having and caring for this child pulled their family unit together and made them stronger (Patterson & Leonard, 1994). This response may reflect the processes of coping and adaptation via shared social construing described in this article.

Chronic Illness and Level-Three Meanings

Disastrous events shatter expectations and goals and even world views. Uncertainty and ambiguity result. Individuals turn to their significant others in search of emotional comfort and explanation for what is happening. A loss of a sense of personal control leads to joining more closely with others. Steinglass and Horan (1987) report that families often pull together—giving up individual world views for a shared one.

The process of restructuring the family is often associated with changes in the family's orientation to those outside of the family, and to life itself. Most children with chronic illnesses or disabilities need an array of specialized services, often including education and social services as well as health services. Learning about the child's health and education needs, finding services to meet these needs, determining eligibility, determining who will pay and for how long is a laborious, confusing process for many families. A lack of clear information, discrepant information from different professionals, getting the "run around," being discounted "as only a parent," are all experiences parents describe that may lead to cynicism, a lack of trust in "powerful others," or to a commitment to "do something about the system." Some parents become attuned to the injustices of health policies and eventually join together with other families to advocate for change. The uncertainty inherent in many chronic illnesses is particularly challenging for many families (Jessop & Stein, 1985) and, for some, it leads to a stronger orientation to live in the present because the future is too uncertain. Goals for life achievement (career, possessions, travel) may become redirected toward revaluing simpler, more basic experiences (a smile, a flower in bloom, a quiet evening).

Some families experience stigmatization and isolation within their communities. This marginalizing experience may lead to a new view of community. Families report that they learn who their "real" friends are. Others find a new or renewed commitment to religious beliefs as a way to accept what cannot be explained. Cultural, religious, and spiritual beliefs shape the world views held by families. Community attitudes and beliefs about chronic illness and disability influence the meanings that families attribute to their situation. Parents who find that their religious and neighborhood communities welcome their child despite his or her impairments often report feeling supported by these groups. In addition, parents often report that positive attitudes and beliefs in the community (inclusion and acceptance of differences) facilitate their adjustment to the chronic condition. In contrast, parents who encounter negative attitudes and beliefs struggle to make sense of the situation and feel isolated from their communities.

Culture is powerful in influencing and shaping the world view held by families. Persons with chronic illness or disability and their family members acknowledge that there is a culture of disability that is separate from mainstream culture (Patterson & Blum, 1993). Many families living with chronic illness or disability find their way into this culture, or at least feel its influence. Part of the coping process involves enlarging the context: "We are not just a family that has a member with a disease, but a family with a history, an identity, and values that has a member with a disease, and we live in relationships with significant others and in a world where others have this disease too."

Relationship Between Meanings, Behaviors and Emotions

It is in the domains of meaning (cognition), behavior, and emotion that change occurs—changes in behaviors (actively living with and managing the illness); changes in emotions as the work of grieving takes place; changes in beliefs about self, relationships, work, and priorities; and even changes about the meaning of life. Whether changes in meaning precede behavioral change or vice versa varies across individuals and circumstances. There are schools of therapy emphasizing one versus the other (for example, cognitive-behavioral therapy emphasizes behavioral changes as a way to change beliefs, while constructivists focus on meanings as a way to change behavior). Acknowledging and facing emotional reactions are also critical to this process of change in behaviors and meanings. In our study of families with a medically fragile child (Patterson & Leonard, 1994), one explanation for the change in the meaning and purpose of life reported by parents is that they may have needed a world view that would be consonant with the reality of their behavioral and emotional investment in their child. There would be too much cognitive dissonance for parents to spend time and energy caring for a medically fragile child if they viewed this as an investment in an undesirable person or set of circumstances.

Another observation about the coping and adaptation process in families who have a medically fragile child is that families experienced real limits in how much they could change their situation. In other words, coping by reducing demands had its limits because they wanted their child at home, and that meant an ongoing set of chronic care demands had to be managed. Coping by increasing resources also had its limits, primarily because of policies that limited the amount and kind of service provided, and because there were limits on who would pay for these services. Parents and families were left with coping by changing the way they thought about their situation—about their child and themselves. This led to changes in their definitions of relationships and to changes in their world views.

CONCLUSIONS

The process of family adaptation to stressful life events is strongly influenced by meaning making. Stress and coping scholars like Richard Lazarus (Lazarus, 1966; Lazarus & Folkman, 1984) have long emphasized the importance of appraisal of the situation in coping with stress. However, it is our view that families adapting to *chronic* stress go deeper into this meaning-making process. In addition to situational meanings, their view of themselves as a family and their world view influence how they adapt to stress. In turn, these three levels of family meaning may be changed by the process of adaptation. Family meanings have implications for clinicians working with families who have a member with chronic illness and for researchers studying family adaptation to chronic illness.

Implications for Clinical Work

Three premises regarding family meanings underlie recommendations for clinicians working with families living with chronic illness. First, the meaning of an event influences behavioral responses to that event. Second, meanings can be changed by the very act of responding to an event. Third, meaning is a social construction. Adapting to chronic illness is a process that evolves over time, during which meanings, behaviors, and emotions reciprocally influence each other. Furthermore, these interactions between meanings, behaviors, and emotions happen in the social context of the family. One way clinicians can facilitate better patient and family adaptation to chronic illness is to pay more attention to the meaning-making process and support patients and their families in making these processes more explicit and hopefully more adaptive. Family attributions about the causes and consequences of illness (situational meanings) often set a kind of trajectory for family response over time. Working with families to develop shared situational meanings that reduce guilt and blame and that include shared responsibility for managing the condition are most adaptive. Early interventionists working with children and families with special needs emphasize the importance of family empowerment as a way to strengthen the competence of the family, and this family sense of mastery ultimately benefits the child (Dunst, Trivette, & Deal, 1988). From our theoretical perspective, this would be an example of constructing situational meanings that increase family capabilities. Empowerment is also consistent with the increasing emphasis on resilience in individuals and families. Clinicians promote resilience when they attend to family strengths and resources at least as much as (and preferably more than) they do to their problems or deficits.

At the second level of family meanings, clinicians should support the family in developing an identity that keeps both the illness and the family unit in balance. In other words, structuring family roles, rules, routines, and rituals in a way that allows for normal developmental processes in families to continue, while simultaneously incorporating the illness-related needs, promotes better health outcomes for all family members. This kind of family balance is one of the major themes in the multiple family discussion group protocol developed by Steinglass and his colleagues (Gonzalez et al., 1989). As mentioned earlier, there is a growing awareness of the importance of family routines and rituals for the maintenance of healthy family functioning (Bennett et al., 1988; Imber-Black et al., 1988). Clinicians can be instrumental in supporting families to develop and maintain rituals that support their values and their sense of who they are. In addition, clinicians working with the whole family are more likely to learn how illness needs may have skewed family process, thereby sacrificing the needs of other family members and the family as a whole. One way that clinicians may inadvertently undermine family identity is

when they myopically focus only on the illness needs and become overly directive in telling the family that they "must" adhere to all aspects of treatment regimens. Overly compliant families may lose their sense of integrity and their identity as they let others take over more and more domains of their family life. This was a particularly salient issue in our study of medically fragile children who often had professional caregivers in their homes for one or more 8-hour shifts a day. Home care has the potential of invading family life. Relationships with professionals was one of the major sources of strain for these families and was associated with high levels of parental distress (Patterson & Leonard, 1994).

A clinician who is aware that a family's world view may also be changed in the process of adapting to chronic illness can support this need by connecting the family with community resources that will empower the family and provide validation for its views and values. In addition, the clinician should be challenged to be respectful of the family's choices and behaviors—which may not be congruent with his or her own—such as its changed priorities, assertiveness with service providers, or advocating for policy changes. Rolland (1993), in his model of working with families experiencing chronic and life-threatening illness, has emphasized the importance of the family's belief system and how it may be discrepant with the belief system of those providing services. Understanding a family's world view is particularly important in the provision of culturally competent care. As we strive to understand more about the health care needs and preferences of persons of color and of different ethnic beliefs, clinicians must pay more attention to the role of world view in shaping family responses to chronic illness and disability (Groce & Zola, 1993).

Future Research Directions

There is a need for more empirical studies to further our understanding of these levels of family meanings, particularly with families of diverse cultural, ethnic, and racial backgrounds. Much of this research will call for qualitative methods because of the subjective nature of meaning making. Careful attention also needs to be given to the development of standardized measures for assessing family meanings so that the relationship of family meanings to health outcomes and other outcomes of interest can be assessed with large samples.

Particularly important are studies in which the total family system is the unit of analysis. For example, David Reiss and his colleagues measure the family paradigm with the card sort procedure. Family members, as a unit, are asked to do a laboratory problem-solving task, and their score is derived directly from their interaction (Reiss, 1981). In our research, we have used audiotaped, conjoint family interviews, and qualitative procedures to analyze the language of the total family system. These two methods are examples of what Ransom (1986) has called Type III family data in his classification of different methods for operationalizing family variables. In contrast, his Type II measures are obtained from individual family member self-report data about the family. Relational scores can be obtained by combining two or more family members' self-reports, but this procedure is still distinct from an outsider's observations of family interaction in a naturalistic or laboratory setting (Ransom, 1986).

We need more longitudinal studies in which the natural processes by which families change meanings in response to the diagnosis and presence of chronic illness can be understood as well as how the different levels of meanings are related. In addition, studies of the relationship between meanings at the different levels and outcomes of interest need to be expanded. The work of Ransom et al. (1992), relating the world view of a sample of parents to health outcomes, is one such example. Another example is the work of Reiss, Gonzalez, and Kramer (1986) who have examined the relationship between the family paradigm and mortality in persons with end-stage renal disease.

Intervention studies designed to support families in the development of meanings that contribute to healthy adaptation to chronic illness also are needed. The protocol developed by Gonzalez et al. (1989) for a multiple family discussion group in which maintenance of a family's chosen identity is emphasized needs to be tested in clinical trials to determine its effectiveness.

Families are complex social units that vary widely in their adaptive capacities. One of the challenges social scientists face is to extend our understanding

by describing the range of this variability. One of the most interesting questions still facing us is why some families develop positive, adaptive beliefs and meanings and others do not. Further studies are needed to understand how families share and construct meanings about illness and disability. In addition to continuing to build family stress theory, such findings would contribute to improved practices in working with families who are adapting to chronic stress, particularly the presence of disability or chronic illness.

NOTE

1. *Family* should be thought of in the broadest possible sense as that group of persons with whom one shares a bond of connection by virtue of blood, marriage, adoption, or long-term commitment. Any person is likely to have membership in more than one family over the life course. For example, we are born into a family of origin; we create a new family of procreation at the time of marriage; and maybe create a stepfamily at the time of remarriage, and so on. In the case of chronic illness and disability, it is also quite probable that a *caregiving family* may emerge that is distinct from and separate from these other families. The prevalence of AIDS in our society has taught us that persons marginalized from others by virtue of their illness may, in fact, form new bonds of commitment that should be included in any definition of family. Our point here is that most people have several families, and the discussion that follows is relevant to the widest definition of family structure.

REFERENCES

Antonovsky, A. (1979). *Health, stress, and coping.* San Francisco: Jossey-Bass.

——— (1987). *Unraveling the mystery of health: How people manage stress and stay well.* San Francisco: Jossey-Bass.

Bennett, L. A., Wolin, S. J., & McAvity, K. J. (1988). Family identity, ritual, and myth: A cultural perspective on lifecycle transitions (pp. 211-234). In C. J. Falicov (ed.), *Family transitions: Continuity and change over the life cycle.* New York: Guilford Press.

Bennett, L. A., Wolin, S. J., Reiss, D., & Teitelbaum, M. A. (1987). Couples at risk for the transmission of alcoholism: Protective influences. *Family Process 26:* 111-129.

Berger, P. L., & Luckmann, T. (1966). *The social construction of reality*. New York: Doubleday.

Boss, P. G. (1977). A clarification of the concept of psychological father presence in families experiencing ambiguity of boundary. *Journal of Marriage and the Family 39:* 141-151.

——— (1987). Family stress (pp. 695-723). In M. B. Sussman & S. Steinmetz (eds.), *Handbook of marriage and the family*. New York: Plenum Press.

——— (1988). *Family stress management*. Newbury Park CA: Sage Publications.

Bossard, J., & Boll, E. (1950). *Ritual in family living*. Philadelphia: University of Pennsylvania Press.

Dell, P. F. (1985). Understanding Bateson and Maturana: Toward a biological foundation for the social sciences. *Journal of Marital and Family Therapy 11:* 1-20.

Dunst, C., Trivette, C., & Deal, A. (1988). *Enabling and empowering families: Principles and guidelines for practice*. Cambridge MA: Brookline Books.

Garwick, A. (1991). Shared family perceptions of life with dementia of the Alzheimer's type. Doctoral dissertation, University of Minnesota. *Dissertation Abstracts International*, 5205A, 1098.

Garwick, A., Detzner, D., & Boss, P. (1994). Family perceptions of living with Alzheimer's disease. *Family Process 33:* 327-340.

Garwick, A., Patterson, J. M., Blum, R., & Bennett, F. C. (1993). Family caregivers' perceptions of Down syndrome versus congenital heart disease. Poster presentation at conference on "Physical Illness, Psychologic Development and How the Twain Shall Meet," Keystone CO, June.

Gonzalez, S., Steinglass, P., & Reiss, D. (1989). Putting the illness in its place: Discussion groups for families with chronic medical illnesses. *Family Process 28:* 69-87.

Groce, N. E., & Zola, I. K. (1993). Multiculturalism, chronic illness, and disability. *Pediatrics 91:* 1048-1055.

Hill, R. (1949). *Families under stress*. New York: Harper.

——— (1958). Generic features of families under stress. *Social Casework 49:* 139-150.

Imber-Black, E., Roberts, J., & Whiting, R. (eds.). (1988). *Rituals in families and family therapy*. New York: W. W. Norton.

Janoff-Bulman, R., & Frieze, I. H. (1983). A theoretical perspective for understanding reactions to victimization. *Journal of Social Issues 39:* 1-17.

Jessop, D. J., & Stein, R. E. K. (1985). Uncertainty and its relation to the psychological and social correlates of chronic illness in children. *Social Science and Medicine 20:* 993-999.

Kobasa, S., Maddi, S., & Kahn, S. (1982). Hardiness and health: A prospective study. *Journal of Personality and Social Psychology 42:* 168-177.

Lazarus, R. S. (1966). *Psychological stress and the coping process*. New York: McGraw-Hill.

Lazarus, R. S., & Folkman, S. (1984). *Stress, appraisal, and coping*. New York: Springer Publishing Co.

Levenson, H. (1981). Differentiating among internality, powerful others, and change (pp. 15-63). In H. Lefcourt (ed.), *Research with the locus of control construct. Vol. 1: Assessment methods*. New York: Academic Press.

McCubbin, H. I., & Patterson, J. M. (1982). Family adaptation to crises (pp. 26-47). In H. I. McCubbin, A. E. Cauble, & J. M. Patterson (eds.), *Family stress, coping, and social support*. Springfield IL: Charles C. Thomas.

——— (1983a). Family stress and adaptation to crises: A double ABCX model of family behavior (pp. 87-106). In D. H. Olson & B. C. Miller (eds.), *Family studies review yearbook* (Vol. 1). Beverly Hills CA: Sage Publications.

——— (1983b). The family stress process: The double ABCX model of family adjustment and adaptation. *Marriage and Family Review 6:* 7-37.

Patterson, J. M. (1993). The role of family meanings in adaptation to chronic illness and disability (pp. 221-238). In A. D. Turnbull, J. M. Patterson, S. K. Behr, et al. (eds.). *Cognitive coping research and developmental disabilities*. Baltimore: Paul Brookes.

Patterson, J. M. (1985). Critical factors affecting family compliance with home treatment for children with cystic fibrosis. *Family Relations 34:* 79-89.

——— (1988). Families experiencing stress. *Family Systems Medicine 6:* 202-237.

——— (1989a). The family stress model: The family adjustment and adaptation response (pp. 95-118). In C. N. Ramsey, Jr. (ed.), *Family systems in medicine*. New York: Guilford Press.

——— (1989b). Illness beliefs as a factor in patient-spouse adaptation to treatment for coronary artery disease. *Family Systems Medicine 7:* 428-442.

Patterson, J. M., & Blum, R. (1993). A conference on culture and chronic illness in childhood: Conference summary. *Pediatrics 91:* 1025-1030.

Patterson, J. M., Budd, J., Goetz, D., & Warwick, W. (1993). Family correlates of a ten-year pulmonary health trend in cystic fibrosis. *Pediatrics 91:* 383-389.

Patterson, J. M., & Leonard, B. J. (1994). Caregiving and children (pp. 133-158). In E. Kahana, D. E. Biegel, & M. Wykle (eds.), *Family caregiving across the life span*. Newbury Park CA: Sage Publications.

Patterson, J. M., Leonard, B. J., & Titus, J. M. (1992). Home care for medically fragile children: Impact on family health and well-being. *Developmental and Behavioral Pediatrics 13:* 248-255.

Patterson, J. M., McCubbin, H. I., & Warwick, W. (1990). The impact of family functioning on health changes in children with cystic fibrosis. *Social Science and Medicine 31:* 159-164.

Ransom, D. C. (1986). Research on the family in health, illness and care—State of the art. *Family Systems Medicine 4:* 329-336.

Ransom, D. C., Fisher, L., & Terry, H. E. (1992). The California family health project: II. Family world view and adult health. *Family Process 31:* 251-267.

Reiss, D. (1981). *The family's construction of reality.* Cambridge: Harvard University Press.

——— (1989). The represented and practicing family: Contrasting visions of family continuity (pp. 191-220). In A. Sameroff & R. Emde (eds.), *Relationship disturbances in early childhood: A developmental approach.* New York: Basic Books.

Reiss, D., Gonzalez, S., & Kramer, N. (1986). Family process, chronic illness, and death: On the weakness of strong bonds. *Archives of General Psychiatry 43:* 795-804.

Reiss, D., & Oliveri, M. E. (1980). Family paradigm and family coping: A proposal for linking the family's intrinsic adaptive capacities to its responses to stress. *Family Relations 29:* 431-444.

Reiss, D., Oliveri, M. E., & Curd, K. (1983). Family paradigm and adolescent social behavior (pp. 77-92). In H. Grotevant & C. Cooper (eds.), *Adolescent behavior in the family: New directions for child development.* San Francisco: Jossey-Bass.

Reiss, D., Steinglass, P., & Howe, G. (1993). The family's organization around the illness (pp. 173-213). In R. Cole & D. Reiss (eds.), *How do families cope with chronic illness?* Hillsdale NJ: Lawrence Erlbaum Associates.

Rolland, J. S. (1993). Mastering family challenges in serious illness and disability (pp. 444-473). In F. Walsh (ed.), *Normal family processes* (2nd ed.). New York: Guilford Press.

Steinglass, P., Bennett, L. A., Wolin, S. J., & Reiss, D. (1987). *The alcoholic family.* New York: Basic Books.

Steinglass, P., & Horan, M. (1987). Families and chronic medical illness. *Journal of Psychopathology and the Family 3:* 127-142.

Taylor, S. (1983). Adjustment to threatening events: A theory of cognitive adaptation. *American Psychologist 38:* 624-630.

Thompson, S., & Janigian, A. (1988). Life schemes: A framework for understanding the search for meaning. *Journal of Social and Clinical Psychology 7:* 260-280.

Wamboldt, F. S., & Reiss, D. (1989). Defining a family heritage and a new relationship identity: Two central tasks in the making of a marriage. *Family Process 28:* 317-335.

Wamboldt, F. S., & Wolin, S. J. (1988). Reality and myth in family life: Changes across generations. *Journal of Psychotherapy & the Family 4:* 141-165.

Weisz, J. R., Rothbaum, F. M., & Blackburn, T. C. (1984). Standing out and standing in: The psychology of control in America and Japan. *American Psychologist 39:* 955-969.

Wolin, S. J., & Bennett, L. A. (1984). Family rituals. *Family Process 23:* 401-420.

Wolin, S. J., Bennett, L. A., Noonan, D., & Teitelbaum, M. (1980). Disrupted family rituals: A factor in the intergenerational transmission of alcoholism. *Journal of Studies in Alcoholism 41:* 199-214.

PART 2

MODELS AND THEORIES

Articles in Part 2 were selected to stimulate critical thinking in preparation for new directions for research-based theory development. I refer you to *Family Stress Management* (*FSM*) for an explanation of the contextual model of family stress (Boss, 2002). Included here is an article representing a competing model, the Double ABCX, and its testing (Lavee, McCubbin, & Patterson, 1985). Using a military sample, Lavee and his colleagues found support for the idea of stress pileup and for the importance of appraisal. It is noteworthy that since the 1985 test of the Double ABCX model, these researchers shifted to a focus on meaning, appraisal, or coherence. Might it be that complex models and sophisticated analyses cannot elicit the deeper essence of what stress and coping *mean* to people? To enhance your critical thinking about meaning and perceptions, we also include a series of interdisciplinary discussions about integrating family stress theory and measurement around negative family stressors such as loss. Stress-resistant attributes (resources) are discussed, leading us once again to think of resilience. Psychologists Hobfoll and Spielberger (1992) present their conservation of resource theory. Boss (1992) in family social science and family therapy and Kazak (1992) in pediatric oncology respond. Hobfoll and Spielberger (1992) get the last word. There is considerable discussion about "perception" and its centrality in family stress management. How much does perception matter? The answer is debated.

If this collection of articles on models and theories raises more questions for you than it answers, that was intended. Innovative ideas about theories and measurement are more likely to emerge during times of questioning.

In addition, we also recommend reading Crystal L. Park and Susan Folkman's (1997) article, "Meaning in the Context of Stress and Coping."

REFERENCES

Boss, P. (2002). *Family stress management* (2nd ed.). Thousand Oaks, CA: Sage.

Park, C. L., & Folkman, S. (1997). Meaning in the context of stress and coping. *Review of General Psychology, 1*(2), 115-144.

9

THE DOUBLE ABCX MODEL OF FAMILY STRESS AND ADAPTATION

An Empirical Test by Analysis of Structural Equations With Latent Variables

YOAV LAVEE
HAMILTON I. MCCUBBIN
JOAN M. PATTERSON

This study examines the relationships among the major variables of the Double ABCX model of family stress and adaptation. The theoretical model is translated into an empirically testable model using data on Army families' adaptation to the crisis of relocation overseas, and the data is analyzed by structural equation models with latent (unobserved) variables. The results support the notion of pile-up of demands, in that previous family life events significantly influence the postcrisis strain. Family system resources and social support are both found to facilitate adaptation, but in different ways: family system resources affect adaptation directly, whereas social support appears to have a buffering role in that it reduces the postcrisis strain. This study demonstrates the applicability of structural equation modeling approach (LISREL VI program) for theory building.

Reprinted from the *Journal of Marriage and the Family,* November 1985, 811-25. Copyright © 1985 by the National Council on Family Relations, 3989 Central Ave. NE, Suite 550, Minneapolis, MN 55421. Reprinted by permission. The research project upon which this study is based—One Thousand Army Families: Strengths, Coping, and Supports—was jointly sponsored and supported by the Department of the Army and the University of Minnesota. The findings presented are those of the authors and do not represent the official viewpoints of the Department of the Army or the University of Minnesota.

123

Efforts to understand and explain family response to stressful situations traditionally have been concentrated on the relations among three basic phenomena: the stressful event(s) and its associated hardships; the outcome of stress (crisis and adaptation); and the intervening factors between the two. The central question is, How much and what kinds of stressors, mediated by what family resources and processes, shape the course and ease of family adaptation?

Review of theory building and empirical studies in the 1970s (McCubbin et al., 1980) and the first half of the 1980s suggest that, parallel to the interest in theory building (e.g., Boss, 1980; Burr, 1973; Hansen and Johnson, 1979; McCubbin and Patterson, 1982, 1983a, 1983b), researchers have studied family processes, the mediating effects of various family resources, coping patterns and perception, and adaptation to both normative transitions and nonnormative events.

In concluding their decade review of family stress and coping literature, McCubbin and associates (1980:866-867) suggest that, "as we increase the number of variables in the family stress equation, we need to develop research paradigms which include techniques such as path analysis, so we can begin to obtain a clearer picture of the ordering of these variables and, in turn, advance theory construction in this area of research."

In response to this challenge, the present investigation was designed to examine the relations among some of the major variables of the Double ABCX model (McCubbin and Patterson, 1982, 1983a, 1983b) by using maximum likelihood analysis of structural equations with latent (unobserved) variables. This statistical approach, while highly compatible with the process of theory development and testing, has been used rarely in family studies. Therefore, we discuss some of its advantages and illustrate its applicability, after briefly presenting the theoretical model to be examined. The theoretical model then is translated into an empirically testable model, and the results are presented and discussed.

THE THEORETICAL MODEL

The Double ABCX model of family stress and adaptation (McCubbin and Patterson, 1982, 1983a, 1983b), shown in Figure 9.1, builds on Hill's (1949, 1958) ABCX model of family stress and crisis. It redefines precrisis variables and adds postcrisis variables in an effort to describe (a) the additional life stressors and strains, prior to or following the crisis-producing event, which result in a pile-up of demands; (b) the range of outcome of family processes in response to this pile-up of stressors (maladaptation to bonadaptation); and (c) the intervening factors that shape the course of adaptation: family resources, coherence and meaning, and the related coping strategies.

Pile-up (the aA Factor)

The pile-up of demands refers to the cumulative effect, over time, of pre- and postcrisis stressors and strains. Mechanic (1974) and Hansen and Johnson (1979) have suggested that stress be viewed as a process, a complex set of changing conditions that have a history and future, rather than a short-term, single stimulus. The clustering effect of normative and nonnormative events also has been noted by others (e.g., Hill and Joy, 1979; Mederer and Hill, 1983; Patterson and McCubbin, 1983). Additional stressors—such as required role changes, prior unresolved strains, intrafamily boundary ambiguity (Boss, 1977, 1980)—all may be demands for change and sources of strain that the family faces while struggling with the major stressor event.

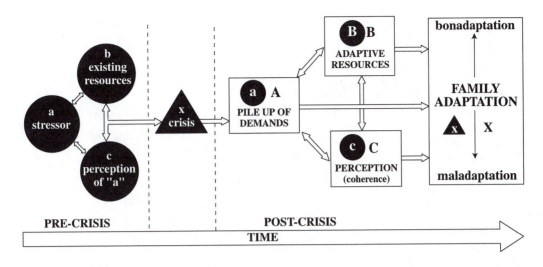

Figure 9.1   The Double ABCX Model
SOURCE: Adapted from McCubbin and Patterson (1983a).

Family Adaptive Resources (the bB Factor)

Adaptive resources refer both to existing resources and to expanded resources that are developed and strengthened in response to the demands posed by the stressor event. These resources mediate between the pile-up of demands and adaptation. As such, they can either reduce the impact of demands on the family and/or help the family adapt to the required changes.

Family adaptive resources may include (a) *personal resources*—i.e., characteristics of individual family members such as self-esteem, knowledge, and skills which are potentially available to the family in times of need (George, 1980; Pearlin and Schooler, 1978); (b) *family system resources*—i.e., internal attributes of the family unit such as cohesion, adaptability, and communication (Olson and McCubbin, 1982; Olson et al., 1983); and (c) *social support*—i.e., capabilities of people or institutions outside the family on which the family can draw or a network in which the family is cared for and loved, is esteemed and valued, and where it feels that it belongs (Cobb, 1976, 1979; Pilisuk and Parks, 1981, 1983).

Perception and Coherence (the cC Factor)

This factor refers to the family's general orientation to the overall circumstances. Antonovsky (1979) describes this orientation as the pervasive, enduring, though dynamic feeling of confidence that internal and external environments are predictable. It reflects a sense of acceptance and understanding of the situation, a framework within which definition of the situation is made and within which perceptions are judged. When applied to the family unit (McCubbin and Patterson, 1983a, 1983b), coherence is dynamically influenced by the experiences of the family—both its internal environment (such as perceived strengths) and the cumulative effect of experiences (positive and negative) with the external environment. In turn, it shapes the meaning the family gives to the total crisis situation, including the stressor event, added sources of strain (pile-up), and the resources the family has for meeting the demands. Coherence, then, is an intervening factor between crisis and adaptation and is another facilitator of the family's adaptive power.

Family Adaptation (the xX Factor)

Family adaptation is the outcome of the family's processes in response to the crisis and pile-up of demands. As Burr (1973) notes, adaptation does not mean that disorganization or change in the system have not occurred; it merely means that the system has resumed its routine level of operation after having to cope with change.

Family adaptation is a continuous variable, ranging from maladaptation to bonadaptation (McCubbin and Patterson, 1983a, 1983b). Maladaptation, the negative end of the continuum, is defined as continued imbalance between the pile-up of demands and the family's capabilities for meeting those demands. It may be characterized by deterioration of family integrity, of family members' sense of well-being, and of their physical and/or psychological health. Bonadaptation, the positive end of the continuum, is defined as a minimal discrepancy between the pile-up of demands and the family's capabilities, so as to achieve a balance in family functioning. It is characterized both by maintenance or strengthening of family integrity and by family members' sense of well-being.

The following propositions are derived from the Double ABCX model of family adaptation to stressful situations: (a) the severity of strain associated with a crisis situation is influenced by other sources of demand (stressors and strains) on the family, and this is a positive relationship; (b) the level of adaptation of the family to the crisis situation is influenced by the severity of the pile-up of stressors and strains, and this is a negative relationship; (c) the amount of personal resources, family system resources, and social support the family has influences its adaptation to the pile-up of stressors and strains, and this is a positive relationship; (d) the amount of personal resources, family system resources, and social support influences the severity of strain created by the pile-up of demands, and this is a negative relationship; and (e) the level of the family's sense of coherence regarding the total situation (demands and capabilities) influences its adaptation, and this is a positive relationship.

In an attempt to examine these propositions, we examined the effect of various sources of demand on one another and on adaptation (propositions a and b), as well as the mediating effect of resources and sense of coherence (propositions c, d, and e). Of particular interest was the way by which these intervening factors mediate between stress and adaptation: Do they influence the family's adaptation *directly*, as in proposition c; or do they mainly serve their purpose indirectly, by buffering the stressor from creating stress, as in proposition d?

To achieve these goals, we examined the influence of two distinct sources of demand (aA factor), two characteristics of family resources (bB factor), and perception and coherence (cC factor) on each other and on adaptation (xX factor).

EXPLORING CAUSAL RELATIONS AMONG STRESSORS, RESOURCES, PERCEPTION, AND ADAPTATION

Causal Modeling

In general, causal modeling attempts to provide an explanation of phenomena (effects) as a result of previous phenomena (causes). The notion of causality is controversial in social science research, even more so within the framework of family systems thinking. Specifically, it has been suggested that unless variables are measured in some temporal order, an inference of causality cannot be validly made. In contrast, Bentler (1980:420) has argued that "it is not necessary to take a stand on the meaning of 'cause' to see why the modeling process is colloquially called causal modeling (with latent variables). The word 'cause' is meant to provide no philosophical meaning beyond designation for a hypothesized unobserved process, so that phrases such as 'process' or 'system' modeling would be viable substitute labels for 'causal modeling.'"

Statistical approaches to analysis of causal models share several advantages: (a) they analyze simultaneous relations among the variables in the model; (b) they estimate the model's parameters so as to determine the significance of each hypothesized path and achieve an estimate of the relative strength of paths in relation to others; (c) they enable the investigator to differentiate between *direct* effects of independent on dependent variables and *indirect* effects of the former on the latter through some intervening variables. Furthermore, investigators can determine joint (spurious) effects due to relations with a common cause. In discussing the issue of fit between research methods and theories in family studies, Miller, Rollins and Thomas (1982:860) argued that "it is not enough to merely submit to empirical test a given number of bivariate relationships implied by the model. Multiple tests of bivariate relationships cannot adequately assess the 'nexus' of the multiple propositions nor the 'inferential form' implied by the theoretical model." It is for this reason that causal models' analysis techniques were found useful in studying more complex theoretical models, in which multiple variables are proposed to influence one another in some order.

Until recently, causal models were studied in the social and behavioral sciences most frequently by path analysis, a series of progressive multiple regression analyses. While having the advantages mentioned above, the validity of path analysis has been questioned lately (Schumm et al., 1980; Pedhazur, 1982). The main criticism has been that path analysis is based on a set of restrictive assumptions that rarely are met in social and behavioral studies, particularly in survey research. Specifically, the assumptions of measures without error and uncorrelated residuals are difficult to meet in a scientific field where many measures are not perfectly reliable and residuals are often correlated. In addition, many variables are unobservable, complex constructs which are difficult to capture validly and reliably with single indicators.

Structural Equation Models

Structural equation modeling, on the other hand, permits the analysis of causal relationships with latent (unobserved) variables, thus enabling theory testing. It is primarily for this reason that Bentler (1980) considered it to be an approach that held the greatest promise for furthering behavioral science.

Structural equation models are analyzed most frequently by statistical packages like Linear Structural Relationships (LISREL) (Jöreskog, 1973, 1977). Such programs enable the analysis of causal models with multiple indicators of latent variables, nonrecursive causation, measurement errors, and correlated residuals. LISREL's estimation of the model consists of two parts: (a) the relations of observed measures to latent variables, or "constructs" (measurement model), and (b) the relations among the constructs (structural model).

The specification of latent variables in terms of their indicators (observed variables) is done in the *measurement model* by confirmatory factor analysis. Each hypothetical construct is extracted as a common factor that underlies the set of theoretically

related, a priori specified, observed variables. Each observed variable, in turn, also has a residual—its unique variance and error term. Unlike the commonly used (exploratory) factor analysis, the factor solution in confirmatory factor analysis is unique. Furthermore, a powerful test is provided of the relations of the observed variables to the constructs.

The estimation of causal relationships among the latent variables in the *structural model* is based on maximum likelihood statistical theory: model parameters are optimally estimated so that the variance-covariance matrix implied by the model is as close as possible to the observed (sample) variance-covariance matrix. The magnitude of discrepancies between the observed and predicted (by the model) variances/covariances is estimated via a "goodness of fit" test (chi-square), with degrees of freedom equal to the difference between the number of known relationships and unknown parameters.[1] The goodness of fit of the whole model also can be judged by two other measures—the goodness-of-fit index (GFI), a measure of the relative amount of variances and covariances jointly accounted for by the model, and the root mean square residual (RMR), a measure of the average residual variances and covariances.

In addition, LISREL provides other information that may be useful in analyzing the model: (a) parameter estimates, which provide an indication of the importance of each parameter to the model as a whole; (b) matrices of residuals, i.e., differences between observed and implied variances/covariances; and (c) first-order derivatives and modification indices for the fixed parameters, which may suggest changes in specification of the model that would improve the model's fit to data. LISREL, therefore, has been evaluated as the best available systematic development of statistical procedures to handle the dual inferential problems of simultaneously assessing measurement and theoretical models (Miller, Rollins, and Thomas, 1982).

To apply structural equations analysis (with latent variables) using LISREL for theory testing, the researcher is called upon to translate the theoretical model into an empirically testable model, i.e., specify the indicators predicted to define each latent variable (construct) and specify the predicted causal paths among these variables.

THE DOUBLE ABCX MODEL AS AN EMPIRICALLY TESTABLE MODEL

The empirical testing of the Double ABCX model in this study is based on an examination of Army families' adaptation to the transitional crisis of relocation in a foreign country.

Relocation is probably an aspect of military life most clearly reflecting the plight of families, particularly those of enlisted personnel (McCubbin et al., 1976; McCubbin and Marsden, 1978). Besides the associated financial hardships, the military family pays social-psychological costs. Being isolated from the traditional supports of extended family, close friends, and stable community relationships, members of military families often experience emotional and interpersonal difficulties. For military children problems in school, with friends, and at home have been noted and correlated with separation and relocation. For military members' spouses, educational and career ambitions are normally curtailed.

With overseas assignments these difficulties may become even more problematic. Not only are the financial costs greater, but families are challenged to accommodate to a foreign culture, learn a language and social customs, manage different currency, get accustomed to a new transportation system and traffic laws, and so on. In addition, there are some unique associated hardships such as getting a passport and immunizations, selling a home or a car, leaving close relatives behind, getting housing upon arrival, buying new household goods, etc.

Since all the families in our sample had experienced the same stressor event (relocation to a foreign country), we attempted to study families' adaptation to the strains and hardships associated with it (i.e., leaving the home in the U.S. and settling down overseas), as well as the effect of recent family life changes (pile-up of demands). At the same time, we attempted to study the mediating effect of family system resources, social support, and the family's sense of coherence regarding the overall circumstances.

The general empirical model for this study is outlined in Figure 9.2. The circles in Figure 9.2 represent the latent variables, or constructs, and the rectangles represent the measured variables. The arrows demonstrate the proposed causal relationships among the latent variables, and the signs denote the hypothesized direction of effects (i.e., positive or negative effect).

The model contains two pile-up (aA) variables: *relocation* strains, which are hardships specifically related to the stressor event (relocation) under study, and *family life events,* which represent residual strains due to significant events in the family's life during the year prior to relocation. There are two resource (bB) variables—*family system resources* and *social support*—and a perception (cC) variable—*coherence.* Finally, *adaptation* is the model's outcome measure (xX).

In general, variables in a causal model can be either exogenous (i.e., independent, external to the model) or endogenous ("caused" by other variables in the model). In our model the two resources (family resources and social support) are assumed to be exogenous, i.e., they are not to be explained or "caused" by the model. Family life events also are represented as an exogenous variable, since these changes are perceived as "natural" causes which are not likely to be explained by other variables in the model. Coherence, relocation strain, and adaptation are endogenous variables, in that they are each being influenced by other variables in the model.

We operationally defined "family adaptation" as a composite of family members' (i.e., military member and spouse) sense of well-being; satisfaction with the family lifestyle in the Army; and low incidence of health, emotional, marital, and legal problems in the family. The model allows us to test the *hypothesis that the level of adaptation is positively influenced by family system resources, social support, and coherence and negatively influenced by the stress experiences (relocation strains and family life events).* In addition, it is proposed that the two "resource" variables (family system resources and social support) influence adaptation indirectly by affecting other variables (relocation strain, coherence). This permits the testing of additional hypotheses which will be discussed later in this section.

The *severity of strain associated with relocation is hypothesized to be (a) positively influenced by previous family life events, and (b) negatively influenced by both family system resources and social support.* The hypothesized effect of family life

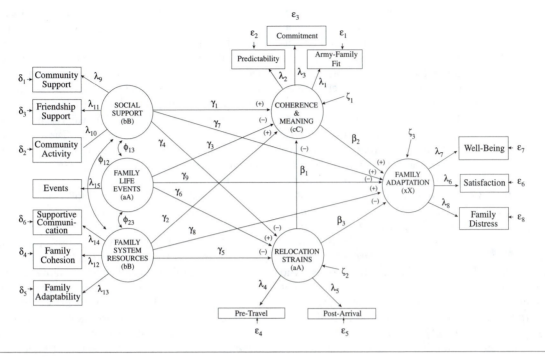

Figure 9.2   Empirical Causal Model for Testing the Double ABCX Model

events on relocation strain is guided by the pile-up hypothesis, namely, that the effect of two or more sources of strain is cumulative and that the severity of strain associated with a crisis situation is directly influenced by other sources of strain. At the same time, we hypothesize that the severity of relocation strain would be buffered (i.e., reduced) by family system resources and social support.

"Coherence" is operationally defined as a composite of family members' commitment to the Army mission, their sense of predictability, and their perception of "fit" between the family and the Army lifestyle. These three variables appear to capture the concept of coherence as a general framework wherein the overall situation is perceived and judged. *It is hypothesized that this sense of coherence is positively influenced by the two "resource" variables—social support and family resources— and negatively influenced by the two "stressor" variables—family life events and relocation strain.*

The variable "family system resources" is operationally defined as a composite of family cohesion,

family adaptability, and family supportive communication. Family cohesion and adaptability are two variables proposed to influence family vulnerability to stress and its regenerative power (Burr, 1973) which have been studied most frequently by family stress researchers (McCubbin et al., 1980). Family supportive communication is considered to be a major facilitating factor of family cohesion and adaptability (Caplan, 1976; Olson and McCubbin, 1982; Olson et al., 1983). It is hypothesized that *"family system resources" influence adaptation directly, and also indirectly through their effect on coherence and on relocation strain.* The direct effect on adaptation is suggested by Hansen's (1965) and Burr's (1973) propositions regarding family regenerative power; the indirect effect, through reducing the severity of relocation strain, is suggested by Hansen's and Burr's propositions regarding family vulnerability to stress. Though Hansen's (1965) and Burr's (1973) propositions apply to families facing a stressor event (precrisis), they can be applied to a postcrisis situation as well. Thus, the model permits us to test the hypothesis that family resources influence the ease of family adaptation to postcrisis pile-up of demands. Furthermore, it allows examination of the specific function of these resources either as being part of the family's adaptive power (affecting adaptation directly) or as buffers (affecting the severity of strain).

"Social support" is defined operationally as a composite of the family's perception of the community as supportive and safe, as a network of important friends, and as a locus for activity and involvement in community life. Based on the model, it is hypothesized that *social support,* like family system resources, has *both a direct effect on the family's adaptation to the pile-up of demands and an additional indirect effect by buffering the relocation strain and by positively influencing the sense of coherence.*

To conclude, the empirical model enables us to test simultaneous relationships among the major variables of the Double ABCX model using multiple indicators of theoretical constructs. It allows us to (a) test empirically the notion of pile-up of demands and (b) examine the relative magnitude of effects of family resources, social support, and coherence on family adaptation to stress. In addition, it enables us to gain some insight into the role of family resources as influencing the family's vulnerability to stress and its adaptive power.

Sample and Data Collection

Sample

The sample for this study was drawn from the total population of U.S. Army families who were located in West Germany in May 1983. The initial sample of 1,227 officer and enlisted families selected for the Army Family Survey was drawn by a proportionate stratified method with two related and overlapping layers of stratification. Type of military unit (combat, combat support, and combat service support) was one layer used to get a representative slice of U.S. Army families. The second layer, size of military community (which also related to urban vs. rural German communities), assisted us in obtaining representation of living experiences in a foreign country (McCubbin et al., 1983).

The sample consisted entirely of intact marriages and families. Families in all stages of the family life cycle, from newlywed to empty nest, were surveyed. Both military members and their spouses completed questionnaires which were designed to tap a broad range of experiences and attitudes related to the relocation and adaptation to the Army-family lifestyle in a foreign country. Participation was voluntary, and complete anonymity was assured. Questionnaires were self-administered, completed by military members and their spouses at home and returned within 24 hours.

The overall return rate was 86%, and almost all (98%) of the returned questionnaires were usable. A total of 53 surveys were excluded when *family* data was incomplete (one spouse's questionnaire was missing), critical data (rank) was missing, or when the military member was a female. Nine such families with female military members were excluded to achieve homogeneity of the sample.

The data analysis in the present study is based on 288 families (husbands and wives) of *enlisted personnel* (ranks Private E2 to Sergeant Major E9) who completed *all* items and scales used for the analysis. The mean age of military members and spouses was 30.9 and 29.6, respectively (range from below 20 to 50 years). The "typical" enlisted military member was a high school graduate or had some college or vocational-technical education and had been in the Army for more than 6 years. The "typical" spouse of an enlisted soldier was a high school graduate or at least had attended high school. Nearly one-third of the families belonged to a minority group. The majority (80%) of the families were in their first marriage, and close to 50% had been married between 4 to 10 years. Three-fourths (75%) of the families had either preschool children or children in school, and nearly one-fourth (23%) had adolescents or were in the launching stage of the family life cycle. Only 2% of the sample consisted of couples with no children. About one-half of those surveyed were on their first European tour. At the time the survey was conducted, nearly one-half of the families had been in Europe for one to two years.

This sample of enlisted soldiers and their spouses approximated the profile of married personnel in the U.S. Army and was representative of accompanied enlisted military personnel in the U.S. Army in Europe (McCubbin et al., 1983).

Measures

Fifteen measures were used to study the relationships among the model's six latent variables:

1. *Relocation strain* was measured by two scales designed to assess the severity of strains created by leaving the U.S. and those created by arrival and settling down in Germany. (a) *Pretravel strain* included 15 items (rated on a 4-point severity scale) related to leaving kids, relatives, and close friends behind; interruption of an educational program or medical care; giving up a job; selling a home or an automobile before relocation; and getting a passport, immunizations, etc. (b) *Postarrival hardships* included 12 items (rated on a 4-point severity scale) related to demands in a foreign country such as getting a driver's license, learning the language, using transportation, as well as strains created by delay in getting housing, major purchases, cost of moving, and temporary duty assignments upon arrival.

2. *Family life events* was defined by a single indicator, a 12-item scale (McCubbin et al., 1981) designed to assess the occurrence and perceived severity (on a 3-point scale) of major events in the family in the year prior to relocation (e.g., marriage; birth of a child; major financial changes; health problems; death of a family member, close relative, or friend, etc.).

3. *Family system resources* was composed of three scales. (a) *Family cohesion* is a 16-item scale (Olson et al., 1982) that measured the emotional bonding that family members have toward one another around dimensions of time, space, friends, interests and recreation. (b) *Family adaptability* is a 14-item scale (Olson et al., 1982) that measured the ability of the family system to change its power structure, role relationships, and relationship rules in response to situational and developmental needs. (c) *Supportive communication* was measured by two items that tap respondent's perception of being listened to, understood, and supported by other family members.

4. *Social support* was defined by three scales (McCubbin et al., 1981). (a) *Community support* was a 6-item scale that measured the extent to which the family feels it can depend upon the community, feels secure and safe, and can depend upon help and support for their children. (b) *Friendship support* was a 5-item scale that measured the extent to which the family feels it has a network of important friends who value and care for them. (c) *Community activity* was a 3-item scale that measured the extent to which the family is active and involved and feels part of the community.

5. *Coherence and meaning* was composed of three scales (McCubbin and Patterson, 1983c). (a) *Family-army fit* was a 5-item scale that measured the degree to which the respondent feels the family is part of Army life, that the Army takes care of its families, and that help will be given if needed. (b) *Predictability* was a 3-item scale that measured the degree to which the respondent feels the family can predict the immediate future in terms of work and family schedule. (c) *Commitment* was a 4-item scale that measured the degree to which the family is committed to the Army lifestyle and to the feeling that the Army can be good for family life.

6. *Adaptation* was operationalized by three measures. (a) *General well-being* measured the degree (using an 11-point semantic differential scale) to which the respondent feels energized, peppy, vital, cheerful, healthy, relaxed, calm, and happy. (b) *Satisfaction* measured the degree (on a 4-point scale) to which the respondent is satisfied with family life and with Army life in Germany (two items). (c) *Family distress* was a checklist of emotional, marital, health, financial, and legal problems the family may have struggled with during the past three months. Family distress score reflects the number of symptoms checked.

Data for pretravel strains and family distress were collected from military members (husbands) only. Data for postarrival hardships, family life events, and family cohesion and adaptability were collected from wives only. Data for all other measures were collected from both family members, and mean family scores were used in subsequent phases of the data analysis.

ANALYSES AND RESULTS

The correlation matrix of the observed variables (Table 9.1) was analyzed using LISREL VI program (Jöreskog and Sörbom, 1984).[2] Three consecutive analyses were conducted by changing the model's specifications, using the model presented in Figure 9.2 as the basic empirical model.

In order to examine the effect of pile-up of stressors and strains, the model in Figure 9.2 was first analyzed with paths γ_3, γ_6 and γ_9 fixed to 0, i.e. without the effect of life events on relocation, coherence, and adaptation. The chi-square measure of goodness of fit of the model was 187.8 with 79 degrees of freedom ($p < .01$). While this relatively high chi-square (compared with the number of degrees of freedom) may suggest bad fit of the model to data, it could not be a valid test statistic for the whole model since a standardized covariance matrix was analyzed and not all the observed variables were assured of having a multivariate normal distribution (see note 1). Other measures of the model's goodness of fit, such as goodness-of-fit index (GFI) and root mean square residual (RMR) can be judged only relatively. The GFI, which is independent of the sample size and relatively robust against departure from normality, was .914 (normal range: 0 to 1.0). The RMR was .068, compared with a root mean square correlation of .273 between the observed variables (off-diagonal), indicating a relatively small residual. Taken together with other indicators (such as absence of the clear indicators of bad fit, magnitude of normalized residuals, and plotting of the normalized residuals against normal quantiles), these results may be interpreted as representing a *moderate* model's fit.

As noted earlier, the chi-square measure of goodness of fit could be used most validly in a comparative way, i.e., in comparing the model with an alternative model and measuring the change in the magnitude of chi-square relative to the change in the number of degrees of freedom (see note 1). Thus, the significance of this change (improvement in the model's fit) can be tested. As Jöreskog and Sörbom (1984) and others (e.g., Bentler, 1980) suggest, the model can be improved by freeing fixed parameters as assessed by the first-order derivatives or the modification indices of the program. While this procedure may indeed improve the model's fit, these

modifications may not be theoretically justified. Instead, we chose to test the alternative model by freeing the γ_3, γ_6 and γ_9 parameters, i.e., allowing family life events to "cause" relocation strain, coherence, and adaptation as proposed in the basic empirical model (Figure 9.2).

Analysis of this second model resulted in a chi-square of 156.6 with 76 degrees of freedom. The change in chi-square compared with the first model is 31.2 with 3 degrees of freedom, indicating a significant ($p < .001$) improvement in the model's fit. In addition, the goodness-of-fit index has increased (GFI = .929), and the mean square residual has decreased (RMR = .059) to indicate further the improvement of the model.

While the model's fit has improved indeed, examination of other LISREL estimates indicated that it did not account for all of the observed data. First, modification indices suggested that some observed variables could have loaded on more than one latent variable. For example, the model's fit would have improved had we allowed satisfaction with Army-family lifestyle to load not only on adaptation but also on coherence. Second, few normalized residuals were significant (larger than 2 in magnitude), indicating that the corresponding data points were not sufficiently accounted for by the model's specifications. Third, it was indicated by the data (first-order derivatives and correlation of estimates) that the model's fit to data could have been improved if we had allowed residuals of some of the exogenous measures to correlate. Carefully examining each of these indices, we chose *not* to make modifications in the specifications of the model (i.e., allowing measures to load on more than one factor or allowing residuals to correlate) because we had no theoretical basis for such modifications. As Bentler (1980) and Jöreskog and Sörbom (1984) noted, adding paths, such as those representing correlations between errors, works well in practice by improving fit to data; but it is recommended only when it makes sense from a substantive point of view, or else tests can capitalize on chance associations in the data.

The rest of this section focuses, therefore, on the parameter estimates of this second model. We turn first to the measurement model (confirmatory factor analysis). Table 9.2 presents results of LISREL

Table 9.1   Correlation Matrix of Indicator Variables

Variables	1	2	3	4	5	6	7	8	9	10	11	12	13	14	15
1. Army-family fit	—														
2. Predictability	.548	—													
3. Commitment	.436	.367	—												
4. Pretravel	-.242	-.291	-.259	—											
5. Postarrival	-.332	-.315	-.146	.306	—										
6. Satisfaction	.590	.581	.332	-.299	-.376	—									
7. General well-being	.388	.387	.146	-.204	-.328	.464	—								
8. Family distress	-.222	-.229	-.084	.187	.170	-.293	-.361	—							
9. Community support	.591	.419	.362	-.226	-.300	.509	.325	-.138	—						
10. Community activity	.395	.222	.207	-.113	-.138	.350	.216	-.094	.447	—					
11. Friendship support	.259	.204	.106	-.064	-.050	.209	.245	-.065	.427	.316	—				
12. Cohesion	.098	.006	-.012	.026	-.091	.102	.278	-.241	.108	.024	.098	—			
13. Adaptability	.027	-.047	-.016	.096	-.008	.046	.176	-.133	.076	.014	.136	.693	—		
14. Communication	.032	.063	-.026	.055	-.095	.120	.308	-.259	.027	.009	.149	.592	.524	—	
15. Family life events	-.271	-.269	-.104	.176	.345	-.230	-.268	.245	-.154	-.158	-.101	-.090	.032	-.185	—
Mean	15.43	6.04	4.29	12.31	8.92	2.74	49.97	1.70	23.02	7.86	20.56	63.40	38.93	11.63	2.65
SD	5.59	3.64	2.46	7.65	5.92	1.40	13.03	1.30	8.24	2.75	4.34	10.20	7.61	2.88	2.74

Table 9.2   LISREL Estimates for Measurement Model (relations of indicator variables to latent variables)

Construct	Indicator	Path	Unstandardized Coefficient	Standardized Coefficient	Residual	Variance
Coherence	Army-family fit	λ_1	(1.000)	.810	ε_1	.344*
	Predictability	λ_2	.869*	.704	ε_2	.505*
	Commitment	λ_3	.609*	.493	ε_3	.757*
Relocation	Pretravel	λ_4	(1.000)	.474	ε_4	.775*
	Postarrival	λ_5	1.361*	.645	ε_5	.584*
Adaptation	Satisfaction	λ_6	(1.000)	.786	ε_6	.382*
	Well-being	λ_7	.780*	.613	ε_7	.624*
	Distress	λ_8	-.506*	-.398	ε_8	.842*
Social support	Community support	λ_9	(1.000)	.883	δ_1	.220*
	Community activity	λ_{10}	.594*	.524	δ_2	.725*
	Friendship support	λ_{11}	.539*	.476	δ_3	.774*
Family resources	Cohesion	λ_{12}	(1.000)	.883	δ_4	.221*
	Adaptability	λ_{13}	.882*	.779	δ_5	.393*
	Communication	λ_{14}	.768*	.667	δ_6	.541*
Life events	Life events	λ_{15}	(1.000)	1.00	—	—

NOTE: Parenthesized coefficients are fixed reference indicators.
*$p < .01$.

estimates of the relations of the observed variables to the latent variables, and the residuals for the observed variables. The loadings of observed variables on latent variables are represented by the lambda (λ) coefficients. For each latent variable one (arbitrarily selected) observed variable is fixed to 1.0 in order to give the latent variable a referent, and the others are freely estimated.[3] The residuals of the observed measures are represented by epsilon (ε) for the indicators of the endogenous (dependent) latent variables and by delta (δ) for the indicators of the exogenous (independent) latent variables.

As can be seen in Table 9.2, the constructs seem reasonably well defined: all the loadings of the observed measures (not fixed as reference indicators) on latent variables were significant. Also, all the residuals were significant, suggesting that differences exist between the measures and the constructs underlying them.

Turning now to the structural model, Table 9.3 shows (a) variances of and covariances among latent exogenous variables (phi, ϕ), (b) path coefficients between latent exogenous and latent endogenous variables (gamma, γ), (c) path coefficients among latent endogenous variables (beta, β), and (d) residuals of the latent endogenous variables (zeta, ζ).

As the results in Table 9.3 indicate, adaptation—the model's outcome variable—appears to be directly and positively influenced by both family system resources ($\gamma_8 = .202$, $t = 3.76$) and coherence ($\beta_2 = .720$, $t = 3.91$) and directly and negatively affected by relocation strain ($\beta_3 = -.537$, $t = -2.01$). The coefficients of the direct effects of social support and life events on adaptation are not significant. Over 90% of the variance of adaptation is explained by the other five latent variables of the model, with a nonsignificant residual variance ($\zeta_3 = .60$, $t = 1.18$). Coherence appears to be positively affected by social support ($\gamma_1 = .546$, $t = 5.70$) and negatively affected by relocation ($\beta_1 = -.593$, $t = -2.50$) but not by family resources and life events. Relocation strain is positively affected by previous life events ($\gamma_6 = .195$, $t = 4.41$) and negatively influenced by social support ($\gamma_4 = -.228$, $t = -3.97$). The effect of family system resources on relocation strain is not significant.

As a final analysis, we deleted the nonsignificant paths to test the hypothesis that these paths did not contribute to the fit of the model. This revised model is presented in Figure 9.3. Figure 9.3 also shows the modified paths' unstandardized and standardized (in parentheses) coefficients.

The goodness-of-fit measure of the revised model is $\chi^2 = 158.6$ with 81 degrees of freedom. This represents an increase in χ^2 by 2.0 with 5 degrees of freedom, an insignificant ($p > .80$) change in the model's overall fit. The other two measures of goodness of fit (GFI and RMR) remained unchanged.

An examination of Figure 9.3 reveals that, of the two types of resources, only family system resources have a direct effect on adaptation. However, while social support has no such direct effect, it does affect adaptation indirectly by positively affecting coherence and also by negatively affecting the strain of relocation. Relocation, in turn, has both a direct effect on adaptation and an indirect effect through its negative effect on coherence. Table 9.4 summarizes the direct, indirect, and total effects of the model's variables on adaptation.

Relocation strain appeared to have a major total effect on adaptation; and that was, as expected, a negative effect. Coherence and social support seem to affect adaptation positively and strongly: the former by its direct effect and the latter by its combined indirect effects. The total effects of life events and family system resources appear to be less than those of the other three variables, though both are significant effects.

DISCUSSION

In that empirical testing of theoretical models is part and parcel of the process of family theory construction (Burr et al., 1979), this study contributes to the continuous work of refining family stress theory (McCubbin and Patterson, 1982, 1983a, 1983b). While numerous studies have supported hypothesized relations between pairs of variables in the Double ABCX model of family stress and adaptation (McCubbin et al., 1980), the present study examined the model as a whole.

Table 9.3 LISREL Estimates for Structural Model (relations among latent variables)

Variance-Covariance of Exogenous Latent Variables (Phi Matrix)[a]		Social Support	Family Resources	Life Events
Social support	(ϕ_1)	.780 (1.000)		
Family resources	(ϕ_2)	.097 (.124)	.779 (1.000)	
Life events	(ϕ_3)	−.166 (−.189)	−.079 (−.089)	1.000 (1.000)

Path Coefficients Between Latent Variables	Path	Unstandardized Coefficient	Standardized Coefficient	Residual	Variance
Social support — Coherence	γ_1	.546**	.595	ζ_1 (Coherence)	.190**
Family resources — Coherence	γ_2	−.038	−.041	ζ_2 (Relocation)	.133**
Life events — Coherence	γ_3	−.048	−.059	ζ_3 (Adaptation)	.060
Social support — Relocation	γ_4	−.228**	−.424		
Family resources — Relocation	γ_5	.018	.034		
Life events — Relocation	γ_6	.195**	.411		
Social support — Adaptation	γ_7	−.065	−.073		
Family resources — Adaptation	γ_8	.202**	.227		
Life events — Adaptation	γ_9	.047	.060		
Relocation — Coherence	β_1	−.593*	−.347		
Coherence — Adaptation	β_2	.720**	.742		
Relocation — Adaptation	β_3	−.537*	−.324		

a. Standardized estimates are shown in parentheses.

*p < .05, **p < .01.

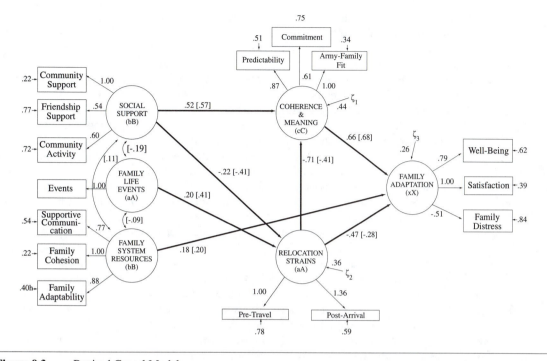

Figure 9.3   Revised Causal Model

NOTE: Unstandardized coefficients shown. Parenthetical figures denote standardized path coefficients. All path coefficients are significant ($p < .05$).

Table 9.4   Direct, Indirect, and Total Effects of Model's Latent Variables on Adaptation (unstandardized estimates)

	Effect on Adaptation		
Variables	*Direct Effect*	*Indirect Effect*	*Total Effect*
Life events	—	−.181	−.181
Relocation	−.466	−.465	−.931
Coherence	.656	—	.656
Family resources	.181	—	.181
Social support	—	.548	.548

The Effect of Stressors, Resources, and Coherence on Family Adaptation

The results confirmed the hypothesis that the severity of strain associated with a transitional crisis situation is intensified by the pile-up of sources of family strain before the transitional crisis (relocation) occurs. The analysis showed that, when the effect of previous family life events was added to the model, it significantly improved the model's overall fit. Furthermore, this improvement could be almost solely explained by the effect of family life events on relocation strain, since their effect on coherence and on adaptation was insignificant. It appears that the family struggles not only with the transitional crisis situation itself but with an accumulation of demands that stem from current as well as previous, unresolved family life changes. The results also confirmed the hypothesis that this pile-up of demands negatively influences the level of adaptation. In other words the greater the accumulation of stressors with a resulting intensification of strains, the less family members are satisfied with the family lifestyle; the less their personal well-being; and the greater the probability of health, emotional, and relational problems in the family. These findings are consistent with the family and individual research literature on life stress and illness (see Coddington, 1972; Dohrenwend and Dohrenwend, 1974; Patterson and McCubbin, 1983).

This negative effect of pile-up of demands on the family's level of adaptation does appear to be buffered by certain resources. As proposed by the model, family system resources, social support, and a sense of coherence have a positive effect on the family's level of adaptation. The results, however, show that these resources have differential effects and, therefore, possess different buffering qualities. Intrafamily system resources proved to be part of the family's *adaptive power* in that they directly enhance family adaptation. Specifically, the results suggest that families who are more cohesive, who communicate support to their members better, and whose systems are more flexible are better able to adapt to the pile-up of stressors and strains. In many respects the findings of this study are consistent with earlier studies of families under stress (Angell, 1936; Cavan and Ranck, 1938; Hill, 1949) which pointed to the powerful influences of family bonds of unity (cohesion) and flexibility in facilitating the family's recovery from crisis situations.

However, while we tend to endow positive family characteristics such as cohesion and flexibility with seemingly magical properties to reduce the strains associated with a crisis situation, our hypothesis that family system resources would also buffer the family against the severity of the strain was not supported.

Social support did not emerge as part of the family's adaptive power as was hypothesized. It appears, however, that it has a significant *indirect* role in family adaptation to stress. First, the findings of this investigation suggest that involvement in the community, community support, and friendship networks tend to ease the perceived stressfulness of the situation. In that sense social support plays an important *buffering role.* Second, the more the community and friendship networks are supportive of the family, the more the situation as a whole is coherent and is interpreted in positive terms—there is more commitment, better perception of "fit," and stronger feelings that things are predictable and under control. These findings support Cobb's (1979) suggestion that, while esteem and emotional supports (such as in our notion of family resources) contribute to adaptation, network support leads to a sense of participation (i.e., fit) and control.

The findings also support the hypothesis that the family's coherence and meaning are influenced by its experience of demands and resources. It appears, however, that the *external* environment, as the family experiences it, is more influential than the family's internal resources. Specifically, our analysis suggests that coherence is not as affected by family system (internal) resources as it is by both negative experiences (pile-up of demands) and positive experiences of the external environment (social support). This ability to perceive the overall situation as coherent, as one that "makes sense," and to perceive a "fit" between the family and the circumstances, in turn, is of great value to the family in facilitating its adaptation.

The Application of Structural Equation Models

This study has demonstrated the applicability of structural equation models (specifically, the LISREL model) to theory testing; the examination of several simultaneous relationships among theoretical constructs was possible. Additionally, because complex variables such as "family system resources," "social support," "adaptation," or "coherence" are not likely to be captured by any one of their indicators alone, the use of multiple indicators to define these constructs was also important.

There are two additional observations worthy of note. First, examination of the results revealed that some of the measures' residuals were nonrandom errors and that they tended to covary. This is not surprising given that our measures were—as in many family studies—self-reports (for instance, see Thomson and Williams, 1984). LISREL enables the investigator to detect nonrandom, systematic errors, and to obtain estimates of their magnitude and covariances, while the latent variables themselves are maintained free of these errors.

Second, examination of the modification indices of the confirmatory factor analysis suggested stronger ties between coherence and adaptation than were proposed by our empirical model. These clues may be investigated further in future research and ultimately may facilitate refining the original Double ABCX model (Lavee and McCubbin, 1985).

While the present study attempts to clarify the relations among the major variables of the Double ABCX model, the task has not yet been completed. First, changes in the model's specifications, as suggested by the results of this study, can be introduced and empirically tested. For example, once the strong causal effect of family life events on relocation has been confirmed, would the model fit better if a new latent variable, say pile-up, replaced the two separate stressor variables in our model? Second, not all of the theoretical constructs of the Double ABCX model were measured and, consequently, not all were entered into our structural model. For instance, personal resources and coping strategies were not included. Future research can estimate not only their adaptive and buffering roles but also their relations to other resources. Finally, future research should examine the relationships among stressors, resources, perception, and adaptation in other sets of pile-up of demands and in other populations.

NOTES

1. This "goodness of fit" test, and its associated probability level, may not be valid as a likelihood ratio test statistic of the whole model in most practical cases, especially when not all the observed variables have a multivariate normal distribution and the analysis is based on a standardized covariance matrix (Jöreskog and Sörbom, 1984). However, it is a useful index in assessing the value of the causal model: the lower the chi-square relative to the degrees of freedom, the better the model's fit. This statistic is more useful in comparative model fitting, i.e., in comparing alternative models and assessing the model's improvement by the change in chi-square relative to the change in degrees of freedom.

2. As a general rule, the covariance matrix should be analyzed. However, if the units of measurement in the observed variables have no intrinsic meaning (as in our measures), a correlation matrix can be analyzed as long as the data are cross-sectional and the model is tested within a single population (for example, see Jöreskog and Sörbom, 1984; Kenny, 1979; Long, 1976).

3. Alternatively, the exogenous variables can be standardized by fixing the diagonal elements (variances) of the phi matrix to unity. We have chosen to define these variables' measurement units by assigning reference indicators as in the endogenous variables.

REFERENCES

Angell, R. C.
1936 The Family Encounters the Depression. New York: Charles Scribner's Sons.

Antonovsky, A.
1979 Health, Stress and Coping. San Francisco: Jossey Bass.

Bentler, P. M.
1980 "Multivariate analysis with latent variables: causal modeling." Annual Review of Psychology 31:419-456.

Boss, P. G.
1977 "A clarification of the concept of psychological father presence in families experiencing ambiguity of boundary." Journal of Marriage and the Family 39:141-151.

———
1980 "Normative family stress: family boundary changes across the life span." Family Relations 29:445-450.

Burr, W. R.
1973 Theory Construction and the Sociology of the Family. New York: John Wiley & Sons.

Burr, W. R., Hill, R., Reiss, I. L. and Nye, F. I. (Eds.)
1979 Contemporary Theories About the Family (Vol. 1). New York: The Free Press.

Caplan, G.
1976 "The family as a support system." Pp. 19-36 in G. Caplan and M. Killilea (Eds.), Support Systems and Mutual Help. New York: Grune & Stratton.

Cavan, R. S. and Ranck, K. H.
1938 The Family and the Depression. Chicago: University of Chicago Press.

Cobb, S.
1976 "Social support as a moderator of life stress." Psychosomatic Medicine 38:300-314.

———
1979 "Social support and health through the life

course." In M. W. Riley (Ed.), Aging From Birth to Death. Boulder, CO: Westview Press.

Coddington, R. D.
1972 "The significance of life events as etiologic factors in diseases of children, II: a study of a normal population." Journal of Psychosomatic Research 16:205-213.

Dohrenwend, B. S. and Dohrenwend, B. P. (Eds.)
1974 Stressful Life Events, Their Nature and Effects. New York: John Wiley & Sons.

George, L.
1980 Role Transitions in Later Life. Belmont, CA: Brooks/Cole.

Hansen, D.
1965 "Personal and positional influence in formal groups: compositions and theory for research on family vulnerability to stress." Social Forces 44: 202-210.

Hansen, D. and Johnson, V.
1979 "Rethinking family stress theory: definitional aspects." Pp. 582-603 in W. Burr, R. Hill, I. Reiss and F. I. Nye (Eds.), Contemporary Theories About the Family (Vol. 1). New York: The Free Press.

Hill, R.
1949 Families Under Stress. New York: Harper and Row.

———
1958 Generic features of families under stress. Social Casework 39:139-150.

Hill, R. and Joy, C.
1979 "Conceptualizing and operationalizing category systems for phasing of family development." Unpublished manuscript, University of Minnesota.

Jöreskog, K. G.
1973 "A general method for estimating a linear structural equation system." Pp. 85-112 in A. S. Goldberg and O. D. Duncan (Eds.), Structural Equation Models in the Social Sciences. New York: Seminar Press.

———
1977 "Structural equation models in the social sciences: specification, estimation and testing." Pp. 265-287 in P. R. Krishnaiah (Ed.), Application of Statistics. Amsterdam: North-Holland.

Jöreskog, K. G. and Sörbom, D.
1984 LISREL VI: Analysis of Linear Structural Relationships by the Method of Maximum Likelihood (3rd ed.). Mooresville, IN: Scientific Software.

Kenny, D. A.
1979 Correlation and Causality. New York: John Wiley and Sons.

Lavee, Y. and McCubbin, H. I.
1985 "Adaptation in family stress theory: theoretical and methodological considerations." Paper presented at the Theory Construction and Research Methodology Workshop, National Council on Family Relations annual meeting, Dallas, TX (November).

Long, J. S.
1976 "Estimation and hypothesis testing in linear models containing measurement error: a review of Jöreskog's model of analysis of covariance structures." Sociological Methods and Research 5:157-206.

McCubbin, H. I., Dahl, B. B. and Hunter, E. J.
1976 "Research on the military family: a review." Pp. 291-319 in H. I. McCubbin, B. B. Dahl and E. J. Hunter (Eds.), Families in the Military System. Beverly Hills, CA: Sage Publications.

McCubbin, H. I., Joy, C., Cauble, A., Comeau, J., Patterson, J. and Needle, R.
1980 "Family stress, coping and social support: a decade review." Journal of Marriage and the Family 42:855-871.

McCubbin, H. I. and Marsden, M. A.
1978 "The military family and the changing military profession." Pp. 207-221 in F. D. Margiotta (Ed.), The Changing World of the American Military. Boulder, CO: Westview Press.

McCubbin, H. I. and Patterson, J. M.
1982 "Family adaptation to crisis." Pp. 26-47 in H. I. McCubbin, A. Cauble and J. Patterson (Eds.), Family Stress, Coping and Social Support. Springfield, IL: Charles C. Thomas.

———
1983a "The family stress process: the Double ABCX model of adjustment and adaptation." Pp. 7-37 in H. I. McCubbin, M. B. Sussman and J. M. Patterson (Eds.), Social Stress and the Family: Advances and Developments in Family Stress Theory and Research. New York: The Haworth Press.

———
1983b "Family stress and adaptation to crises: a Double ABCX model of family behavior." Pp. 87-106 in D. H. Olson and B. C. Miller (Eds.), Family Studies Review Yearbook (Vol. 1). Beverly Hills, CA: Sage Publications.

McCubbin, H. I. and Patterson, J. M.
1983c Family Index of Coherence. St. Paul, MN: University of Minnesota, Family Social Science.

McCubbin, H. I., Patterson, J. M. and Glynn, T.
1981 Social Support Index. St. Paul, MN: University of Minnesota, Family Social Science.

McCubbin, H. I., Patterson. J. M. and Lavee, Y.
1983 One Thousand Army Families: Strengths, Coping and Supports. St. Paul, MN: University of Minnesota, Family Social Science.

McCubbin, H. I., Patterson, J. M. and Wilson, L.
1981 FILE: Family Inventory of Life Events and Changes. St. Paul, MN: University of Minnesota, Family Social Science.

Mechanic, D.
1974 "Social structure and personal adaptation: some neglected dimensions." Pp. 32-44 in G. V. Coelho, D. A. Hamburg and J. E. Adams (Eds.), Coping and Adaptation. New York: Basic Books.

Mederer, H. and Hill, R.
1983 "Critical transitions over the family life span: theory and research." Pp. 39-60 in H. I. McCubbin, M. B. Sussman and J. M. Patterson (Eds.), Social Stress and the Family: Advances and Developments in Family Stress Theory and Research. New York: Haworth Press.

Miller, B. C., Rollins, B. C. and Thomas, D. L.
1982 "On methods of studying marriages and families." Journal of Marriage and the Family 44:851-873.

Olson, D. H. and McCubbin, H. I.
1982 "Circumplex model of marital and family systems, V: application to family stress and crisis intervention." Pp. 48-68 in H. I. McCubbin, A. E. Cauble and J. M. Patterson (Eds.), Family Stress, Coping and Social Support. Springfield, IL: Charles C. Thomas.

Olson, D. H., McCubbin, H. I., Barnes, H., Larsen, A., Muxen, M. and Wilson, M.
1983 Families: What Makes Them Work. Beverly Hills, CA: Sage Publications.

Olson, D. H., Portner, J. and Bell, R.
1982 Family Adaptability and Cohesion Scales (FACES II). St. Paul, MN: University of Minnesota, Family Social Science.

Patterson, J. M. and McCubbin, H. I.
1983 "The impact of family life events and changes on the health of a chronically ill child." Family Relations 32:255-264.

Pearlin, L. and Schooler, C.
1978 "The structure of coping." Journal of Health and Social Behavior 19:2-21.

Pedhazur, E. J.
1982 Multiple Regression in Behavioral Research (2nd ed.). New York: Holt, Rinehart & Winston.

Pilisuk, M. and Parks, S. H.
1981 "The place of network analysis in the study of supportive social associations." Basic and Applied Social Psychology 2:121-132.

———

1983 "Social support and family stress." Pp. 137-156 in H. I. McCubbin, M. B. Sussman and J. M. Patterson (Eds.), Social Stress and the Family: Advances and Developments in Family Stress Theory and Research. New York: Haworth Press.

Schumm, W. R., Southerly, W. T. and Figley, C. R.
1980 "Stumbling block or stepping stone: path analysis in family studies." Journal of Marriage and the Family 42:251-262.

Thomson, E. and Williams, R.
1984 "A note on correlated measurement error in wife-husband data." Journal of Marriage and the Family 46:643-649.

10

FAMILY STRESS

Integrating Theory and Measurement

STEVAN E. HOBFOLL
CHARLES D. SPIELBERGER

Family stress theory and family stress measurement were critically reviewed. After Hill's (1949) original formulation, 4 factors in family stress were examined: the stressor, family resources, family perceptions, and stress outcomes. The research findings clearly indicate that change per se can no longer be viewed as the essence of family stress and that the focus should be on negative changes and, in particular, loss. Family resources, such as cohesiveness, flexibility, social support, and shared family values, were evaluated as key stress-resistance attributes. Resource conservation and utilization models were applied in explaining the origins of stress for families and how existing resources aid families during stressful circumstances. One stress model, termed the *conservation of resources* theory, was applied to the family stress context. The popular concept of resource fit was also challenged and revised.

The study of family stress has a long history. Although recent work in this field is often linked to the seminal research of Hill (1949) on separation and reunion during and after World War II, it is infrequently recognized that Hill's work was part of a broader revolution in psychology, family sociology, and community psychiatry that has emphasized adjustment to crises (Caplan, 1964; Lindemann, 1944). Earlier work had focused primarily on psychopathology; the family's role was examined primarily from the perspective of the things parents (especially mothers) did wrong.

Reprinted from the *Journal of Family Psychology* 6 (1992): 99-112. Copyright © 1992 by the American Psychological Association. Reprinted with permission.

Hill and others who shared his view, including Caplan (1964) and Jahoda (1958), were interested in what individuals and families did right in successfully adjusting and adapting to the normal and unusual demands placed on people through the natural life course. Central to this approach are the following suppositions: (a) that stress and even crises are normative, (b) that stress sometimes places extraordinary demands on individuals and families, (c) that most people adapt reasonably well to stress, (d) and that if they do not initially fare well, more negative sequelae will follow. In this context, stress has come to be defined as a state in which individuals' resources are challenged by the environment in a way that overtaxes their coping ability and endangers their well-being (Hobfoll, 1989; Lazarus & Folkman, 1984). Family stress may be defined as an extension of individual stress applied to the family domain. Family stress, as such, can be defined as the state in which family members (Boss, 1987) and the family as a unit (H. P. McCubbin & Patterson, 1982) are challenged by the environment in a way that overtakes their individual or collective resources and threatens the well-being of the family.

In the present article we first examine the common elements in models of family stress, how these core constructs fit in the greater scheme of the theories, and how they are measured. New models and emerging elements of interest are especially highlighted. In particular, the resources of the family and how these resources can best be assessed receive attention as one of the most promising areas of family stress research. The special contributions of family systems theory is also addressed, and evolving notions about family systems are considered. We also challenge those elements of the early stress models that continue to be highlighted in new models but that lack empirical support: for example, the assumption that change is itself stressful. Finally, suggestions for future research on family stress are presented.

ESSENTIAL ELEMENTS OF FAMILY STRESS THEORY

Hill's legacy in the area of family stress has been unusually long-standing in comparison to most

scientific contributions. Indeed, some aspects of his thinking such as the importance of cultural diversity and conflicting roles, which have only recently been studied, are now critical areas for future concern. His central contribution, however, is the ABC-X stress model.

The A factor in Hill's theory pertains to the stressor, which consists of life events or occurrences that, as Hill postulated, are of sufficient magnitude to create change in the family system. The B factor stands for the resources or strengths of the individual or system. These are the mechanisms that are used to combat the demands placed on the family by stressful events and circumstances. The C factor refers to the perceptions of family members, which determine the meaning of the event for the family. The X factor is the stress outcome or crisis that follows as a reaction to stressful events and the coping process.

The Stressor

A focus on stressors is central in virtually all theories of family events, but different theorists envisaged different conceptions of the nature of stressors. For Hill (1949), stressors were events that placed pressure for change on the family system. A double ABC-X model was later introduced by H. I. McCubbin and Patterson (1983). In addition to the original crisis, this model emphasized the pattern of follow-up in responding to the original stressful event and its sequelae (hence "double").

Consistent with Hill's theoretical approach, H. I. McCubbin and his colleagues conceptualized stressors as events or circumstances that place pressure for change on the family system. However, Olson and McCubbin (1982) also theorized that it is the buildup of change that is stressful, suggesting that although families can withstand some change, repeated demands for change would overly tax family resources. A similar conception of change as the central element in family stress has been proposed by Boss (1987) and more recently by Buehler (1990).

In this article, we challenge the notion that change is itself stressful. As previously noted, the assumption that change per se is stressful has its roots in Hill's (1949) study of separation and reunion among families after World War II, in which the changes that these families had to make were emphasized. This perspective was reinforced by the influential original work of Holmes and Rahe (1967), who devised a conveniently administered life-change scale. Emphasis on the significance of change was also consistent with systems theory, which assumes that systems seek balance.

Change theories were actually borrowed from biology, where it has long been recognized that systems demand growth and revitalization and not simply balance or equilibrium. Unfortunately, the items in the Holmes-Rahe scale mixed clearly negative items, such as "death of a spouse," with items that were quite ambiguous, such as "change at work," which could indicate either positive or negative change. By including positive, negative, and ambiguous change items in the same scale, the relationship between stressful events and outcomes was clouded.

Stressful Effects of Desirable and Undesirable Change

Thoits (1983) conducted a careful review of the research literature on the kinds of life events that influenced psychological distress. Of 20 studies that compared the effects of undesirable change versus change itself, only 3 failed to find that undesirable change was more strongly related to psychological disturbance than change alone. Even more compelling, several studies demonstrated that the relationship between change and disturbance dropped to nearly zero when the effects of undesirable events were partialed out. Indeed, Cohen and Hoberman (1983) reported that positive change can act as a stress buffer, offsetting the negative sequelae that might otherwise follow negative change. Thus, positive change was not only not stressful but had a positive impact on adjustment. We should note, however, a possible exception to our argument in regard to health effects related to physical exhaustion. Here, unrelenting change may, indeed, tax biological systems to the point at which breakdown occurs. However, biological processes are very different from the social-psychological processes that are addressed in family stress theory.

Because most of the studies that Thoits (1983) reviewed focused on individual responses to stress,

it is possible that families react to change more negatively than individuals do. Therefore, in order not to bias our search, we examined those studies by family stress researchers that are often cited as supporting the assumption that change equals stress. The findings of research on moving to a new location, for example, are typically cited as evidence that change causes family stress. However, Brett (1982) found that families who move were no more distressed than static families. Moreover, positive changes in job status (typically a salary increase and greater prestige) were unrelated to distress, providing further evidence that change per se was not the stressful element in the move.

Munton (1990) also investigated the stressful impact of job relocation. Although several of Munton's items were somewhat ambiguous (e.g., "disruption to family home") as to whether they indicated change only or negative change, whenever a clear differentiation was possible only negative change had deleterious consequences, and the more negative the change, the greater the adverse effects. For example, moving shorter distances was generally less stressful because there was less negative change. On such moves, people lose fewer friends and spend less time searching for a new home. If a spouse experienced job loss or had problems finding a new job, this negative consequence further exacerbated the stress of moving.

Divorce is another life event in which the notion that change per se is stressful has been argued, but even those who hold this view have reported contrary findings. For example, Buehler and Langenbrunner (1987) found that the most disruptive changes stemming from divorce were all related to some form of loss, such as economic deterioration, a negative relationship with the individual's former spouse, feeling out of control, and moving. In contrast, items that indicated positive changes resulting from divorce were generally least disruptive or had little influence (e.g., economic improvement). Although we have argued that the stress of moving seems to depend on how the consequences of the event are perceived, moving appears to be particularly disruptive for women after divorce, because women have fewer financial resources and must adapt to worse circumstances (Caldwell, Bloom, & Hodges, 1984).

In a study of the stressful effects of parenting on parental warmth and firmness or strictness (Roberts, 1989), major losses (e.g., death of a spouse) and minor losses (e.g., failing an exam) were both found to be stressful. In this same study, however, changes such as a spouse beginning or discontinuing work, the birth of a child, or relocation to another town were unrelated to the outcome variables. Thus, change itself was not stressful, but the negative consequences of change were.

In sum, the trend in the family literature is similar to that noted in the individual stress literature. Specifically, the only indication in family stress studies that change is stressful occurs either when ambiguous items are used (e.g., family disruption) or when neutral items (e.g., a move) are mixed with negative items (e.g., spouse could not find work) and a total score is presented. Nor is equating change with stress merely a matter of semantics. To do so is misleading because attention is distracted from the critical challenge to families, namely, the accumulation of negative changes.

The measurement of family stress and the importance of family resources, including social support, are considered next. The role of family perceptions and values are examined in the following section.

Measurement of Family Stress

An important implication of the preceding discussion for the measurement of family stress is that stressor measures that combine neutral, negative, and positive items will produce misleading findings. The outcome effects of positive and negative changes are confounded or masked when such measures are used. Because the best and currently most widely used stressor scales have some of these problems, efforts to break down scales into subcategories are helpful (H. I. McCubbin & Thompson, 1991). Given our present state of knowledge, dividing stressful events into acute and chronic stressors, major and minor stressors, and ongoing family strains is a critical requirement.

It is also important to separate events or circumstances that occur to families (e.g., job layoffs, dual-career demands) from those that come from the family itself (e.g., parent-child strains, family violence). Both types of events and circumstances are important for study, but they lie at very different places in family stress theories. For example, according to Olson's (1991) circumplex model, job layoffs are outside events, whereas family violence is both an event and an outgrowth of family problems, stemming perhaps from the family's lack of differentiation.

A related measurement issue is the problem of intraitem variability that may result from varying interpretations of the meaning of key words in stressor scale items. For example, divorce in the Holmes-Rahe (1967) scale can mean a wanted divorce, an unwanted divorce, a divorce that leads to rags or riches, or the pain that occurred years earlier when the divorce was initiated. If such items mean many different things to respondents, the results will provide little insight into the family stress and adaptation processes that are of central interest (Brown & Harris, 1989). B. P. Dohrenwend, Raphael, Schwartz, Steuve, and Skodol (in press) developed a structured event probe that avoids this problem and has exciting potential for use in future family stress research.

We have used the concept of loss to refer to a critical component of most stressful life events, but this point deserves further discussion. Earlier research simply described the types of "undesirable" events that were stressful (Thoits, 1983), but undesirable seems to translate more clearly into events or circumstances in which losses occur or are threatened (see Brown & Harris, 1989; B. P. Dohrenwend, Link, Kern, Shrout, & Markowitz, 1990; Hobfoll, 1988, 1989). In a broad overview of findings from stress research, it is clear that the most stressful events all involve tangible loss or circumstances that threaten loss (e.g., death of a spouse, divorce, loss of freedom through imprisonment). The next most powerful stressors are losses such as lowered health status and loss of income. Similarly, McCollum (1990) found that the most stressful elements in relation to moving involved some form of loss.

Although microstressors or hassles have not yet been closely examined in relation to the attribute of loss, there is evidence that hassles have an aggregate negative effect when they accumulate to produce larger losses. In the literature on burnout, for example, it has been found that small work hassles do not have much effect until they aggregate to make individuals feel that work is hopeless or that one cannot have any real impact (Pines, Aronson, & Kafry, 1981; Shirom, 1989). In stress reactions to hassles, perception plays an exceedingly important role (Boss, 1988). Moreover, the effects of many microstressors may be largely attributed to underlying personality dispositions that influence perception and not the stressful event (B. S. Dohrenwend, Dohrenwend, Dodson, & Shrout, 1984; Spielberger, 1972, 1979).

Resource Factor

A significant emerging trend in the family stress literature is the increased focus on family resources, which were included as a major component (factor B) in Hill's original ABC-X model. Family resources were subsequently incorporated in a more complex and sophisticated manner in the double ABC-X model by H. I. McCubbin and Patterson (1982). In general, resources may be defined as the strengths of individuals, families, or larger systems that are valued or that act as a vehicle for obtaining that which is valued. The double ABC-X model assumes that family resources are not only used to combat stressors but that they are themselves transformed in the stress process. Resource theory and, in particular, the acknowledgment of the ecological context of resource utilization has been the hallmark of Moos's work on the family (1974, 1984). In particular, this has led Moos to examine family climate on the dimensions of supportiveness and openness of communication.

One of the most significant contributions of research on family stress has been the concept of systems level resources, which has received scant attention in the individual and traumatic stress literatures. Although systems level resources have been of interest in regard to organizational stress, this interest has been accompanied by relatively little research (Shirom, 1989). A handful of family resources have been identified as especially important in coping with stressful events. Among these are (a) flexibility/adaptability versus rigidity; (b) cohesion versus separateness; (c) communication versus privacy; (d) boundary ambiguity versus boundary clarity; and (e) order and mastery versus

chaos and helplessness (Boss, 1987; Epstein, Bishop, & Baldwin, 1982; H. I. McCubbin & Patterson, 1983; Moos, 1984; Olson & McCubbin, 1982; Reiss, 1981).

In emphasizing the dialectical nature of many resources, Boss (1987) raised a very interesting point that has meaning for both theory and measurement. This dialectic can be related, for example, to Olson's (1991) circumplex model. The circumplex model has three dimensions—(a) cohesion, (b) adaptability, and (c) communication—that in Olson's latest revision exist in a spherical space. A very complex theory, one of its central tenets states that "Balanced systems will generally function more adequately than Unbalanced (Extreme) systems" (p. 11). After noting that families who do a good job in resisting stress's harmful effects are high on cohesion, flexibility, and communication, Olson concluded that cohesion must not sacrifice separateness, flexibility must also allow for stability, and communication must be open but not limit privacy. These resources clearly focus attention on the fact that antithesis is inherent in synthesis (e.g., flexibility and rigidity tend to be opposite in their effects, but both must be present and integrated for healthy functioning).

As a family resource, *cohesion* is generally defined as the connectedness among members of a family. Sometimes referred to as *integration,* this construct depicts the family's common interests, affection, and economic interdependence (H. I. McCubbin & Patterson, 1982). *Adaptability* and *flexibility* refer to the ability of a family to change with changing demands (Olson, 1991), which implies flexibility in the power structure and in rules and role relationships. Communication refers to the ability to exchange information in terms of both content and emotional relevance (Olson & McCubbin, 1982). It also includes the notion that communication should be empathic and supportive and not disqualifying or double binding (Olson, 1972).

Boss (1987) emphasized the importance for the family of boundary ambiguity, which she described as the degree of clarity of who is included in the family. Unlike cohesion, it is not how close family members are but rather the degree to which the status of a family member is known. High ambiguity tends to upset rules and family relationships and makes goal setting and achievement more difficult.

Order and mastery (Pearlin & Schooler, 1978; Reiss & Oliveri, 1980) are factors that have been identified as individual and organizational stress-resistance factors. For example, mastery (and related concepts) has been found to buffer the deleterious effects of stress for individuals facing health and work challenges (Hobfoll & Lerman, 1988; Kobasa & Puccetti, 1983). Similarly, Iscoe (1974) talked about the competent community, suggesting that the need for order and mastery is a stress-resistance resource that bridges all levels of social systems. Order and mastery not only provide a means to address stressful events directly but also facilitate the assignment of meaning to events. The importance of meaning is less evident in research but has been a common element in stress and coping theories about individuals (Antonovsky, 1979), families (Reiss & Oliveri, 1980), and organizations (French, Caplan, & Harrison, 1982). It appears that people have a need to assign meaning to the world around them, and when meaning is lost a cornerstone in the motivational process breaks down. We address meaning further when evaluating the perception factor in the ABC-X model.

Although self-esteem is viewed as an important stress-resistance factor in the individual stress literature (Hobfoll & Leiberman, 1987; Kobasa, 1987), family self-esteem has received less attention. *Family esteem* can be defined as the extent to which the family feels that they are deserving of love, affection, and positive regard. Olson and his colleagues (Olson, Russel, & Sprenkle, 1989) hypothesized that families who are more extreme on his circumplex dimensions will nevertheless fare well if they are satisfied with the family structure. Satisfaction with the family is tangentially related to family esteem, but esteem implies positive regard of the family and its members.

A theoretical issue with important measurement implications arises in relation to the question of whether the resources described previously are independent dimensions or components of a global construct. Family stress research has found that a number of the resource dimensions are reasonably independent. Lavee and Olson (1991), for example, found a fairly equal distribution of the four major

family types in the circumplex model. This study is especially helpful for examining the question of multiple resource dimensions because it has large sample size (1,140 families) distributed over a broad spectrum of life stages (i.e., newly married to retirement). Unfortunately, most of these resources have not as yet been studied together so carefully. It is important in family stress research to examine multiple resources and to use advanced statistical techniques, such as multiple regression and structural modeling, to distill the active ingredients and remove areas of overlap (see Bloom, 1985).

Fitting Resources, Not Resource Fit

Organizational stress researchers have been concerned about the fit of resources with tasks (French et al., 1982; French, Rodgers, & Cobb, 1974). Fit theory maintains that it is not whether a resource is good or not, but whether it fits the current task demands (Cutrona, Cohen, & Igram, 1990). Waldren, Bell, Peck, and Sorrel (1990) applied fit theory in the family context. They hypothesized that postdivorce remarried families would benefit more than first-marriage families from cohesion and adaptability. The more complex structure of remarried families, issues of membership, and demands from parents, relatives, and the prior biological family make for greater demands and perhaps a greater need for the family resources of adaptability and cohesion. In fact, Waldren et al. (1990) found that lower levels of family stress were related to cohesion and adaptability for remarried families, but not for first-marriage families. Because this kind of research adds precision to more general theory, it provides important insights for future investigations as well as for clinical work.

Hobfoll and Vaux (in press) introduced a new concept of fit using *fit* as an active verb. Resources do not fit demands; rather, people adapt (or fit) their resources to meet demands (i.e., more adaptable families mold their resources to meet changing demands). This is easily understood with money, where the same amount of money can be used to meet different financial demands through careful budgeting. Like any team, if the whole is to be greater than the sum of its parts, then the parts must be fit together in ways that maximize their potential. A family may, for example, use social support from friends for help with certain problems but may rely on intimate family members when addressing other concerns. The resources of two families might be the same, but how they are used to meet different tasks will often determine the outcome.

Fit is also an ongoing process, as stressful events and their consequences evolve over time. The idea that fitting resources to need is an active process is buttressed by work by M. McCubbin (1989), who found that single-parent families are higher on adaptability than two-parent families. It is unlikely that their greater adaptability led to divorce. Rather, it seems more likely that single-parent families became more adaptive in their coping efforts to meet the greater demands placed on them.

Social Support

One key family resource, social support, is quite different than the family resources already discussed. Social support is, in part, a dimension of family communication as suggested by Olson et al. (1989), but it also comes largely from outside of the family. Whether from family, colleagues, or friends, social support is the major vehicle for the provision of resources outside of the self.

Social support has been defined a number of ways. Rather than a single construct, as it is often used in the family stress literature, it is probably best seen as a metaconstruct. This construct includes a related set of resources that, when taken together, encompass social support (Vaux, 1988). Caplan (1974) suggested that social support was the product of social activities that enhanced people's sense of mastery through sharing tasks, providing material and cognitive assistance, and providing emotional comfort. Other theorists suggested that social support was the product of beliefs that one was esteemed and cared for. Over the past 15 years, research on social support has identified three major factors: (a) support network resources; (b) supportive behavior; and (c) the subjective appraisals of support (Hobfoll & Vaux, in press). All three aspects of social support are important and have different causes and influences.

There has been intensive interest in the family stress literature in all three aspects of social support

(H. I. McCubbin, Cauble, & Patterson, 1982). The concept of a cohesive, supportive, positively communicating family is central to many family stress theories (Boss, 1987; H. I. McCubbin & Patterson, 1982; Moos, 1974, 1984; Olson et al., 1989). Greater family support is related to a lower risk of potential coronary heart disease in children (Woodall & Matthews, 1989); better psychological adjustment among adolescents (Burt, Cohen, & Bjorck, 1988); lower rates of posttraumatic stress disorder after psychiatric breakdown in combat (Solomon, Mikulincer, Freid, & Wosner, 1987); better family adjustment when a child in the family has a chronic, serious illness (Kazak, 1989); and better postdivorce adjustment (Wilcox, 1986).

It is difficult to separate the concept of social support from other family resources. For example, family cohesiveness, family communication, and family adaptability are all related to social support. It is important for future research to differentiate these concepts from the behaviors that constitute support. Cohesiveness, for instance, could be related to well-being because family members are closely linked. This does not mean, however, that they will help each other in a particular stressful instance. Because cohesiveness, adaptability, and communication can be seen as factors that underlie social support, families that are high on these dimensions are more likely to offer family members social support during stressful circumstances.

Research on the *process* of social support may help clarify what social support actually does for families. Hobfoll and Lerman (1988) showed, for instance, that social support becomes taxed during persistently stressful family circumstances, such as when a child is chronically ill. Over time, the value of social support is reduced, and differences between those who originally received support and those who did not may become less meaningful. Furthermore, other resources previously linked to receiving social support become less influential. These findings suggest that cohesiveness might be more strongly related to initial social support in confronting acute family stress than to support dealing with long-term family stress. As stress becomes chronic, the ability for the cohesive family to rally and mobilize support may become worn down by the ongoing call for help. At this point, the family may have to rely increasingly on the internal resources of its members, such as their sense of self-esteem and mastery.

It is misleading to consider social support as always positive. Dense family networks may actually be related to greater distress among parents of handicapped children (Kazak, 1989). Family members may have an investment in sustaining the family, even when this is to the detriment of the individual, as was found to be the case with battered women (Mitchell & Hodson, 1983). Similarly, Hirsch (1980) found that women benefitted from less dense social networks that contained confidants outside of the family. Indeed, women low in self-esteem were actually found to be hampered by social support, whereas women who were high in self-esteem benefitted from greater support (Hobfoll, Nadler, & Leiberman, 1986), suggesting that family members need strong internal resources to benefit from social support.

Julien and Markman (1991) reported that the greater the marital distress, the more husbands and wives mobilized outside support, indicating that support may actually increase as marital problems become more severe. Under stressful circumstances, social support may also result in stress contagion (Riley & Eckenrode, 1986) or a pressure-cooker effect (Hobfoll & London, 1986). Because those who are close share both the stress and the social support, the weight of the stress is sometimes predominant over the benefit of the support. This may especially be the case for persons with low self-esteem, because they either use support unwisely (e.g., becoming overly dependent) or their need surpasses what support can offer.

There are a number of good measures of social support (see Barrera, 1986; Sarason, Sarason, & Pierce, 1989; Vaux, 1988), but it is essential for researchers to identify the specific aspects of social support in which they are interested. Different measures are appropriate when one is asking, say, about the importance of strong versus weak ties or the size of a family's social network. Brown and Harris (1978) emphasized the importance of a few intimate others. In contrast, when a family is relocating after a job layoff, it seems likely that a large number of loose ties will be most helpful in regaining

employment, finding suitable housing, and integrating children in new schools (Wellman, 1981).

It is important to note that social support is nested in a number of instruments within broader surveys of stressful events (Holyrod, 1988). This practice makes examination of the effect of social support difficult because common method variance is likely to increase when individuals respond to stress items along with social support items. Such instruments might also mislead researchers into thinking that social support itself has been assessed rather than as a component of the broader concept. In addition, it is important to emphasize that stress is a process that affects support systems and changes them (H. I. McCubbin & Patterson, 1982).

Family Perceptions, Values, and Meaning: The C Factor

A number of theorists pointed to the importance of shared values and meaning as a stress-resistance resource. The origins of the study of the relationship between values, meaning, and stress resistance can be found in the early work of May (1958) and Frankl (1963). In his studies of concentration camp survivors, Frankl found that the emergence of personal meaning in the context of these horrible events was related to more successful adjustment.

Following Frankl's lead, Antonovsky (1979) replicated Frankl's findings on a sample of concentration camp survivors some years later. Hill's (1949) early work on family stress also emphasized the importance of family perception and meaning (his C factor) in stress resistance and adaptation, and this factor has been particularly emphasized in the family stress literature by Boss (1988).

Reiss and Oliveri (1980) postulated that a shared family paradigm was a major resource in the success of the family in coping with stressful events. When severe stressors are encountered, however, the family is often forced to challenge this basic set of shared values and beliefs. If the family can successfully rally around a new set of values and beliefs, they may emerge with a heightened sense of family potency. This model further emphasizes that family values and meaning are influenced by an underlying set of resources that include a sense of family mastery, solidarity, and openness to novel responses.

Reiss and Oliveri (1991) reported that a family's values and meaning paradigms will be influenced by their congruence with the values and meaning paradigms of the community. When the two are congruent, the family will enjoy community support; when they are incongruent, community support will not be forthcoming. This is an exciting new approach that deserves further attention.

Although an emphasis on shared values and meaning seems quite reasonable, this view is not widely accepted in practice. Reiss and Oliveri (1980) argued that family scholars have focused on conflict, which on a face-valid level belies that there are shared values. They contended, however, that even conflicted families have a broad set of shared values and must agree on what is important to have a shared battlefield for conflict. Lazarus and Folkman (1984) also emphasized individual differences as a major focus for stress research, as have a number of family stress researchers (Buehler, 1990). Although Lazarus and Folkman's notions have considerable value, they can be overstated. Specifically, what they depict as individual differences often reflect family and community paradigms (i.e., shared conceptualizations within the social group rather than idiosyncratic differences between individuals).

The family's own perception of the stressfulness of an event and the resources they have to cope with the event is very important (Boss, 1988; Imig & Imig, 1986; Lavee, McCubbin, & Patterson, 1985; Meeks, Arnkoff, Glass, & Nortarius, 1986), especially on a clinical level where even small differences in the evaluation of the meaning of an event may have clinical significance. Investigators need to be aware, however, that there is broad consensus about the stressfulness of specific life events and the resources that are needed to meet these challenges. If it were otherwise, the research on family stress would not have been so successful in identifying key family resources.

Coping Behavior

Following the work of Lazarus (1966), there has been considerable interest in the role of coping behavior in adjustment to stress. Coping is a multidimensional concept that includes the behavioral, emotional, and cognitive activities that individuals and families engage in to adjust and adapt to stressful events and circumstances (H. I. McCubbin & Patterson, 1983; Moos, 1984). Menaghan (1983) emphasized that, from theoretical and assessment perspective, it is critical to distinguish between the use and the effectiveness of coping strategies. Much coping is not effective.

Research has typically focused on three types of coping: cognitive or appraisal focused, problem focused, and emotion focused. Boss (1987) pointed out that although coping research has emphasized active versus passive dimensions, it has left the social versus nonsocial dimension unstudied. Similarly, Hobfoll and Dunahoo (1992) developed a dual-axis model of coping (Figure 10.1) that includes active-passive and prosocial-antisocial dimensions. Studying gender and role differences in coping, Dunahoo (1991) found traditional men relied more on active-antisocial coping, whereas traditional women relied more on passive-prosocial coping. Moreover, a nontraditional gender role orientation and a high sense of mastery were related to more active-prosocial coping strategies.

Family research might especially benefit from this dual-axis model. For families, it is a question not only of active or passive coping but whether coping supports other family members or ignores or belittles them. Previous research identified men as higher than women in problem-focused coping (Folkman & Lazarus, 1980), but such coping may have been in these men's own best interests, independent of its harm or benefit to the family. As a multicultural perspective becomes increasingly valued, we must recognize that individually based and socially based coping strategies are not only different but are often in direct conflict (Jackson & Meadows, 1991).

In general, theory and measurement relating to family coping lags behind other areas of family stress study. Although the discussion sections of many articles on family stress are filled with rich ideas, these need to be translated into hypotheses, models, and careful empirical investigation. Part of the problem in the studies of coping stems from the weakness of the available instruments in this field

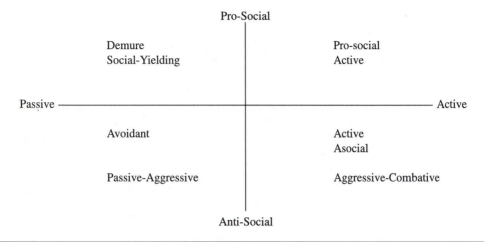

Figure 10.1   The Dual-Axis Model of Coping

and how they are used (see Stone, Greenberg, Kennedy-Moore, & Newman, 1991). Attempts to construct more reliable coping measures, such as those of Carver, Scheier, and Weintraub (1989), will prove helpful.

The Crisis or Outcome: Factor X

The X factor has been conceived as the crisis or stress-outcome component of the ABC-X model. Stress and crisis are not, however, one and the same. Crisis is usually considered to encompass an extreme stress response in a situation in which personal or familial coping resources are overwhelmed (Boss, 1988; Caplan, 1964). Studies of individual stress have focused primarily on the psychological and emotional well-being of individuals (Goldberger & Breznitz, in press). Similarly, family stress research has been most attentive to individual trait or state variables, such as depression, anxiety, and physical well-being. However, family stress research has also addressed the systems level when examining outcomes of stressful circumstances. Among the more commonly measured systems constructs are marital distress and family satisfaction.

There has been increased interest in resources themselves as outcome variables (Hobfoll, 1990; M. McCubbin & McCubbin, in press), which parallels the increased attention given to stress resistance as a process. For example, stressful events tax

resources such as family mastery, and the loss of mastery is itself an important outcome. Loss or preservation of resources will ultimately branch out into a broad web of other outcomes such as family discord and the emotional and health problems of individual family members. Our focus should be directed not at breakdown but at resiliency, as M. McCubbin and McCubbin (in press) have recently suggested.

In the ABC-X system, the outcome variables chosen for study are as varied as the questions that researchers and clinicians wish to ask. Family conflict, the psychological distress of family members, and whether or not families stay in counseling are all legitimate outcome variables. Because the number of potential outcome variables can be exceedingly large, it is imperative for investigators to state their questions clearly and avoid confounding the stressor event with the outcome. They should also rely on prospective designs with multiple points of measurement.

It is highly desirable to study multiple outcome variables, especially because these may be related to the nature of the stressor event and its aftermath. For example, job layoffs should be examined in the context of how they affect family mastery, financial status, depression in family members, and job search activity. Because the possible sequences are complex, applying family stress models will be especially informative. Findings in the individual stress literature, such as the relations between stress, anger, and heart disease (Spielberger & London, 1982, 1990), are illustrative of possible avenues of investigation.

Before concluding our discussion of the outcome factor in ABC-X models of family stress, we should note that such models are highly consistent with Lazarus's (1966) conception of stress as a complex transactional process. In Lazarus's view, the term *stressor* refers to situations or circumstances that are objectively characterized by some degree of physical or psychological danger or threat (Spielberger, 1972). Individuals who perceive or appraise a particular situation or circumstance as potentially harmful or dangerous will experience an anxiety reaction (Spielberger, 1979). Individuals who perceive that they are being attacked or treated unfairly by others are likely to react with anger.

The impact of negative change on the behavior of family members is markedly influenced by their emotional reactions, which are mediated by their perceptions and appraisals of stressful circumstances. The intensity of these emotional states will be a function of the individual's personality traits and coping skills as well as the resources of the family as a social system. Thus, emotional states and their consequences are important outcomes in the family stress process. Consequently, research on family stress should take into account the personality traits and emotional states of family members, for which well-validated measures of anxiety and anger are available (Spielberger, 1983, 1988).

CONSERVATION OF RESOURCES THEORY

Hobfoll (1988, 1989) developed a theory of stress that seems applicable as a framework for family stress research. This model, called conservation of resources (COR) theory, depicts resources as a product of widely shared values and meaning as to what is valuable to people. The role of resources is the pivotal construct in COR theory, in which the central tenet is that individuals (alone and in systems) strive to maximize resource gain and minimize resource loss. Therefore, major sources of stress are (a) threat of loss of resources; (b) actual loss of resources; or (c) the failure to gain resources after

significant resource investment. Seen in this way, events are stressful to the extent that they threaten or result in loss of critical family resources. To the extent that an event threatens or results in a loss in family cohesiveness, depletes family mastery, or attacks family order, families will react to the event as stressful.

Resources are defined as those things that people value or that act as a means of obtaining or protecting that which they value. COR theory posits four principal resource categories: (a) object resources (e.g., transportation and home); (b) condition resources (e.g., good marriage and tenure); (c) personal resources (e.g., self-esteem and social aplomb); and (d) energy resources (e.g., money and credit). The theory further proposes that all that a family has to offset resource loss is other resources. For example, a family may use its sense of mastery to offset threats to order or family cohesiveness. Other family stress models have uniformly thought of the stressor as challenging the family but have been somewhat tautological. It is commonly held that events are stressful to the extent they make demands that outstrip resources and that resources are those things that are used to meet demands. COR theory states more directly that stress occurs with resource loss, even if resources are not outstripped. Furthermore, such loss makes families more vulnerable because they have fewer resources available to deal with future stressors that will inevitably occur.

Just as stressors pile up, loss of resources can be cumulative as well. Resource loss sets up an adverse cycle whereby further loss is more likely. After initial loss, fewer resources are available for stress resistance. Hence, the family is less resilient and more vulnerable. Moreover, this cycle is likely to occur with increasing velocity, as the family is bombarded with demands for resource mobilization against a resource pool that is decreasingly robust. After resource gain, an opposite positive cycle is also predicted (i.e., future gain is more likely). By successfully meeting the challenge of a straightforward transition, the family feels more confident in their ability to address more stressful challenges.

COR theory posits that loss and gain cycles do not have equal intensity or velocity because losses are more highly weighted by individuals than are gains (Hobfoll, Lilly, & Jackson, 1992). Extending this notion to families, the same should hold true. We predict that loss cycles will have greater intensity and momentum than gain cycles and that loss cycles will be harder to interrupt and reverse than gain cycles. Such thinking might be helpful in guiding family stress research as it places greater emphasis on resource models.

Boss (1987) independently arrived at a number of family stress resistance principles that appear to be quite consistent with COR theory. She wrote (Boss, 1987, p. 702):

> The family's resources, therefore, are the sociological, economic, psychological, emotional, and physical assets on which the members can draw in response to a single stressor event or an accumulation of events. However, having resources does not imply how the family will use them. . . . If the family has few resources, individually and collectively, the coping process may never begin, and crisis may result.

Boss's (1987) resource utilization model and COR theory, with its emphasis on the overweighting of loss versus gain, may aid researchers and clinicians in examining the process by which resources are used by families in responding to the demands of stressful circumstances.

FAMILY STRESS THEORY AND MEASUREMENT ISSUES

There are a number of general issues and questions that should be addressed when examining the integration of theory and measurement in the study of family stress. The first of these questions pertains to determining the correct target for research attention. Much family research has relied on the accounts of individual family members. A number of investigators argued the importance of developing a familial accounting. Still others relied on clinicians' observations of family processes (see Buehler, 1990). The question of which of these provides the best perspective is probably less important than whether the locus of attention is appropriate for the particular research or clinical question. Boss (1987, p. 704) argued that "the family as a group is not coping if

even one member manifests distress symptoms." If this stringent criterion is adopted, then both individual and familial loci are of critical importance in the study of family stress.

Closely related to this first issue is the question of how individual scores are best treated. Researchers will again find that different methods result in different strengths and problems. Averaging minimizes the effect of within-family variability, but treating scores individually may result in confounding the family forest with the individual trees (i.e., the unit of family is lost). New statistical methods, such as structural equation modeling, may help in this regard because they extract the common element in diverse measurements of a single construct (Bentler, 1989). However, this currently popular statistical method also minimizes the effects of differences between family members. Future research will benefit from developing and comparing both individual and familial models of adaptation and adjustment. Research on obtained differences with different loci and levels of measurement will itself be informative.

Overall, family stress research has greatly benefitted from a very close tie between theory and measurement. No other area of stress research has models and measurements so closely connected. One negative consequence of this state of affairs is that researchers have had to shoulder the burden of producing measures to assess every facet of their model, which inevitably results in a plethora of scales whose reliability and validity are mixed. To their credit, however, family stress researchers have been extremely forthcoming with studies of the reliability and validity of their measures. The FACES test, for example, has gone through numerous revisions and refinements (Olson, 1991), and there will probably be further improvements as well.

A number of our conclusions may be controversial. A primary assertion of this article is that change per se is not stressful in itself. Rather, we see loss, threat of loss, and failure to gain as underpinnings of the stress process. We review the literature critically to make this point. It is our conclusion that the belief that change itself is stressful can no longer fit the accumulation of literature. We think it has remained a part of family stress models because it was integral to early theories and because of the ambiguity in questionnaires that assessed change. Thoits (1983) carefully reviewed the literature comparing studies that assessed positive and negative changes and found that only negative change had a significant impact. Thoits was among the first to make this assertion, and we find that the literature since her germinal article reifies her interpretation of the data. Some may argue that our conclusion is premature or even different from how they would interpret the literature. It is hoped that this controversial point will spur further research on the topic.

The family stress literature has increasingly emphasized perception (Boss, 1988) rather than the event as the major contributor to stress outcomes. We agree that appraisal is very important but suggest that appraisal is not as idiographic as Boss suggested (see Boss, 1987, and her response to this article for an alternative viewpoint). Indeed, many studies of family stress have focused on clear stressors, such as illness or divorce, and not on ambiguous events. This, we think, is a response to the conclusion that both the perception and the actual nature of the stressor is critical and to earlier findings that strongly suggested that stress reactions and neurosis are often confounded when perception is overemphasized and the importance of objective circumstances is not adequately emphasized (B. S. Dohrenwend et al., 1984). Lazarus and Folkman (1984) made the important point that the more ambiguous the event, the greater the influence of perception. We emphasize the other end of this continuum; that is, for events of importance, individuals' unique perceptions play an increasingly smaller role. Rather, shared common perceptions that would be held by most who experience the stressor will assume preeminence. Clearly, however, we hope that investigators examine these two interacting factors more closely.

In conclusion, we must emphasize that further refinement of family stress measures is critical for assessing the increasing exactitude of the family stress models that are being developed. This course of theory building, measurement construction and refinement, and model testing and revising is both the strength and the future of family stress research. Given the need for continued examination, there is nevertheless much to learn from the family stress literature. Implications and lessons for intervention

and prevention already abound. Clear progress has been made in our knowledge base, and few areas offer more potential for affecting people's needs because stress is such a critical phenomenon in family life.

REFERENCES

Antonovsky, A. (1979). *Health, stress, and coping.* San Francisco: Jossey-Bass.

Barrera, M., Jr. (1986). Distinctions between social support concepts, measures and models. *American Journal of Community Psychology, 14,* 413-445.

Bentler, P. M. (1989). *EOS structural equations program manual.* Los Angeles: BMDP.

Bloom, B. B. (1985). A factor analysis of self report measures of family functioning. *Family Process, 24,* 225-240.

Boss, P. (1987). Family stress. In M. B. Sussman & S. K. Steinmetz (Eds.), *Handbook of marriage and the family* (pp. 695-723). New York: Plenum Press.

Boss, P. (1988). *Family stress management.* Newbury Park, CA: Sage.

Brett, J. M. (1982). Job transfer and well-being. *Journal of Applied Psychology, 67,* 450-463.

Brown, G. W., & Harris, T. O. (1978). *The social origins of depression: The study of psychiatric disorder in women.* New York: Free Press.

Brown, G. W., & Harris, T. O. (1989). *Life events and illness.* New York: Guilford Press.

Buehler, C. (1990). Adjustment. In J. Touliatas, B. F. Perlmutter, & M. A. Strauss (Eds.), *Handbook of family measurement techniques* (pp. 493-574). Newbury Park, CA: Sage.

Buehler, C., & Langenbrunner, M. (1987). Divorce-related stressors: Occurrence, disruptiveness, and area of life changes. *Journal of Divorce, 11*(l), 25-50.

Burt, C. E., Cohen, L. H., & Bjorck, J. P. (1988). Perceived family environment as a moderator of young adolescents' life stress adjustment. *American Journal of Community Psychology, 16*(l), 101-122.

Caldwell, R. A., Bloom, B. L., & Hodges, W. F. (1984). Sex differences in separation and divorce: A longitudinal perspective. In A. U. Rickel, M. Gerrard, & I. Iscoe (Eds.), *Social and psychological problems of women* (pp. 103-120). New York: Hemisphere.

Caplan, G. (1964). *Principles of preventive psychiatry.* New York: Basic Books.

Caplan, G. (1974). *Support systems and community mental health: Lectures on concept development.* New York: Behavioral Publications.

Carver, C. S., Scheier, M. F., & Weintraub, J. K. (1989). Assessing coping strategies: A theoretically based approach. *Journal of Personality and Social Psychology, 56,* 267-283.

Cohen, S., & Hoberman, H. M. (1983). Positive events and social supports as buffers of life change stress. *Journal of Applied Social Psychology, 13,* 99-125.

Cutrona, C. E., Cohen, B. B., & Igram, S. (1990). Contextual determinants of the perceived supportiveness of helping behaviors. *Journal of Social and Personal Relationships, 7,* 553-562.

Dohrenwend, B. P., Link, B. G., Kern, R., Shrout, P. E., & Markowitz, J. (1990). Measuring life events: The problem of variability within event categories. *Stress Medicine, 6,* 179-187.

Dohrenwend, B. P., Raphael, K., Schwartz, S., Steuve, A., & Skodol, A. (in press). The structured event probe and narrative rating method for measuring life events. In L. Goldberger & S. Breznitz (Eds.), *Handbook of stress: Theoretical and clinical aspects* (2nd ed.). New York: Free Press.

Dohrenwend, B. S., Dohrenwend, B. P., Dodson, M., & Shrout, P. E. (1984). Symptoms, hassles, social support, and life events: Problem of confounded measures. *Journal of Abnormal Psychology, 93,* 222-230.

Dunahoo, C. (1991). Gender differences in professional versus interpersonal coping strategies. Unpublished master's thesis, Kent State University, Kent, OH.

Epstein, N. B., Bishop, D. S., & Baldwin, L. M. (1982). McMaster model of family functioning: A view of the normal family. In F. Walsh (Ed.), *Normal family process* (pp. 136-162). New York: Guilford Press.

Folkman, S., & Lazarus, R. S. (1980). An analysis of coping in a middle-aged community sample. *Journal of Health and Social Behavior, 21,* 219-239.

Frankl, V. E. (1963). *Man's search for meaning.* Boston: Beacon Press.

French, J. R. P., Jr., Caplan, R. D., & Harrison, R. V. (1982). *The mechanisms of job stress and strain.* London: Wiley.

French, J. R. P., Rodgers, W. L., & Cobb, S. (1974). Adjustment as person-environment fit. In G. V. Coelho, D. A. Hamburg, & J. E. Adams (Eds.), *Coping and adaptation* (pp. 316-333). New York: Basic Books.

Goldberger, L., & Breznitz, S. (in press). *Handbook of stress: Theoretical and clinical aspects* (2nd ed.). New York: Free Press.

Hill, R. (1949). *Families under stress: Adjustment to the crisis of war, separation and reunion.* New York: Harper & Row.

Hirsch, B. J. (1980). Natural support systems and coping with major life changes. *American Journal of Community Psychology, 8,* 159-172.

Hobfoll, S. E. (1988). *The ecology of stress.* Washington, DC: Hemisphere.

Hobfoll, S. E. (1989). Conservation of resources: A new attempt at conceptualizing stress. *American Psychologist, 44,* 513-523.

Hobfoll, S. E. (1990). The importance of predicting, activating and facilitating social support. *Journal of Social and Personal Relationships, 7,* 435-436.

Hobfoll, S. E., & Dunahoo, C. (1992). *Are we studying coping strategies or piecemeal behavior?* Paper presented at the Centennial Meeting of the American Psychological Association, Washington, DC.

Hobfoll, S. E., & Leiberman, Y. (1987). Personality and social resources in immediate and continued stress resistance among women. *Journal of Personality and Social Psychology, 52,* 18-26.

Hobfoll, S. E., & Lerman, M. (1988). Personal relationships, personal attributes and stress resistance: Mothers' reactions to their children's illness. *American Journal of Community Psychology, 16,* 565-589.

Hobfoll, S. E., Lilly, R. S., & Jackson, A. P. (1992). Conservation of social resources and the self. In H. O. F. Veiel & U. Baumann (Eds.), *The meaning and measurement of social support* (pp. 125-141). Washington, DC: Hemisphere.

Hobfoll, S. E., & London, P. (1986). The relationship of self-concept and social support to emotional distress among women during war. *Journal of Social and Clinical Psychology, 4,* 189-203.

Hobfoll, S. E., Nadler, A., & Leiberman, J. (1986). Satisfaction with social support during crisis: Intimacy and self-esteem as critical determinants. *Journal of Personality and Social Psychology, 51,* 296-304.

Hobfoll, S. E., & Vaux, A. (in press). Social support and social context. In L. Goldberger & S. Breznitz (Eds.), *Handbook of stress: Theoretical and clinical aspects* (2nd ed.). New York: Wiley.

Holmes, T. H., & Rahe, R. H. (1967). The social readjustment rating scale. *Journal of Psychosomatic Research, 11,* 213-218.

Holyrod, J. (1988). A review of the criterion validation research on the questionnaire on resources and stress-for families with chronically ill or handicapped members. *Journal of Clinical Psychology, 44,* 335-354.

Imig, D., & Imig, G. (1986). Influences of family management and spousal perceptions on stressor pile-up. *Family Relations, 34,* 227-232.

Iscoe, I. (1974). Community psychology and the competent community. *American Psychologist, 29,* 607-613.

Jackson, A. P., & Meadows, F., Jr. (1991). Getting to the bottom to understand the top. *Journal of Counseling and Development, 70,* 72-76.

Jahoda, M. (1958). *Current concepts of positive mental health.* New York: Basic Books.

Julien, D., & Markman, H. J. (1991). Social support and social networks as determinants of individual and marital outcomes. *Journal of Social and Personal Relationships, 8,* 549-568.

Kazak, A. E. (1989). Families of chronically ill children: A systems and social-ecological model of adaptation and challenge. *Journal of Consulting and Clinical Psychology, 57*(l), 25-30.

Kobasa, O. S. C. (1987). Stress responses and personality. In R. C. Barnett, L. Biener, & G. K. Baruch (Eds.), *Gender & stress* (pp. 308-329). New York: Free Press.

Kobasa, O. S. C., & Puccetti, M. C. (1983). Personality and social resources in stress resistance. *Journal of Personality and Social Psychology, 45,* 839-850.

Lavee, Y., McCubbin, H. I., & Patterson, J. (1985). The double ABCX model of family stress and adaptation: An empirical test by analysis of structural equations with latent variables. *Journal of Marriage and the Family, 47,* 811-825.

Lavee, Y., & Olson, D. H. (1991, August). Family types and response to stress. *Journal of Marriage and the Family, 53,* 786-798.

Lazarus, R. (1966). *Psychological stress and the coping process.* New York: McGraw-Hill.

Lazarus, R. S., & Folkman, S. (1984). *Stress, appraisal, and coping.* New York: Springer.

Lindemann, E. (1944). The symptomatology and management of acute grief. *American Journal of Psychiatry, 101,* 637-641.

May, R. (1958). Contributions of existential psychotherapy. In R. May, E. Angel, & H. F. Ellenberger (Eds.), *Existence: A new dimension in psychiatry and psychology* (pp. 37-91). New York: Basic Books.

McCollum, A. T. (1990). *The trauma of moving: Psychological issues for women.* Newbury Park. CA: Sage.

McCubbin, H. I., Cauble, A. E., & Patterson, J. M. (Eds.). (1982). *Family stress, coping, and social support.* Springfield, IL: Charles C Thomas.

McCubbin, H. I., & Patterson, J. M. (1982). Family adaptation to crisis. In H. McCubbin, A. Cauble, & J. Patterson (Eds.), *Family stress, coping and social support* (pp. 26-47). Springfield, IL: Charles C Thomas.

McCubbin, H. I., & Patterson, J. M. (1983). The family stress process: The double ABCX model of adjustment. *Marriage and Family Review, 6*(1-2), 7-37.

McCubbin, H. I., & Thompson, A. (Eds.). (1991). *Family assessment inventories for research and practice* (2nd ed.). Madison: University of Wisconsin.

McCubbin, M. (1989). Family stress and family strengths: A comparison of single- and two-parent families with handicapped children. *Research in Nursing & Health, 12,* 101-110.

McCubbin, M., & McCubbin, H. I. (in press). Family coping with illness: The resiliency model of family stress, adjustment and adaptation. In C. Danielson, B. Hammel-Bissel, & P. Winstead-Fry (Eds.), *Families health and illness.* St. Louis, MO: Mosby.

Meeks, S., Arnkoff, D., Glass, C., & Nortarius, C. (1986). Wives' employment status, hassles, communication, and relational efficacy: Intra- versus extrarelationship factors and marital adjustment. *Family Relations, 34,* 249-255.

Menaghan, E. G. (1983). Individual coping efforts: Moderators of the relationship between life stress and mental health outcomes. In H. B. Kaplan (Ed.), *Psychological stress: Trends in theory and research* (pp. 157-191). New York: Academic Press.

Mitchell, R. E., & Hodson, C. A. (1983). Coping and domestic violence: Social support and psychological health among battered women. *American Journal of Community Psychology, 11,* 629-654.

Moos, R. (1974). *Family environment scales and preliminary manual.* Palo Alto, CA: Consulting Psychologists Press.

Moos, R. H. (1984). Context and coping: Toward a unifying conceptual framework. *American Journal of Community Psychology, 12,* 5-25.

Munton, A. G. (1990). Job relocation, stress, and the family. *Journal of Organizational Behavior, 11,* 401-406.

Olson, D. H. (1972). Empirically unbinding the double bind: Review of research and conceptual formulations. *Family Process, 11,* 69-94.

Olson, D. H. (1991, November). *Three-dimensional (3D) circumplex model: Theoretical & methodological advances.* Paper presented at the National Council of Family Relations Theory Construction and Research Methodology Workshop, Denver, CO.

Olson, D. H., & McCubbin, H. I. (1982). Circumplex model of marital and family systems V: Application to family stress and crisis intervention. In H. I. McCubbin, A. E. Cauble, & J. M. Patterson (Eds.), *Family stress, coping, and social support* (pp. 48-68). Springfield, IL: Charles C Thomas.

Olson, D. H., Russel, C. S., & Sprenkle, D. H. (Eds.). (1989). *Circumplex model: Systematic assessment and treatment of families.* New York: Haworth Press.

Pearlin, L. I., & Schooler, C. (1978). The structure of coping. *Journal of Health and Social Behavior, 19,* 2-21.

Pines, A., Aronson, E., & Kafry, D. (1981). *Burnout: From tedium to personal growth.* New York: Free Press.

Reiss, D. (1981). *The family's construction of reality.* Cambridge, MA: Harvard University Press.

Reiss, D., & Oliveri, M. E. (1980). Family paradigm and family coping: A proposal for linking the family's intrinsic adaptive capacities to its responses to stress. *Family Relations, 29,* 431-444.

Reiss, D., & Oliveri, M. E. (1991). The family's conception of accountability and competence: A new approach to the conceptualization and assessment of family stress. *Family Process, 30,* 193-214.

Riley, D., & Eckenrode, J. (1986). Social ties: Subgroup differences in costs and benefits. *Journal of Personality and Social Psychology, 51,* 770-778.

Roberts, W. L. (1989). Parents' stressful life events and social networks: Relations with parenting and social competence. *Canadian Journal of Behavioral Science, 21,* 133-146.

Sarason, B. R., Sarason, I. G., & Pierce, G. R. (1989). *Social support: An interactional viewpoint.* New York: Wiley.

Shirom, A. (1989). Burnout in work organizations. In C. L. Cooper & I. Robertson (Eds.), *International review of industrial and organizational psychology* (pp. 26-48). New York: Wiley.

Solomon, S., Mikulincer, M., Freid, B., & Wosner, Y. (1987). Family characteristics and posttraumatic stress disorder: A follow-up of Israeli combat stress reaction casualties. *Family Process, 26,* 383-394.

Spielberger, C. D. (1972). Anxiety as an emotional state. In C. D. Spielberger (Ed.), *Anxiety: Current trends in theory and research* (Vol. 1, pp. 23-49). New York: Academic Press.

Spielberger, C. D. (1979). *Understanding stress and anxiety.* New York: Harper & Row.

Spielberger, C. D. (1983). *Manual for the State-Trait Anxiety Inventory (Form Y).* Palo Alto, CA: Consulting Psychologists Press.

Spielberger, C. D. (1988). *Professional manual for the State-Trait Anger Expression Inventory (STAXI)* (research ed.). Odessa, FL: Psychological Assessment Resources.

Spielberger, C. D., & London, P. (1982). Rage boomerangs: Lethal type-A anger. *American Health, 1,* 52-56.

Spielberger, C. D., & London, P. (1990, January/February). Blood pressure & injustice. *Psychology Today,* pp. 48-51.

Stone, A., Greenberg, M. A., Kennedy-Moore, E., & Newman, M. G. (1991). Self-report, situation-specific coping questionnaires: What are they measuring? *Journal of Personality and Social Psychology, 4,* 648-658.

Thoits, P. A. (1983). Dimensions of life events that influence psychological distress: An evaluation and synthesis of the literature. In H. B. Kaplan (Ed.), *Psychosocial stress* (pp. 33-103). San Diego, CA: Academic Press.

Vaux, A. (1988). *Social support: Theory, research and intervention.* New York: Praeger.

Waldren, T., Bell, N., Peck, C. W., & Sorrel, G. (1990). Cohesion and adaptability in post-divorce remarried and first married families: Relationships with family stress and coping styles. *Journal of Divorce and Remarriage, 14*(1), 13-28.

Wellman, B. (1981). Applying network analysis to the study of support. In B. H. Gottlieb (Ed.), *Social networks and social support* (pp. 171-200). Beverly Hills, CA: Sage.

Wilcox, B. L. (1986). Stress, coping, and the social milieu of divorced women. In S. E. Hobfoll (Ed.), *Stress, social support, and women* (pp. 115-133). Washington, DC: Hemisphere.

Woodall, K. L., & Matthews, K. A. (1989). Familial environment associated with type A behaviors and psychophysiological responses to stress in children. *Health Psychology, 8,* 403-426.

11

PRIMACY OF PERCEPTION IN FAMILY STRESS THEORY AND MEASUREMENT

PAULINE BOSS

A selection of interdisciplinary family stress literature is cited to illustrate that perceptions, even more than resources, predict which families manage high stress and which fall into crisis. Paraphrasing symbolic interactionist W. I. Thomas (1928), if family members define their helplessness as real, then their helplessness is real in its consequences. Cautions are given about measuring only shared common perceptions. Giving preeminence to a common perception may obscure gender and generational differences in families and could be ethically problematic. Research on boundary ambiguity is presented as an example of measuring individual and shared perceptions in distressed families.

I am delighted to accept Ron Levant's invitation to comment on the Hobfoll and Spielberger (1992) article and to have family stress the focal point in this issue of the *Journal of Family Psychology*. Starting with sociologist Reuben Hill, family stress researchers and theorists have built

their work on the primarily psychological literature on individual stress. It is fitting, then, that interdisciplinary links continue to complete the circle. What is new, however, is that there is now another discipline—family studies—that is being included in this process of accumulating knowledge about

Reprinted from the *Journal of Family Psychology* 6 (1992): 113-19. Copyright © 1992 by the American Psychological Association. Reprinted with permission.

Support of research on which this commentary is based was provided by the National Institute of Aging (P01-AG06309-01) and the University of Minnesota Experiment Station.

stressed families. It is primarily within this newer discipline that I have worked as a researcher, theorist, and family therapist. In 1973, I presented my first paper on family stress—"Psychological Father Absence in Intact Families"—at the National Council on Family Relations. This marked the beginning of my inquiry into the phenomenon of ambiguous loss as a major family stressor. This work has continued to the present, moving from clinical observation to inductive theory development to instrument development to empirical testing and qualitative study to clinical application and back again.

My assumptions, based on a contextual use of systems theory, are that families manage stress in diverse ways but that they are not managing optimally as long as even one member of that system remains depressed, scapegoated, demoralized, somaticized, or immobilized in any other way. The units of analysis for my research, therefore, include the individual and the family system as a whole plus the interactional process between them. My major theoretical premise is that families are most highly stressed by losses that are ambiguous. That is, family members do not know whether a loved one is absent or present. The "lost" person may be physically present but psychologically absent or physically absent but psychologically present. When family members cannot obtain clear facts surrounding their loss, the system is frozen into place; structural reorganization is blocked; systemic boundaries cannot be maintained. Individuals remain immobilized until they are able to construct a new reality of who is in and who is out of their family. When a loss remains ambiguous, this process depends on perceptions (Boss, 1980, 1987, 1988, 1990, 1993; Boss & Greenberg, 1984).

It is from this perspective that I comment on the Hobfoll and Spielberger (1992) article, first and only briefly regarding resources theory and then centering on family stress theory for the major discussion.

CONSERVATION OF RESOURCES THEORY

Hobfoll and Spielberger (1992) set out to integrate family stress theory and measurement with a focus on resources. They made a broad sweep and, in so doing, may have overwhelmed the newcomer; or

they may, as I hope, have stimulated family psychologists to join an ongoing effort to understand the complexity of family stress. There is an extensive body of family stress literature that has accumulated over decades stimulated by the Great Depression, World War II, and the Vietnam War. More recently, the focus has been on families coping with chronic physical and mental illnesses, chronic disabilities, divorce and remarriage, missing children, and political hostages.

What I like best about the conservation of resources (COR) theory is that it avoids focusing on the family's symptom and instead centers on a general variable that cuts across all families regardless of the stressor event. I applaud family stress researchers and family therapists who move beyond labeling families by their situation or symptom bearer and instead study the dynamic that builds up (or reduces) pressure in families. Resources represent such a variable.

First, however, there are some critical questions to consider. What are considered resources, and why are they more important than perceptions? How can resources be separated from perceptions? Hobfoll and Spielberger (1992) stated that "resources are defined as those things that people value or that act as a means of obtaining or protecting that which they value" (p. 108). Even with a construct that appears to be that straightforward, the question remains: Why do people with ample resources (from the perception of the researcher or therapist) not always use them? Resources are clearly not independent from perceptions.

Another question that has been raised is why people without resources do not just work harder and acquire them? Although resource theory may be helpful in tidying up the operationalization of family stress variables, the theory's underlying assumptions may not take into account disenfranchised families or disempowered family members. Politically, many families and individuals lack the resources and power to make decisions concerning their own destinies. Decision making and resource management are skills that were, for example, not highly cultivated in Communist countries. The caution about using resource theories to understand family stress centers on the need to include such variables as power, control over one's destiny, and the availability of choices without which families cannot act on or develop their resources. Indeed, "mastery" is an important representation of this idea (Pearlin, Menaghan, Lieberman, & Mullam, 1981), but I am referring here to something even more ecological or contextual in nature, more like Antonovsky's (1979) sense of coherence. Families will not develop resources or act on them without a sense that their actions will make a difference. Issues of power and oppression are therefore relevant. I refer readers to a further discussion on this topic in Boss (1988, chap. 6 and 7) and to a comprehensive review by Sabatelli and Shehan (in press), who merge psychological and family research and theories concerning resources. Other readings that may be of interest concerning resources are Converse, Foa, and Foa (in press), Foa and Foa (1980), Rettig and Bubolz (1983), Sabatelli (1988), Sabatelli and Shehan (in press), and Thibaut and Kelley (1959).

FAMILY STRESS THEORY

From the perspective of family stress theory, I agree with Hobfoll and Spielberger (1992) on many points, but I do not agree with them that "change per se is not stressful" (p. 109). Our disagreement, however, may be an issue of definitions. I define *family stress* as "pressure or tension . . . disturbance in the steady state of the family. . . . It is normal and even desirable at times. . . . With change comes disturbance, pressure—what we call stress" (Boss, 1988, p. 12). Stress, therefore, is neutral. Given this definition, I disagree with the authors' statement that change itself is not stressful, but I agree that change is not *dis*tressful (negative valence). Said another way, change does not automatically lead to negative stress—*strain, hassle,* or *crisis* (terms not synonymous but all representing different degrees of negative stress)—nor does it automatically lead to positive stress. Change is, however, by its very nature a disturbance in the status quo and thereby, at minimum, neutrally stressful.

I could agree with Hobfoll and Spielberger (1992) if they were to say that change per se does not cause the family to be strained or *dis*tressed (the neutrality is now gone). Indeed, some changes may not trouble the family—they may welcome them—but other

changes, such as loss, as the authors pointed out, are more often problematic. Loss is change and loss upsets most families. The family's level of stress could increase to the point of strain or crisis, or it could merely rise slightly and momentarily. It depends on a number of other variables.

Here, then, I raise a question to Hobfoll and Spielberger's (1992) premise that lack of resources is the primary cause of negative stress. Few family stress researchers today would support that idea. For example, Patterson (1988) found that the ratio between resources and stressor is the critical issue, not simply the lack of resources. Clinicians also report seeing numerous families with abundant resources who are nevertheless in crisis. Also they see families with few apparent resources who are managing well. If researchers make resources the prime focus, they will miss key intervening variables that are more powerful than the depletion of resources in predicting which families remain resilient and which fall into crisis.

Family stress theorists, therefore, have not uniformly thought of stressor events or situations as negative challenges to families even though family resources are taxed. I think of events such as a family performing a flying trapeze act, a mate taking a major examination or running a marathon, or a child preparing for a solo performance at school. Although any one of these events will challenge a family's resources, none will predictably outstrip them. It depends on the family's definition of the event even more than on the depth of their resources. Some of the most vulnerable families I see in therapy are those in which there is absolutely no stress. Nothing is going on. No one is being challenged. Resources are available, but no decisions are being made. Everyone is quiet and immobilized. There is no interaction. These are "flat-liner" families, and the prognosis for avoiding crisis is not good.

Although I agree with Hobfoll and Spielberger (1992) that "events are stressful to the extent they make demands" (p. 108), I do not agree that these demands will inevitably deplete resources. Family life can go on positively in spite of a heavy burden. For example, in my research with families experiencing the ambiguous loss of living with an Alzheimer's disease patient, I see this positive outlook repeatedly.

Trouble surfaces only when pressures on the family structure outweigh resources. Yet even when the ratio of resources to burden remains the same, some family members may reach a turning point where they cannot bear the load any longer. The question we ask is, Why? If these two variables did not change, what did? One place to find the answer lies in the family's perceptions, meanings, or appraisals. All fit under Hill's (1949) C factor (definition of the event), not under the B factor (resources). Indeed, perceptions influence how one sees or uses resources, but the sequence begins and ends with perceptions. This is not a new idea. In 1928, symbolic interactionist W. I. Thomas said that if people define things as real, they are real in their consequences.

The existing research will not support Hobfoll and Spielberger's (1992) statement that negative stress "occurs with resource loss, even if resources are not outstripped. Furthermore, such loss makes families more vulnerable because they have fewer resources available to deal with future stressors that will inevitably occur" (p. 108). That model is too mechanistic for human systems. What researchers have found instead is that families who have coped successfully with past stressors are better able to do so again. The process is self-reinforcing. Families as a whole and the individuals in them learn how to cope by coping successfully. The process is synergistic. The greatest lessons for coping with stress and preventing crisis, therefore, may be learned in families of origin or from significant persons who taught and modeled problem solving and mastery rather than helplessness and hopelessness. The more a person observes and experiences successful coping and managing, the more invulnerable they will be to the next challenge, whatever it turns out to be.

Examples of research that support this idea come from various disciplines. Masten and Garmezy studied children who came from dysfunctional families but who nevertheless remained resilient and competent (Masten, 1989). Research on soldiers who were prisoners of war documents that those who survived drew on coping strategies and resources that had been useful to them even before captivity (Figley, 1989; Hunter, 1991). Although physical contact with loved ones was impossible, many prisoners and more recent political hostages said that keeping their loved ones present in their minds kept them going. Also, those who used mastery as a coping skill before captivity remained masterful, to the degree that they could, even in the unjust context of captivity. Media accounts tell us that journalist Terry Anderson, 7 years (1985-1992) a hostage in Beirut, Lebanon, used mastery skills not only to keep himself alive but also to keep his fellow prisoner, Tom Sutherland, alive.

As readers may already have surmised, my conceptualization of family stress theory links the ideas of learned helplessness (Seligman, 1975), just-world theory (Lerner, 1971), and mastery (Pearlin et al., 1981) to better understand how families construe their realities as they experience negative stress. Ideally, measures of individual perceptions plus the collective family perception as well as an outside observer's assessment are needed. Congruence scores will yield data that can guide interventions. When an illness cannot be cured, a disability is permanent, or a body cannot be found, the focus on perceptions is especially useful because this provides the only window for change and for lowering the family's stress level. For example, Patterson and Leonard (in press) reported the importance of perceptual shifts in their research on families caring for medically fragile children at home where there are real limits (because of policy) to the resources that families are able to access. Boss, Caron, Horbal, and Mortimer (1990) found perceptions to be the strongest predictor of caregiver depression when an elderly dementia patient was being cared for at home.

This primary focus on the family's construction of reality marks researchers as symbolic interactionists, a perspective that I find especially useful for assessing family interaction and process when negative stress persists. (See also Berger & Luckman, 1966; Blumer, 1969; Burgess, 1926; Goffman, 1974; Handel, 1985; Hill, 1949; Mead, 1934; Reiss, 1981; Thomas, 1928.)

Symbolic interactionist researchers believe in the social construction of reality. The family is conceptualized as a socially interacting group that arrives at "a more-or-less shared sense of the world . . . a shared set of goals, values, beliefs and norms" (see LaRossa & Reitzes, in press). Sometimes, of course, we see families that are collectively delusional, what was called "a folie a famille" by Pollner and McDonald-Wikler (1985). Even in such cases, however, perceptions must be listened to and taken into account before interventions will be effective.

Symbolic interactionists insist that meanings emerge from the interaction between subject and object. One family member begins to anticipate the other's response and behaves accordingly. The process continues. Past patterns of interaction influence the family's definition of what is taking place in the present.

Although resources are important, they are most often overpowered by perceptions, perceptions that the resources they have will do no good, that the situation is hopeless, that there are no options. Seligman (1975) discussed uncontrollability as a precursor of the subject's helplessness, hopelessness, and subsequent depression. This research and theory from psychology and the symbolic interactionism from sociology formed the base for my family stress research regarding situations of ambiguous loss. Findings indicate that although the lack of mastery (perceptions of helplessness) leads to depression, the lack of mastery is predicted by the degree of ambiguity in the family member's perception of the lost person (Boss, Caron, Horbal, & Mortimer, 1990). To be sure, mastery is a resource, but it is the family members' perception of it even more than its availability that ultimately matters in preventing depression. Paraphrasing Thomas (1928), if family members define their helplessness as real, then their helplessness is real in its consequences.

Coming from different root disciplines, researchers and clinicians look at the family from different angles; some see individual symptoms first, whereas others see the larger context first. However we approach distressed families, we need to note the context surrounding their situation, including the degree of ambiguity in what they are experiencing. To discover this information, we listen to their story of what is happening to them, their meaning of the situation, individually and collectively.

Given these cautions, I support Hobfoll and Spielberger's (1992) focus on the depletion of family resources as critical in the stress-management process. Resource losses are increasing at an alarming rate for our nation's families, certainly for the poor but also for the middle class. As chronic stressor situations pile up to dangerous levels for families, the COR model, with its emphasis on exhaustion of resources, may be especially timely.

The COR theory emphasizes overweighing depletion versus gain in resources and could indeed aid researchers and clinicians in assessing the *process* by which resources are used by families responding to the demands of stressful circumstances. However, in assessing resources, it is the family's appraisal of them that is predictive of outcome. Whether or not a change is labeled as *loss* or as *gain* is determined by the subject's perception. Except for instances such as child abuse, incest, or other life-threatening situations, it is not up to the researcher or clinician to decide what troubles a family. We need to listen to their meanings. Moving may be a negative event for some individuals and families and positive for others. Divorce may be positive for some and negative for others. Even the death of a loved one may be perceived as positive by the family if it occurs after a long and terrible illness. Differences in how events are perceived may relate to gender, generation, ethnicity, or race. Not until we listen to family members' interpretations of their reality, individually and collectively, will we understand why some families remain resilient whereas others collapse.

This raises an issue of measurement. I was concerned by the Hobfoll and Spielberger (1992) words used to end their article: "Individuals' unique perceptions play an increasingly *smaller* [emphasis added] role. Rather, shared common perceptions that would be held by most who experience the stressor will assume preeminence" (p. 110). I suggest that the authors reexamine that premise. Using only the shared perception obscures gender and generational differences within families. We need data on such differences—or the lack of them—to determine the intricacies of family process under pressure. Giving preeminence to the common perception (the one held by most family members) not only obscures data but could be ethically problematic. The runaway child in an incestuous family may be the only family member who perceives the situation as wrong and immobilizing. Are family researchers and therapists going to discount the outliers and look only at majority perception? I hope not.

Assuming as I do that the family as a whole is not coping optimally if even one member manifests distress symptoms, the unit of analysis, therefore, needs to be both individual family members and the family as a whole. Critical scores will be the degree of congruence among individual family members' perceptions and between a family member and the group as a whole. If we examine only the common perception held by the majority of family members, we are likely to overlook the least powerful person in that family and may inadvertently reinforce a dysfunctional dynamic. Newcomers to family stress research, especially those skilled at psychometrics, are needed to develop better methods of measuring this intricate process of family stress and coping, but at the outset the question is this: What is being measured and why?

The variable of boundary ambiguity was developed as one attempt to measure family and individual perception. Quantitative instruments measure the family members' perceptions of who is in or who is out of the family (Boss, Greenberg, & Pearce-McCall, 1990). Qualitative methods, using family sculpture and family stories, assess individual and collective perceptions of who is absent or present in the family. The theoretical premise is that the higher the boundary ambiguity in the family and individual perceptions, the higher the family conflict and individual depression. This premise has been generally supported with different populations, and it continues to be tested.

Having researched ambiguous losses, I was drawn to Hobfoll and Spielberger's (1992) statement that "many studies of family stress have focused on clear stressors, such as illness or divorce, and not on ambiguous events" (p. 109). I do not agree that illness and divorce are clear-cut stressors. They too have high potential for ambiguity. Here again, we need to determine how family members perceive the situation. Even when there is clear and legal documentation of an event (a divorce decree, a medical diagnosis, a death certificate, a pink slip, a judgment of driving while intoxicated), we cannot be sure of how this information is perceived or cognitively accepted. There may be individual or collective denials in situations that appear clear to professionals. However, there are also many situations in everyday

family life in which ambiguity is never completely resolved; divorce, remarriage, immigration, relocation, and chronic illness are examples. Ambiguous losses are not uncommon in family life. Understanding more about the process of how families adapt to them is useful information for prevention as well as therapy.

This premise leads me to question strongly the idea that stress reactions and neurosis are often confounded when perception is overemphasized. It is just as likely that stress reactions and behavior disorders are confounded if perception is *under*emphasized. I agree with Lazarus and Folkman (1984), who stated that "whenever there is ambiguity, person factors shape the understanding of the situation, thereby making the interpretation of the situation more a function of the person than of objective stimulus constraints" (p. 104). I go one step further and apply this idea to families: Very few events in family life are clear-cut. Even normative events such as deciding to have a baby, getting married, launching an adolescent, or caring for aged parents are full of ambiguity regarding who is in and who is out of the family. Lately, I cannot even ask how many children a couple has and get a clear answer. I cannot agree, therefore, with Hobfoll and Spielberger (1992), who said that "for events of importance, individuals' unique perceptions play an increasingly smaller role" (p. 110). Who is to say what is important? I see couples in which one thinks an extramarital affair is important and the other says it is not. Who is right? It is unethical for us as researchers and therapists to say that the perceptions of the people we work with are not valid data. For example, health-care providers in the Twin Cities find it useful to hear a Hmong family's perception of the source of their child's illness to understand and therefore ameliorate their resistance to Western medicine. Cultural, gender, race, and generational differences in perceptions of stressor events surface if we listen to the families we are trying to help. This does not mean we always accept their definition of the event but rather that we listen to them so that we know how to intervene more effectively.

Perception matters, but of course it is not all that matters. In this belief, Hobfoll, Spielberger, and I may not be that far apart. We may only disagree on the sequencing or weighting given to perceptions versus resources.

I commend Hobfoll and Spielberger for introducing family stress theory to the readers of this journal. The measurement skills of psychologists are needed for this complex research. As new researchers join this effort, however, they need to be aware that the literature about family stress theory and research is scattered in journals from several disciplines: sociology, family studies, social work, nursing, family therapy, counseling, and others. That is the nature of family stress research. It crosses disciplines and is therefore challenging to track. In addition, family stress articles appear in empirical, theoretical, and applied journals. This diversification makes it difficult to keep up with the literature on family stress, but for the scholars who track it down, they will find role models for doing such work, documenting the process from clinical observation, induction, empirical testing, application, and back again to refinement of theory. Hobfoll and Spielberger (1992) have now entered into this process and, I hope, will now operationalize and test their model to determine its usefulness for understanding and helping troubled families. I look forward to reading more from these two scholars.

REFERENCES

Antonovsky, A. (1979). *Health, stress and coping.* San Francisco: Jossey-Bass.

Berger, P., & Luckman, T. (1966). *The social construction of reality.* Garden City, NJ: Doubleday.

Blumer, H. (1969). *Symbolic interactionism: Perspective and method.* Englewood Cliffs, NJ: Prentice Hall.

Boss, P. (1980). Normative family stress: Family boundary changes across the life-span. *Family Relations, 29,* 445-450.

Boss, P. (1987). Family stress: Perception and context. In M. Sussman & S. Steinmetz (Eds.), *Handbook on marriage and the family* (pp. 695-723). New York: Plenum Press.

Boss, P. (1988). *Family stress management.* Newbury Park, CA: Sage.

Boss, P. (1990). Ambiguous loss. In F. Walsh & M. McGoldrick (Eds.), *Living beyond loss: Death and the family* (pp. 164-175). New York: Norton.

Boss, P. (1993). Boundary ambiguity: A block to cognitive coping. In A. P. Turnbull, J. Patterson, S. K. Behr,

D. L. Murphy, J. Marquis, & M. Blue-Banning (Eds.), *Cognitive coping, families, and disability: Participatory research in action.* Baltimore: Brookes.

Boss, P., Caron, W., Horbal, J., & Mortimer, J. (1990). Predictors of depression in caregivers of dementia patients: Boundary ambiguity and mastery. *Family Process, 29,* 245-254.

Boss, P., & Greenberg, J. (1984). Family boundary ambiguity: A new variable in family stress theory. *Family Process, 23,* 535-546.

Boss, P., Greenberg, J., & Pearce-McCall, D. (1990). *Measurement of boundary ambiguity in families* (Station Bulletin 593-1990, Item AD-SB-3763). St. Paul: University of Minnesota Experiment Station Publication.

Burgess, E. (1926). The family as a unity of interacting personalities. *The Family, 7,* 3-9.

Converse, J. M., Foa, U. G., & Foa, E. B. (Eds.). (in press). *Resource theory: Explorations and applications.* San Diego, CA: Academic Press.

Figley, C. R. (1989). *Helping traumatized families.* San Francisco: Jossey-Bass.

Foa, E. B., & Foa, U. G. (1980). Resource theory: Interpersonal behavior as exchange. In K. J. Gergen, M. S. Greenberg, & R. H. Willis (Eds.), *Social exchange: Advances in theory and research* (pp. 77-94). New York: Plenum Press.

Goffman, E. (1974). *Frame analysis: An essay on the organization of experience.* New York: Harper & Row.

Handel, G. (1985). *The psychosocial interior of the family.* Chicago: Aldine-Atherton.

Hill, R. (1949). *Families under stress.* Westport, CT: Greenwood.

Hobfoll, S. E., and Spielberger, C. D. (1992). Family stress: Integrating theory and measurement. *Journal of Family Psychology, 6,* 99-112.

Hunter, E. (1991). Prisoners of war: Readjustment and rehabilitation. In R. Gal & A. D. Mangelsdorff (Eds.), *Handbook of military psychology* (pp. 741-757). New York: Wiley.

LaRossa, R., & Reitzes, D. C. (in press). Symbolic interactionism and family studies. In P. Boss, W. J. Doherty, R. LaRossa, W. R. Schumm, & S. K. Steinmetz (Eds.), *Sourcebook of family theories and methods.* New York: Plenum Press.

Lazarus, R. S., & Folkman, S. (1984). *Stress, appraisal, and coping.* New York: Springer.

Lerner, M. J. (1971). Justice, guilt, and veridical perception. *Journal of Personality and Social Psychology, 20,* 127-135.

Masten, A. S. (1989). Resilience in development: Implications of the study of successful adaptation for developmental psychopathology. In D. Cicchetti (Ed.), *The emergence of a discipline: Rochester symposium on developmental psychopathology* (Vol. 1, pp. 261-294). Hillsdale, NJ: Erlbaum.

Mead, G. H. (1934). *Mind, self, and society.* Chicago: University of Chicago Press.

Patterson, J. (1988). Families experiencing stress. *Family Systems Medicine, 6*(2), 202-237.

Patterson, J., & Leonard, B. J. (1994). Caregiving and children. In E. Kahana, D. E. Biegel, & M. Wykle (Eds.), *Family caregiving across the lifespan.* Thousand Oaks, CA: Sage.

Pearlin, L. I., Menaghan, E. G., Lieberman, M. A., & Mullam, J. T. (1981). The stress process. *Journal of Health and Social Behavior, 22,* 337-356.

Pollner, M., & McDonald-Wikler, L. (1985). The social construction of unreality: A case study of a family's attribution of competence to a severely retarded child. *Family Process, 24*(2), 241-254.

Reiss, D. (1981). *The family's construction of reality.* Cambridge, MA: Harvard University Press.

Rettig, K., & Bubolz, M. (1983). Perceptual indicators of family well-being. *Social Indicators Research, 12,* 417-438.

Sabatelli, R. M. (1988). Measurement issues in marital research: A review and critique of contemporary survey instruments. *Journal of Marriage and the Family, 50,* 891-913.

Sabatelli, R. M., & Shehan, C. L. (in press). Exchange and resource theories. In P. Boss, W. Doherty, R. LaRossa, W. Schumm, & S. Steinmetz (Eds.), *Sourcebook of family theories and methods.* New York: Plenum Press.

Seligman, M. (1975). *Helplessness: On depression, development and death.* San Francisco: Freeman.

Thibaut, J. W., & Kelley, H. H. (1959). *The social psychology of groups.* New York: Wiley.

Thomas, W. I. (1928). The behavior pattern and the situation. *Publication of the American Sociological Society, 22,* 1-13.

12

STRESS, CHANGE, AND FAMILIES

Theoretical and Methodological Considerations

ANNE E. KAZAK

In response to issues raised in Hobfoll and Spielberger (1992, this issue), additional theoretical and methodological concerns are discussed. Specifically, differentiating types of changes and the impact of change on individuals within the family are discussed. The relationship between change and loss is presented with respect to the loss involved in all changes, positive and negative. The long-term implications of change and methodological concerns in assessing the impact of change on family systems are also presented.

amily and *stress* are two broad concepts that are used liberally across clinical work, research, and casual conversation. Singularly, each word has multiple meanings and connotations. For example, *family* may represent children and parents as individuals, dyads, or triads; many generations of a family system; or affective bonds not necessarily dependent on biological or legal relatedness. *Stress* (and stressors) can be acute or chronic, major or minor, and manageable or devastating.

Stress is often used rather indiscriminately to describe irritants in daily life, often without clarifying what is stressful and what outcomes are considered indicative of stress.

The combination of these two concepts into the phrase *family stress* is fraught with the difficulties of merging two very familiar but often poorly specified notions. Hobfoll and Spielberger (1992) reviewed a large number of studies in a strong effort to promote important linkages between theory and measurement

Reprinted from the *Journal of Family Psychology* 6 (1992): 120-24. Copyright © 1992 by the American Psychological Association. Reprinted with permission.

in this area. One of the major arguments made is that, contrary to much clinical experience, it is negative change, rather than change itself, that is stressful for families. This is a provocative and interesting argument, worthy of strong consideration. However, in this commentary, some additional theoretical issues are presented, and attention to important methodological concerns is recommended to generate more data on these issues.

THEORETICAL ISSUES: STRESS AND CHANGE

A critical underlying issue is the relationship between stress and change. Hobfoll and Spielberger (1992) defined stress as "a state in which individuals' resources are challenged by the environment in a way that overtaxes their coping ability and endangers their well-being" (p. 99). Family stress is the extension of this overtaxing threat to the family. Within the conservation of resources theory, "events are stressful to the extent that they threaten or result in loss of critical family resources" (p. 108).

Change is an implicit part of the challenges (events) that are associated with stress. However, Hobfoll and Spielberger (1992) argued that change itself is not stressful. They used a distinction between negative changes and nonnegative changes to conclude that it is the negative aspects of changes that are stressful. The implicit assumption is that nonnegative changes do not overtax the individual (or family) and, therefore, are not stressful.

In this article, I present some additional considerations related to change (and stress) that may be important in the next steps of understanding the impact of change and stress on families. Change is the fabric of growth and development for individuals and families and is inextricably related to some degree of stress. The changes and stressors that affect families vary widely in type and in terms of how they are perceived by individuals within the family. It is not necessarily clear what is a negative or a nonnegative change. Perhaps most important, all changes, positive and negative, involve loss. The measurement of family stress, taking these issues into account, is very complex.

Developmental and Nondevelopmental Changes

There are many different types of change. One basic type of change is developmentally inherent to processes of growth that necessitate periods of disorganization followed by reorganization, as in the changes accompanying, for example, birth, adolescence, and menopause. Other types of changes are unexpected occurrences. These may be catastrophic and feared (as in losing one's home in a flood or fire; an unexpected death of a previously healthy friend or family member), or spectacular and anticipated (winning a large lottery; adopting a long-awaited child).

We know that some aspects of all developmental changes are stressful, and this understanding is the underpinning of much family stress research. In a negative versus nonnegative dichotomy, developmental changes such as birth, adolescence, and menopause defy easy categorization. The birth of a child, although a positive event, is not necessarily a uniformly positive occurrence for a family. The actual birth and uncomfortable aspects of pregnancy and childbirth represent stressful and negative aspects of the process as well. Somewhat longer term issues such as changes in the mother's employment and sibling reactions to a new child represent potentially negative reverberations of a positive life event. The question of whether menopause is negative or nonnegative similarly rests on what aspects of the change are considered. It also probably depends on who is asked to describe the experience and how our societal values about older women are integrated into the meaning that an individual and family make of the event.

An important question, then, concerns the possible impact of developmental versus nonnormative life events in terms of the stress outcome for an individual or family. Life-event scales mix these types of changes and have not addressed potential differences.

Choices, Control, and Changes

Some changes are voluntary (e.g., accepting a promotion to a desirable locale), whereas others are not (e.g., being transferred to a less desirable location in order not to be laid off). Although both may be stressful, the underlying dimensions of choice and control are ones known to be associated with psychological outcome.

The extent to which one can control changes and the amount of choice involved may mediate psychological distress. Although the dichotomy of negative versus nonnegative change is problematic in some ways (see later discussion), the issue of choice may be helpful. For any change or life stress, the question may be asked as to whether there are choices and, if so, whether they are acceptable ones.

The issue of choice in change highlights the permeable boundary between the family and other systems and also focuses on issues of power and control within the family. In the example of job relocation, one individual may want to accept a relocation. For this person, relocation is desirable professionally and is exciting. For others in the family, there may be choices (e.g., not moving), but these may be unacceptable in view of additional stress on the family and violation of family rules. Thus, the power structure of the family may mediate the choices involved for individuals and the extent to which a given life change is stressful for individuals and the family as a whole.

Classifying Changes

The preceding discussions underscore the difficulty of establishing negative or nonnegative changes. Developmental changes, assessing choices and control, and examining whose perspective of change is reported illustrate the complexity of classifying changes. Classifying a change as negative or nonnegative implies a value judgment. Just as it is usually the researchers' perspectives and values that influence the questions asked and the ways in which they are answered, we must be cautious not to assume certainty or generalizability in terms of the meaning of life changes.

Change and Loss

Almost any change involves loss. Loss, although basic to human existence, is negative in the pain experienced. At the same time, one's individual and collective (family) resources, coping skills, and interpretation of loss allow for positive processes of resolution and integration of loss experiences. The adaptive use of resources to cope with loss occurs across all changes and allows, in part, for the competence seen in many individuals and families as they cope with change.

In events such as work layoffs and deaths, it is clear that loss is present. Even generally nonnegative changes such as a new job and marriage involve losses. The losses are seen as ones for which there is relatively little mourning. That is, the decision to marry is usually predicated on the belief that one's life will be better for being married. Nonetheless, the marriage does represent a change and a loss of a life before marriage that may have been very positive. Because some life events are defined as nonnegative, therapists may fail to provide people with opportunities to validate the losses that they feel (e.g., missing peer relationships with persons who are now subordinates, missing time with spouse and children in a more demanding position).

Conversely, events that clearly entail loss may also represent nonnegative change. Divorce, representing the end of a marriage, is a loss. However, as the freedom from an abusive relationship and a chance to start over, it may be positive. Similarly, coping with a difficult crisis and getting through it successfully can contribute to positive self-esteem and feelings of competence without negating the adverse nature of the event.

Theoretically, the interrelatedness of change and loss can be understood from the perspective of attachment theory. Any relationship carries with it attachment bonds and the threat of losing the relationship. Attachments can be to individuals, places, communities, or ideas and can vary widely in their type and quality. Changes that result in alterations of attachment bonds may be stressful to individuals and families. Rolland (1990) discussed the nature of "anticipatory loss" for families with an ill member. The notion that loss includes early and possibly subtle changes as well as the anticipation of what may be lost in the future is important in considering the complex interrelatedness of stress and change.

Long-Term Implications of Change

Hobfoll and Spielberger (1992) addressed the implications of multiple stressors and the "pile-up" effects that may result. However, in general, the research they reviewed examines the impact of a discrete event at one point in time. Ultimately, it will be important to develop models for understanding and predicting the outcome of changes over time. For example, within a few months of the diagnosis of cancer in an adolescent, parents tend to look psychologically distressed, and there is a high probability of finding clinical symptoms of reactive depression or anxiety in the adolescent. Clinically, we believe that adaptive family reorganization, combined with utilization of coping strategies, will contribute to a more positive adaptation at some point during treatment or after treatment ends. However, existing research has not clearly documented this process and contributes relatively little to our understanding of the impact of time on adjustment.

Related to the impact of changes over time is the potential interrelatedness of changes. For example, divorce may be associated with alcoholism in a spouse, long-term conflicts in the family, a geographic relocation that was unsatisfying for one partner, or unresolved issues concerning relationships with the partners' families of origin. It will be important to develop models that begin to examine the multifaceted nature of related events rather than assuming that one pivotal event is the stressor most related to psychological outcome.

MEASUREMENT ISSUES: FAMILIES AND CHANGE

Although Hobfoll and Spielberger (1992) presented a strong argument for their positions, ultimately meta-analyses and other quantitative approaches should be considered to evaluate the cumulative results of a very diverse literature. Related to this are a few important methodological considerations particularly pertinent to family research.

Conceptualizing Family as a Unit of Measurement

Approaching the family as a unit of measurement has remained fraught with unresolved difficulties. Many family self-report scales actually reflect individuals' perceptions of the family. Family research

has been conducted on the basis of one individual's perceptions, on multiple individuals either separately or using statistical combinations of individual-level data, and using videotaped interactions of whole families. In addition, Q sorts and other methodologies provide alternate ways of assessing the multifaceted nature of families. Combining results from studies that conceptualize and measure family in diverse ways is very complicated and fraught with difficulties.

It may be useful in conceptualizing and measuring family stress to give careful consideration to the level of analysis for which data are collected. There are many configurations of data available. For example, using the example of marital separation, data at an individual level could be collected from spouses as individuals reporting on (a) themselves; (b) each other as individuals; (c) their children; or (d) the family as a whole. Each of these may provide a different assessment of the stress experienced.

At a family level of analysis, family interaction data can be collected, or a method of combining individual data could be determined that would take into account the interrelatedness of family members and their shared history. How individuals' resources, interpretation, and outcomes combine in reacting to a stressor is an area of needed investigation.

At larger levels of analysis, one might ask how interactions outside the family (e.g., with social support resources) or perspective of others outside the immediate family (neighbors, extended family, and teachers) may help shed light on describing family stress more clearly. A contextual approach necessitates studying the individual, the family, and the demands and resources of the environment. The point is not that one level of analysis or approach may be better than others but that attention to methods that promote a multifaceted approach to family stress may be helpful in understanding the impact of change on families.

Identifying the Respondent and the Underlying Model of "Family"

A major complication in much of the literature on family stress concerns clear articulation of whose view of the family is being reported. Related to this is the underlying model of family that is being used as a standard for understanding the broad concept of family stress.

For some life changes, we know that the impact of gender is considerable. In the example of divorce, Carter (1988) proposed the notion of "his" and "her" divorces. The reactions of mothers and fathers to parenting a disabled or chronically ill child differ (Kazak, 1987), all underscoring the importance of considering gender in family stress research (Kazak & Segal-Andrews, 1992).

Perhaps more insidious and subtle are studies that clearly assess men and women separately but that at the same time describe only one type of family structure while generalizing data to families more broadly. For example, the Brett (1982) article cited by Hobfoll and Spielberger assesses husbands' and wives' perceptions of change related to the husbands' job relocation. The family being described is White, includes children, and has two parents who are presumed heterosexual, and the woman's work is less career oriented than the husband's. Although these are important data, they are not comprehensive. Thus, in their discussion of Brett (1982), Hobfoll and Spielberger's statement that "families who move were no more distressed than static families" (p. 101) should be qualified in accord with the sample from which the data were obtained. Whether these conclusions can be generalized to single-parent, dual-career, or non-White families should be addressed in future research.

These concerns also pertain to the issue of ambiguous and objective events. Without clearly stating whose view of the event is defining it, it is difficult to evaluate the objectiveness or ambiguity of a stressor. Although all members of a family may be distressed by the objective signing of final divorce papers, the nature of the distress and the meaning attached to the divorce is likely to differ for the ex-wife, ex-husband, and the children. Recommendations for nonsexist research (e.g., Eichler, 1988) can be used proactively to avoid assuming an androcentric perspective in conceptualizing and measuring family stress.

SUMMARY

Although family stress is a key concept in understanding family functioning, considerable further refinement, both conceptually and methodologically, is necessary. In particular, the role of loss in the relationship between change and stress warrants further consideration, along with inclusion of other dimensions along which changes may be understood. With respect to measurement, an understanding of the ways in which individuals' perspectives are included, assessed, and interpreted is important before generalizing about family stress.

REFERENCES

Brett, J. (1982). Job transfer and well-being. *Journal of Applied Psychology, 67,* 450-463.

Carter, B. (1988). Divorce: His and hers. In M. Walters, B. Carter, P. Papp, & O. Silverstein (Eds.), *The invisible web* (pp. 253-271). New York: Guilford Press.

Eichler, M. (1988). *Nonsexist research methods.* Winchester, MA: Allen & Unwin.

Hobfoll, S. E., & Spielberger, C. D. (1992). Family stress: Integrating theory and measurement. *Journal of Family Psychology, 6,* 99-112.

Kazak, A. (1987). Families with disabled children: Stress and social networks in three samples. *Journal of Abnormal Child Psychology, 15,* 137-146.

Kazak, A., & Segal-Andrews, A. (1992). Women and families: Individual and family systems issues related to theory, therapy, and research. *Journal of Family Psychology, 5,* 360-378.

Rolland, J. (1990). Anticipatory loss: A family systems developmental perspective. *Family Process, 29,* 229-244.

13

PROCESS OF FAMILY STRESS

A Response to Boss (1992) and Kazak (1992)

STEVAN E. HOBFOLL
CHARLES D. SPIELBERGER

We emphasize that family stress is not an event or internal state but an ongoing process that especially affects and is affected by individuals' personal and social resources. This process entails both objective and subjective factors. However, we argue that the subjective factors are largely a product of the actual event. This differs from others who accentuate individual differences rather than classes of differences that are common to like stressful circumstances.

We appreciate the opportunity to respond to Anne Kazak and Pauline Boss on their reactions to our article in this issue. These researchers offer rich perspectives based on their knowledge of and contributions to the family stress literature. Rather than arguing the points on which we disagree, we have chosen to highlight areas of common ground between their and our treatises. We also suggest some foci for research that follow from these points. Clearly, there are differences in our perspectives, but we do not believe that research on family stress has developed sufficiently to confirm any particular perspective.

STRESS AS A PROCESS

One key issue that emerges from this dialogue is that stress is not an event or internal state but an ongoing process. Lazarus and Folkman's (1984) transactional

Reprinted from the *Journal of Family Psychology* 6 (1992): 125-27. Copyright © 1992 by the American Psychological Association. Reprinted with permission.

model is instructive in this regard. Events occur both independent of individual and family actions and as a consequence of those actions.

After any event that initiates the stress process, a complex sequence of events follows. Indeed, this sequence can be so complicated that one is tempted to resort to chaos theory (Gleick, 1987), which posits that multidetermined interactions of numerous contributing factors can result in an inestimable near-random pattern. Predicting the course of water rushing in a stream over thousands of rocks is an example of such a phenomenon. As an alternative to the chaos of unpredictability, theorists, researchers, and clinicians rely on some subset of factors and try to understand how they operate. The complexity of the patterns that emerge when considering merely three or four factors is humbling, but progress has occurred in understanding some important aspects of the stress process.

It is indeed possible to select a different starting point for the analysis of the stress process. This analysis could begin with any of the factors in the Hill (1949) or McCubbin and Patterson (1983) double-ABC-X models. Rather than beginning with a precipitating event, for example, one could begin with the perceptions of family members and examine how these lead to certain stressor events, building or loss of resources, or emotional reactions. The fact that most research has begun with events as a starting point is rather arbitrary, although choosing this starting point has helped clarify a number of research questions.

We agree with Boss and Kazak on another significant point about the stress process but must add that this point should not be mistakenly interpreted as a criticism of our article or of conservation of resource (COR) theory. Specifically, we agree that it is critical to differentiate major general events into event sequences. As they emphasize, general events such as divorce, marriage, job loss, and relocation are best seen as markers for smaller sequences of events. For example, divorce implies arguments that occurred in the family, financial problems that resulted from litigation, pain caused to the children, and the joy, elation, depression, and fear that may have followed in divorce's wake. Each divorce will have its own particular sequence.

We emphasize that it is the loss aspects of the sequence that are stressful (or distressful, to use Boss's somewhat different lexicon). Indeed, the positive aspects of change are not only not stressful, but they also contribute to better coping and more positive emotional and health outcomes. Kazak is correct in emphasizing that change is often necessary for growth, and we agree that growth may emerge from either gain or loss. Kazak also reminds us that many positive changes contain hidden losses. One must look onward in the stress chain and examine how successfully the family ultimately coped with the change. Consequently, a marriage may be joyously awaited but nevertheless mean a loss of freedom.

MASTERY AS A KEY RESOURCE

Mastery and control are key constructs in our article and in the comments of both Boss and Kazak. According to COR theory, mastery is conceptualized as a critical management resource. This executive resource most certainly affects people's perceptions of events around them, the adequacy of other resources, and their ability to use these resources. High-mastery individuals have more resources at their disposal and use these resources more effectively (Bandura, 1977; Hobfoll, 1988; Kobasa & Puccetti, 1983).

We caution, however, that it is important not to overestimate perceptions. Although high-mastery individuals perceive themselves as more capable (Kobasa, 1979), they are also, in fact, more capable (Bandura, 1982; Ozer & Bandura, 1990). They even attract more social support from others, who are attracted to being associated with one who successfully copes (Dunkel-Schetter, Folkman, & Lazarus, 1987). Contemporary research theory has tended to emphasize perceptions and, in so doing, may not give sufficient attention to the actual abilities that people bring to the family in the service of coping. Imagine that a father perceives himself to be an effective communicator. To what extent will this help the family if he is, in fact, domineering and unempathic? Perceptions should be considered in the context of the family system and situation. On that base, perceptions become one of the important denominators.

Boss makes another cogent point we wish to underscore. When stressors are objectively ambiguous, and many stressors are, then perceptions and appraisal become increasingly important. Many neutral changes that families experience fit in this category. For example, when young children develop more independent identities in adolescence, the meaning of this change for the family is almost exclusively in the realm of perception. Personal and social resources of family members, nevertheless, affect these perceptions. Parents with high self-esteem and families who are flexible will be more likely to experience positive perceptions of change than families whose members have poor self-esteem and who are inflexible.

There is some confusion in regard to our meaning of resources as taken by Boss. When she argues that many families in crisis are rich in resources, she implies that financial or material resources are what we meant in the resource concept. Our views are, indeed, more congruent when we clarify the meaning of this concept to note that mastery, self-esteem, and communication skills are also important resources. On this issue, there seems to be good agreement between us. When events cause or threaten resource loss, COR theory holds that those with stronger resource reservoirs are less likely to experience loss spirals and the negative psychosocial and health sequelae that occur in the wake of these spirals.

LOSS AND GAIN SPIRALS

It is important to reemphasize that resource-rich and resource-poor families have different likelihoods of experiencing loss and gain spirals. Events that have major impact on resource loss and gain will also be most likely to have subsequent impact on psychological and physical well-being. Once loss or gain spirals are initiated, they develop their own energy and momentum.

Boss (1992) argued that events do not inevitably decrease resources, and we acknowledge that this is an important point. People must invest their resources to offset resource loss or contribute to resource gain, but this does not necessarily result in further resource loss. Schönpflug (1985) showed, however, that coping demands resource investment. Even self-esteem and mastery must, in this sense, be invested in efforts to cope with stressful circumstances. If coping is successful, however, it is likely to contribute to enhanced self-esteem or mastery (Ozer & Bandura, 1990). However, when coping efforts are unsuccessful, mastery and self-esteem are likely to decrease (Pearlin, Leiberman, Menaghan, & Mullan, 1981).

The process by which coping results in resource enhancement should be viewed cautiously. Repeated coping efforts, even successful ones, may at times dangerously deplete resources. Although successful coping may contribute to an increased sense of efficacy, once efficacy is established, continued assault by a threatening environment can deplete the very resources that emerged as a product of earlier experience (Hobfoll & Walfisch, 1986). Here it is important not to confuse everyday challenges with major stressful events, because the former may continue to mold mastery if successfully confronted, whereas the latter kinds of events may not.

In conclusion, we find that the evolution of theory and research on examination stress or test anxiety (Spielberger, 1980; Spielberger, Anton, & Bedell, 1976) serves as an excellent model for the development of theory and research on family stress. Individuals differ widely in test anxiety as a function of their abilities and personalities. Differences in these personal resources result in different perceptions about the meaning of a particular examination.

An individual's cognitive abilities (i.e., the intellectual resources they bring to the event) in large part determines whether the test will be at all stressful for them. All this occurs against a common backdrop of the perception of tests as more or less stressful for most individuals. Thus, research on test anxiety highlights the common nature of many perceptions while demonstrating the importance of cognitive skills, situational factors (nature of the test, e.g., history or mathematics), and special knowledge (e.g., special knowledge and attitude about mathematics). Similarly, each of the elements in the family stress process needs to be considered in research in this field. Greater understanding of the family stress process will result from rigorous research on the essential elements of this process guided by the rich framework that is provided by clearly articulating competing theoretical conceptualizations.

REFERENCES

Bandura, A. (1977). Self-efficacy: Toward a unifying theory of behavioral change. *Psychological Review, 84,* 191-215.

Bandura, A. (1982). Self-efficacy mechanisms in human agency. *American Psychologist, 37,* 122-147.

Boss, P. (1992). Primacy of perception in family stress theory and measurement. *Journal of Family Psychology, 6,* 113-119.

Dunkel-Schetter, C., Folkman, S., & Lazarus, R. S. (1987). Social support received in stressful situations. *Journal of Personality and Social Psychology, 53,* 71-80.

Gleick, J. (1987). *Chaos: Making a new science.* New York: Penguin Books.

Hill, R. (1949). *Families under stress: Adjustment to the crisis of war, separation, and reunion.* New York: Harper & Row.

Hobfoll, S. E. (1988). *The ecology of stress.* Washington, DC: Hemisphere.

Hobfoll, S. E., & Spielberger, C. D. (1992). Family stress: Integrating theory and measurement. *Journal of Family Psychology, 6,* 99-112.

Hobfoll, S. E., & Walfisch, S. (1986). Stressful events, mastery, and depression: An evaluation of crisis theory. *Journal of Community Psychology, 14,* 183-195.

Kazak, A. E. (1992). Stress, change, and families: Theoretical and methodological considerations. *Journal of Family Psychology, 6,* 120-124.

Kobasa, S. C. (1979). Stressful life events, personality, and health: An inquiry into hardiness. *Journal of Personality and Social Psychology, 37,* 1-11.

Kobasa, S. C., & Puccetti, M. C. (1983). Personality and social resources in stress resistance. *Journal of Personality and Social Psychology, 45,* 839-850.

Lazarus, R. S., & Folkman, S. (1984). *Stress, appraisal and coping.* New York: Springer.

McCubbin, H. I., & Patterson, J. M. (1983). The family stress process: The Double ABCX model of adjustment. *Marriage and Family Review, 6,* 7-37.

Ozer, E. M., & Bandura, A. (1990). Mechanisms governing empowerment effects: A self efficacy analysis. *Journal of Personality and Social Psychology, 58,* 472-486.

Pearlin, L. I., Leiberman, M. A., Menaghan, E. G., & Mullan, J. T. (1981). The stress process. *Journal of Health and Social Behavior, 22,* 337-356.

Schönpflug, W. (1985). Goal directed behavior as a source of stress: Psychological origins and consequences of inefficiency. In M. Frese & J. Sabini (Eds.), *The concept of faction in psychology* (pp. 172-188). Hillsdale, NJ: Erlbaum.

Spielberger, C. D. (1980). *Test Anxiety Inventory: Preliminary professional manual.* Palo Alto, CA: Consulting Psychologists Press.

Spielberger, C. D., Anton, W. D., & Bedell, J. (1976). The nature and treatment of test anxiety. In M. Zuckerman & C. D. Spielberger (Eds.), *Emotions and anxiety: New concepts, methods and applications* (pp. 317-345). New York: Erlbaum/Wiley.

PART 3

DEFINITIONS:
A GUIDE TO FAMILY STRESS THEORY

The discussion in *Family Stress Management* (*FSM*; Boss, 2002) about definitions and constructs is enriched by reading this classic article by Reuben Hill (1958), unquestionably "the father of family stress theory." Although we disagree with his use of *stress* and *crisis* as synonyms, we want scholars to know the richness of his early work. It influences our work—still. Sociologists don't often think of Rueben Hill as developing theory for practitioners, but he did. As written in *FSM*, his last conversation with me was about linking his ideas with those in family therapy, a theoretical task not unlike his 1958 presentation to social workers about generic features of families under stress. He reminisced that as a new University of Wisconsin Ph.D. and a newlywed who couldn't find work due to the Great Depression, he organized a men's group at the Memorial Union on campus for new husbands and fathers unable to find work. Perhaps this is why he too wanted family stress theory to be useful. In *FSM,* I discuss the adaptations needed in Hill's model regarding the addition of contexts and differentiating stress from crisis, but we still encourage the scientist-practitioner to go back and read about the original ABCX model. It is useful heuristically.

Philip Cowan, a psychologist, wrote in 1991 a chapter (not included but recommended) titled "Individual and Family Life Transitions: A Proposal for a New Definition." His point is that major life transitions (e.g., a parent going to war; pregnancy) often overlap and create a situation in families where stability and change are always in flux. There are ebbs and flows, so family life is never "quiescent." Because researchers for the most part have been "the sole definers of transitions," Cowan calls for asking families how *they* see change. Is it stressful? Chaotic? Cowan's call for studying family adaptation (resilience) by focusing on family transitions is akin to what Boss (1980) in her article on normative stress proposes (see Part 4, this volume). She suggests that entries and exits across the family boundary are periods of change that are potentially stressful for families, not because they are developmental *stages* but because of the boundary ambiguity during such transitional *processes* resulting from losses and acquisitions. Both Cowan and Boss refer back to Hill's original ABCX model.

REFERENCES

Boss, P. (2002). *Family stress management* (2nd ed.). Thousand Oaks, CA: Sage.

Cowan, P. A. (1991). Individual and family life transitions: A proposal for a new definition. In P. A. Cowan & E. M. Hetherington (Eds.), *Family transitions* (pp. 3-30). Hillsdale, NJ: Lawrence Erlbaum.

14

GENERIC FEATURES OF FAMILIES UNDER STRESS

REUBEN HILL

Two streams of research concerned about social stresses and the family have been running parallel for some time. This conference should stimulate their early convergence. I refer to the research on crisis-proneness in families carried out by family sociologists and the cumulating work of latter-day social work researchers on the properties of the "multi-problem family." To facilitate further the merger of these two professional groups, I shall undertake in this paper to summarize the major issues and findings in family crisis research as seen by family sociologists. I shall first attempt to provide the broad outlines of the conceptual framework most used by family sociologists in the study of family crisis. Second, I shall attempt to catalog stressful events that have been studied and those that remain unstudied, using classifications developed to differentiate crises into types. Third, our chief findings to date will be listed, indicating types of families which thrive and which wilt under stress. Fourth, the generic phases and modes of adjustment to stress will be demonstrated. Fifth, the short-run and long-run effects of stress on families will be assessed. I shall conclude with speculations about the implications of these findings for agency policies and practices.

A CONCEPTUAL FRAMEWORK FOR VIEWING FAMILIES IN CRISIS

The conceptual scaffolding on which the research to be summarized in this paper has been built makes frequent use of three variables: family, crisis-provoking event, and meaning attached to the event. Let us begin by identifying the major conceptual properties of the family.

The Family as an Interacting and Transacting Organization

Family sociologists have come to view the family as a small group, intricately organized internally into paired positions of husband-father, wife-mother,

Reprinted from *Social Casework,* 49 (1958): 139-50. Reprinted by permission: Families in Society. Copyright © 2002. This article was part of a larger chapter that included other articles. Only references that pertain to this article have been included.

son-brother, and daughter-sister. Norms prescribing the appropriate role behavior for each of these positions specify how reciprocal relations are to be maintained as well as how role behavior may change with changing ages of the occupants of these positions.

Viewed externally, the family often appears to be a "closed corporation," particularly in urban areas where the nuclear group of father, mother, and their children is clearly differentiated from the kinship extensions of maternal and paternal grandparents and collateral relatives. Such a family performs like a closed corporation in presenting a common front of solidarity to the world, handling internal differences in private, protecting the reputation of members by keeping family secrets, and standing together under attack. Nevertheless, the closed nature of the family is selectively opened for transacting business with other agencies, including kin and professionals. These agencies can be ranked on their accessibility to the interior of the family: immediate kin highest, family friends and neighbors next, the family physician, the family pastor, the family lawyer, and so on. Other agencies enter the family with greater difficulty and often through the intermediation of individual family members who act as liaisons for the family: the school, the employer, the health clinic, the casework agency, and other such formal agencies. Recent research has suggested that the more open the community (as in the modern city), the more likely the family is closed in form; and the more closed the community (as in the isolated mountain village), the more open are the doors and windows of the family to non-family members.[1]

Compared with other associations in the society, the average family is badly handicapped organizationally. Its age composition is heavily weighted with dependents, and it cannot freely reject its weak members and recruit more competent team mates. Its members receive an unearned acceptance; there is no price for belonging. Because of its unusual age composition and its uncertain sex composition, it is intrinsically a puny work group and an awkward decision-making group. This group is not ideally manned to withstand stress, yet society has assigned to it the heaviest of responsibilities: the socialization and orientation of the young, and the meeting of the major emotional needs of all citizens, young and old.

When the family is viewed historically, we can see that it is more dependent today than it was formerly on other agencies in society for fulfilling its purposes. Once a self-contained economic and social unit buttressed by kinship supports, the family now has interdependent relations with many other associations in working out its problems. I have elsewhere (55) described the ways in which the family functions in equilibrating troubles of its members:

The modern family lives in a greater state of tension precisely because it is the great burden carrier of the social order. In a society of rapid social change, problems outnumber solutions, and the resulting uncertainties are absorbed by the members of society, who are for the most part also members of families. Because the family is the bottleneck through which all troubles pass, no other association so reflects the strains and stresses of life. With few exceptions persons in work-a-day America return to rehearse their daily frustrations within the family, and hope to get the necessary understanding and resilience to return the morrow to the fray.

Thus, the good family today is not only the focal point of frustrations and tensions but also the source for resolving frustrations and releasing tensions. . . . Through its capacity for sympathy, understanding, and unlimited support, the family rehabilitates personalities bruised in the course of competitive daily living. In that capacity the family is literally love in action.

In sum, the concept of the family which we have identified above is that of an arena of interacting personalities, intricately organized internally into positions, norms, and roles. When viewed externally it can be seen as an organized group engaged in transactions with other associations. It is not new to trouble. Indeed, problems and exigencies beset American families from wedding day to dissolution day. Most families have had a long history of troubles and have worked out procedures and a division of responsibility for meeting problematic situations as they arise. These can be viewed broadly as the family's repertory of resources for dealing with crises which we shall have occasion to return to later.

The Crisis-Precipitating Event

The second major concept in our scaffolding is the *stressor*, or crisis-provoking event. A stressor in this context is a situation for which the family has had little or no prior preparation and must therefore be viewed as problematic.(132) It is often difficult empirically to disentangle the problematics and the hardships of the stressful event from the definitions the family makes—the meaning aspect of the event. To make the distinction conceptually is one step in the direction of doing so empirically. Actually the hardships of the event lie outside the family and are an attribute of the event itself, constituting a distinct variable requiring separate attention.

No crisis-precipitating event is the same for any given family; its impact ranges according to the several hardships that may accompany it. We might take, as an illustration, the dismemberment of a family through conscription of the husband-father into the armed services in wartime—an event that appeared to be uniform, striking, as it did, hundreds of thousands of families in America in World War II. Hill and Boulding,[2] studying this phenomenon, found the number of hardships accompanying the event ranging from none to six, including sharp changes in income, housing inadequacies, enforced living with in-laws or other relatives, illness of wife or children, wife's having to work and be both mother and father, and child-discipline problems stemming from the father's absence. There were, on the other hand, families where the war separation event produced father-substitutes who were an improvement on the absentee, improved housing, increased income, and a more relaxed family life. Similarly the catastrophic event of a tornado strikes unevenly as a crisis-precipitating event. Some families lose not only property but life and limb too; many experience reduced income only, still others suffer fright and anxiety, but in the short run make net gains financially because of the moratorium on debts and the grants from relief agencies which often accompany severe catastrophes.(56) Clearly, the stressor event must be seen as a variable rather than as a constant in family crisis research.

Since no stressor event is uniformly the same for all families, but varies in striking power by the hardships that accompany it, the concept of hardship itself requires some additional attention. Hardships may be defined as those complications in a crisis-precipitating event which demand competencies from the family which the event itself may have temporarily paralyzed or made unavailable.

Definition of the Event as Stressful

It has always puzzled observers that some families ride out the vicissitudes of floods and disasters without apparent disorganization, whereas most families are at least temporarily paralyzed by such catastrophes. The key appears to be at the "meaning" dimension. Stressors become crises in line with the definition the family makes of the event.

A boy caught stealing in one neighborhood may be ostracized and bring his family shame and disgrace, while a boy in a different social grouping may well achieve standing within his family and in his neighborhood through an identical act. To transform a stressor event into a crisis requires an intervening variable that has been variously termed, "meaning of the event" or "definition of the event."

Placing this final variable in an equation with the other elements in our conceptual framework, we get a formula as follows: A (the event) → *interacting* with B (the family's crisis-meeting resources) → *interacting* with C (the definition the family makes of the event) → *produces* X (the crisis). The second and third determinants—family resources and definition of the event—lie within the family itself and must be seen in terms of the family's structures and values. The hardships of the event, which go to make up the first determinant, lie outside the family and are an attribute of the event itself.

This threefold framework enables us to ask the proper questions to account for crisis-proneness in families, identifying as it does the interplay of the most important explanatory variables. We turn now to our findings about the stresses studied to date, the properties of the crisis-prone, and the phases of adjustment characteristic of families under stress.

A CLASSIFICATION OF STRESSOR EVENTS

Three systems of classification of family troubles have been used by investigators in cataloging crises:

(1) by source, whether extra-family or intra-family, (2) by effects upon the family configuration, which combine dismemberment, accession, and demoralization, and (3) by type of event impinging on the family.

Source of Trouble

If the blame for the stressor can be placed outside the family, the stress may solidify rather than disorganize the family. Crises differ in their sources—some originate within, others outside the family. Crises that arise as a result of economic depression or of war, both of which are beyond the individual family's control, present quite different problems from the crises arising out of the interpersonal relations within the family such as infidelity, non-support, or alcoholism. The loss of life's savings due to bank failure during a depression will induce a crisis for most families, but consider the impact created by the loss of life's savings through the improvidence of an alcoholic father, which event was in turn precipitated by a serious rift in the affectional relations within the family. It is not the loss of life's savings in this instance so much as it is the interpersonal relations which constitute the matrix of trouble.

Classified by source of trouble, stressor events divide into three categories: (1) extra-family events which in the long run tend to solidify the family, such as war bombings, political persecutions, religious persecutions, floods, tornadoes, hurricanes, and other "acts of God," defined as stressful but solidifying because external to the family; (2) intra-family events such as illegitimacy, non-support, mental breakdown, infidelity, suicide, and alcoholism, which are defined as stressful but usually are more disorganizing to the family because they arise from troubles that reflect poorly on the family's internal adequacy; and (3) some extra-family events that are often not defined as critically stressful and are assimilable because other persons are in the same situation or worse, or events similar to others the family has previously undergone, such as some war separations, some war reunions, loss of home in a disaster, forced migration, sudden decrease in income during a depression, and premature births (see especially Caplan [18]).

Combinations of Dismemberment-Accession and Demoralization

A second type of classification first suggested by Eliot (27) and expanded by Hill (132) involves the combination of loss of family member (dismemberment) or addition of an unprepared-for member (accession) and loss of morale and family unity (demoralization), or all three. (In Table 14.1, crises that have already been studied are bulleted, suggesting areas in which there is demonstrable need for further research.)

Closely allied with this classification are stressor events that do not result in dismemberment in the sense of a change in the plurality pattern of the family, but do bring marked changes in the family configuration. Those family situations where roles are involuntarily vacated through illness, or are not fulfilled at all as in families with mentally retarded children, might be cited as examples (see the work of Bernard Farber and his associates in the Institute for Research on Exceptional Children, the University of Illinois). Families experience significant strains when members become diabetics, rheumatic fever patients, or experience congestive heart failure and demand special considerations over prolonged periods. Such illnesses require a reallocation of the patient's roles to others within the family and a standardization of his role on a more or less indefinite basis.(93)

Most crises of dismemberment, accession, and crippling illness sooner or later involve *de-moralization,* since the family's role patterns are always sharply disturbed. Dismemberment creates a situation in which the departed one's roles must be reallocated, and a period of confusion-delay ensues while the members of the family cast learn their new lines. The addition of a new member resulting from the marriage of a divorced or widowed person strains the resources of a family that "closed ranks" too well.(8, 46)

Types of Impact of Stressor Events

Ernest W. Burgess (16) has added two categories for further classifying family crisis: (1) sudden change in family status, and (2) conflict among family members in the conception of their roles.

Table 14.1   A Classification of Family Crises of
Dismemberment-Accession and
Demoralization

Dismemberment Only

- Death of child, spouse, or parent
- Hospitalization of spouse
- War separation

Accession Only

   Unwanted pregnancy
   Deserter returns
   Stepfather, stepmother additions
- Some war reunions
- Some adoptions, aged grandparents, orphaned kin

Demoralization Only

- Nonsupport
   Infidelity
- Alcoholism
   Drug addiction
   Delinquency and events bringing disgrace

Demoralization Plus Dismemberment or Accession

- Illegitimacy
   Runaways
- Desertion
- Divorce
   Imprisonment
   Suicide or homicide
- Institutionalization for mental illness

A sudden upturn in economic and social status may constitute a crisis quite as disruptive as that of economic loss or social disgrace. The price of upward mobility for some families may be family breakdown. We are only beginning to learn something of the conditions under which the family survives or goes to pieces when there is a swift change from poverty to riches or from obscurity to fame. More usually we think of stressor events bringing sudden changes downward in status. The variety of crises of this type is well known. The large number starred in the list below suggests that many of these crises have already been studied systematically by family sociologists.

Types of Stresses Involving Status Shifts

- Sudden impoverishment
- Prolonged unemployment
  Sudden wealth and fame
- Refugee migrations, political and religious
- Disasters, tornadoes, floods, explosions
- War bombings, deprivations
- Political declassing, denazification

Many of the difficulties that build up into crises involve differences in conception of their respective roles by family members. Conflicts between parents and children should be understood and studied in terms of their differences in role expectations. Koos (71) finds the adolescent-parent relationships to be a focal point of crisis in the middle-class family. In upward-mobile families, the appropriate roles for wife and mother differ by socioeconomic groups, and the work-a-day housekeeper roles of one's original class may have to be unlearned and the hostess roles of the next class may have to be learned to fit the changed expectations of husband and children.

The current crisis of desegregation in the South is a stressful event for both white and Negro families, largely because of the great differences in role expectations held by parents and children. As the schools are integrated, children of both groups tend to forget color as the individual personality shines through. They make friends on the basis of congeniality rather than color alone. Parents and some teachers lag behind the children in this respect. Parents try to limit friendships and home associations, thus producing conflict with their volatile adolescents. Dating, dancing, and contact games become focal points of disagreement, since these activities violate the Southern mores which parents feel obliged to perpetuate. The children may only partially accept these mores and resent their parents' restrictions. Conflicts develop between families whose restrictions differ, since styles for adolescents are often set by the freedoms that the most permissive parents allow their children. Thus the full-blown dimensions of a family crisis are experienced until a new set of norms accepted by both generations develops.(54)

With this background of the range of types of stressful events spelled out, we turn to a consideration of the factors making for crisis-proneness and freedom from crisis among families. It has been suggested that crisis-proneness runs in families as does accident-proneness. What support can be adduced for such a proposition? We know that some families can handle stress better than other families. In what ways do they differ from the crisis prone?

FACTORS MAKING FOR CRISIS-PRONENESS IN FAMILIES

We can profitably take advantage now of an equation that summarizes the conceptual framework of most of the family crisis research I am reporting: A (the event) → *interacting* with B (the family's crisis-meeting resources) → *interacting* with C (the definition the family makes of the event) → *produces* X (the crisis). Crisis-proneness is in effect the phenomenon of experiencing stressor events (A) with greater frequency and greater severity and defining these (C) more frequently as crises. In other words, crisis-prone families appear to be more vulnerable to stressor events of the types we have just cataloged, and more likely because of meager crisis-meeting resources (B) and failure to have learned, from past experience with crisis, to define these events as crisis-provoking. The explanation for crisis-proneness therefore lies primarily in the B and C factors in our equation.

Note the differences in vulnerability when families are assessed on a class basis alone. To the lower-class family, living up to and even beyond its income, there may be a quality of desperation in a financial crisis that is lacking for the middle-class family with reserves upon which it can draw. The lower-class family not only is restricted in income, but in health, energy, space, and ideas for coping with crisis— owing to its hand-to-mouth existence, it lacks defense in depth. Conversely, the lower-class family with little to lose in the way of prestige or status and little opportunity to climb upward may be able to react more favorably to endangered reputation than can the respectability-focused, middle-class family.

Crisis-Meeting Resources, the B Factor

The vulnerability of the lower-class family, however, is no greater to certain stressor events than that of the middle-class family. Each has its characteristic Achilles heel. Robert C. Angell (5) was the first among family sociologists to seek for the B factor in our equation, a set of resources in family organization which, by their presence or absence, kept the family from crisis or urged it into crisis. His findings go beyond the points of vulnerability identified above by class. He employed two concepts—family integration and family adaptability. By the first he meant the "bonds of coherence and unity running through family life, of which common interests, affection, and a sense of economic interdependence are perhaps the most prominent." By the second he referred to the family's capacity to meet obstacles and shift courses as a family. He was trying to get at the family's latent predisposition to action in the face of challenges to its usual mode of existence. These latent action patterns, which are most clearly observable at times of crisis, are integrated, in turn, by the values held by the family. Angell found it possible to explain the different reactions of crisis-proof and crisis-prone families to sharp decreases in income during the Depression by these twin factors of integration and adaptability, with a restudy of the cases suggesting the greater importance of family adaptability.

Cavan and Ranck (19) and Koos (72) used somewhat different concepts but were in essential agreement. To these researchers a crisis-proof family must have agreement in its role structure, subordination of personal ambitions to family goals, satisfactions within the family obtained because it is successfully meeting the physical and emotional needs of its members, and goals toward which the family is moving collectively. Having all of these, the family is adequately organized. Lacking them, the family is inadequately organized and likely to prove vulnerable to crisis-precipitating events. In both the Cavan-Ranck and Koos studies, the B factor is, in effect, adequacy-inadequacy of family organization.

Social workers have long employed the term "problem family" to designate the crisis-prone family. Early social work viewed problem families primarily as reactors to the conditions of poverty, and saw a shoring up of the economic resources as all-important. Subsequently the shift to a more psychological emphasis established that parents and children in problem families were maladjusted individuals in need of individual treatment. Problem families became not so much victims of a poor distributive order as aggregates of neurotic or psychopathic individuals. More recently the work of Community Research Associates with problem families emphasizes the importance of the distortions of the marital axis, the incompatible combinations of personalities which make for divided and incompetent family headship.(22) Such families are "disorganized" social failures when judged against generally accepted family objectives (23), and tend to be *multi-problem* families collecting attention and services from public and private agencies all out of proportion to their number in the community.

English researchers have written considerably on problem families, labeling them as deviant, antisocial, and lower class. Irvine (60) stated that "Problem families can be most usefully defined as socially defective families characterized by child neglect and squalor, which defeat current efforts at rehabilitation." Stephens (125) observed that the most obvious common feature of these families is the disorder of their lives. Baldamus and Timms (7) see them as having defective standards of behavior: "The more extreme cases of disorganization and inefficiency in problem families approach a situation of retreatism, as defined by Robert Merton. Conformity to established values is virtually relinquished, especially in respect to standards of behavior."

Max Siporin (121), in summarizing the work on the problem family, has made the cogent observation that present-day American social workers and sociologists, in contrast to our English colleagues, have preferred to concentrate on the processes of family maladjustment rather than to focus on the stereotyping of families with the use of such epithets as hard-core, inadequate, and disordered. Behind the use by these Americans of terms like "disorganized" is a theory of disorganization and recovery which they seek to study further. This is evident in the attempt we shall make below to link together crisis-meeting resources of family organization and the definitions the family makes of a stressor event in accounting for its crisis-proneness.

Family Definitions, the C Factor

The C factor in our equation has received attention only recently from students of the family. Hill and Boulding,[2] studying war separation and reunion crises, perceived three possible definitions of the crisis-precipitating event: (1) an *objective* definition, formulated by an impartial observer, (2) a *cultural* definition, formulated by the community, and (3) a *subjective* definition, provided by the family. The most relevant definition in determining a family's crisis-proneness is the third, that provided by the family. The researcher and the community stand outside the situation looking in, but the family members are on the inside, and the family's attitudes toward the event are all-important in this connection.

A family's definition of the event reflects partly the value system held by the family, partly its previous experience in meeting crises, and partly the mechanisms employed in previous definitions of events. This is the *meaning* aspect of the crisis, the interpretation made of it.

Not infrequently families with objective resources adequate to meet the hardships of sickness or job loss crack under the stress because they define such hardship situations as insurmountable. Accident-proneness is disproportionately high among individuals who lack self-confidence and are characterized by anxiety. Crisis-proneness in families also proves related to outlook to whether or not the event is defined as challenging or crisis-provoking.

Crisis-Proneness, a Function of Both B and C Factors

If we combine deficiency in family organization resources (the B factor) and the tendency to define hardships as crisis-producing (the C factor) into one concept of family inadequacy, we may analyze its major features in a polygon wheel of interacting forces which we reproduce in Figure 14.1 is from the work of Koos and Fulcomer.(73) As they explain it, there is sometimes an initial cause that tends to create

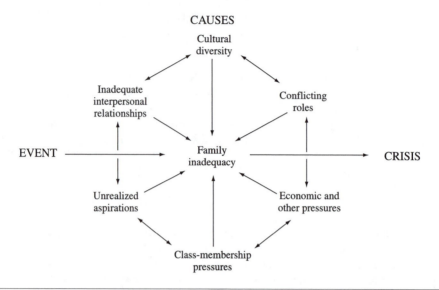

Figure 14.1   A Schema for Depicting the Interplay of Stressor Event, Contributing Hardships, and Family Resources in Producing a Family Crisis

tensions in other areas of family life, which, in turn, become conflicts themselves. For example, cultural disparity may cause a lack of sexual satisfaction because of the differing ideas and standards of sex behavior, which in turn may lead to suspicion of the mate and lack of co-operation as breadwinner or homemaker, which in turn may create conflicting roles in the family and draw individual members into new positions of responsibility in the family at the expense of other members. The accumulation of these tensions so weakens the affectional relationships and integration of the family as to render it unable to meet even a simple departure from its ordinary life patterns. The result, when an out-of-ordinary event occurs, is a crisis.

ADJUSTMENT TO CRISIS

Koos and Fulcomer's ingenious diagram, if carried another step into the adjustment of the family to the crisis, would reveal again an interplay of many of the same factors reflecting family adequacy-inadequacy which made families prone to crisis originally. Causation is just as complex in adjustment as it is in the definition of, or sensitivity to, crisis.

Adjustment to a crisis that threatens the family depends upon the adequacy of role performance of family members. As we have already shown in our discussion of the conceptual framework, the family consists of a number of members interacting with one another, and each member is ascribed roles to play within the family. The individual functions as a member of the family largely in terms of the expectations that other members place upon him; the family succeeds as a family largely in terms of the adequacy of role performance of its members. One major effect of crisis is to cause changes in these role patterns. Expectations shift, and the family finds it necessary to work out different patterns. In the process the family is slowed up in its affectional and emotion-satisfying performances until the new patterns are worked out and avenues for expressing affection are opened once more.

The Course of Adjustment

What can we say about the course of adjustment to crisis? We know that it varies from family to family and from crisis to crisis, but the common denominator may be charted in the truncated form of

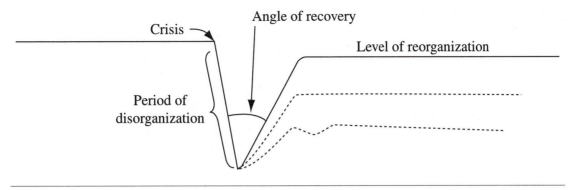

Figure 14.2

a roller-coaster [Figure 14.2]. As a result of meeting a crisis, the family members are collectively numbed by the blow. They may meet friends, at first, as if the blow had not fallen. Then, as the facts are assimilated, there follows a downward slump in organization, roles are played with less enthusiasm, resentments are smothered or expressed, conflicts are expressed or converted into tensions that make for strained relations. As the nadir of disorganization is reached, things begin improving, new routines arrived at by trial-and-error or by thoughtful planning and sacrificing are put into effect, and some minimum agreements about the future are reached. The component parts to the roller-coaster profile of adjustment to crisis are: crisis → disorganization → recovery → reorganization.

Refinements of this basic pattern have been worked out by Hill (55) on adjustments to war separation and by Jackson (61) on adjustments to alcoholism. Jackson identifies seven stages of adjustment: (1) attempts to deny the problem, (2) attempts to eliminate the problem, (3) disorganization, (4) attempts to reorganize in spite of the problem, (5) efforts to escape the problem: the decision to separate from the alcoholic spouse, (6) reorganization of the family without spouse, (7) reorganization of the entire family. These stages parallel closely the stages of adjustment and recovery to bereavement. An analysis of what happens as the family breaks old habits and organizes new routines during the downhill and uphill part of the roller-coaster figure

above shows some interesting changes in family organization.

Generic Effects of Crisis on Family Behavior

In one of the most sensitive areas of family life, the sexual area, sharp changes are noted. The frequency and pattern of sexual relations change, ceasing altogether for some couples.(70) In crises involving interpersonal recriminations, where the crisis is regarded as the fault of any one member, the position of that member is greatly devaluated.(71) Personality changes in members reflect the anxiety and feelings of insecurity engendered by the crisis, and in a sense each responsible member experiences a roller-coaster pattern of personal shock, disorganization, recovery, readjustment. Particularly is this evident in bereavement, where the adjustments of family members follow a course of disbelief → numbness → mourning → trial-and-error adjustments → renewal of routines → recovery.

Changes in parent-child relations are frequently reported in adjustment to crisis. In well-integrated families, Angell (5) found few changes in relative position of parents and children as a result of the crisis of impoverishment, but did find changes in less well-integrated but more adaptable families.

In summarizing the impressions of disaster workers and making inferences from the relatively scanty firsthand information from families experiencing such catastrophes as tornado, hurricane, or flood, we find a confirmation of the roller-coaster pattern at the beginning of the crisis experience. In the immediate recovery period, however, there is an almost euphoric increase in family solidarity (with high solidarity also in the network of neighbors and friends) in the first weeks after the disaster.(56)

Inter-family activities vary as a result of crisis. Some families withdraw from all activities until the "shame" is over and become more than ever closed systems. Others become quite outgoing in their open-window policy during the troubled period.(5)

These are all *short-time* effects of crisis. The evidence concerning the long-time effects of crisis on families is conflicting. Cavan (19) found that, if the families were well organized before the crisis of impoverishment, they tended to remain well organized; moreover, it seemed that previous successful experiences with crisis were predictive of recovery in a new crisis. Angell (5) found well-integrated and adaptable families invulnerable to crisis; that is, they took it in stride without marked changes in their organization or role structure. Helmut Shelsky (119), studying post–World War II German families who had experienced severe bombing and the post-war deprivations of denazification and underemployment, found families in general more solid as a consequence. He explains the phenomenon of higher family solidarity as a reaction to the unstable larger society in which home and family are made into a haven from the uncertainty and insecurity of the post-war world. Kent Geiger (39), studying refugee families from the U.S.S.R. in Europe and the U.S., found families that had been terrorized politically by the regime to be more frequently solidified than disorganized by the experience. The impact of economic deprivation on these families, however, was seen to be detrimental to interpersonal solidarity within the family. Thus, from Geiger's study, political persecution appears to be positively, and deterioration of material living conditions to be negatively, related to family unity. Koos, focusing on the troubles of low-income families in New York City over a two-year period, found among those initially disorganized by crisis evidence of permanent demoralization, a blunting

of the family's sensitivity, and a tendency to be more vulnerable in future exposures. "Once having been defeated by a crisis, the family appears not to be able to marshal its forces sufficiently to face the next event; there is, in other words, a permanent defeat each time."(72)

If the conflicting evidences were to be reconciled, the synthesis would follow these lines: Successful experience with crisis tests and strengthens a family, but defeat in crisis is punitive on family structure and morale.(53)

TYPES OF FAMILIES BEST EQUIPPED TO MEET TROUBLES

In this brief discussion of family adjustment to stress, there may be some merit in listing the attributes of family organization, modes of adjustment, and factors making for adjustment which have grown out of the studies of families in crisis and which have been confirmed in an entirely new context by Hill in an analysis of family adjustments to war separation and reunion. In it the findings of earlier studies were treated as hypotheses to be tested in the as-yet-unstudied crises of war separation and reunion. The findings of this analysis divide between factors making for adjustment to crisis and a confirmation of generalizations about modes of adjustment that work out best in the face of crisis (see especially Table 28 in Hill [55]).

Factors Conducive to Good Adjustment to Crisis

Family adaptability, family integration, affectional relations among family members, good marital adjustment of husband and wife, companionable parent-child relationships, family council type of control in decision-making, social participation of wife, and previous successful experience with crisis were all confirmed as important factors in enabling families to adjust to crisis.

Rather fully corroborated within the new contexts of war separation and reunion were the following generalizations from previous studies:

1. Crisis-proneness, the tendency to define troubles as crises, is distributed disproportionately among families of low family adequacy.

2. The course of adjustment is a roller-coaster pattern of disorganization-recovery-readjustment (corroborated as modal pattern for separation but not for reunion).

3. Family reactions to crisis divide between short-time immediate reactions and secondary long-time adjustments.

4. Demoralization following a crisis usually stems from incipient demoralization before the crisis.

5. The length of time a family continues to be disorganized as a result of crisis is inversely related to its adequacy of organization.

6. Unadaptable and unintegrated families are most likely of all to be unpredictable deviants in adjusting to crisis.

7. Foreknowledge and preparation for a critical event mitigates the hardships and improves the chances for recovery.

8. The effects of crisis on families may be punitive or strengthening depending on the margin of health, wealth, and adequacy possessed by the family.

IMPLICATIONS FOR AGENCY POLICIES AND PRACTICE

My statement of implications for agency policies and practices is offered most tentatively. It attempts to answer two questions: (1) How does research on families under stress change our views of family organizational needs? (2) How might practices be changed in line with these needs?

Family Organizational Needs

We find families increasingly vulnerable as they are shorn of kin, neighbors, and friends. Centered as they are about the husband and wife and their one or two children, modern American families are highly mobile, precariously small, and poorly structured units to survive life's stresses—death, unemployment, war separations, infidelity, desertion, and so on.

The goal of self-sufficiency, of families being capable of surviving by themselves, may have had some merit in pioneer days when the family groups were large and included several relatives besides the children. Today the myth of family self-sufficiency requires discrediting. To replace it we bring the concept of interdependence of families within communities. This concept will need to be implemented in our communities with appropriate organization, to be sure, if it is to have any meaning to people.

In my war-separation study the families who adjusted least well and most slowly were frequently solitary families characterized by past mobility and transiency, or they were families whose relationships with relatives and neighbors had become tenuous. In either case, these families lacked the nests of supporting families with which to share their troubles and were, therefore, forced to live *alone* in an enforced anonymity. Left to their own devices, crisis-stricken families in a new neighborhood withdraw into their narrow family circles and fester inwardly rather than risk being rebuffed.

Several studies have offered evidence that families whose economic well-being is marginal are more vulnerable to crisis. Koos (72) eloquently portrays the marginality of living in such families:

As the investigator strips off the outer layers of low-income urban existence he becomes increasingly aware of its hand-to-mouth quality. Only the things that must be done managed to get done. There are no sheltered reservoirs within which man can store up his surplus thoughts, energies and products—and not surprisingly, because for people living under these conditions there are no surplus thoughts and energies and products. They need all of their energies and every cent they can earn in order to meet the day-by-day demands, and they know that their environment will make endless demands upon them whichever way they turn. Life under such conditions takes on a nip-and-tuck urgency that belies our culture's middle-class *ethos* of a reasoned calculation of one's future.

Individuals and whole families of individuals suffer from these pressures. Housewives lament that they can buy only for the next meal because there is no place in which to store additional foods. Wage earners know that every cent they make is mortgaged in advance simply to keep up with basic expenditures, and they curse and worry because they cannot save for a rainy day. Adolescent girls have no place in which to entertain the "boy friend" because home offers no opportunity for privacy. Only the youngest members of the family can dawdle and dream beyond life's immediacies, and they, too, suffer indirectly.

IMPLICATIONS FOR FAMILY SERVICES NEEDED

The high mobility of young families results in feelings of "aloneness" as they move into new communities or join the stream moving out of the central city into the suburbs. Separated from kin and hometown neighbors, to whom do they turn for counsel and help when they want to spill their troubles? How do they become integrated into a new neighborhood or community? The challenge for social work is to develop institutions less commercial than the "welcome wagon" and more neighborhood oriented. We need community organization and neighborhood development activities in this direction, such as Milwaukee supported in its department of health for a time. We need to institutionalize the status of "newcomers" and utilize it to provide orientation and welcoming activities into neighborhood and community.

It is noteworthy that those families that best succeeded in meeting the crisis of wartime separation made frequent mention of accessibility of relatives, neighbors, and friends. They rarely mentioned, we are sad to report, the churches, the family agencies, or other welfare groups that claim in their annual bid for contributions from the community that they provide services of this kind to families in trouble.

In shaping a community program that is more family-centered, we need to face the fact that many families that once received help and comfort from kin and neighbors have now lost contact with them and live in anonymity. We must recognize that their problems are often such that they do not know which, if any, social agency could or would help if asked. We need to reorganize our agency offerings to meet families at their own level of need. As we have seen the need among the families in the studies reviewed here, help might often have consisted simply of providing an opportunity to ventilate their anxieties, share their woes, and ask for reassuring, simple advice about problems occasioned by the absence of the husband and father, or the changed regulations for children attending schools in double shifts. There are, at the present time, few agencies to which families willingly turn for help on the more superficial levels of life.

Even if social workers were willing to extend such superficial services broadly, there are only a few hundred family service agencies in the entire United States, and marriage counseling services are limited to the metropolitan centers and to a few college campuses. The professional services for non-indigent families in trouble must be drawn mainly from the family physician, the teacher, the minister, the family lawyer, and the occasional child welfare worker with the public welfare department. To these professionals, the following suggestions from the researches I have summarized appear justified:

1. Professional services will make their greatest contribution if they are made with the total family context in mind. Particularly is this true in the case of crises of dismemberment and demoralization.

2. Families, like combat teams and other collectivities, have a morale and *esprit de corps* to maintain if they are to be effective. Physicians have found that illnesses that yesterday were called psychosomatic are today regarded as products of family aggravations.

The helping professionals will need to approximate family group workers, serving the child's family *as a family* rather than serving the child solely as a personality. This involves becoming an artist in relationship therapy, keeping all the family relationships healthy.

3. Families need to be kept intact and relatively self-sustaining.

Both war separations and peacetime separations render a net disservice to most families, although many ride them out successfully. Voluntary separations should not be undertaken without serious thought as to the consequences. Employers should know that transferring an employee to a position in a distant community where tight housing prevents his taking the family along is doing the employee a serious disservice. However, if separation is forced upon the family, our research shows that it is much more easily assimilated if prepared for well in advance. Making this fact known widely may greatly mitigate the untoward effects of separation because of employment, hospitalization, institutionalization, and even imprisonment.

4. Counseling and casework become patchwork remedies unless a strong program of preventive social work and education is undertaken by agencies.

We know that families of various types are capable of meeting crises, that we do not have to stamp out uniform models. Successful families, however, share the resources of good marital adjustment, family adaptability, and, to a lesser degree, family integration. Their communicative lines must be kept open through frank discussions and the use of the consultative process in arriving at family decisions. Case-workers will see the challenge to train young people, and they will seize the opportunity through parent education to reach young parents, to encourage the development of patterns of family organization which make for survival in the face of trouble. To date, few programs have attempted, even experimentally, to produce students competent to exercise family leadership in flexible family organizations of this sort. Here lies the challenge of preventive social work and family life education of tomorrow.

NOTES

1. In this connection, see the reports of European research by C. D. Saal of Holland and Elizabeth Bott of England, in *Recherches Sur La Famille,* published by UNESCO Institute of Social Science, Cologne, 1956, pp. 29-69, 229-247.

2. In *Families Under Stress* (55), Chapt. IV, pp. 50-97.

REFERENCES

5. Angell, R. C., *The Family Encounters the Depression,* Charles Scribner's Sons, New York, 1936.

7. Baldamus, W., and Timms, N., "The Problem Family: A Sociological Approach," *British Journal of Sociology,* Vol. VI, No. 2 (1955), pp. 318-327.

8. Bernard, J., *Remarriage,* Dryden Press, New York, 1956.

16. Burgess, E. W., "The Family and Sociological Research," *Social Forces,* Vol. XXVI, No. 1 (1947), pp. 1-6.

18. Caplan, G. and Associates, Harvard School of Public Health, "Some comments on family functioning in its relation to mental health," unpublished, 1956.

19. Cavan, R. S., and Ranck, K. H., *The Family and the Depression,* University of Chicago Press, Chicago, 1938.

22. Community Research Associates, *Classification of Disorganized Families for Use in Family Oriented Diagnosis and Treatment,* New York, 1954.

23. Community Research Associates, *The Prevention and Control of Disordered Behavior in San Mateo County, California,* New York, 1954.

27. Eliot, T. D., "Handling Family Strains and Shocks," in *Family, Marriage and Parenthood,* H. Becker and R. Hill (eds.), D. C. Heath, Boston, 2nd ed., 1955, p. 617.

39. Geiger, K., "Deprivation and Solidarity in the Soviet Urban Family," *American Sociological Review,* Vol. XX, No. 1 (1955), pp. 57-68.

46. Goode, W. J., *After Divorce,* The Free Press, Glencoe, IL, 1956.

53. Hill, R., "The American Family: Problem or Solution?" *American Journal of Sociology,* Vol. LIII, No. 2 (1947), pp.125-130.

54. Hill, R., "Families and the Prospect of Educational Integration," in *The Implications of Desegregation for Family Life in Virginia,* Virginia Council on Family Relations, Richmond, VA, 1955, pp. 2-10.

55. Hill, R., *Families Under Stress,* Harper & Brothers, New York, 1949.

56. Hill, R., and Rayner, J., "Observations of Family Adjustments in the Kansas City Tornado," unpublished memorandum in preparation, 1957.

60. Irvine, E. E., "Research Into Problem Families: Questions Arising From Dr. Blacker's Investigations," *British Journal of Psychiatric Social Work,* Vol. IX (1954), p. 32.

61. Jackson, J. K., "The Adjustment of the Family to Alcoholism," *Marriage and Family Living,* Vol. XVIII, No. 4 (1956), pp. 361-369.

70. Komarovsky, M., *The Unemployed Man and His Family,* Dryden Press, New York, 1940.

71. Koos, E. L., "Class Differences in Family Reactions to Crisis," *Marriage and Family Living,* Vol. XII, No. 3 (1950), pp. 77-78.

72. Koos, E. L., *Families in Trouble,* King's Crown Press, New York, 1946.

73. Koos, E. L., and Fulcomer, D., "Families in Crisis," in *Dynamics of Family Interaction,* E. M. Duvall and R. Hill (eds.), Women's Foundation, New York, 1948 chapt. 8 (mimeographed).

93. Parsons, T., and Bales, R. F., *Family, Socialization and Interaction Process,* The Free Press, Glencoe, IL, 1955.

119. Shelsky, H., *Wandlunger in der Deutschen Familien in der Gegenwart,* Enke-Verlag, Stuttgart, 1954.

121. Siporin, M., "The Concept of the Problem Family," Baylor University College of Medicine, Texas Medical Center (unpublished), 1956.

125. Stephens, T., *Problem Families,* William S. Heinman, New York, 1947.

132. Waller, W. W., "The Family: A Dynamic Interpretation," in *Family Crises and Family Adjustment,* rev. by R. Hill, Chapt. 21, Dryden Press, New York, 1951.

PART 4

Boundary Ambiguity: A Risk Factor in Family Stress Management

Included are two articles of the many now available on boundary ambiguity in various situations. Boss (1980) writes a conceptual paper about normative family stress as people enter and exit the family system across the life span. The major assumption is that family boundaries will change over the life course and that these changes, whether losses or acquisitions, will create stress. Caron, Boss, and Mortimer's (1999) article is one of several tests of the boundary ambiguity theory—in this case, with a sample of caregivers coping with the chronic illness of Alzheimer's disease. This study used the Boundary Ambiguity Scale, and findings showed a reciprocal relationship between caregiver and patient. That is, caregiver closeout (distancing themselves from patient) predicted an increase in patient behavior problems. We hope this study stimulates further research about boundary ambiguity during various situations of ambiguous loss.

The first journal publication on boundary ambiguity was Boss (1977), "A Clarification of the Concept of Psychological Father Presence in Families Experiencing Ambiguity of Boundary." I did not include this paper because in it, I mistakenly used the constructs of *ambiguity* and *ambivalence* synonymously. The paper may, however, be of historical interest. In 1984, Jan Steven Greenberg and I wrote a theoretical paper titled "Family Boundary Ambiguity: A New Variable in Family Stress Theory." I recommend reading it but could not include it due to space limitations. For a conceptual summary, see Boss's (1999) *Ambiguous Loss*.

REFERENCES

Boss, P. (1977). A clarification of the concept of psychological father presence in families experiencing ambiguity of boundary. *Journal of Marriage and the Family, 39*(1), 141-151.

Boss, P. (1999). *Ambiguous loss.* Cambridge, MA: Harvard University Press.

Boss, P., & Greenberg, J. S. (1984). Family boundary ambiguity: A new variable in family stress theory. *Family Process, 23*(4), 535-546.

15

NORMATIVE FAMILY STRESS

Family Boundary Changes Across the Life-Span

PAULINE G. BOSS

Normative stress in families results whenever components are added to or subtracted from a family system. From birth to death, family boundaries change and remain ambiguous during the process of reorganization after acquisition or loss of a member. The family's perception of who is inside or outside the family system is significantly related to the interaction within that system as well as between that system and the outside world. It is proposed that due to the process of family boundary maintenance, there is little similarity in family structures across time: family structures are constantly changing to facilitate the accomplishment of functions while maintaining family boundaries.

All families, functional and dysfunctional, experience stress—that is, change at various times throughout the family life cycle. However, the question remains as to *why* some families recover from the stress of change and, in fact, become stronger, whereas other families cannot cope and are caught in a downward spiral toward increasing dysfunction.

Issues related to this question were addressed decades ago in the contexts of non-normative crises encountered by families: Angell (1936) and Cavan and Ranck (1938) on effects of the depression; DuVall (1945), Hill (1949), and Boulding (1950) on the effects of separation and reunion. In the 1970s a number of studies were conducted at the Center for Prisoner of War Studies in San Diego on the effects

Reprinted from *Family Relations* 29 (1980): 445-50. Copyright © 1988 by the National Council on Family Relations, 3989 Central Ave. NE, Suite 550, Minneapolis, MN 55421. Reprinted by permission.

of military separation (for a review, see McCubbin, Dahl, and Hunter, 1976).

NORMATIVE FAMILY STRESS AND FAMILY BOUNDARIES

Normative life-span stress for the family has been studied much less extensively. Rhona Rapoport's work (1963) represents a classic in that sparse literature. Though her research centered on the stress of change resulting from "getting married," she focused theoretically on other critical transition points in normal family development: the birth of the first child, children going to school for the first time, death of a spouse, or adolescents leaving home (Rapoport, 1963). These she called "points-of-no-return" which lead either to resolution and growth or to maladaptation and subsequent deterioration of the system. She wrote:

> It is postulated that the way these normal "crisis" or status transitions are handled or coped with, will affect outcome—both in terms of the mental health of the individuals and in terms of the enduring family relationship (Rapoport, 1963, p. 69).

Later Stierlin (1974) referred to family types and the adolescent's struggle to move out of the family system if the dominant family type is binding and closed, the adolescent's attempt to unbind himself will be crisis-producing for the family, at least for a time. Stierlin sees this struggle for independence as functional for parents as well as adolescents and illustrates this point with the analogy of Martin Luther who forced the sixteenth century church to reform and strengthen itself "while he, in separating himself from it, bore the onus of rebel . . ." (Stierlin, 1974, p. 174).

More recently, Kantor and Lehr (1975) addressed the issue of the dimensions of family space or boundaries. They defined boundaries as ". . . all the interface rings that constitute the totality of family process interactions . . ." and stated:

> Families that adopt the closed-type homeostatic ideal define their boundaries in terms of the fixed constancy feedback patterns. . . . Families that seek the random

ideal define their boundaries in terms of variety loops rather than constancy loops. . . . Disequilibrium is the random homeostatic ideal. Families that adopt an open homeostatic ideal opt for a mixture of equilibrium and disequilibrium. . . . Open family boundaries are defined in terms of a combination of constancy and variety loop patterns, employed to maximize the potential for a joint negotiation of distance regulation issues at interface (Kantor & Lehr, 1975, pp. 116-117).

Although Kantor and Lehr's boundary types are not classified as either enabling or disabling, Boss proposes that a high degree of boundary ambiguity in *any* family system may cause dysfunction (Boss, 1975, Note 1; 1977, 1980). If a family member is perceived as psychologically present but is, in reality, physically absent for a long time, the family boundary is ambiguous and cannot be maintained. The reverse also manifests boundary ambiguity: physical presence with psychological absence, as in some intact families where a parent is consistently preoccupied with outside work (Boss, McCubbin, & Lester, 1979). Operationalization is based on whether or not roles are still being assigned to the absent person and whether or not the absent member is still perceived as present. Thus the premise is based on role theory and symbolic interaction.

This premise of boundary ambiguity plus the works of Kantor and Lehr reflect the influence of earlier works by Piaget and Inhelder (1956), who investigated space as a central aspect of individual perception and cognition. Using this spatial metaphor from early developmentalists, Kantor and Lehr also focused on structuralism for family boundary maintenance as the family responds to everyday life.

> At each stage of development in a family's life cycle, new distance-regulation crises appear, stimulating new images and reemphasizing older ones. The development of family and individual strategies at each stage continues to be dependent on the interaction of family and individual image hierarchies . . . (Kantor & Lehr, 1975, p. 249).

Therefore, in Kantor and Lehr's terms the perception of family boundary (who is inside or outside the family system) is a distance-regulation or space-bounding issue. But even before Kantor and Lehr, family therapists proposed the critical nature of both real and perceived family boundaries. Boszormenyi-Nagy and Spark (1973, p. 84) referred to boundaries between the family and the larger world formed by "invisible loyalties" such as family values. From a more microscopic perspective, Minuchin (1974) used boundaries within family subsystems in clinical assessment of family functioning. He believed that for proper family functioning, the boundaries of subsystems must be clear.

> [Boundaries] must be defined well enough to allow subsystem members to carry out their functions without undue interference, but they must allow contact between the members of the subsystem and others. The composition of subsystems organized around family functions is not nearly as significant as the clarity of system boundaries. A parental subsystem that includes a grandmother or a parental child can function quite well, so long as lines of responsibility and authority are clearly drawn (Minuchin, 1974, p. 54).

Concomitantly, Minuchin (1974) referred to "diffuse boundaries" (p. 61) as indicators of dysfunctional families. For example diffuse boundaries are found in "enmeshed" families where mother and children are in coalition against the father-husband. In such families, boundaries between the generations, both real and symbolic, remain ambiguous.

ACCOMMODATION TO FAMILY STRESS

Based on the perspective of family therapists and earlier developmentalists and on the initial testing by this author of the boundary ambiguity propositions, it is proposed that individual and family life span perceptions of who is inside or outside the family system are significantly related to the interaction within that system and between that system and the outside world. The specific theoretical proposition is that *the greater the boundary ambiguity at various developmental and normative junctures throughout the family life-cycle, the higher the family and individual dysfunction.* Resolution of the ambiguity is necessary before the family system can reorganize

and move on toward new functioning at a lower level of stress. Nonresolution of boundary ambiguity holds the family at a higher stress level by blocking the regenerative power to reorganize and develop new levels of organization. Boundaries of the system cannot be maintained, so the viability of the system is blurred. Dysfunction results.

Change in Family Boundaries

Obviously, some families resolve the stress of membership change much more quickly than do others. For example, roles and tasks may be quickly reassigned when a new baby joins a family. The father takes over the cooking; grandmother or father or a friend takes over the housework temporarily. The theoretical proposition refers operationally to task accomplishment through role performances (function) within the family structure across time. That is, boundaries are maintained after the birth of a baby by a major shifting of roles and tasks within the family system. Furthermore, interaction of the family with the outside world may be altered: grandmother or a professional support person temporarily becomes active within the system while the new mother temporarily may not be employed outside the home. The latter alone is a major boundary change for many new mothers who are accustomed to daily interaction with colleagues or friends in their outside work world. The task of redefining her family roles after having a new baby is complicated for an employed woman when boundaries remain unclear—in this case, when she isn't sure if she's in or out of the family with respect to her roles and perceptions. She may want to be out in the work world, but she may feel she should be with her new baby, or vice versa. Until she and her family clarify how she is in and how she is out, both perceptually and physically, the family system cannot fully reorganize after the impact of acquiring a new member. Needless to say, the same clarity is necessary to redefine the new father's role.

To emphasize the recurrence and complexity of such situations of change in family systems across time, some examples of Change in Family Boundaries Over the Life-Span are presented in Figure 15.1. The major assumptions in this model

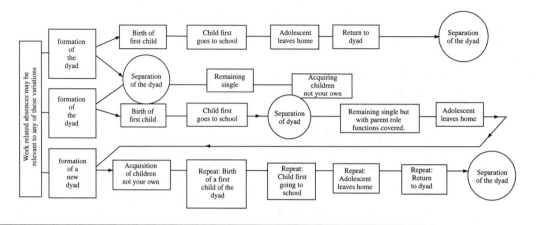

Figure 15.1   Selective Examples of Changes in Family Boundaries Over the Life-Span

are that *family system boundaries will change over the life-span.* Furthermore, boundary changes resulting from adding and/or losing family members cannot be predicted normatively for diverse American families beyond initial pairing and final separation. Hence, various family structural patterns may be exhibited as families progress throughout the life cycle.

Variability in Family Structures for Boundary Maintenance

With an obvious focus on normative function more than on normative structure, it is suggested that there may be no universals in family structural boundaries beyond the original formation of the boundary and its eventual dissolution through family separation. Between these two stages, it is variance more than universality that allows for coping and functional adaptation across the life-span. Varied structures across *and* among families may support the accomplishment of functions that are necessary for family survival and growth over time. In other words, there may indeed be more than one way for families to reach the same end goal (von Bertalanffy, 1968; pp. 40, 132; Buckley, 1967; Hill, 1971).

The Black American family is an excellent example of adaptive boundary maintenance in the face of severe stress from both inside and outside the family. Such families survived only because of adaptations to the normative family structure, as the television epic

Roots so clearly illustrated. The Haley family added and exited people as they needed regardless of societal norms or biological destiny. There was no doubt that Chicken George was still the father and husband in his family and that he still performed the necessary functions for his family even though he remained up North for many years. The family boundary stretched, because of necessity, to retain him as a viable member of the system. Indeed, he actively performed the role of provider and purchaser of freedom for the rest of his family system. It was precisely such boundary elasticity that permitted this Black family to perceive his membership within the system despite great physical distance.

To provide examples of the types of boundary changes families appear to encounter in their everyday life over time, selected representative research is noted in Table 15.1. The boundary changes listed are derived from the classic Rapoport (1963) article, but with these revisions: first, because the "formation of the dyad" is not always synonymous with "marriage," the former term is used. Second, because the "death of a spouse" is not the only recognized way to break up a dyad, "loss of a spouse," which can include death, divorce, or desertion, is used in Table 15.1. Third, the "acquisition of children not your own" is added because of the frequency of this phenomenon today in remarried or blended families and, traditionally, in the Black American subculture. Fourth, "formation of a new

Table 15.1 Selected References to Illustrate Normative Life-Span Boundary Changes

Type of Life-Span Family Boundary Changes	*Boundary Stressors Related to Physical and Psychological Membership in the System*
Formation of the dyad Rapoport, 1963	– acquisition of a mate – acquisition of in-laws – realignment with family of orientation – incorporating or rejecting former friendships
Birth of the first child LeMasters, 1957 Russell, 1974 Pridham, Hansen, & Conrad, 1977	– acquisition of a new member – possible separation from extra-familial work world – if so, loss of working colleagues, etc.
Children first going to school Anderson, 1976 Klein & Ross, 1958	– separation of child from the family system to the world of school – acquisition of child's teacher, friends, and peers, i.e., acceptance of them as part of the child's world
Job-related parent/spouse absence or presence Hill, 1949 Boulding, 1950 Boss, 1975, 1980 McCubbin et al., 1976 Boss, McCubbin, & Lester, 1979 Hooper, 1979	– fluctuating acquisition *and* separation due to extra-familial role, i.e., military service, routine absence of the corporate executive, etc. Stress results from repeated exit and re-entry of the member. Also includes job changes such as return of mother to college or work after she's been a full-time homemaker or retirement of father from work back into the home.
Adolescent children leaving home Stierlin, 1974 Boss & Whitaker, 1979	– separation of adolescent from the family system to his peers, school or job system – acquisition of the adolescent's peers and intimates/same and opposite sex
Taking in child(ren) not your own or blending children from different dyads Duberman, 1975 Visher & Visher, 1978, 1979	– acquisition of another's offspring into the family system, i.e., stepchildren, grandchildren, other nonrelated children

Loss of a spouse (through death, divorce, etc.)
Parkes, 1972
Lopata, 1973, 1979
Bohannan, 1970
Wallerstein & Kelly, Studies from 1974
  through 1977
Weiss, 1975
Hetherington & Deur, 1971;
  Hetherington, Cox, & Cox, 1976
Boss & Whitaker, 1979
	– separation of mate from the dyad, therefore dissolution of the marital dyad. Note: In case of divorce, the dyad may continue and function on other levels, such as co-parenting, etc.

(continued)

Table 15.1 (continued)

Type of Life-Span Family Boundary Changes	Boundary Stressors Related to Physical and Psychological Membership in the System
Loss of parent(s) Sheehy, 1976 Silverstone & Hyman, 1976 Levinson, 1978	– separation of child from parent(s) (child may likely be an adult)
Formation of a new dyad: remarriage Bernard, 1956 Messinger, 1976 Westoff, 1977 Whiteside & Auerbach, 1978 Roosevelt & Lofas, 1976	– acquisition of a new mate – acquisition of a new set of in-laws – realignment with family of orientation and former in-laws, children of former marriage, etc. – incorporating or rejecting former friendships, former spouses, etc., former spouse may still be in partnership with a member of the new dyad regarding parenting.
Remaining single Stein, 1976	– realignment with family of orientation – if previously married, realignment with former in-laws – acquisition of friends, intimates, colleagues, etc.

dyad" is added because of the high rate of remarriage today. Finally, "work-related absence" is added to Table 15.1 because it occurs in so many variations of American families today.

SUMMARY

If it can be assumed that family structural adaptations have been made for the survival of the organism, then these adaptations must be recognized and documented before scientists can proceed toward valid explanation of why some families can cope with the stress of normative membership change whereas others cannot.

Stress continues in any family until membership can be clarified and the system reorganized regarding (a) who performs what roles and tasks, and (b) how family members perceive the absent member. Challenges to the family's capacity for boundary maintenance come not only from outside forces, but also from normal developmental maturation throughout the life cycle. Such challenges are met by families by varying their structure to maintain functions. Recognizing and investigating variability in structure

for boundary maintenance offers one promising approach to study the original question of why some families can cope with everyday life stresses whereas others cannot.

REFERENCES

Anderson, L. S. When a child begins school. *Children Today*, August 1976, 16-19.

Angell, R. C. *The family encounters the Depression.* New York: Scribner's & Sons, 1936.

Bernard, J. *Remarriage.* New York: Holt, Rinehart, and Winston, 1956.

Bohannan, P. *Divorce and after.* Doubleday, 1970.

Boss, P. G. A clarification of the concept of psychological father presence in families experiencing ambiguity of boundary. *Journal of Marriage and the Family,* 1977, 39, 141-151.

Boss, P. G. The relationship of psychological father presence, wife's personal qualities and wife/family dysfunction in families of missing fathers. *Journal of Marriage and the Family,* 1980, 42, 541-549.

Boss, P. G. Psychological father absence and presence: A theoretical formulation for an investigation into family systems interactions. University of Wisconsin doctoral dissertation. Madison, WI, August, 1975.

Boss, P. G., McCubbin, H. I., & Lester, G. The corporate executive wife's coping patterns in response to routine husband-father absence. *Family Process,* 1979, 18, 79-86.

Boss, P. G., & Whitaker, C. Dialogue on separation. *The Family Coordinator,* 1979, 28, 391-398.

Boszormenyi-Nagy, I., & Spark, G. M. *Invisible loyalties.* Hagerstown, MD: Harper & Row, 1973.

Boulding, E. Family adjustment to war separation and reunion. *Annals of the American Academy of Political and Social Science,* 1950, 272, 59-88.

Buckley, W. *Sociology and modern systems theory.* Englewood Cliffs, NJ: Prentice-Hall, 1967.

Cavan, R. S., & Ranck, K. H. *The family and the Depression.* Chicago: University of Chicago Press, 1938.

Duberman, L. *The reconstituted family: A study of remarried couples and their children.* Chicago: Nelson-Hall, 1975.

DuVall, E. M. Loneliness and the serviceman's wife. *Marriage and Family Living,* August 1945, 77-81.

Hetherington, E. M., & Deur, J. The effects of father absence on child development. *Young Children,* 1971, 26, 233-248.

Hetherington, E. M., Cox, M., & Cox, R. Divorced fathers. *The Family Coordinator,* 1976, 25, 417-428.

Hill, R. *Families under stress.* Connecticut: Greenwood Press, 1949.

Hill, R. Modern systems theory and the family: A confrontation. *Social Science Information,* 1971, 72, 7-26.

Hooper, J. O. My wife, the student. *The Family Coordinator,* 1979, 28, 459-484.

Kantor, O., & Lehr, W. *Inside the family.* San Francisco: Jossey-Bass, 1975.

Klein, D. C., & Ross, A. Kindergarten entry: A study of role transition. In M. Krugman (Ed.), *Orthopsychiatry and the school.* New York: American Orthopsychiatric Association, 1958.

LeMasters, E. E. Parenthood as crisis. *Marriage and Family Living,* 1957, 29, 352-355.

Levinson, D. J. *The seasons of a man's life.* New York: Ballantine Books, 1978.

Lopata, H. I. *Widowhood in an American city.* Cambridge, MA: Schenkman, 1973.

Lopata, H. I. *Women as widows.* New York: Elsevier, 1979.

McCubbin, H., Dahl. B., & Hunter, E. Research in the military family: A review. In H. McCubbin, B. Dahl, & E. Hunter (Eds.), *Families in the military system.* Beverly Hills: Sage, 1976.

Messinger, L. Remarriage between divorced people with children from previous marriages. *Journal of Marriage and Family Counseling,* 1976, 2, 193-200.

Minuchin, S. *Families and family therapy.* Cambridge, MA: Harvard University Press, 1974.

Parkes, C. M. *Bereavement: Studies of grief in adult life.* New York: International Universities Press, Inc., 1972.

Piaget, J., & Inhelder, B. *The child's conception of space.* London: Routledge & Kegan Paul, 1956.

Pridham, K. F., Hansen, M., & Conrad, H. H. Anticipatory care as problem solving in family medicine and nursing. *Journal of Family Practice,* 1977, 4, 1077-1081.

Rapoport, R. Normal crises, family structure, and mental health. *Family Process,* 1963, 2, 68-80.

Roosevelt, R., & Lofas, J. *Living in step: A remarriage manual for parents and children.* New York: McGraw-Hill, 1976.

Russell, C. Transition to parenthood: Problems and gratifications. *Journal of Marriage and the Family,* 1974, 36, 294-302.

Silverstone, B., & Hyman, H. *You and your aging parent.* New York: Pantheon, 1976.

Sheehy, G. *Passages: Predictable crises of adult life.* New York: Dutton, 1976.

Stein, P. *Single.* Englewood Cliffs, NJ: Prentice-Hall, 1976.

Stierlin, H. *Separating parents and adolescents.* New York: Quadrangle, 1974.

Visher, E., & Visher, J. Common problems of step parents and their spouses. *American Journal of Orthopsychiatry,* 1978, 48(2), 252-282.

Visher, E., & Visher, J. *Stepfamilies: A guide to working with step-parents and step-children.* New York: Brunner-Mazel, 1979.

von Bertalanffy, L. *General systems theory* (revised edition). New York: George Braziller, 1968.

Wallerstein, J. S., & Kelly, J. B. The effects of parental divorce: The adolescent experience. In E. J. Anthony & C. Koupernik (Eds.), *The child and his family: Children at psychiatric risk III.* New York: Wiley, 1974.

Wallerstein, J. S., & Kelly, J. B. The effects of parental divorce: Experiences of the preschool child. *American Academy of Child Psychiatry,* 1975, 14(4), 600-616.

Wallerstein, J. S., & Kelly, J. B. The effects of parental divorce: Experiences of the child in early latency. *American Journal of Orthopsychiatry,* 1976a, 46, 20-32.

Wallerstein, J. S. &. & Kelly, J. B. The effects of parental divorce: Experiences of the child in later latency. *American Journal of Orthopsychiatry,* 1976b, 46, 258-269.

Wallerstein, J. S., & Kelly, J. B. Divorce counseling: A community service for families in the midst of divorce. *American Journal of Orthopsychiatry,* 1977a, 47, 4-22.

Wallerstein, J. S., & Kelly, J. B. Brief intervention with children in divorcing families. *American Journal of Orthopsychiatry,* 1977b, 47, 23-37.

Weiss, R. *Marital separation.* New York: Basic Books, 1975.

Westoff, L. A. *The second time around: Remarriage in America.* New York: Viking, 1977.

Whiteside, M., & Auerbach, L. Can the daughter of my father's new wife be my sister? Families of remarriage in family therapy. *Journal of Divorce,* 1978, 1, 271-283.

16

FAMILY BOUNDARY AMBIGUITY PREDICTS ALZHEIMER'S OUTCOMES

WAYNE CARON
PAULINE BOSS
JAMES MORTIMER

This study examines caregiver and patient relationship characteristics in the etiology of behavior problems in Alzheimer's disease. Seventy-two caregivers and patients were assessed twice, 12 months apart. Cross lag panel analysis was used to test for one-way or reciprocal causal links among caregiver variables, patient impairment measures, and patient behavior problems. Caregiver distancing from patients (closeout) predicted increases in the frequency of behavior problems, including activity disturbances, paranoia, and anxiety. These behaviors in turn led to increased closeout of the patient by the caregiver. The reciprocal causal associations found in this study suggest that dysfunctional family interactions may underlie patient behavior problems and caregiver distress.

Although research in Alzheimer's disease (AD) has focused predominantly on cognitive and functional impairments associated with the disorder, increasing attention is being paid to the behavioral disturbances that accompany this illness (Teri et al. 1991). Behavioral disturbances are highly prevalent in AD with estimates of 30% to 87% reported in the literature (Baker, Kokmen, Chandra, and Schoenberg 1991; Eisdorfer et al. 1992; Mendez, Martin, Smyth, and Whitehouse 1990; Rubin, Morris, and Berg 1987; Teri, Borson, Kiyak, and Yamagishi 1989; Wragg and Jeste 1989).

Reprinted from *Psychiatry, 62* (1999): 347-56 with permission of The Guilford Press. This research was funded by National Institute of Aging Grant 1 PO1-AG06309, Psychosocial Impact of Dementia on Caregivers and Family Project, Pauline Boss, Principal Investigator.

These behaviors have serious consequences. They impact quality of life negatively (Callahan 1992; Whitehouse and Rabins 1992); are associated with higher levels of strain in caregivers (Boss, Caron, Horbal, and Mortimer 1990; Reddy and Pitt 1993), impacting the relationship between caregivers and patients (Deimling and Bass 1986); result in earlier institutionalization (Chenowith and Spencer 1986; O'Donnell et al. 1992); and are associated with faster rates of disease progression (Fenn, Luby, and Yesavage 1993; Mortimer, Ebbitt, Jun, and Finch 1992; Wragg and Jeste 1989) as well as increased mortality (Burns, Lewis, Jacoby, and Levy 1991; Walsh, Welch, and Larson 1990).

Although a variety of categorization schemes and measurement instruments have been proposed for behavioral disturbances (Deutsch and Rovner 1991; Mendez et al. 1990; Rubin et al. 1987; Teri et al. 1989), their development is hindered by a lack of agreement regarding the basic dimensions of behavioral problems and the relationships between behavioral symptoms. Another area in which knowledge is lacking is the etiology of behavioral disturbances. Overall, there is a general increase in the prevalence of behavior problems with the progression of disease (Baker et al. 1991; Reisberg, Frassen, Solar, Kluger, and Ferris 1989; Rubin et al. 1987), which lends support to the idea that behavior problems are a consequence of disease progression. However, when specific behaviors are examined, there is less evidence for a direct link between behavioral symptoms and cognitive decline (Merriam, Aronson, Gaston, Wey, and Katz 1988; Teri et al. 1989). Although increasing prevalence of behavior problems with progression of the illness may seem to establish a causal link, it should be remembered that persons with AD experience a variety of life changes as their dementia worsens. Relationships with family and friends undergo dramatic changes, participation in former interests and activities becomes difficult, and ultimately the place of residence changes. It is impossible to establish through analysis of behavioral problem prevalence across time whether increases are due to disease progression or changing psychosocial factors. In addition, it is a common clinical observation that some behavioral problems may come and go. In this way, they differ from cognitive and functional impairments, which once established, never remit in a significant way.

Theories that focus solely on biochemical or neurological factors to account for the preponderance of behavioral problems in AD appear to discount alternative explanations that rely on psychological or interpersonal factors. One potentially important set of factors in the development of behavioral disturbances, those relating to interpersonal relations, has received much less attention (Lyman 1989).

Boss (Boss 1977, 1987, 1988; Boss and Greenberg 1984) has proposed a theory of boundary ambiguity that describes the dilemmas families face. Boundary ambiguity occurs in situations where there is a lack of certainty about whether a person is inside or outside the family system. It arises in specific situations where either there is psychological presence in the face of physical absence, or psychological absence in the face of physical presence. The latter situation occurs with AD. Family caregivers are uncertain about whether the person with dementia is in or out of the family since the patient is emotionally absent but physically present. This uncertainty of their absence or presence hinders the family's ability to adapt to the changes brought on by the illness (Boss, Caron, and Horbal 1988) and therefore to reorganize in the face of the progressive loss of the AD patient's personality and intellectual functioning. The caregiver may become immobilized, unable to organize new behaviors and responses to match the changing needs of the patient. Distortions may arise in the way in which family members relate to the person with AD, either overcompensating or undercompensating for the impairments present.

Earlier analyses established boundary ambiguity as a central mediating factor in the relationship between problem behaviors in dementia and caregiver depressive symptoms (Boss, Caron, Horbal, and Mortimer 1990). That analysis was limited by the cross-sectional nature of the data, which precluded an assessment of the causal direction of the links between caregiver factors and patient behaviors. In the present article the relationship between caregiver depression and patient behavior problems is examined utilizing a longitudinal data set. Building on an empirically derived taxonomy of behavior symptoms, the hypothesis tested is that reciprocal causal links exist between the caregiver and the patient's attitudes and behaviors, which lead to progressive worsening of the relationship and an increase in both patient and caregiver problems.

RESEARCH METHOD

Sample

Seventy-two caregivers and patients were initially interviewed as part of their involvement in a longitudinal research study. Patients were included if they satisfied criteria from the third edition of the *Diagnostic and Statistical Manual of Mental Disorders* (DSM-III-R; American Psychiatric Association 1980) for primary degenerative dementia, lived in the community, had a family caregiver, had a minimum score of 8 on the Mini-Mental State Exam (MMSE; Folstein, Folstein, and McHugh 1975), and had mild to moderate cognitive impairment as defined by Reisberg's Global Deterioration Scale, Stage 3, 4, or 5 (Reisberg et al. 1989). Patients were excluded if they had a history of alcohol or drug abuse within the last 5 years. Of the initial 72 patient/caregiver dyads, 60 (83%) were also assessed at 1-year followup.

Eighty-six percent of the caregivers were spouses to the person with AD, while 8% were children, 4% siblings, and 2% close friends. Seventy-eight percent of the patients were male, while 79% of the caregivers were female. The mean caregiver age was 63.57 ($SD = 8.94$, range = 30-84); the average age of the person with AD was 68.26 ($SD = 8.44$, range = 53-90). Caregivers had an average of 13.17 years of education ($SD = 2.98$, range = 8-20), while patients had an average of 12.8 years ($SD = 3.5$, range = 5-22). Mean age of onset, estimated from history provided by the family, was 63.8 years ($SD = 8.5$, range = 49-89) and mean symptom duration at the time of initial evaluation was 3.4 years ($SD = 2.5$, range = 1-13).

Measures

Patients' behavior problems were assessed through caregiver reports using the BEHAVE-AD instrument (Reisberg et al. 1989). This instrument requires the caregiver to rate each of 24 behaviors on a scale of 0 to 3, with 0 meaning the behavior is not present and 1 to 3 indicating the behavior is present and rating the level of severity. A final item gives an overall rating of behavior problem severity. Scores range from 0 to 75. The ratings were obtained considering behaviors present during the 6 weeks prior to administration of the instrument.

The patient's cognitive impairment was assessed with the MMSE (Folstein et al. 1975). This test administered by a trained psychometrician assesses the patient's orientation to time and place, recent and remote memory functions, and other aspects of cognitive performance. The maximum score is 30.

Patients' functional abilities were assessed by caregiver reports on the Instrumental Activities of Daily Living Scale (Lawton 1983). This is an 8-item scale that has caregivers rate the patient's ability to perform activities necessary for daily living in the community. Behaviors rated include ability to use the telephone, shopping, meal preparation, housekeeping, responsibility for own medication, handling own finances, doing own laundry, and independently using public transportation. Scores range from 8 to 31, with higher scores indicative of greater functional impairment.

The caregiver's level of depressive symptoms was assessed using their self-report on the Zung Depression Scale (Zung 1965). Respondents rated how frequently in the last week they experienced 20 depressive symptoms. Scores range from 20 to 80, with high scores indicative of depression.

Caregivers' sense of mastery versus helplessness was assessed by the Pearlin Mastery Scale (Pearlin, Menaghan, Mullan, and Leiberman 1981). This 7-item scale asks caregivers to indicate their level of agreement with statements indicative of feelings of mastery or feelings of helplessness in their lives. Scale scores range from 7 to 28, with high scores indicative of high mastery.

Caregivers' boundary ambiguity was measured with the Boundary Ambiguity Scale for Dementia (Boss, Greenberg, and Caron 1990). The Boundary Ambiguity Scale (Table 16.1) is a 21-item self-report instrument developed for this study. It is intended

Table 16.1   Boundary Ambiguity Subscales

Scale 1: Immobilization[a]

1. I feel guilty when I get out of the house to do something enjoyable while _____ remains at home.
2. I feel it will be difficult if not impossible to carve out my own life as long as _____ needs my help.
3. I feel incapable of establishing new friendships right now.
4. I feel I can't go anywhere without first thinking about _____'s needs.
5. I feel I have no time to myself.
6. I'm not sure what I should expect _____ to do around the house.
7. I often feel mixed up about how much I should be doing for _____.
8. I put _____'s needs before my own.
9. When I'm not with _____ I wonder how s/he is getting along.
10. I have already resigned myself to _____ no longer being the person I used to know.
11. I think about _____ a lot.

Scale 2: Patient Closeout[b]

1. I continue to keep alive my deepest hope that _____ will be like his/her old self again.[c]
2. I feel I have adjusted to _____'s dependency on me.[c]
3. I continue to seek meaningful responses from _____.[c]
4. _____ has specific jobs around the house.[c]
5. Sometimes I'm not sure where _____ fits in as part of the family.
6. My family and I often have disagreements about my involvement with _____.
7. Family members tend to ignore _____.
8. I sometimes tend to ignore _____.
9. _____ no longer feels like my spouse/parent/sibling.
10. I think about _____ a lot.[c]
11. _____ is no longer involved in family gatherings such as birthdays and holidays.

a. Alpha for initial interview ($n = 72$) = .78; alpha for second interview ($n = 60$) = .80.
b. Alpha for initial interview ($n = 72$) = .70; alpha for second interview ($n = 60$) = .70.
c. Indicates item with inverted scoring.

to measure the degree to which the caregiver is preoccupied with the patient. The scale was modified from an instrument used in initial boundary ambiguity studies of missing-in-action families (Boss 1977, 1980; Boss, Greenberg, and Pearce-McCall 1990). The items derive from a theory of stress induced by ambiguous family boundaries (Boss 1987, 1988; Boss and Greenberg 1984). Two factors representing boundary ambiguity have been identified: caregiver immobilization and caregiver closeout. The immobilization factor includes items related to feelings of being trapped and overwhelmed in the caregiving role (Boss 1987, 1988). The closeout factor consists of items indicating emotional disengagement from the patient (Boss 1977).

Procedures

Patients and caregivers were assessed in face to face interviews at two time points 12 months apart. To identify the dimensions of behavioral disturbance, a principal components factor analysis was performed on the BEHAVE-AD data from the initial assessment. Only those items that were endorsed by at least 20% of the sample were included in this analysis. To maximally differentiate between the factors, repeated factoring was done, retaining those items that had a factor loading of at least .40 on one factor and a minimal difference between loadings on different factors of at least .25.

To estimate the magnitude of the reciprocal links between variables, cross lag panel analysis was used. This technique draws causal inferences by

Table 16.2   Factor Scores for BEHAVE-AD

	Factor 1: Activity Disturbances	Factor 2: Depression	Factor 3: Paranoia	Factor 4: Anxiety
Purposeless activity	.752	.060	.058	.119
Inappropriate behaviors	.683	.041	.270	.013
Agitation	.697	.192	.065	.230
Day/night disturbance	.655	−.150	−.003	−.151
Tearfulness	.173	.787	−.036	.078
Depressed mood	−.107	.798	.121	.102
Delusions of stealing	.004	.001	.803	−.069
Suspiciousness	.190	−.139	.651	.409
Verbal aggression	.194	.247	.624	.163
Anxiety about upcoming events	−.009	.045	.131	.751
General anxiety	.091	.153	.037	.791

examining and comparing measures of association within each time period, across time periods for the same variable and across time periods for different variables. To avoid interpreting spurious associations based on correlated error variance across time (Rogosa 1980), two-wave least squares was used to estimate the cross lag coefficients (Plewis 1985).

RESULTS

Factor Analysis of BEHAVE-AD Instrument

Of the 24 behaviors assessed by the BEHAVE-AD instrument, 11 met the criteria of occurring in at least 20% of the sample. Responses to these items were subjected to a principal components factor analysis with varimax rotation. A scree test indicated that a four-factor model accounted for a substantial portion of the variance. The items and their factor loadings are presented in Table 16.2. Factor 1 consists of items relating to activity disturbances. Factor 2 consists of two items linked with depressed mood. Factor 3 consists of items from the Paranoia subscale as well as the item on verbal aggression. The association of verbal aggression with suspiciousness and delusions about stealing indicates that

verbal outbursts may be less strongly related with task failure for this group (the catastrophic reaction theory) and more associated with paranoid or suspicious thoughts. Finally, Factor 4 consists of two items indicating anxiety.

Cross Lag Analysis Results

The estimated cross lag coefficients characterize the relationship between initial scores on predictor variables and increases or decreases in the dependent variables.[1] The cross lag parameters are partial correlations estimated using two-stage least squares analysis in which the autocorrelation function for each variable is controlled (Plewis 1985). Thus the correlation estimates the relationship between the score at Time 1 for one variable with the change in the second variable over the 12-month period.

Tables 16.3-16.6 summarize the cross lag correlation estimates for each of the BEHAVE-AD factors. Estimates are presented as squared partial correlations to aid in interpretation. Associated p values are provided for each parameter estimate. To control for multiple comparison error rates, only parameters with $p < .001$ will be considered as significantly different from 0.

Table 16.3   Cross Lag Analysis Results for Patient Paranoia

Initial Score Predictive Variable	12-Month Change Dependent Variable	Partial r^2	Significance
Caregiver depression →	Patient paranoia	.06	< .05
Patient paranoia →	Caregiver depression	.06	< .05
Caregiver immobilization →	Patient paranoia	.06	< .05
Patient paranoia →	Caregiver immobilization	.08	< .05
Caregiver closeout of patient →	Patient paranoia	.30	< .001
Patient paranoia →	Caregiver closeout of patient	.11	< .01
Caregiver mastery →	Patient paranoia	.01	ns
Patient paranoia →	Caregiver mastery	.01	ns
Patient MMSE →	Patient paranoia	.08	< .05
Patient paranoia →	Patient MMSE	.02	ns
Patient IADLS →	Patient paranoia	.04	ns
Patient paranoia →	Patient IADLS	.05	ns

NOTE: MMSE = Mini-Mental State Exam; IADLS = Instrumental Activities of Daily Living Scale.

Table 16.4   Cross Lag Analysis Results for Patient Activity Disturbances

Initial Score Predictive Variable	12-Month Change Dependent Variable	Partial r^2	Significance
Caregiver depression →	Patient activity disturbances	.03	ns
Patient activity disturbances →	Caregiver depression	.14	< .01
Caregiver immobilization →	Patient activity disturbances	.17	< .001
Patient activity disturbances →	Caregiver immobilization	.12	< .01
Caregiver closeout of patient →	Patient activity disturbances	.27	< .001
Patient activity disturbances →	Caregiver closeout of patient	.29	< .001
Caregiver mastery →	Patient activity disturbances	.03	ns
Patient activity disturbances →	Caregiver mastery	.10	< .01
Patient MMSE →	Patient activity disturbances	.54	< .001
Patient activity disturbances →	Patient MMSE	.29	< .001
Patient IADLS →	Patient activity disturbances	.55	< .001
Patient activity disturbances →	Patient IADLS	.25	< .001

NOTE: MMSE = Mini-Mental State Exam; IADLS = Instrumental Activities of Daily Living Scale.

Table 16.3 summarizes the cross lag results for patient paranoia. A substantial predictive relationship exists between initial levels of caregiver closeout of the patient and increases in paranoia over a twelve month period with a trend indicating a possible reciprocal relationship.

Table 16.4 presents the cross lag results for patient activity disturbances. Although there is a trend towards patient activity disturbances leading to increases in caregiver depression, feeling immobilized and helpless (decreased mastery), substantial predictive relationships were observed between caregiver immobilization and closeout of the patient with increases in activity disturbances. The relationship between activity disturbances and patient closeout appears reciprocal.

Table 16.5   Cross Lag Analysis Results for Patient Depressed Mood

Initial Score Predictive Variable	*12-Month Change Dependent Variable*	*Partial r^2*	*Significance*
Caregiver depression →	Patient depressed mood	.14	< .001
Patient depressed mood →	Caregiver depression	.04	*ns*
Caregiver immobilization →	Patient depressed mood	.07	< .05
Patient depressed mood →	Caregiver immobilization	.08	< .05
Caregiver closeout of patient →	Patient depressed mood	.01	*ns*
Patient depressed mood →	Caregiver closeout of patient	.04	*ns*
Caregiver mastery →	Patient depressed mood	.01	*ns*
Patient depressed mood →	Caregiver mastery	.01	*ns*
Patient MMSE →	Patient depressed mood	.01	*ns*
Patient depressed mood →	Patient MMSE	.01	*ns*
Patient IADLS →	Patient depressed mood	.07	< .05
Patient depressed mood →	Patient IADLS	.09	< .05

NOTE: MMSE = Mini-Mental State Exam; IADLS = Instrumental Activities of Daily Living Scale.

Table 16.6   Cross Lag Analysis Results for Patient Anxiety

Initial Score Predictive Variable	*12-Month Change Dependent Variable*	*Partial r^2*	*Significance*
Caregiver depression →	Patient anxiety	.05	*ns*
Patient anxiety →	Caregiver depression	.08	< .05
Caregiver immobilization →	Patient anxiety	.05	*ns*
Patient anxiety →	Caregiver immobilization	.07	< .05
Caregiver closeout of patient →	Patient anxiety	.15	< .01
Patient anxiety →	Caregiver closeout of patient	.10	< .01
Caregiver mastery →	Patient anxiety	.01	*ns*
Patient anxiety →	Caregiver mastery	.01	*ns*
Patient MMSE →	Patient anxiety	.01	*ns*
Patient anxiety →	Patient MMSE	.03	*ns*
Patient IADLS →	Patient anxiety	.14	< .001
Patient anxiety →	Patient IADLS	.01	*ns*

NOTE: MMSE = Mini-Mental State Exam; IADLS = Instrumental Activities of Daily Living Scale.

Finally, there also was evidence of strong reciprocal relationships between activity disturbances and patient cognitive and functional impairments.

Table 16.5 presents the cross lag estimates for patient depressed mood. Only one relationship showed substantial predictive power. Initial levels of caregiver depression were associated with increases in patient depressed mood. The reciprocal relationship did not hold.

Table 16.6 shows the results for patient anxiety. Although there is a trend towards a reciprocal relationship between caregiver closeout of the patient and patient anxiety, the only substantial predictive relationship is between patient functional impairment and increases in patient anxiety.

DISCUSSION

Factor Structure of Behavior Problems

The BEHAVE-AD instrument was developed to provide a rating system that is appropriate for persons with Alzheimer's disease. Through chart review and clinical observation 24 behaviors were identified. However, many of these behaviors are infrequently seen in a sample of mildly to moderately demented patients. Understanding the nature of behavior problems in this population requires focusing on those behaviors that affect a meaningful portion of the group. Restricting the factor analysis to these behaviors provides greater homogeneity of variance across items, avoiding the spurious influence of items with highly skewed distributions. The resulting factors are similar to patterns of psychiatric symptoms found in nondemented populations. Ownby and Seibal (1990), for example, identified six dimensions in a cluster and factor analytic study of the Brief Psychiatric Rating Scale in a nondemented elderly population. Three of these factors—Motor Disturbances, Depressive Symptoms, and Paranoid Symptoms—correspond quite closely with the first three factors found in this sample. It may be that behavior problems in AD are more appropriately seen as psychiatric disorders associated with the disease rather than unique symptom patterns resulting from the illness. It is also interesting to note that one behavior commonly described as agitation related (verbal aggression) was found to covary with paranoid delusional symptoms in this study.

Cross Lag Panel Results

This study confirmed findings of other researchers (Merriam et al. 1988; Teri et al. 1989) that the level of cognitive and functional impairment shows little relationship with the degree of paranoia or suspiciousness. The strongest predictor accounting for 30% of the partial variance associated with change in these symptoms was the caregiver endorsement of items indicating emotional closeout of the patient. The psychological extrusion of the patient from the family system is one method of dealing with ambiguous family boundaries when the person is physically present but psychologically absent. This is not unlike how families of physically missing members have been found to cope (Boss 1977, 1980; Boss et al., 1988).

The results show changes in activity disturbances to be multiply influenced by both the progressive impairment in cognitive and functional abilities and caregiver attitudes. Reciprocal relations exist between activity disturbances and both cognitive and functional decline indicating that the activity disturbances symptoms both result from and predict disease progression. Reciprocal relationships with activity disturbances were also found for caregiver closeout of patient and to a lessor extent caregiver immobilization. This would suggest that once activity disturbances begin, forces within the dyadic relationship may serve to reinforce and maintain these behaviors over time.

There was only one substantial predictive relationship for patient depressive symptoms. They tend to be preceded by higher levels of caregiver depression. This suggests a sensitivity of the AD patient to the distress experienced by the caregiver. It is interesting to note patient depression did not appear to influence caregiver variables.

The strongest influence on changes in patient anxiety was the level of functional impairment. This suggests that anxious behaviors may result from experiences of task failure. There was a trend towards reciprocal influence between patient anxiety and caregiver closeout of the patient, implying that caregivers may cope with patient anxiety by emotional disengagement.

Overall, it is striking to find the influence of caregiver closeout of the patient across multiple symptom patterns. This finding, which holds for all behaviors except depression, suggests that increased emotional distance between patients and their familial caregivers may impact negatively on the patients' sense of self. More attention to the internal experience of the demented and especially the process of depersonalization that occurs for them seems warranted.

Focusing on the results from the perspective of the caregiver, it is striking how little impact caregiver mastery had on behavioral symptoms. More mastery-oriented coping styles within caregivers may do little to change the relationship dynamics producing behavioral symptoms. More striking was the mutual amplification between caregiver factors, such as their closeout of the patient and their immobilization, and patient behaviors including paranoia and activity disturbances. The common theme is that the emotional adjustment and response of each party in the dyad affects the other in ways that may mutually increase strain in the relationship. Future research needs to examine whether attention to the difficult emotional relationship issues that develop between caregiver and patient can lead to more effective interventions for behavioral disturbances than interventions which focus on developing active coping responses in caregivers.

Study Limitations

The limitations of this study are important to acknowledge both in terms of understanding how to interpret the results and identifying further areas of study. The sample used in this study consisted of volunteers who made a significant commitment to participate in a 5-year longitudinal project. The screening protocols excluded those with alcohol or drug abuse problems. Thus, there is reason to believe that this sample may have been healthier and more altruistic than the general population of Alzheimer patients and their caregivers. This is supported by the smaller proportion of significantly depressed caregivers than those reported in other studies (George and Gwyther 1986). It is not clear without further research whether our results would apply to more dysfunctional couples.

The use of a two-wave panel design limits the ability to specify the causal sequence to one link for each variable. A more powerful approach would be to collect data across multiple time points, with shorter intervals between, to more clearly capture the reciprocal influences between caregiver and patient attitudes and behaviors. However, such a design would have placed more of a burden on families and perhaps have led to greater attrition.

Because the major predictor and outcome variables were based on data collected from caregivers, estimates of the relationships between these might be inflated by response sets or other forms of method variance. Further research using independent ratings for both caregiver and patient variables is needed.

NOTE

1. Specification of the cross lag model involved estimating three parameters: the synchronous correlations between variables within each time period, the autocorrelation within each variable across time periods and the cross lag correlations between variables across time. Only the cross lag parameters are presented here. Full specifications of the models' parameters are available from the first author on request.

REFERENCES

AMERICAN PSYCHIATRIC ASSOCIATION. *Diagnostic and Statistical Manual of Mental Disorders*, 3rd ed. American Psychiatric Association, 1980.

BAKER, F., KOKMEN, E., CHANDRA, V. and SCHOENBERG, B. Psychiatric symptoms in cases of clinically diagnosed Alzheimer's disease. *Journal of Geriatric Psychiatry and Neurology* (1991) 4: 71-78.

BOSS, P. A clarification of the concept of psychological father presence in families experiencing ambiguity of boundary. *Journal of Marriage and the Family* (1977) 39:141-51.

BOSS, P. The relationship of wife's sex role perceptions, psychological father presence and functioning in the ambiguous father-absent MIA family. *Journal of Marriage and the Family* (1980) 42:541-9.

BOSS, P. Family stress: Perception and context. In M. Sussman and S. Steinmetz, eds., *Handbook on Marriage and the Family* (pp. 695-723). Plenum, 1987.

BOSS, P. *Family Stress Management.* Sage, 1988.

BOSS, P., CARON, W. and HORBAL, J. Alzheimer's disease and ambiguous loss. In C. Chillman, E. Nunnally, and F. Cox, eds., *Chronic Illness and Disability: Vol. 2. Families in Trouble* (pp. 123-40). Sage, 1988.

BOSS, P., CARON, W., HORBAL, J. and MORTIMER, J. Predictors of depression in caregivers of dementia: Boundary ambiguity and mastery. *Family Process* (1990) 29:245-54.

BOSS, P. and GREENBERG, J. Family boundary ambiguity: A new variable in family stress theory. *Family Process* (1984) 23:535-46.

BOSS, P., GREENBERG, J. and CARON, W. Boundary ambiguity scale for caregivers of patients with Alzheimer's disease. In P. Boss, J. Greenberg, and D. Pearce-McCall, eds., *The Measurement of Boundary Ambiguity* (p. 20). University of Minnesota Agriculture Experiment Station Publication, 1990.

BOSS, P., GREENBERG, J. and PEARCE-McCALL, D. *The Measurement of Boundary Ambiguity.* University of Minnesota Agricultural Experiment Station, Publication, 1990.

BURNS, A., LEWIS, G., JACOBY, R. and LEVY, R. Factors affecting survival in Alzheimer's disease. *Psychological Medicine* (1991) 21:363-70.

CALLAHAN, S. Ethics and dementia: Current issues— Quality of life. *Alzheimer's Disease and Associated Disorders* (1992) 6:138-44.

CHENOWITH, B. and SPENCER, B. Dementia: The experience of family caregivers. *The Gerontologist* (1986) 26:267-72.

DEIMLING, G. and BASS, D. Symptoms of mental impairment among elderly adults and their effects on family caregivers. *Journal of Gerontology* (1986) 41:778-84.

DEUTSCH, L. and ROVNER, B. Agitation and other noncognitive abnormalities in Alzheimer's disease. *Psychiatric Clinics of North America* (1986) 14: 341-51.

EISDORFER, C., COHEN, D., PAVEZA, G., ASHFORD, J., LUCHINS, D., GORELICK, P., HIRSCHMAN, R., FREELS, S., LEVY, P., SEMLA, T. and SHAW, H. An empirical evaluation of the Global Deterioration Scale for staging Alzheimer's disease. *American Journal of Psychiatry* (1992) 149:190-4.

FENN, H., LUBY, V. and YESAVAGE, J. Subtypes in Alzheimer's disease and the impact of excess disability: Recent findings. *International Journal of Geriatric Psychiatry* (1993) 8:67-73.

FOLSTEIN, M., FOLSTEIN, S. and McHUGH, P. Mini-Mental State: A practical method for grading the cognitive state of patients for the clinician. *Journal of Psychiatric Research* (1975) 12:189-98.

GEORGE, L. and GWYTHER, L. Caregiver's well-being: A multi-dimensional examination of family care-givers of demented adults. *The Gerontologist* (1986) 26:253-9.

LAWTON, P. Assessment of behaviors required to maintain residence in the community. In T. Crook, S. Ferris, and R. Bartus, eds., *Assessment in Geriatric Psychopharmocology* (pp. 119-36). Mark Powley Associates, 1983.

LYMAN, K. Bringing the social back in: A critique of the biomedicalization of dementia. *The Gerontologist* (1989) 29:597-605.

MENDEZ, M., MARTIN, R., SMYTH, K. and WHITE-HOUSE, P. Psychiatric symptoms associated with Alzheimer's disease. *Journal of Neuropsychiatry* (1990) 1:28-33.

MERRIAM, A., ARONSON, M., GASTON, P., WEY, S. and KATZ, I. The psychiatric symptoms of Alzheimer's disease. *Journal of the American Geriatrics Society* (1988) 36:7-12.

MORTIMER, J., EBBITT, B., JUN, S. and FINCH, M. Predictors of cognitive and functional progression in patients with probable Alzheimer's disease. *Neurology* (1992) 42:1689-96.

O'DONNELL, B., DRACHMAN, D., BARNES, H., PETERSON, K., SWEARER, J. and LEW, R. Incontinence and troublesome behaviors predict institutionalization in dementia. *Journal of Geriatric Psychiatry and Neurology* (1992) 5:45-52.

OWNBY, R., and SEIBAL, H. Empirical clusters of disordered behavior among older psychiatric patients. *Journal of Gerontology: Psychological Sciences* (1990) 45:28-32.

PEARLIN, L., MENAGHAN, E., MULLAN, J., and LEIBERMAN, M. The stress process. *Journal of Health and Social Behavior* (1981) 22:337-56.

PLEWIS, I. *Analyzing Change: Measurement and Explanation Using Longitudinal Analysis.* Wiley, 1985.

REDDY, S. and PITT, B. What becomes of demented patients referred to a psychogeriatric unit? An approach to audit. *International Journal of Geriatric Psychiatry* (1993) 8:175-80.

REISBERG, B., FRASSEN, E., SOLAR, S., KLUGER, A. and FERRIS, S. Stage-specific incidence of potentially remediable behavioral symptoms in aging and Alzheimer's disease: A study of 120 patients using the BEHAVE-AD instrument. *Bulletin of Clinical Neuroscience* (1989) 54:95-112.

ROGOSA, D. A critique of cross-lag panel analysis. *Psychological Bulletin* (1980) 88:245-58.

RUBIN, E., MORRIS, J. and BERG, L. The progression of personality changes in senile dementia of the Alzheimer's type. *Journal of the American Geriatrics Society* (1987) 35:721-5.

TERI, L., BORSON, S., KIYAK, H., and YAMAGISHI, M. Behavior disturbance, cognitive dysfunction and functional skill: Prevalence and relationship in Alzheimer's disease. *Journal of the American Geriatrics Society* (1989) 37:109-16.

TERI, L., RABINS, P., WHITEHOUSE, P., BERG, L., SUNDERLAND, T., EICHELMAN, B., REISBERG, B. and PHELPS, C. *Management of behavior problems in Alzheimer's disease: Current status and future directions.* Paper presented at the Behavior Management Workshop of the Treatment Committee of the Alzheimer's Association's Medical and Scientific Advisory Board, Chicago, October 1991.

WALSH, J., WELCH, G. and LARSON, E. Survival of outpatients with Alzheimer type dementia. *Archives of Internal Medicine* (1990) 113:429-34.

WHITEHOUSE, P. and RABINS, P. Quality of life and dementia. *Alzheimer's Disease and Associated Disorders* (1992) 6:135-7.

WRAGG, R. and JESTE, D. Overview of depression and psychosis in Alzheimer's disease. *American Journal of Psychiatry* (1989) 146:577-87.

ZUNG, W. A self rating depression scale. *Archives of General Psychiatry* (1965) 12:63-70.

PART 5

THE LINK BETWEEN AMBIGUITY AND AMBIVALENCE IN FAMILY STRESS THEORY

This section represents a new direction in family stress theory development. In *Family Stress Management* (Boss, 2002), ideas were merged from sociology and psychology to provide clinically useful links to explain why ambiguous loss so often leads to ambivalent feelings when a loved one is missing physically or psychologically. With sociological ambivalence as a central construct, Luescher and Pillemer (1998) present a new approach to help us understand the normalcy of tensions in intergenerational relations. There is also a study by Campbell and Demi (2000) on adult children of pilots still missing in Southeast Asia. You will want to read Campbell's personal note at the end of the article. Also note their analysis of family hardiness.

For contrast, see the essay written by Francine du Plessix Gray (2000), describing her struggle to resolve the loss of her missing father, a French Resistance pilot shot down during World War II.

REFERENCES

Boss, P. (2002). *Family stress management* (2nd ed.). Thousand Oaks, CA: Sage.
du Plessix Gray, F. (2000). The work of mourning. *The American Scholar, 69,* 7-13.

17

INTERGENERATIONAL AMBIVALENCE

A New Approach to the Study of Parent-Child Relations in Later Life

KURT LUESCHER
KARL PILLEMER

Social scientific interest in intergenerational relationships between adults has increased in recent years. However, there is a lack of theoretical work that allows for the integration of research findings. Further, there has been a tendency to interpret intergenerational relationships within limited frameworks that emphasize either intergenerational solidarity or conflict. In contrast, we propose that ambivalence is a more useful organizing concept for understanding intergenerational relations. In this article, we argue that relationships between the generations in families are structured such that they generate various types of ambivalence. We then discuss three aspects of intergenerational relationships that are likely to be ambivalent and propose an agenda for future research.

Interest in intergenerational relations among adults within the family has grown dramatically over the past three decades, as demonstrated by research reviews and edited volumes from both sides of the Atlantic, all of which contain extensive bibliographies of recent publications (Attias-Donfut, 1995a; Finch & Mason, 1993; Hareven, 1996; Lye, 1996; Lüscher & Schultheis, 1993;

Reprinted from the *Journal of Marriage and the Family* 60 (1998): 413-25. Copyright © 1998 by the National Council on Family Relations, 3989 Central Ave. NE, Suite 550, Minneapolis, MN 55421. Reprinted by permission. The order of authorship is alphabetical; both authors contributed equally to this article.

Suitor, Pillemer, Bohannon & Robison, 1995). Indeed, the amount of empirical work on this topic has made it one of the more vigorous research areas in contemporary sociology and psychology. The development of theory to integrate the host of findings, however, has not kept up with empirical productivity. Research on aging and the family has tended to respond to obvious social problems (such as caregiving for impaired relatives, housing, grandparents raising grandchildren), rather than consider theoretical issues (Lye, 1996).

Perhaps the most popular organizing framework for understanding family relationships in later life is that which highlights intergenerational solidarity. A number of prominent researchers responded to Talcott Parsons's (1942, 1944) concern about the isolation of the nuclear family by proposing that extensive family solidarity actually existed (Litwak, 1965; Shanas et al., 1968; Sussman, 1959). Since the early 1970s, Bengtson and colleagues have continued and expanded this tradition in an influential series of articles and books (cf. Bengtson & Harootyan, 1994; Roberts, Richards, & Bengtson, 1991; Silverstein & Bengtson, 1997; Treas & Bengtson, 1988). The solidarity perspective has been taken up by other researchers in the United States (Rein, 1994; Rossi & Rossi, 1990) and is also a reference point for European authors, although not without critical overtones (Attias-Donfut, 1995b; Bawin-Legros, Gauthier, & Strassen, 1995; Coenen-Huther, Kellerhals, & von Allmen, 1994; Donati, 1995; Finch & Mason, 1993).

Some scholars have criticized the overly positive and consensual bias of the solidarity perspective. Research within the solidarity framework typically assumes that individuals' personal feelings—such as affection, attraction, and warmth—serve to maintain cohesion in the family system (Sprey, 1991). Marshall, Matthews, and Rosenthal (1993) state that even the term "solidarity" indicates an emphasis on consensus. European writers have pointed out the value-laden origins of the term in proletarian movements and in religious social doctrine (Kleine, 1992; Lüscher, 1997). As Roberts et al. (1991) themselves note, solidarity "has been treated as the engine driving the pursuit of the common good within families"

(p. 12). Negative aspects of family life typically are interpreted in this view as an absence of solidarity. Research in this tradition has tended to emphasize shared values across generations, normative obligations to provide help, and enduring ties between parents and children.

However, at the same time that scholars in the solidarity tradition have emphasized mutual support and value consensus, another line of research has focused on isolation, caregiver stress, family problems, conflict, and abuse (Marshall et al., 1993). The perception of weakened family ties and the abandonment of aged persons also remains strong in popular opinion and in portrayals of the family in contemporary fiction and theater. Thus, some scholars, as well as the general public, appear to be unwilling to accept that intergenerational relationships are characterized by shared values and reciprocal help. As Marshall and colleagues have succinctly put it, "the substantive preoccupations in gerontology over the past 30 years point to a love-hate relationship with the family" (p. 47).

We argue in this article that the study of parent-child relations in later life must move beyond this "love-hate relationship." The vacillation between images of mistreatment and abandonment, on the one hand, and comforting images of solidarity, on the other, are not two sides of an academic argument that will ultimately be resolved in favor of one viewpoint. Rather, we hold that societies and the individuals within in them are ambivalent about relationships between parents and children in adulthood.

Therefore, we propose ambivalence as an alternative to both the solidarity and conflict perspectives models for orienting sociological research on intergenerational relations. We can sum up our fundamental point in the following axiom. Intergenerational relations generate ambivalences. That is, the observable forms of intergenerational relations among adults can be social-scientifically interpreted as the expression of ambivalences and as efforts to manage and negotiate these fundamental ambivalences.

The major goal of this article is a straightforward one: We wish to make the case for ambivalence as a theoretically and empirically useful approach to the study of intergenerational relations. We should be clear that it is not our intention to provide a comprehensive theoretical formulation of intergenerational ambivalence. Indeed, such a formulation would not be appropriate at this point, given the state of knowledge. Instead, following Aldous (1990), we propose ambivalence as a "general orientation" to the subject of intergenerational relationships, rather than as a formal theory. We suggest the types of variables that researchers should consider, and we demonstrate the potential insights that result from this more complex view of parent-child relations.

We begin with a discussion of the concept of ambivalence and review its theoretical antecedents in several related sociological and psychological literatures. Following this discussion, we propose a working definition of intergenerational ambivalence. Next, we offer three illustrations, each of which treats a different aspect of intergenerational ambivalence. In each case, we provide a detailed analysis of one or more exemplary studies from the social sciences that demonstrate a particular type of ambivalence in parent-child relations. We conclude with suggestions for future work on this topic.

Dimensions of Intergenerational Ambivalence

The term "ambivalence" is almost absent in the social science literature on parent-child relations in later life. For example, a search of the Socio-File and PsychLit databases uncovered no articles on this topic with the key word "ambivalence." A few scholars, however, have applied the term to other social relations. In addition, several theoretical approaches in family studies have employed closely related concepts. These literatures suggest that there are two dimensions of ambivalence that are relevant to the study of intergenerational relations: sociological ambivalence, which is evident in social-structural positions, and psychological ambivalence, which is experienced on the individual level. We believe that both of these dimensions are important to the study of parent-child relations in adulthood.

Sociological ambivalence was given its classic formulation in an article by Merton and Barber

(1963) and in Coser's (1966) expansion of their argument. In Merton and Barber's view, sociological ambivalence focuses on "incompatible normative expectations of attitudes, beliefs, and behavior" (pp. 94-95). These incompatible expectations may be assigned to or incorporated into a particular status (or set of statuses) within a society or even within a single role of a single status. In this way, "the core-case of sociological ambivalence puts contradictory demands upon the occupants of a status in a particular relation" (p. 96). Sociological ambivalence in their perspective refers to "opposing normative tendencies in the social definition of a role" (p. 99). Thus, as Coser notes, sociological ambivalence is "built into the structure of statuses and roles" (p. 175).

Merton and Barber encourage social scientists to examine social roles not only in terms of their dominant attributes (which, we note, has been the case in the study of intergenerational relations), but also as a dynamic organization of norms and counter-norms that in combination produce ambivalence. Ambivalence results when these norms require contradictory attitudes and actions. Merton and Barber use the role of the physician as an example. A doctor is called on to be both professionally detached as well as compassionate and concerned for the patient. More recent sociological work has continued to emphasize conflicting commitments within an individual's role systems, examining contradictions in the objective demands of roles (O'Neil & Greenberger, 1994; see also the interchange with Marks, 1994).

Two increasingly influential theoretical orientations also have highlighted the potential for sociological ambivalence (although they do not typically use the term, itself). These are what have come to be known as postmodernist theory and feminist theory of the family. These views share a distrust of dualistic thinking and, instead, deal explicitly with contradiction and paradox in social relations.

An overarching theme of the postmodern perspective is that, in contemporary society, fixed relationships have weakened, and societal guidance about how these relationships should be carried out has nearly disappeared. The condition of postmodernity is characterized by a dramatically accelerated pace of change and the enormous scale on which it occurs. These developments have had a major impact on human relationships, resulting in a sense of fragmentation and discontinuity, of confusion and uncertainty regarding how social relations should be conducted (Denzin, 1991; Gergen, 1991).

This analysis of contemporary social conditions suggests that more complex theoretical models are needed to understand the family, including intergenerational relations. In the postmodernist view, family life is now characterized by plurality (Baber & Allen, 1992; Gubrium & Holstein, 1994) and by a multiplicity of forms, such as divorce, remarriage, "blended" families, and same-sex partnerships. In Stacey's (1990) explicitly postmodern perspective, "contemporary family relationships are diverse, fluid, and unresolved" (p. 17). Sociological work is needed that can interpret "today's deeply polarized discourse on American family life" (p. 19). Thus, the postmodern emphasis on heterogeneity and paradox and its rejection of reductionistic theories and dualistic thinking suggest that ambivalence can be a useful tool to analyze intergenerational relations.

Most relevant to our discussion here is the postmodern emphasis on the intensification of internal contradictions in society. Indeed, analysts of postmodernity agree that a hallmark of contemporary social life is that individuals are confronted with directly countervailing ideas and pressures on a wider scale than ever before. Van der Loo and van Reijen (1992) have dealt most clearly with this issue, noting that fundamental contradictions have appeared between personal autonomy and the demands of community and between a desire for freedom of action and a simultaneous desire for support from institutions. Families are clearly not exempt from such "multiple reality claims" (Holstein & Gubrium, 1995; see Stacey, 1990, for numerous empirical examples).

The second body of theory was developed by feminist scholars to analyze family life. Feminist theory challenges the assumption that a harmony of interests exists among all members of a family. Thus, feminist scholars' treatment of a variety of issues, from reproductive control to the household division of labor and parenthood, has alerted us to fundamental (and not entirely resolvable) conflicts within contemporary families (Thorne, 1992). Ferree (1990) notes that the feminist approach to the family involves a critique of the concept of solidarity, by which is meant "the conventional conceptualization of 'the family' as a unitary whole" (p. 867). When the notion of an undifferentiated "family interest" and the conventional view of family unity are challenged, internal contradictions can take center stage.

For example, evidence of sociological ambivalence comes from the feminist literature on household labor or what many have termed the "politics of housework." Feminist scholars have identified a contradiction built into women's family roles, in which domestic labor is both exhausting and resented, but also viewed as an expression of love and caring (Thorne, 1992). As DeVault (1991) has noted, a central characteristic of feminist writing on the family "results from potentially contradictory insights about family work: family work is burdensome and oppressive, but also meaningful because it serves as a means for connecting with others" (p. 232).

Feminist scholars also have pointed out contradictions involved in women's caring activities. In this context, Abel and Nelson (1990) have highlighted the interconnected themes of autonomy and nurturance. They note that caring for children or impaired relatives can be seen as leading to maturity and self-development and fostering a sense of self-integrity and connectedness. Giving care is humanizing, meaningful, and fulfilling. Simultaneously, however, the fact that caregiving is part of the structure of women's roles is seen as potentially oppressive. Women can be overwhelmed by caregiving responsibilities and can become isolated from the larger society, including the world of work. The caregiving role, in this view, forces women into boring and repetitive tasks. Thus, feminist research on the family suggests that sociological ambivalence permeates family relations, particularly for women.

Ambivalence also has been used to describe the psychological experience of individuals, particularly in the clinical and psychological literature on human development. For Bleuler (1911), who apparently originated the term, and Freud (1913) and later psychoanalysts (see Eidelberg, 1968; Rycroft, 1973), ambivalence generally is viewed as simultaneous feelings of love and hate toward the same individual (typically a parent). Erikson's (1994) influential epigenetic theory of psychosocial development also has ambivalence at its core. Conflicts between two countervailing tendencies (for example, autonomy vs. shame in young children) lead to the next stage of development and are shaped by relations between parents and children.

Within recent sociological thought, ambivalence on the individual level has received some attention in literature on the sociology of emotions. A detailed discussion is offered by Weigert (1991), who expands the definition of the term to "the experience of contradictory emotions toward the same object" (p. 21). According to Weigert, ambivalence also can be observed in individual motivations: that is, "simultaneous attraction to and repulsion from pursuing a particular line of action" (p. 19). In everyday speech, the term has this connotation of holding two contradictory emotions, motivations, or values at the same time. An example of research in this area is Dressel and Clark's (1990) work on "emotive dissonance" regarding caring activities (primarily for children and spouses). Respondents reported mixed emotions about care provision, when warmth, tenderness, and delight coexisted with frustration, disappointment, and resentment.

We propose a working definition of ambivalence for the purposes of the discussion that follows. This definition includes both ambivalence at the social structural level, as well as the contradictory perceptions and subjective experiences of individuals. As a general concept, we use the term "intergenerational ambivalence" to designate contradictions in relationships between parents and adult offspring that cannot be reconciled. The concept has two dimensions: (a) contradictions at the level of social structure, evidenced in institutional resources and requirements, such as statuses, roles, and norms and (b) contradictions at the subjective level, in terms of cognitions, emotions, and motivations.

This definition distinguishes ambivalence from two other related concepts. First, we differentiate our approach from the focus on intergenerational conflict. Simply emphasizing negative perceptions in intergenerational relationships does not constitute an analysis of ambivalence. Instead, the critical component is the presence of both positive and negative perceptions by an individual. Thus, an individual who experiences the relationship with a parent as incorporating both affection and resentment would be identified as ambivalent. We also distinguish the concept of ambivalence from that of ambiguity. This term connotes uncertainty and unclarity in a family situation where the family system is not secure or well defined and in which family members cannot get the facts required to take appropriate action (Boss, 1988). It is possible that ambiguity contributes to ambivalence, but it does not necessarily imply opposed perceptions or emotions. Indeed, in close relationships, it has been argued that when a relationship becomes well defined, the coexistence of positive and negative feelings begins to play a larger role (Thompson & Holmes, 1996).

To summarize, a variety of theoretical perspectives suggest that ambivalence is a useful concept and that it is relevant to an analysis of family relationships. To date, however, ambivalence has never been proposed as a general approach to the study of intergenerational relationships. Why focus on ambivalence in the study of parent-child relations in later life? Ultimately, the question is an empirical one. What does the research show about the dynamics of actual intergenerational relationships among adults? Are they essentially positive, supportive, or harmonious, so that solidarity can be fundamentally assumed in intergenerational relations? Or is there evidence that parent-child relations in later life are characterized by ambivalence and by attempts to manage such ambivalence?

Our reading of the literature suggests three aspects of parent-child relations in later life that are especially likely to generate ambivalence. These are: (a) ambivalence between dependence and autonomy, (b) ambivalence resulting from conflicting norms regarding intergenerational relations, and (c) ambivalence resulting from solidarity.

These examples are aimed at clarifying the concept of ambivalence in the context of intergenerational relations and at making a case for its usefulness for empirical research. In each example, we provide a reinterpretation of one empirical study that illustrates the type of ambivalence in question. This is not meant to be a comprehensive typology. A high priority for future investigations is the identification of types of intergenerational ambivalence.

DEPENDENCE VERSUS AUTONOMY

There is a sound basis on which to argue that ambivalence between the two poles of autonomy and dependence characterizes intergenerational relations in contemporary society. Indeed, this dilemma appears to be built into the structure of the paired statuses of parent and adult child. Specifically, in adulthood, ambivalence exists between the desire of parents and children for help, support, and nurturance and the countervailing pressures for freedom from the parent-child relationship (cf. Cohler, 1983; Cohler & Altergott, 1995; Moss & Moss, 1992). Cohler and Grunebaum (1981) describe this ambivalence succinctly:

> There is a paradox in contemporary society where, on the one hand, it is believed that adults will strive to become both psychologically and economically autonomous and self-reliant, while, on the other, findings from systematic investigations of family life show that dependence across the generations is the typical mode of intergenerational relations, including the interdependence of very old parents on their middle-aged offspring. (p. 10)

An empirical study by Cohler and Grunebaum (1981) convincingly documented ambivalence over dependence and autonomy. They conducted a detailed, naturalistic study of the mother-daughter relationship in four urban Italian-American families. Adult daughters in their study desired closeness to their mothers. This lack of separateness was fostered by women's "kin-keeping" functions within families and by the shared status of mother by both generations. Daughters looked to mothers for socialization to the parent role. However, the daughters' desire for support and care from their mothers conflicted with the mothers' developmental stage. The older women were coming to terms with their own aging and were trying out new roles as workers or volunteers. They wished to help their daughters and to feel "solidarity" with them, but simultaneously resented incursions on their autonomy.

Thus, there is fundamental ambivalence in relations between adult daughters and their mothers. When daughters have children, they come into closer contact with their mothers, and their bond with mothers deepens. This increased closeness, however, carries with it the seeds of tension and conflict. At times, mothers in the study attempted to dominate their daughters' lives, especially in the realm of childrearing. More common, however, was the "feeling among members of the grandparental generation that their young adult offspring expect advice and assistance, which they are unwilling to provide, and the feeling of young adult offspring that their need for help and advice is rebuffed by their parents" (p. 38).

One example must suffice here to illustrate the inability of an exclusive focus on solidarity to account for family dynamics in this study. Two of the mothers appear to have close relationships with their daughters. They live near one another, they call each other every day, they engage in a wide range of mutual assistance, they report high levels of emotional closeness, and they share similar values. However, the relationships are also a source of tremendous stress to both women:

> Mrs. Limpari and Mrs. Giorgio view their daughters' proffered help as a means by which their daughters can control their mothers' lives. Rather than enjoying the help and attention their daughters wish to bestow on them, these grandmothers make considerable effort to avoid such help. It is probable that each of these grandmothers is aware of the motive underlying this desire to be of greater help, for each of the two daughters . . . seeks to have her unfulfilled dependency needs met through a continuing close relationship with her own mother. Given both the strength of the daughters' needs and the nature of their own mothers' personalities, disappointment and frustration are likely to be the only result for both generations. (p. 197)

It is of interest to observe the contrast between this study and those that have used solidarity as a general approach. All four of the families in the Cohler and Grunebaum study would have scored high on most or all of the solidarity measures used by Bengtson & Harootyan (1994) and Rossi and Rossi (1990). However, the relationships actually were characterized by conflict and anxiety. In contrast to a relationship that phenomenologically is experienced as "solidarity," Cohler and Grunebaum's mothers are caught between daughters' needs for closeness and support and their own desires for self-fulfillment and independence. Daughters, in turn, struggle with their ambivalent desire to remain daughters, but also to be independent wives and mothers.

Cohler and Grunebaum's respondents share two special characteristics: They are mother-daughter dyads, and they are in close, regular contact with one another. Researchers have found similar themes in other family constellations. Nydegger and Mitteness (1991) found considerable ambivalence in close father-son relationships in later life. Fathers and sons show solidarity but also "inherent, sustained tensions" (p. 257) as fathers simultaneously push sons toward independence, but also resist relinquishing authority. Further, Eisenhandler (1992) studied parent-child relationships in which the degree of mutual involvement was considerably less intense than in those described by Cohler and Grunebaum. Nevertheless, Eisenhandler found that there was ambivalence over issues of visiting, advice giving, and helping during crises.

CONFLICTING NORMS REGARDING INTERGENERATIONAL RELATIONSHIPS

Norms entail widely accepted rules that specify appropriate behavior in particular circumstances. These rules state how individuals in certain social positions are obligated to think or act. Further, norms imply a degree of social consensus about the content of the norm and the required degree of adherence to it (Rossi & Rossi, 1990). To the extent that social scientists who are concerned with intergenerational relations have examined norms, they have tended to document dominant normative structures, such as filial responsibility, commitment to assist members of another generation, or obligation to kin. The intergenerational ambivalence approach, however, encourages the investigation of conflict between norms, the way in which such conflict is managed, and the effects of the resulting ambivalence on individuals. The study of family caregiving that we review here clearly shows the existence of conflicting norms, as well as the resulting ambivalence on the part of both parents and children.

George's (1986) analysis is one of the few that explicitly focuses on conflicting norms in the provision of care to disabled older persons. She focuses on two incompatible, powerful normative structures: the norm of reciprocity, which suggests that profit and loss should be equitable between relationship partners, and the norm of solidarity, which implies that individuals should give close family members whatever help they need without concern for a "return on investment." In George's view, "providing care to a chronically ill older adult . . . leads to a long-term imbalance in adherence to these norms and creates personal discomfort and the conclusion that one has behaved badly—regardless of which norm is adhered to most strongly" (p. 68). Over the course of long-term caregiving to a chronically ill person, the caregiver is likely to feel inadequate in the performance of one of the two norms.

George's research indicates that, although caregivers experience feelings of solidarity, they become distressed when previously established exchange relationships are disrupted. However, despite the distress, the caregivers cannot simply give up, for in so doing, they would violate the norm of solidarity. This dynamic leads to a classically ambivalent situation. The care recipients are also likely to feel ambivalent. Although they expect support from children, based on the norm of solidarity, they also feel guilty and helpless about their inability to reciprocate.

In a study of persons caring for relatives with Alzheimer's disease, George found greater normative conflict on the part of adult children than among persons caring for their spouses. Children were forced into the dilemma of when to stop providing care, and they often longed for the time when rewards were more equally distributed. They also reported conflicts between loyalty to the parent, on the one hand, and to their spouse and children, on the other. Many felt that there was no way to resolve the contradiction between the demands of solidarity and the desire for reciprocity, and they were left with profound feelings of guilt. A quote from one of George's respondents illustrates the resulting ambivalence:

I want to take care of my dad, but I have my own family, too. My husband doesn't say much, but I know he wonders when it will end. My kids are coming to hate old people. They don't understand why Grandpa screams and won't call them by their names. If I put Dad in a nursing home, I'll be miserable. But I'm miserable now, too. (p. 84)

Thus, rather than a simple relationship between the effort of caregiving and distress, George's study shows a complex and ambivalent situation. Indeed, one can posit conflicting feelings here among (a) biologically based factors (parent-child attachment), (b) socialization factors (the fact that most caregivers are women who have been socialized into nurturing and supportive roles), (c) competing roles (daughter vs. wife and mother), and (d) countervailing social norms (solidarity vs. reciprocity). It is perhaps no wonder that caregivers experience elevated rates of psychological distress (Schulz, Williamson, Morcyz, & Biegel, 1990).

George's research provides compelling evidence in support of normative ambivalence in intergenerational relations. Is such normative conflict, however, inherent only in caregiving relationships, or is it also apparent in parent-child relationships more generally? Farber's (1989) study of conflicting norms provides an example of a quantitative study that found striking ambivalence in kin relations. Although Farber focused not only on parents and children, but also on other family relationships, the findings are relevant here. Farber posits the existence of a norm of "amity," which specifies that individuals should act in ways that promote the welfare of their family members. This rule of "prescriptive altruism" is analogous to George's norm of solidarity. Farber suggests that this norm is found across societies and is probably universal.

Two large-scale surveys in the U.S. and Hungary, however, revealed a surprising finding. Although a norm of amity was, indeed, present, it existed independently beside a contradictory norm: that of distrust of kin. Factor analyses demonstrated that amity and distrust of kin are two separate factors, which exist as a duality in the minds of the respondents. That is, in assessing the items on the amity scales, Farber suggests that the respondents used two different reference points, with the norm of amity as one basis for evaluating certain items, but with the norm of distrust as the basis for evaluating others.

Farber's theoretical explanation for these ambivalent attitudes is relevant to normative intergenerational ambivalence. He suggests that, if people took the axiom of amity literally, everyone would distribute all of their resources to kin. However, this would be dysfunctional because it would exhaust some relatives and allow other kin to contribute nothing and live off the generosity of others. For this reason, the axiom of distrust serves as a "brake for limiting the extent of redistribution" (p. 320). There is thus a dynamic relationship in which the axiom of amity generates altruistic acts, and the norm of distrust limits the scope of such acts.

This generalization helps explain the contradictions that caregivers experience. Given unlimited adherence to solidarity, adult children would exhaust themselves in the care of their parents and would neglect responsibilities to the family of procreation and to other social roles. It is possible that the competing norms serve a useful function in routine family interactions, but they become problematic in situations that involve chronic stress. The norms of amity and distrust coexist in a way that allows for family ties without dangerous overcommitment but that leads to distress when an excess of help is demanded. Similar conclusions can be drawn from the reconstruction of the processes of negotiation by Finch and Mason (1993), who emphasize the relativistic character of moral obligations.

SOLIDARITY AND AMBIVALENCE

As the studies by Cohler and Grunebaum (1981) and George (1986) demonstrated, families in which solidarity of all kinds exists (for example, coresidence or close proximity, extensive mutual dependency for help, frequent interaction) are especially likely to contain solidarity's opposites: deep dissatisfaction about the relationship, struggles for independence, and serious conflict. These findings are supported by the literature on romantic relationships, which suggests that interdependence tends to increase the likelihood of conflict (Braiker & Kelley, 1979). The gerontological literature, however, typically has not considered this possibility. We review here a set of studies on the abuse of older persons that illustrates this tendency toward conflict resulting from solidarity itself.

The concept of violence against aged persons appears at first consideration to be at odds with the solidarity perspective. Indeed, the popular image of physical abuse, in which a relatively unattached child (who also may be neglectful) has few scruples in attacking the aged parent, might be thought to be inversely related to solidarity. In fact, research on violence against the elderly does not support this view. Studies have shown a "web of mutual dependency" between parents and children in situations where elder abuse occurs (Wolf & Pillemer, 1989). Most investigations show that parents who experience violence from their children typically have some degree of physical impairment and receive at least occasional help from the abusive child.

More striking, however, is the dependence of the violent child on the parent. In two separate studies, Pillemer conducted case-comparison analyses of parent-adult child dyads in which violence had and had not occurred (Pillemer, 1985, 1993). In both studies, he found that the abusive children were heavily dependent on the parent whom they were victimizing. Abusers were found to be substantially more dependent on their parents for housing (most lived as dependents in their parents' homes), for financial assistance, and for help with instrumental activities such as transportation than were nonabusers.

Extensive qualitative data, collected in both studies, were consistent with the quantitative findings. In the majority of cases, the data showed that the mutual dependency of the adult child and the parent was a key dynamic in the abuse. The victims heavily supported children who maltreated them. The children often were individuals who had difficulty separating from their parents and establishing an independent life. Indeed, Pillemer (1985, 1993) found that the physical abuse stemmed directly from the sense of dependency and powerlessness experienced by the abuser.

Parents were caught up in ambivalence when they tried to resolve the situation. Most of the parents felt trapped by a sense of family obligation and, therefore, did not leave the situation or eject the abuser. Some parents stressed the formal relationship and justified exposing themselves to the risk of abuse because of normative obligations to help their children. Equally common were feelings of love and affection for the child, despite the abuse. Many parents explicitly referred to feeling "torn" or "of two minds" about the positive and negative aspects of the relationship with the child.

We have selected these research findings, which have been confirmed in European studies (cf. Ogg, 1993), to highlight the limitations of the solidarity model in representing the actual experience of families. As in the Cohler and Grunebaum study (1981), many of the abusive families would have scored high on the measures of solidarity (as, indeed, they did on comparable measures used in the study). However, these were fundamentally ambivalent family situations that contained a complex mix of elements of solidarity, conflict over power and resources, and violence.

FUTURE PROSPECTS FOR THE STUDY OF INTERGENERATIONAL AMBIVALENCE

We began by pointing out that the study of intergenerational relations has been dominated by a paradigm that emphasizes intergenerational solidarity and a less well articulated focus that highlights conflict and abandonment. We proposed ambivalence as an alternative general approach to understanding intergenerational relations among adults. We provided evidence for the value of this approach, both from theoretical work in the social sciences, as well as in detailed examples from research that point to relationships between the generations that are ambivalent, rather than characterized by solidarity. These studies provide a clear argument against the dualistic, solidarity-versus-conflict view. Instead, they demonstrate that countervailing positive and negative forces characterize intergenerational relationships and that the focal point of interest is the way in which ambivalence is mediated and managed.

The question then arises: What type of research should be conducted to explore intergenerational ambivalence? Although a detailed answer to this question is beyond the scope of this article, the ambivalence approach suggests a number of important steps for future researchers.

Measurement

The ambivalence perspective reveals the need for new and more sensitive measures of intergenerational relations. Specifically, the types of measures employed by researchers in the solidarity tradition are not adequate to address the more complex nature of the questions raised by intergenerational ambivalence. The most commonly used measures make it impossible to explore contradictory feelings within the same relationship. In the research by Bengtson and colleagues, for example, "affectual solidarity" is measured by scales of "the type and degree of positive sentiments held about family members" (Roberts et al., 1991). In a recent study, Silverstein and Bengtson (1997) took an even more minimalist approach and operationalized affectual solidarity using the single measure: "In general, how close do you feel to your [relative]?" with three response categories ("very close," "somewhat close," and "not at all close"). Such measures are not likely to reflect the range of family members' contradictory feelings about one another.

Similarly, Rossi and Rossi (1990) employed a scale to measure affectual solidarity that asks respondents to rate relationships on a scale from 1 to 7. The low end of the scale represents relationships that are *tense and strained,* and the high end those that are *close and intimate.* This measure, of course, does not allow the study to capture persons who feel both ways (Marshall et al., 1993). As Mangen (1995) notes, the positive bias in measures like these cannot account for families who score high on both positive and negative dimensions. To address such shortcomings, researchers should begin to include measures of conflicting attitudes, motivations, or emotions. The Farber (1989) study is a good example. Rather than measuring only solidarity, items about distrust of kin also were included. Similarly, George (1986) obtained information about competing normative structures, rather than only one. Analytic strategies then can be employed to explore patterns of dilemmas and conflicting factors.

In the early stages of studying intergenerational ambivalence, triangulation of various methods appears to be a sound strategy. For example, Cohler and Grunebaum (1981) used methods that could be applied to the study of ambivalence: repeated in-depth interviews over time, semistructured questionnaires, observation of parents and children, and clinical techniques such as projective tests. The four families in the study were selected from a larger survey, which allowed for comparisons between the case studies and a more representative group. The families also were selected according to theoretically defined criteria: joint versus separate living arrangements and high or low scores on a measure of the appropriateness of the mother's attitude toward closeness to the adult child. This type of approach is likely to uncover the complexity of family life implied by the intergenerational ambivalence perspective.

Quantitative measures of intergenerational ambivalence also should be developed, and possible adaptation of existing measures should be explored. One of the few direct measures of ambivalence in close relationships was developed by Braiker and Kelley (1979). They asked respondents involved in romantic relationships general questions such as, "How confused were you about your feelings toward [the other person]?" and "How ambivalent or unsure were you about continuing the relationship with [the other person]?" As a first step, general questions like these could be used to describe the parameters of intergenerational ambivalence. However, this type of approach may not be meaningful to some respondents because it requires them to be consciously aware of the ambivalence.

An improvement on this method has been developed by Thompson and Holmes (1996), who adapted measures from the study of ambivalent attitudes (Thompson, Zanna, & Griffin, 1995). To study ambivalence in romantic relationships, they asked respondents to carry out separate assessments of positive and negative components of attitudes toward the partner. Respondents were asked first to focus only on the positive aspects of an attribute of the partner and to rate each one on a scale from *not at all* to *extremely positive.* Then they asked the respondent to focus only on the negative aspects of the same attribute and to rate the degree of negativity.

For example, using the Thompson et al. method, one could ask an adult child: "Focus only on the best aspects of helping your mother. To what extent do you believe helping her is beneficial to your relationship?" The paired negative question would substitute "worst" for "best" and "harmful" for "beneficial." It is possible to compare the degree to which the situation is seen as both positive and negative, using one of several computational formulae. (See Thompson et al., 1995, for a review of estimation methods.) Whether or not this approach will be effective in studying intergenerational ambivalence remains to be tested. Most important is that such a precedent exists in the literature on close relationships and can point the way toward measurement strategies.

Ambivalence as a Dependent or an Independent Variable

In the studies we reviewed, ambivalence was investigated fruitfully as both an independent and a dependent variable. Cohler and Grunebaum's (1981) work focused on ambivalence as a dependent variable. They examined factors such as family history and shared living arrangements as sources of ambivalence. George (1986) treated normative ambivalence as an independent variable and explored the role of ambivalence as a source of negative affect among caregivers. Similarly, Pillemer (1985, 1993) identified ambivalence regarding dependency as a predictor of elder abuse.

In considering intergenerational ambivalence as a dependent variable, researchers can explore its antecedents in earlier phases of the relationship. For example, some investigators have linked ambivalence in close relationships to early patterns of parent-child attachment (cf. Hazan & Shaver, 1987). Further, it would be useful to determine the degree to which subgroups of the population differ in their experience of ambivalence. As a beginning step, studies of variations in intergenerational ambivalence according to gender, race, and socioeconomic status should be conducted.

The effects of intergenerational ambivalence also should be investigated. It might be assumed that ambivalence is invariably a negative experience, leading to psychological distress. However, Thompson and Holmes (1996), in an analysis of romantic relationships, suggest that having both positive and negative attitudes toward another person may not always indicate personal disturbance. Instead, they suggest, "a moderate level of ambivalence may be indicative

of a balanced, realistic assessment of a partner" (p. 502). Such a view is consistent with Farber's (1989) study. Up to a certain point, a degree of ambivalence may serve a protective function. The impact of ambivalence on both psychological well-being and behavior would be a fruitful area for study.

It is too early in our understanding of intergenerational ambivalence to attempt a formal conceptual model of its causes and consequences. However, Figure 17.1 presents a simple illustrative model. As Figure 17.1 indicates, conflicts within norms or within positions in the social structure are seen as resulting in feelings of ambivalence, which, in turn, have an impact on psychological well-being, as well as on decisions made to relieve the ambivalence. Further, the arrows between the first two domains indicate that conflicts may occur between norms and social-structural positions.

To provide a simple example, consider a researcher who is interested in the impact of late-life divorce on intergenerational relationships. The researcher could hypothesize that older women who remarry will be likely to experience ambivalence between the social positions of parent and that of new wife. Children may feel that it is inappropriate for their mother to remarry, may worry that they will lose her attention, and may be concerned about the safety of their inheritance. The new husband, on the other hand, may make traditional demands on his wife's attention and expect her to separate from her adult children. The resulting ambivalence might lead to psychological distress and to a decision to reduce contact with children.

Mechanisms

Mechanisms for managing intergenerational ambivalence merit attention. Separation of the generations is one possible mechanism identified by family historians. Divided spheres of life are allowed to develop between old and young, reinforced by residential segregation. (See for example Graff, 1995; Stearns, 1986.) When segmentation by place and time is impossible, Coser (1966) and others (Boehm, 1989; Foner, 1984; Marshall et al., 1993) point to the importance of ritual and etiquette

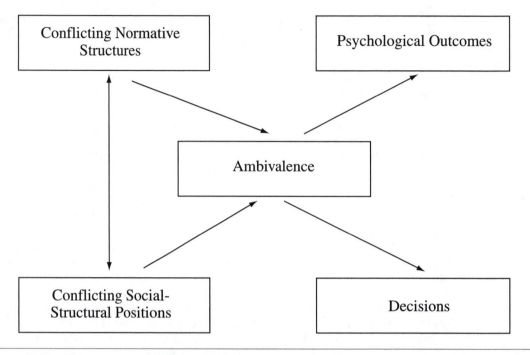

Figure 17.1   Illustrative Model for Research on Intergenerational Ambivalence

as tension-reducing mechanisms. In contemporary society, the absence of some of the segregating and insulating mechanisms, as well as the rites of passage of traditional societies, may serve to increase ambivalence.

Life Course Approach

The study of intergenerational ambivalence requires a dynamic life course focus. Coser (1966) proposes that ambivalence will be particularly strong during status transitions because in "changing from one status position to another, conformity with the requirements of one of these positions implies nonconformity with the requirements of the other" (p. 184). The literature on close relationships supports this view. For example, research indicates that ambivalence may characterize the early stages of a romantic relationship but then subside later on (Braiker & Kelley, 1979). Boss (1988) notes that major family transitions over the life course have an ambivalent quality; they

typically involve losses and gains. For example, when a child is launched from the parental home, "the family *loses* a dependent child, but *gains* an independent young adult" (p. 79).

Therefore, we predict heightened ambivalence around the time of status transitions (for example, retirement or widowhood) and lower levels in periods of stability. Studies of the relationships between mid-life women who returned to college and their mothers (Suitor, 1987) and of adult children shortly after they became family caregivers (Pillemer & Suitor, 1996) provide evidence to support this view. Status transitions provide perhaps the best laboratory for the study of intergenerational ambivalence.

In conclusion, we have attempted to establish ambivalence as a theoretically and empirically useful approach to the study of intergenerational relations. Developing innovative qualitative and quantitative strategies for understanding the causes and consequences of ambivalence will prove an exciting challenge for future researchers. As methods and measures are developed and refined, ambivalence is likely to become an even more powerful general approach to research on parent-child relations in later life.

REFERENCES

Abel, E. K., & Nelson, M. K. (1990). *Circles of care: Work and identity in women's lives.* New York: State University of New York Press.

Aldous, J. (1990). Family development and the life course: Two perspectives on family change. *Journal of Marriage and the Family, 52,* 571-583.

Attias-Donfut, C. (Ed.). (1995a). *Les solidarités entre générations* [Solidarities between generations]. Paris: Nathan.

Attias-Donfut, C. (1995b). Le double circuit des transmissions [The twofold circle of transmissions]. In C. Attias-Donfut (Ed.), *Les solidarités entre générations* [Solidarities between generations] (pp. 41-81). Paris: Nathan.

Baber, K. M., & Allen, K. R. (1992). *Women and families: Feminist reconstructions.* New York: Guilford Press.

Bawin-Legros, B., Gauthier, A., & Strassen, J.-F. (1995). Les limites de l'entraide intergénérationelle [The limits of intergenerational helping]. In C. Attias-Donfut (Ed.), *Les solidarités entre générations* [Solidarities between generations] (pp. 117-130). Paris: Nathan.

Bengtson, V. L., & Harootyan, R. A. (1994). *Intergenerational linkages: Hidden connections in American society.* New York: Springer.

Bleuler, E. (1911). *Dementia praecox oder Gruppe der Schizophrenien* [Dementia Praecox or the Group of Schizophrenias]. Leipzig und Wien: Franz Deuticke.

Boehm, C. (1989). Ambivalence and compromise in human nature. *American Anthropologist, 91,* 921-939.

Boss, P. (1988). *Family stress management.* Newbury Park, CA: Sage.

Braiker, H. B., & Kelley, H. H. (1979). Conflict in the development of close relationships. In R. L. Burgess & T. L. Huston (Eds.), *Social exchange in developing relationships* (pp. 135-168). New York: Academic Press.

Coenen-Huther, J., Kellerhals, J., & von Allmen, M. (1994). *Les réseaux de solidarité dans la famille* [Networks of solidarity in the family]. Lausanne: Réalités Sociales.

Cohler, B. (1983). Autonomy and interdependence in the family of adulthood. *The Gerontologist, 23,* 33-39.

Cohler, B., & Altergott, K. (1995). The family of the second half of life: Connecting theories and findings. In R. Blieszner & V. Hilkevitch (Eds.), *Handbook of aging and the family* (pp. 59-94). Westport, CT: Greenwood Press.

Cohler, B. J., & Grunebaum, H. (1981). *Mothers, grandmothers, and daughters: Personality and childcare in three-generation families.* New York: Wiley.

Coser, R. L. (1966). Role distance, sociological ambivalence, and transitional status systems. *American Journal of Sociology, 72,* 173-187.

Denzin, N. (1991). *Images of postmodern society.* London: Sage.

DeVault, M. L. (1991). *Feeding the family.* Chicago: University of Chicago Press.

Donati, P. (1995). *Quarto rapporto sulla famiglia in Italia* [Fourth report on the family in Italy]. Cinisello Balsamo: Edizione San Paolo.

Dressel, P. L., & Clark, A. (1990). A critical look at family care. *Journal of Marriage and the Family, 52,* 769-782.

Eidelberg, L. (1968). *Encyclopedia of psychoanalysis.* New York: Free Press.

Eisenhandler, S. (1992). Lifelong roles and cameo appearances: Elderly parents and relationships with adult children. *Journal of Aging Studies, 6,* 243-257.

Erikson, E. H. (1994). *The life cycle completed.* New York: Norton.

Farber, B. (1989). Limiting reciprocity among relatives: Theoretical implications of a serendipitous finding. *Sociological Perspectives, 32,* 307-330.

Ferree, M. M. (1990). Beyond separate spheres: Feminism and family research. *Journal of Marriage and the Family, 52,* 866-884.

Finch, J., & Mason, J. (1993). *Negotiating family responsibilities.* London: Tavistock/Routledge.

Foner, N. (1984). *Ages in conflict.* New York: Columbia University Press.

Freud, S. (1913). *Totem and taboo* (A. A. Brill, Trans.). New York: New Republic.

George, L. K. (1986). Caregiver burden: Conflict between norms of reciprocity and solidarity. In K. Pillemer & R. Wolf (Eds.), *Elder abuse: Conflict in the family* (pp. 67-92). Dover, MA: Auburn House.

Gergen, K. J. (1991). *The saturated self.* New York: Basic.

Graff, H. J. (1995). *Conflicting paths: Growing up in America.* Cambridge, MA: Harvard University Press.

Gubrium, J. F., & Holstein, J. A. (1994). Grounding the postmodern self. *The Sociological Quarterly, 34,* 685-703.

Hareven, T. K. (1996). *Aging and generational relations: Life-course and cross-cultural perspectives.* New York: Aldine De Gruyter.

Hazan, C., & Shaver, P. (1987). Romantic love conceptualized as an attachment process. *Journal of Personality and Social Psychology, 52,* 511-524.

Holstein, J. A., & Gubrium, J. F. (1995). Deprivatization and the construction of domestic life. *Journal of Marriage and the Family, 57,* 894-908.

Kleine, T. (1992). Solidarität als Prozeß [Solidarity as process]. Tübingen. Fachbereich kathologische Theologie.

Litwak, E. (1965). Extended kin relations in a democratic industrial society. In E. Shanas & G. Streib (Eds.), *Social structure and the family* (pp. 290-323). Englewood Cliffs, NJ: Prentice-Hall.

Lüscher, K. (1997). Solidarische Beziehungen: Das "neue" Problem der Generationen [Solidarity in relationships: The "new" problem of generations]. In K. Gabriel, A. Herth, & K. P. Strohmeier (Eds.), *Modernität und Solidarität* [Modernity and solidarity] (pp. 59-77). Freiburg: Herder.

Lüscher, K., & Schultheis, F. (1993). *Generationenbeziehungen in "postmodernen" Gesellschaften* [Intergenerational relations in "postmodern" societies]. Konstanz: Universitätsverlag.

Lye, D. N. (1996). Adult child-parent relationships. *Annual Review of Sociology, 22,* 79-102.

Mangen, D. J. (1995). Methods and analysis of family data. In R. Bliezner & V. H. Bedford (Eds.), *Handbook of aging and the family* (pp. 148-177). Westport, CT: Greenwood Press.

Marks, S. R. (1994). What is a pattern of commitments? *Journal of Marriage and the Family, 56,* 112-115.

Marshall, V. W., Matthews, S. H., & Rosenthal, C. J. (1993). Elusiveness of family life: A challenge for the sociology of aging. In G. L. Maddox & M. P. Lawton (Eds.), *Annual review of gerontology and geriatrics: Focus on kinship, aging, and social change.* New York: Springer.

Merton, R. K. & Barber, E. (1963). Sociological ambivalence. In E. Tiryakian (Ed.), *Sociological theory: Values and sociocultural change* (pp. 91-120). New York: Free Press.

Moss, M. S., & Moss, S. Z. (1992). Themes in parent child relationships when elderly parents move nearby. *Journal of Aging Studies, 6,* 259-271.

Nydegger, C. N., & Mitteness, L. S. (1991). Fathers and their adult sons and daughters. In S. K. Pfeifer & M. B. Sussman (Eds.), *Families: Intergenerational and generational connections* (pp. 250-266). Binghamton, NY: Haworth Press.

Ogg, J. (1993). Researching elder abuse in Britain. *Journal of Elder Abuse and Neglect, 5,* 37-54.

O'Neil, R., & Greenberger, E. (1994). Patterns of commitment to work and parenting: Implications for role strain. *Journal of Marriage and the Family, 56,* 101-118.

Parsons, T. (1942). Age and sex in the social structure of the United States. *American Sociological Review, 8,* 604-616.

Parsons, T. (1944). The social structure of the family. In R. N. Anshen (Ed.), *The family: Its function and destiny* (pp. 173-201). New York: Harper.

Pillemer, K. (1985). The dangers of dependency: New findings on domestic violence against the elderly. *Social Problems, 33,* 146-158.

Pillemer, K. (1993). The abused offspring are dependent. In R. J. Gelles & D. Loeseke (Eds.), *Controversies in family violence* (pp. 237-249). Newbury Park, CA: Sage.

Pillemer, K., & Suitor, J. J. (1996). It takes one to help one: Effects of status similarity on well-being. *Journal of Gerontology, 51B,* S250-S257.

Rein, M. (1994). *Solidarity between generations: A five-country study of the social process of aging.* Vienna, Austria: Institut für Höhere Studien; Reihe Politikwissenschaft.

Roberts, R. E. L., Richards, L. N., & Bengtson, V. L. (1991). Intergenerational solidarity in families: Untangling the ties that bind. In S. K. Pfeifer & M. B. Sussman (Eds.), *Families: Intergenerational and generational connections* (pp. 11-46). Binghamton, NY: Haworth Press.

Rossi, A., & Rossi, P. (1990). *Of human bonding: Parent-child relationships across the life course.* Hawthorne, NY: Aldine de Gruyter.

Rycroft, C. (1973). *A critical dictionary of psychoanalysis.* Totowa, NJ: Littlefield Adams.

Schulz, R., Williamson, G. M., Morcyz, R., & Biegel, D. E. (1990). Psychiatric and physical morbidity effects of caregiving. *Journals of Gerontology: Psychological Sciences, 45,* 181-191.

Shanas, E., Townsend, P., Weddeburn, D., Friis, H., Milhoj, P., & Stehouwer, J. (1968). *Old people in three industrial societies.* New York: Atherton Press.

Silverstein, M., & Bengtson, V. L. (1997). Intergenerational solidarity and the structure of adult child-parent relationships in American families. *American Journal of Sociology, 103,* 429-460.

Sprey, J. (1991). Studying adult children and their parents. In S. K. Pfeifer & M. B. Sussman (Eds.), *Families: Intergenerational and generational connections* (pp. 221-235). Binghamton, NY: Haworth Press.

Stacey, J. (1990). *Brave new families: Stories of domestic upheaval in late twentieth century America.* New York: Basic Books.

Stearns, P. N. (1986). Old age family conflict: The perspective of the past. In K. Pillemer & R. S. Wolf (Eds.), *Elder abuse: Conflict in the family* (pp. 1-24). Dover, MA: Auburn House.

Suitor, J. J. (1987). Mother-daughter relations when married daughters return to school: Effects of status similarity. *Journal of Marriage and the Family, 49,* 435-444.

Suitor, J. J., Pillemer, K., Bohanon, K. S., & Robison, J. (1995). Aged parents and aging children: Determinants of relationship quality. In V. Bedford & R. Blieszner (Eds.), *Handbook of aging and the family* (pp. 223-242). Westport, CT: Greenwood Press.

Sussman, M. B. (1959). The isolated nuclear family: Fact or fiction. *Social Problems, 6,* 333-347.

Thompson, M. M., & Holmes, J. G. (1996). Ambivalence in close relationships: Conflicted cognitions as a catalyst for change. In R. M. Sorrentin & E. T. Higgins (Eds.), *Handbook of motivation and cognition, Vol. 3: The interpersonal context* (pp. 497-530). Houston, TX: The Guilford Press.

Thompson, M., Zanna, M., & Griffin, D. (1995). Let's not be indifferent about (attitudinal) ambivalence. In R. E. Petty & A. Krosnick (Eds.), *Attitude strength: Antecedents and consequences* (pp. 361-386). Hillsdale, NY: Erlbaum.

Thorne, B. (1992). Feminism and the family: Two decades of thought. In B. Thorne & M. Yalom (Eds.), *Rethinking the family* (pp. 3-30). Boston: Northeastern University Press.

Treas, J., & Bengston, V. L. (1988). The family in later years. In M. B. Sussman & S. K. Steinmetz (Eds.), *Handbook of marriage and the family* (pp. 625-648). New York: Plenum Press.

van der Loo, H., & van Reijen, W. (1992). *Modernisierung: Projekt und Paradox* [Modernization: Project and paradox]. Munich: Universitätsverlag.

Weigert, A. J. (1991). *Mixed emotions: Certain steps toward understanding ambivalence.* Albany: State University of New York Press.

Wolf, R. S., & Pillemer, K. (1989). *Helping elderly victims: The reality of elder abuse.* New York: Columbia University Press.

18

ADULT CHILDREN OF FATHERS MISSING IN ACTION (MIA)

An Examination of Emotional Distress, Grief, and Family Hardiness

CATHY L. CAMPBELL

ALICE S. DEMI

This study investigated the relationships among emotional distress, grief, and family hardiness in adult children of missing in action (MIA) fathers using the Resiliency Model of Family Stress, Adjustment and Adaptation. Quantitative and qualitative data were collected in telephone interviews of twenty adult children. Results indicated that 25 years after notification of their father's MIA status, participants still had unresolved grief. Findings provide some support for family hardiness as a strength that facilitated family bonadaptation.

When the Vietnam War ended militarily in 1973, there were 2,453 men listed as missing in action (MIA) (Doyle, 1992). "A military service member is in a missing (missing in action) status if not at his duty location due to apparent involuntary reasons as a result of hostile action and his location is not known" (Department of Defense POW/MIA Newsletter, 1996, p. 5).

Reprinted from *Family Relations* 49 (2000): 267-76. Copyright © 2000 by the National Council on Family Relations, 3989 Central Ave. NE, Suite 550, Minneapolis, MN 55421. Reprinted by permission. The research reported in this paper was supported in part by a grant from the Georgia Nurses Foundation. The paper was presented at the 1998 Southern Nursing Research Society meeting. This research is dedicated to the first author's father, Colonel William E. Campbell, missing in action since 1969 from the Vietnam War.

Three criteria currently guide accounting for missing personnel by the Defense Prisoner of War/Missing Personnel Office: (1) the return of a live American; (2) the return of identifiable remains; and (3) provision of convincing evidence why the first two criteria are not possible (personal communication, June 19, 1998). In 1998 the National League of Families of American Prisoners and Missing in Southeast Asia reported 2,089 men remain still missing and unaccounted for from the Vietnam War: 1,559 in Vietnam (North, 566; South, 993); 447 in Laos; 75 in Cambodia; and 8 in Peoples Republic of China territorial waters. The MIA issue fueled intense political debates in the United States government and sparked dramatic stories in the Hollywood film industry (Leonard, 1993).

Experiencing the loss of a loved one during the Vietnam War was difficult for all families. Impact of war challenged a family system to regain its normal functioning (Hogancamp & Figley, 1983). Many families continue to wrestle with resolution of losses that occurred during the Vietnam War (Berkseth, 1988). Circumstances of the death, the lack of concrete evidence, the inadequate support available, and the conflicted social environment associated with the Vietnam War contributed to family difficulty in resolving the loss (Provost, 1989). Families of those missing in military action experience tremendous stress from the lack of confirmation of the death, the continuing absence of the loved one, and the demand for an end of mourning (Rando, 1993). Complicated mourning in these families has resulted from having to "know without knowing" and "to live without knowing" (Rando, 1993, p. 397). Resolution of their grief is complicated by boundary ambiguity and ambiguous loss (Boss, 1999).

Twenty-five years later, how have families of these men, and especially their children, who are now adults, lived with the MIA issue? The purpose of this descriptive, correlational study was to examine relationships among emotional distress, grief, and family hardiness in adult children of MIA fathers from the Vietnam War. Questions investigated in the study included:

1. What is the level of emotional distress related to their father's MIA status, in adult children whose fathers are still unaccounted for from the Vietnam War?

2. What current grief manifestations do these adult children report?

3. What is the reported level of family of origin hardiness in these adult children?

4. What are the relationships among emotional distress, grief, and family hardiness in these adult children?

While this study utilizes a quantitative design rather than a naturalistic design, it is important to note that the first author of this article is an adult child of an MIA father. Thus while a positivist paradigm was used, the study, from original conception to completion, was influenced by the first author's experience (see Personal Thoughts at end of paper).

The findings of this study may contribute to development of interventions that will help promote resilience in family members who experience ambiguous loss. Describing how children of a military family have dealt with the ambiguous loss of an MIA father may help others in similar situations to deal with their loss.

REVIEW OF THE LITERATURE

In the early 1970s, the Center for Prisoner of War Studies (CPWS) was established at the Naval Health Research Center in San Diego, California. The Family Studies Branch of the CPWS interviewed families of Prisoners of War (POW) and MIA men during the Vietnam War. A sample of 215 Army, Navy, and Marine Corps families was studied to describe adjustment problems (McCubbin, Hunter, & Metres, 1974a; McCubbin, Hunter, & Dahl, 1975; McCubbin, Dahl, Lester, Benson, & Robertson, 1976; McCubbin & Dahl, 1976). The Air Force did not participate in these family studies. The majority of children in the CPWS family studies were between the ages of 8 and 15 years with a range of ages from less than 1 year to 25 years (Hunter, 1988). Most of the studies from 1971 to 1978 focused on the wife's reactions to her POW/MIA husband's prolonged and unknown length of absence.

Several studies on children of POW/MIA fathers from the Vietnam War were conducted in the 1970s. Hall and Simmons (1973) examined case studies of two POW/MIA support groups and concluded that separation anxiety, role distortion, and sleep disorders were common in these children. In a study conducted by McCubbin, Hunter, & Metres (1974b), they reported that mothers viewed their children as vulnerable and wanted to protect them from the trauma of dealing with the fathers' absence. The researchers referred to the children as "children in limbo."

Dahl, McCubbin, & Lester (1976) examined children from three types of families to assess their adjustment: reunited families (fathers returned from Vietnam); non-reunited families (fathers did not return); and reconstituted families (fathers did not return and mothers remarried). The California Test of Personality was administered to determine the children's level of social and personality development. Findings showed children of reunited parents, when compared with the reconstituted families, were significantly better adjusted in the areas of school and community relations and displayed a general freedom from withdrawal tendencies, nervous symptoms and anti-social tendencies. Findings on children of non-reunited families were described in a subsequent paper (Dahl, McCubbin, & Ross, 1977). Significant differences on the total adjustment scores were not found between the non-reunited families and reunited families. The children of non-reunited families, however, did show significant differences on two subscale scores measuring freedom from nervous symptoms and community relations.

McCubbin, Dahl, Lester, & Ross (1977) described negative and positive factors, which affected the parent-child relationship following a POW father's release from captivity. Negative factors included the severity of mental and physical abuse suffered by the POW father, the wife's relationship with her parents, and the wife's involvement with POW/MIA activities. A positive factor was the father's preparation of his family for the war separation.

Following the CPWS family studies project, Hunter (1982, 1983, 1986, 1988; Hunter-King, 1993, 1998) continued her assessment of the children of POW/MIA fathers. She found that how well the children adjusted and coped often reflected how well the mother handled the stress. Some mothers were so preoccupied with their own ambiguous situation as a POW/MIA wife that the children were ignored (Hunter, 1983). Limitations of the CPWS project included a limited sample (findings which were based only on Navy POW families), MIA families were not followed after 1973 when POWs returned during Operation Homecoming, and incomplete data analysis when the project and its funding ended in 1978 (Hunter, 1986). Important factors in the children's later adjustment to their ambiguous, unresolved grief were the mother's resolution of the stress and their age when the father left for Vietnam (Hunter, 1988). A small pilot study used The 1988 Survey of Vietnam-Era MIA Children developed by Hunter with 82 MIA children who were members of the National League of Families of American Prisoners and Servicemen Missing in Southeast Asia. Based on written comments from the mailed survey, findings indicated that having an MIA father produced both negative and positive effects. Negative effects included: living with the nature of a prolonged, ambiguous stressor; fear of abandonment in close relationships, especially for daughters of MIA fathers; lack of a male role model as husband/father, especially for sons of MIA fathers; and mistrust of the government. The children viewed the following effects as positive: financial assistance to obtain higher degrees; closer family relationships; greater, earlier maturity; and increased valuing of life itself (Hunter-King, 1993, 1998).

Boss (1977, 1980) studied the concept of psychological father presence (PFP) in a sample of MIA families. In families experiencing a physically absent father, a high level of PFP was a strong predictor of family dysfunction. Ambiguous losses were complicated by boundary ambiguity in which the family did not know with certainty "who is in" and "who is out" of the family system (Boss, 1991). Wertsch (1991) described a military child whose father became MIA in the early years of Vietnam. Closure for the child, now a man, has been difficult. Due to the nature of his father's work, there was not even time for a goodbye, let alone the opportunity for a funeral. The man is "locked in an emotional Vietnam which he can neither win nor abandon" (Wertsch, 1991, p. 81).

A review of literature by Jensen & Shaw (1993) on the effects of war-related events and processes on children and their families revealed more research is needed to determine how age, development, family, and community factors influence adaptation following the aftermath of war. Long-term effects of living with the MIA status of men from the Vietnam War are not known, specifically, how the children of these men handled the ambiguous loss.

THEORETICAL PERSPECTIVE

The Resiliency Model of Family Stress, Adjustment and Adaptation (McCubbin & McCubbin, 1996) provided the theoretical framework for the study. The model is an outgrowth of the evolution in family stress theory dating back to Reuben Hill's research on war-induced crises in World War II families. Using the Resiliency Model, researchers attempt to discover which family properties, behaviors, and capabilities buffer the impact of stressful life events on recovery. Furthermore, researchers seek to understand why some families survive (and thrive) and other families do not.

The Resiliency Model of Family Stress, Adjustment and Adaptation consists of two phases, adjustment and adaptation. A stressor produces tension in a family system that calls for management and initiates the process. In this study the stressor is conceptualized as notification of the father's MIA status. According to the theory, in the first phase of the model, adjustment, a family manages the stressor with relative ease. Minor adjustments or changes in the established patterns of family functioning are made. Bonadjustment, a term used to describe successful adjustment, occurs when the needs of individual family members and the functioning of the family system and its transactions with the community are met. However, a stressor as powerful as the ambiguous loss of a father produces a pile-up of demands and the family becomes increasingly vulnerable. The family then moves into the second phase of the Resiliency Model, the adaptation phase. During this phase, a family engages in dynamic relational processes to introduce changes in existing patterns of functioning which help resolve stressors. The family's efforts in adaptation attempt to bring "fit" at two levels: individual-to-family fit and family-to-community fit.

Critical for family recovery are four domains of family systems functioning which help the family regain harmony and balance in the face of adversity:

(a) interpersonal relationships; (b) development, well-being, and spirituality; (c) community relationships and nature; and (d) structure and function. Family levels of appraisal influence these domains of family systems functioning, which, in turn, affect patterns of functioning and problem solving and coping. The five levels of family appraisal include: (a) stressor appraisal; (b) situational appraisal; (c) paradigms (shared expectations as to how the family will function in areas of child rearing, discipline, etc.); (d) coherence (dispositional view of the family's sense of order, trust, predictability and manageability); and (e) schema (family-shared values and beliefs). Family adaptation is achieved over time with the continuum of family adaptation ranging from optimal bonadaptation to maladaptation (Lavee, McCubbin, & Patterson, 1985; McCubbin & McCubbin, 1996). In this study, adaptation is conceptualized as the level of resolution of emotional distress related to the father's MIA status and the level of resolution of grief reported by the adult child of the MIA father.

According to the Resiliency Model of Family Stress, Adjustment and Adaptation, family hardiness is one of the strengths of a family system. Family hardiness is characterized by the family working together to solve problems, having a sense of control over outcomes of life events, a view of change as beneficial and growth producing, and an active rather than passive orientation in managing stressful situations (McCubbin, 1993). Thus, for this study, family resiliency was conceptualized as family hardiness.

METHOD

Sample and Setting

A nonprobability sample of adult children of MIA fathers from the Vietnam War was recruited using a snowball sampling strategy with those participants recruited identifying additional eligible people (Henry, 1990). Criteria for inclusion in the study were that the adult child's father was listed as MIA during the Vietnam War and continues in an unaccounted for status up to the present time. Initial identification of study participants was facilitated by a notice posted on the Air Force POW/MIA Internet home page and contact with the National League of Families of American Prisoners and Missing in Southeast Asia.

Potential participants contacted one of the researchers by email or telephone. If, after explaining the study to them, they wanted to participate a telephone interview was scheduled. During the telephone interviews, verbal informed consent was obtained and recorded on audiotape; then demographic data were obtained and the questionnaires administered. The first author of this paper conducted all interviews. The 20 participants resided in 12 states in diverse areas of the country. The mainly White sample, whose average age was 37 years with a range of 29 to 48 years, included 10 males and 10 females. These adult children ranged in age from less than one year to 18 years old when their father, most of whom (75%) were Air Force pilots, became MIA. Sixty percent of their mothers had remarried, and three of the mothers were deceased at the time of the study. (See Table 18.1 for further demographic data.)

MEASURES

Impact of Event Scale (IES)
(Horowitz, Wilner, & Alvarez, 1979)

The Impact of Event Scale was used to assess the participants' emotional distress related to the father's MIA status. The 15-item IES is designed to assess intrusive thoughts and avoidance related to a specific stressful life event. A 4-point Likert scale (*not at all* = 1, *rarely* = 2, *sometimes* = 3, and *often* = 4) assesses how often the respondent experienced the item over the past week. The responses are weighted as 0, 1, 3, and 5; items are then totaled to obtain the scale score. The 7-item Intrusion subscale assesses intrusively experienced ideas, images, feelings, and bad dreams related to the stressful event. The 8-item Avoidance subscale assesses consciously recognized avoidance of certain ideas, feelings, or situations (Zilberg, Weiss, & Horowitz, 1982). Cronbach's alpha for the Intrusion subscale is reported as .79 and for the Avoidance subscale as .82 (Zilberg et al., 1982). The instrument has been used widely to assess responses to diverse catastrophic events.

Bereavement Experience
Questionnaire Short Form (BEQ-24)
(Guarnaccia & Hayslip, 1998)

The 24-item Bereavement Experience Questionnaire Short Form is designed to assess grief manifestations. The BEQ-24 is based on a longer instrument, the Bereavement Experience Questionnaire (Demi & Schroeder, 1989). The shorter form was selected because of its stronger psychometric properties. The BEQ-24 contains three subscales, Existential Loss/Emotional Needs, Guilt/Blame/Anger, and Preoccupation with Thoughts of the Deceased (Alphas .86, .83, and .81, respectively). The structure of the subscales is supported by factor analysis (Guarnaccia & Hayslip, 1998). Respondents rate the frequency with which they experienced specific behaviors in the past month on a 4-point Likert scale (*never* = 1, *sometimes* = 2, *often* = 3, *almost always* = 4). The mean score for the scales are then computed.

Family Hardiness Index (FHI)
(McCubbin, McCubbin, & Thompson, 1986)

The 20-item Family Hardiness Index was used to assess resilience in the adult child's family of origin. The FHI contains three subscales, Commitment, Challenge, and Control. Responses are scored on a 4-point scale (*false* = 0, *mostly false* = 1, *mostly true* = 2, and *true* = 3). Negative items are reversed; a total score for Family Hardiness is obtained by summing the scores on the items. The internal reliability for the Family Hardiness Index is .82 and test-retest reliability is .86 (McCubbin et al., 1986). Prior to administering the FHI, participants were told: "Please listen to each statement and decide to what degree each describes your family. By family I mean yourself, your mother, and any other siblings you had when your father became MIA in the Vietnam War."

Data Analysis

Quantitative data were entered into a data file and were analyzed using the Statistical Package for the Social Sciences (SPSS, Inc., 1993). Descriptive statistics were used to analyze the demographic data and to describe the participants' responses to the

Table 18.1 Selected Characteristics of the Adult Children, MIA Fathers, and Mothers of the Adult Children (*n* = 20)

Adult Children	M	SD
Present age	37.40	5.38
Age when father became MIA	8.49	5.78
Years of education	15.68	1.45
	n	*%*
Sex		
Male	10	50.0
Female	10	50.0
Race		
White	18	90.0
Other	2	10.0
Marital Status		
Single	5	25.0
Married	12	60.0
Divorced	3	15.0

MIA Fathers	M	SD
Father's age at time of MIA status	34.60	6.78
	n	*%*
Year of father's MIA		
1965-1968	10	50.0
1969-1972	10	50.0
Place of father's MIA		
Laos	11	55.0
North Vietnam	4	20.0
South Vietnam	5	25.0
Father's service branch		
Air Force	15	75.0
Army	1	5.0
Navy	2	10.0
Marine Corps	1	5.0
Civilian pilot	1	5.0

Mothers of Adult Children	M	SD
Mother's present age	60.00	*
Mother's age when husband became MIA	31.90	6.73
	n	*%*
Mother remarried		
Yes	12	60.0
No	8	40.0

* Three mothers of the adult children were deceased.

Table 18.2   Impact of Event Scale, Bereavement Experience Questionnaire–Short Form, and Family Hardiness Index (*n* = 20)

Instrument	Items	Alpha	M	SD	Range
Impact of Event Scale	15	.83	28.0	12.8	0-75
Intrusion	7	.89	16.7	8.6	0-35
Avoidance	8	.66	11.3	6.9	0-23
Bereavement Experience questionnaire–Short Form	24	.90	1.97	.44	1-4
Existential Loss/Emotional Needs	9	.79	1.82	.49	1-4
Guilt/Blame/Anger	9	.76	1.68	.44	1-4
Preoccupation with Thoughts of Deceased	6	.80	2.62	.63	1-4
Family Hardiness Index	20	.87	44.3	8.0	0-60
Commitment	8	.85	19.1	4.0	0-24
Challenge	5	.64	10.7	2.3	0-15
Control	6	.39	11.9	2.3	0-18

questionnaires, and Pearson Correlation Coefficients were used to assess the relationships among the variables. Participants' comments during the interview were transcribed and used to further describe the participants' experiences.

FINDINGS

The participants' level of emotional distress (IES), grief manifestations (BEQ-24), and family hardiness (FHI) are presented in Table 18.2. The alpha reliabilities for the scales and subscales were within the acceptable range (.64-.90) for all but one scale, the Family Hardiness subscale, Control. Participants scored relatively higher on the IES Intrusion scale than on the IES Avoidance scale (item mean score 2.38 vs. 1.41). On the BEQ-24, the participants scored higher on Preoccupation with Thoughts of the Deceased than on Existential Loss/Emotional Needs and Guilt/Blame/Anger (item mean score 2.62 vs. 1.82 and 1.68); while on the Family Hardiness Index, participants scored higher on the Commitment subscale than on the Challenge and Control subscales (item mean score 2.39 vs. 2.15 and 1.98). Comparing participants by gender revealed no significant difference in scores on the Bereavement Experience Questionnaire nor on the Impact of Event Scale; however, women tended to score higher on the Family Hardiness Index (total score 47.7 vs. 40.9, *p* = .056).

Pearson Correlation Coefficients for the IES, BEQ-24, and the FHI subscales are presented in Table 18.3. IES Intrusion was positively correlated with Guilt/Blame/Anger and Preoccupation with Thoughts of the Deceased, and IES Avoidance was positively correlated with all three BEQ-24 subscales and negatively correlated with two of the FHI subscales, Commitment and Control. In addition, the BEQ-24 Existential Loss was negatively correlated with two of the FHI subscales, Challenge and Control. The participants' current age and age at time of the family's notification of the father's MIA status were correlated with the IES, BEQ-24, and FHI scales and subscales, and no significant correlations were found.

DISCUSSION

The scores on the IES Intrusion scale and the BEQ-24 Preoccupation with Thoughts of the Deceased scale indicate that 25 or more years after their fathers were reported as MIA, the participants continue to have unresolved grief and emotional distress related to their fathers' MIA status. This finding is congruent with Boss's (1999) theory of ambiguous loss in which she proposes the survivors of an ambiguous loss experience persistent preoccupation with thoughts of the loss and lingering psychological presence. Further, the findings indicate that the higher the family hardiness characteristics of

Table 18.3 Pearson Correlation Coefficients Among the Subscales of the Impact of Event Scale, Bereavement Experience Questionnaire–Short Form, and Family Hardiness Index

Variables	IES Total	IES Intrus	IES Avoid	BEQ–SF Avg	BEQ–SF Exist Loss	BEQ–SF Guilt	BEQ–SF Preoccup	FHI Total	FHI Commit	FHI Challenge	FHI Control
IES Total	1.00										
Intrusion		1.00			.350	.697*	.504*		.213	.034	−.074
Avoidance		.354	1.00		.766**	.613**	.627**		−.471*	−.376	−.492*
BEQ–SF Avg				1.00							
Exist Loss					1.00	.697**	.520*		−.437	−.497*	−.618**
Guilt						1.00	.723**		−.244	−.122	−.168
Preoccupation							1.00		.009	−.073	−.188
FHI Total								1.00			
Commitment									1.00	.630**	.510*
Challenge										1.00	.728**
Control											1.00

*$p < 0.05$. **$p < 0.01$.

Challenge and Control, the less Guilt/Blame/Anger and Preoccupation with Thoughts of the Deceased, and the higher the family hardiness characteristics of Control and Commitment, the less avoidance of thoughts, events, and places that stimulate recall of the stressful event, their fathers' MIA status.

When compared with survivors of other stressful life events, the participants in this study scored considerably higher on Intrusiveness, while they were similar on Avoidance. Horowitz, Field, & Classen (1993) reported the mean IES Intrusion score as 12.8 and 12.3 for Avoidance for 26 different samples. The participants in this study had an Intrusion score of 16.7 and an Avoidance score of 11.3. Mardi Horowitz (1986), author of the IES, proposes that after a serious life event, an individual typically experiences a stress response syndrome that consists of outcry, denial and numbing, intrusion, working through, and completion. These participants appeared to be stuck in the intrusion and working through stages of the stress response syndrome. This response is congruent with Boss's (1999) findings of immobilization and frozen grief in other situations of ambiguous loss.

In response to open-ended questions, many of the participants reported that they frequently had intrusive thoughts about the loss. One woman stated: "There are little things—the way that it keeps popping up—like occasionally getting the government notifications saying that it was finally recognized that when he went down he was killed in action." Two participants talked about how films stimulated intrusive thoughts. A woman reported her un-nerving experience of seeing a film entitled BAT-21: "I had no idea at the beginning of the movie they were going to show the shoot down of my dad's plane; so here I am sitting in the middle of a crowded theater and watching how my dad may have died; and crying my eyes out, of course. And it was very, very emotional. Still is." One man said:

> What I am talking about is *Forest Gump*, . . . I walked out, and I thought, why in the hell is anybody nostalgic about that period. That period sucked, you know. And it did, it did. I mean, I lived next door to most of the things that went on in that movie and, whether it was intentional or not, I felt like my reaction to that movie was very different from most of the people

coming out of the theater. They were all reveling in the nostalgia of it all. I did not feel that way. I thought, well, you know, that is why I try to forget about that time, because it was pretty bad.

A few participants reported how they tried to avoid thoughts of their loss. One man stated: "I built one hell of a wall up and it took many, many years to finally—I think it is about half way down, I don't think it will ever fully come down." A woman stated:

> The strength is also the weakness. I think I first noticed it the day I learned that dad had been shot down, because, rather than feel defeated or even feel the loss, . . . [I] immediately started coping with the loss. . . . By not dealing with the issues, by coping too well, by being too resilient at that particular episode, I actually buried the wound rather than actually allowing it to heal.

Another man told about his efforts to avoid dealing with his grief:

> I would not admit that there was a loss until I was 18ish and then . . . I left home and was living on my own from then until now. And I was struggling so intensely day-to-day that I was using that struggle as a shield to protect me from dealing with those issues. And from those days until now, I have been almost maniacally involved with the day-to-day planning, and making things happen. Very little rest, vacation, any of those things, just kind of a drivenness to be—not effective I guess—to have an impact. . . . And I think that is what I have done, I have used that as a shield against actually dealing with the issue. . . .

In a combined sample of 734 adult participants who had experienced the death of a family member or close friend within the past 10 years, the mean score on Existential Loss was 1.84 (SD = .54), Guilt/Blame/Anger was 1.39 (SD = .43) and Preoccupation with Thoughts of the Deceased was 1.73 (SD = .61) (Guarnaccia & Hayslip, 1998). The participants in this study were similar on Existential Loss (M = 1.82, SD = .49) higher on Guilt/Blame/Anger (M = 1.68, SD = .44), and much higher on Preoccupation with Thoughts of the Deceased (M = 2.62, SD = .63). The higher score on Preoccupation with Thoughts of the Deceased is striking considering the length of time since notification of the MIA status, 25 or more years, while in the Guarnaccia & Hayslip study the maximum length of time since bereavement was 10 years.

Some examples of participants' preoccupation with thoughts of the deceased follow. One man said:

I get out the slide projector because he . . . liked taking pictures. . . . So I pull out the slide projector and sit there and go through the slides, and look at the ones of him; then, I will set the slide projector just as far back as I can to bring him up to life size on the screen, and I go up there and just pick out every detail I can about him.

Another said:

I kind of try to think like he did—try to wonder how he thought, I guess. Of course there's no way to do it. I do fortunately have a reel-to-reel tape of his voice, of him talking; although I don't remember him because I was six when he left. I do have a voice, an audiotape, which to me is very unique . . . I can't say it doesn't sound like him because I don't remember . . . I get that out every now and then; although he is talking about whatever, I just sit there and listen to his voice. I couldn't tell you what he said on the tape other than just trivial talk. But just the fact that I do still have his voice on there, as well as my mother's, and I still do, it's an everyday thought of my life, everyday thought.

A third participant stated: "[My son] is literally named after my father. That is why he is always in my thoughts. Every waking and even sleeping moment. He is in my thoughts, because my son is named after him." And another stated:

Nothing really truly helps; nothing takes the pain away. There is not a single living, waking moment that I don't think about him but I think, gee, I wish you were here for this. When my sister got married and my mom had to walk her down the aisle, when I got married and my mom had to walk me down the aisle, when I had my son, when my sister had her boy—nothing really gets you over it, because there is that constant little reminder that takes you back to what is missing.

What was most striking was the strong feelings of anger toward and blame of the government.

Following are two of the many examples of this anger and blame.

I have a lot of anger toward the government because I feel like these people put their lives—gave their lives for their country—and the country did not support them. And I feel like, because of some political decisions that were made, you know, a lot of this happened. I feel like just—government decisions could have been made differently to avoid this having been dragged out this many years. I mean, I am not saying they might not have been prisoners in the beginning, you know, but you know, I think this could have been handled a long time ago.

Another participant stated that what made him angry was:

The government's assumption that he is dead. The government's assumption that he rode the airplane and went down with it. . . . Their lack of commitment; their lack of full bore, 110% trying to do something. For example, they go out there—we have small underwater remote control video cameras. I am sure you have seen them on National Geographic, you know, the tiny robot things—remote control, they are very small. You know, I asked them to go out there and check it out, and what do they do, they, you know, some guy—one of the military people peeled his shirt off and takes three dives with no goggles, and no nothing and tried to feel around the bottom if he can see something. Tell me, what kind of effort is that? That is halfhearted, that is bogus . . . I mean this so typical of what, you know, the government is doing.

The participants' scores on the Family Hardiness Index were compared with other samples reported in the literature and were found to be similar. The FHI score of 44.3 was comparable to the FHI score of 47.4 for a sample of 304 families associated with a large nationally recognized insurance company (McCubbin et al., 1986). The researchers also reviewed studies of families with a member who had a chronic illness since it was felt that these families also live with an ambiguous situation. Comparison of these data again showed similarities in the mean total FHI score (45.1 chronic illness/44.3 MIA) and mean Commitment subscale score (19.5 chronic illness/19.1 MIA). However, differences were noted in the mean Challenge subscale score (12.3 chronic illness/10.7 MIA) and mean Control subscale score (13.5 chronic illness/11.9 MIA). Control, according to McCubbin et al. (1986), is defined as a belief that one can influence the course of events. Given the long-term ambiguous nature of their father's MIA status and their inability to influence the government, it is not surprising to find slightly lower mean scores for the Challenge and Control subscales in these adult children.

There was some support for family hardiness as a strength that would facilitate bonadaptation. While the total score on the FHI was not correlated with the total score on either the IES or BEQ-24, all three FHI subscales were correlated with one or more of the IES and BEQ-24 subscales. The more the Commitment and Control the participant reported, the less the Avoidance; and, the more Challenge and Control, the less the Existential Loss/Emotional Needs. Intrusive thoughts and Preoccupation with Thoughts of the Deceased were not correlated with any of the family hardiness scales. Thus, it seems that, regardless of the level of family hardiness, participants experience intrusive thoughts and preoccupation with thoughts of the deceased. While in other circumstances this would be perceived as pathological grief, as Boss (1999) states, "complicated grieving can be a normal reaction to a complicated situation and is not [due to] internal personality defects" (p. 10).

Several participants talked about the strengths (hardiness) in their families, particularly in their mothers, and how that had helped them cope with their loss. One participant said: "For a time there, all it was in our lives, was us three kids with my mother; and, I'm sure the world existed, and we had friends and neighbors, but it was us four against the world. I mean there's tight blood within the four of us." Another participant said:

> You know, [mom] really controlled how we dealt with it . . . I know I've never questioned that. That was intrinsic in my body, that we were just going to go on. . . . Mom would even show us families that were dealing with it correctly and not correctly—not as well as we did—and say, you know, I don't want that for you girls. This Vietnam War was an awful, horrible thing that happened, and it is not going to ruin your lives too.

Another reported about his mother's strength:

> [What helped?] Mostly my mom. She just never let it occur to us that we wouldn't go on. We were so little, and she just said, you know, she always said, ah, you can just crumple up in a heap, or you can go on with your life, and our family is going to go on with our lives. So I guess that is probably it.

Many reported a lack of family strengths [hardiness]. Two participants gave dramatic examples of how their families were unable to provide for their needs. One participant said:

> I feel like, with the disarray that my family suffered through the years because of my father's absence, there was not a great family structure. There was a lot of individualism in our family. We had to learn how to take care of ourselves at an early age because my mom suffered a great deal; and, she was, at a lot of time through those years, wrapped up with her own personal problems, I guess you can say, because it affected her greatly. And so there was a big gap in all of our lives; and, as the youngest member of the family, I guess I sort of took on the experiences that my mother, my older brothers and sisters went through, and learned from their mistakes . . . and I think a lot of that had to do with the fact that there was no strong family structure there.

Another participant echoed this feeling of growing up alone:

> Ever since I was 13 or 14 years old, I basically was on my own, and I moved out of the house at an early age, at 17, and it feels like difficulty in life for me was having to grow up on my own without having a fatherly figure really to help teach me about life. I think that is what a father can do for his children, is build strong support systems and values for the children, so they do the right things in life; hopefully that is the way it's supposed to be. That was certainly absent in my life, so it was difficult to grow up, be proper and not get involved in the wrong kind of things and, you know, try to come out as an adult and be successful and not be on some drug trip, or be some alcoholic.

LIMITATIONS/STRENGTHS

Several limitations of the study need to be noted. First, the personal bias of the first author needs to be acknowledged. Since she is an adult child of an MIA father from the Vietnam War it is likely that this influenced the research process; however, it was a benefit in gaining access to the population and in obtaining valid information. Further, the sample was largely the adult children of White Air Force pilots. During the Vietnam War, there were few non-White Air Force pilots; thus, this sample reflects the racial composition of military pilots at that time. A great majority of the sample was highly educated and had the resources and knowledge to access information from the Internet. Since they were contacted through Internet sites that deal with MIA issues, they obviously were interested. Sample size was small, and the retrospective approach required participants to answer questions in relation to an event that happened long ago. All of these factors limit the generalizability of the findings to other samples of adult children whose fathers are reported as MIA.

IMPLICATIONS FOR PRACTICE

Boss (1991) proposed five strategies for support and clinical intervention with family members experiencing an ambiguous loss: (a) label the ambiguity as a major stressor for family members; (b) provide a setting and structure for family meetings so that family members of several generations can sit together and hear one another's perceptions of the situation and what meaning they are making of it; (c) provide as much information as possible about the situation, technical as well as psychosocial; (d) provide families with sources and choices of support for their situation, peer as well as professional; and (e) encourage family members to find some meaning in their loss and provide a format within which they can work (pp. 168-169).

In 1999, Boss further emphasized the need to find meaning in an ambiguous loss. Some ways she suggested for family members to find meaning are through participating in rituals and celebrations, developing one's spirituality, developing an optimistic way of thinking, learning to live with uncertainty, avoiding self-blame, avoiding blaming others, seeking information, and reminiscing. These guidelines for dealing with any type of ambiguous loss are relevant for adult children of MIA fathers.

In addition to the general intervention guidelines proposed by Boss, these adult children should be told about resources specifically designed for family members who have had someone MIA, such as the Defense POW/Missing Personnel Office, the National League of Families of American Prisoners and Missing in Action in Southeast Asia, the POW Network, and Sons and Daughters in Touch (see Table 18.4). They should also be told about what helped the participants in this study go on in life knowing their father was MIA.

Following are some ways that participants found meaning in the loss of their father. One woman who was 2 years old when her father become MIA said: "I got to a certain point in my life where I just became very proud of what he did and that gives me a lot of satisfaction of who he was and what he did."

A man who was 3 years old when his father became MIA said:

> . . . I finally realized I was living a life similar to what my father lived in that he was married, he had children, and he was a young father like I was. And so I was able to project myself into his shoes and he into mine . . . [I] have a better understanding of what he did, not as a soldier, but as a husband and a father and a man who lived just 30 years. . . . There's some part of him in me that guides . . . and motivates me. . . .

Another man who was 16 years old when his father became MIA stated:

> Yes, I do miss my dad. I wish he were here. I wish I could talk to him. But I also tell [people] that he died doing what he liked to do. And he could have died in a car wreck . . . or choked on his eggs or died of a heart attack or died of cancer. Would the loss be any different? That's the way I become to look at it.

Other participants credited their father's influence in their decision to "go on in life." One woman who was 9 years old when her father become MIA said:

> About 10 years ago, almost 20 years after his death, I was talking about my dad and somebody said to me, 'You know, he would not have wanted you to be upset for this long'. . . . It was like a switch went off in my head saying that was very true. He would not have wanted us to be this upset this long.

Table 18.4   Resources for Family Members Who Have Had Someone Reported as Missing in Action

Defense POW/Missing Personnel Office (DPMO) (http://www.dtic.mil/dpmo/) (703-602-2102) sponsor Family Member Updates that consist of informal briefings followed by a question and answer period for families of Americans unaccounted for from the Vietnam War, Cold War, and Korean War. Additional information is available from the respective casualty offices:

Air Force	1-800-531-5501	http://www.afpc.randolph.af.mil/
Army	1-800-892-2490	http://www.perscom.army.mil/
Civilians	202-647-6769	http://travel.state.gov
Marine Corps	1-800-847-1597	http://www.usmc.mil/
Navy	1-800-443-9298	http://www.persnet.navy.mil/

National League of Families of American Prisoners and Missing in Southeast Asia (http://www.pow-miafamilies.org) (202-223-6846–Main number) (202-659-0133–Update Line for current information 24 hours a day) has a threefold goal: the return of all prisoners, the fullest possible accounting for those still missing, and the repatriation of all recoverable remains of those who died serving our nation in Southeast Asia.

POW Network (http://www.asde.com/~pownet) is an electronic newsletter of the National Alliance of Families (http://www.nationalalliance.org). This organization is committed to the return of America's missing servicemen from World War II, Korea, Cold War, and Vietnam.

Sons and Daughters in Touch (SDIT) (http://www.sdit.org) (1-800-984-9994) is an organization whose mission is to unite and provide support to sons, daughters, family members, and friends of those lost, and those who remain missing, in Southeast Asia.

One man who was 16 years old when his father became MIA stated: " . . . For a long time we all grieved very heavily. . . . I thought about it for a while, and then I said, if my dad comes back, he would kick my butt all over the place if I am sitting around like this. He would have expected me to go on."

A person's way of thinking, and one's view of how the world works, influences how meaning is found in an ambiguous loss (Boss, 1999). Following are some examples of participants' ways of thinking, and views of the world that helped them cope with their loss. A woman who was 6 months old when her father became MIA said: "I feel what I learned early on is you could drive yourself crazy asking 'what if,' and so I don't do that." Another woman who was 13 when her father became MIA stated: "I don't know where this well of optimism comes from, but from some source, I have an ability to never, ever, ever give up, quit, say die, or feel defeated. Even when I am whipped, I just never give in." A man who was 6 years old when his father became MIA said: "I try to see everything in a positive way—try to see how things come out, and hopefully it helps people. If it helps one person, it is worth it."

While many of these participants have been able to move on with their lives and find meaning in their ambiguous loss, others are still stuck in acute grief and have not been able to receive the help they need. Some of their pain might have been alleviated if counselors and other care providers were more cognizant of the needs of survivors of ambiguous loss. As one participant stated: ". . . to this day I cannot find a therapist, or social worker, or counselor of any type who knows how to deal with this kind of grief." Therapists and other health care providers who follow Boss' (1991, 1999) guidelines should be able to address this unmet need.

PERSONAL THOUGHTS BY
CATHY CAMPBELL, DAUGHTER
OF COLONEL WILLIAM E. CAMPBELL
(MIA IN LAOS, 1969)

Interviewing other adult children of MIA fathers for this study has been a healing experience for me. I heard variations of my own family story repeated and was amazed at how similar they were to my experience. This study was triggered by the unexpected death of my mother who died in her sleep at the age of 64. Her death made me realize how comforting it could be to see and touch a dead body and to go through the rituals surrounding a funeral. The experience of my mother's death, however, also reawakened feelings about what had happened to my father.

During the Vietnam War in January 1969, my father's F4-D Phantom fighter plane was hit by a ground-to-air missile in Laos. My father and the co-pilot were declared MIA. I was 17, the oldest of four children, when this happened. We children were told not to cry because of the possibility that he might be a POW. Our family waited, hoped, and held in our grief. My father was not among the POWs returned during Operation Homecoming in 1973. Five years later, in 1978, my mother decided that he was probably killed in action, and the Air Force sponsored a memorial service for him. I remember thinking the service was "dumb," and I did not cry. For over ten years, there was very little mention of my father. We all tried to go on with our lives the best we could. We rarely spoke about him. Then starting in 1989, we began receiving bits and pieces of information after a Laos villager took my father's college ring to a military installation in order to exchange the ring and information about the ring's owner for money. Following two years of negotiations, the ring was returned to my mother in 1991. We were given photographs in 1993 of the pistol and leather holster issued to my father, which were on display in the Hanoi War Museum. My mother died two years later in 1995, at which time I became the "primary next of kin" and received all correspondence from the government. In 1996, my family was asked to provide a blood sample for mitochondrial DNA testing on some bones and teeth being stored in Hawaii which, perhaps, belonged to my father. Two years later, we learned there was not a DNA match between the remains and the blood sample. As recently as 1998, material recovered during investigations of crash sites in Laos has been determined insufficient to establish an exclusive connection to my father's aircraft.

Looking back, I realize I shut down emotionally at age 17 when we received the news of his plane being shot down. There was very little communication in my family about what had happened. In contrast to the opinions of many survivors, I believe that throughout the past 30 years, the government has done an adequate job in sending us what information they could about my father. But I remember thinking at times that I wished they would leave us alone. Every time a brown manila envelope arrived in the mail from the Air Force, it would re-open wounds for me. For several years, I placed the envelopes, unopened, in a file. I did not want to deal with whatever might be in the envelopes because there was never good news about my father. As primary next of kin, annually I receive a Christmas card from the White House with its brief note (from the current president) about current MIA accountability issues. It is a bittersweet honor and an annual reminder of the loss of my father. It became easier to talk about my father after my mother's death. While she was alive, I felt that I had to watch what I said about him in order not to upset or anger her. Twenty-six years after his plane was shot down, for the first time, I talked with my sister and two brothers about what had happened to our father. I learned things about the perceptions of my siblings in relation to our father's loss that I never knew. The four of us are very close to one another now. With both parents gone, it is almost as if we are "parenting" one another.

When I conducted a literature review on parental death during childhood for an earlier paper, the most important thing I learned was the need to somehow honor and remember a parent who has died. I realized I had never done this. This led me to honor and remember my father in the following ways: on special occasions I fly a POW/MIA flag (available from U.S. Veteran Dispatch at 1-800-452-8906) along with an American flag; I took apart a long necklace of beads from Thailand that my father gave me and used the beads to make jewelry for people I care about; and on Veterans Day, I placed a photograph of my father in the local newspaper with a message saying "we remember you" and signed the names of his children.

The death of my mother and this study has helped me to reach a better understanding and acceptance of the loss of my father. It still hurts at times, and probably always will, but I am living more comfortably with the reality that I will probably never know, with certainty, what happened to my father. I have learned to live with ambiguity.

REFERENCES

Berkseth, J. K. (1988). Legacy of Vietnam. *Journal of Psychosocial Nursing, 26*(6), 24-27.

Boss, P. (1977). A clarification of the concept of psychological father presence in families experiencing ambiguity of boundary. *Journal of Marriage and the Family, 39,* 141-151.

Boss, P. (1991). Ambiguous loss. In F. Walsh & M. McGoldrick (Eds.), *Living beyond loss: Death in the family* (pp. 164-175). New York: W. W. Norton & Company.

Boss, P. (1999). *Ambiguous loss: Learning to live with unresolved grief.* Cambridge, MA: Harvard University Press.

Boss, P. G. (1980). The relationship of psychological father presence, wife's personal qualities and wife/family dysfunction in families of missing fathers. *Journal of Marriage and the Family, 42,* 541-549.

Dahl, B. B., McCubbin, H. I., & Lester, G. R. (1976). War-induced father absence: Comparing the adjustment of children in reunited, non-reunited and reconstituted families. *International Journal of Sociology of the Family, 6,* 99-108.

Dahl, B. B., McCubbin, H. I., & Ross, K. L. (1977). Second generational effects of war-induced separations: Comparing the adjustment of children in reunited and non-reunited families. *Military Medicine, 142*(42), 146-151.

Demi, A. S., & Schroeder. M. A. (1989). *Bereavement Experience Questionnaire: Development and testing.* Unpublished manuscript: Georgia State University, School of Nursing; Atlanta, Georgia.

Department of Defense POW/MIA Newsletter. (1996, Spring). Washington, DC: Defense Prisoner of War/Missing in Action Office.

Doyle, R. C. (1992). Unresolved mysteries: The myth of the missing warrior and the government deceit theme in the popular captivity culture of the Vietnam War. *Journal of American Culture, 15*(2), 1-18.

Guarnaccia, C. A., & Hayslip, B. (1998). Factor structure of the Bereavement Experience Questionnaire: The BEQ-24, a revised short form. *Omega, 37,* 303-316.

Hall, R. C., & Simmons, W. C. (1973). The POW wife: A psychiatric appraisal. *Archives of General Psychiatry, 29,* 690-694.

Henry, G. T. (1990). *Practical sampling—Applied social research methods series: Volume 21.* Newbury Park, California: Sage.

Hogancamp, V. E., & Figley, C. R. (1983). War: Bringing the battle home. In C. R. Figley & H. I. McCubbin (Eds.), *Stress and the family: Volume 2. Coping with catastrophe* (pp. 148-165). New York: Brunner/Mazel, Inc.

Horowitz, M. J. (1986). Stress-response syndromes: A review of posttraumatic and adjustment disorders. *Hospital and Community Psychiatry, 37,* 241-249.

Horowitz, M., Wilner, N., & Alvarez, W. (1979). Impact of Event Scale: A measure of subjective stress. *Psychosomatic Medicine, 41,* 209-218.

Horowitz, M. J., Field, N. P., & Classen, C. C. (1993). Stress response syndromes and their treatment. In L. Goldberger & S. Breznitz (Eds.), *Handbook of stress: Theoretical and clinical aspects* (pp. 757-773). New York: The Free Press.

Hunter, E. J. (1982). *Families under the flag: A review of military family literature.* New York: Praeger.

Hunter, E. J. (1983). Captivity: The family in waiting. In C. R. Figley & H. I. McCubbin (Eds.), *Stress and the family. Volume II: Coping with catastrophe* (pp. 166-184). New York: Brunner/Mazel.

Hunter, E. J. (1986). Families of prisoners of war held in Vietnam: A seven-year study. *Evaluation and Program Planning, 9,* 243-251.

Hunter, E. J. (1988). Long-term effects of parental wartime captivity on children: Children of POW and MIA servicemen. *Journal of Contemporary Psychotherapy, 18,* 312-328.

Hunter-King, E. J. (1998). Children of military personnel missing in action in Southeast Asia. In Y. Danieli (Ed.), *International handbook of multigenerational legacies of trauma* (pp. 243-256). New York: Plenum.

Hunter-King, E. J. (1993). Long-term effects on children of a parent missing in wartime. In F. W. Kaslow (Ed.), *The military family in peace and war* (pp. 48-65). New York: Springer.

Jensen, P. S. & Shaw, J. (1993). Children as victims of war: Current knowledge and future research needs. *Journal of the American Academy of Child and Adolescent Psychiatry, 32,* 697-708.

Lavee, Y., McCubbin, H., & Patterson, J. (1985). The double ABCX model of family stress and adaptation: An empirical test by analysis of structural equations with latent variables. *Journal of Marriage and the Family, 47,* 811-825.

Leonard, F. A. (1993). Prisoners of war, missing in action. In J. S. Olson (Ed.), *The Vietnam War: Handbook of the literature and research* (pp. 469-454). Westport, Connecticut: Greenwood Press.

McCubbin, H. I., & Dahl, B. B. (1976). Prolonged family separation in the military: A longitudinal study. In H. I. McCubbin, B. B. Dahl, & E. J. Hunter (Eds.),

Families in the military system. Beverly Hills, CA: Sage.

McCubbin, H. I., Dahl, B. B., Lester, G. R., Benson, D., & Robertson, M. L. (1976). Coping repertoires of families adapting to prolonged war-induced separations. *Journal of Marriage and the Family, 38,* 461-471.

McCubbin, H. I., Dahl, B. B., Lester, G. R., & Ross, B. (1977). The prisoner of war and his children: Evidence for the origin of second generational effects of captivity. *International Journal of Sociology of the Family, 7*(1), 25-36.

McCubbin, H. I., Hunter, E. J., & Dahl, B. B. (1975). Residuals of war: Families of prisoners of war and servicemen missing in action. *Journal of Social Issues, 31*(4), 95-109.

McCubbin, H. I., Hunter, E. J., & Metres, Jr., P. J. (1974a). Adaptation of the family to the POW/MIA experi-ence: An overview. In H. I. McCubbin, B. Dahl, P. Metres, Jr., E. Hunter, & J. Plag (Eds.), *Family sepa-ration and reunion: Families of prisoners of war and servicemen missing in action.* Washington, DC: U.S. Government Printing Office.

McCubbin, H. I., Hunter, E. J., & Metres, Jr., P. J. (1974b). Children in limbo. In H. I. McCubbin, B. Dahl, P. Metres, Jr., E. Hunter, & J. Plag (Eds.), *Family sepa-ration and reunion: Families of prisoners of war and servicemen missing in action.* Washington, DC: U.S. Government Printing Office.

McCubbin, M. A. (1993). Family stress theory and the development of nursing knowledge about family adaptation. In S. L. Feetham, S. B. Meister, J. M. Bell, & C. L. Gilliss (Eds.), *The nursing of families: Theory/research/education/practice* (pp. 46-58). Newbury Park: Sage.

McCubbin, M. A., & McCubbin, H. I. (1996). Resiliency in families: A conceptual model of family adjustment and adaptation in response to stress and crises. In H. I. McCubbin, A. I. Thompson, & M. A. McCubbin (Eds.), *Family assessment: Resiliency, coping and adaptation-inventories for research and practice* (pp. 1-64). Madison: University of Wisconsin System.

McCubbin, M. A., McCubbin, H. I., & Thompson, A. I. (1986). Family Hardiness Index (FHI). In H. I. McCubbin, A. I. Thompson, & M. A. McCubbin (Eds.), *Family assessment: Resiliency, coping and adaptation-inventories for research and practice* (pp. 239-305). Madison: University of Wisconsin System.

National League of Families of American Prisoners and Missing in Southeast Asia. (1998). Status of the POW/MIA issue: June 6, 1998. Washington, D.C.

Provost, P. K. (1989). Vietnam: Resolving the death of a loved one. *Archives of Psychiatric Nursing, 3*(1), 29-33.

Rando, T. A. (1993). *Treatment of complicated mourning.* Champaign, Illinois: Research Press.

SPSS, Inc. (1993). *SPSS base system syntax reference guide.* Old Tappans, NJ: Prentice-Hall Publishers.

Wertsch, M. E. (1991). *Military brats: Legacies of child-hood inside the fortress.* Bayside, New York: Aletheia Publications.

Zilberg, N. J., Weiss, D. S., & Horowitz, M. J. (1982). Impact of Event Scale: A cross-validation study and some empirical evidence supporting a conceptual model of stress response syndromes. *Journal of Consulting and Clinical Psychology, 50,* 407-414.

PART 6

FAMILY VALUES AND BELIEF SYSTEMS: INFLUENCES ON FAMILY STRESS MANAGEMENT

The article chosen to illustrate family values and beliefs comes from the field of transcultural psychiatry. Kirmayer, Boothroyd, Tanner, Adelson, and Robinson (2000) discuss the Cree of James Bay in Quebec and present a culturally sensitive epidemiological study that also includes a qualitative focus on family values and beliefs. With consideration for differences in gender and generation, they focus on health, recommending more tailor-made interventions rather than a universal strategy. When reading this article, note the high number of losses experienced by the Cree Indians in James Bay. Also note the association between spending more time "in the bush" and reporting less psychological distress depending on gender and age. Coping strategies used by the Cree such as spending time in the bush—hunting, fishing, and trapping; living outside in nature; relating spiritually to animals; eating traditional foods; and participating in traditional tribal activities—are rarely found on current coping questionnaires. It is hoped that this article will stimulate further research on cultural loss, an area of study akin to family stress but still lacking our attention. A question to ponder is whether getting back to or retaining cultural roots and some of the "old ways" might strengthen resilience for all families.

19

Psychological Distress Among the Cree of James Bay

Laurence J. Kirmayer
Lucy J. Boothroyd
Adrian Tanner
Naomi Adelson
Elizabeth Robinson

The object of this study was to identify potential risk and protective factors associated with psychological distress among the Cree of James Bay, through a secondary analysis of data on 1136 Cree (aged 15-85) from a random general population health survey in 1991. In multiple linear regression models, factors significantly associated with reporting more distress in the past week included: younger age, female gender, early loss of a parent or close relative, more life events in the year before the survey, a serious illness or drinking problem in the past year, ever having used cannabis, having more than elementary education, having fewer than five close friends/relatives and residing in an isolated or inland region. Having a good relationship with others in the community and spending more time in the bush were both associated with less distress. The relative importance of these factors varied across age/gender cohorts. We conclude that gender and generational differences should be considered when planning mental health promotion strategies for this population. In addition to more conventional approaches to reduce alcohol abuse, improve coping with loss and increase social support, targeted programs should be developed addressing the impact of education and role strain for women.

Reprinted by permission of Sage Publications from *Transcultural Psychiatry* 37 (2000): 35-56. Copyright © 2000 McGill University.

Introduction

Among Native peoples in North America, there is wide variation in the levels of mental health and illness in different nations and communities. Likely due to the effects of economic disparity, discrimination, loss of culture and even cultural genocide, some aboriginal groups show evidence of severe psychological distress (with high rates of depression, suicide, violence, alcoholism and substance abuse) (H. Armstrong, 1993; Kirmayer, 1994). Retention of traditional cultural practices has been related to well-being and community wellness in ethnographic studies (Adelson, 1998) but there are few epidemiological data that address these issues (Chandler & Lalonde, 1998).

In 1991, Santé Québec, a provincial health authority, conducted a large-scale survey in all the Cree communities in the James Bay region (Santé Québec, 1994). The survey included a series of 14 questions to assess level of psychological distress during the past week; a similar instrument was used in a general population survey carried out in Quebec in 1992. We used data from the 1991 survey to study the possible association of psychological distress level with a number of social factors identified from the literature, as well as from clinical and research experience. The factors included the following survey items: socio-demographic characteristics, alcohol and substance use variables, significant life events, participation in traditional activities, indicators of social support, and medical and psychiatric history. Given the recent history of the James Bay Cree, different age cohorts have had substantially different social experiences. Consequently, we repeated our global analyses for cohorts defined according to gender and age.

Background

The Cree of James Bay, who currently number about 13,500 persons (MSSS, 1999), live in nine communities in the subarctic northwestern region of Quebec, Canada (an area of about 3000 km^2). They represent about 25% of the total aboriginal population in Quebec (Atkinson & Magonet, 1990). Over a span of 250 years, the Cree have undergone radical transformations of their way of life. The Cree have lived in the James Bay region for at least 5000 years according to archeological records. Before the arrival of Europeans, they relied on hunting bear, caribou and other smaller game, with emphasis placed on self-sufficiency, oral tradition and extended family structure (Salisbury, 1986). Hunting followed a specific patterned use of resources with circular routes, which brought them back into contact with other family members (and later, traders at posts), most often in the summer. Sharing, acute sensitivity to natural cycles and systems, clear separation of roles along gender lines, and preservation of family and kinship were core traditional values. Hunting and fishing had significance at many levels—economic, cultural, social and spiritual (Tanner, 1979).

The arrival of European fur traders in the James Bay region in the late 1600s led to a trading relationship with the Cree and the establishment of company posts. Christian missions were set up in the region in the mid-1800s and later were in charge of residential schools; in the 1950s and 1960s many James Bay Cree were sent to residential schools in Ontario. Permanent villages were established and biomedical services were developed in the region, with a hospital being opened in one community in 1930. Settlement at trading post sites and living in close quarters led to epidemics of infectious diseases which caused many deaths in the first half of the twentieth century (Sturtevant, 1981; T. K. Young, 1994).

In 1975, the James Bay and Northern Quebec Agreement enabled vast hydroelectric development, with resultant flooding of traditional lands, in exchange for monetary compensation, a formal land claims settlement, provisions for environmental and traditional activity protection and a degree of Cree control of various sectors including education, health and social services (Salisbury, 1986). The Cree have continued to be politically active and have successfully challenged provincial government plans for further hydroelectric development. Local self-government of the Cree communities was legislated in 1984 with the Cree-Naskapi (of Quebec) Act.

The Cree population has been growing in size and is younger than the Quebec population as a whole; 35% of the James Bay Cree are under 15 years compared with 16% of the Quebec population, and the median age among the Cree is 20.8 (versus 34.2 for Quebec; Santé Québec, 1994). Currently, youth are educated within the communities through high school. There is some out-migration for employment or education outside the region, but a large proportion of those who leave for schooling return to their communities at a later time. The region has a mixed subsistence and wage economy, with three main groups: full-time hunters and trappers, full-time wage earners (employed either by Cree agencies or private companies), and those with casual or seasonal waged work. Hunting and living in the bush are important to all three of these groups.

Little has been published about mental health and illness among the Cree of the James Bay region (Prince, 1993). A study of mental health service use between 1986 and 1988 found that depression was the most common psychiatric illness, at 16.5%, among 242 Cree receiving help from nursing and medical personnel in the region (Lavallée, Robinson, & Laverdure, 1991). When gender-specific rates were examined, depression remained the most common problem for females, while alcohol abuse was the most prevalent for males. Only 13% of Cree trappers and hunters received mental health services although they make up 35% of the population. This observation could reflect either lower rates of mental health problems in this group or simply lower use of services. The study did not allow any conclusions to be made about the prevalence of psychiatric problems in the general population.

Unlike many other aboriginal populations in Canada, including some other Cree and Ojibway groups, the James Bay Cree have a suicide rate no higher than that among non-aboriginal Canadians (Kirmayer, 1994; Petawabano, Gourdeau, Jourdain, Palliser-Tulugak, & Cossette, 1994). Studies of completed suicides during 1975-1981 (Robinson, 1985) and 1982-1986 (Courteau, 1989) did not find greater mortality among the James Bay Cree, nor do death statistics from 1982-1991 (Barss, 1998a), which showed that one person completed

suicide each year on average. The 10-year study did find about eight times as many hospitalizations for suicide attempts as deaths, and estimated that as many as 18 other attempts could have occurred for each hospitalized case. A general population survey carried out in the region in 1991 found that 5% of respondents reported suicidal thoughts in their lifetime and 4% reported a previous suicide attempt (Santé Québec, 1994); when age-standardized, the prevalence of attempts was not statistically different from that for the rest of Quebec in a 1987 survey, and the prevalence of ideation was significantly lower. The 10-year study by Barss (1998b), however, found that James Bay Cree, who are more likely to have guns in their homes than other Canadians, were 2.5 times more likely to die and nine times more likely to be hospitalized from a gunshot wound than the general Quebec population. Firearm-related injuries included suicides and attempts, homicides and assaults, and unintentional shootings. It is not clear whether these statistics reflect a higher level of violence in the region or can be accounted for by the greater accessibility to guns. Deaths from injuries were significantly higher among the James Bay Cree than in the general Quebec population for the period 1987-1992, particularly in the case of drownings and motor vehicle accidents (Saint-Pierre, 1995).

METHOD

Sample

Data for this study came from the Santé Québec Health Survey among the Cree of James Bay. This survey was designed to collect data on the physical, psychological and social health of the Cree population in the region, which numbered 1716 private households and about 9300 persons in 1991. The survey methods are described in detail elsewhere (Santé Québec, 1994). Briefly, 400 households in nine communities were sampled during the summer of 1991. The sample was stratified in proportion to the size of the individual communities; in each community, systematic sampling was then carried out using the list of household addresses. Of the 400 households approached, a total of 354

(1999 persons) agreed to participate in the survey. Permission to conduct secondary analysis of the data was obtained from both Santé Québec and the Cree Board of Health and Social Services of James Bay (the Cree institution responsible for health care in the region). To ensure anonymity for respondents from these small communities, we received a dataset from which community identification had been removed. Data were available for 1136 persons 15 years of age and older who answered the confidential questionnaire containing the psychological distress items.

Measures

The instruments used by Santé Québec included an interviewer-assisted confidential questionnaire for those aged 15 years and older, a face-to-face interview with an individual questionnaire for those aged 15 years and older, and a face-to-face household questionnaire for a designated adult respondent. The health survey was translated into Cree in as standardized a manner as possible for use with unilingual Cree-speakers. All of the interviewers were Cree and the survey instruments were administered in the respondent's choice of English or Cree (or both).

Psychological Distress. The measure of psychological distress was based on a 14-item index adapted by Santé Québec from the Ilfeld Psychiatric Symptom Index (Boyer, Préville, Légaré, & Valois, 1993; Ilfeld, 1976). The Santé Québec (1994) index contained 14 statements addressing psychological symptoms experienced in the previous week (Figure 19.1). The distress measure was subjected to focus group discussion with representatives of the Cree community to test its content validity (Santé Québec, 1994); however, the only adaptation made to the index was the rewording of one question ('how often have you felt lonely?' was replaced with 'how often have you felt like being alone?').[1]

Each item had four possible responses coded as: 0 = never, 1 = once in a while, 2 = fairly often and 3 = very often. The index score was calculated by summing the responses to the questions answered, dividing the sum by the number of questions

answered multiplied by a factor of 3 (the highest response value), and then multiplying this result by 100. The valid score thus ranged from a minimum of 0 to a maximum of 100. Reliability and factor analysis of these items among the Cree respondents showed high internal consistency (Cronbach's alpha = 0.94), with one factor accounting for 54.7% of the variance. In terms of validation of the index, significant positive associations were found between psychological distress level and previous suicidal ideation, previous suicide attempt, stress level associated with a number of significant life events in the past year and feeling 'not too happy' at the time of the survey.

Socio-demographic Characteristics. 'Unemployed' included those collecting unemployment insurance or welfare, as well as those who specified that they were 'unemployed,' 'looking for a job,' 'out of school' or '[doing] nothing.' Persons attending school, retired persons and homemakers were not considered as unemployed. 'Working full- or part-time' included those with full-time, part-time or occasional work, as well as the self-employed and hunters/trappers receiving income security.

Although individual community identification was removed from the dataset, Santé Québec classified the respondents according to whether they resided in one of the four inland communities or one of the five coastal communities of James Bay. Secondly, the respondents were classified according to whether they resided in an isolated region not accessible by road except in winter in some cases or in a nonisolated area accessible by road throughout the year. Each of the four inland communities is road-accessible and nonisolated; one of the coastal communities is also accessible by road. The educational level of each respondent was coded in a dichotomous manner to indicate those with primary (elementary) school education or no formal schooling versus those with at least some secondary school education.

Alcohol and Substance Use. A respondent was considered to have had a drinking problem in the past year if he/she reported at least one incident resulting from alcohol use in the previous 12 months (includ-

In the past week, did you . . .

- feel hopeless about the future
- have your mind go blank
- feel down or blue
- feel tense or under pressure
- lose your temper
- feel bored or have little interest in things
- feel fearful or afraid
- have trouble remembering things
- cry easily or feel like crying
- feel nervous or shaky inside
- feel critical of others
- feel easily annoyed or irritated
- get angry over things that are not too important
- feel like being alone

Figure 19.1   Items in the Psychological Distress Measure

ing failure to carry out personal duties at school or work, health problems or injury, drunk driving, hospitalization or admittance to a treatment center, and social or relationship problems) *and* answered 'yes' to at least two of the following questions: (i) 'Have you had a drink first thing in the morning to calm nerves or a hangover in the past year?' (ii) 'Have you ever been criticized by people around you because of your drinking?' (iii) 'Have you ever felt you should cut down on your drinking?' (iv) 'Have you ever felt bad/guilty about your drinking?' These four questions form the CAGE index, used to identify drinkers at risk for alcohol dependence, and previously implemented in the 1987 Santé Québec survey (Mayfield, McLeod, & Hall, 1974).

With respect to substance use, respondents were asked whether they had ever used cocaine or crack (labeled as 'cocaine' in Tables 19.1-19.4) and marijuana or hashish ('cannabis' in Tables 19.1-19.4). They were also asked if they had ever tried to 'get high' by sniffing glue, gasoline or any other solvents ('solvents' in Tables 19.1-19.4). These three variables were coded in a dichotomous manner: whether the substance had ever been consumed or not.

Significant Life Events. Respondents were asked if they had experienced any of six different significant life events in the previous 12 months: a move away from family, loss of a job, rejection or disapproval from the community, death of a spouse, death of someone else 'very close' to the respondent, or a serious physical or mental illness in a household member. Early loss was represented by the experience of the death of a parent or close family member when the respondent was a child, under the age of 12 years.

Participation in Traditional Activities. Respondents were asked how many weeks they had spent in the bush in the past year.

Social Support. Participants were asked 'Other than on special occasions, such as weddings, funerals or baptisms, how often did you attend services or meetings connected with your religion in the past 12 months?' Those who responded with 'at least once a week' or 'at least once a month' were classified as regular church attenders. It should be pointed out that this question did not explicitly ask about traditional and spiritual healing practices.

In response to the question 'How would you describe your relationship with other people in your community?' the following options were available: 'very satisfactory,' 'somewhat satisfactory,' 'somewhat unsatisfactory' and 'very unsatisfactory.' Respondents were considered to have a good relationship with the community if they answered 'very satisfactory.' The number of people (friends or family members) to whom the respondent could turn if he/she needed help or had a problem was retained in the dichotomous format used by Santé Québec, namely 0-4 persons versus 5 or more persons.

Medical and Psychiatric History. Data on chronic medical illness and psychiatric problems came from the household questionnaire answered by an adult representative. A chronic medical illness in an individual's lifetime included having any one of a list of 23 health problems, such as anemia, allergies, arthritis or rheumatism, cancer, diabetes, digestive problems, heart disease, hearing troubles, incapacity due to being overweight and migraine or recurring headaches. A lifetime psychiatric symptom or problem included having experienced any of the following: depression, periods of excessive nervousness or irritability, periods of confusion or memory loss, hearing voices, having visions or being afraid without reason for 6 months or more, or believing his/her mind was affected by a curse.

Data Analysis

Differences in means between two independent groups were tested with the Student's *t*-test. A Pearson correlation coefficient was calculated for the association between two continuous variables. Simple linear regression models containing one independent variable were used to measure the association between possible risk or protective factors and psychological distress (the dependent variable) in terms of a beta coefficient. To determine which variables to include in subsequent multivariate models for the age/gender cohorts, a less restrictive *p*-value of .10 or less (two-tailed) was used to indicate a statistically significant result. Multivariate linear regression was used to identify the factors that were most strongly associated with the level of psychological distress. Stepwise backward selection was used to eliminate non-significant independent variables from the regression models. Interpretation of results was aided by extensive ethnographic fieldwork in the region by Adelson and Tanner guided by the epidemiological research findings, as well as by discussions with

representatives of the Public Health Module—Cree Region.

RESULTS

Table 19.1 describes the characteristics of the study sample. We present unadjusted frequencies for the 1136 respondents included in our study; weighted population frequencies have been reported previously by Santé Québec in their survey report, and differed only by 1.3% on average (minimum: 0.1%, maximum: 3.2%) from our figures (Santé Québec, 1994). Continuous variables are not included in Table 19.1, but are described below.

The average age of the respondents was 33.1 years (± 15.3). Forty-seven percent of the study subjects reported at least one significant life event in the last year including: death of a spouse or close friend/family member (27%); moving away from their family (13%); serious illness in the household (10%); rejection/disapproval from the community (7%); or losing their job (3%). The number of persons in the household varied from a minimum of two to a maximum of 13 with an average of 6.5 persons (± 2.5). The average number of weeks spent in the bush in the past year was 8.5 (± 10.8); for those who spent at least some time in the bush (81% of the study sample), the total number of weeks varied from 0.5 to 48 weeks with an average of 9.6 (± 11.0).

A total of 21 factors were selected from the questionnaire items and analyzed with respect to psychological distress level for the 1111 subjects who answered all 14 of the distress questions. Table 19.2 presents the results of regression analyses, with psychological distress level as the dependent variable. A large number of factors was significant in simple linear regression models. Although the substantial number of factors studied increases the possibility of falsely positive tests, the use of a restrictive Bonferroni correction to the significance levels (where the corrected *p*-value = .05/21 or .0024) still resulted in 11 statistically significant results.

For the 833 persons with complete data, all of the factors were entered as independent variables in a multivariate linear regression model, with

Table 19.1 Characteristics of the Study Sample (*n* = 1136)

	% (unadjusted)
Gender (% female)	52.0
Married or common-law	54.4
Occupational status	
Student	4.5
Working full- or part-time	67.2
Homemaker	13.4
Retired	2.1
Unemployed/welfare	10.7
More than elementary education	68.0
Resides in inland region	33.6
Resides in isolated region	34.7
Attended church less than once a month in past year	52.8
Alcohol and drug use	
Drinking problem in past year	28.3
Used cannabis in lifetime	38.2
Used cocaine in lifetime	7.4
Used solvents in lifetime	10.2
Serious illness in past year	6.2
Chronic medical illness in lifetime*	39.0
Psychiatric problem in lifetime*	3.1
Death of a close relative when under 12 years old	57.4
Good relationship with community	46.0
Has five or more friends	41.0

* According to household respondent.

psychological distress level as the dependent variable. Backward selection was used to remove all nonsignificant independent variables (*p* > .05) in a stepwise manner. The reduced model, which contained 12 independent variables, explained 28% of the variance in level of distress. The following variables were associated with a higher level of psychological distress (*p* < .05): female gender, having more than elementary (primary) education, residing in an inland region, residing in an isolated region, having a drinking problem in the past year, use of cannabis in lifetime, death of a close relative when a child, having fewer than five friends (i.e., close contacts) and a greater number of life events in the past year. Age, type of relationship with others in the community and time in the bush were negatively associated

with psychological distress; older age, having a good relationship with the community and more time spent in the bush in the past year were associated with a lower level of distress.

Following the above analysis on the entire sample, the study sample was divided into eight groups by gender and age (15-24 years, 25-44 years, 45-64 years or 65 years and older). Table 19.3 shows the results of bivariate analyses carried out with 19 factors (no age or gender variables) in each of the eight groups or cohorts. The cells of the table present, for dichotomous factors, the percentage of persons with each attribute listed; for continuous variables, the Pearson correlation coefficient is presented.

The factors found to be significant in the bivariate tests were analyzed further with multivariate linear

Table 19.2   Results of Simple and Multivariate Regression Analyses on Entire Sample

Factors	Simple Regression	Multivariate regression (reduced model[a])		
	n = 1111	n = 833		
	β	β	SE	p-value
Age	−.31‡	−.89[b]	.041	.03
Female gender	2.30†	2.82	.91	.002
Single	4.27‡			
Unemployed	4.23†			
More than elementary education	9.91‡	5.93	1.34	< .001
Resides in inland region	2.58†	4.39	1.12	< .001
Resides in isolated region	NS	3.77	1.11	< .001
Attended church less than once a month in past year	3.19‡			
Drinking problem in past year	8.89‡	4.83	1.06	< .001
Used cannabis in lifetime	8.21‡	2.10	1.07	.05
Used cocaine in lifetime	6.54‡			
Used solvents in lifetime	8.36‡			
Serious illness in past year	4.99†			
Chronic medical illness in lifetime[c]	−2.83†			
Psychiatric problem in lifetime[c]	NS			
Death of a close relative when under 12 years old	NS	2.04		.03
Good relationship with community	−7.53‡	−3.61		< .001
Has fewer than five friends	1.63*	2.36		.009
Number of significant life events in past year	3.44‡	2.82[d]		< .001
Number of persons in household	NS			
Number of weeks spent in the bush in past year	−.29‡	−1.07[e]		.004
Constant	NA	23.02	3.34	< .001
				$R^2 = .28$

NA, not applicable; NS not significant; *$p < .10$; †$p < .01$; ‡$p < .001$.

a. β, SE (standard error of β), and p noted only if significant.
b. For each increase of 10 years.
c. According to household respondent.
d. For each additional life event.
e. For each increase of 8 weeks.

regression models. Owing to the small numbers, the two groups of persons aged 65 years and older were not included in this analysis. For each of the six remaining age/gender cohorts, all of the significant factors in Table 19.3 (with $p \leq .10$) were included as independent variables in regression models, except if the attribute was present in < 5% of the respondents. In addition, three factors of interest (number of life events in the past year, educational level and number of weeks spent in the bush) were included as independent variables in each full model, regardless of their bivariate significance level, since it is possible

that an association could be masked in the bivariate analysis. Stepwise backward selection was used to remove nonsignificant independent variables, resulting in reduced models.

Table 19.4 presents the reduced models for each cohort. For males 15-24 years old, four factors were independently associated with psychological distress level. Having experienced while a child the death of a close relative and having fewer than five close friends or relatives were both associated with an increase in psychological distress level. Each additional life event experienced in the year before

Table 19.3   Summary of Bivariate Analysis in Each Age/Gender Cohort: Association Between Psychosocial and Socio-Demographic Factors and Level of Psychological Distress

| Factor | Percentage of Respondents With Factor or Pearson Correlation coefficient ($r =$) | | | | | | | |
| | 15-24 Years | | 25-44 Years | | 45-64 Years | | 65 Years and Older | |
	Males $n = 194$	Females $n = 228$	Males $n = 228$	Females $n = 228$	Males $n = 97$	Females $n = 109$	Males $n = 26$	Females $n = 26$
Single	83	75*	32	24	8.3	22	19	54
Unemployed	16	16	10	7.8	5.2	6.5	0	0
More than elementary education	90*	93†	78	77	20§	13§	3.8	0
Resides in inland region	37	32	31	32†	33	42*	35	38
Resides in isolated region	29	34‡	35	33	38	33	50	46
Attended church less than once a month in past year	68	51	58	36	28	21	19	32
Drinking problem in past year	54†	35§	37§	13‡	14	8.3	7.7	3.8
Used cannabis in lifetime	41	52‡	59‡	31§	4.2‡	2.9§	0	0
Used cocaine in lifetime	12*	8.6	17*	2.4*	0	0	0	0
Used solvents in lifetime	20*	19‡	11	5.7	0	0	0	0
Serious illness in past year	8†	7.6‡	5.0	5.1	7.3	4.6	15	0
Chronic medical illness in lifetime[a]	16	26	28	45	47	74	50	85
Psychiatric problem in lifetime[a]	1.1	1.8	0	4.1	6.2	11	0	3.8
Death of a close relative when under 12 years old	52§	58§	59	52	80	81	64	77
Good relationship with community	42‡	36‡	44§	44	70†	65§	77	54
Has fewer than five friends	50†	60†	40	57	52	60	67	88
Number of life events in past year	$r = .27$§	$r = .33$§	$r = .09$	$r = .15$†	$r = .23$†	$r = -.14$	$r = -.05$	$r = .56$‡
Number of persons in household	$r = -.04$	$r = -.004$	$r = -.09$	$r = -.08$	$r = -.15$	$r = -.08$	$r = .14$	$r = -.008$
Number of weeks spent in the bush in past year	$r = -.12$	$r = -.09$	$r = -.13$*	$r = -.11$	$r = -.28$‡	$r = -.09$	$r = .14$	$r = .02$

*$p \leq .10$; †$p \leq .05$; ‡$p \leq .01$; §$p \leq .001$ for the comparison of psychological distress level in those with the factor versus those without the factor or the correlation between psychological distress level and a count (mean level of distress higher for those with the factor indicated for all significant comparisons except where a negative correlation coefficient was observed).
a. According to household respondent.

Table 19.4   Results of Multivariate Regression Analyses in Age/Gender Cohorts

Significant Factors in Reduced Model	Beta Coefficient	Significance Level
Males, 15-24 years	$N = 140$	adj. $R^2 = 18.0$
Death of a close relative when under 12 years old	6.62	.005
Good relationship with community	−4.67	.041
Has fewer than five friends	4.70	.038
Number of significant life events in past year	4.46	.001
Number of weeks spent in the bush in past year	−1.54	.087
Other factors in full model: more than elementary education, drinking problem in past year, used cocaine in lifetime, used solvents in lifetime, serious illness in past year		
Females, 15-24 years	$N = 167$	adj. $R^2 = 26.1$
Death of a close relative when under 12 years old	6.04	.010
Good relationship with community	−4.26	.078
Has fewer than five friends	7.11	.002
Number of significant life events in past year	5.24	< .001
More than elementary education	8.51	.056
Resides in isolated region	6.50	.010
Drinking problem in past year	6.09	.014
Other factors in full model: single, used cannabis in lifetime, used solvents in lifetime, serious illness in past year, number of weeks spent in the bush in past year		
Males, 25-44 years	$N = 200$	adj. $R^2 = 12.0$
Drinking problem in past year	6.27	.001
Good relationship with community	−5.64	.003
Number of weeks spent in the bush in past year	−1.29	.074
Other factors in full model: more than elementary education, used cannabis in lifetime, used cocaine in lifetime, number of significant life events in past year		
Females, 25-44 years	$N = 194$	adj. $R^2 = 11.6$
Drinking problem in past year	7.76	.012
More than elementary education	4.36	.079
Resides in inland region	3.98	.083
Used cannabis in lifetime	6.48	.003
Other factors in full model: number of life events in past year, number of weeks spent in bush in past year		
Males, 45-64 years	$N = 94$	adj. $R^2 = 18.9$
More than elementary education	8.95	< .001
Good relationship with community	−4.63	.019
Other factors in full model: drinking problem in past year, number of significant life events in past year		

(continued)

Table 19.4 (continued)

Significant Factors in Reduced Model	Beta Coefficient	Significance Level
Females, 45-64 years	$N = 101$	adj. $R^2 = 15.3$
More than elementary education	8.64	.010
Good relationship with community	−7.78	< .001
Other factors in full model: resides in inland region, drinking problem in past year, number of significant life events in past year, number of weeks spent in the bush in past year		

the survey was associated with an increase of 4.5 units in distress level. Having a good relationship with others in the community was associated with significantly less distress. In addition, there was a trend for the number of weeks spent in the bush in the past year to be negatively associated with distress, so that each additional 8 weeks in the bush decreased distress level by 1.5 units.

For females 15-24 years old, a similar pattern was seen with early loss, having fewer close friends/relatives and a greater number of life events being associated with more distress. Unlike males in this age group, time spent in the bush did not remain in the reduced model for females, and there were additional significant associations: distress level increased by 6.5 units for those residing in an isolated region and by 6.1 units for those with a drinking problem. Having more than elementary education was associated with more distress with a *p*-value of .056.

The two groups of 25–44-year-olds in the multivariate analyses were similar in that a drinking problem was associated with more psychological distress for both genders. As for the younger cohorts, there was a trend for more time spent in the bush to be associated with lower levels of distress for males, while more education was correlated with higher levels of distress for females. Having a good relationship with others in the community was significantly associated with less distress for males. Distress level was higher for those females who reported using cannabis in their lifetime. Residing in the inland region also tended to be correlated with more distress for females.

For the 45–64-year-old age group a strong association was found for both genders between

having at least some secondary education and higher psychological distress, and between having a good relationship with others in the community and lower distress. None of the other factors considered for these analyses were significant in the reduced models.

DISCUSSION

This secondary analysis of respondents in the Santé Québec Cree survey identified personal and social factors associated with psychological distress. When the sample as a whole ($N = 833$ with complete data) was analyzed in a multivariate linear regression model (controlling for age and gender), the following factors were significantly associated with reporting greater distress in the past week: younger age, female gender, having more than elementary education, residing in an inland region, residing in an isolated region, having a drinking problem in the past year, ever having used cannabis, early loss of a close relative, not having a good relationship with the community, having fewer than five close friends/relatives, having had more significant life events in the year before the survey and spending less time in the bush in the past year. Although it is clear that other factors, not tested here, could play a role in determining psychological distress, the multivariate model explained 28% of the variation in distress level.

The association of psychological distress with female gender, early loss, life events and lack of social support is consistent with much previous research on these factors in other populations. The gender association may be partly due to a reluctance to disclose distress among males which is a feature both of Cree culture and the larger North American society (Darnell, 1981). The effect of early loss was observed only for those aged 15-24. This may reflect a recency effect either in memory or impact of events. The negative effect of drinking problems was found particularly for younger females, and for males and females aged 25-44. The protective effects of social support cut across age groups. The higher level of distress among the young and the associations with a higher level of education and less time in the bush are distinctive for this population and require further comment.

The higher levels of distress among Cree youth parallel similar findings on distress with other Canadian aboriginal groups (Kirmayer, 1994; Petawabano et al., 1994). In many communities, youth face a great discrepancy between the world portrayed in the mass media, expectations placed on them by elders and the options open to them locally. There are few wage-earning jobs and many obstacles to pursuing higher education. Cultural transmission from elders has been disrupted, leaving youth without a clear sense of identity and direction to their lives (Wintrob & Sindell, 1972). These problems, which have had devastating effects in some communities, may be mitigated for the Cree by very active signs of cultural revitalization and political empowerment.

The association between spending more time in the bush and reporting less psychological distress was observed in both bivariate and multivariate analyses with the whole sample of respondents. When the sample was divided into age/gender cohorts, this association appeared to be more relevant for males between the ages of either 15 and 24 or 25 and 44. Although female respondents also spent time in the bush (and, in fact, 16% of them were trappers by occupation), going to the bush, particularly for extended periods, is more common among male James Bay Cree. The average length of time spent in the bush by the male respondents was 10.9 weeks versus 8.3 weeks for the females ($p < .001$). Of the 124 persons who reported that they did not spend any time in the bush in the year before the survey, 67% were female and 76% had more than elementary education. Thus, men are

more likely to experience whatever beneficial effects are associated with time in the bush. Also, men's and women's experience in the bush tends to differ in that men are primarily concerned with hunting while women are in charge of preparation of the meat (and other foods) which may be time-consuming and physically challenging.

The income-security program for Cree hunters and trappers is a unique system that was set up to subsidize traditional land use and allow families to continue living on their traditional hunting grounds, as part of the James Bay and Northern Quebec Agreement in 1975. Participants must maintain a long-term pattern of going to the bush and spend a minimum number of days on the land each year. However, the Cree do not go into the bush solely to obtain an income, in terms of furs for trade and meat for subsistence. Bush living is a valued activity in itself that involves the extended family as a whole. The Cree of the James Bay region are noteworthy among northern aboriginal peoples in the degree to which entire families still go to the bush. The school calendar is arranged so that hunting breaks, particularly the spring 'goose break,' are at a time most advantageous for families to get together in hunting camps.[2]

Most Cree agencies shut down during the hunting breaks to allow their employees to spend time in the bush. The Cree sharing ethic means that employees living in the villages obtain bush food, and provide the full-time hunters some of the things needed in the bush that require cash.[3] Full-time employees tend to have the equipment that allows them access to the bush; a number of them spend evenings, weekends and vacation in bush camps, often visiting those of relatives or friends who are income-security recipients. Seasonal or casual laborers also tend to spend time in the bush when there is no work available.

A large part of bush life involves contact with nature, spiritual relations with animals, consumption of valued foods and participation in other traditional activities. Increased time in the bush may confer mental health benefits by increasing family solidarity and social support, reinforcing cultural identity, improving physical health with nutritious bush foods and exercise, or providing respite from the pressures of settlement life. Alternatively, individuals who are less distressed may find it easier (physically, economically and socially) to participate in bush life.

Another possible mental health benefit of time in the bush for those who have a history of abuse problems may be the degree to which access to alcohol and other substances is limited. While it is possible to carry these substances to the bush, or even to manufacture home brew, a different ethic that limits substance use is generally in effect in the bush. Similarly, while living in the bush does not prevent family violence, it does establish a situation in which people are much more aware of the behavior of everyone else in the group; violence may thus be more readily discouraged by social pressures than it is in the villages.

Surprisingly, having had at least some secondary education was significantly associated with more psychological distress in the entire sample. Education may increase expectations for employment that are difficult to meet in the Cree context. Alternatively, those with more education may tend to have more stressful jobs, perhaps because they involve longer working hours, travel away from the family or are less traditional careers. We examined whether being a 'professional' could account for the education/distress relationship, by entering an occupation variable in the final age/gender cohort models containing the education variable. In each case, the education variable retained a similar beta coefficient as in a model not containing the occupation variable, and the occupation variable did not achieve statistical significance. The only age/gender group for whom the occupation factor approached significance was females aged 45-64, where being a professional increased distress level by 6.9 units with a *p*-value of .091. For this group, then, occupation may play a role but it does not explain the association of distress with higher education.

Across each age/gender cohort analyzed with multivariate regression, the education factor appeared to be more relevant for the female groups. It is possible that having a higher education leads to distress due to the additional pressures placed on women to fulfill job/career aspirations and financial responsibilities, at the same time as having children and being in charge of a household. Cree women tend to start families at a young age and even those who work continue to carry the major burden of domestic tasks.

This explanation would account for the negative impact of education in women aged 15-44; however, the association between higher education and psychological distress was significant for both males and females in the 45-64 age group, suggesting that factors other than the strain of multiple roles may be important for this group.

The effect of education on distress may also reflect a cohort effect. Men and women 45-64 years of age who had at least some secondary school education likely attended residential schools. In addition to prolonged and often painful separations from their families, they may have suffered systematic devaluation and suppression of their language and culture (Miller, 1996). Recent literature has documented the harsh conditions in many of these schools, including a high prevalence of physical and sexual abuse (Haig-Brown, 1988; Knockwood, 1992; Royal Commission on Aboriginal Peoples, 1996). Exposure to this environment may have long-term effects and may account, in part, for the association between a history of more education and higher levels of emotional distress. Unfortunately, the survey did not include questions about residential school experience so this interpretation remains conjecture.

We found some regional differences in levels of distress but these are difficult to interpret. Living inland (as opposed to in coastal communities) and in a relatively isolated community (as opposed to a community with access by road) were both significantly associated with distress in the multivariate analysis of the whole sample. Women aged 15-24 in an isolated region reported more distress, which may reflect feelings of entrapment, frustration or boredom related to the lack of year-long road access. For women aged 25-44, distress was more closely related to living in an inland region. All of the villages in the inland region are also 'non-isolated' (that is, accessible by road all year). The proximity of the road to larger non-Native towns with bars could in part contribute to increased stress among women aged 25-44 whose male spouses may access these urban centers for drinking. It is also possible that these differences do not reflect any consistent geographical effect but variations in level of distress in a few communities due to other local social circumstances. Communities differ in their political structure, religious activities and social problems.

This study has important limitations that stem from the design of the original survey. The index of psychological distress provides only an indirect measure of psychiatric disorder in a population (Santé Québec, 1994; Perrault, 1987). The only measure of psychiatric history used in the Santé Québec survey was a small number of questions about problems experienced by each household member which were answered by the household respondent. Other personal and social factors that could have an impact on distress were absent from the survey, such as drinking by parents and other family members, spousal abuse and fragmented caregiver history (i.e., multiple home placements). The measure of distress was not culturally adapted and its sensitivity to the range of expression of distress across gender and age cohorts is unknown (Manson, Shore, & Bloom, 1985; O'Nell, 1996; Timpson et al., 1988). The survey did not examine other traditional pursuits besides time in the bush (e.g., healing practices, dream interpretation) which may also have importance (Prince, 1993; Tanner, 1979; D. E. Young, 1989). The cross-sectional nature of the data should be kept in mind when interpreting the results since both the independent and dependent variables were collected at one point in time. However, the psychological distress measure referred to the past week only and most of the independent factors reflected longstanding or prior characteristics.

These findings have implications for mental health promotion among the Cree of James Bay. The differences in factors contributing to distress across age and gender suggest that an approach targeted to specific age/gender cohorts is needed. Further qualitative research may clarify the observed association between higher education and more distress for younger females (15-24 and 25-44 years old) and identify the specific challenges faced by these women. Interviews with women from the two age-groups represented, preferably linked to the development of mental health promotion strategies, should address what level of stress they are experiencing, how they are dealing with their everyday lives, and whether they have developed any stress reduction tactics of their own. Qualitative research may also clarify the role of time in the bush in modulating psychological distress.

Conventional mental health promotion programs, such as those that serve to help people overcome addictions, are needed in the James Bay region (Kirmayer, Boothroyd, Laliberté, & Laronde Simpson, 1999; Mrazek & Haggerty, 1994; Tudor, 1996). Programs that make living in the bush more accessible appear to have been beneficial for the mental health of some individuals. The income-security program has likely been important in reducing the level of psychological distress among older adults, especially men, but living in the bush may not be effective for everyone. There is a wide range of different lifestyles and attitudes toward waged work, bush life and education in the communities. Accordingly, it is important that mental health promotion includes programs that provide a range of options for making life in the villages more satisfactory, or for allowing work or pursuit of educational opportunities outside the villages. Innovative programs could be developed for specific age and gender groups using qualitative research methods.

ACKNOWLEDGMENTS

This work was supported by grants from the Conseil québécois de la recherche sociale and the Fonds de la recherche en santé du Québec. We thank Santé Québec and the Cree Board of Health and Social Services of James Bay for their collaboration. We also thank Robert Imrie, Jill Torrie, and especially Caroline Oblin for valuable feedback on this article.

NOTES

1. The reason for this change was unclear and would seem to shift the meaning of the item from predominantly sadness or distress to irritability and social withdrawal (cp. O'Nell, 1996).

2. During the school year children stay in the community, often living with relatives while their parents are in the bush.

3. Depending on the community of residence and family ties, a person's traditional hunting grounds may be a considerable distance away from his or her home. The costs of transportation and hunting/camping equipment can limit some people's access to the bush.

REFERENCES

Adelson, N. (1998). Health beliefs and the politics of Cree well-being. *Health, 2*(1), 5-22.

Armstrong, I. E., Robinson, E. J., & Gray-Donald, K. (1998). Prevalence of low and high birthweight among the James Bay Cree of Northern Quebec. *Canadian Journal of Public Health, 89*(6), 419-420.

Atkinson, H. B., & Magonet, G. (Eds.). (1990). *The James Bay experience: A guide for health professionals working among the Crees of northern Quebec.* Quebec, Canada: Government of Quebec.

Barss, P. (1998a). *Suicide and parasuicide among the Cree of eastern James Bay, Canada: Circumstances and prevention.* Montreal, Canada: Cree Board of Health & Social Services of James Bay and Régie régionale de la santé et des services sociaux.

Barss, P. (1998b). *Injuries from guns in Cree communities of Eeyou Istchee, Quebec, Canada: A ten year study.* Montreal, Canada: Cree Board of Health & Social Services of James Bay and Régie régionale de la santé et des services sociaux.

Boyer, R., Préville, M., Légaré, G., & Valois, P. (1993). La détresse psychologique dans la population du Québec non institutionnalisée: résultats normatifs de l'enquête Santé Québec. *Revue canadienne de psychiatrie, 38,* 339-343.

Chandler, M. J., & Lalonde, C. (1998). Cultural continuity as a hedge against suicide in Canada's First Nations. *Transcultural Psychiatry, 35*(2), 191-219.

Courteau, J.-P. (1989). *Mortality among the James Bay Cree of northern Quebec: 1982-1986.* MSc thesis, Department of Epidemiology and Biostatistics. Montreal, Canada: McGill University.

Darnell, R. (1981). Taciturnity in Native American etiquette: A Cree case. *Culture, 1*(2), 55-60.

Haig-Brown, C. (1988). *Resistance and renewal: Surviving the Indian residential school.* Vancouver, Canada: Tillacum Library.

Ilfeld, F. W. (1976). Further validation of a psychiatric symptom index in a normal population. *Psychological Reports, 39,* 1215-1228.

Kirmayer, L. J. (1994). Suicide among Canadian Aboriginal peoples. *Transcultural Psychiatric Research Review, 31*(1), 3-58.

Kirmayer, L. J., Boothroyd, L. J., Laliberté, A., & Laronde Simpson, B. (1999). *Suicide prevention and mental health promotion in First Nations and Inuit communities* (Report No. 9). Montreal, Canada: Culture & Mental Health Research Unit, Institute of Community & Family Psychiatry, Sir Mortimer B. Davis—Jewish General Hospital.

Knockwood, I. (1992). *Out of the depths: The experiences of Mi'kmaw children at the Indian residential school at Shubenacadie, Nova Scotia.* Lockeport, Canada: Roseway Publishing.

Lavallée, C., Robinson, E., & Laverdure, J. (1991). Description de la clientèle et des services de santé mentale au sein de la population crie du nord québécois. *Santé Culture Health, 8*(3), 265-284.

Manson, S. M., Shore, J. H., & Bloom, J. D. (1985). The depressive experience in American Indian communities: A challenge for psychiatric theory and diagnosis. In A. M. Kleinman & B. Good (Eds.), *Culture and depression* (pp. 331-368). Berkeley: University of California Press.

Mayfield, D., McLeod, G., & Hall, P. (1974). The CAGE questionnaire: Validation of a new alcoholism screening instrument. *American Journal of Psychiatry, 131,* 1121-1123.

Miller, J. R. (1996). *Shingwauk's vision: A history of Native residential schools.* Toronto, Canada: University of Toronto Press Inc.

Mrazek, P., & Haggerty, R. J. (Eds.). (1994). *Reducing risks for mental disorders: Frontiers for prevention research.* Washington, DC: National Academy Press.

MSSS (1999). *Info-Pop: bulletin d'information sur les données de population du MSSS.* Bulletin no. 8. Quebec, Canada: Ministère de la Santé et des Services sociaux, Government of Quebec.

O'Nell, T. D. (1996). *Disciplined hearts: History, identity and depression in an American Indian community.* Berkeley: University of California Press.

Perrault, C. (1987). *Mental health instruments methodology: Scope and limitations.* Technical Manual 87-06. Quebec, Canada: Ministère de la Santé et des Services sociaux, Government of Quebec.

Petawabano, B., Gourdeau, E., Jourdain, F., Palliser-Tulugak, A., & Cossette, J. (1994). *Mental health and Aboriginal people of Quebec.* Montreal, Canada: Gaëtan Morin Éditeur.

Prince, R. H. (1993). Psychiatry among the James Bay Cree: A focus on pathological grief reactions. *Transcultural Psychiatry Research Review, 30*(1), 3-50.

Robinson, E. (1985). Mortality among the James Bay Cree, Quebec 1975-1982. In R. Fortuine (Ed.), *Circumpolar health 84* (pp.166-169). Seattle: Washington Press.

Royal Commission on Aboriginal Peoples (RCAP) (1996). Residential schools. In *Report of the Royal Commission on aboriginal peoples* (pp. 333-385). Ottawa: Canada Communication Group.

Saint-Pierre, M.-H. (1995*). Mortalité de la population des huit villages cris de la Baie James 1987-1992.*

Montreal, Canada: Module de santé publique région crie de la Baie James and Régie régionale de la Santé et des Services sociaux de Montréal-Centre.

Salisbury, R. F. (1986). *A homeland for the Cree: Regional development in James Bay, 1971-1981.* Montreal, Canada: McGill-Queen's University Press.

Santé Québec (1994). *A health profile of the Cree: Report of the Santé Québec Health Survey of the James Bay Cree 1991.* Quebec, Canada: Ministère de la Santé et des Services sociaux, Government of Quebec.

Sturtevant, W. C. (Ed.). (1981). *Handbook of North American Indians. Volume 6: Subarctic.* Washington, DC: Smithsonian Institution.

Tanner, A. (1979). *Bringing home animals: Religious ideology and mode of production of the Mistassini Cree hunters.* Social and Economic Studies No. 23. St. Johns, Canada: Memorial University Institute of Social and Economic Research.

Timpson, J., McKay, S., Kakegamic, S., Roundhead, D., Cohen, C., & Matewapit, G. (1988). Depression in a Native Canadian in Northwestern Ontario: Sadness, grief or spiritual illness. *Canada's Mental Health* (June), 5-8.

Tudor, K. (1996). *Mental health promotion: Paradigms and practice.* London: Routledge.

Wintrob, R., & Sindell, P. (1972). Culture change and psychopathology: The case of Cree adolescent students in Quebec. In J. W. Berry & G. J. S. Wilde (Eds.), *Social psychology: The Canadian context.* Toronto, Canada: McClelland & Stewart.

Young, D. E. (1989). *Cry of the eagle: Encounters with a Cree healer.* Toronto, Canada: University of Toronto Press.

Young, T. K. (1994). *The health of Native Americans.* New York: Oxford University Press.

PART 7

THE FAMILY'S EXTERNAL CONTEXT

The first article by Hardy and Laszloffy (1995) presents an exercise in cultural competence for the readers of this book. Whether scientist or practitioner, cultural sensitivity and awareness are enhanced when you explore your own cultural history. This article provides one example of how to do this.

Also in this section are two articles each representing stress-producing external contextual factors: economics and racial discrimination. Since *FSM* (Boss, 2002) was published, I see that *chronic discrimination* must be added to the list of external factors in the contextual model of family stress. Simply suggesting that discrimination fits under the existing five external factors (Boss, 2002, p. 40) is not enough. An explicit sixth factor, labeled *chronic discrimination,* should be added to the contextual model of family stress.

The articles by Murry, Brown, Brody, Cutrona, and Simons (2001) on racial discrimination and Conger, Rueter, and Elder (1999) on economic distress illustrate stressors that emanate from outside the family. In addition, each article illustrates a complex methodology and analysis that reflects the complexity of family life in an environment of outside forces. The Murry et al. sample consists of African Americans from Iowa and Georgia, whereas the Conger et al. sample is White and rural but also from Iowa. Murry et al. focused on contextual factors such as neighborhood and found that chronic racial discrimination amplifies the effects of other ongoing stressors. Racial discrimination, according to Murry et al., is a unique contextual stressor experienced by African American families. These researchers develop new measures, generate hypotheses, and raise important new questions. Conger et al. do this also by bringing to our attention the variable of economic hardship as a risk factor for emotional distress, which in turn increases the risk for marital distress. They found that strong marital support increases emotional resilience during economically hard times. Too often, therapists leave out the reality of economic hardship in their assessment of anxiety, depression, and marital conflict. Conger et al. give us a research-based family stress model that links economic stress and marital relations. With deftness in methods and analysis, both Murry et al. and Conger et al. provide us with research-based family stress models that focus on factors from the family's *external* context.

REFERENCE

Boss, P. (2002). *Family stress management* (2nd ed.). Thousand Oaks, CA: Sage.

20

THE CULTURAL GENOGRAM

Key to Training Culturally Competent Family Therapists

KENNETH V. HARDY
TRACEY A. LASZLOFFY

Training programs committed to the development of culturally competent family therapists must discover ways to raise cultural awareness and increase cultural sensitivity. While awareness involves gaining knowledge of various cultural groups, sensitivity involves having experiences that challenge individuals to explore their personal cultural issues. This article outlines how the cultural genogram can be used as an effective training tool to promote both cultural awareness and sensitivity.

To meet the demands of a changing world, it will be imperative for family therapy training programs to devote greater attention to preparing culturally competent therapists. Unfortunately, current efforts to prepare culturally competent therapists are skewed heavily toward promoting cultural "awareness" while neglecting the importance of cultural "sensitivity." This occurs primarily through the use of multicultural training models that rely heavily on providing trainees with multicultural content, with far less emphasis upon promoting meaningful multicultural experiences.

Although it is beneficial for trainees to receive exposure to content highlighting the unique aspects of

From *Journal of Marital and Family Therapy* 21 (1995): 227-37. Copyright © 1995, American Association for Marriage and Family Therapy. Reprinted with permission.

various cultural groups, it is rare that such knowledge readily translates into sensitivity. The content-focused approach to multicultural education overemphasizes the characteristics of various cultural groups while ignoring the importance of the trainees' perceptions of and feelings toward their respective cultural backgrounds. As a result, trainees are rarely challenged to examine how their respective cultural identities influence understanding and acceptance of those who are both culturally similar and dissimilar.

AWARENESS AND SENSITIVITY

Training programs devoted to preparing culturally competent therapists must recognize and attend to the distinction between awareness and sensitivity. Awareness is primarily a cognitive function; an individual becomes conscious of a thought or action and processes it intellectually. Sensitivity, on the other hand, is primarily an affective function; an individual responds emotionally to stimuli with delicacy and respectfulness. Although these functions appear unique and separate, each is shaded with nuances of the other. Essentially, awareness involves a conscious sensitivity, and sensitivity involves a delicate awareness.

Although most individuals possess varying degrees of awareness and sensitivity, training programs devoted to preparing culturally competent therapists must facilitate a greater interface between these functions. This article describes how the genogram can be used as a training tool to promote cultural awareness and sensitivity.

Human service professionals from a range of disciplines have cited various clinical applications of the genogram. It has been used to facilitate joining between client and therapist (Carter & Orfandis, 1976; Guerin & Pendagast, 1976; Pendagast & Sherman, 1977) and to gain insight into the client's psyche (Wachtel, 1982). Family practitioners have used it as a data-gathering device (Doherty & Baird, 1983; Jolly, Froom, & Rosen, 1980; Milhorn, 1981; Rogers & Durkin, 1984; Sproul & Gallagher, 1982), and family therapists have used it as an assessment tool (Hartman, 1977; Kramer, 1985; McGoldrick & Gerson, 1985).

Although not reflected in the family therapy literature, the genogram also has been used widely as a training tool. Bahr (1990) explains that as a training tool, the objective of the genogram is to help both illustrate and clarify family systems concepts and to help trainees get in touch with their personal emotional family-of-origin issues. Using the genogram for training differs from using it as a clinical tool. As a training tool, "the objective is to help students visualize and *understand* their family system and their own place within it, rather than to change it" (Bahr, 1990, p. 243).

THE CULTURAL GENOGRAM

The primary goal of the cultural genogram is to promote cultural awareness and sensitivity by helping trainees to understand their cultural identities. Through this process, trainees gain greater insight into and appreciation for the ways in which culture impacts their role as therapists and influences the lives of clients in treatment. The cultural genogram is designed to accomplish its primary goal by (a) illustrating and clarifying the influence that culture has on the family system; (b) assisting trainees in identifying the groups which contribute to the formation of their cultural identity; (c) encouraging candid discussions that reveal and challenge culturally based assumptions and stereotypes; (d) assisting trainees in discovering their culturally based emotional triggers (i.e., unresolved culturally based conflicts); and (e) assisting trainees in exploring how their unique cultural identities may impact their therapeutic style and effectiveness.

CULTURE AND ETHNICITY

One of the major conceptual challenges associated with completing a cultural genogram involves understanding the relationship between "culture" and "ethnicity." There is widespread confusion regarding the relationship between these two concepts. Within the family therapy literature, for example, some authors consider culture to be more expansive than ethnicity (Falicov, 1988) while others use them synonymously

(McGoldrick & Gerson, 1985; Preli & Bernard, 1993).

The cultural genogram is based on the assumption that culture and ethnicity are both interrelated and distinct. Culture is a broad multidimensional concept that includes but is not limited to ethnicity, gender, social class, and so forth. Ethnicity, on the other hand, refers to the group(s) from which an individual has descended and derives the essence of her/his sense of "peoplehood." Therefore, when all of the dimensions that contribute to culture converge (e.g., ethnicity, social class, gender), they form the whole of an individual's cultural identity. It is this whole in which the cultural genogram is ultimately interested.

Culture represents the principal focus of the cultural genogram; however, ethnicity is an integral part of the process and serves as a primary vehicle for promoting understanding of one's cultural identity. Using ethnicity as a means toward understanding culture is an approach used commonly by other educators and trainers of cultural diversity. For instance, Falicov (1988) notes that "one way for trainees to learn to think *culturally* [italics added] is for them to interview a non-clinical family of a distinct *ethnic* [italics added] or socioeconomic group" (p. 339). Thus, ethnicity constitutes a means to an end rather than *the* end.

PREPARING A CULTURAL GENOGRAM

Preparing a cultural genogram requires careful thought and planning. The following section outlines the steps necessary for constructing and presenting a comprehensive cultural genogram.

Getting Organized

Defining One's Culture of Origin. The first critical step in preparing a cultural genogram involves defining one's culture of origin. For the purposes of this exercise, culture of origin refers to the major group(s) from which an individual has descended that were the first generation to come to the United States (except for Native Americans). For example, an individual may have been born and raised in America, but if her/his grandparents were Irish and Greek, then the culture of origin consists of these two groups.

Organizing Principles and Pride/Shame Issues. The next step in preparing a cultural genogram is identifying the major organizing principles of each group that comprises the trainee's culture of origin. Organizing principles are fundamental constructs which shape the perceptions, beliefs, and behaviors of members of a group. They are the basic structures upon which all other aspects of a culture are predicated. Identifying organizing principles serves to establish a framework, which is an essential step in organizing and constructing an effective cultural genogram presentation.

Trainees also should identify pride/shame issues for each group associated with their culture of origin. Pride/shame issues are aspects of a culture that are sanctioned as distinctively negative or positive. They derive their meaning from organizing principles. Understanding the distinction between organizing principles and pride/shame issues is important. They are similar in that both organize the perceptions, beliefs, and behaviors of group members. However, the critical distinction between the two is that pride/shame issues punctuate behaviors as negative or positive, while organizing principles do not. For instance, in Jewish culture, fear of persecution is an organizing principle, and educational achievement is a pride/shame issue. Although both of these organize Jewish people, educational achievement, unlike fear of persecution, punctuates the individual behavior of Jews as either positive or negative.

Identifying organizing principles and pride/shame issues requires trainees to utilize a variety of sources. These sources may include drawing from one's personal knowledge of a group, conducting interviews with members from a particular group, or reviewing reference materials, such as films, books, or cultural artifacts.

Creating Symbols. Symbols should be designed by the trainee to denote all pride/shame issues. They should be placed directly on the cultural genogram to depict graphically the prevalence of pride/shame issues and to highlight their impact on family

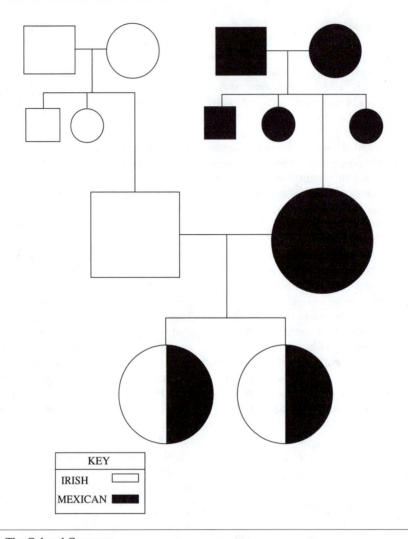

Figure 20.1 The Cultural Genogram

functioning. The use of symbols is a form of analogic communication that allows the presenter to express the intuitive and affective aspects of cultural issues which are sometimes difficult to capture with words. Essentially, using symbols provides trainees with a means for communicating the nonrational, emotional dimensions of cultural issues which often defy verbal expression.

Selecting Colors. A different color should be selected to represent each group comprising a trainee's culture of origin. The colors are used to identify different groups and to depict how each group contributes to the cultural identity of each individual. For instance, if a female is half Swedish (yellow), a quarter Ugandan (red), and a quarter Venezuelan (blue), then the circle that identifies her on the genogram would be color-coded half yellow, a quarter red, and a quarter blue.

The configuration of colors provides a graphic snapshot of the overall cultural composition of the family system and of each individual's unique cultural identity. The initial "color snapshot" inspires a variety of initial hypotheses about the family system and the trainee. For instance, genograms that are dominated by a single color reveal that the family system is characterized by a high degree of cultural homogeneity. On the other hand, genograms which are a collage of colors quickly reveal the multiculturalism of the family system. From these initial observations, numerous questions can be generated to guide further exploration, interpretation, and understanding of the trainees' unique cultural issues and identities.

Identifying Intercultural Marriages. Intercultural marriages represent a blending of cultures and hence a blending of organizing principles and pride/shame issues. Cultural differences in marriage often have a significant influence on the nature of the relationship and on children. Therefore, in addition to identifying where intercultural marriages occur, trainees should also (a) explore how divergent cultural issues were/are negotiated and (b) trace the intergenerational consequences of the intercultural union. Trainees should use the (~) symbol to denote intercultural marriages.

Putting It Together

Cultural Framework Charts. Establishing cultural framework charts (CFC) is the next crucial step in the cultural genogram process. The CFC is to the cultural genogram as a legend is to a map. In other words, it provides the keys for interpreting the genogram. A CFC is necessary for each group comprising one's culture of origin. It should list the major organizing principles and the pride/shame issues with their corresponding symbols.

Genogram. The final preparatory step involves constructing at least a three-generation family genogram and adding the following elements to it: the (~) symbol to identify intercultural marriages, colors to illustrate the cultural composition of each person's cultural identity, and the symbols denoting pride/shame issues.

Questions to Consider. It is also recommended that trainees answer the questions outlined in Table 20.1:

"Questions to Consider While Preparing for the Presentation." Trainees' familiarity with the answers to these questions can facilitate an informed dialogue about the various sociological factors (e.g., race, religion, regionality, class) that contribute to cultural identity. Through addressing these questions they will be encouraged to appreciate the complexity of cultural identity formation.

INTERPRETATION AND PRESENTATION

The cultural genogram presentation should begin with an introduction of the trainee's cultural framework chart(s). This portion of the process is primarily didactic. Trainees introduce, and discuss in detail, organizing principles, pride/shame issues, and the colors and symbols they have selected.

After presenting the cultural framework chart(s), the next step involves using the genogram as a means to illustrate the issues delineated in the chart(s). Essentially, trainees use their genograms to identify and trace the presence or absence of the various pride/ shame issues defined on their chart(s). It is recommended that trainees begin exploring the transmission of cultural issues from the oldest generation on their genogram through the subsequent generations. This portion of the process is primarily experiential and involves considerable interaction and discussion.

SYNTHESIS

The cultural genogram experience should culminate in an analysis of a trainee's cultural background, highlighting how it shapes her/his cultural identity and impacts her/his role as a therapist. The synthesis stage enables trainees to reflect upon, further explore, and integrate the various aspects of the entire process. It is during this stage that trainees are encouraged to think critically about themselves as cultural beings. They should be challenged to describe and analyze at least one critical incident from each stage of the cultural genogram process (i.e., "Getting Organized," "Putting It All Together," etc.).

There are two basic tasks associated with this stage. The first is retrospective self-reflection, which encourages trainees to ponder the impact of

Table 20.1   Questions to Consider While Preparing for the Cultural Genogram Presentation

Please consider these questions for *each* group constituting your culture of origin, as well as considering the implications of the answers in relation to your overall cultural identity.

1. What were the migration patterns of the group?
2. If other than Native American, under what conditions did your family (or their descendants) enter the United States (immigrant, political refugee, slave, etc.)?
3. What were/are the group's experiences with oppression? What were/are the markers of oppression?
4. What issues divide members within the same group? What are the sources of intragroup conflict?
5. Describe the relationship between the group's identity and your national ancestry (if the group is defined in terms of nationality, please skip this question).
6. What significance does race, skin color, and hair play within the group?
7. What is/are the dominant religion(s) of the group? What role does religion and spirituality play in the everyday lives of members of the group?
8. What role does regionality and geography play in the group?
9. How are gender roles defined within the group? How is sexual orientation regarded?
10. a) What prejudices or stereotypes does this group have about itself?
    b) What prejudices and stereotypes do other groups have about this group?
    c) What prejudices or stereotypes does this group have about other groups?
11. What role (if any) do names play in the group? Are there rules, mores, or rituals governing the assignment of names?
12. How is social class defined in the group?
13. What occupational roles are valued and devalued by the group?
14. What is the relationship between age and the values of the group?
15. How is family defined in the group?
16. How does this group view outsiders in general and mental health professionals specifically?
17. How have the organizing principles of this group shaped your family and its members? What effect have they had on you?
18. What are the ways in which pride/shame issues of each group are manifested in your family system?
19. What impact will these pride/shame issues have on your work with clients from both similar and dissimilar cultural backgrounds?
20. If more than one group comprises your culture of origin, how were the differences negotiated in your family? What were the intergenerational consequences? How has this impacted you personally and as a therapist?

the cultural genogram process ex post facto. The central question germane to successful completion of this task is "now that it's over, what did I learn from it?" The second task is integration, which involves inspiring trainees to search for the goodness of fit between thoughts and feelings, content and process, and their personal and professional identities, as each of these has been shaped by the cultural genogram process. It is through completion of these interrelated tasks that trainees incorporate what they have gained from the exercise into their clinical work.

The synthesis process occurs over an extensive period of time. However, it may be necessary and even desirable for trainers to establish artificial benchmarks to represent a point of closure for the cultural genogram process. Thus, the synthesis stage, as described here, is a ritual which symbolizes an end to the cultural genogram process and the beginning of an ongoing process of cultural self-exploration and integration.

THE ROLE OF THE FACILITATOR

The facilitator assumes a crucial role in the overall success of the cultural genogram experience. It is necessary for the facilitator to support the trainees

Table 20.2   Questions to Answer in Synthesis Paper

1. What are your family's beliefs and feelings about the group(s) that comprise your culture of origin? What parts of the group(s) do they embrace or reject? How has this influenced your feelings about your cultural identity?
2. What aspects of your culture of origin do you have the most comfort "owning," the most difficulty "owning"?
3. What groups will you have the easiest time working with, the most difficult?
4. What did you learn about yourself and your cultural identity? How might this influence your tendencies as a therapist?
5. Was the exercise valuable, worthwhile? Why or why not?

emotionally during this self-exploratory process while remaining detached enough to challenge them intellectually. As with any experience of this type, successful execution of the facilitator's role is largely dependent on the extent to which her/his emotional involvement in the overall process is managed effectively. It is only through achieving an appropriate balance between engagement and disengagement that the facilitator can create the emotional climate necessary to stimulate emotional sharing and intellectual exploration.

An effective facilitator (a) clarifies the goals of the exercise and evaluates trainees' attainment of the goals; (b) determines what factors impeded or stimulated trainees' abilities to accomplish their goals; (c) demonstrates sensitivity to and respect for differences and the numerous ways in which differences are manifested, for example, how trainees learn and process information; (d) takes an active role in creating a milieu that promotes emotional safety and risk taking; (e) encourages trainees to challenge respectfully racial, ethnic, and ultimately cultural stereotypes and biases; and (f) demonstrates a tolerance for and an ability to manage escalating levels of anxiety, anger, and fear.

Because of the hypersensitivity that often characterizes cross-cultural interactions, it is important for the facilitator to remain comfortable with and even encourage interactions that often result in increased anxiety, fear, and frustration. The facilitator's overt display of comfort (or lack thereof) becomes either the catalyst for, or impediment to, heightened risk taking, meaningful sharing, and cultural sensitivity. Since trainees are often hesitant to discuss cultural differences openly for fear of "saying the wrong thing," the facilitator must assume the interrelated roles of interaction catalyst and broker of permission.

It is primarily through these roles that trainees will be inspired and challenged to gain the essence of the cultural genogram process.

Table 20.3 outlines sample questions facilitators might ask to help guide the cultural genogram presentations and related discussions.

IMPLICATIONS FOR TREATMENT AND RESEARCH

Clinical Implications

Several family therapists (Hardy, 1990; Lappin, 1983) have emphasized the importance of therapists knowing their respective cultures before attempting to work cross-culturally. Lappin (1983) asserts that "knowing thy own culture is perhaps the most difficult aspect of conducting effective cross cultural therapy" (p. 135). To facilitate this process, Lappin recommended that the first step one must take is to develop a three-generational cultural genogram.

The cultural genogram not only helps therapists become more conversant with their cultural identities but also highlights culturally linked issues that may impede effective treatment. The didactic portion of the cultural genogram provides valuable contextual information about specific groups that can be beneficial in treatment. This is particularly true of groups with whom the therapist has had no previous contact. Rather than using the information as the basis for perpetuating stereotypes, it allows therapists to generate culturally based hypotheses that can help shape the course of treatment.

The presentations and discussions associated with the cultural genogram are valuable and have strong implications for clinical practice. The exercise can

Table 20.3   Questions for Facilitators to Consider During the Presentation

1. a) What does the content of the presentation teach about the presenter's culture of origin?
    b) What does the process of the presentation teach about the presenter's culture of origin?
    c) What parallels, if any, exist between the presenter's style and the cultural content disclosed?
2. Are family-of-origin and culture-of-origin issues appropriately differentiated?
3. Do the colors and symbols chosen by the presenter have special cultural relevance? How were these chosen?
4. Is there a disproportionate number of pride or shame issues? What is the presenter's rationale for the schism?
5. When there are multiple groups comprising a trainee's culture of origin, how are they presented/negotiated?
6. How comfortable is the presenter in engaging in an open dialogue about inter- and/or intragroup prejudices and stereotypes?
7. What issues appear too uncomfortable for the presenter to discuss?
8. What impact did the presentation have on other trainees? What are the hypotheses regarding why such reactions were generated?
9. What relevance or insights did the presenter have as a result of this experience?
10. What was the process by which the information for the cultural genogram was gathered?

be instrumental in assisting therapists to identify unresolved culturally based issues. Resolution of these issues allows therapists to work more effectively cross-culturally, as well as with clients who are culturally similar.

Culturally unresolved therapists experience considerable difficulty demonstrating sensitivity to clients from similar and dissimilar backgrounds. For example, a therapist of Brazilian descent who rejects her/his heritage may find it difficult to work with Brazilian clients. This therapist may either express inappropriate affect toward any aspect of the client's background that appears unequivocally Brazilian, or efforts may be made to coerce the client indirectly to embrace her/his heritage more fully. In either case, it is the therapist's unresolved cultural issues that become a major organizing principle in treatment.

The cultural genogram experience also helps to shape the worldview of therapists. Rather than embracing the theoretical myth of sameness (the belief that all families are the same), therapists develop a genuine appreciation of and respect for the differences that exist between and among families. It is through this process therapists learn, for example, that there are some families for whom Saturday is not an appropriate day for therapy appointments or for whom it does make a difference whether they are thought of as Puerto Rican or Hispanic.

Research Implications

McGoldrick and Gerson (1985) and Lewis (1989) have emphasized the need for more empirical research on the genogram. The cultural genogram could benefit from empirical inquiry regarding its effectiveness. Outcome data gathered from training and clinical settings could enhance reliability and validity of the cultural genogram as an effective training tool for promoting culturally competent family therapists.

As family therapy programs continue to struggle with how to integrate multiculturalism into their curricula, data obtained from the cultural genogram could serve as a useful guide. The cultural genogram could be used as an instrument to collect aggregate data from training programs to highlight implications for how multiculturalism might (or might not) be incorporated into MFT curricula. Programs would have not only a wealth of rich trainee data to draw upon but also a variety of experiences with a myriad of teaching methodologies.

The cultural genogram, although conceived of as a training tool, may have some clinical applicability as well. Future research may determine that the instrument can be modified to use clinically in two significant ways: (a) as a basis for collecting/analyzing therapists' cultural competence in cross-cultural family therapy and (b) as an assessment instrument in working with cross-cultural families where the blending of cultural issues is the presenting problem or related to it.

The need and implications for further research are enormous. Questions regarding the specifics of such research should remain part of an open and continuing dialogue.

REFLECTIONS ON THE CULTURAL GENOGRAM

The cultural genogram is a practical instrument for assisting trainees in becoming more familiar with their culturally constructed realities. The process of developing, using, and refining the instrument has assisted the authors in this goal as well. The cultural genogram has been instrumental in heightening our awareness of our cultural biases and the numerous ways in which these are deeply embedded in the cultural genogram process. Thus, we wish to admonish trainers and trainees that the instrument and recommended process are only as objective as our cultural lenses would permit us to be. Everything we have described, recommended, or chosen to include or ignore has been "tarnished" by our Westernized view of the world.

For example, a Hindu trainee from Southern India pointed out the cultural bias ingrained in our assumption that a complete family system can be mapped out in a single two-dimensional diagram. She explained that in her culture, the definition of family is much more expansive than in Western society. In constructing her cultural genogram, she was forced by the limitations of the standardized genogram format to leave out many individuals who were significant in defining her cultural context and identity. As an example of how large familial networks are in her culture, she explained that 900 relatives attended her sister's wedding, and her mother and sisters personally wrote thank-you notes to all of them.

Another one of our assumptions is that trainees will have knowledge of the groups from which they have descended. However, many trainees of African American descent, for example, may experience difficulty tracing their roots as a result of the historical legacy of slavery.

Another cultural bias has to do with our conceptualization of marriage. The cultural genogram asks trainees to identify intercultural marriages, but the term *marriage* is ambiguous. In Western cultures, marriage refers to a legally sanctioned union, but in other cultures the definition of marriage (and of legal) varies. The failure to make this distinction constitutes a bias.

These brief descriptions highlight the caution that should be exercised before attempting to fit "a square peg in a round hole," an attempt that characterizes most cross-cultural interactions. It is our hope that the cultural genogram, despite its cultural biases, will assist trainees and trainers alike in better knowing what it is they do not know. We believe that this process will contribute to the development of future generations of family therapists who will possess the cultural awareness and sensitivity necessary to meet the needs of an increasingly diverse clinical population.

REFERENCES

Bahr, K. (1990). Student responses to genogram and family chronology. *Family Relations, 39*(3), 243-249.

Carter, E. A., & Orfandis, M. (1976). Family therapy with only one person and the therapist's own family. In P. Guerin (Ed.), *Family therapy* (pp. 197-199). New York: Gardner.

Doherty, W. J., & Baird, M. A. (1983). *Family therapy and family medicine.* New York: Guilford.

Falicov, C. J. (1988). Learning to think culturally. In H. Liddle, D. Breulin, & D. Schwartz (Eds.), *Handbook of family therapy training and supervision* (pp. 335-357). New York: Guilford.

Guerin, P. J., & Pendagast, E. G. (1976). Evaluation of family system and genogram. In P. J. Guerin (Ed.), *Family therapy* (pp. 450-464). New York: Gardner.

Hardy, K. V. (1990). Effective treatment of minority families. *Family Therapy News, 21*(5), 5.

Hartman, A. (1977). Diagrammatic assessment of family relationships. *Social Casework, 59,* 465-476.

Jolly, W., Froom, J., & Rosen, M. G. (1980). The genogram. *The Journal of Family Practice, 10*(2), 251-255.

Kramer, J. R. (1985). *Family interfaces: Transgenerational patterns.* New York: Brunner/Mazel.

Lappin, J. (1983). On becoming a culturally conscious family therapist. In C. J. Falicov (Ed.), *Cultural perspectives in family therapy* (pp. 122-136). Rockville, MD: Aspen.

Lewis, K. G. (1989). The use of color-coded genograms in family therapy. *Journal of Marital and Family Therapy, 15,*169-176.

McGoldrick, M., & Gerson, R. (1985). *Genograms in family assessment.* New York: W. W. Norton.

Milhorn, H. T. (1981). The genogram: A structured approach to the family history. *Journal of the Mississippi State Medical Association, 10,* 250-252.

Pendagast, E. G., & Sherman, C. O. (1977). A guide to the genogram. *The Family, 5,* 101-112.

Preli, R., & Bernard, J. M. (1993). Making multiculturalism relevant for majority culture graduate students. *Journal of Marital and Family Therapy, 19,* 5-16.

Rogers, J., & Durkin, M. (1984). The semi-structured genogram interview: I Protocol; II. Evaluation. *Family Systems Medicine, 2*(l), 176-187.

Sproul, M. S., & Gallagher, R. M. (1982). The genogram as an aid to crisis intervention. *The Journal of Family Practice, 14*(5), 959-960.

Wachtel, E. F. (1982). The family psyche over three generations: The genogram revisited. *Journal of Marital and Family Therapy, 8,* 334-343.

21

Racial Discrimination as a Moderator of the Links Among Stress, Maternal Psychological Functioning, and Family Relationships

Velma McBride Murry
P. Adama Brown
Gene H. Brody
Carolyn E. Cutrona
Ronald L. Simons

This study focuses on the links between social contexts and normative family patterns to identify factors at the societal, community, family, and individual levels that enhance African Americans' ability to overcome stressful life events and foster positive family relationships. The Mundane Extreme Environmental Stress Model was used to explore these links. From urban and rural areas in Iowa and Georgia, 383 families with 10- or 11-year-old children were recruited. Structural equation modeling was used to test the hypotheses.

Reprinted from *Journal of Marriage and Family* 63 (2001): 915-26. Copyright © 2001 by the National Council on Family Relations, 3989 Central Ave. NE, Suite 550, Minneapolis, MN 55421. Reprinted by permission. This research was supported by the National Institute of Mental Health through funding for the Center for Family Research in Rural Mental Health (Grant MH48165) at Iowa State University. Additional funding was provided by the National Institute on Drug Abuse, the National Institute on Alcohol Abuse and Alcoholism, and the Iowa Agriculture and Home Economics Experiment Station (Project 3320).

Maternal psychological distress was linked with parent-child relationship quality both directly and indirectly through its association with intimate partnership quality. When racial discrimination was greater, stronger links emerged between stressor pileup and psychological distress, as well as between psychological distress and the quality of both intimate partnerships and parent-child relationships. Future research on African American family processes should include the effects of racial discrimination.

The situations among African Americans at the beginning of the 21st century can best be described as paradoxical. Many African American families and communities are in crisis, confronting high unemployment, poverty, crime, drug abuse, HIV/AIDS, teenage pregnancy and parenthood, and single motherhood (Bennett, 1995; Taylor, Chatters, Tucker, & Lewis, 1990). Conversely, the number of college-educated, middle-, and upper-middle-class African Americans is greater than in any other historical period (U.S. Bureau of the Census, 1992).

Research on African American families is also paradoxical. Although the number of published reports about African American adults and children is increasing, large gaps remain in the literature addressing basic questions about African American family functioning, particularly in two-adult families. This study was designed to help fill these gaps by describing the implications of racial discrimination for family processes. We specifically examined the moderating effect of racial discrimination on the linkages among contextual stress, psychological functioning, intimate partnership quality, and parent-child relationship quality.

Several theories contributed to the current study's design and the analysis of the data it yielded. The family stress theories that McCubbin, Joy, Cauble, Comeau, Patterson, & Needle (1980) and Conger and associates (1990) formulated maintain that an overload of contextual stressors overwhelms family members' coping capacities. This results in compromised psychological functioning, which, in turn, helps to make intimate partnerships and parent-child relationships less supportive and more conflicted. Little empirical information is available on the interrelationships among these processes in African American families. Brody & Flor (1997) and Brown, Brody, and Stoneman (2000) documented links between financial stress and impaired psychological functioning among African American wives. Specifically, African American parents who experienced more depressive symptoms had less supportive marital interactions and engaged in less coparental cooperation. McLoyd, Jayarate, Cebello, & Borquez (1994), Brody & Flor (1998), and Taylor (2000) have demonstrated similar links for single African American mothers. Single mothers who reported more depressive symptoms were less involved in their children's lives (McLoyd, 1990; Taylor, Roberts, & Jacobson, 1997), whereas mothers with more optimistic outlooks used more supportive and involved parenting practices (Brody & Flor, 1997; Brody, Stoneman, Flor, & McCrary, 1994). The empirical literature, however, has not examined the mechanisms through which contextual stress, particularly perceived racial discrimination, cascades through African American families to affect mothers' psychological functioning, their intimate partnerships, and their relationships with their children. This study addresses these issues. Because prior studies and theoretical models for family stress research have been based on female caregiver's reports of family functioning, our study includes only mother reports.

CONSEQUENCES AND EFFECTS OF RACISM AND STRESS ON AFRICAN AMERICAN FUNCTIONING

A multitude of stressors have been linked to both individual and family well-being (Horwitz &

Scheid, 1999). Chronic stressors, such as poverty, and more discrete stressors, such as negative life events, note the proliferation of stress. One source of stress that is unique to the African American experience is racial discrimination. Although racial discrimination has been long recognized as a social and historical problem, few empirical tests of its affects on African American family functioning have been documented (Sigelman & Welch, 1991). The majority of studies that exist highlight the deleterious consequences of perceived racial discrimination for African American physical and psychological health. For instance, in study of hypertension among African American men, James, LaCroix, Kleinbaum, and Strogatz (1984) found that blood pressure was higher for those who attributed their lack of success to racism. Findings from Krieger's (1990) comparative study of Black and White women suggests that African American women who passively accepted racial discrimination were more likely to have high blood pressure than those who used more effective means to cope with it. In addition to its adverse physical health implications, studies show that racial discrimination is significantly and negatively correlated with psychological adjustment (Jackson, Brown, Williams, Torres, Sellers, & Brown, 1996; Kessler, Mickelson, & Williams, 1999). Furthermore, external stressors such as racism interfere with African Americans' life opportunities because of disparities between African Americans and White Americans in economic and political power, civil rights, and accessibility to resources. These disparities have stimulated scientific inquiry into the ways in which African American families contend with the pressures associated with racism (Allen, 1995; Jones, 2000; McAdoo, 1997; Peters & Massey, 1983; Williams & Williams-Morris, 2000).

Despite the challenges and family stress associated with racism (DuBois, 1967; Peters & Massey, 1983), the family is hypothesized to serve as a sanctuary that protects African Americans from impact of racism and provides support that is often unavailable in the wider society (Neighbors & Jackson, 1984). Although a particular encounter with racism may be an individual experience, sharing the experience with family members transforms it into a family issue that elicits support from family members

(Feagin & Spikes, 1994). In the process the family places the racial experience in a wider social context, linking race-related stressors to historic issues such as slavery (Billingsley, 1968, 1992). Racism is thereby defined as a global social injustice rather than a response to an individual's personal characteristics (Pearlin, 1983).

Consideration of African American families' social systems is important in understanding their ability to overcome adversity. Families constitute social subsystems that interact mutually with other subsystems in the community and the wider society (Billingsley, 1968), responding to their demands and benefitting from their resources (Allen, 1978). For example, the church has historically buffered African American families from the effects of racism by serving as a source of spiritual and emotional support (McAdoo, 1997; Pool, 1990; Tatum, 1997), as well as providing for social welfare services, such as banking, housing, health care, employment, and legal assistance, which often are difficult for members to obtain in the larger social system (Billingsley, 1992). Although African Americans' everyday life experiences cannot be understood adequately without systematically assessing the interrelationships between families and other social systems, empirical studies of these dynamics are sparse. Most do not acknowledge the daily hassles associated with simply being *Black* in America. In our study, we focused on the links between social contexts and normative family patterns to identify factors at the societal, community, family, and individual levels that enhance African Americans' ability to overcome stressful life events and foster positive family relationships.

CONCEPTUAL MODEL OF STRESS AND AFRICAN AMERICAN FAMILY FUNCTIONING

The Mundane Extreme Environmental Stress model (MEES; Peters & Massey, 1983) served as the primary guide for this study. In this model, racism is conceptualized as a ubiquitous, continuous contextual variable in African Americans' lives. Both subtle and overt forms of discrimination are hypothesized to amplify other forms of contextual stress, resulting in stronger negative associations among contextual stressors, mothers' psychological functioning, intimate partnerships, and parent-child relationships. The Family Stress model, which integrates individual and family subsystem variables to explain family functioning, was also incorporated into the research. This model has heuristic value for the study of African American family patterns because it treats stress as a social contextual variable that does not arise from unique circumstances or unfortunate individual experiences (Pearlin, 1983). Rather, stress is conceptualized as the consequence of engagement with social institutions, the structure and functions of which engender and sustain patterns of conflict and distress (Guelkow, Bird, & Koball, 1991; Pearlin, 1983). Both the MEES and Family Stress models thus provided theoretical guidance for examining the link between stress and subsystem functioning within African American families. We included only women in the test of our model because the underlying empirical and theoretical bases for most family stress models have been developed almost exclusively from women's reports of family functioning, family relationship quality, and the interplay between depressive symptoms and marital quality. Furthermore, most of the primary caregivers in the larger research project from which our study was drawn were the target children's biological mothers. We do not intend to disregard the significant effect of fathers' functioning on family processes and child development, but less is known about these associations among men (Heim & Snyder, 1991; Olin & Fennell, 1989; Phares & Compas, 1992).

Stressor pileup in the form of job loss, financial strain, and stressful life events was hypothesized to be linked with compromised maternal psychological functioning. Maternal distress, in turn, was expected to be associated with lower quality relationships with intimate partners, which will impact negatively the nature and quality of mothers' relationships with their children. The study also takes into account the ongoing toll of racial discrimination in the lives of African Americans. Thus, we hypothesized that the links would be strongest among female caregivers experiencing the most racial discrimination.

The predicted associations of stressor pileup with mother-reported depression and anxiety presumably arise from the stress and loss of control over one's own life that are associated with confronting multiple stressors (Brody & Flor, 1997, 1998; Conger et al., 1990; McLoyd et al., 1994). Psychological distress in mothers induces negative emotionality that compromises their relationships with their partners and children; romantic relationships become less satisfying and more conflicted (Beach, Smith, & Fincham, 1994; Brody et al., 1994; Conger, Conger, Elder, Lorenz, Simons, & Whitbeck, 1992; Davila, Bradbury, Cohan, & Tochluk, 1997; Karney & Bradbury, 1995), and parenting becomes less nurturant and involved (Brody & Flor, 1997; McLoyd et al., 1994). Consistent with the MEES and Family Stress theories, the link between maternal psychological distress and parenting quality was hypothesized to be partially mediated by the quality of adults' intimate relationships. Such negativity has been shown to spill over into interactions with children, compromising parent-child relationship quality (Brody & Forehand, 1986; Conger et al., 2000). Under these circumstances, stressor-induced psychological distress would be linked with less nurturing mother-child relationships, both directly and indirectly, through its association with lower quality intimate relationships.

Using the MEES model to analyze the contributions of racist experiences to family functioning derived the expectation that racial discrimination would moderate the associations included in the conceptual model. From this perspective, racist experiences impact psychological well-being, which influences relationship quality in all family subsystems. The observations that Peters and Massey (1983) incorporated into the MEES model were validated by research on African Americans, which indicated that experiencing racial discrimination was linked to heightened psychological and physiological stress responses (Anderson, McNeilly, & Myers, 1991; Clark, Anderson, Clark, & Williams, 1999; Dressler, 1991). This developing literature does not yet include an empirical analysis of the amplification effects that racism may have on the daily stressors and negative life events that African American parents experience. We hypothesized that when mothers reported experiencing higher levels of racial discrimination, the links between stressor pileup and psychological distress and between psychological distress and family relationship quality would be stronger.

METHOD

The hypotheses were tested using the first wave of data from the Family and Community Health Study (FACHS), a multisite, two-wave panel study of neighborhood and family effects on health and development. Participants in this large-scale study of African American children and their caregivers included 897 families, 475 in Iowa and 422 in Georgia. Each family included a child who was 10 or 11 years old when recruited; families with children of this age were chosen for study because systematic analyses of developmental and family processes among this population are rare.

Sampling Strategy

A central goal of the larger study was to investigate the effects of neighborhood characteristics on the functioning of adults and children. We recruited families from neighborhoods that varied on demographic characteristics to obtain a sample that reflected the diversity of African American families. In selecting neighborhoods from which to draw the sample, we examined neighborhood characteristics at the level of block group areas (BGAs), which are clusters of blocks within census tracts. Each census tract typically includes four or five BGAs. In constructing BGAs, the Census Bureau strives to use naturally occurring neighborhood boundaries, such as major thoroughfares or rivers, whenever possible. During the 1990 census, BGAs averaged 452 housing units with 1,100 residents. Using the 1990 data, we identified BGAs in Iowa and Georgia in African American families made up 10% or more of the population. Families were recruited from 259 BGAs, 144 in Iowa and 115 in Georgia.

In Iowa, BGAs in Waterloo (population 65,000) and Des Moines (population 193,000) that met the sampling criteria were identified. Families with African American children between the ages of 10 and 12 were identified through the public schools, which provided rosters of all African American students in grades four through six. In Georgia, BGAs that met the criteria were identified in small towns and a suburban area adjacent to Atlanta; community members who served as liaisons between the University of Georgia researchers and the neighborhood residents compiled rosters of children who met the sampling criteria. Families were randomly selected from these rosters and contacted to determine their interest in participation. Those who declined were removed from the rosters, and other families were randomly selected until the required number of families from each BGA had been recruited. Recruitment rates did not differ significantly across sites, ranging from 61% to 68%.

Interview Procedure

To enhance rapport and cultural understanding, African American university students and community members served as field researchers to collect data from the families. They received one month of training in the administration of the self-report instruments. Before data collection began, four focus groups in Iowa and four in Georgia examined and critiqued the instruments. Each group was composed of 10 African American women who lived in neighborhoods similar to those from which the study participants were recruited. They suggested modification of items that they perceived to be culturally insensitive, intrusive, or unclear. After these revisions were incorporated into the instruments, the protocol was pilot tested on eight families from each site. Researchers took extensive notes on the participants' reactions to the questionnaires and offered suggestions for further changes.

The research protocol included a two-part interview administered during two separate sessions. Questionnaires administered during the interviews assessed neighborhood quality, stressful life events, personal characteristics, coping, social support, participation in religious activities, and psychological functioning. The measures were administered via computer-assisted personal interviews (CAPI), in which questions appeared in sequence on a laptop computer screen and were read aloud to the participant. Both the interviewer and the participant could see the screen. Interviewers entered participants' responses into the computer immediately following each question, using CASES, a special program designed for conducting research interviews.

Most (84%) of the primary caregivers included in the FACHS were the children's biological mothers, 6% were fathers, 6% were grandmothers, 3% were foster or adoptive parents, 2% were other relatives, 1% were stepparents, and less than 1% were non-relatives such as babysitters. Overall, 93% of the primary caregivers were women. Their mean age was 37.1 years ($SD = 8.18$) and ranged from 23 to 80 years. Education among participants ranged from less than high school (19%) to advance graduate degrees (3%). The mode was a high school diploma (41%). Of the primary caregivers, 92% identified themselves as African American. The remaining 8% identified themselves as ethnically mixed or belonging to another ethnic group.

Our study included a subsample of 386 families from the larger FACHS sample, in which the adults were either married or cohabiting. The mean age of the mothers in the subsample was 35 years, and 44.5% of them had at least a high school education. They resided in households in which the mean per capita income was $27,000 ($SD = \$24,000$). On average, the women in this subsample had at least three children.

Measures

Stressor pileup was operationalized as a latent construct measured by four indicators used to assess the stressful life events that the families experienced. *Negative life events* included a number of relatively severe, chronic stressors that families experienced during the previous 12 months. They were assessed using a 29-item checklist that included events such as criminal victimization, serious illness or injury to oneself or an immediate family member, legal problems, the death of a loved one, and marital separation or divorce. *Chronic financial stressors* were assessed using Conger and Elder's (1994) Unmet Material Needs, Can't Make Ends Meet, and Financial Adjustments subscales, which assess, respectively, the specific needs that families could not meet because of financial hardship (e.g., "not enough money for to buy the food we need"; Cronbach's alpha = .69), family members' general perceptions of financial distress (Cronbach's alpha = .59), and specific ways in which the family tried to economize (Cronbach's alpha = .76). Job stress was assessed further using two more items developed for this project, by which respondents indicated the extent to which their jobs

involved the threat of illness or injury and their concerns about losing their jobs ($r = .34$). Finally, *racial discrimination* was assessed using the Experiences of Discrimination Scale, which was developed for this study (see Appendix). Respondents indicated how often they experienced 13 types of racial discrimination (e.g., "How often has someone suspected you of doing something wrong just because you are African American?"). Response options ranged from 1 (*never*) to 4 (*several times*). Coefficient alpha for the scale was .92.

Psychological functioning was assessed using two subscales from the Mini-Mood and Anxiety Symptom Questionnaire (Mini-MASQ; Clark & Watson, 1997). The five-item general distress-depression subscale assessed nonspecific depressive symptoms, and the three-item general distress-anxiety subscale assessed nonspecific anxiety-related symptoms. Cronbach's alpha was .80 for the depression subscale and .76 for the anxiety subscale.

Intimate relationship quality was operationalized as a latent construct measured by two indicators that assessed relationship stability and relationship satisfaction. *Relationship stability* was assessed using a five-item scale that Booth, Johnson, and Edward (1983) developed. Sample items include "Within the last 3 months have you suggested the idea of ending the relationship"; "Discussed ending the relationship with a friend"; and "Thought the relationship might be in trouble." Cronbach's alpha was .88. *Relationship satisfaction* was measured using two items developed for the project: "How happy are you with your relationship with your partner?" and "How satisfied are you with your relationship with your partner?" ($r = .87$).

Mother-child relationship quality was operationalized as a latent construct measured by two indicators describing the mother's relationship with the target child. The four-item *mother-child relationship satisfaction* measure indicated the extent to which the mother enjoyed, was satisfied, and was happy about raising the target child along with her overall experiences in raising the child (Cronbach's alpha = .72). Indicators of *nurturant-involved parenting* were constructed by summing standardized scores from scales used to assess mothers' warmth, inductive reasoning, communication, and monitoring. These scales have been used in previous studies (Brody et al., in press; Ge, Brody, Conger, Simons, & Murry, 2000), and the combination of these variables has been found to be related consistently to children's conduct problems and affiliation with deviant peers (Simons et al., 1994).

RESULTS

Correlations, Means, and Standard Deviations

t tests comparing the means for the study variables at the two sites, including demographic characteristics, indicate the sample did not differ by site. We therefore combined the sample for subsequent analyses. Table 21.1 presents the correlations, means, and standard deviations for all study variables. The results from the bivariate correlations confirm the expected association between stress and psychological functioning. For example, negative life events were significantly and positively associated with general anxiety and depression. In addition, respondents who reported financial setbacks and high levels of job stress were also more likely to experience poorer psychological functioning.

Female caregivers who reported high levels of distress were also more likely to report dissatisfaction and instability in their intimate partnerships, as well as poor relationships with their children. For instance, general depression was negatively and significantly correlated with intimate relationship stability, relationship satisfaction, and with caregiver-child relationship quality. The relation between general anxiety and intimate partnership quality was also significant and in the expected direction. As expected, the correlations also revealed that mother-child relationship quality was better in families where mothers had stable, content intimate partnerships.

In addition, women who reported high levels of perceived racial discrimination were more likely to suffer numerous stressful life events, financial setbacks, and psychological distress. Intimate relationship quality and caregiver-child relationships were also greatly diminished for those who experienced discrimination.

Structural Equation Models

Structural equation modeling (SEM) was used to test the hypothesized relationships among the study variables as presented in the conceptual model. Maximum likelihood estimates based on covariance matrices were obtained using LISREL VIII (Bollen, 1989; Jöreskog & Sörbom, 1993). Two research questions were addressed in this study. First, we sought to determine whether stress pileup would be linked with psychological adjustment and, in turn, with the quality of intimate partnerships and parent-child relationships. LISREL analyses were executed in which the links among stressful conditions, psychological distress, and mother-child relationship quality were examined. The findings are presented in Figure 21.1. As expected, stressor pileup was significantly associated with poorer psychological functioning, explaining 44% dns ($\beta = .66$, $t = 6.51$) of the variance in psychological functioning. In turn, poorer psychological functioning was associated with less nurturant mother-child relationships, explaining 21% ($\beta = -2.30$, $t = -3.94$) of the variance in mother-child relationship quality. The overall goodness of fit indices, presented in Figure 21.1, is well within the suggested parameters, as noted by the precision of the GFI and AGFI, having values close to 1.0, .98, and 95, respectively (Byrne, 1998, p. 116).

We also were interested in determining how racial discrimination would impact African American women's ability to manage stress, function psychologically, and maintain family relationships. More specifically, we wanted to see whether the associations we hypothesized would differ for respondents who had experienced higher levels of racial discrimination. We used a series of stacked models to test this moderational hypothesis (see Table 21.2). The sample was split into two groups at the median of the distribution for reported incidences of racial discrimination. We first constrained all paths to be equal between the two groups (baseline model) and then released each path in turn to determine if the groups differed. This analysis revealed that both psychological functioning and intimate partnership quality were poorer among mothers who had experienced more racial discrimination. For example, the coefficient for the path between stressor pileup and

Table 21.1 Correlations, Means, and Standard Deviations for Variables in the Analysis

	1	2	3	4	5	6	7	8	9	10
1. Life events	—									
2. Negative financial events	.40**	—								
3. Job stress	.12*	.24**	—							
4. Depression	.38***	.34***	.21**	—						
5. Anxiety	.25***	.25***	.10	.58**	—					
6. Relationship stability	-.27***	-.17***	-.04	-.20**	-.17**	—				
7. Relationship satisfaction	-.28***	-.15***	-.09	-.27***	-.26***	.61**	—			
8. Caregiver-target relationship quality	-.19***	-.15***	-.13*	-.25***	-.24***	.19***	.26**	—		
9. Caregiver-target nurturing relationship quality	-.09	-.08	-.07	-.25***	-.25***	.12***	.23***	.55**	—	
10. Perceived discrimination	.24***	.27***	.05	.14***	.16**	-.15***	-.12*	-.13*	-.12*	—
M	2.47	2.57	9.95	6.22	4.25	17.21	4.28	14.25	54.61	19.66
SD	2.54	2.99	2.42	1.49	1.32	4.31	1.79	1.58	5.50	6.65*

*p < .05. **p < .01.

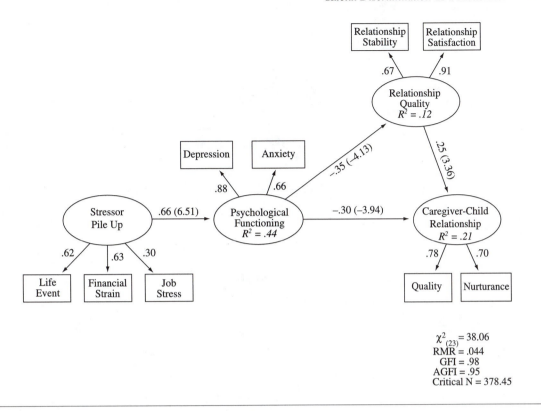

Figure 21.1 Parameter Estimates for Proposed Model

psychological functioning was .75 for the high discrimination group and .41 for the low discrimination group. This finding suggests that African American mothers who encountered high levels of racial discrimination were more likely to experience psychological distress when faced with a multitude of stressful conditions. The impact of psychological functioning on intimate relationship quality also varied by group. The standardized β weight was −.47 for the high discrimination group and −.15 for the low discrimination group. These results suggest that the link between psychological distress and intimate partnership quality is stronger for women who report more experiences with discrimination. Similarly, the relationship between caregivers' psychological functioning and the relationship with the target child were more adversely affected if the caregiver reported higher levels of discrimination (β = −.40 versus −.34 for those who reported fewer episodes of discrimination). Surprisingly, among

those who experienced greater levels of racism, there was little difference between intimate relationship quality and caregiver-target relationships. The stacked model analyses comparing each hypothesized relationship support the aforementioned differences.

DISCUSSION

Few studies have addressed the associations between stressor pileup and relationship quality in African American families. This study specifies the ways in which stressors identified in Peters and Massey's (1983) theoretical analyses of African American family functioning are linked both directly and indirectly with family relationships. Our findings, which are based on data collected from several hundred African American families, were consistent with our theoretical model. We hypothesized that

Table 21.2 Stacked Model Analyses Comparing Each Hypothesized Relationship of High and Low Perceived Discrimination Groups Against the Baseline Model

	χ^2	df	$\Delta\chi^2$	Δdf	GFI	CFI	RMR	CN
1. Baseline model (paths constrained to be equal)	84.96	51	—	—	.94	.94	.060	313.46
2. Stressor pileup → Psychological Distress	76.85	48	17.11**	3	.95	.97	.060	373.47
3. Psychological distress → Relationship Quality	75.23	48	9.73**	3	.95	.96	.060	336.93
4. Psychological distress → Relationship Quality	68.59	48	16.37**	3	.95	.97	.060	369.46
5. Relationship quality → Caregiver-Target Relationship	77.82	48	7.14**	3	.95	.95	.060	325.78

$**p < .01$.

stressor pileup would be associated with mothers' psychological distress. The analyses supported this hypothesis; mothers and female caregivers experiencing higher levels of a variety of stressors reported more symptoms of depression and anxiety. These results are consistent with previous findings for African American families headed by married couples (Brody et al., 1994) and single mothers (Brody & Flor, 1997) living in the rural South. In addition, Pearlin (1983) found that an accumulation of stressors such as those examined in our study create high levels of distress in families because they have the potential to exacerbate existing strain or generate new strain, thus increasing parental anxiety and depression.

Links from maternal psychological distress to relationship quality also emerged as hypothesized. Maternal distress was linked directly to the quality of both mother-child relationships and intimate partnerships; it was also linked indirectly with mother-child relationships through its association with intimate partnership quality. These findings are similar to those that have emerged from studies of contemporary middle-class White families (Conger et al., 1992) and Depression-era White families (Elder, 1974). Although elements of the model tested in this study have been examined in other studies involving African American families (Brody et al., 1994; McLoyd et al., 1994; Murry & Brody, 1999), prior research has not examined all of the components in combination.

The second purpose of this study was to determine whether racial discrimination would amplify the effects of stressor pileup on maternal psychological distress and family relationships. When mothers reported experiencing higher levels of racial discrimination, stronger links emerged between stressor pileup and psychological distress, as well as between psychological distress and the quality of the mothers' relationships with their children and intimate partners. These findings support the hypothesis advanced in the MEES model that chronic racial discrimination amplifies the effects of other ongoing stressors in African American families, as indicated by heightened psychological stress responses (Anderson et al., 1991).

Berkowitz's (1989) reformulation of the frustration-aggression hypothesis provides some theoretical understanding of this process. According to Berkowitz, frustrating and painful events induce emotional arousal and negative affect that can lead to depression and anger. From our perspective, ongoing racial discrimination induces negative emotionality and frustration that contribute to heightened reactivity to negative life situations. The sequelae of this reactivity include a distressed parent and family relationships that are more conflicted and less nurturing. Understanding the range of psychological consequences associated with racism and oppression is significant as efforts are undertaken to develop interventions for improving African Americans' quality of life.

Great variation exists, of course, in the ways in which African Americans cope with experiences of racial discrimination (Krieger, 1990; Murry, 2000). Differences in the coping strategies that individuals employ in response to racist events may account for individual variation in the stress-enhancing effects of racial discrimination. This hypothesis should be tested in future research. A clearer understanding of the buffering effects of intimate partnership quality on stress management among African Americans is also needed. The results of our study suggest that in stressful situations, a relationship with an intimate partner may reduce the likelihood that mothers will become depressed or anxious (Feagin & Spikes, 1994; Vincent, Friedman, Nugent, & Messerly, 1979). Thus, having a satisfying and stable partnered relationship appeared to play a protective or buffering role against contextual stressors (Cutrona, Russell, Hessling, Brown, & Murry, 2000), including racism.

Limitations

Several limitations of this study and some caveats must be noted. First, the proposed model is not intended to be exhaustive. Models that include different parameters than those included in our model could also account for variation in family relationship quality. Second, although the paths in the model may imply causality, at this point we can only test the extent to which the observed variables can be predicted from the hypothesized model without respect to direction of effects. Obviously, the results presented here need to be replicated with an even larger sample of African American families from both metropolitan and nonmetropolitan areas.

Another liability is the cross-sectional design of the study. As a consequence, the direction of all bivariate relations is ambiguous. Models in which family and intimate relationship stressors increase mothers' sensitivity to racial discrimination are also plausible. Understanding the complexity of such reciprocal relations will provide considerable challenge in future research studies.

Our findings nevertheless demonstrate that research on African American family processes should consider racial discrimination. Furthermore, the positive effects of a supportive and stable relationship with one's intimate partner indicated a clear pattern of protection or buffering and should be included in future studies of African American women's mental health. Such studies would provide valuable information for understanding the unique contextual influences on the life courses of African American parents and their children.

REFERENCES

Allen, W. R. (1978). Black family research in the U.S.: A review, assessment, and extension. *Journal of Comparative Family Studies, 9,* 167-189.

Allen, W. R. (1995). African American family life in societal context: Crisis and hope. *Sociological Forum, 10,* 569-592.

Anderson, N. B., McNeilly, M., & Myers, H. (1991). Autonomic reactivity and hypertension in Blacks: A review and proposed model. *Ethnicity and Disease, 1,* 154-170.

Beach, S. R. H., Smith, D. A., & Fincham, F. D. (1994). Marital interventions for depression: Empirical foundation and future prospects. *Applied and Preventative Psychology, 3,* 233-250.

Bennett, C. E. (1995). *The Black population in the United States: March 1994 and 1993. U.S. Bureau of the Census* (Current Population Reports, P20-480). Washington, DC: U.S. Government Printing Office.

Berkowitz, L. (1989). Frustration-aggression hypothesis: Examination and reformulation. *Psychological Bulletin, 106,* 59-73.

Billingsley, A. (1968). *Black families in White America.* Englewood Cliffs, NJ: Prentice-Hall.

Billingsley, A. (1992). *Climbing Jacob's ladder.* New York: Simon and Schuster.

Bollen, K. A. (1989). *Structural equations with latent variables.* New York: Wiley.

Booth, A., Johnson, D., & Edward, J. N. (1983). Measuring marital instability. *Journal of Marriage and the Family, 48,* 381-387.

Brody, G. H., & Flor, D. L. (1997). Maternal psychological functioning, family processes, child adjustment in rural, single-parent, African American families. *Developmental Psychology, 33,* 1000-1011.

Brody, G. H., & Flor, D. L. (1998). Maternal resources, parenting practices, and child competence in rural, single-parent African American families. *Child Development, 69,* 803-816.

Brody, G. H., & Forehand, R. (1986). Maternal perceptions of child maladjustment as a function of the combined influence of child behavior and maternal depression. *Journal of Consulting and Clinical Psychology, 54,* 237-240.

Brody, G. H., Ge, X., Conger, R. D., Gibbons, R. X., Murry, V. M., Gerrard, M., & Simons, L. (in press). The influence of neighborhood disadvantage, collective socialization and parenting on African American children's affiliation with deviant peers. *Child Development.*

Brody, G. H., Stoneman, Z., Flor, D., & McCrary, C. (1994). Religion's role in organizing family relationships: Family process in rural, two-parent African American families. *Journal of Marriage and the Family, 56,* 878-888.

Brown, A. C., Brody, G. H., & Stoneman, Z. (2000). Rural Black women and depression: A contextual analysis. *Journal of Marriage and the Family, 62,* 187-198.

Byrne, B. M. (1998). *Structural equation modeling with LISREL, PRELIS, and SIMPLIS: Basic concepts, applications, and programming.* Mahwah, NJ: Erlbaum.

Clark, L. A., & Watson, D. (1997). *The Mini Mood and Anxiety Symptom Questionnaire (Mini-MASQ).* Unpublished manuscript, University of Iowa.

Clark, R., Anderson, N. B., Clark, V. R., & Williams, D. R. (1999). Racism as a stressor for African Americans: A biopsychosocial model. *American Psychologist, 54,* 805-816.

Conger, R. D., Conger, K. J., Elder, G. H., Lorenz, F. O., Simons, R. L., & Whitbeck, L. B. (1992). A family process model of economic hardship and adjustment of early adolescent boys. *Child Development, 63,* 526-541.

Conger, R. D., Ebert-Wallace, L., Sun, Y., McLoyd, V. C., Brody, G. H., & Simons, R. L. (2000). *Economic pressure in African American families: A replication and extension of the Family Stress Model.* Manuscript submitted for publication.

Conger, R. D., & Elder, G. H. (1994). *Families in troubled times: Adapting to change in rural America.* New York: Aldine de Gruyter.

Conger, R. D., Elder, G. H., Lorenz, F. O., Conger, K., Simons, R. L., Whitbeck, L. B., Huck, S., & Melby, J. N. (1990). Linking economic hardship to marital quality and instability. *Journal of Marriage and the Family, 52,* 643-656.

Cutrona, C. E., Russell, D. W., Hessling, R. M., Brown, P. A., & Murry, V. M. (2000). Direct and moderating effects of community context on the psychological well-being of African American women. *Journal of Personality and Social Psychology, 79,* 1088-1101.

Davila, J., Bradbury, T. N., Cohan, C. L., & Tochluk, S. (1997). Marital functioning and depressive symptoms: Evidence for stress generation model. *Journal of Personality and Social Psychology, 73,* 849-861.

Dressler, W. W. (1991). Social class, skin color, and arterial blood pressure in two societies. *Ethnicity and Disease, 1,* 60-77.

DuBois, W. E. B. (1967). *The Philadelphia Negro: A social study.* New York: Schocken.

Elder, G. H., Jr. (1974). *Children of the great depression: Social change in life experience.* Chicago: University of Chicago Press.

Feagin, J. R., & Spikes, M. P. (1994). *Living with racism: The Black middle-class experience.* Boston: Beacon.

Ge, X., Brody, G. H., Conger, R. D., Simons, R. L., & Murry, V. M. (2000). *Contextual amplification of pubertal transition effects on deviant peer affiliation and externalizing behavior among African American children.* Manuscript submitted for publication.

Guelkow, M. B., Bird, G. W., & Koball, E. H. (1991). An exploratory path analysis of the stress process of dual career men and women. *Journal of Marriage and the Family, 53,* 151-164.

Heim, S. C., & Snyder, D. K. (1991). Predicting depression from marital distress and attributional processes. *Journal of Marital and Family Therapy, 17,* 67-72.

Horwitz, A. V., & Scheid, T. L. (1999). *A handbook for the study of mental health: Social context, theories, & systems.* Cambridge, MA: Cambridge University Press.

Jackson, J. S., Brown, T. N., Williams, D. R., Torres, M., Sellers, S. L., & Brown, K. (1996). Racism and the physical and mental health status of African Americans: A thirteen-year national panel study. *Ethnicity and Disease, 6,* 132-147.

James, S. A., LaCroix, A. Z., Kleinbaum, D. G., & Strogatz, D. S. (1984). John Henryism and blood pressure differences among Black men: II. The role of occupational stressors. *Journal of Behavioral Medicine, 7,* 259-275.

Jones, C. P. (2000). Levels of racism: A theoretic framework and a gardener's tale. *American Journal of Public Health, 90,* 1212-1215.

Jöreskog, K., & Sörbom, D. (1993). *LISREL 8: User's reference guide.* Chicago: Scientific Software.

Karney, B. R., & Bradbury, T. N. (1995). The longitudinal course of marital quality and stability: A review of theory, method, and research. *Psychological Bulletin, 111,* 3-34.

Kessler, R., Mickelson, K. D., & Williams, D. R. (1999). The prevalence, distribution, and mental health correlates of perceived discrimination in the United States. *Journal of Health and Social Behavior, 40,* 208-230.

Krieger, N. (1990). Racial and gender discrimination: Risk factors for high blood pressure? *Social Science and Medicine, 30,* 1273-1281.

McAdoo, H. P. (1997). Upward mobility across generations in African American families. In H. P. McAdoo (Ed.), *Black families* (pp. 139-162). Thousand Oaks, CA: Sage.

McCubbin, H. I., Joy, C. B., Cauble, A. E., Comeau, J. K., Patterson, J. M., & Needle, R. H. (1980). Family stress and coping: A decade review. *Journal of Marriage and the Family, 41,* 237-244.

McLoyd, V. C. (1990). The impact of economic hardship on Black families and children: Psychological stress, parenting, and socioemotional development. *Child Development, 61,* 311-346.

McLoyd, V. C., Jayarate, T. E., Cebello, R., & Borquez, J. (1994). Unemployment and work interruptions among African American single mothers: Effects on parenting and adolescent socioemotional functioning. *Child Development, 65,* 562-589.

Murry, V. M. (2000). Challenges and experiences of Black American families. In P. C. McKenry & S. J. Price (Eds.), *Families and change: Coping with stressful events* (2nd ed., pp. 333-358). Thousand Oaks, CA: Sage.

Murry, V. M., & Brody, G. H. (1999). Self-regulation and self-worth of Black children reared in economically-stressed, rural, single, mother-headed families: The contribution of risk and protective factors. *Journal of Family Issues, 20,* 458-484.

Neighbors, H., & Jackson, J. (1984). The use of informal and formal help: Four patterns of illness behavior in the Black community. *American Journal of Community Psychology, 12,* 629-644.

Olin, G. V., & Fennell, D. L. (1989). The relationship between depression and marital adjustment in a general population. *Family Therapy, 16,* 11-20.

Pearlin, L. I. (1983). Role strains and personal stress. In H. P. Kaplan (Ed.), *Psychological stress: Trends, theory, and research* (pp. 3-32). New York: Academic Press.

Peters, M. F., & Massey, G. C. (1983). Mundane extreme environmental stress in family stress theories: The case of Black families in White America. *Marriage and Family Review, 6,* 193-218.

Phares, V., & Compas, B. E. (1992). The role of fathers in child and adolescent psychopathology: Make room for daddy. *Psychological Bulletin, 111,* 387-412.

Pool, T. G. (1990). Black families and the black church: A sociohistorical perspective. In H. E. Cheatham & J. B. Stewart (Eds.), *Black families* (pp. 33-48). New Brunswick, NJ: Transition.

Sigelman, L., & Welch, S. (1991). *Black Americans' views of racial inequality: The dream deferred.* Cambridge, MA: Harvard University Press.

Simons, R. L., Whitbeck, L. B., Beaman, J., & Conger, R. D. (1994). The impact of mother's parenting, involvement of nonresidential fathers, and parental conflict on the adjustment of adolescent children. *Journal of Marriage and the Family, 56,* 356-374.

Taylor, R. D. (2000). An examination of the association of African American mothers' perceptions of their neighborhoods with their parenting and adolescent adjustment. *Journal of Black Psychology, 26,* 267-287.

Taylor, R., Chatters, L. M., Tucker, B. M., & Lewis, E. (1990). Developments in research on Black families: A decade review. *Journal of Marriage and the Family, 52,* 993-1014.

Taylor, R. D., Roberts, D., & Jacobson, L. (1997). Stressful life events, psychological well-being, and parenting in African American mothers. *Journal of Family Psychology, 4,* 436-446.

Tatum, B. D. (1997). Out there stranded: Black families in White communities. In H. P. McAdoo (Ed.), *Black families* (pp. 214-233). Thousand Oaks, CA: Sage.

U.S. Bureau of the Census. (1992). *The Black population in the United States: March 1992* (Current Population Reports, P20-471). Washington, DC: U.S. Government Printing Office.

Vincent, J. P., Friedman, L. C., Nugent, J., & Messerly, L. (1979). Demand characteristics in observations of marital interaction. *Journal of Consulting and Clinical Psychology, 47,* 557-566.

Williams, D. R., & Williams-Morris, R. (2000). Racism and mental health: The African American experience. *Ethnicity and Health, 3,* 243-269.

APPENDIX

EXPERIENCES OF RACISM SCALE

Scale: 1 = never, 2 = once or twice, 3 = a few times, 4 = several times.

1. How often has someone said something derogatory or insulting to you just because you are African American?	1	2	3	4
2. How often has a store owner, sales clerk, or person working at a place of business treated you in a disrespectful way just because you are African American?	1	2	3	4
3. How often have the police hassled you just because you are African American?	1	2	3	4
4. How often has someone ignored you or excluded you from some activity just because you are African American?	1	2	3	4
5. How often has someone suspected you of doing something wrong just because you are African American?	1	2	3	4
6. How often has someone yelled a racial slur or racial insult at you?	1	2	3	4
7. How often has someone threatened to harm you physically just because you are African American?	1	2	3	4
8. How often have you encountered Whites who are surprised that you, as an African American person, did something really well?	1	2	3	4

9. How often have you been treated unfairly because you are African American instead of White?	1	2	3	4
10. How often have you encountered Whites who did not expect you to do well just because you are African American?	1	2	3	4
11. How often has someone discouraged you from trying to achieve an important goal just because you are African American?	1	2	3	4
12. How often have close friends of yours been treated unfairly just because they are African American?	1	2	3	4
13. How often have members of your family been treated unfairly just because they are African American?	1	2	3	4

22

COUPLE RESILIENCE
TO ECONOMIC PRESSURE

RAND D. CONGER
MARTHA A. RUETER
GLEN H. ELDER, JR.

Over 400 married couples participated in a 3-year prospective study of economic pressure and marital relations. The research (a) empirically evaluated the family stress model of economic stress influences on marital distress and (b) extended the model to include specific interactional characteristics of spouses hypothesized to protect against economic pressure. Findings provided support for the basic mediational model, which proposes that economic pressure increases risk for emotional distress, which, in turn, increases risk for marital conflict and subsequent marital distress. Regarding resilience to economic stress, high marital support reduced the association between economic pressure and emotional distress. In addition, effective couple problem solving reduced the adverse influence of marital conflict on marital distress. Overall, the findings provided substantial support for the extended family stress model.

C lear evidence exists to support the proposition that stressful life events and conditions can disrupt both personal well-being and the quality of marital and other close relationships (Aneshensel, 1992; Cohan & Bradbury, 1997; Conger, Lorenz, Elder, Simons, & Ge, 1993; Coyne & Downey, 1991; Hammen, 1991; Karney & Bradbury, 1995; Pearlin, 1989; Turner, Wheaton, &

Reprinted from the *Journal of Personal and Social Psychology,* 76 (1999): 54-71. During the past several years support for this research has come from multiple sources, including the National Institute of Mental Health (Grants MHOO567, MH19734, MH43270, MH48165, and MH51361), the National Institute on Drug Abuse (Grant DA05347), the Bureau of Maternal and Child Health (Grant MCJ-109572), the MacArthur Foundation Research Network on Successful Adolescent Development Among Youth in High Risk Settings, and the Iowa Agriculture and Home Economics Experiment Station (Project No. 3320).

Lloyd, 1995). One of the most significant stressors in married life involves the inability to meet basic economic needs (Albrecht, Bahr, & Goodman, 1983). When spouses experience economic hardship, they may suffer both personally and as a couple (Conger et al., 1990; Conger & Elder, 1994; Conger, Ge, Elder, Lorenz, & Simons, 1994; Liem & Liem, 1990; Liker & Elder, 1983).[1] As for stressful life conditions in general, then, the adverse influence of economic hardship for individuals and marital relationships has been well established. Not so well understood, however, are either (a) the mechanisms through which financial problems effect the quality or course of marriage or (b) the personal or relationship characteristics that might protect against the disruptive influence of economic stress (e.g., Conger et al., 1990; Karney & Bradbury, 1995; Menaghan, 1991; Vangelisti & Huston, 1994).

The present article seeks to improve understanding of these issues by examining the association between economic stress and change in the quality of marital relations. The research proceeds in two stages. First, we propose and evaluate a family stress model that hypothesizes a series of intervening processes through which economic stress is expected to effect changes in the quality of marriage across time (see also Conger & Elder, 1994). This aspect of the inquiry involves investigation of hypothesized main and mediated effects of economic stress on marital relations. Second, we examine specific dyadic-interactional properties of marriages that we hypothesize should enhance couple resilience to the negative influence of economic stress at different points in the proposed theoretical model. Here interest turns to moderating effects; that is, dimensions of marital interactions predicted to buffer the adverse consequences of economic stress.

Societal economic problems in North America, such as the Depression of the 1930s, the severe recession of the 1980s, and the current economic uncertainty of the 1990s, have tended to increase scientific interest in the impact of economic hardship on marital and family relations (Conger & Elder, 1994; Voydanoff, 1990). Research findings from the 1930s through the 1980s indicate that involvement in a satisfying marriage may help each spouse cope more successfully with financial problems; however, this early evidence also suggests that even a strong marital relationship will likely suffer under the weight of serious and continuing financial deprivation (Angell, 1965; Cavan & Ranck, 1938; Komarovsky, 1940; Liem & Liem, 1990; Liker & Elder, 1983). Despite the importance of this earlier work, it has serious limitations in that the research findings do not clearly identify (a) the processes or mechanisms through which economic stress affects the quality of marriage or (b) the specific interactional properties of marital relationships that may promote couple resilience to the adverse influences of economic problems. More recent studies have begun to address these issues and those investigations have led to the development of the conceptual framework that guided the present inquiry.

A FAMILY STRESS MODEL OF ECONOMIC PRESSURE AND MARITAL DISTRESS

Research conducted during the past decade has merged the interests of the work described above with a more careful delineation of the psychological and interactional attributes of couples that may be influenced by financial troubles and that may lead to problems in a marriage. For instance, in a study of 74 Midwestern couples, Conger and his colleagues (1990) demonstrated that economic problems appear to affect marital quality and stability by decreasing the positive and increasing the negative behaviors that husbands and wives demonstrate in their interactions with one another. On the basis of these preliminary empirical findings and on a theoretical framework suggested by Berkowitz (1989), Conger and Elder (1994) proposed a family stress model of economic influence on marital relations. A slightly modified version of this model guided the present study (see Figure 22.1). In the following discussion, we first consider the theoretical basis and previous empirical support for the main and mediated effects of economic pressure (a specific form of economic stress) proposed in the model. We then turn to the same issues regarding hypothesized protective or moderating effects of social support and effective problem solving at specific points in the proposed economic stress process.

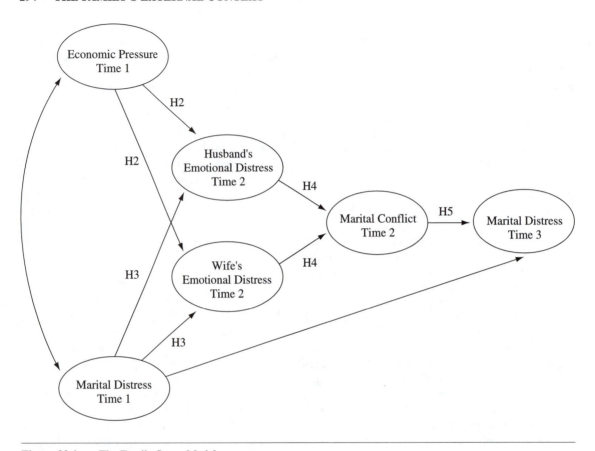

Figure 22.1   The Family Stress Model

NOTE: The indirect, or mediational, hypotheses are as follows: H1—Economic pressure at Time 1 will be positively related to change in marital distress from Time 1 to Time 3. H6—The association between economic pressure at Time 1 and Time 3 marital distress will be mediated by emotional distress and marital conflict. H1, H2, H3, H4, H5, and H6 refer to Hypotheses 1, 2, and so on.

Hypothesized Main and Mediated Effects of Economic Pressure

Economic Pressure, Marital Distress, and Emotional Distress. In path diagrams of the type illustrated in Figure 22.1, both omitted and included paths indicate specific hypotheses for model testing (Dwyer, 1983). Thus, even though the proposed model does not include a direct path from economic pressure at Time 1 to marital distress at Time 3, consistent with the research just reviewed, the first hypothesis for the present study is that economic stress at Time 1, in the form of economic pressure, will be positively related to change in marital distress from Time 1 to

Time 3. Prediction of change is indicated by the inclusion of both Time 1 and Time 3 measures of marital distress in the theoretical model (Dwyer, 1983). By implication, the model in Figure 22.1 proposes that the influence of economic pressure on change in marital distress will be mediated or explained by spouses' emotional distress and marital conflict. We first consider each of the intervening steps in the model and then return to this mediational hypothesis.

The theoretical underpinnings for the family stress model derive primarily from Berkowitz's (1989) reformulation of the frustration-aggression hypothesis. Berkowitz demonstrated that many stressful, frustrating, punishing, or painful events and conditions are lawfully related to increased emotional arousal or negative affect that varies from despondency to anger in both humans and other animal species. For the model guiding the present study, economic pressure provides the primary impetus for the emotional response to aversive events and conditions proposed by Berkowitz (Conger et al., 1992; Conger & Elder, 1994). Economic pressure is a construct that reflects the kinds of painful or frustrating experiences hypothesized by Berkowitz to increase emotional distress. It uses indicators such as being unable to purchase basic necessities or pay bills or having to reduce normal expenditures to meet increasing financial demands to capture the daily stressful and aversive experiences that follow from limited income or high financial demands. It is important to note that economic pressure also expands on the concept of economic strain which, although similar to economic pressure, typically provides a more truncated assessment of the daily difficulties created by financial hardships (e.g., Vinokur, Price, & Caplan, 1996). We discuss differences between the constructs of economic pressure and economic strain more specifically later in the measurement section of this report. Whether one uses the concept of economic pressure or economic strain, however, there is significant empirical support for their hypothesized relationship to emotional arousal and distress (Conger et al., 1990, 1992; Conger, Ge, Elder, et al., 1994; Huston & Lucchetti, in press; Kessler, Turner, & House, 1988; Vinokur et al., 1996).

Consistent with Berkowitz's (1989) reformulation of the frustration-aggression hypothesis, then, the theoretical model for the present study proposes a direct path from economic pressure at Time 1 to the emotional distress (i.e., depressed mood, symptoms of anxiety, and angry or hostile feelings) of husbands and wives at Time 2 (Figure 22.1). Thus our second hypothesis is that economic pressure at Time 1 will be positively related to emotional distress at Time 2 for husbands and wives in the study.

Also consistent with Berkowitz's (1989) perspective, the model in Figure 22.1 proposes that marital distress at Time 1 will influence emotional distress at Time 2. That is, we propose that, like economic pressure, experiencing marital distress will be an aversive condition for married couples (see

Christensen & Walczynski, 1997). This expectation leads to our third hypothesis—that marital distress at Time 1 will be positively associated with emotional distress at Time 2 for the couples in the study. This hypothesis receives preliminary support from previous research which has shown that problems in a marriage are positively associated with the emotional distress of married partners (e.g., Beach & O'Leary, 1993; Davila, Bradbury, Cohan, & Tochluk, 1997; Gotlib & McCabe, 1990). The additional path in the model from Time 1 marital distress to Time 3 marital distress simply recognizes the frequently observed tendency for various qualities of marriages to be relatively stable across time (Karney & Bradbury, 1995). It is important to note that, in the present study, marital distress refers to negative evaluations of the marriage by both spouses (e.g., thinking their marriage is in trouble or considering a divorce or separation). In using the term *marital distress,* we follow a recent suggestion by Fincham, Beach, and Kemp-Fincham (1997) who proposed that evaluations of marriage that are highly negative and not positive indicate what they call a distressed marriage.

From Emotional Distress to Marital Conflict. The next step in the hypothesized economic stress process (Figure 22.1; i.e., the proposed paths from husband and wife emotional distress to marital conflict) follows from Berkowitz's (1989) hypothesis that the negative affect or emotional distress resulting from aversive experiences will "produce aggressive inclinations and the primitive experience of anger" (p. 71). This observation leads to our fourth hypothesis, that emotional distress at Time 2 will be positively related to marital conflict at Time 2. Marital conflict involves criticism, defensiveness, escalations in negativity, angry withdrawal, and insensitivity. Empirical support for this hypothesis comes from a growing body of research evidence which shows that psychological problems can lead both to angry interactions and also to withdrawal in close relationships (Davila et al., 1997; Conger, Ge, Elder, et al., 1994; Conger, Ge, & Lorenz, 1994; Downey & Coyne, 1990; Gotlib & McCabe, 1990).

From Marital Conflict to Marital Distress. The final step in this "chain of events" model involves the path from marital conflict to marital distress. Consistent with this path, our fifth hypothesis proposes that marital conflict at Time 2 will be positively related to marital distress at Time 3. This prediction follows from Gottman's (1993) theory of marital dissolution in which he proposes that, over time, conflict and negativity in marital interactions will lead to negative evaluations of the relationship, including thoughts or even actions related to divorce or separation. Although some studies have failed to demonstrate this hypothesized connection between marital conflict or negativity and marital distress, most research on this issue has produced findings consistent with the hypothesis (e.g., Christensen & Walczynski, 1997; Conger et al., 1990; Gottman, 1993; Gottman, Coan, Carrere, & Swanson, 1998; Karney & Bradbury, 1995; Matthews, Wickrama, & Conger, 1996).

Mediating Mechanisms. Following from the intervening steps in the model that were just described, the sixth hypothesis derived from Figure 22.1 is that the association between economic pressure at Time 1 and change in marital distress from Time 1 to Time 3 will be explained or mediated by emotional distress and marital conflict, in accordance with the definition of statistical mediation proposed by Baron and Kenny (1986). Important corollaries of this mediational hypothesis are the predictions that (a) emotional distress will mediate the influence of both economic pressure and marital distress on marital conflict at Time 2 and (b) marital conflict will mediate the influence of emotional distress on marital distress at Time 3.

Additional Results and Limitations of Earlier Research Related to the Family Stress Model. In addition to the empirical support already cited for specific linkages in the conceptual framework (e.g., between economic pressure and emotional distress), several studies have evaluated most of the hypothesized main and mediating effects in the family stress model (Conger et al., 1990; Conger, Ge, & Lorenz, 1994; Huston & Lucchetti, in press; Vinokur, Price, & Caplan, 1996). Results from these studies have generally been consistent with the theoretical model. There are significant limitations in this earlier work, however. For instance, three of the supporting studies (Conger et al., 1990; Conger, Ge, & Lorenz, 1994; Huston & Lucchetti, in press) included only cross-sectional data, thus limiting inferences about proposed causal relationships when compared with longitudinal, prospective investigations (Dwyer, 1983). Moreover, two of the studies had only self-report information regarding couple interaction processes (Huston & Lucchetti, in press; Vinokur et al., 1996), a measurement strategy that has been questioned in terms of the accuracy with which it assesses actual interactions between romantic partners (Karney & Bradbury, 1995; Lorenz, Conger, Simons, Whitbeck, & Elder, 1991).

The one longitudinal study in this set of investigations also was limited by the fact that it assessed the positive and negative behaviors of only one member of a marital or cohabiting romantic dyad (Vinokur et al., 1996), thus providing incomplete information regarding interactions between partners, an important element in the family stress model. A final limitation of all of these studies is that they did not examine interactional processes related to couple resilience to economic pressure. That is, they did not consider the possibility that some couples would be more or less vulnerable than others to economic stress. The present investigation addresses these limitations and extends the basic mediational model by considering specific dimensions of marital interactions hypothesized to protect against the adverse influences of economic pressure.

Marital Interactions and Couple Resilience to Economic Pressure

In addition to the main and mediated effects of economic pressure illustrated in Figure 22.1, we proposed that social support in marriage and effective couple problem solving would reduce the adverse consequences of economic pressure at two specific points in the proposed mediational model. Figure 22.2A indicates our seventh hypothesis that high levels of social support between spouses will buffer the negative influence of economic pressure on emotional distress. Figure 22.2B illustrates the eighth hypothesis that couples high in effective problem-solving skills will be less likely to experience marital distress as a result of marital conflict. We discuss the rationale for each of these hypotheses in turn.

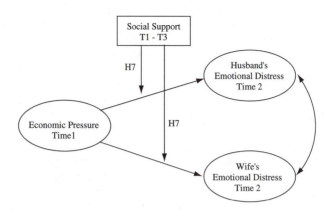

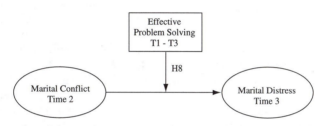

Figure 22.2 Proposed Moderating Effects of Social Support (Panel A) and Effective Problem Solving (Panel B)
NOTE: H7 and H8 refer to Hypotheses 7 and 8. T1 = Time 1; T3 = Time 3.

Social Support in Marriage. In recent years, several investigators have suggested the importance of studying social support processes in marriage, either as a direct influence on maintaining marital quality over time (Acitelli, 1996;. Canary & Stafford, 1994; Julien & Markman, 1991; Rusbult, Drigotas, & Verette, 1994; Vangelisti & Huston, 1994) or, consistent with the focus of the present inquiry, as a source of couple resilience to stressful life events or conditions (see especially Cohan & Bradbury, 1997; Cutrona, 1996). Cutrona, for example, observed that "couples who are able to provide support to one another during times of duress may be able to prevent significant emotional withdrawal by either partner" (p. 175). She also noted that "social support may prevent conflict and relationship deterioration in times of duress through its impact on individual well-being" (p. 176).

Cutrona (1996), then, describes a process similar to that depicted in Figure 22.2: Under conditions of duress (economic pressure in the present case), supportive couple relationships may protect against the exacerbation of individual distress. We expected that Gottman's (1993; Gottman et al., 1998) concept of couple "soothing" through positive marital interactions likely accounts for this hypothesized protective effect. According to Gottman, the exchange of emotionally supportive behaviors or positive affect between partners in a marriage will reduce the emotional or physiological arousal that may result from stress or tensions in their lives. This view is consistent with perspectives offered by other theorists who have proposed that when outside threats like economic pressure exist, behaviors indicative of reassurance of worth, expressions of affection, and careful listening in a marital relationship should enhance feelings of well-being and reduce the level of emotional distress experienced by spouses (Pearlin & McCall, 1990; Weiss, 1990). Because marital support, but not effective problem solving, would be expected to have this soothing effect on emotional response to economic pressure, we predicted that effective couple problem solving would not buffer the hypothesized negative influence of economic pressure on emotional distress.

Drawing on these ideas, we developed a measure of social support in marriage. Marital support refers to the tendency of each spouse to (a) listen to the other's cares and concerns, (b) maintain a cooperative and helpful posture in relation to expressed concerns, (c) indicate sensitivity to the partner's point of view, and (d) express approval of the partner's qualities and characteristics. Couples high in this interactional style also express willingness to make changes in their own behavior to help meet the needs of the spouse. To assure that the degree of supportiveness was a relatively stable characteristic of the couple, we combined scores on this attribute over the years of the study (see Figure 22.2). Also, we assessed couple supportiveness using trained observers, avoiding possible measurement confounds between self-reports of mood and behavioral interactions that may occur when only perceptual measures of social support are used (Acitelli, 1996; Lorenz et al., 1991; Pearlin & McCall, 1990).

Effective Problem Solving. According to our eighth and final hypothesis, couples who demonstrate effective problem-solving skills, compared to less skillful couples, should suffer less marital distress in response to marital conflict (see Figure 22.2). In the present study we drew especially on the work of Levinger and Huston (1990) and Gottman (1979, 1993) who suggest that conflict occurs in all marriages at some time and that it is the means couples use to resolve disputes that distinguishes more successful from less satisfying relationships. In many instances, couples will engage in conflict as a contest that results in a winner and a loser, or they will withdraw from disagreements, leaving the underlying dispute as a nagging and unresolved issue in the marriage. In contrast to these destructive styles of dealing with conflict, Levinger and Huston (1990)

proposed that "collaborating to resolve a problem jointly is the principal way to go beyond a zero-sum conception of an interpersonal conflict" (p. 51). Gottman (1979) noted, however, that in distressed marriages collaboration can be reduced to repeated proposals and counter-proposals for resolving a problem that never lead to a mutually agreed upon solution. That is, couples in distressed marriages may be able to identify many potential solutions to problems, but they have difficulty reaching agreement on which solutions to implement.

Drawing on these ideas, we developed a concept called effective problem solving. Couples demonstrating this attribute work effectively together to develop or identify realistic and nonexploitive solutions to conflicts they experience. However, they do not propose either the highest or lowest number of such solutions; rather, they fall in the mid-range for these behaviors, thus indicating that they can both identify possible avenues for resolving a disagreement and also avoid getting caught in endless loops of solution generation that never lead to conflict resolution. We proposed that couples who demonstrated such problem solving skills would be most resilient to the negative influence of marital conflict on marital distress as shown in Figure 22.2. As with the marital support measure, observer ratings for effective problem solving were combined over three years to assure stability in this interactional style and observer ratings rather than self-reports were used to assess the construct. In addition, we expected that marital support would not moderate the relationship between marital conflict and marital distress. Specifically, we proposed that internal family stressors such as marital conflict require more than understanding to reduce their negative influence on family relationships. Without some degree of resolution they will be a continuing threat to family well-being. Later analyses evaluate the empirical validity of the hypotheses generated by the family stress model.

Summary of Hypotheses

Hypothesis 1. Economic pressure at Time 1 will be positively related to change in marital distress from Time 1 to Time 3.

Hypothesis 2. Economic pressure at Time 1 will be positively related to emotional distress at Time 2 for husbands and wives.

Hypothesis 3. Marital distress at Time 1 will be positively related to husbands' and wives' emotional distress at Time 2.

Hypothesis 4. Husbands' and wives' emotional distress at Time 2 will be positively related to marital conflict at Time 2.

Hypothesis 5. Marital conflict at Time 2 will be positively related to change in marital distress from Time 1 to Time 3.

Hypothesis 6. The association between economic pressure at Time 1 and marital distress at Time 3 will be mediated by emotional distress and marital conflict at Time 2.

Hypothesis 7. The magnitude of the positive relationship between economic pressure and husbands' and wives' emotional distress will be reduced among those in marriages with high levels of social support compared to those in marriages with low levels of social support.

Hypothesis 8. The magnitude of the positive relationship between marital conflict and marital distress will be reduced among couples with effective problem-solving skills compared to those with ineffective problem-solving skills.

METHOD

Sample

The couples in this study were participants in a larger investigation of family economic stress.[2] When first interviewed in 1989, the sample consisted of 451 white, lower-middle and middle class families living in north central Iowa. During the next three years, 44 families withdrew from the study. Up to 18 additional families were deleted from some of the following analyses because of missing data. Each family in the original sample included two married parents (average length of marriage = 17.9 years). By Year 3 of the study (Time 3, 1991), nine couples (2% of the original sample) had experienced either divorce or separation. Although all nine of these families remained in the larger investigation, no couple-level data

were available for the six who divorced or separated prior to Time 2 (1990); therefore, they were lost from the present study due to missing data at Time 2. As described later in the *Measures* section, the three couples who divorced or separated between the second and third waves of data collection were retained in the present sample.

Each family also included a seventh-grade adolescent and a male or female sibling who was within four years of age, either older or younger, of the seventh grader. Because of the rural focus of the larger study, all families lived in small towns or the countryside. Specifically, 34% lived on a farm, 12% lived outside a town but not on a farm, and 54% lived in a town with a population no greater than 6,500. The average family size was 4.95 members, and family median income for 1988 was $33,399 (range = −61,474.00 to $257,000.00). The retention rate for each year of data collection (1989, 1990, 1991) was about 95%. Families who withdrew from the study were, in most respects, not significantly different from those who remained in the study; however, husbands who dropped out averaged 12.74 years of education whereas those who remained in the study averaged 13.58 years ($p < .05$). Other longitudinal studies of families with adolescents also report greater attrition of less-educated parents (e.g., Flanagan & Eccles, 1993).

Procedures

The families in the study were recruited from all 34 public and private schools with a seventh grade class in communities of 6,500 or less in eight Iowa counties. After receiving a letter explaining the research project, families were contacted by telephone and asked to participate. About 78% of the eligible families agreed to take part in the study. Although we have no specific information concerning families who did not participate, the broad range of economic circumstances in the final sample suggests sufficient variability to study the economic stress processes of interest. Each participating family member was paid approximately $10 per hour of participation.

In each year of the study, families were visited twice in their homes. During the first visit, each of the four family members completed a set of questionnaires focusing on, among other things, family member characteristics and patterns of family interaction. The second visit occurred within two weeks of the first. A trained interviewer began the second visit by asking both parents and the two children to complete checklists designed to identify current family disagreements or conflicts. Potential areas of disagreement between parents and children included household chores, homework, transportation, and so forth. Potential areas of disagreement between the marital couple included money, relatives, drug or alcohol use, and so forth. After completing the checklists, family members were asked to gather around a table for the videotaping of four different structured interaction tasks.

For the first interaction task (Task 1, 30 min) family members were given a set of cards containing questions about their family life (e.g., activities they do together) that were designed to elicit family interactions. Family members reviewed and discussed the one or two questions on each card in sequence and one at a time. As in all four tasks, the interviewer explained the task procedures, completed a practice card with the family, and checked the video recording equipment before leaving the room for another part of the house.

The problem-solving task (Task 2, 15 min) began shortly after the completion of Task 1. During this task, parents and children discussed and attempted to resolve three problems identified on the previously completed checklist. Families were asked to first discuss the problem that created the most difficulties and disagreements between parents and children. They were told to go on to the second and third problems only after resolving the first problem. Data for the measures of problem-solving behavior were collected while the family addressed the first problem. Across the 3 study years, the amount of time taken to resolve the first problem ranged from 1 min 16 s to 15 min ($M = 6$ min 43 s; $Mdn = 5$ min 59 s). The time spent on Problem 1 was minimally correlated with the other study variables (range of correlations: $-.09$ to $.15$). Husbands' report of marital distress at Time 1 and Time 3 and wives' report at Time 1 were not significantly related to time spent discussing the first problem. Wives' report of marital distress at Time 3 had a small but significant

association with time spent on the first problem ($r = .11$, $p < .05$), which suggests that the more distressed couples at Time 3 may have spent slightly more time attempting to resolve disagreements.

The third task involved only the siblings and lasted 15 min. The two children discussed topics such as things they do together, school activities, and their plans for the future. During the sibling interaction task, the parents completed questionnaires in another room. For the fourth task, the husband and wife spent 25 min discussing several topics including the history and status of their relationship, areas of agreement or disagreement, and their plans for the future. Meanwhile, the two children worked on questionnaires in another room. The analyses reported here used both observational data (from Tasks 2 and 4) and survey data collected during the study's first, second, and third years.

The videotaped family interactions were rated by trained observers who used the Iowa Family Interaction Rating Scales (Melby et al., 1990) to rate styles of family interaction of theoretical interest. Before they began rating videos, all observers received 200 hr (20 hr per week for 10 weeks) of training and passed extensive written and viewing reliability tests. Once reliable, all observers attended at least two rater training sessions each week to ensure continued reliability. To assess interobserver reliability, 12% of all videotaped tasks in Year 1 and 25% in Years 2 and 3 were assigned to be rated by a second, independent observer. The primary and secondary ratings were then compared using intraclass correlations (Suen & Ary, 1989). An observer rating manual with a complete description of all rating and task procedures as well as definitions for all rating scales is available from Rand D. Conger.

Measures

Two important theoretical and methodological concerns influenced the selection and construction of measures in the present study. First, we were interested in distinguishing between individual and dyadic phenomena in the analyses (cf. Huston & Lucchetti, in press and Thompson & Walker, 1982). For that reason, emotional distress, which reflects a frequently covert, intrasubjective state, was evaluated at the individual level. All other constructs reflected couple characteristics involving the degree of mutual support, joint problem solving, shared concerns with the marriage, marital conflict, or experienced economic pressure and thus were assessed at the dyadic level.[3] Second, to reduce method variance that can result in strong associations among theoretical constructs that are, at least in part, a function of a single reporter's dispositional characteristics (Bank, Dishion, Skinner, & Patterson, 1989; Lorenz et al., 1991), we gathered information from several informants, using multiple methods of data collection. A description of each measure follows.

Economic Pressure. Economic pressure represents the daily irritations and difficulties created by the inability to pay one's bills or to finance economic necessities, and the need to continually reduce expenditures (see Conger et al., 1992; Conger, Ge, Elder, et al., 1994). This construct expands upon the concept of economic strain (Conger & Elder, 1994) by: (a) measuring a broad range of specific economic experiences rather than a small number of global economic evaluations (e.g., Kessler et al., 1988) and (b) assessing recent, actual economic events or conditions rather than expectations regarding future economic circumstances (e.g., Vinokur et al., 1996). Other, presumably objective indicators of economic hardship such as low income and job loss have been shown to have their impact on individual and family functioning primarily through the actions or experiences included within the economic pressure construct (e.g., Broman, Hamilton, & Hoffman, 1990; Conger, Ge, Elder, et al., 1994; Kessler et al., 1988). Analyses of the data used in the present study, but not reported here, also demonstrate this mediational role for economic pressure.

Economic pressure was measured in the study's first year using three indicators. For the first indicator, *can't make ends meet,* husbands and wives were independently asked if they had enough money to meet their expenses (1 = *strongly agree,* 5 = *strongly disagree*), had difficulty paying monthly bills (1 = *no difficulty at all,* 5 = *a great deal of difficulty*), and had any money left over at the end of the month (1 = *more than enough,* 4 = *not enough*). Responses

to these three items were standardized and summed. The correlation between the spouses' summed indexes was substantial ($r = .64$); therefore they were combined to produce the first indicator of economic pressure ($\alpha = .86$). Each spouse was also asked if his or her family had the money needed to purchase clothing, household items, a home, a car, food, medical care, and recreational activities (1 = *strongly agree,* 5 = *strongly disagree*). The summed husbands' and wives' indexes were significantly correlated ($r = .54$) and were combined to form the *material needs* indicator of economic pressure ($\alpha = .91$). To create the final indicator of economic pressure, *economic adjustments,* husbands and wives independently responded (0 = *no,* 1 = *yes*) to a list of 16 possible cutbacks in expenditures (e.g., giving up medical insurance) made during the past year in response to financial difficulties. The husbands' and wives' scores were significantly correlated ($r = .59$) and were combined into a single index or indicator ($\alpha = .89$). For instances in which both spouses responded in the affirmative to a specific item, the index increased only by one rather than two, resulting in a possible range of 0 to 16.

The means, standard deviations, ranges, and intercorrelations for each of the three indicators of economic pressure are reported in Table 22.1. Table 22.1 also contains this information for all of the study variables.

Marital Distress. The multi-item scale we chose to reflect problems in the marriage was originally developed as a measure of marital stability, that is, it reflects the degree to which spouses have considered divorce or separation (Booth, Johnson, & Edwards, 1983). Marital stability, however, is usually concerned with actual separation or divorce rather than with their contemplation alone (Karney & Bradbury, 1995; Lewis & Spanier, 1979). For that reason, we used the term *marital distress* for the Booth measure, a concept that follows from Fincham et al. (1997) who have applied this descriptor to marriages that are highly negatively evaluated in terms of their quality.

We measured marital distress during the study's first and third years. The two indicators of marital distress were developed from (a) the husbands' and

Table 22.1   Correlations, Means, Standard Deviations, and Ranges for All Study Variables

Variable	1	2	3	4	5	6	7	8	9	10	11	12
Time 1												
1. Ends meet	—											
2. Material needs	.73**	—										
3. Economic adjustments	.68**	.64**	—									
4. Husband's depression	.19**	.15**	.15**	—								
5. Husband's hostility	.11*	.11*	.12*	.61**	—							
6. Husband's anxiety	.09	.06	.06	.73**	.55**	—						
7. Transactional conflict	.12*	.02	.08	.00	.03	-.02	—					
8. Tense silence	.03	.08	.01	.00	.00	.00	.24**	—				
9. Brittle relationship	.14**	.11*	.08	.04	.12*	.03	.49**	.43**	—			
10. Wife's depression	.26**	.30**	.22**	.04	.04	.03	.11	.11*	.09	—		
11. Wife's hostility	.27**	.27**	.22**	.06	.03	.06	.13*	.08	.10	.57	—	
12. Wife's anxiety	.29**	.32**	.24**	.04	.01	.04	.08	.14**	.12*	.68**	.50**	—
13. Marital distress, husband report	.11*	.08	.10*	.20*	.25**	.11*	.25**	.17**	.22**	.10	.09	.10*
14. Marital distress, wife report	.15**	.11	.11*	.02	.09	.03	.28**	.19**	.29**	.31**	.23**	.27**
Time 2												
15. Husband's depression	.18**	.17**	.15**	.65**	.43**	.55*	.03	.03	.03	.06	.05	.02
16. Husband's hostility	.12*	.11*	.11**	.42**	.52**	.39**	.08	-.01	.06	.05	.06	-.02
17. Husband's anxiety	.11*	.07**	.10**	.51**	.33**	.60**	-.00	.02	.03	.02	.05	-.04
18. Wife's depression	.27**	.28**	.29**	.06	.03	.02	.10*	.14**	.13**	.60**	.39**	.44*
19. Wife's hostility	.24**	.26**	.25**	-.03	-.02	-.05	.11*	.07	.11**	.46**	.50**	.38**
20. Wife's anxiety	.24**	.25**	.21**	.02	.01	.03	.06	.11*	.07	.50**	.31**	.56**
21. Transactional conflict	.11*	.08	.12*	.02	.12*	.04	.47**	.04	.32**	.06	.16*	.03
22. Tense silence	.10	.17**	.15**	-.04	.01	-.04	.19**	.23**	.30**	.09	.08	.04
23. Brittle relationship	.10*	.11*	.09	.05	.10	.04	.27**	.20**	.45**	.11*	.08	.07
24. Marital distress, husband report	.13*	.08	.07	.17**	.20**	.12*	.18**	.13**	.22**	.05	.11*	.05
25. Marital distress, wife report	.20**	.14**	.14*	.03	.09	.01	.24**	.14**	.25**	.18**	.20*	.17**
Moderator variables												
26. Social support	-.11*	-.14**	-.08	.04	-.02	.00	-.21**	-.26**	-.53**	-.07	-.08	-.04
27. Effective problem-solving	.05	.05	.00	.02	.09	.05	.02	-.09	-.14	-.02	.00	.01
M	-.11	35.27	5.02	4.29	1.50	2.02	2.51	1.63	2.61	5.21	1.66	2.23
SD	4.77	9.78	3.69	3.20	1.44	2.11	.88	.82	.88	3.37	1.33	2.15
Range	-10.8-11.3	14-67	0-13	0-12	0-6	0-10	1-5	1-5	1-5	0-13	0-6	0-10

Table 22.1 Continued

Variable	13	14	15	16	17	18	19	20	21	22	23	24	25	26	27
Time 1															
1. Ends meet															
2. Material needs															
3. Economic adjustments															
4. Husband's depression															
5. Husband's hostility															
6. Husband's anxiety															
7. Transactional conflict															
8. Tense silence															
9. Brittle relationship															
10. Wife's depression															
11. Wife's hostility															
12. Wife's anxiety															
13. Marital distress, husband report	—														
14. Marital distress, wife report	.54**	—													
Time 2															
15. Husband's depression	.15**	.04	—												
16. Husband's hostility	.16**	.03	.57**	—											
17. Husband's anxiety	.11*	.01	.70**	.50**	—										
18. Wife's depression	.12*	.32**	.10*	.07	.04	—									
19. Wife's hostility	.12*	.24**	.07	.06	.06	.62**	—								
20. Wife's anxiety	.08	.25**	.07	.04	-.01	.68**	.53**	—							
21. Transactional conflict	.22**	.21**	.07	.13**	.05	.06	.11*	.04	—						
22. Tense silence	.14**	.20**	.04	.08	.06	.10*	.17**	.05	.29**	—					
23. Brittle relationship	.20**	.28**	.11*	.14**	.11*	.15**	.19**	.15**	.43**	.36**	—				
24. Marital distress, husband report	.50**	.33**	.26**	.27**	.19**	.16**	.17**	.13**	.20**	.18**	.23**	—			
25. Marital distress, wife report	.35**	.52**	.11*	.12*	.02	.22**	.29**	.20**	.19**	.16**	.22**	.66**	—		
Moderator variables															
26. Social support	-.04	-.14**	.00	-.01	.00	-.10*	-.15**	-.06	-.19**	-.26**	-.52**	-.16**	-.20**	—	
27. Effective problem-solving	-.08	-.04	.09	-.06	-.04	-.01	-.10*	-.01	.02	-.06	-.17**	-.10*	-.09	.23**	—
M	7.45	7.74	3.24	1.16	1.38	4.35	1.38	1.83	2.27	1.41	2.76	6.39	6.61	75.11	31.72
SD	2.82	3.10	3.22	1.31	1.79	3.33	1.18	2.08	.94	.75	.85	2.99	33.6	9.42	7.28
Range	5-20	5-20	0-12	0-6	0-10	0-13	0-6	0-10	1-15	1-15	1-15	5-20	5-20	53-105	12-50

$*p < .05.$ $**p < .01.$

303

(b) the wives' responses to the Booth et al. (1983) five-item scale. In 1989, both spouses used a 4-point scale (1 = *never,* 2 = *yes, prior to the last three years,* 3 = *yes, within the last three years,* 4 = *yes, within the last three months*) to report the degree to which they had (a) thought their marriage might be in trouble, (b) thought of getting a divorce or separation, (c) discussed divorce or separation with a close friend, (d) ever seriously suggested the idea of divorce, or (e) talked about consulting a lawyer regarding divorce or separation ($\alpha = .82$ for husband report, $\alpha = .85$ for wife report). During Year 3, the possible responses were *not in the past year, within the past year, within the last six months,* and *within the past three months* ($\alpha = .82$ for husband report, $\alpha = .87$ for wife report). This altered response set allowed us to predict change in marital distress occurring between Years 1 and 3 of the study. As described later in the Results section, each summed indicator was transformed to reduce skewness and kurtosis by taking its natural log. Prior to the third wave of data collection, three couples divorced or separated, and no data on Time 3 marital distress was available for them. Both the husband and wife in these couples were assigned the maximum score of 20 on marital distress.

Emotional Distress. To measure symptoms of emotional distress, each husband and wife completed the depression, anxiety, and hostility subscales of the SCL-90-R (Derogatis, 1983) during the study's first and second years. For each subscale, the husbands and wives reported whether they had experienced the symptoms listed (0 = *not at all* to 4 = *extremely*) during the past week. Responses greater than zero were recoded to equal 1. Scale items were summed to create three indexes of the number of symptoms experienced. Internal consistency for the indicators ranged from $\alpha = .72$ (wives' Time 1 hostility) to $\alpha = .88$ (husbands' Time 2 depression).

Marital Conflict. Three observational ratings assessed during the first- and second-year marital interaction tasks (Task 4) served as indicators of marital conflict. Observers rated each couple's verbal and nonverbal behavior using a five-point scale (1 = *the behavior is not at all characteristic of the individual,* 5 = *the behavior is very characteristic*

of the individual). The first rating, *transactional conflict,* measured the extent to which the couple engaged in reciprocal exchanges of hostility that became progressively more negative. The *tense silence* indicator measured the extent to which the couple engaged in protracted silences that were tense and uncomfortable. A high score on the third observational rating, relationship quality (reverse coded), reflected a *brittle relationship* that was unhappy and high in conflict. Interobserver reliability (intraclass correlations) for these observational ratings ranged from .61 (tense silence, Time 2) to .83 (transactional conflict, Time 1).

Social Support. To assure that the measure assessed a relatively stable characteristic of the couple, we measured marital support during the study's first, second, and third years using observational ratings from Task 2 (the family problem solving task) and Task 4 (the marital interaction task). Thus, couples showing a high level of marital support exhibited supportive behavior toward one another while confronting a problem as well as during the more relaxed, general marital discussion. Six observational ratings (three measuring the husband's behavior and three measuring the wife's behavior) from each of the two tasks were used to measure marital support in each year of the study. Observers used a 5-point scale (1 = *the behavior is not at all characteristic of the individual,* 5 = *the behavior is very characteristic of the individual*) to rate the husbands' and wives' verbal and nonverbal behavior.

With the first rating, *prosocial behavior,* observers assessed the extent to which husbands and wives were cooperative, helpful, and sensitive toward one another. The second rating, *listener responsiveness,* assessed the husband's and the wife's ability to listen attentively to one another. The *endearments* rating assessed the extent to which the partners expressed personalized and unqualified approval of one another. These three ratings of the wives' and of the husbands' behaviors were then summed within tasks. The wives' and husbands' behaviors were significantly correlated (from .46 for Task 4 at Time 1 to .61 for Task 2 at Time 2); thus, their separate ratings were combined across tasks and across the 3 years of the study into a single measure of marital support ($\alpha = .85$). Interobserver reliability (intraclass correlations) for the ratings included in this measure averaged .56.

Effective Problem Solving. As for marital support, effective problem solving was assessed during each year of the study. Four observational ratings were used to evaluate the couple's demonstrated ability to generate a number of useful solutions to a problem. Task 2 (the problem solving task) observers rated both the husband and wife on the number of solutions each proposed for the problem they were discussing (1 = *no solutions identified*, 5 = *4 or more solutions identified*) and on the quality of the proposed solutions (1 = *no solutions identified*, 5 = *at least one solution identified that is reasonable, non-exploitive, realistic, achievable, and specifically stated*). Across the 3 years of the study, interobserver reliability (intraclass correlations) for these ratings averaged .75. The husband and wife ratings were significantly correlated (from .22 at Time 3 to .29 at Time 2) and internal consistency ($\alpha = .71$) for the scale, summed across spouses for all three years, was adequate.

RESULTS

Prior to evaluating the study hypotheses, we examined the data to assure adherence to the structural equation modeling (SEM) assumption of multivariate normality for maximum likelihood estimation (Bollen, 1989). Measures of multivariate kurtosis and skewness showed that the Time 3 measures of husbands' and wives' marital distress were potential threats to multivariate normality. To alleviate this problem, these variables and the corresponding Time 1 measures of marital distress were transformed by taking their natural log. After these transformations, the data showed nonsignificant values for both multivariate skewness and multivariate kurtosis. Therefore, all further analyses were run using transformed marital distress data. Visual inspection of each variable's distribution suggested the absence of outliers. However, to be more certain of this, we ran the initial analyses with and then without the five cases showing the largest values of Mardia's coefficient (Bentler, 1995). The analyses with and without the five cases showed virtually no

differences in model parameters; therefore, the following analyses were run with the entire sample.

Table 22.2 provides the intercorrelations among study constructs used in the following SEM analyses. These latent constructs or variables are based on multiple indicators as described in the measurement section. The LISREL 8 computer program (Jöreskog & Sörbom, 1996) generated these correlations using maximum likelihood estimation. Almost all of the zero-order correlations were statistically significant and consistent with expectations. Most important, and following from the first study hypothesis, Time 1 economic pressure was significantly related to Time 3 marital distress ($r = .09$, $p < .05$). In addition, and consistent with the second study hypothesis, economic pressure was significantly correlated with both husband ($r = .28$) and wife ($r = .37$) emotional distress at Time 2. Similar support for other predictions from the family stress model is apparent throughout Table 22.2. On the basis of this promising correlational evidence, we pursued more formal tests of the theoretical model (Figure 22.1).

SEM Analyses of the Mediational Model (Hypotheses 1-6)

Hypothesis 1 proposes that economic pressure at Time 1 will be positively related to change in marital distress from Time 1 to Time 3. The standardized regression coefficients provided in Figure 22.3 are consistent with this hypothesis. They indicate that, even after controlling for the initial level of marital distress, economic pressure was significantly related to later marital distress ($\beta = .11$, $p < .05$). This simple change model provides a good fit with the data (e.g., adjusted goodness-of-fit index [AGFI] = .99) and all factor loadings were significantly related to their respective latent variables. Finally, the regression coefficient of .56 in Figure 22.3 shows that marital distress was relatively stable across time.

The next step in the analyses was to test the empirical credibility of the remaining main (Hypotheses 2-5) and mediational (Hypothesis 6) effects proposed in the theoretical model (Figure 22.1).[4] We took two different approaches to evaluating these hypothesized relationships. First, it may be the case that the interrelationships among economic

Table 22.2 Correlations Among the Latent Constructs in the Theoretical Model

Latent Construct	1	2	3	4	5	6	7	8	9
1. Economic pressure (Time 1)	—								
2. Husband's emotional distress (Time 1)	.19*	—							
3. Marital conflict (Time 1)	.14*	.04	—						
4. Wife's emotional distress (Time 1)	.32*	.06	.17*	—					
5. Marital distress (Time 1)	.12*	.08	.43*	.37*	—				
6. Husband's emotional distress (Time 2)	.28*	.74*	.04	.08	.05	—			
7. Wife's emotional distress (Time 2)	.37*	.08	.17*	.70*	.36*	.14*	—		
8. Marital conflict (Time 2)	.15*	.11*	.65*	.18*	.31*	.15*	.22*	—	
9. Marital distress (Time 3)	.09*	.06	.32*	.22*	.57*	.05	.22*	.31*	—

*$p < .05$.

306

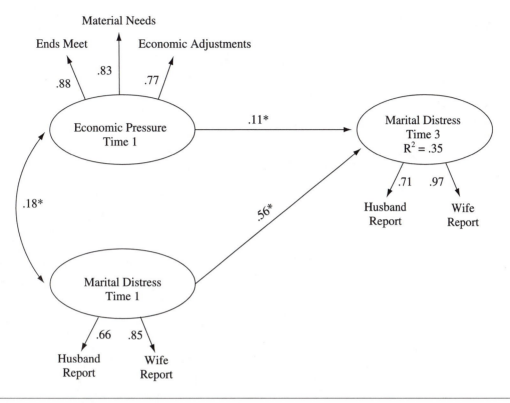

Figure 22.3   Economic Pressure Predicting Change in Marital Distress From Time 1 to Time 3

NOTE: Standardized regression coefficients, maximum likelihood estimation, and parallel residuals across time are correlated. For example, the residual for husband's report of marital distress, Time 1, is correlated with the residual for husband's report of marital distress, Time 3; $\chi^2(9, N = 407) = 4.13$, $p = .94$; adjusted goodness-of-fit index = .99, *$p < .05$.

pressure, emotional distress, and marital conflict proposed in Figure 22.1 reflect a system in equilibrium (Dwyer, 1983). That is, economic pressure may represent a chronic stressor that maintains high levels of emotional distress or conflict across time, but these responses to chronic stress are not continuing to change even though their elevated levels have a deteriorating influence on the course of the marriage. In this form of the model, change in marital distress from Time 1 to Time 3 is predicted by controlling for Time 1 marital distress in the analyses. However, because change is not predicted for emotional distress or marital conflict, Time 1 controls are not included in the model for these variables. A second, stronger form of the model predicted continuing change in the intervening or mediational variables by including controls for earlier emotional

distress and marital conflict. In this model, significant prediction would suggest change over time in emotional distress and marital conflict as a result of economic pressure. The following analyses test both the equilibrium and change forms of the model.

The results provided in Figure 22.4 are consistent with expectations regarding both the equilibrium and change versions of the theoretical model. Coefficients outside parentheses relate to the equilibrium model. Those within parentheses relate to the change analyses. In the latter instance, Time 1 emotional distress is controlled in predictions of Time 2 emotional distress and Time 1 marital conflict is controlled in predictions of Time 2 marital conflict. These Time 1 exogenous variables were allowed to correlate with one another and with Time 1 economic pressure and marital distress. Although

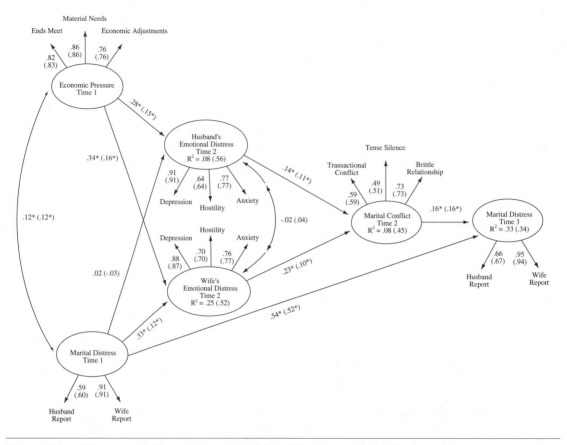

Figure 22.4   Maximum Likelihood Estimation of the Equilibrium and Change Versions of the
Family Stress Model

NOTE: Standardized regression coefficients are in parentheses for the change version of the model. Parallel residuals across time are correlated. For example, the residual for husband's report of marital distress, Time 1, is correlated with the residual for husband's report of marital distress, Time 3. For the equilibrium model, $\chi^2(94, N = 389) = 162.89$ ($p = .00$), adjusted goodness-of-fit index = .93; for the change model, $\chi^2(242, N = 389) = 310.12$ ($p = .01$), adjusted goodness-of-fit index = .92. *$p < .05$.

their stability coefficients from Time 1 to Time 2 were statistically significant and were included in the analyses, they were not significantly related to any other of the endogenous variables. For that reason, none of the paths from these variables to the other endogenous variables was included in the estimation of the change form of the conceptual model.

Consistent with Hypothesis 2, the standardized regression coefficients show that economic pressure was significantly related to Time 2 emotional distress for husbands (.28) and wives (.34) and to change in emotional distress for husbands (.15) and

wives (.16). In accord with Hypothesis 3, marital distress at Time 1 predicted both level (.33) and change (.12) in wives' Time 2 emotional distress; however, the hypothesis was not supported with regard to husbands' distress. The results also supported Hypothesis 4, which proposed that husbands' and wives' emotional distress would be significantly related to marital conflict. Finally, the significant regression coefficient (.16) from marital conflict to marital distress provides support for Hypothesis 5. Because change in marital distress as a result of marital conflict is predicted by both the change and equilibrium versions of the conceptual model, the path coefficients for the two forms of the model were exactly the same. The results also indicate a reasonably good fit between both the equilibrium and the change versions of the model and the data (e.g., AGFI = .93 for the equilibrium analyses and .92 for the change analyses). In addition, all factor loadings were statistically significant and were almost identical for both sets of analysis.

Hypothesis 6 proposed that the main effect of economic pressure on Time 3 marital distress would be explained or mediated by emotional distress and marital conflict. We tested this hypothesis in two ways. First, for both the equilibrium and change versions of the model evaluated in Figure 22.4, we tested an alternative model which added a direct path from economic pressure to marital distress at Time 3. Contrary to the original, statistically significant bivariate association between economic pressure and change in marital distress ($\beta = .11$, $p < .05$; see Figure 22.3), and consistent with the mediational hypothesis, this path was not statistically significant ($\beta = .05$; Baron & Kenny, 1986). Second, we tested the significance of the indirect effect of economic pressure on Time 3 marital distress through emotional distress and marital conflict (Bollen, 1989). This indirect pathway was statistically significant ($p < .05$) for both the equilibrium and change analyses, also consistent with the mediational hypothesis.

Two important corollaries of Hypothesis 6 were that (a) Time 2 emotional distress would mediate the influence of Time 1 economic pressure and marital distress on Time 2 marital conflict and (b) that Time 2 marital conflict would mediate the influence of Time 2 emotional distress on Time 3 marital distress. The same two-step procedure just described was used to evaluate these predictions. First, the zero-order correlations between Time 2 marital conflict and Time 1 economic pressure ($r = .15$, $p < .05$) and marital distress ($r = .31$, $p < .05$) were positive and statistically significant, as expected (see Table 22.2). Alternative models were estimated that added direct paths from earlier economic pressure and marital distress to Time 2 marital conflict. Neither of the alternative paths was statistically significant (economic pressure: $\beta = .01$, marital distress: $\beta = .14$). Second, for both the equilibrium and change forms of the

theoretical model, the indirect effect of Time 1 economic pressure on Time 2 marital conflict was statistically significant ($p < .05$). The indirect effect for Time 1 marital distress was significant only for the equilibrium model. These findings also support the mediational hypothesis.

Similarly, the zero-order correlations between Time 3 marital distress and husbands' ($r = .05$, *ns*) and wives' ($r = .22$, $p < .05$) Time 2 emotional distress were positive, as predicted. Alternative models were tested that added direct paths from Time 2 emotional distress to Time 3 marital distress. When this was done, the relationship between husbands' emotional distress and later marital distress remained nonsignificant and the relationship for wives became nonsignificant ($\beta = .04$). In addition, the indirect effect of husbands' and wives' Time 2 emotional distress on Time 3 marital distress through marital conflict was statistically significant ($p < .05$) for the equilibrium but not the change model, also consistent with one form of the mediational hypothesis. A final fully recursive alternative to the proposed family stress model (i.e., all possible paths originally held to zero were allowed to be estimated) also was tested. This final alternative did not significantly improve the fit of either the change or equilibrium versions of the model; therefore, it was rejected in favor of the more parsimonious theoretical model (Bollen, 1989).

Testing for Protective Influences (Hypotheses 7 and 8)

The next step in the analyses concerned the evaluation of the hypothesized protective influences of marital support (Hypothesis 7) and effective problem solving (Hypothesis 8) at different points in the proposed economic stress process. Because it has been shown that ordinary least squares regression analysis has greater power than the usual two-group SEM procedure for detecting the types of statistical interaction effects of interest (Stone-Romero & Anderson, 1994), we used ordinary least squares (OLS) regressions for the next phase of the investigation (Cohen & Cohen, 1983).[5] For all of these analyses, we included as predictors (a) all variables exogenous to the dependent variable, including the independent variable predicted to interact with either social support or effective problem solving, (b) the protective variable of interest, and (c) the product term for the hypothesized interaction. In earlier analyses, latent constructs were estimated using multiple indicators. The variables for the following analyses were created by summing the indicators for each SEM construct to create a single measure. For example, after being standardized, the *can't make ends meet, material needs,* and *economic adjustments* indicators of economic pressure were summed. Because they were based on the same response categories, the remaining sets of indicators were summed without standardization. The interaction product term was formed by first centering each variable of interest by subtracting its mean and then multiplying the two variables to produce the interaction term. If the standardized regression coefficient for the interaction term was statistically significant and the form of the interaction was as predicted, we interpreted the findings as supportive of the study hypotheses.

The Protective Influence of Marital Support (Hypothesis 7). We turn first to the proposed buffering effect of marital support on the connection between economic pressure and emotional distress. This interaction effect was tested separately for husbands and wives. As just described, we tested for this hypothesized protective effect by regressing Time 2 emotional distress on the full set of Time 1 exogenous variables (economic pressure, marital distress, marital conflict, husband emotional distress, wife emotional distress), plus social support, plus the product term for social support and economic pressure. The results of these regression analyses showed that the interaction between economic pressure and social support was statistically significant for both wives ($\beta = -.10$, $p < .01$) and husbands ($\beta = -.06$, $p < .05$). These results are consistent with the study hypothesis.

Further support for the prediction of a protective influence is provided in Figure 22.5, which graphically portrays these findings. This figure was produced using procedures outlined by Aiken and West (1991) which consider all members of a sample in determining the form of a statistical interaction effect. Specifically, the relationship between economic pressure and change in emotional distress

was computed as a function of couples scoring 1 *SD* above the mean and 1 *SD* below the mean on social support. The equation also controlled for all other exogenous variables, which were set to their mean. As can be seen in Figure 22.5, the dashed lines, which represent the relationship between economic pressure and emotional distress for couples with low social support, have a steeper slope than the solid lines, which represent the relationship between economic pressure and emotional distress at high levels of social support.

We also had hypothesized that different interactional processes would be protective at different points in the proposed model of economic stress (Figure 22.2). Consistent with this expectation, statistical tests of the type just reported indicated that effective couple problem solving did not significantly interact with economic pressure in predicting Time 2 emotional distress for either husbands or wives.

The Protective Influence of Effective Couple Problem Solving (Hypothesis 8). The final set of analyses evaluated the statistical interaction between effective problem solving and Time 2 marital conflict in predicting change in Time 3 marital distress. We hypothesized that the relationship between Time 2 marital conflict and Time 3 marital distress would be strongest for couples exhibiting ineffective problem-solving skills (i.e., receiving very high or very low scores on solution generation) and weakest among those with effective problem-solving skills (i.e., scoring toward the middle of the range on solution generation). To test this interaction, we created a dummy variable that assigned a value of 0 to couples whose problem solving scores fell either below the 25th percentile or above the 75th percentile (less effective problem solvers) and a value of 1 to couples scoring within the middle 50% of the range on problem solving (more effective problem solvers).

Following the same approach described for evaluating the interaction between marital support and economic pressure, marital distress at Time 3 was regressed on all Time 1 exogenous variables (economic pressure, marital distress, marital conflict, husbands' emotional distress, wives' emotional distress), plus Time 2 endogenous variables (marital

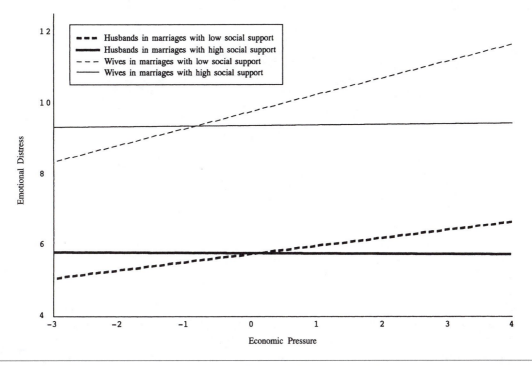

Figure 22.5 The Interaction of Social Support and Economic Pressure in Predicting Husbands' and Wives'
Emotional Distress

conflict, wives' emotional distress, husbands' emotional distress), plus effective problem solving, plus the product term for problem solving and marital conflict at Time 2. The results of these analyses showed that the interaction between problem solving and marital conflict was statistically significant ($\beta = -.16$, $p < .05$), consistent with Hypothesis 8.[6] Figure 22.6 illustrates the significant interaction by separately regressing Time 3 marital distress on Time 2 marital conflict for the ineffective and effective problem-solving groups. The figure shows that the slope describing the relationship between marital conflict and marital distress for the less effective problem-solving couples (the solid line) is quite a bit steeper than the slope for the more effective problem-solving couples (the dashed line). Indeed, the latter slope is almost a flat line, consistent with the hypothesis of a protective influence for effective couple problem solving.

The results of additional analyses also supported our expectations regarding differential protective

influences. The final set of regression analyses showed that the couple's level of marital support did not significantly interact with Time 2 marital conflict in predicting distress in the marriage at Time 3.

DISCUSSION

In this article, we have attempted to shed new light both on the mechanisms through which economic stress may affect marital relations and on particular interactional characteristics of spouses that might reduce the cumulative harm produced by these stress processes. The initial impetus for the research derives from earlier investigations during the 1930s and 1980s which produced suggestive evidence that economic stress has an adverse influence on marital quality and that spouses with strong marriages may be less likely to suffer either personally or as a family when they experience economic hardship (Angell, 1965; Cavan & Ranck, 1938; Komarovsky, 1940;

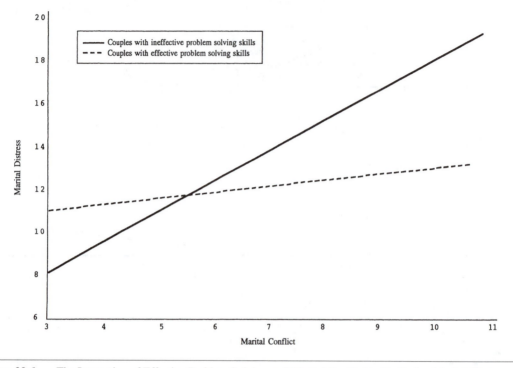

Figure 22.6   The Interaction of Effective Problem Solving and Marital Conflict in Predicting Marital Distress

Liem & Liem, 1990; Liker & Elder, 1983). This earlier research, however, had several conceptual and methodological weaknesses, the most significant of which was the failure to identify and evaluate specific personal or interactional mechanisms through which economic stress might influence romantic partners. Research during the past decade has improved upon this previous work by attempting to identify the intraindividual and interindividual characteristics of spouses that may be affected by economic stress and, in turn, influence the course of marriage (e.g., Conger, Ge, & Lorenz, 1994; Vinokur et al., 1996). As yet, however, this research has not led to the identification of particular marital characteristics that might explain why some couples are relatively resilient in the face of family economic stress and others are not.

Information regarding specific styles of marital interaction that are protective in the face of financial difficulties as well as other stressful events and conditions has both theoretical and practical importance (Cohan & Bradbury, 1997). Not only does the identification of such mechanisms advance basic understanding of human behavior and close relationships, it also facilitates the application of basic research knowledge to the development of intervention programs that can assist families during troubled times. Moreover, for maximum theoretical and practical benefits, specific patterns of marital interaction need to be linked to the particular points in the economic stress process where they will have a protective influence.

In response to these issues, the present study had two primary goals. The first was to replicate and extend earlier research related to the family stress model (Figure 22.1 and Hypotheses 1-6) which hypothesizes that, through a series of intervening processes, economic pressure increases risk for marital distress over time. The present investigation extended this earlier work by overcoming several of its methodological limitations by (a) using a prospective, longitudinal study design, (b) using observer ratings of marital interactions, and (c) including behavioral information for both husbands and wives, thus allowing a test of the complete mediational model. The second goal of the study was to extend earlier research by proposing and testing specific dimensions of marital interaction that might increase couple resilience to the economic stress processes proposed in the family stress model (Hypotheses 7 and 8). Earlier investigations have not studied these hypothesized protective mechanisms in couple response to economic stress.

Findings Regarding the Family Stress Mediational Model of Economic Pressure and Marital Distress (Hypotheses 1-6)

The results were generally supportive of the process model proposed in Figure 22.1. Most of the postulated direct and indirect effects (Hypotheses 1 through 6) were statistically significant as were factor loadings for the indicators of the various constructs. Moreover, the overall goodness-of-fit indexes were quite robust. The findings were essentially the same whether a change version of the model, which controlled for earlier levels of emotional distress and marital conflict, or an equilibrium model, which did not include such controls, was tested. The results were consistent with the study hypothesis that economic pressure will be associated with emotional distress for both husbands and wives. As expected, these emotional problems were positively associated with conflict in the marriage which, in turn, was related to relatively greater marital distress over time.

Also as predicted, the association between Year 1 economic pressure and later marital distress was not statistically significant with the proposed mediating variables in the analyses. That is, economic pressure was associated with relatively higher levels of marital distress through its covariation with personal distress and marital conflict. Moreover, just as the association between economic pressure and marital distress was not statistically significant with the mediating variables in the equations, the same was true for the relationship between economic pressure

and marital conflict. Finally, a number of alternative models were evaluated, none of which improved upon the fit of the proposed and more parsimonious theoretical model. To the extent that these findings have causal implications, we conclude that economic pressure likely has its most significant impact on marriage through its exacerbation of wives' and husbands' emotional problems.

Only three findings were inconsistent with the proposed mediational model. First, Time 1 marital distress did not predict husbands' Time 2 emotional distress, and Time 1 marital distress was not indirectly related to change in marital conflict from Time 1 to Time 2. These findings underscore the relative importance of economic pressure which was directly related to both husbands' and wives' emotional distress and indirectly related to both level and change in marital conflict. They also suggest that economic problems may be an even more important source of stress for a couple than are difficulties in their marriage. In addition, the indirect effect from emotional distress at Time 2 to marital distress at Time 3, through marital conflict, was not statistically significant for the change version of the model. We interpret this as a relatively minor negative finding that does not significantly reduce empirical support for the overall mediational model.

These findings add to the growing empirical support for the basic set of hypotheses derived from the family stress model of economic stress influences on marital relations. Despite differences in measurement strategies and some small variations in results, several different studies now report findings in accord with the mediational model (Conger et al., 1990; Conger, Ge, & Lorenz, 1994; Huston & Lucchetti, in press; Vinokur et al., 1996). The present investigation has extended this earlier work by (a) replicating longitudinally earlier cross-sectional findings, (b) demonstrating that the results hold even when observed rather than self-reported measures of marital interaction are used in the analyses, and (c) evaluating the full model by assessing behavioral interactions between spouses rather than the behaviors of just one romantic partner. Thus, predictions consistent with the model have now been reported for both cross-sectional and longitudinal studies, for observer and self-reports of couple interactions, for both spouses or partners in a romantic union, and for couples living in rural and urban settings. We conclude that there is reasonably strong empirical support for the family stress model of economic stress and marital relations. But are there specific couple characteristics that can protect against these economic stress processes?

Couple Resilience to Economic Stress (Hypotheses 7 and 8)

We predicted that specific types of interactional skills in marriage would be protective at different points in the basic mediational model. Specifically, we proposed that understanding and support would be most protective against an external threat to the marriage (i.e., economic pressure), and that problem-solving skills would be most protective in response to internal family stressors (i.e., marital conflict). We consider the results and implications regarding these hypotheses in turn.

Marital Support (Hypothesis 7). Several researchers have suggested that supportive behaviors exchanged between couples should protect against the adverse influence of stressful life events or conditions, especially stressors external to the marital relationship (e.g., Cohan & Bradbury, 1997; Cutrona, 1996; Pearlin & McCall, 1990; Weiss, 1990). We hypothesized that these supportive interactions likely create a "soothing" effect, consistent with Gottman's (1993; Gottman et al., 1998) proposal that positive affect exchanged between partners will soothe or reduce the emotional or physiological arousal that may result from stress or tensions in couples' lives. Hypothesis 7, then, proposed that highly supportive couples would experience less emotional distress in response to economic pressure than would less supportive couples. Our measure of marital support involved the observed tendency of both spouses to demonstrate concern, caring, affection, sensitivity, and helpfulness to one another during two videotaped interaction tasks. The findings were supportive of the hypothesis. For both husbands and wives, the interaction between marital support and economic pressure was statistically significant, indicating that the positive association between economic

pressure and emotional distress was of greater magnitude for less supportive compared to more supportive couples. Also consistent with the notion that it is the soothing nature of social support that protects against external stressors, other analyses found that couple problem-solving skills did not moderate the relationship between economic pressure and emotional distress.

Effective Problem Solving (Hypothesis 8). Once the source of stress for couples involves difficulties within the family itself, we hypothesized that other interactional skills would be needed to reduce the potentially adverse impact of such stressors. Drawing on the work of Levinger and Huston (1990) and Gottman (1979, 1993), we proposed that couples with strong problem-solving skills would be most able to effectively respond to marital conflict, reducing its impact on later marital distress. As noted, we also predicted that marital support would do little to moderate the relationship between marital conflict and marital distress. The findings were consistent with these hypotheses. Couples who demonstrated the ability to generate realistic and nonexploitive solutions to their conflicts and disagreements, and who did not engage in protracted solution generation to the neglect of actually resolving a disagreement, were less likely to suffer distress in their marriages as a result of such conflicts compared with less capable couples. Also consistent with expectations, the level of couple supportiveness did not moderate the relationship between marital conflict and marital distress. These findings suggest that, when faced with an internal family stressor, couples need to do more than provide sensitivity and concern. They need to be able to negotiate, bargain, and reach agreement on realistic solutions to internal family matters.

Some Additional Implications of the Findings on Protective Processes. These results provide suggestive new information regarding specific properties of marriages that may be protective in the face of economic stress. They begin to tell us what couples might actually do that has a protective influence, rather than simply indicating that those who are happy with their marriages are more resilient in the face of economic difficulties than those who are not. Specifically, these findings suggest that, when faced with an immediate external stressor such as economic pressure, couples who engage in the nurturant and soothing behaviors included within the marital support construct are likely to be more resilient than those who do not. When couples experience internal stressors such as marital conflict, however, the ability to generate and agree on realistic solutions appears to be especially important for promoting resilience. To test the generalizability of these findings, future research should be directed toward replicating and extending these results not only for economic pressure and marital conflict, but also for other internal and external stressors experienced by romantic partners. In any case, these promising results should encourage current research interest in social support processes in marriage (Acitelli, 1996; Cohan & Bradbury, 1997; Cutrona, 1996; Julien & Markman, 1991).

Also important, data such as these regarding specific behavioral interactions provide the type of information needed to assist in the development of interventions for stressed couples. Presumably, the types of behaviors included within the marital support construct can be taught to and applied by couples who, as a result, should increase their degree of resilience to outside threats such as economic pressure. Similarly, almost all couples will experience periods of conflict in their relationships. As with marital support, we expect that problem-solving skills are teachable and can be used in programs designed to help couples develop strategies for promoting more satisfying relationships and resolving significant disagreements.

An Overview and Study Limitations

The findings reported here have implications for at least three important areas of contemporary research on marital relations. First, they obviously enhance our understanding of the processes through which economic stress may influence husbands and wives and the quality of their relationships. Second, because economic stress represents one of the many social-contextual factors that are drawing increasing attention from marital and family researchers

(e.g., Cohan & Bradbury, 1997; Karney & Bradbury, 1995; Menaghan, 1991), the present findings also inform research that seeks to increase understanding of how marriages change in response to the social contexts in which they exist. And third, the present findings inform research on social support in marriage (e.g., Acitelli, 1996; Cutrona, 1996). Our results suggest that research in this area should focus on the specific interactional qualities and individual spouse or romantic partner characteristics that either promote resilience or increase vulnerability to difficult life conditions. This type of research would go beyond earlier work that has dealt primarily with perceptions of satisfaction and closeness in family relationships by identifying the particular behaviors of spouses that likely help to account for both relationship satisfaction and possible protective effects.

Interventions involving such marital interactions, of course, represent only one of many strategies for reducing the adverse consequences of economic pressure. The possibilities for helping families range from social structural, such as the provision of alternative means for augmenting income, to individual therapy for the alleviation of personal distress. Thus, a wide range of methods can play an important role in assisting families facing financial difficulties.

The present study, of course, requires additional replication with urban as well as rural families both within and outside the United States. Moreover, these findings need confirmation with other ethnic groups, with other family forms (e.g., childless married partners), and with couples in short- as well as long-term marriages. It is also important to note that these findings are correlational and, thus, might be dependent on third variables. For example, they may result from unspecified domains of relationship history or early attachment experiences that could not be directly evaluated in these analyses. Despite these limitations, we can conclude that the present findings add to an increasing base of empirical support for the family stress model of economic stress and marital relations. Moreover, the initial findings on couple resilience provide promising leads for future research on interactional processes in marriage that may protect against many of life's important stresses and strains.

NOTES

1. Throughout the article, terms such as economic stress, financial troubles, economic strain, economic hardship, economic problems, and so forth, will be used interchangeably to indicate a situation in which a family's economic resources do not meet its basic material needs or financial obligations. More precisely defined constructs will be used in later tests of a theoretical model relating economic stress to marital and individual distress.

2. There have been numerous research publications from this sample, most of which have examined family influences on adolescent development. Only one previous article has been published on economic pressure and marriage (Conger, Ge, & Lorenz, 1994). The present article is a longitudinal extension of that earlier, cross-sectional analysis. Other investigations of marital relations with these data have been concerned with issues other than economic pressure or hardship (Lorenz, Conger, Simons, & Whitbeck, 1995; Matthews, Conger, & Wickrama, 1996; Matthews, Wickrama, & Conger, 1996; Melby, Conger, Ge, & Warner, 1995a; Melby, Conger, Ge, & Warner, 1995b).

3. Using this dyadic approach, the highest scores on economic pressure, marital support, marital conflict, marital distress, and effective problem solving occur when both partners score at a high level on these variables. This measurement approach is consistent with our assumption that, for example, the most economically stressed couples will be those in which there is agreement by both spouses that the family is experiencing high levels of economic pressure. Similarly, the highest levels of social support, and thus, the highest levels of couple resilience, are expected to occur when both partners are highly supportive of one another, and so on. Although the effects of differences on these constructs within couples may play a role in these processes, they are not the focus of the present investigation.

4. It is possible, of course, that the causal processes proposed in the theoretical model are in the opposite direction. That is, emotional distress, marital conflict, and marital distress might predict change in economic pressure rather than or in addition to the reverse. To evaluate this possibility, in separate analyses we regressed Time 3 economic pressure on Time 2 emotional distress and marital conflict and on Time 1 marital distress, controlling for Time 1 economic pressure. With the exception of the stability coefficient from Time 1 to Time 3 economic pressure, none of the resulting regression coefficients was statistically significant. Thus, the proposed causal direction from economic pressure to change in marital distress is most consistent with these data. In addition, it may be

the case that current economic pressure (i.e., at Time 3) may be a stronger predictor of Time 3 marital distress than Time 1 economic pressure. The difficulty with this approach, however, is that a strong relationship between the two constructs at a single point in time begs the question of temporal order, is economic pressure leading to marital distress or is it the reverse? Researchers revert to the time-lagged relationships such as those used in the present analyses to sort out this question (e.g., Vinokur et al., 1996). We believe that this is the most conservative and reliable approach and use it here.

5. Lubinski & Humphreys (1990) point out that researchers often overlook the existence of significant quadratic effects when testing interaction effects and thus misinterpret the relationships among the data. Therefore, in addition to testing for curvilinear relationships between each independent variable and each dependent variable, we also tested for the existence of quadratic and cubic relationships between the moderator variables and the dependent variables prior to examining the interaction effects. In all cases, no curvilinear effects were found.

6. We also tested this interaction using the LISREL multiple group comparison option. This comparison produced results that also indicated the presence of a statistically significant interaction effect.

REFERENCES

Acitelli, L. K. (1996). The neglected links between marital support and marital satisfaction. In G. R. Pierce, B. R. Sarason, & I. G. Sarason (Eds.), *Handbook of social support and the family* (pp. 83-103). New York: Plenum.

Aiken, L. S., & West, S. G. (1991). *Multiple regression: Testing and interpreting interactions.* Newbury Park, CA: Sage Publications.

Albrecht, S., Bahr, H. T., & Goodman, K. (1983). *Divorce and remarriage: Problems, adaptations, and adjustments.* Westport, CT: Greenwood.

Aneshensel, C. S. (1992). Social stress: Theory and research. *Annual Review of Sociology, 18,* 15-38.

Angell, R. C. (1965). *The family encounters the Depression.* Gloucester, MA: Charles Scribner.

Bank, L., Dishion, T. J., Skinner, M., & Patterson, G. R. (1989). The glop problem in structural equation modeling. In G. R. Patterson (Ed.), *Family social interaction* (pp. 247-280). Hillsdale, NJ: Erlbaum.

Baron, R., & Kenny, D. (1986). The moderator-mediator variable distinction in social psychological research: Conceptual, strategic, and statistical considerations. *Journal of Personality and Social Psychology, 51,* 1173-1182.

Beach, S. R. H., & O'Leary, K. D. (1993). Marital discord and dysphoria: For whom does the marital relationship predict depressive symptomatology? *Journal of Social and Personal Relationships, 10,* 405-420.

Bentler, P. M. (1995). *EQS structural equation program manual.* Encino, CA: Multivariate Software, Inc.

Berkowitz, L. (1989). Frustration-aggression hypothesis: Examination and reformulation. *Psychological Bulletin, 106,* 59-73.

Bollen, K. A. (1989). *Structural equations with latent variables.* New York: Wiley.

Booth, A., Johnson, D., & Edwards, J. N. (1983). Measuring marital stability. *Journal of Marriage and the Family, 38,* 387-394.

Broman, C. L., Hamilton, V. L., & Hoffman, W. S. (1990). Unemployment and its effects on families: Evidence from a plant closing study. *American Journal of Community Psychology, 18,* 643-659.

Canary, D. J., & Stafford, L. (1994). Maintaining relationships through strategic and routine interaction. In D. J. Canary & L. Stafford (Eds.), *Communication and relational maintenance* (pp. 3-22). San Diego, CA: Academic Press.

Cavan, R. S., & Ranck, K. M. (1938). *The family and the Depression.* Chicago: University of Chicago Press.

Christensen, A., & Walczynski, P. T. (1997). Conflict and satisfaction in couples. In R. J. Sternberg & M. Hojjat (Eds.), *Satisfaction in close relationships* (pp. 249-274). New York: Guilford Press.

Cohan, C. L., & Bradbury, T. N. (1997). Negative life events, marital interaction, and the longitudinal course of newlywed marriage. *Journal of Personality and Social Psychology, 73,* 114-128.

Cohen, J., & Cohen, P. (1983). *Applied multiple regression/ correlation analyses for the behavioral sciences* (2nd ed.). Hillsdale, NJ: Erlbaum.

Conger, R. D., Conger, K. J., Elder, G. H., Jr., Lorenz, F., Simons, R., & Whitbeck, L. (1992). A family process model of economic hardship and influences on adjustment of early adolescent boys. *Child Development, 63,* 526-541.

Conger, R. D., & Elder, G. H., Jr. (1994). *Families in troubled times: Adapting to change in rural America.* New York: Aldine de Gruyter.

Conger, R. D., Elder, G. H., Jr., Lorenz, F., Conger, K., Simons, R., Whitbeck, L., Huck, S., & Melby, J. (1990). Linking economic hardship to marital quality and distress. *Journal of Marriage and the Family, 52,* 643-656.

Conger, R. D., Ge, X., Elder, G. H., Jr., Lorenz, F. O., & Simons, R. L. (1994). Economic stress, coercive family process, and developmental problems of adolescents. *Child Development, 65,* 541-561.

Conger, R. D., Ge, X., & Lorenz, F. O. (1994). Economic stress and marital relations. In R. D. Conger & G. H. Elder, Jr. (Eds.), *Families in troubled times: Adapting to change in rural America* (pp. 187-203). New York: Aldine de Gruyter.

Conger, R. D., Lorenz, F. O., Elder, G. H., Jr., Simons, R. L., & Ge, X. (1993). Husband and wife differences in response to undesirable life events. *Journal of Health and Social Behavior, 34,* 71-88.

Coyne, J. C., & Downey, G. (1991). Social factors and psychopathology: Stress, social support, and coping processes. In M. R. Rosenzweig & L. W. Porter (Eds.), *Annual review of psychology* (Vol. 42, pp. 401-425). Palo Alto, CA: Annual Reviews, Inc.

Cutrona, C. E. (1996). Social support as a determinant of marital quality: The interplay of negative and supportive behaviors. In G. R. Pierce, B. R. Sarason, & I. G. Sarason (Eds.), *Handbook of social support and the family* (pp. 173-194). New York: Plenum.

Davila, J., Bradbury, T. N., Cohan, C. L., & Tochluk, S. (1997). Marital functioning and depressive symptoms: Evidence for a stress generation model. *Journal of Personality and Social Psychology, 73,* 849-861.

Derogatis, L. R. (1983). *SCL-90-R administration, scoring, and procedures manual-II.* Towson, MD: Clinical Psychometric Research.

Downey, G., & Coyne, J. C. (1990). Children of depressed parents: An integrative review. *Psychological Bulletin, 108,* 50-76.

Dwyer, J. H. (1983). *Statistical models for the social and behavioral sciences.* New York: Oxford University Press.

Fincham, F. D., Beach, S. R. H., & Kemp-Fincham, S. I. (1997). Marital quality: A new theoretical perspective. In R. J. Sternberg & M. Hojjat (Eds.), *Satisfaction in close relationships* (pp. 275-304). New York: Guilford Press.

Flanagan, C. A., & Eccles, J. S. (1993). Changes in parents' work status and adolescents' adjustment at school. *Child Development, 64,* 246-257.

Gotlib, I. H., & McCabe, S. B. (1990). Marriage and psychopathology. In F. D. Fincham & T. N. Bradbury (Eds.), *The psychology of marriage: Basic issues & applications* (pp. 226-257). New York: Guilford Press.

Gottman, J. M. (1979). *Marital interaction: Experimental investigations.* New York: Academic Press.

Gottman, J. M. (1993). A theory of marital dissolution and stability. *Journal of Family Psychology, 7,* 57-75.

Gottman, J. M., Coan, J., Carrere, S., & Swanson, C. (1998). Predicting marital happiness and stability from newlywed interactions. *Journal of Marriage and the Family, 60,* 5-22.

Hammen, C. (1991). *Depression runs in families: The social context of risk and resilience in children of depressed mothers.* New York: Springer-Verlag.

Huston, T. L., & Lucchetti, A. (in press). The impact of economic hardship on marital stability and satisfaction: Testing a mediational model. *Journal of Marriage and the Family.*

Jöreskog, K. G., & Sörbom, D. (1996). *LISREL 8: User's reference guide.* Chicago, IL: Scientific Software International, Inc.

Julien, D., & Markman, H. J. (1991). Social support and social networks as determinants of individual and marital outcomes. *Journal of Social and Personal Relationships, 8,* 549-568.

Karney, B. R., & Bradbury, T. N. (1995). The longitudinal course of marital quality and stability: A review of theory, methods, and research. *Psychological Bulletin, 118,* 3-34.

Kessler, R. C., Turner, J., & House, J. S. (1988). Effects of unemployment on health in a community survey: Main, modifying, and mediating effects. *Journal of Social Issues, 44,* 69-85.

Komarovsky, M. (1940). *The unemployed man and his family.* New York: Dryden Press.

Levinger, G., & Huston, T. L. (1990). The social psychology of marriage. In F. D. Fincham & T. N. Bradley (Eds.), *The psychology of marriage: Basic issues & applications* (pp. 19-58). New York: Guilford Press.

Lewis, R. A., & Spanier, G. B. (1979). Theorizing about the quality and stability of marriage. In W. R. Burr, R. Hill, F. I. Nye, & I. L. Reiss (Eds.), *Contemporary theories about the family: Research-based theories* (Vol. 1, pp. 268-294). New York: The Free Press.

Liem, J. H., & Liem, G. R. (1990). Understanding the individual and family effects of unemployment. In J. Eckenrode & S. Gore (Eds.), *Stress between work and family* (pp. 175-204). New York: Plenum Press.

Liker, J. K., & Elder, G. H., Jr. (1983). Economic hardship and marital relations in the 1930s. *American Sociological Review, 48,* 343-359.

Lorenz, F. O., Conger, R. D., Simons, R. L., & Whitbeck, L. B. (1995). The effects of unequal covariances and reliabilities on contemporaneous inference: The case of hostility and marital happiness. *The Journal of Marriage and the Family, 57,* 1049-1064.

Lorenz, F. O., Conger, R. D., Simons, R. L., Whitbeck, L. B., & Elder, G. H., Jr. (1991). Economic pressure and marital quality: An illustration of the method variance problem in the causal modeling of family processes. *Journal of Marriage and the Family, 53,* 375-388.

Lubinski, D., & Humphreys, L. G. (1990). Assessing spurious "moderator effects": Illustrated substantively with the hypothesized ("synergistic") relationship between spatial and mathematical ability. *Psychological Bulletin, 107,* 385-393.

Matthews, L. S., Conger, R. D., & Wickrama, K. A. S. (1996). Workfamily conflict and marital quality: Mediating processes. *Social Psychology Quarterly, 59,* 62-79.

Matthews, L. S., Wickrama, K. A. S., & Conger, R. D. (1996). Predicting marital instability from spouse and observer reports of marital interaction. *Journal of Marriage and the Family, 58,* 641-655.

Melby, J. N., Conger, R. D., Book, R., Rueter, M., Lucy, L., Repinski, D., Ahrens, K., Black, D., Brown, D., Huck, S., Mutchler, L., Rogers, S., Ross, J., & Stavros, T. (1990). *The Iowa family interaction rating scales.* Ames, IA: Iowa Youth and Families Project.

Melby, J. N., Conger, R. D., Ge, X., & Warner, T. (1995a). The importance of task in evaluating positive marital interactions. *Journal of Marriage and the Family, 57,* 981-994.

Melby, J. N., Conger, R. D., Ge, X., & Warner, T. (1995b). The use of structural equation modeling in assessing the quality of marital observations. *Journal of Family Psychology, 9,* 280-293.

Menaghan, E. G. (1991). Work experiences and family interaction processes: The long reach of the job? *Annual Review of Sociology, 17,* 419-444.

Pearlin, L. I. (1989). The sociological study of stress. *Journal of Health and Social Behavior, 30,* 241-256.

Pearlin, L. I., & McCall, M. E. (1990). Occupational stress and marital support: A description of microprocesses. In J. Eckenrode & S. Gore (Eds.), *Stress between work and family* (pp. 39-60). New York: Plenum Press.

Rusbult, C. E., Drigotas, S. M., & Verette, J. (1994). The investment model: An interdependence analysis of commitment processes and relationship maintenance phenomena. In D. J. Canary & L. Stafford (Eds.), *Communication and relational maintenance* (pp. 115-139). San Diego, CA: Academic Press.

Stone-Romero, E. F., & Anderson, L. E. (1994). Relative power of moderated multiple regression and the comparison of subgroup correlation coefficients for detecting moderating effects. *Journal of Applied Psychology, 79,* 354-359.

Suen, H. K., & Ary, D. (1989). *Analyzing quantitative behavior observation data.* Hillsdale, NJ: Erlbaum.

Thompson, L., & Walker, A. (1982). The dyad as a unit of analysis: Conceptual and methodological issues. *Journal of Marriage and the Family, 44,* 889-900.

Turner, R. J., Wheaton, B., & Lloyd, D. A. (1995). The epidemiology of social stress. *American Sociological Review, 60,* 104-125.

Vangelisti, A. L., & Huston, T. L. (1994). Maintaining marital satisfaction and love. In D. J. Canary & L. Stafford (Eds.), *Communication and relational maintenance* (pp. 165-186). San Diego, CA: Academic Press.

Vinokur, A. D., Price, R. H., & Caplan, R. D. (1996). Hard times and hurtful partners: How financial strain affects depression and relationship satisfaction of unemployed persons and their spouses. *Journal of Personality and Social Psychology, 71,* 166-179.

Voydanoff, P. (1990). Economic distress and family relations: A review of the eighties. *Journal of Marriage and the Family, 52,* 1099-1115.

Weiss, R. S. (1990). Bringing work stress home. In J. Eckenrode & S. Gore (Eds.), *Stress between work and family* (pp. 17-37). New York: Plenum Press.

PART 8

SUMMARY AND FUTURE DIRECTIONS

For future directions, we include an article by David Reiss and Mary Ellen Oliveri, who present a new approach for the conceptualization and assessment of family stress. Although their publication is dated 1991, what *remains* new is their idea that a family's meaning about an event is defined by their social community. Rather than continuing to assess individual or family perceptions or meanings, Reiss and Oliveri say we should assess the external community's appraisal. How does the neighborhood, religious group, or tribe, for example, define a family's situation? In family therapy, for example, I have at times included priests, tribal matriarchs or patriarchs, extended kin, teachers, neighborhood friends, Scout leaders, and, once, a woman's bridge club. In unique ways, each social group provided an external definition of the situation that enlightened. Working with multicultural families in New York's lower Manhattan after the September 11, 2001, attacks on the World Trade Center, we saw that each family's perception of their situation (a missing family member) was shaped by their spiritual community's conception of whether there could be a funeral without a body. How the ethnic and religious community defined their unique situation of loss often determined the meaning and thus outcome for surviving families. The importance of diversity at all levels of human relational experience requires future scholars in family stress management to assess external influences on the meaning a family or its individual members—male, female, old, and young—have for their situation of stress, crisis, or trauma.

While we honor diversity and multiculturalism, we must at the same time continue the search for commonalities across communities, societies, cultures, and international borders. As evidence mounts to show that different kinds of families can achieve the same ends—strong families with strong children—it is hoped that moral overtones about one kind of "normal family" will diminish.

For future directions worldwide in family trends, problems, and dilemmas, I refer you to Florence Kaslow's (2001) article, "Families and Family Psychology at the Millennium." This is her list:

Sociopolitical changes that affect family dynamics and power alignments; the changing nature of male-female relationships; increase in domestic violence, quest for effective child-rearing and socialization practices; rising divorce rates and their implications; the search for identity: balancing I, Thou, and We; a longing for greater spirituality and a coherent belief system; the increasing magnitude of addictions; the proliferation of wars, starvation, persecution, and other national disasters; the escalation of crime and violence; stealing people: child snatching and adult kidnapping; homelessness and throwaway children; huge waves of immigration lead to more cultural pluralism and often more prejudice; different family branches relocate to different countries: massive uprooting; adoption of foreign-born children: another contribution to multicultural diversity; the advent of cyberspace and new media influences; other global trends [e.g., spread of HIV/Aids and other illnesses]. (pp. 37-43)

Just as in the 1970s scientists and practitioners shifted from a focus on the individual to families, Kaslow (2001) states that scientists and practitioners must now again "expand the scope" to include "larger socioeconomic and political contexts" (p. 44). We agree with her views and those of Reiss and Oliveri, who call for more focus on the community and context in which each family and its members reside.

Finally, my concern that family stress researchers and theorists have meandered away from practice can be abated by using postmodern and positivist approaches that are mindful of application. Family therapists and other clinicians are essential collaborators on research teams if we are to develop useful theory that will guide those who work directly, not abstractly, with distressed families. Social workers, nurses, family therapists, psychologists, clergy, teachers, hospice workers, health care workers, disaster workers, and family caregivers are hungry for research-based models to guide their difficult work. It is hoped that this book of readings has stimulated your thinking about new directions to ease the stress of contemporary families—wherever they have come from and whatever their community now.

REFERENCE

Kaslow, F. (2001). Families and family psychology at the millennium. *American Psychologist, 56*(1), 37-46.

23

THE FAMILY'S CONCEPTION OF ACCOUNTABILITY AND COMPETENCE

A New Approach to the Conceptualization and Assessment of Family Stress

DAVID REISS
MARY ELLEN OLIVERI

Clinicians and researchers have a strong interest in understanding how families respond to stress. Often, they begin their analyses by attempts to estimate the seriousness or magnitude of the stressful events impinging on the families they observe. Until now, they have relied on two strategies. First, they attempt to develop objective or external indicators of the magnitude of the stress of the events. The problem here is that the family's own perceptions and experiences are not properly weighted. The second strategy depends heavily or exclusively on the family's perceptions of the events. However, these perceptions are often a product of the family's efforts to cope with the stress since the organization and perception of meaning in events is a fundamental part of family coping. Thus, this approach cannot disentangle the stress inherent in the events from the family's efforts to cope with it. This article explores a third alternative. The social community in which the family lives often provides a coherent frame of meanings for most events. It not only defines the magnitude of the event but it also defines how accountable the family is for producing the event in the first place. A method for assessing these community frameworks is presented. Initial results suggest that there is not only a coherent community framework attributing magnitude and family accountability to a large number of stressful events impinging the family but, also, that these community attributions are embedded in a community concept of family development.

Reprinted from *Family Process*, 30 (1991): 193-214. Reproduced with permission of Family Process Inc. This research was supported by Grant RO1-MH26711 to Dr. Reiss from the National Institute of Mental Health.

Family stress is a matter of great importance to family researchers but is of even more importance to families themselves. Just as researchers do, families can observe the occurrence of stress in themselves as well as in other families. And as researchers do, they can observe their own response to stress; they can observe how families they know respond to stress, and they can form their own conclusions about the consequences for themselves and for other families of those responses. Most importantly, families, like researchers, can develop theories to explain their responses and those of others. It seems likely that these intuitive theories of family stress are part of an amalgam of perceptions, values, theories, and philosophies families develop about themselves and the social world in which they live.

If we consider any community of families (a small town; a neighborhood; a small, homogeneous and enclosed primitive culture), we can distinguish two kinds of these intuitive theories. First, there are theories that are relatively unique to each family in the community, theories that are a product of the family's own development and history. For any family, these are visions, values, world views, and subjective convictions that are, more or less, shared by all its members but not necessarily by all or even most other families in the same community. There have been several well-known attempts to distinguish among families on the basis of the form or quality of these theories. For example, Farber and Jenne (10) distinguished between child- and career-centered families; Kantor and Lehr (18) distinguished the meaning systems of families as open, closed, or random; and our research group has empirically defined a coherent world view, characteristic for each family, which we (20) have labeled the *family paradigm.*

For some of these informal theories, family members may be fully aware of the principles or perspectives that typify their own family unit; at other times, these informal theories must be inferred by the outside observer because the family cannot describe them in words but enacts them through patterned routines, problem-solving patterns, and rituals (21, 28). We have reported evidence that these efforts by families to understand the social world in which they live include their efforts to understand other families (23). Our data suggested that members of a family do indeed discuss and formulate together the characteristics and motives of other families they know. The data also suggested that these discussions reveal, for each family, aspects of its underlying paradigm about how its social world is constructed.

It seems likely, however, that the concepts that families develop about other families do not remain entirely idiosyncratic. There are many opportunities for families to compare their concepts about family life with other families in their community: informal discussion, reading, television, and through a variety of forms of social participation. We might expect, then, that in any community of interacting families these views of family life achieve some consensus through a continuing process of comparison and reconciliation among families. At this level, a consensus among families is akin to what Goffman (12) called *primary frameworks,* sets of common social assumptions in the community by which its members readily construe the cause, probable intent, and consequence of any conspicuous social act. In a recent review, drawing on ethnographic accounts of family responses to natural disasters, Boss (5) applies this perspective to understanding family stress along lines that parallel our own.

These conceptions of family life, shared by families in the same community, can be referred to as *community-level* concepts, in contrast to conceptions that are shaped by the individual circumstances of a particular family, which can be called *family-level* concepts. The level, then, refers to the *subject* of the concept not its *object*. Heider (15) was the first to study systematically these community-level conceptions about motives that laypeople attribute to individuals. He called them "naive psychologies," although a less pejorative term might be *intuitive psychologies.* Correspondingly, when families struggle to understand the patterns and motives in other families, they are constructing their own *intuitive family sociologies.*

In this current article, we focus on one aspect of this community-level, intuitive sociology of family life: how families understand the impact of stress on family life. The article deals sequentially with five logically interrelated components of this process:

1. We posit some of the forms these community-level views about family stress may take.

2. We show how this approach to understanding family stress improves the precision and clarity of assessing, in any community, which events are stressful for families and which are not.

3. We present a simple and straightforward quantitative method for assessing these community-level conceptions of family stress.

4. We report results of the first use of this method. These results show a consistency across families in how they understand the impact of life events and circumstances on families. Moreover, these results reveal a consensus among families in their conceptualization of two processes that also lie at the heart of many professional theories about families: family boundaries and family development. Indeed, these results suggest that the families in our sample used their concepts of family boundaries and family development to understand the impact of life events on family process.

5. We illustrate how these findings may be useful in understanding the impact of personal and community disasters, how they may help to identify high-risk and alienated families within any specified community, and how they may explain difficulties in establishing relationships between therapist and family.

INTUITIVE SOCIOLOGICAL CONCEPTIONS OF FAMILY STRESS

A variety of historical and anthropological analyses suggest that community-level concepts about family stress may vary along two dimensions: the *accountability* of a family for producing or exacerbating the stressor situation in the first place, and its *competence* in protecting itself from disruption in the face of the stressor, whether the family can be held accountable for it or not.

Family Accountability

By accountability we mean how an intuitive sociology conceives of family dynamics or family process. We suggest that families in all communities share some notions about causal sequences of interactional events in families: what kind of family interactions and role relationships lead to what kind of consequences for the family as a whole, for its individual members, and for the community. Perhaps the most universal concerns in this regard are child development and health and illness. Community-level concepts may be distinguished by their attributions concerning the family's influence and power over these processes. For example, for child development, historical analyses are most instructive. Aries, in *Centuries of Childhood* (4), argues that in Europe during the Middle Ages there was no conception of childhood as an extended and vulnerable phase of human development. Quite the contrary, the child was—at an early age—perceived as a little adult whose development unfolded within the social forces of general public life. During that period, to ask a family whether it or any other family could influence this development was to inquire about not only the impossible but also the inconceivable. In striking contrast, as detailed by Demos (8), in Puritan communities the family was charged with full responsibility for the community's children, not just the social and emotional development but their academic and occupational training as well. Sameroff and Feil (26) have shown that intuitive sociologies may be discriminated on much subtler grounds; for example, parents in traditional Mexican communities in the United States view child development as determined by single, simple causes such as good or bad discipline, whereas higher-SES families, fully acculturated to American life, conceive of a variety of interacting and conditional causes for child development, some originating in the family and some without, which may change across the life span.

Two major features of intuitive sociologies emerge from these reports. First, subject families can readily conceive, at least on an implicit level, of an average or typical family in their culture or community, and develop opinions, views, perspectives, or behavior in accord with this community or culture-based notion of a typical family. Second, these lay conceptions of accountability can shape the family's view of the cause of a broad range of stressful life events or circumstances. For example, if a child was caught stealing in the European Middle Ages, it was unlikely that the family would be held accountable. However, in Puritan New England, the family would be held fully accountable not only for these instances of moral turpitude but for an even broader range of educational and occupational failures as well.

Family Competence

By competence we mean distinctions among community-level conceptions in how the community views the family's competence or hardiness in the face of stress. This includes views of how disruptive a given circumstance should be on family life; that is, the community's estimate of the magnitude of the impact of a stressful circumstance on a typical family reflects its conception of the typical or ordinary family's competence to withstand it. Current data suggest that intuitive sociologies address competence in two closely related ways.

First, they shape an understanding of the *seriousness of the event* or circumstance for the typical family in the community. Intuitive sociologies recognize that, for the average family in its community, some events are more disruptive than others. Scotch's (27) study of high blood pressure in the Zulus illustrates this process. His analysis sought to understand variations in social circumstances that would lead to variations among Zulus in elevated blood pressure. His data revealed that in traditional, rural Zulu communities the number of children a woman had was unrelated to her blood pressure, but the onset of menopause often produced sharply elevated levels. In striking contrast, in urban communities—into which Zulus had migrated in large numbers—the reverse was true: each new child brought the risk of more elevated blood pressure, but menopause was not a risk factor at all. It was clear to Scotch that the birth of a child in traditional Zulu communities was framed by a traditional intuitive sociology as a blessed event assuring the continuity of clan and the community. In urban settings a child was another mouth to feed in a desperately poor and ravaged community; thus, the urban intuitive sociology conceived of the birth of a child as a major disruptive event for the mother and her family.

Intuitive sociologies also conceive of the expectable *hardiness of families* in the face of serious stressful events. For example, we (19) have tried to reconstruct the family theories of those families who braved the rigors and isolation in settling the Great Plains in the mid-19th century. Primarily from literary sources, for example, Hamlin Garland (11), Laura Ingalls Wilder (30), and Willa Cather (6), it was possible to recognize a shared belief that individual families could be entirely self-sufficient in the face of almost any conceivable threat. Boss, in her recent review (5), paints a very different picture for Turkish families facing natural disaster. In these communities, a pervasive fatalism construes the families as having little power to resist the enormous disruptions of floods and earthquakes.

ANALYTIC ADVANTAGES OF MAPPING COMMUNITY CONCEPTIONS OF FAMILY STRESS

Our community-based approach to understanding family stress is designed to fill two gaps in current theory and empirical work in this area. First, it offers the prospect of a theoretically coherent, empirically based definition of family stress. According to this new perspective, family stress is defined as an event that by community standards is high in the capacity to disrupt ordinary family routines. This permits us to avoid a partially tautological definition now current in the field, an approach that—following Hill (16)—defines a stressful event according to the meaning of the event as the family itself sees it. Elsewhere (20), we have pointed out that this more typical approach fails to recognize that the family's experience of an event is better regarded as a central part of its coping response rather than as inherent in the event itself. For example, consider a family in rural Zulu culture. Let us suppose that the family perceives the wife's menopause as an expectable transition and takes comfort in the children that have already been born, rather than being terrified about those that, after this transition, will never be born. This family is actively framing its own meaning of an event in a way that contrasts sharply with the surrounding culture. If, in this family, our definition of stress depended on the *family's* rather than the *community's* definition of stress, we would be tempted to say simply that the family is not undergoing much stress. By not taking account of the *contrast* between the family and community definitions, we would miss the extraordinary competence of the family's coping effort. In other words, the active reframing is itself a central part of the coping effort.

Second, this new approach offers the opportunity for a rational, empirically based distinction between stress arising from processes internal to the family and that arising from forces external to the family. As many critics have pointed out, it is often meaningless to use stressful life events as independent variables in seeking explanations for the development of psychopathology in individual members or the development of relationship disturbances in families. This is because most life-events scales, and the theories underlying them, cannot clearly distinguish between events that themselves may be *indices* of psychopathology or of relationship disturbances, and events that may *cause* these disturbances. For example, several research programs attempt to measure stress on families by determining which events, from a standardized list, have happened to the family recently. Several of these lists contain, for example, the item "child's engagement is broken." This event might be a cause of marital distress in the child's parents or a cause of psychopathology in the mother. On the other hand, it might reflect a general level of disturbance and distress in the family. Along with

mother's psychopathology or marital distress, it might be only an index rather than a cause of family disruption. Here again, community-based definitions offer considerable conceptual and empirical leverage. Researchers would not have to make arbitrary or intuitive distinctions about "outside" or "inside" circumstances but could rely on those distinctions inherent in the cultural or community definitions of reality.

Hypotheses

These concepts of an intuitive sociology of families, developed by families, generate four testable hypotheses:

1. In any relatively homogeneous community, there should be consensus or uniformity concerning the impact of events on the family and the accountability of families for producing those events in the first place.

2. The importance of families for these concepts should be evidenced in two ways: (a) the community-wide consensus should be preserved when we inquire about events stressful to *families* and about the competence of families, each considered as a unitary group, to respond to those events; (b) the consensus should also be preserved if we query families, as whole groups, about their views on stress rather than querying individuals one at a time.

3. This consensus of families about families should hold both for accountability and competence of the average family.

4. If families are serving as *informants* about the perceptions of their culture or community rather than as *expressors* of their own views, then their perceptions of events should be relatively uninfluenced by characteristics that distinguish them within their community. Of particular interest are the idiosyncratic philosophies, visions, values, and world views that are a unique product of their own history.

Two other hypotheses are conspicuous derivatives of these considerations but are not tested in this study. First, these concepts or intuitive theories of families' responses to stress should vary in predictable fashion from one defined culture or community to another. Second, the community's own social apparatus for assisting families facing stress should be predictable from its intuitive sociology. For example, we might expect more informal support systems for traditional Zulu women facing menopause and more for urban Zulu women bearing children. Alternatively, if support enters the community from the outside (Federal disaster relief to a rural community or Federal health services for Indian reservations), it will be accepted to the extent that it conforms with the community's intuitive sociology about family needs.

Strategies for Measurement

To anticipate, our method represents a relatively straightforward extension of a method first used by Holmes and Rahe (17) in their studies of stress, and later perfected by Dohrenwend and colleagues (9). As they did, we ask our respondents to assign numerical ratings to a broad variety of stressful events and examine the consensus among them. We regard high levels of consensus among many families as evidence that there is a shared or common community conception of stressful circumstances. Masuda and Holmes (19) recognized early that this approach would be sensitive to community and cultural differences, and they published data showing striking differences between Japanese and American respondents; unfortunately, these illuminating cultural differences were never pursued systematically.

By using this procedure, we can extend our observations beyond straightforward tests of the hypotheses we have listed. We can explore the *pattern* of the ratings our families make. We can ask whether there are underlying themes or contours in these shared images of competence and accountability of families in the face of stress. Even more interesting will be an examination of events using the dimensions of competence and accountability simultaneously. What events, for example, do the families regard as very disruptive but for which the family is not to be held accountable? Will these ratings reveal some underlying assumptions about how families operate?

Our approach to measurement is different from previous ones in four respects. First, we have developed systematically a set of *circumstances most likely to be stressful to the family as a group* rather than to individuals. Second, we ask *families to provide ratings* by responding as a group. Third, we not only ask questions about how disruptive events would be—as did Holmes and Rahe and Dohrenwend et al.—but we also ask *how accountable the family is for the event in the first place*. Finally, to make the task more vivid, we use a variant of *Q-sort methodology*. In this initial study we use a convenience sample to explore the feasibility and initial yield of our new approach.

METHODS

Sample

In this first study, we recruited 45 White, two-parent step- and nondivorced families with a minimal marital duration of 7 years from two high-school districts in the suburban ring around Washington DC. High-school Parent-Teacher Associations (PTAs) were used in each district as the basis for recruiting families, but families varied greatly in their level of participation in the PTA or other school-based activities. From our informal observation, the cultural perspectives on family life in this ring are relatively uniform. In general, families are at least second-generation Americans, White, middle class, and their employment is often in the Federal government or in the myriad of firms and businesses that serve the government. To the extent that there is more heterogeneity in this mix than these simple indices suggest, the use of this sample will work against the possibility of confirming our first hypothesis.

As Table 23.1 shows, this sample is squarely in the middle class, with relatively narrow ranges of income and occupational rating. The subsamples from each of the high schools were similar to each other on all demographic measures, and thus we pooled the two for all analyses. We always worked with a family triad: both parents and the high-school student.

Procedures

Three steps were required by our measurement strategy. First, we needed to produce a set of events

Table 23.1 Characteristics of the Sample

Variable	Mean	SD
Father, years of education	17.4	2.9
Mother, years of education	15.2	2.2
Father, income in thousands	37.6	17.8
Mother, income in thousands	10.9	11.1
Father, Duncan SES rating	73.6	14.9
Employed mothers, Duncan SES rating	67.5	15.4
Father, age	47.7	6.4
Mother, age	45.6	6.0
Marital duration, years	20.7	5.9
Father, Shipley-Hartford intelligence (maximum score = 80)	66.4	13.1
Mother, Shipley-Hartford intelligence	65.3	11.2
Child, Shipley-Hartford	70.0	12.7

that are perceived as happening to families as groups rather than to individuals. Second, these events had to be described in general terms so that a family could judge how disruptive it might be for a typical family without having to know specific details about the event or about the family to whom it was happening. Third, we had to design a procedure for family triads to work together as unitary groups to rate these events on the dimensions of accountability and competence. In effect, we were making it possible for families to serve as cultural informants in a way somewhat analogous to the field procedures of many anthropologists.

Step 1: Eliciting Events. Each family was invited to our research offices for a structured interview in which we asked them to describe events during the last year that in some way had had an impact on their family. After an initial probe, we systematically explored six separate areas of family life: health, jobs, family activities, school, extended-family life, and the family's neighborhood. The family discussion was recorded and transcribed verbatim. Each family produced many events and, at the conclusion of interviewing, 45 families had provided a total of 469 family events. These events, of course, were very specific: "Aunt Sally was in a car accident"; "Fred dropped out of high school"; "Ferris Junior High School is going to close."

Step 2: Translating Events From the Specific to the General. We, as researchers, had to "translate" these particular events into general terms so that they could be rated by families who did not know Aunt Sally or her relationship to her family. If our overall notions about intuitive sociologies are true, then a translation process of this kind is one that must go on in all cultures. In order for an intuitive sociology or for a community frame to work effectively, there must be common symbols or understandings by which particular or idiosyncratic events are coded into common terms. Goffman (12) used the concept of "keying" to refer to this process. This informal translation process would itself be of great interest in ethnographic investigations. Since an ethnographic investigation of this kind was beyond the scope of this initial study, we followed the next best course: to develop an intuitively based set of translation procedures that would follow specific rules. We hoped these rules would be similar to how ordinary families key or code events. It was also important that, in our work, we verified that these translation rules could be reliably applied by our coding staff.

A major objective of the coding was to reduce the original list of 469 highly specific events to a much smaller set that was phrased in more general terms. The coding procedure had three steps. First, the "translator" scanned the verbatim typescripts of all 45 original interviews to demarcate descriptions of actual events. Second, whenever possible, the event description was divided into a noun phrase and a verb phrase or their nearest equivalents, that is, who did what and what was done. For example, "Grandmother [noun phrase] went to the hospital [verb phrase]." Third, each phrase was translated into more general terms. We limited almost all of the noun phrases to the following nine categories: family member, mother, father, child, parent, relative, friend, neighbor, and pet. We did this with a heavy heart since it involved blurring such critical distinctions as "grandparent" and "aunt." However, retaining this distinction would have expanded our list of events well beyond 200. We also tried to make systematic distinctions between short- and long-term events, and to distinguish events that arose from direct or immediate experience from events that were learned about indirectly or in advance (for example, as in the distinction between "child's school closes" and "family learns that child's school may close"). Fourth, all events were phrased in the present tense.

Two coders jointly coded 5 (11%) of the type-scripts. An agreement was counted if both derived the identically worded event from the typescript. A disagreement was counted when one coder derived an event that was not matched by the other coder (kappa for each jointly coded typescript = 0.7); 170 items were retained for the next phase of the study. Conceptually, most could be grouped into the same six categories as specified in the original interview; however, 57 items fell into a range of other categories including major life-cycle events, moves, experiences with crime, and several items on abortion and miscarriage.

Step 3: Rating Events. We invited the same 45 families back to serve as judges of the entire set of 170 translated items. Each family triad was asked to judge the items as a group. (In some families the ratings were done after full discussion and careful consensus-building; in others a single member dominated decision making. We did not test systematically the effect on our ratings of these different styles of reaching a family decision.) Each item was typed on a separate card. The order of the cards was the same for each family triad but the items were randomized throughout the card deck without making

any effort to preserve the logical categories into which they could be grouped.

Family triads rated the events two ways. First, in order to assess competence, was a rating of the magnitude of events. Here, families rated events according to their capacity to disrupt a typical family. This rating reflects the community-level conception of both the salience of the event being rated for the typical family in the community as well the hardiness of the typical family to withstand disruption from that event. Second, we asked our family triads to rate the typical family's accountability for producing the event in the first place. An event for which the family is not held accountable is called an external event. There were, as a result, two dimensions for the family triad to use in rating: *magnitude and externality.*

Families were first asked to rate the magnitude of each item by placing the cards on one of nine ruled columns. They were asked to consider families they knew and were given this specific instruction: "How much impact would the event have on the average family?" As we anticipated in our theory of intuitive sociologies, no family seemed to experience any difficulty in conceiving of the "average family" and using this conception as a ready basis for judgment. The first, third, fifth, seventh, and ninth columns were labeled "minimal or none," "mild," "moderate," "substantial," and "severe," respectively. Unlike conventional Q-sorts, families could place as many cards in each column as they wanted; in effect, the task was equivalent to rating each item on a 9-point Likert scale. Most families assigned one person the role of the "card placer" who acted on behalf of the whole family.

After each of the cards was placed, the same deck was again presented to the family for ratings of externality with these instructions: "What kind of factors lead to the event's occurrence?" A new set of sorting columns was placed in front of the family with the first, third, fifth, seventh, and ninth columns labeled as follows: "*Only* factors *internal* to a family," "*Predominantly* factors *internal* to the family," "A *balance* between internal and external factors," "*Predominantly* factors *external* to a family," and "*Only* factors *external* to a family."

The most critical test of our basic hypothesis is the level of consensus achieved *among* all family triads on these two ratings. If there were no consensus on all or most of the items, then there would be little basis to believe in a cultural or community frame that shapes families' perceptions of events and their impact. However, as we will show, the achievement of consensus does not, by itself, support the notion of a community framework. For example, it may be an artifact of agreement among families on just the most severe or trivial items. Indeed, in order to confirm our hypothesis, it is necessary to show that there is consensus on items across the full range of magnitude and externality, and that there are well-structured patterns in actual ratings of items that achieve high consensus.

Card-Sort Procedure

In addition to procedures for rating events (steps 1-3), each of the families in the sample was assessed for characteristics that might strongly influence their perception of these events; these assessments served as an initial exploration of hypothesis four. The test of this hypothesis is not, of course, a strong one since it can be confirmed only by the *absence* of associations between these measures and the ratings.

The Card-Sort Procedure measures three aspects of families' beliefs about the social world. Collectively, these shared beliefs have been called the family's paradigm; a family paradigm is an excellent example of family-level conception about the social world. A detailed explanation of the procedure and its theoretical rationale is available (20). The procedure is administered to family members who are isolated in booths where they can talk to each other over a telephone-like apparatus but cannot see each other. The procedure is divided into two phases. In the first, family members work alone to sort a deck of 16 cards into as many as seven different piles. In the second phase the members receive a somewhat different deck and are encouraged to talk to one another. Many families recognize that the cards can be sorted logically according to the patterns of letters on each. For example, they can see that these two sequences are alike: PMSVK and PMSMSMSMSVK. Other families use more superficial sorting systems.

Three measures are derived from this procedure. *Configuration* reflects the family's success in identifying the logical patterns in the cards. A broad range of research has demonstrated that this behavior reflects the family's shared view that the world is patterned and masterable. *Coordination* reflects the level of cooperation and communication during the second phase of the procedure, and, according to past research, reflects the family's belief that they are a single unit rather than separate, loosely federated individuals. *Closure* reflects the family's flexibility in the face of new information. Do they stick with the same pattern as they examine each card in turn or does the system evolve or change as new information is reviewed? High or delayed closure reflects the family's openness to new experience. If ratings made by the families in this study reflect their own philosophies rather than their role as cultural informants, then we might expect to find significant correlations between these variables and the event ratings. For example, high-configuration families might see a number of events as less disruptive and high-coordination families might hold families more accountable for their circumstances. In other research, the Card Sort Procedure has reflected a variety of family views about how families and groups function. The absence of significant correlations in this study would support our idea that when we instruct the family to do so, it does serve as a cultural informant.

In addition, as Table 23.1 indicates, this relatively homogeneous sample still displays a broad range of variation on a number of social status indicators that are ordinarily correlated with social attitudes. Again, an absence of correlation between these variables and the event ratings would support the argument that family ratings are influenced by community rather than family factors.

RESULTS

Analysis

Each item was scored according to the column number in which it was placed. Thus, an item would receive a magnitude rating of 9 if it were placed under the heading "severe," or an externality rating of 6 if it were placed in the column between "A *balance* between internal and external factors" and "*Predominantly* factors *external* to a family."

In order to assess the overall agreement among all families on all items, we used an intraclass correlation coefficient, which is essentially a one-way analysis of variance, using item number as the independent variable, ratings as the dependent variables, and families as "judges" or "cases." A highly significant coefficient reflects high levels of variance between items in comparison to variance within items, which in turn suggests that families were relatively similar to each other in their ratings.

More revealing is an analysis of those items that are rated with particularly high consensus. Here we assess the families' ratings of magnitude and externality. There are two analytic tasks involved. The first was to determine differences among items in the levels of consensus. This enabled us to focus on items that were rated with moderate or high consensus; these items are, presumably, the best reflection of the community-level intuitive sociology that guided the item ratings. In other words, in order to delineate the content of the community's intuitive sociology, we needed to identify which items achieved reasonably high consensus ratings from our informant families. The second analytic task stemmed from hypothesis four. Here we wanted to know whether salient differences among families in the sample influenced their ratings of items.

In order to accomplish the first task, we needed an estimate of the consensus among families on each item. There is no widely agreed-upon method for this assessment on an item-by-item basis; thus, we adapted the chi-square test for this purpose. We reasoned that if, for any item, there were no agreement among families on the rating of either magnitude or externality, the ratings would tend to distribute themselves equally across all nine categories. (A knowledge of the actual sampling distribution of item ratings must await the study of many communities.) Increasing agreement would be reflected in a non-chance concentration of ratings in just a few of the categories. Chi-squares were computed comparing the actual distribution of items against a distribution in which items were equally distributed across all nine categories. Thus, high chi-squares would reflect substantial agreement

among families that the items should be placed in just a small subset of the available categories. There is one exception: bi- or multimodal distributions of ratings. For example, a high chi-square could be obtained if 15 families rated an item in the lowest category, another 15 rated it in the middle category, and yet another 15 rated it in the highest. Thus, we discounted all items with other than unimodal distributions of ratings and regarded them as unreliably rated no matter what the magnitude of chi-square.

A second analysis of items related each to measures of family paradigm as well as selected indicators of family status. Here we used simple bivariate correlations.

For both analyses we applied the Bonferroni procedure with a liberal overall Type-I error rate of 0.2. This liberal level reduces the chances of a Type-II error, a more serious error in an exploratory investigation of this kind. It further reflects our conservative decision to use the entire 170-item set in our computation of the Bonferroni inequality with no effort to subgroup the items into subsets (13); the inequality was computed separately for magnitude and externality ratings. Computations yielded a minimum chi-square of 25 and a minimum bivariate r of 0.48 (for both, $p = 0.001$).

Findings

Levels of Consensus and Item Analyses. The first three hypotheses, all concerning levels of consensus among families, were tested by the overall intraclass correlations for magnitude (the inverse of competence) and externality (the inverse of accountability), as well as a detailed inspection of consensus among families for each of the items. The intraclass correlation coefficient for the magnitude ratings was 0.51 ($p < .0001$), and for the externality ratings even higher: 0.61 ($p < .00001$).

Findings for the item analysis for magnitude ratings by the families showed that of the total of 170 items, 61 failed to achieve unimodal chi-squares above 25. As expected, all of these low consensus items had mean ratings in the mid-range, from 3.1 to 6.5, since the ratings were, by definition, scattered across most of the 9 rating categories. Table 23.2 shows examples of low-consensus items.

Table 23.2   Examples of Low-Consensus Items

Item Number	Item Content
Items low on consensus for both magnitude and externality	
69.	Married child gets pregnant
103.	Family learns that parent will take an extended business trip
156.	Family member develops short-term illness, condition, or disability
Some items low on consensus for magnitude	
2.	Demands of parent's job increase
36.	Family learns that neighborhood schools may close
45.	Property near family's home is sold for development
100.	Subway station opens in family's neighborhood
117.	Relative gets separated or divorced from spouse
161.	Mother enters menopause
170.	Relative gets in trouble with the law
Some items low on consensus for externality	
32.	Married child has a baby
50.	Mother has a miscarriage
92.	Family member learns about a member's medical problems
125.	Family member is convicted of a crime

However, there were a large number of mid-range items on which families showed high levels of consensus. For example, of the 122 items that were rated less than 7 or more than 2, 61 achieved unimodal chi-square scores above 25. Even among the 42 highest consensus items—those achieving unimodal chi-squares of above 50—12 were rated lower than 7 or higher than 2. Of these 42, only 3 were rated 2.5 in magnitude or less. Thus, our family judges showed substantial agreement on the items across the full range of magnitude ratings, but with a dip in consensus in the middle ranges and a substantial increase in consensus at the upper end. It is, of course, impossible to say whether the higher consensus achieved at each extreme—particularly the upper end—of the magnitude ratings was due to the pervasiveness of a community frame or because the high magnitude items were so self-evidently disruptive that *any* group of families would have agreed on them. But it is clear from the large number of mid-range items that achieve high consensus that our high levels of overall agreement among families, as shown by the high intraclass correlations, is not due simply to

high levels of agreement on just a few items that are conspicuously stressful or trivial.

The patterns of item agreements are even more pronounced for externality ratings. Here only 28 items of the 170 failed to achieve unimodal chi-squares of 25 or more. These items were all mid-range items with mean externality ratings of 3.2 to 6.5; 82 items achieved unimodal chi-squares of 50 or greater, 24 of which were rated less than 7 or greater than 2. Of these 82 items, only 8 were rated 2.5 or less, again demonstrating that high-consensus items tend to be mostly the very highly rated ones. Table 23.2 shows examples of items achieving low consensus on externality ratings.

We examined the bivariate correlations among the three dimensions of family paradigm and the families' magnitude and externality ratings on all the items. Of these 1,020 correlations, only 2 exceeded the Bonferroni threshold. We next examined more traditional indicators of social status for both mothers and fathers: education, income, and Duncan occupational rating. We also correlated the mean score for the family threesome on the Shipley-Hartford

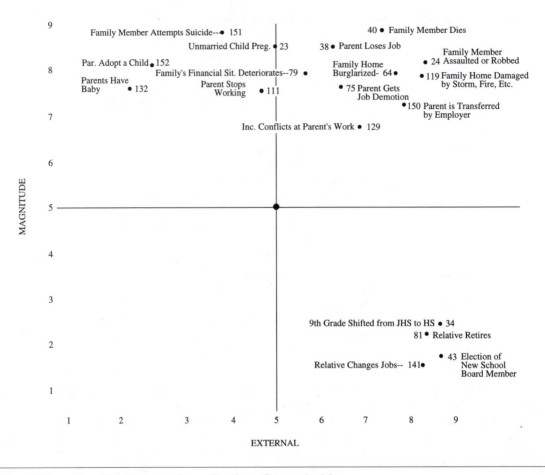

Figure 23.1   Very High-Consensus Items: Charting a Community Map

intelligence scale, using separate scores for the verbal and abstract portions. Of these 2,720 correlations, only 15 were above threshold. Although seemingly very scattered, there was one pattern to note: of these 15 significant correlations, 10 are for mothers and they are all inverse. In general, mothers who have more education and a better income are located in families that see events as generally of lesser magnitude and the family as more accountable (lower externality) for producing them in the first place. There is no consistent influence of father characteristics on these ratings.

Pattern of Item Ratings: Delineating Intuitive Sociology. The central task of the analysis is to

draw a map of the community's concept of family competence and accountability that our family informants have provided. We do so in four steps, as illustrated in Figures 23.1 through 23.4. The basic strategy is to construct a two-dimensional map, using the mean of the magnitude ratings across families as one dimension and the mean of the externality ratings as the other (as shown in Figure 23.1). This creates four broad regions: (a) events perceived as having high impact on the family but for which they are not held accountable; (b) high-impact events for which the family is held accountable; (c) low-impact events for which the family is and (d) is not held accountable. The map can be organized by using the highest consensus items first;

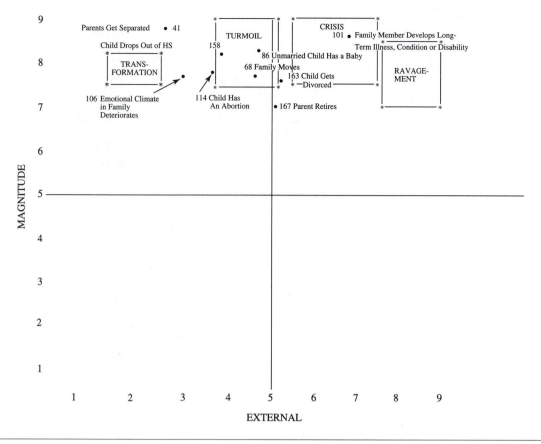

Figure 23.2   Zones of Family Calamity

then its details can be sketched in using items that achieved somewhat lower levels of consensus, for the most part, but still exceeded Bonferroni thresholds on *both* magnitude and externality ratings.

Figure 23.1 locates the 18 highest consensus items, those that achieved chi-squares of above 50 on both magnitude and externality ratings. We assume these are the most secure indicators of the community's conception of families and stress, and hence may be the basis for defining critical subzones within the four broad regions of our map. Indeed, there do appear to be five subzones that are almost naturally defined in this graph: four in the high magnitude regions and one in the low.

Farthest to the left (family accountability is very high for these events) are the events "parents have a

baby" and "parents adopt a child." Hansen and Hill (14) would have called these accession stresses. However, to anticipate subsequent figures, this zone may be called *Family Transformation*. This term fits the special nature of the events in this zone and suggests the central role, as the community ascribes it, the family plays in these events.

A second subzone is just to the right, implying equal magnitude but less clear family accountability. Here we find the events "family member attempts suicide," "unmarried child gets pregnant," and "parent stops working." It is conceivable that the community recognizes all these events as indicative of intense family turmoil for which they are to be held at least partially accountable; hence this may be identified as the subzone of *Family Turmoil*. All

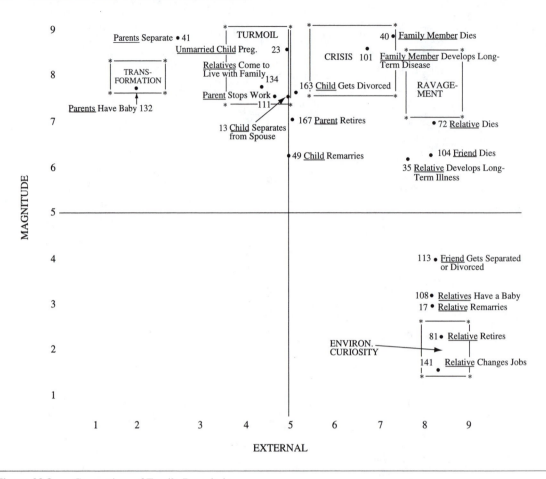

Figure 23.3   Conceptions of Family Boundaries

three of these items are phrased as happening to an individual member of the family. There are two possible mechanisms that may account for why our family raters attributed these events to "factors inside the family." One possibility is that they saw these events as arising out of a matrix of family patterns. In this instance they would be operating as many family therapists do. A second possibility is that the family may rate the event as due to factors inside the family because the act in the event is committed by a "family member" or an "unmarried child" or a "parent." All of these labels, on the cards they are sorting, refer to people inside the family. Thus, our raters may have been swayed by these labels rather than by a family-systems perspective.

A third zone contains "family's financial situation deteriorates," "parent loses job," and "parent gets job demotion." As do several items, "family member dies" lies at the border, but because of its qualitative distinctions from the next set we place it here as well. The item "increased conflicts at parent's work" may be too low in magnitude to fit into this subzone. Here, our informants are telling us, are events that are bound to produce serious family crisis, but for which the family cannot be held very accountable. To distinguish the lesser responsibility, we can call this the subzone of *Family Crisis.*

A fourth zone has four high-magnitude items for which the family is not held accountable: "family home burglarized," "family member assaulted or

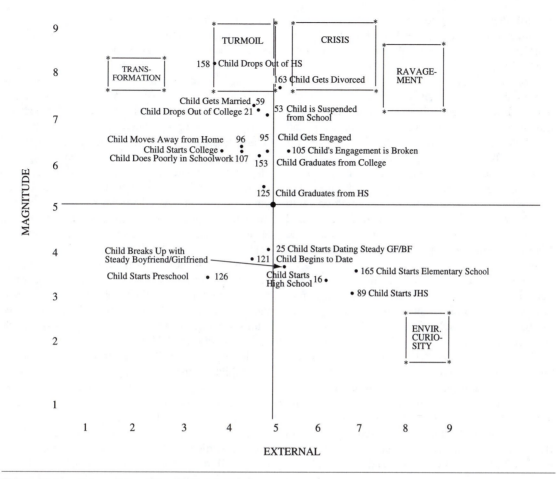

Figure 23.4   Conceptions of Family Development

robbed," "parent is transferred by employer," and "family home damaged by storm, fire, etc." To emphasize the view that these are completely external afflictions, we can call this the subzone of *Family Ravagement.*

A fifth zone is identified by four high-consensus items that all cluster in a small area in the right, lower quadrant. Because they are perceived as having so little impact on the family and are clearly regarded as arising from the environment and not the family, we can term this the subzone of *Environmental Curiosity.*

In Figure 23.2, we have drawn squares to indicate the approximate regions of these subzones so that they embrace the high-consensus items that seem to define the meaning of the zone. We then added all

the remaining high-magnitude items that met the Bonferroni criterion for magnitude and externality. Our definition of the zones seemed confirmed for the most part by these additional items. Thus, two items reflecting major internal changes in the family ended up near the Transformation Zone: "parents get separated" and "emotional climate in the family deteriorates."

Four serious events happening to individuals ended up near or in the Turmoil Zone: "child has an abortion," "child drops out of high school," "child gets divorced," and "unmarried child has a baby." These are events over which individuals may be said to have some control and for which they, and perhaps their families, are being held to account. The fact that a fourth item referring to the whole family, "family moves," is grouped here further suggests that our families see these individual misfortunes as equivalent to the misfortune of the entire family group.

One more item ends up in the Family Crisis zone: "family member develops long-term illness, condition, or disability." Families rate this as only slightly less in magnitude than "family member dies," and also hold the family slightly more accountable for the event. Its placement here, along with the placement of other high-consensus items in this zone shown in Figure 23.1, suggests that our family raters see both major reverses in health and employment in similar ways: they are sure to generate a crisis and yet the family cannot be completely exonerated from responsibility for producing or contributing to these events in the first place.

An examination of the remaining Bonferroni items begins to fill out a picture not only of family calamity but also of the structure and development of the family itself. Figure 23.3 shows all Bonferroni items in which an event ascribed to a member of the family, "child," or "parent" is also ascribed to a "relative" or "friend." We made one exception to the Bonferroni restrictions by adding, for completeness, the item "relative develops long-term illness," which achieved the Bonferroni threshold for externality but just missed achieving a Bonferroni chi-square for magnitude ($\chi^2 = 24$, $p = 0.002$). While, as we have noted, the term "relative" is somewhat ambiguous, all subject families were told that this was someone outside the household other than a child. Thus, it must have been clear to all our families that the items discriminated between nuclear family members and all others.

Two patterns in these items can be observed. First, an item happening to a relative is always considerably to the right and below the comparable event happening to parent or child; that is, it is seen as being much less disruptive and much less under the influence of the family. Many of the "relative" items are in or near the zone of Environmental Curiosity. The one exception to this pattern is the item "relative comes to live with family," which is not too distant from other severe Turmoil items such as "unmarried child becomes pregnant" and "child drops out of high school," and even surprisingly close to "family member attempts suicide." This pattern of ratings strongly suggests a community conception of family boundaries as firmly fixed around the nuclear household: the family has little influence over "relatives" and in many cases is barely disrupted by major events in the lives of relatives. When relatives break this boundary by coming to live with the nuclear family, it is clearly a crisis.

Against this background of perceived firmness of family boundaries, the ratings depicted in Figure 23.4 take on added interest. Here we have displayed all items that relate to major developmental achievements of children in childhood, adolescence, and young adulthood. These items are organized developmentally in Table 23.3, which shows that we added, again for completeness, three items that failed to achieve Bonferroni thresholds.

Figure 23.4 shows that these items cluster in two groups. In the top cluster are, primarily, normative and non-normative transitions of considerable importance. The non-normative ones—those associated with some stigma and psychological pain—are at the top of the cluster: "child drops out of high school," "child gets divorced," "child drops out of college," and "child is suspended from school." The bottom cluster is made up entirely of normative transitions into a new status rather than out of a current status; these are seen as much less problematic for families.

Compare these results to those in Figure 23.3 and note, in particular, the ratings of items that refer to adult children: "child gets married," "child gets divorced," "child gets engaged," and "child's engagement is broken." In this late-marrying subculture, these "children" are probably perceived as in their 20s and 30s and, for the most part, as living away from home. However, our family triads place these items as part of a cluster that includes items such as: "child does poorly in school work." This item, and others like it, must be perceived as a stressful event for a much younger child who is still clearly a household resident. Taking these ratings together, our informants seem to be saying that the tight family boundary, noted in the ratings shown in Figure 23.3, stretches to include the major transitions of young adults who are living outside the home. However, as soon as these adult children have their own children, their own "parents" may be extruded from the inner or nuclear family. That is, when their children have their own children, "parents" become "grandparents."

Table 23.3 Items Describing Developmental Achievements and Setbacks for Children at Various Stages of Development

Developmental Achievements		Developmental Setbacks	
Item Number	Content	Item Number	Content
Childhood			
12.	Child starts preschool*	53.	Child suspended from school
165.	Child starts elementary school		
Adolescence			
89.	Child starts junior high school	107.	Child does poorly in school work
16.	Child starts high school	158.	Child drops out of high school
121.	Child begins to date		
25.	Child starts dating steady boyfriend/girlfriend	137.	Child breaks up with steady boyfriend/girlfriend*
125.	Child graduates high school*		
Young adulthood			
62.	Child starts college*	21.	Child drops out of college
153.	Child graduates from college		
96.	Child moves away from home		
95.	Child is engaged	105.	Child's engagement is broken
59.	Child gets married	163.	Child gets divorced

* Ratings of these items did not exceed Bonferroni thresholds.

As "grandparents" they may suffer the same fate as other "relatives" whose major life transitions end up in or near the zone of Environmental Curiosity from the perspective of the family of procreation.

DISCUSSION

Practical and Clinical Import

These findings do suggest an intricate concept of family competence and accountability that achieves high levels of consensus within the community. These concepts seem embedded within even more sophisticated concepts of family calamities, family boundaries, and family development. These intriguing findings from this one community already suggest practical and clinical uses of data of this kind.

First, they allow us to take a much more accurate reading of the relative role of the family and the community in managing events of great stress.

When most members of a community agree that a stressful event is both external and of great magnitude, we might expect the community to establish or support agencies or mechanisms for support of families dealing with this event. Consider, for example, the enormous stress engendered by severe, chronic medical illness in a parent. In the face of the enduring demands of the illness, a broad range of ordinarily trivial events have the potential for major disruption, and such events can feel as if they are beyond the afflicted family's control. For example, the entry of child into elementary school may pose a mixture of practical and emotional problems with which burdened families cannot cope. Their ratings for this event would show it as both very disruptive and very external. However, since this is at variance with the community rating, the family is, we would suspect, left alone to cope without the built-in or institutionalized mechanisms for support. One might regard the difference between community readings of events and those of a beleaguered subset of families as central to the isolation and alienation of these beleaguered families.

In contrast are circumstances where there is a high level of synchrony between the family and the community. For example, consider the reading of events that might occur during or after a natural disaster that has equally affected an entire community. In this instance, we might expect families to be brought together with unusual force and intensity—rather than to be forced into a position of alienation and full self-reliance. Families, then, would become part of a community of unusual solidarity, welded together by intense, vivid, and *shared* conceptions of the calamities before them. Some histories of the impact of World War II on Britain suggest precisely these transformations. The more routine and distinct readings of events that kept British social classes distinct prior to the outbreak of war became unified in the face of the Blitz.

A second and related use of tools of this kind helps us to spot the minority or alienated family groups whose world of calamity feels to them unique and isolating. Family self-help groups are born from such a matrix. For example, Darling (7) studied the reading of events that were unique to families of children with spina bifida, a brain and spinal cord congenital abnormality that can be severely disabling. The attractiveness of these groups for families was that other families in the group shared their perception of the magnitude and disruptive potential of even simple events. Further, the group helped its member families to perceive clearly that they could not be held accountable for the fact of spina bifida itself or for the disruptiveness of many events that occurred in its wake. Indeed, these groups developed high levels of consensus that the medical and political systems were to be held accountable for many of the stresses they endured. As a consequence, they became highly effective political action groups.

Finally, as implied by the discussion above, tools of this kind are helpful in understanding the therapeutic process. For example, therapists comprise their own communities with their own beliefs about issues such as family boundaries and development. Almond (2) and Reiss, Costell, and Almond (22) have shown how, for example, psychiatric wards function as communities with their own values and

perspectives; these perspectives, partially unique to each unit, tend to shape the technical options woven into therapeutic regimens. Much of the initial tangle between a therapist and family may involve clashes in these fundamental concepts. Reiss and colleagues (24) have shown that family members who do not see themselves as enclosed by firm boundaries—when being treated by a therapeutic team that seems to hold exactly such a conception of most families—are at risk of dropping out of therapy.

Toward Improved Delineation of Intuitive Sociologies

The validity and utility of this procedure depends on two research design decisions: the selection of items for rating and the selection of families to do the rating.

Items Selected for Rating. At least four changes in the items used in this study would be useful for future work. First, the exploration of the intuitive concept of family boundary could be much more thorough if finer-grained distinctions among "relatives" were used. For example, in future work, it would seem useful to single out grandparents from other "relatives," and even distinguish among paternal and maternal grandparents. These two sets of grandparents may take on very different functions in the life of the family, and those differences may be important and distinctive to our cultural informants. For example, families may be closer to the maternal grandparents because of the particularly strong bonds between adult mothers and their own mothers. The special ties between nuclear families and the maternal extended family have been amply documented (1, 3, 25, 29). Thus, families—as raters—may report that events in the lives of maternal grandparents are likely to have a bigger impact on and seem less external to the families in their communities.

Second, new items might make the procedure more sensitive to perceived gender differences in children and adults. Indeed, mothers and girls may be seen as more central and boys and men more at the periphery of family life. For example, we did have an item "unmarried daughter gets pregnant" (which received very nearly the maximum score on magnitude) but did not have a corresponding item "unmarried son gets his girlfriend pregnant." Interestingly, the failure of the second item to occur reflects the fact that not a single family mentioned that item in our original structured interviews. This in itself might presage a sizeable gender effect, with many calamities being perceived as more disruptive and more internal when they happen to mothers and daughters, in contrast to fathers and sons.

Third, the community's intuitive concepts of development could be explored more systematically, with a greater range of items covering developmental achievements and setbacks across the life span. These would enable us to examine more closely how development is conceived in the intuitive family sociologies we are tracing.

Fourth, we might explore the difference between rare and common events. For example, might rare events—particularly if they are unexpected—be seen as more disruptive and external?

Families Selected as Raters. Obviously, the selection of particular groups of subjects as raters has a big impact on the ratings. For example, strict comparisons among cultures or among communities—clearly a next step for work of this kind—would require systematic, random sampling of larger samples of families. This has already been achieved by Dohrenwend et al. (9) for individual informants. Also, we have only assumed that our ratings take on a special coloration because we have family triads working as a group to do the ratings. We have assumed we are, thereby, tapping into an intuitive sociology constructed by families in order to regulate—on a community level—the relationships among families. But surely these conceptions held by families shade into systems more developed by individual family members. This contrast could be explored by systematic comparisons among different sets of raters: families versus individuals or, among individuals, parents versus adolescents or mothers versus fathers. Such an examination would provide an alternative, and complementary, perspective on the developmental and gender issues that are addressed in part by ratings of selected classes of items. It may also provide a means of studying boundaries within the family, by identifying family subgroups that are defined by patterns of similarity and dissimilarity in judgments of the meaning of salient events in the life of the family.

REFERENCES

1. Adams, B. N. *Kinship in an urban setting.* Chicago: Markham Publishing, 1968.
2. Almond, R. *The healing community: Dynamics of the therapeutic milieu.* New York: Jason Aronson, 1974.
3. Anspach, D. & Rosenberg, S. Working class matricentricity. *Journal of Marriage and the Family, 34:* 437-442, 1972.
4. Aries, P. *Centuries of childhood.* New York: Random House, 1962.
5. Boss, P. G. Family stress: Perception and context. In M. Sussman & S. Steinmetz (eds.), *Handbook on marriage and the family.* New York: Plenum Press, 1987.
6. Cather, W. *My Antonia.* New York: Houghton Mifflin, 1949.
7. Darling, R. B. *Families against society.* Beverly Hills CA: Sage Publications, 1979.
8. Demos, J. *A little commonwealth: Family life in Plymouth colony.* London: Oxford University Press, 1970.
9. Dohrenwend, B. S., Krasnoff, L., Askenasy, A. R. & Dohrenwend, B. P. Exemplification of a method for scaling life events: The PERI Life Events Scale. *Journal of Health and Social Behavior, 19:* 205-229, 1978.
10. Farber, B. & Jenne, W. C. Family organization and parent child communication. *Monographs of the Society for Research in Child Development, 28:* 1-78, 1963.
11. Garland, H. *A son of the middle border.* New York: Macmillan, 1914.
12. Goffman, E. *Frame analysis: An essay on the organization of experience.* Cambridge: Harvard University Press, 1974.
13. Grove, W. M. & Andreasen, N. C. Simultaneous tests of many hypotheses in exploratory research. *Journal of Nervous and Mental Disease, 170:* 3-8, 1982.
14. Hansen, D. & Hill, R. Families under stress. In H. T. Christensen (ed.), *Handbook of marriage and the family.* Chicago: Rand McNally, 1964.
15. Heider, F. *The psychology of interpersonal relations.* New York: John Wiley & Sons, 1958.
16. Hill, R. *Families under stress.* New York: Harper & Row, 1949.
17. Holmes, T. H. & Rahe, R. H. The Social Readjustment Rating Scale. *Journal of Psychosomatic Research, 11:* 213-218, 1967.
18. Kantor, D. & Lehr, W. *Inside the family: Toward a theory of family process.* San Francisco: Jossey-Bass, 1975.

19. Masuda, M. & Holmes, T. H. The Social Readjustment Rating Scale: A cross-cultural study of Japanese and Americans. *Journal of Psychosomatic Research, 11:* 227-237, 1967.

20. Reiss, D. *The family's construction of reality.* Cambridge: Harvard University Press, 1981.

21. Reiss, D. The represented and the practicing family: Contrasting visions of family continuity. In A. J. Sameroff & R. N. Emde (eds.), *Relationship disturbances in early childhood: A developmental approach.* New York: Basic Books, 1989.

22. Reiss, D., Costell, R. & Almond, R. Personal needs, values and technical preferences in the psychiatric hospital: A replicated study. *Archives of General Psychiatry, 33:* 795-804, 1976.

23. Reiss, D., Costell, R., Berkman, H. & Jones, C. How one family perceives another: The relationship between social constructions and problem-solving competence. *Family Process, 19:* 239-256, 1980.

24. Reiss, D., Costell, R., Jones, C. & Berkman, H. The family meets the hospital: A laboratory forecast of the encounter. *Archives of General Psychiatry, 37:* 141-154, 1980.

25. Reiss, D. & Oliveri, M. E. The family's construction of social reality and its ties to its kin network: An exploration of causal direction. *Journal of Marriage and the Family, 45:* 81-92, 1983.

26. Sameroff, A. J. & Feil, L. A. Parental concepts of development. In I. E. Sigel (ed.), *Parental belief systems: The psychological consequences for children.* Hillsdale NJ: Lawrence Erlbaum Associates, 1985.

27. Scotch, N. A. Sociocultural factors in the epidemiology of Zulu hypertension. *Journal of Public Health, 53:* 1205-1213, 1963.

28. Steinglass, P., Bennett, L. A., Wolin, S. J. & Reiss, D. *The alcoholic family.* New York: Basic Books, 1987.

29. Sweetser, D. A. Asymmetry in intergenerational family relationships. *Social Forces, 41:* 346-352, 1963.

30. Wilder, L. I. *On the banks of Plum Creek.* New York: Harper & Row, 1937.

Name Index

Subject Index

About the Editor

Pauline Boss received her Ph.D. in Child Development and Family Studies from the University of Wisconsin-Madison, where she subsequently taught and was tenured. In 1981, she joined the Department of Family Social Science at the University of Minnesota, where she is now Professor and Clinical Supervisor in the doctoral training program in marriage and family therapy. She was appointed Visiting Professor of Psychology at Harvard Medical School, 1995-96. Widely recognized for groundbreaking research and theory development since 1973 on family stress and ambiguity, she summarized part of that work in *Ambiguous Loss: Learning to Live with Unresolved Grief* (Harvard University Press, 1999).

Dr. Boss is a past-president of the National Council on Family Relations (where she also chaired the Research & Theory Section and the Theory Construction & Research Methods Workshop) and is a past-president of the Groves Conference on Marriage and the Family. She is also a member of the Council on Contemporary Families. Known as a pioneer in the interdisciplinary study of family stress, she has worked to connect family science and sociology with family therapy and psychology. She is a Fellow of the American Psychological Association, the American Association of Marriage and Family Therapy (where she chaired the research committee), and the National Council on Family Relations. In addition, she has chaired the research committee of the American Family Therapy Academy and was appointed to serve on the Advisory Board of the Family Research Consortium III on Diversity, funded by the National Institute of Mental Health. Dr. Boss was a coeditor of the *Sourcebook on Family Theories and Methods* (Plenum, 1993). In 2002, she received the Ernest Burgess Award for contributions to family theory.

ABOUT THE AUTHORS

Naomi Adelson, Ph.D., is Associate Professor in the Department of Anthropology at York University, Toronto, Ontario, Canada. Her work as a medical anthropologist has focused extensively on the Cree of northern Quebec and has evolved from an ethnographic analysis of health to the study of the social, cultural, historical, and political parameters of suffering, stress, and social healing in the context of Aboriginal Canada. She is the author of *Being Alive Well: Health and the Politics of Cree Well-Being* (University of Toronto, 2000).

Aaron Antonovsky, Ph.D., (deceased) was Kunin-Lunenfeld Professor of Medical Sociology and chairman of the Department of the Sociology of Health in the Faculty of Health Sciences, Ben Gurion University of the Negev, Beersheba, Israel. He was a medical sociologist who heavily influenced family stress researchers. In his research on stress, Dr. Antonovsky was known internationally as a pioneer in emphasizing health (salutogenesis) rather than pathology.

Lucy J. Boothroyd, M.Sc., at the time the article in this volume, "Psychological Distress Among the Cree of James Bay," was first published, was an epidemiologist and a research assistant for the Culture & Mental Health Research Unit, Jewish General Hospital, Montreal, Quebec. We were unable to locate her for further information.

Gene H. Brody, Ph.D., is Distinguished Research Professor of Child and Family Development, and Director of the Center for Family Research of the Institute for Behavioral Research at the University of Georgia. Major research interests include family influences on children's intellectual, social, and personality development; factors that protect children and adolescents at risk for negative developmental outcomes; the contribution of sibling relationships to children's social and personality development; and the interrelationships among marital quality, parenting, and children's developmental outcomes.

P. Adama Brown is a sociologist interested in mental health, medical sociology, and race, ethnicity, and gender issues. She is also coauthor of an article regarding the effects of community context on the psychological well-being of African American women in the *Journal of Personality and Social Psychology* (2000).

Cathy L. Campbell, Ph.D., RN, is Assistant Professor in the Georgia State University School of Nursing. Her most recent research is in the area of early brain development in the first three years of life and assessment of clinical competency in practicing nurses. Her father's case as a Vietnam War Missing-in-Action Air Force pilot is still open. Dr. Campbell continues to be sensitive to the long-term impact of living with ambiguous loss.

Wayne Caron, Ph.D., is a lecturer in the Department of Family Social Science, College of Human Ecology at the University of Minnesota. His research interests include Alzheimer's disease and aging. He is coauthor of *Alzheimer's Disease: The*

Family Journey (with J. Pattee and O. Otteson, Northridge, 2001).

Rand D. Conger, Ph.D., is Professor of Human Development and Family Studies at the University of California–Davis. His research focuses on social processes and individual characteristics that either increase or reduce risk for problem behavior and mental disorder over time. Of particular importance are the results of the decade-long study of over 500 rural families in Iowa which has been extended to a second generation of rural families and to a study of stress processes in over 800 African American families.

Dr. Conger received the Victor I. Howery Award for significant contributions to rural mental health given by the National Association for Rural Mental Health. Findings from Dr. Conger's research have been published in over 150 books, book chapters, and journal articles.

Carolyn E. Cutrona, Ph. D., is Professor of Psychology and Associate Director of the Institute for Social and Behavioral Research at Iowa State University. Her research has focused on social support, stress, coping, neighborhood context, and depression. She is currently principal investigator on a multi-site longitudinal study of African American parents that focuses on community and individual predictors of mental health. Dr. Cutrona is the author of *Social Support in Couples; Marriage as a Resource in Times of Stress* (Sage, 1996).

Laura DeHaan, Ph.D., is Associate Professor of Psychology at Calvin College. Her research interests focus on adolescent adjustment in rural environments, identity development, and family resilience. In 2001, Dr. DeHann coauthored a chapter examining the effects of economic hardship on rural children and adolescents *in The Last Frontier: Social Problems in Rural America in the Twenty-First Century* (Associated University Press).

Alice S. Demi, RN, DNS, FAAN, is Professor, Acting Director of the School of Nursing, and Associate Dean of the College of Health and Human Sciences at Georgia State University. She has had a long-standing interest in grief and loss and has been instrumental in developing community organizations such as Hospice of Marin (California), Hospice of Metro-Denver (Colorado), The Grief Education Institute (Colorado), and the Georgia Coalition for Youth Suicide Prevention (Atlanta). She is currently a co-investigator on a National Institute of Mental Health (NIMH) funded study of family dynamics and its relationship to medical neglect of children with asthma.

Glen H. Elder, Jr., Ph.D., is Howard W. Odum Distinguished Professor of Sociology at the University of North Carolina, Chapel Hill. He pioneered longitudinal studies of the life course, family, and human development in relation to variations in historical time and place. Projects include an ongoing study of farm and nonfarm youth and their midwestern families, the process by which economic hardship adversely influences the social adjustment of and school of inner-city youth (black and white) in the transition to adulthood, and the investigation of sources of resilient and vulnerable pathways to the adult years. Dr. Elder holds the National Institute of Mental Health (NIMH) Research Scientist and Spencer Senior Scholar Awards. He has authored, coauthored, and edited many books including *Methods of Life Course Research* (Sage, 1998), *Children of the Land: Adversity and Success in Rural America* (University of Chicago, 2000) and the classic *Children of the Great Depression* (University of Chicago, 1974; 1999).

Norman Garmezy, Ph.D., is Emeritus Professor of Psychology at the University of Minnesota. He is known internationally as the pioneer in the area of child competence and human resilience.

Ann Garwick, Ph.D., RN, LMFT, LP, is Associate Professor and Director of the Center for Child and Family Health Promotion Research in the School of Nursing at the University of Minnesota. Her research and clinical interests include the impact of chronic conditions on children and their families, stressors related to family caregiving, and cultural issues in health care. Her work has focused on how families from diverse cultural backgrounds view and manage chronic and disabling conditions. Dr. Garwick coauthored an article about the relationship between uncertainty in preadolescents' chronic health conditions and family distress in the *Journal of Family Nursing* (2002).

Kenneth V. Hardy, Ph.D., is Director of the Center for Children, Families, and Trauma; Ackerman Institute for the Family; New York City and a Senior Clinical Supervisor with the Marriage and Family Therapy Program at Syracuse University. His interests are working with diversity in school systems, family therapy with oppressed populations, and youth aggression and violence. He is coauthor of *Minorities and Family Therapy* (Haworth, 1990) and has published numerous articles devoted to family therapy and training.

Dale R. Hawley, Ph.D., is Family Minister, Woodbury Church of Christ, Woodbury, Minnesota. He serves as adjunct faculty in the Department of Family Social Science, College of Human Ecology, University of Minnesota. A licensed marital and family therapist, he is active in clinical practice and supervision. He has written about clinical implications of family resilience and is coauthor on a forthcoming paper on operationalizing this concept.

Reuben Hill, Ph.D.,(deceased) was Regents Professor of Sociology at the University of Minnesota and known internationally as the "father of family stress theory." He pioneered the study of family stress and family development at the university level. His classic book, *Families Under Stress* (Greenwood, 1971, original work published 1949), about the impact of World War II deployment of servicemen on families, has been reprinted and is still being read.

Stevan E. Hobfoll, Ph.D., is Professor of Psychology and Director of the Applied Psychology Center at Kent State University. He has received over $8 million in federal research grants on stress and health. Dr. Hobfoll has authored and edited numerous books including *Stress, Social Support*

and Women (1986, Hemisphere); *Traumatic Stress* (1995, Plenum); *The Ecology of Stress* (1988, Hemisphere); and *Stress, Culture and Community* (1998, Plenum). In addition he has authored over 140 journal articles and book chapters and has been a frequent workshop leader on stress.

Anne E. Kazak, Ph.D., ABPP, is Director, Department of Psychology at The Children's Hospital of Philadelphia and Professor and Director of Psychology Research in the Department of Pediatrics at the University of Pennsylvania. Using developmental and social ecological perspectives, Dr. Kazak and her research team direct their work toward understanding how children, families, and other systems respond to the demands of serious illness and treatment over time. Her article outlining a social ecological framework for guiding research and practice for the care of children with cancer and their families appeared in *Children's Services: Social Policy, Research and Practice* (2001). Dr. Kazak is also the current editor of the *Journal of Pediatric Psychology*.

Laurence J. Kirmayer, M.D., is Professor and Director, Division of Social and Transcultural Psychiatry, Department of Psychiatry, McGill University, and Editor-in-Chief of *Transcultural Psychiatry.* He also directs the Culture & Mental Health Research Unit at the Department of Psychiatry, Sir Mortimer B. Davis–Jewish General Hospital in Montreal, where he conducts research on the mental health of Canadian Aboriginal peoples, mental health services for immigrants and refugees, consultation-liaison psychiatry, and the anthropology of psychiatry. He is coeditor of *Current Concepts of Somatization* (American Psychiatric Press, 1991) and author of a book in preparation, *Healing and the Invention of Metaphor: Toward a Poetics of Illness Experience.*

Kendra B. Klebba is a graduate student in the clinical psychology program at the University of Buffalo. She received a Master's of Public Health degree specializing in Health Education from Tulane University. Her current research interests include family members' different perspectives and perceptions of family relationships.

Tracey A. Laszloffy, Ph.D., is Associate Professor and Director of the Marriage and Family Therapy Program at Seton Hill University. Her areas of interest include developing oppression-sensitive approaches to clinical training and practice and therapy with troubled adolescents and their families.

Yoav Lavee, Ph.D., is a senior lecturer and director of the doctoral program at the School of Social Work, Faculty of Social Welfare and Health Studies, University of Haifa, Israel, and a senior researcher at the Center for Research and Study of the Family. His interests include family stress and coping, marital dynamics under stress, marital quality in a multicultural context, and family theory and methodology.

Kurt Luescher, Ph.D., is Professor Emeritus, University of Konstanz, Germany, where he held a chair in sociology from 1971-2000 and was director of the Research Center, "Society and Family," founded in 1989. His research, teaching, and publications focus on the sociology of the family, intergenerational relations, law, media, and socialization theory. Dr. Luescher is a member of the Scientific Advisory board to the German Family Ministry and of the Swiss Commission for Family Matters and Family Policy.

Harriette McAdoo, Ph.D., is University Distinguished Professor in the College of Human Ecology at Michigan State University. She is known for her examinations of African American families, people of color, and women in today's society. Dr. McAdoo is the author, editor, and coeditor of thirteen books and monographs and more than 80 scholarly articles and chapters. Her publications include *Black Children: Social, Educational and Parental Environments, Second Edition* (Sage, 2001) and *Family Ethnicity: Strength in Diversity, Second Edition* (Sage,1999).

Hamilton I. McCubbin, Ph.D., is Chief Executive Officer of Kamehameha Schools, Honolulu, Hawaii. He has authored, edited, and coedited 18 books and maintains scholarly research on families over the life cycle and families under stress, with particular emphasis on family postcrisis responses and resiliency.

Bruce D. Miller, M.D., is Professor of Psychiatry and Pediatrics and Chief of the Division of Child and Adolescent Psychiatry at the School of Medicine and Biomedical Sciences, State University of New York at Buffalo. He is also Director of Pediatric Psychiatry and Psychology at the Children's Hospital of Buffalo. Dr. Miller is Principal Investigator on a National Institutes of Health (NIH) funded study, "Effects of Depressive Emotions on Airways in Asthma." He has written many articles on mechanisms by which stress and emotions influence asthma and their families. His work is notable for looking beyond adherence issues while promoting an understanding of the importance of direct effects of stress and emotion on airway function in asthma.

James Mortimer, Ph.D., is the Director of the Institute on Aging, Saunders Professor of Gerontology, and Professor of Epidemiology and Biostatistics at the University of South Florida. An internationally recognized authority on the causes and early detection of Alzheimer's disease, he is the editor of four books and author of more than 200 scientific publications.

Carol Mulligan received her B.S. (summa cum laude) in Family Social Science from the College of Human Ecology, University of Minnesota in 2001. Her interests include family stress surrounding end-of-life issues, family resilience in immigrant populations, and narrative analysis research.

Velma McBride Murry, Ph.D., is Professor of Child and Family Development and Co-Director of the Center for Family Research at the University of Georgia. Her work on the implications of racism for family functioning is important in elucidating the dynamics of this contextual stressor in the everyday life of African Americans. Further, her work helped to define and shape the developing field of African American adolescents' sexuality and normative processes in rural African American families. In addition to her extensive record of publications and presentations at professional meetings, she is one of three co-founders of the National Institute of Mental Health (NIMH) Study Group on Culture, Ethnicity, and Family Process.

Mary Ellen Oliveri, Ph.D., is Chief of the Behavioral Science Research Branch at the National Institute of Mental Health (NIMH), where she is responsible for funding grants to investigators in cognitive science, emotion, personality, social cognition, and biobehavioral processes. Prior to joining NIMH, Dr. Oliveri was on the faculty of George Washington University School of Medicine for twelve years focusing on family interaction research.

Joan M. Patterson, Ph. D., is Associate Professor of Maternal and Child Health in the School of Public Health and Adjunct Associate Professor in Family Social Science, College of Human Ecology at the University of Minnesota. Her research focuses on children with chronic health conditions and their families, with an emphasis on interventions that promote successful psychosocial adaptation and prevent disease progression and functional limitations. Dr. Patterson's publications include articles about integrating family resilience with family stress theory in the *Journal of Marriage and the Family* (2002) and understanding family resilience in the *Journal of Clinical Psychology* (2002).

Karl Pillemer, Ph.D., is Professor of Human Development and Director of the Cornell Gerontology Research Institute (an Edward R. Roybal Center), Cornell University. His interests center on human development over the life course with a special emphasis on family and social relationships in middle age and beyond. Dr. Pillemer studies family members who provide care to Alzheimer's disease victims, examining the relationships among social network structure, social support, and psychological well-being. Other research interests include intergenerational relations in later life.

David Reiss, M.D., is the Vivian Gill Distinguished Research Professor at George Washington University Medical Center and Director of the Division of Research and the Center for Family Research in the Department of Psychiatry and Behavioral Sciences. He is also a Teaching Analyst at the Washington Psychoanalytic Institute. He has received many distinguished research awards, including the coveted National Institute of Mental Health (NIMH) Merit Award. His publications are numerous, spanning the areas of family process and therapy, and over the past decade, genetic and environmental influences in developing psychopathology. Dr. Reiss recently completed *The Relationship Code: Deciphering Genetic and Social Influences on Adolescent Development* (Harvard, 2000).

Elizabeth Robinson, M.D., is a public health physician who has been affiliated with the regional health board of the James Bay Cree of northern Quebec for 25 years. In the past she worked as a family physician in the Cree communities and presently does clinical work in Montreal.

Martha A. Rueter, Ph.D., is Assistant Professor in the Department of Family Social Science, College of Human Ecology, University of Minnesota. Her research interests include rural families, critical transitions, and parent-adolescent problem solving as well as vulnerable rural youth, alcohol use in adolescence, and suicidal behavior among rural adolescents. Her current research projects focus on critical transitions in rural families at risk and the context, comorbidity, and development of suicidal behavior among rural adolescents. In 1999 Dr. Reuter coauthored an article in *the Archives of General Psychiatry* outlining whether parent-adolescent disagreement affects adolescent symptom internalization which, consequently, predicts first onset of a depressive or anxiety disorder.

Ronald L. Simons, Ph.D., is Professor of Sociology and serves as Director of the Institute for Social and Behavioral Research at Iowa State University. His research focuses on domestic violence, determinants of parenting, and the manner in which family, school, and community environments combine to influence child development.

He is author of *Understanding Differences Between Divorced and Intact Families* (Sage, 1996) and is completing a book on families and crime.

Talma Sourani: The article "Family Sense of Coherence and Family Adaptation" in this volume was based on an MSW thesis submitted by Ms. Sourani to the School of Social Work, University of Haifa, Israel, in 1983. We were unable to locate Ms. Sourani to obtain more recent information.

Charles D. Spielberger, Ph.D., is Distinguished Research Professor of Psychology and Director of the Center for Research in Behavioral Medicine and Health Psychology at the University of South Florida. His current research focuses on anxiety, curiosity, depression, and the experience, expression and control of anger; behavioral medicine and health psychology; job stress and stress management; and the effects of stress, emotions and lifestyle factors on the etiology of hypertension, cardiovascular disorders, and cancer. Publications include *Test Anxiety: Theory, Assessment and Treatment* (Hemisphere/Taylor & Francis, 1995) and the continuing 16-volume research series on Stress and Emotion (with I. Sarason, Hemisphere/Taylor & Francis, 1975-1996).

Peter Strang, Ph.D., M.D., was Professor in the Palliative Research Unit, Linköping University, Vrinnevi Hospital, Norrköping, Sweden, at the time the article in this volume, "Spiritual Thoughts, Coping and 'Sense of Coherence' in Brain Tumour Patients and Their Spouses," was first published. We were unable to locate Dr. Strang for further information.

Susan Strang was a nurse in the Department of Oncology, Sahlgrenska University, Gothenburg Hospital, Sweden, when the article in this volume, "Spiritual Thoughts, Coping and 'Sense of Coherence' in Brain Tumour Patients and Their Spouses," was first published. We were unable to locate Ms. Strang for further information.

Adrian Tanner, Ph.D., is Professor of Anthropology at Memorial University, St. John's, Newfoundland. He has published articles and reports on hunting, land claims, ethnic politics,and aboriginal spirituality and is the author of *Bringing Home Animals* (ISER Books, 1979), a book about Cree hunting rituals. He is editor of *The Politics of Indianness* (Institute of Social and Economic Research, Memorial University of Newfoundland, 1983). Dr. Tanner also coauthored a study on aboriginal governance for the Canadian Royal Commission on Aboriginal Peoples. Since 1986 he has also conducted research in Fiji.

Beatrice L. Wood, Ph.D., ABPP, is Associate Professor of Psychiatry and Pediatrics, School of Medicine and Biomedical Sciences, State University of New York at Buffalo. She is also Associate Director of Pediatric Psychiatry and Psychology, Children's Hospital of Buffalo. Dr. Wood is currently involved in an National Institutes of Health (NIH) funded study of stressful family relationship processes and their influence on airway function in children and adolescents with asthma. She has written many articles elucidating integrated individual and family systems models for investigating and treating somatic and emotional illness in children and adolescents.

Lorraine M. Wright, Ph.D., RN, is Director of the Family Nursing Unit and Professor, Faculty of Nursing, at the University of Calgary. Her clinical research focuses on illness beliefs, family interventions, and suffering and spirituality. Dr. Wright co-developed the Calgary Family Assessment and Intervention Models and the Illness Beliefs Model. She is coauthor of *Nurses and Families: A Guide to Family Assessment and Intervention, Third Edition* (F. A. Davis, 2000) and *Beliefs: The Heart of Healing in Families and Illness* (Basic Books, 1996).